Mathematical Methods for Economics and Finance

Mathematical Methods for Economics and Finance

Edited by Hope Bradley

CLANRYE INTERNATIONAL
www.clanryeinternational.com

Clanrye International,
750 Third Avenue, 9th Floor,
New York, NY 10017, USA

ISBN: 978-1-64726-666-0

Cataloging-in-Publication Data

Mathematical methods for economics and finance / edited by Hope Bradley.
p. cm.
Includes bibliographical references and index.
ISBN 978-1-64726-666-0
1. Economics, Mathematical. 2. Business mathematics. 3. Finance--Mathematical models.
4. Economics--Mathematical models. I. Bradley, Hope.
HB135 .M38 2023
330.015 1--dc23

For information on all Clanrye International publications
visit our website at www.clanryeinternational.com

CLANRYE INTERNATIONAL

Contents

Preface.......VII

Chapter 1 **On History of Mathematical Economics: Application of Fractional Calculus**.......1
Vasily E. Tarasov

Chapter 2 **A Deep Neural Network Algorithm for Semilinear Elliptic PDEs with Applications in Insurance Mathematics**.......29
Stefan Kremsner, Alexander Steinicke and Michaela Szölgyenyi

Chapter 3 **Algorithmic Foundations of Economic and Mathematical Modeling of Network Logistics Processes**.......47
Sergey Yevgenievich Barykin, Irina Vasilievna Kapustina, Sergey Mikhailovich Sergeev and Vladimir Konstantinovich Yadykin

Chapter 4 **Macroeconomic Shocks and Changing Dynamics of the U.S. REITs Sector**.......63
Rangan Gupta, Zhihui Lv and Wing-Keung Wong

Chapter 5 **The Impact of Market Condition and Policy Change on the Sustainability of Intra-Industry Information Diffusion**.......75
Chi Dong, Hooi Hooi Lean, Zamri Ahmad and Wing-Keung Wong

Chapter 6 **Organizational Climate and Work Style: The Missing Links for Sustainability of Leadership and Satisfied Employees**.......95
Massoud Moslehpour, Purevdulam Altantsetseg, Weiming Mou and Wing-Keung Wong

Chapter 7 **Does Herding Bias Drive the Firm Value? Evidence from the Chinese Equity Market**.......112
Sayyed Sadaqat Hussain Shah, Muhammad Asif Khan, Natanya Meyer, Daniel F. Meyer and Judit Oláh

Chapter 8 **An Event Study Analysis of Political Events, Disasters and Accidents for Chinese Tourists**.......132
Chia-Lin Chang, Shu-Han Hsu and Michael McAleer

Chapter 9 **A Sustainability-Oriented Enhanced Indexation Model with Regime Switching and Cardinality Constraint**.......209
Zhiping Chen, Xinkai Zhuang and Jia Liu

Chapter 10 **Why are Warrant Markets Sustained in Taiwan but not in China?......223**
Wing-Keung Wong, Hooi Hooi Lean, Michael McAleer and Feng-Tse Tsai

Permissions

List of Contributors

Index

Preface

This book was inspired by the evolution of our times; to answer the curiosity of inquisitive minds. Many developments have occurred across the globe in the recent past which has transformed the progress in the field.

Mathematical finance refers to a branch of applied mathematics that deals with mathematical modeling of financial markets and problems. It is an emerging field that aims to apply mathematical formulas and modeling for creating financial resource values and pricing structures. The disciplines of financial engineering and computational finance are heavily interlinked with mathematical finance. Mathematical economics is the use of mathematical techniques for representing theories and examining issues related to economics. It employs mathematical principles and instruments for developing economic ideas and examines economic quandaries. Mathematics enables the formulation of meaningful, testable hypotheses about broad and complex topics that would be difficult to express informally. Furthermore, it enables the formation of positive and particular claims associated with debatable topics that are otherwise unattainable without the use of mathematics. This book aims to shed light on the applications of mathematical methods for finance and economics. It is a resource guide for experts as well as students.

This book was developed from a mere concept to drafts to chapters and finally compiled together as a complete text to benefit the readers across all nations. To ensure the quality of the content we instilled two significant steps in our procedure. The first was to appoint an editorial team that would verify the data and statistics provided in the book and also select the most appropriate and valuable contributions from the plentiful contributions we received from authors worldwide. The next step was to appoint an expert of the topic as the Editor-in-Chief, who would head the project and finally make the necessary amendments and modifications to make the text reader-friendly. I was then commissioned to examine all the material to present the topics in the most comprehensible and productive format.

I would like to take this opportunity to thank all the contributing authors who were supportive enough to contribute their time and knowledge to this project. I also wish to convey my regards to my family who have been extremely supportive during the entire project.

Editor

1

On History of Mathematical Economics: Application of Fractional Calculus

Vasily E. Tarasov

Skobeltsyn Institute of Nuclear Physics, Lomonosov Moscow State University, Moscow 119991, Russia; tarasov@theory.sinp.msu.ru

Abstract: Modern economics was born in the Marginal revolution and the Keynesian revolution. These revolutions led to the emergence of fundamental concepts and methods in economic theory, which allow the use of differential and integral calculus to describe economic phenomena, effects, and processes. At the present moment the new revolution, which can be called "Memory revolution", is actually taking place in modern economics. This revolution is intended to "cure amnesia" of modern economic theory, which is caused by the use of differential and integral operators of integer orders. In economics, the description of economic processes should take into account that the behavior of economic agents may depend on the history of previous changes in economy. The main mathematical tool designed to "cure amnesia" in economics is fractional calculus that is a theory of integrals, derivatives, sums, and differences of non-integer orders. This paper contains a brief review of the history of applications of fractional calculus in modern mathematical economics and economic theory. The first stage of the Memory Revolution in economics is associated with the works published in 1966 and 1980 by Clive W. J. Granger, who received the Nobel Memorial Prize in Economic Sciences in 2003. We divide the history of the application of fractional calculus in economics into the following five stages of development (approaches): ARFIMA; fractional Brownian motion; econophysics; deterministic chaos; mathematical economics. The modern stage (mathematical economics) of the Memory revolution is intended to include in the modern economic theory new economic concepts and notions that allow us to take into account the presence of memory in economic processes. The current stage actually absorbs the Granger approach based on ARFIMA models that used only the Granger–Joyeux–Hosking fractional differencing and integrating, which really are the well-known Grunwald–Letnikov fractional differences. The modern stage can also absorb other approaches by formulation of new economic notions, concepts, effects, phenomena, and principles. Some comments on possible future directions for development of the fractional mathematical economics are proposed.

Keywords: mathematical economics; economic theory; fractional calculus; fractional dynamics; long memory; non-locality

---

1. Introduction: General Remarks about Mathematical Economics

Mathematical economics is a theoretical and applied science, whose purpose is a mathematically formalized description of economic objects, processes, and phenomena. Most of the economic theories are presented in terms of economic models. In mathematical economics, the properties of these models are studied based on formalizations of economic concepts and notions. In mathematical economics, theorems on the existence of extreme values of certain parameters are proved, properties of equilibrium states and equilibrium growth trajectories are studied, etc. This creates the impression that the proof of the existence of a solution (optimal or equilibrium) and its calculation is the main aim of mathematical economics. In reality, the most important purpose is to formulate economic notions and concepts in mathematical form, which will be mathematically adequate and self-consistent, and then, on their basis to construct mathematical models of economic processes and phenomena. Moreover, it is not enough to prove the existence of a solution and find it in an analytic or numerical form, but it is necessary to give an economic interpretation of these obtained mathematical results.

We can say that modern mathematical economics began in the 19th century with the use of differential (and integral) calculus to describe and explain economic behavior. The emergence of modern economic theory occurred almost simultaneously with the appearance of new economic concepts, which were actively used in various economic models. "Marginal revolution" and "Keynesian revolution" in economics led to the introduction of the new fundamental concepts into economic theory, which allow the use of mathematical tools to describe economic phenomena and processes. The most important mathematical tools that have become actively used in mathematical modeling of economic processes are the theory of derivatives and integrals of integer orders, the theory of differential and difference equations. These mathematical tools allowed economists to build economic models in a mathematical form and on their basis to describe a wide range of economic processes and phenomena. However, these tools have a number of shortcomings that lead to the incompleteness of descriptions of economic processes. It is known that the integer-order derivatives of functions are determined by the properties of these functions in an infinitely small neighborhood of the point, in which the derivatives are considered. As a result, differential equations with derivatives of integer orders, which are used in economic models, cannot describe processes with memory and non-locality. In fact, such equations describe only economic processes, in which all economic agents have complete amnesia and interact only with the nearest neighbors. Obviously, this assumption about the lack of memory among economic agents is a strong restriction for economic models. As a result, these models have drawbacks, since they cannot take into account important aspects of economic processes and phenomena.

2. A Short History of Fractional Mathematical Economics

"Marginal revolution" and "Keynesian revolution" introduced fundamental economic concepts, including the concepts of "marginal value", "economic multiplier", "economic accelerator", "elasticity" and many others. These revolutions led to the use of mathematical tools based on the derivatives and integrals of integer orders, and the differential and difference equations. As a result, the economic models with continuous and discrete time began to be mathematically described by differential equations with derivatives of integer orders or difference equations of integer orders.

It can be said that at the present moment new revolutionary changes are actually taking place in modern economics. These changes can be called a revolution of memory and non-locality. It is becoming increasingly obvious in economics that when describing the behavior of economic agents, we must take into account that their behavior may depend on the history of previous changes in the economy. In economic theory, we need new economic concepts and notions that allow us to take into account the presence of memory in economic agents. New economic models and methods are needed, which take into account that economic agents may remember the changes of economic indicators and factors in the past, and that this affects the behavior of agents and their decision making. To describe this behavior we cannot use the standard mathematical apparatus of differential (or difference) equations of integer orders. In fact, these equations describe only such economic processes, in which agents actually have an amnesia. In other words, economic models, which use only derivatives of integer orders, can be applied when economic agents forget the history of changes of economic indicators and factors during an infinitesimally small period of time. At the moment it is becoming clear that this restriction holds back the development of economic theory and mathematical economics.

In modern mathematics, derivatives and integrals of arbitrary order are well known [1–5]. The derivative (or integral), order of which is a real or complex number and not just an integer, is called fractional derivative and integral. Fractional calculus as a theory of such operators has a long history [6–15]. There are different types of fractional integral and differential operators [1–5]. For fractional differential and integral operators, many standard properties are violated, including such properties as the standard product (Leibniz) rule, the standard chain rule, the semi-group property for orders of derivatives, the semi-group property for dynamic maps [16–21]. We can state that the violation of the standard form of the Leibniz rule is a characteristic property of derivatives of non-integer orders [16]. The most important application of fractional derivatives and integrals of non-integer order is fading memory and spatial non-locality.

The new revolution ("Memory revolution") is intended to include in the modern economic theory and mathematical economics different processes with long memory and non-locality. The main mathematical tool designed to "cure amnesia" in economics is the theory of derivatives and integrals of non-integer order (fractional calculus), fractional differential and difference equations [1–5]. This revolution has led to the emergence of a new branch of mathematical economics, which can be called "fractional mathematical economics."

Fractional mathematical economics is a theory of fractional dynamic models of economic processes, phenomena and effects. In this framework of mathematical economics, the fractional calculus methods are being developed for application to problems of economics and finance. The field of fractional mathematical economics is the application of fractional calculus to solve problems in economics (and finance) and for the development of fractional calculus for such applications. Fractional mathematical economics can be considered as a branch of applied mathematics that deals with economic problems. However, this point of view is obviously a narrowing of the field of research, goals and objectives of this area. An important part of fractional mathematical economics is the use of fractional calculus to formulate new economic concepts, notions, effects and phenomena. This is especially important due to the fact that the fractional mathematical economics is now only being formed as an independent science. Moreover, the development of the fractional calculus itself and its generalizations will largely be determined precisely by such goals and objectives in economics, physics and other sciences.

This "Memory revolution" in the economics, or rather the first stage of this revolution, can be associated with the works, which were published in 1966 and 1980 by Clive W. J. Granger [22–26], who received the Nobel Memorial Prize in Economic Sciences in 2003 [27].

The history of the application of fractional calculus in economics can be divided into the following stages of development (approaches): ARFIMA; fractional Brownian motion; econophysics; deterministic chaos; mathematical economics. The appearance of a new stage obviously does not mean the cessation of the development of the previous stage, just as the appearance of quantum theory did not stop the development of classical mechanics.

Further in Sections 2.1–2.5, we briefly describe these stages of development, and then in Section 3 we outline possible ways for the further development of fractional mathematical economics.

2.1. ARFIMA Stage (Approach)

ARFIMA Stage (Approach): This stage is characterized by models with discrete time and application of the Grunwald–Letnikov fractional differences.

More than fifty years ago, Clive W. J. Granger (see preprint [22], paper [23], the collection of the works [24,25]) was the first to point out long-term dependencies in economic data. The articles demonstrated that spectral densities derived from the economic time series have a similar shape. This fact allows us to say that the effect of long memory in the economic processes was found by Granger. Note that, he received the Nobel Memorial Prize in Economics in 2003 "for methods of analyzing economic time series with general trends (cointegration)" [27].

Then, Granger and Joyeux [26], and Hosking [28] proposed the fractional generalization of ARIMA(p,d,q) models (the ARFIMA (p,d,q) models) that improved the statistical methods for researching of processes with memory. As the main mathematical tool for describing memory, fractional differencing and integrating (for example, see books [29–34] and reviews [35–38]) were proposed for discrete time case. The suggested generalization of the ARIMA(p,d,q) model is realized by considering non-integer (positive and negative) order d instead of positive integer values of d. The Granger–Joyeux–Hosking (GJH) operators were proposed and used without relationship with the fractional calculus. As was proved in [39,40], these GJH operators are actually the Grunwald–Letnikov fractional differences (GLF-difference), which have been suggested more than a hundred and fifty years ago and are used in the modern fractional calculus [1,3]. We emphasize that in the continuous limit these GLF-differences give the GLF-derivatives that coincide with the Marchaud fractional derivatives (see Theorem 4.2 and Theorem 4.4 of [1]).

Among economists, the approach proposed by Gravers (and based on the discrete operators proposed by them) is the most common and is used without an explicit connection with the development of fractional calculus. It is obvious that the restriction of mathematical tools only to the Grunwald–Letnikov fractional differences significantly reduces the possibilities for studying processes with memory and non-locality. The use of fractional calculus in economic models will significantly expand the scope and allows us to obtain new results.

2.2. Fractional Brownian Motion (Mathematical Finance) Stage (Approach)

Fractional Brownian Motion Stage (Approach): This stage is characterized by financial models and the application of stochastic calculus methods and stochastic differential equations.

Andrey N. Kolmogorov, who is one of the founders of modern probability theory, was the first who considered in 1940 [41] the continuous Gaussian processes with stationary increments and with the self-similarity property A.N. Kolmogorov called such Gaussian processes "Wiener Spirals". Its modern name is the fractional Brownian motion that can be considered as a continuous self-similar zero-mean Gaussian process and with stationary increments.

Starting with the article by L.C.G. Rogers [42], various authors began to consider the use of fractional Brownian motion to describe different financial processes. The fractional Brownian motion is not a semi-martingale and the stochastic integral with respect to it is not well-defined in the classical Ito's sense. Therefore, this approach is connected with the development of fractional stochastic calculus [43–45]. For example, in the paper [43] a stochastic integration calculus for the fractional Brownian motion based on the Wick product was suggested.

At the present time, this stage (approach), which can be called as a fractional mathematical finance, is connected with the development of fractional stochastic calculus, the theory fractional stochastic differential equations and their application in finance. The fractional mathematical finance is a field of applied mathematics, concerned with mathematical modeling of financial markets by using the fractional stochastic differential equations.

As a special case of fractional mathematical finance, we can note the fractional generalization of the Black–Scholes pricing model. In 1973, Fischer Black and Myron Scholes [46] derived the famous theoretical valuation formula for options. In 1997, the Royal Swedish Academy of Sciences has decided to award the Bank of Sweden Prize in Economic Sciences in Memory of Alfred Nobel [47] to Myron S. Scholes, for the so-called Black–Scholes model published in 1973: "Robert C. Merton and Myron S. Scholes have, in collaboration with the late Fischer Black, developed a pioneering formula for the valuation of stock options." [47].)

For the first time a fractional generalization of the Black–Scholes equation was proposed in [48] by Walter Wyss in 2000. Wyss [48] considered the pricing of option derivatives by using the time-fractional Black–Scholes equation and derived a closed form solution for European vanilla options. The Black–Scholes equation is generalized by replacing the first derivative in time by a fractional derivative in time of the order $\alpha \in (0,1)$. The solution of this fractional Black–Scholes equation is considered. However, in the Wyss paper, there are no financial reasons to explain why a time-fractional derivative should be used.

The works of Cartea and Meyer-Brandis [49] and Cartea [50] proposed a stock price model that uses information about the waiting time between trades. In this model the arrival of trades is driven by a counting process, in which the waiting-time between trades processes is described by the Mittag–Leffler survival function (see also [51]). In the paper [50], Cartea proposed that the value of derivatives satisfies the fractional Black–Scholes equation that contains the Caputo fractional derivative with respect to time. It should be noted that, in general, the presence of a waiting time and a delay time does not mean the presence of memory in the process.

In the framework of the fractional Brownian motion Stage, a lot of papers [50–71] and books [72,73] were written on the description of financial processes with memory and non-locality.

As a rule, in fractional mathematical finance, fractional dynamic models are created without establishing links with economic theory and without formulating new economic or financial concepts, taking only observable market prices as input data. In the fractional mathematical finance, the main requirement is the mathematical consistency and the compatibility with economic theory is not the key point.

2.3. *Econophysics Stage (Approach)*

Econophysics Stage (Approach): This stage is characterized by financial models and the application of physical methods and equations.

Twenty years ago, a new branch of the econophysics, which is connected with the application of fractional calculus, has appeared. In fact, this branch, which can be called fractional econophysics, was born in 2000 and it can be primarily associated with the works of Francesco Mainardi, Rudolf Gorenflo, Enrico Scalas, Marco Raberto [74–76] on the continuous-time finance.

In fractional econophysics, the fractional diffusion models [74–76] are used in finance, where price jumps replace the particle jumps in the physical diffusion model. The corresponding stochastic models are called continuous time random walks (CTRWs), which are random walks that also incorporate a random waiting time between jumps. In finance, the waiting times measure delay between transactions. These two random variables (price change and waiting time) are used to describe the long-time behavior in financial markets. The diffusion (hydrodynamic) limit, which is used in physics, is considered for continuous time random walks [74–76]. It was shown that the probability density function for the limit process obeys a fractional diffusion equation [74–76].

After the pioneering works [74–76] that laid the foundation for the new direction of econophysics (fractional econophysics), various papers were written on the application of fractional dynamics methods and physical models to describe processes in finance and economics (for example, see [77–84]). The history and achievements of the econophysics stage in the first five years are described by Enrico Scalas in the article [85] in 2016.

The fractional econophysics, as a branch of econophysics, can be defined as a new direction of research applying methods developed in physical sciences, to describe processes in economics and finance, basically those including power-law memory and spatial non-locality. The mathematical tool of this branch of econophysics is the fractional calculus. For example, application to the study of continuous time finance by using methods and results of fractional kinetics and anomalous diffusion. Another example, which is not related to finance, is the time-dependent fractional dynamics with memory in quantum and economic physics [86].

In this stage, the fractional calculus was applied mainly to financial processes. In the papers on fractional econophysics, generalization of basic economic concepts and principles for economic processes with memory (and non-locality) are not suggested.

Unfortunately, economists do not always understand the analogies with the methods and concepts of modern physics, which restricts the possibilities for economists to use this approach. As a result, it holds back and limits both the development and application of the fractional econophysics approach to describing economic processes with memory and non-locality.

It can be said that the time has come for economists and econophysicists to work together on the formulation of economic analogs of physical concepts and methods used in fractional econophysics, and linking them with existing concepts and methods of economic theory. For the development of a fractional mathematical economics, a translation should be made from the language of physics into the language of economics.

2.4. Deterministic Chaos Stage (Approach)

Deterministic Chaos Stage (Approach): This stage is characterized by financial (and economic) models and application of methods of nonlinear dynamics. Strictly speaking, this approach should be attributed to the econophysics stage/approach.

Nonlinear dynamics models are useful to explain irregular and chaotic behavior of complex economic and financial processes. The complex behaviors of nonlinear economic processes restrict the use of analytical methods to study nonlinear economic models.

In 2008, for the first time, Wei-Ching Chen proposed in [87] a fractional generalization of a financial model with deterministic chaos. Chen [87] studied the fractional-dynamic behaviors and describes fixed points, periodic motions, chaotic motions, and identified period doubling and intermittency routes to chaos in the financial process that is described by a system of three equations with the Caputo fractional derivatives. He demonstrates by numerical simulations that chaos exists when orders of derivatives are less than three and that the lowest order at which chaos exists was 2.35. The work [88] studied the chaos control method of such a kind of system by feedback control, respectively.

In the framework of the deterministic chaos stage, many papers [89–99] have been devoted to the description of financial processes with memory. In some papers [100–105], economic models were considered.

We should note that the various stages/approaches of development of fractional mathematical economics did not develop in complete isolation from each other. For example, for the fractional Chen model of dynamic chaos in the economy, Tomáš Škovránek, Igor Podlubny, Ivo Petráš [106] applied the concept of the state space (the configuration space, the phase space) that arose in physics more than a hundred years ago. As state variables authors consider the gross domestic product, inflation, and unemployment rate. The dynamics of the modeled economy in time, which is represented by the values of these three variables, is described as a trajectory in state-space. The system of three fractional order differential equations is used to describe dynamics of the economy by fitting the available economic data. Then *José* A. Tenreiro Machado, Maria E. Mata, Antonio M. Lopes suggested the development of the state space concept in the papers [107–109]. The economic growth is described by using the multidimensional scaling (MDS) method for visualizing information in data. The state space is used to represent the sequence of points (the fractional state space portrait, FSSP, and pseudo phase plane, PPP) corresponding to the states over time.

2.5. Mathematical Economics Stage (Approach)

Mathematical Economics Stage (Approach): This stage is characterized by macroeconomic and microeconomic models with continuous time and generalization of basic economic concepts and notions.

The fractional calculus approach has been used to describe the concept of memory itself for economic processes in [39,40,110–117], and to define basic concepts of economic processes with memory and non-locality in works [118–139].

From a subjective point of view, this stage began with a proposal of generalizations of the basic economic concepts and notions at the beginning of 2016, when the concept of elasticity for economic processes with memory was proposed [132–135]. Then in 2016, the concepts of the marginal values with memory [118–120], the concept of accelerator and multiplier with memory [123,130] and others were suggested [132–136,138]. These concepts are used in fractional generalizations of some standard economic models [140–167] with the continuous time, which were proposed in 2016 and subsequent years [168–189]. These dynamic models describe fractional dynamics of economic processes with memory.

The fractional calculus approach has been used to define basic concepts of economic processes with memory in works [118–139], and to describe dynamics of economic processes with memory [168–189] in the framework of the continuous time models.

It should be noted that formal replacements of derivatives of integer order by fractional derivatives in standard differential equations, which describe economic processes, and solutions of the obtained fractional differential equations were considered in papers published before 2016. However, these papers were purely mathematical works, in which generalizations of economic concepts and notions were not proposed. In these works, fractional differential equations have not been derived, since a formal replacement of integer-order derivatives by fractional derivatives cannot be recognized as a derivation of the equations. Formulations of economic conclusions and interpretations from the obtained solutions are not usually suggested in these papers. Examples of incorrectness and errors in such generalizations are given in the work [189]. In the paper [189], we formulate five principles of the fractional-dynamic generalization of standard dynamic models and then we illustrate these principles by examples from fractional mathematical economics. We can state that in the works with formal fractional generalizations of standard economic equations the Principles of Derivability and Interpretability [189] were neglected. Let us give a brief formulation of the Principles of Derivability and Interpretability.

Derivability Principle: It is not enough to generalize the differential equations describing the dynamic model. It is necessary to generalize the whole scheme of obtaining (all steps of derivation) these equations from the basic principles, concepts and assumptions. In this sequential derivation of the equations we should take into account the non-standard characteristic properties of fractional derivatives and integrals. If necessary, generalizations of the notions, concepts and methods, which are used in this derivation, should also be obtained.

Interpretability Principle: The subject (physical, economic) interpretation of the mathematical results, including solutions and their properties, should be obtained. Differences, and first of all qualitative differences, from the results based on the standard model should be described.

The most important purpose of the modern stage of development of fractional mathematical economics is the inclusion of memory and non-locality into the economic theory, into the basic economic concepts and methods. The economics should be extended and generalized such that it takes into account the memory and non-locality. Fractional generalizations of standard economic models should be constructed only on this conceptual basis. The most important purpose of studying such generalizations is the search and formulation of qualitatively new effects and phenomena caused by memory and non-locality in the behavior of economic processes. In this case, these results in mathematical economics, which are based on fractional calculus, can be further used in computer simulations of real economic processes and in econometric studies.

Let us list some generalizations of economic concepts and fractional generalizations of economic models that have already been proposed in recent years. Using the fractional calculus approach to describe the processes with memory and non-locality, the generalizations of some basic economic notions were proposed in the works [118–139]. The list of these new notions and concepts primarily include the following:

- The marginal value of non-integer order [118–122,190] with memory and non-locality;
- The economic multiplier with memory [123,124];
- The economic accelerator with memory [123,124];
- The exact discretization of economic accelarators and multiplier [125–128] based on exact fractional differences [129];
- The accelerator with memory and crisis periodic sharp bursts [130,131];
- The duality of the multiplier with memory and the accelerator with memory [123,124];
- The elasticity of fractional order [132–135] for processes with memory and non-locality;
- The measures of risk aversion with non-locality [136] and with memory [137];
- The warranted (technological) rate of growth with memory [112,170,174–176,189];
- The non-local methods of deterministic factor analysis for [138,139];

And some other.

The use of these notions and concepts makes it possible for us to generalize some classical economic models, including those proposed by the following well-known economists:

- Henry Roy F. Harrod [140–142] and Evsey D. Domar, [143,144];
- John M. Keynes [145–148];
- Wassily W. Leontief [149,150];
- Alban W.H. Phillips [151,152];
- Roy G.D. Allen [153–156];
- Robert M. Solow [157,158] and Trevor W. Swan [159];
- Nicholas Kaldor [160–162];

And other scientists.

Valentiva V. Tarasova and the author built various economic models with power-law memory, which are generalizations of the classical models. For example, the following economic models have been proposed.

- The natural growth model [168,169];
- The growth model with constant pace [170,171];
- The Harrod–Domar model [172,173] and [112,174–176];
- The Keynes model [177–179];
- The dynamic Leontief (intersectoral) model [86,180–182];
- The dynamics of fixed assets (or capital stock) [170,171];
- The logistic growth model with memory [183,189];
- The model of logistic growth with memory and crises [183];
- The time-dependent dynamic intersectoral model with memory [86,182];
- The Phillips model with memory and lag [185];
- The Harrod–Domar growth model with memory and distributed lag [186];
- The dynamic Keynesian model with memory and lag [187];
- The model of productivity with fatigue and memory [188];
- The Solow–Swan model [189];
- The Kaldor-type model of business cycles (the Van der Pol model) [189];

And some other economic models.

Let us also note works, in which fractional dynamic generalizations of economic models were proposed without introducing new economic notions and concepts.

(1) Michele Caputo proposed some fractional dynamic model of economy [191–200]:

    - In the standard relaxation equation, which describes the relaxation economy to equilibrium, the memory has been introduced in the reactivity of investment to the interest rate.
    - The continuous-time IS–LM model with memory [192];
    - The tax version of the Fisher model with memory for stock prices and inflation rates [199] that can be used to predict nominal and real interest rate behavior with memory.

(2) Mathematical description of some fractional generalization of economic models was proposed by the Kabardino–Balkarian group: Adam M. Nakhushev [201,202], Khamidbi Kh. Kalazhokov [203], Zarema A. Nakhusheva [204].

(3) Mathematical description of some fractional generalization of economic models were proposed by the Kamchatka group: Viktoriya V. Samuta, Viktoriya A. Strelova, and Roman I. Parovik [205], Yana E. Shpilko, Anastasiya E. Solomko., Roman I. Parovik [206] Danil M. Makarov [207].

(4) Shiou-Yen Chu and Christopher Shane proposed the hybrid Phillips curve model with memory to describe the dynamic process of inflation with memory in the work [208].

(5) Rituparna Pakhira, Uttam Ghosh and Susmita Sarkar derived [209–213] some inventory models with memory.
(6) Computer simulation for modeling the national economies in the framework of the fractional generalizations of the Gross domestic product (GDP) model was proposed by Inés Tejado, Duarte Valério, Nuno Valério, Pedro Pires [214–220] in 2014–2019, and by Dahui Luo, JinRong Wang, Michal Feckan in 2018 in the paper [221].
(7) In addition, we may note the works with economic models that were proposed in [100–105] that are related to the deterministic chaos stage.

Let us note that the problems and difficulties arising in the construction of fractional-dynamic analogs of standard economic models by using the fractional calculus are described in [189] with details.

Some of proposed models can be considered as econophysics approach, which are based on fractional generalization of the standard damped harmonic oscillator equation, where the memory has been introduced in the frictional term by using fractional derivative instead of first-orderr derivative.

New principles, effects and phenomena have been suggested for fractional economic dynamics with memory and non-locality (for example, see [174–176,189,222]). Qualitatively new effects due to the presence of memory in the economic process are described in the works [174–176,189,222].

In my opinion, this stage of the development of fractional mathematical economics actually includes (absorbs) approaches based on the ARFIMA model using only the Granger–Joyeux–Hosking fractional differencing and integrating, which in really are the well-known Grunwald–Letnikov fractional differences [39]. This opinion is based on the obvious fact that the new stage allows the AFRIMA approach to go beyond the restrictions of the Grunwald–Letnikov operators, and use different types of fractional finite differences and fractional derivatives of non-integer orders.

Moreover, this stage can include (absorbs) approaches based on the fractional econophysics and deterministic chaos. For the econophysics approach, new opportunities are opening up on the way to formulating economic analogues of physical concepts and notions that will be more understandable to economists. This will significantly simplify the implementation of the concepts and methods of fractional econophysics in economic theory and application.

The most important element in the construction of the fractional mathematical economics as a new theory is the emergence and the formation of new notions, concepts, effects, phenomena, principles and methods, which are specific only to this theory. This gives rise to a new scientific direction (the fractional mathematical economics), since there is something of their own that others do not have.

We have now entered the stage of forming a new direction in mathematical economics and economic theory, when concepts and methods are not borrowed from other sciences and areas, but their own are created.

3. New Future Stages and Approaches

There is a natural question. What stages and approaches will appear and develop in the future? In this section we propose some assumptions about the future use of fractional calculus in economics and discuss the direction of development of fractional mathematical economics.

3.1. Self-Organization in Fractional Economic Dynamics

Self-organization processes play an important role in both the natural and social sciences. In the description of self-organization in economic (and social) processes, it is necessary to abandon the assumption that all economic agents suffer from amnesia. They should be considered as agents with memory that interact with each other. We can consider self-organization with memory [222] in economics and social sciences. Therefore, the fractional mathematical economics and economic theory can be developed by considering the generalization of different economic models of self-organization that are described in the books [223–225].

3.2. *Distributed Lag Fractional Calculus*

The continuously distributed lag has been considered in economics starting with the works of Michal A. Kalecki [163] and Alban W.H. Phillips [151,152]. The continuous uniform distribution of delay time is considered by M.A. Kalecki in 1935 [163], (see also Section 8.4 of [154], (pp. 251–254)) for dynamic models of business cycles. The continuously distributed lag with the exponential distribution of delay time is considered by A.W.H. Phillips [151,152] in 1954. In the Phillips growth models, generalization of the economic concepts of accelerator and multipliers were proposed by taking into account the distributed lag. The operators with continuously distributed lag were considered by Roy G.D. Allen [153,154], (pp. 23–29), in 1956. Currently, economic models with delay are actively used to describe the processes in the economy.

The time delay is caused by finite speeds of processes and therefore it cannot be considered as processes with long memory (for some details about concept of memory, see Section 3.12 of this paper and [29–35,112,113,116,117]). For example, in physics the propagation of the electromagnetic field with finite speed in a vacuum does not mean the presence of memory in this process. In economics and electrodynamics, processes with time delay (lag) are not referred to as processes with memory and effects of time delay are not interpreted as a memory.

Note that the operators with exponentially distributed lag, which were defined in the works of Caputo and Fabrizio [226,227], cannot be interpreted as fractional derivatives of non-integer orders and cannot describe processes with memory. Note that exponential distribution is the continuous analogue of the geometric distribution that has the key property of being memoryless. The Caputo–Fabrizio operators are integer-order derivatives with the exponentially distributed delay time [228]. The fractional generalizations of the Caputo–Fabrizio operator are proposed in [185–187,228].

The distributed lag fractional calculus was proposed by the author and Svetlana S. Tarasova in [228]. To take into account the memory and lag in economic and physical models, the fractional differential and integral operators with continuously distributed lag (time delay) were proposed in [228]. The distributed lag fractional operators are compositions of fractional differentiation or integration and continuously distributed translation (shift). The kernels of these operators are the Laplace convolution of probability density function and the kernels of fractional derivatives or integrals. The random variable is the delay time that is distributed by probability law (distribution) on positive semiaxis. Examples of economic application of the lag-distributed fractional operators have been suggested in the works [185–187], where the economic concepts of accelerator and multipliers with distributed lag and memory were proposed.

3.3. *Distributed Order Fractional Calculus*

In general, the order parameter α, which can be interpreted as the parameter of memory fading [112,113], can be distributed on the interval $[\alpha_1, \alpha_2]$, where the distribution is described by a weight function $\rho(\alpha)$. The functions $\varrho(\alpha)$ describes distribution of the parameter of the memory fading on a set of economic agents. This is important for the economics, since various types of economic agents may have different parameters of memory fading. In this case, we should consider the fractional operators, which depends on the weight function $\rho(\alpha)$ and the interval $[\alpha_1, \alpha_2]$.

The concept of the integrals and derivatives with distributed orders was first proposed by Michele Caputo in [229] in 1995, and then these operators are applied and developed in different works (for example see [230–234]).

Let us note the following three cases.

(1) The simplest distribution of the order of fractional derivatives and integrals is the continuous uniform distribution. The fractional operators with uniform distribution were proposed in [112, 113,129] and were called as the Nakhushev operators. Adam M. Nakhushev [235,236] proposed the continual fractional derivatives and integrals in 1998. The fractional operators, which are inversed to the continual fractional derivatives and integrals, were suggested by Arsen V.

Pskhu [237,238]. In papers [112,113,129], we proved that the fractional integrals and derivatives of the uniform distributed order could be expressed (up to a numerical factor) through the continual fractional integrals and derivatives, which have been suggested by A. M. Nakhushev [235,236]. The proposed fractional integral and derivatives of uniform distributed order have been called in our paper [129] as the Nakhushev fractional integrals and derivatives. The corresponding inverse operators, which contains the two-parameter Mittag–Leffler functions in the kernel, were called as the Pskhu fractional integrals and derivatives [129].

(2) In the papers [112,113], we proposed the concept of "weak" memory and the distributed order fractional operators with the truncated normal distribution of the order. The truncated normal distribution with integer mean and small variance can be used to describe economic processes with memory, which is distributed around the classical case.

(3) As a special case of the general fractional operators, which were proposed by Anatoly N. Kochubei, the fractional derivatives and integrals of distributed order are investigated in the works [239,240].

Fractional differential equations of distributed orders are actively used to describe physical processes. However, at the present time, equations with distributed order operators have not yet been used to describe economic processes. We hope that new interesting effects in economics can be described by using order-distributed fractional operators.

3.4. *Generalized Fractional Calculus in Economics*

Generalized fractional calculus was proposed by Virginia Kiryakova and described in detail in the book [2] in 1994. The brief history of the generalized fractional calculus is given in the paper [10]. Operators of generalized fractional calculus [2,10] can be use to describe complex processes with memory and non-locality in real economy. In the application of the generalized fractional operators, an important question arises about the correct economic (and physical) interpretation of these operators. It is important to emphasize that not all fractional operators can describe the processes with memory. It is important to clearly understand what type of phenomena can be described by a given operator. For example, among these types of phenomena, in addition to memory, we can specify the time delay (lag) and the scaling. Let us give a few examples to clarify this problem.

Example 1. The Abel-type fractional integral (and differential) operator with Kummer function in the kernel, which is described in the classic book [1] (see equation 37.1 in [1], (p. 731)) can be interpreted as the Riemann–Liouville fractional integral (and derivatives) with gamma distribution of delay time [187,228]. Some Prabhakar fractional operators with the three-parameter Mittag–Leffler functions in the kernel can also be interpreted as a Laplace convolution of the Riemann–Liouville (or Caputo) fractional operators with continuously distributed lag (time delay) [186,228].

Example 2. We can state that the Kober fractional integration of non-integer order [1,2,4] can be interpreted as an expected value of a random variable up to a constant factor [241] (see also Section 9 in [228]). In this interpretation, the random variable describes dilation (scaling), which has the gamma distribution. The Erdelyi–Kober fractional integration also has a probabilistic interpretation. Fractional differential operators of Kober and the Erdelyi–Kober type have analogous probabilistic interpretation, i.e., these operators cannot describe the memory. These operators describe integer-order operator with continuously distributed dilation (scaling). The fractional generalizations of the Kober and Erdelyi–Kober operators, which can be used to describe memory and distributed dilation (scaling), were proposed in [228].

Example 3. The Riesz fractional integro-differentiation (See Section 2.10 of [4]) cannot be used to describe memory since this operator violates the causality principle, if it is written in the standard form. For economic and physical processes with memory, the causality can be described by the

Kramers–Kronig relations [116]. The Riesz fractional integro-differentiation can be used to describe power-law non-locality and power-law spatial dispersion.

Therefore, an important part of the application of generalized fractional calculus is a clear understanding of what types of processes and phenomena can describe fractional operators of non-integer order.

3.5. General Fractional Calculus

The concept of general fractional calculus was suggested by Anatoly N. Kochubei [239,240] by using the differential-convolution operators. The works [239,240] describe the conditions under which the general operator has a right inverse (a kind of a fractional integral) and produce, as a kind of a fractional derivative, equations of evolution type. A solution of the relaxation equations with the Kochubei general fractional derivative with respect to the time variable is described [239]. In the works [239,240] the Cauchy problem (A) is considered for the relaxation equation $\left(D_{(k)}X\right)(t) = \lambda X(t)$, where $\lambda < 0$. This Cauchy problem has a solution $X(\lambda, t)$, which is continuous on $\mathbb{R}_{+}$, infinitely differentiable and completely monotone on $\mathbb{R}_{+}$, if the Kochubei conditions (*) are satisfied.

In the economics, various growth models are used to describe real processes in economy. Therefore, it is very important to describe conditions, for which the Cauchy problem (A) for the growth equation $\left(D_{(k)}X\right)(t) = \lambda X(t)$, where $\lambda > 0$, has a solution $X(\lambda, t)$.

The growth equation is considered in [242] for the special case of a distributed order derivative, where it was proved that a smooth solution exists and is monotone increasing. In addition, the solution of the growth equation has been proposed for the case of fractional differential operators with distributed lag in [185–187,228]. The existence of a solution in the growth case has been also proved in 2018 by Chung-Sik Sin [243] for nonlinear equation with a generalized derivative like the Kochubei fractional derivative. The growth equation for physics is discussed in [244].

Solving the problem in the general case will allow us to accurately describe the conditions on the operator kernels (the memory functions), under which equations for models of economic growth with memory have solutions. A paper dedicated to solving this mathematical problem was written by Anatoly N. Kochubei and Yuri Kondratiev [245] in 2019 for the Special Issue "Mathematical Economics: Application of Fractional Calculus" of Mathematics. The application of these mathematical results in economics and their economic interpretation is an open question at the moment.

To understand the warranted (technological) growth rate of the economy, it is important to obtain the asymptotic behavior for solutions of the general growth equation.

In the application of the general fractional operators, it is also important to have correct economic and physical interpretations that will connect the types of operator kernels with the types of phenomena. For example, it is obvious that the kernels of general fractional operators satisfying the normalization condition will describe distributed delays in time (lag), and not memory.

3.6. Partial Differential Equations in Economics

Usually the mathematical formulation of macroeconomic models is reduced to systems of difference equations or ordinary differential equations that describe the dynamics of a relatively small number of macroeconomic aggregates. However, it is known that, in macroeconomics, partial differential equations (PDEs) naturally arise, and they are used in macroeconomics [246,247]. Accounting for non-locality (for example, a power type) in the state space leads us to the necessity of using fractional partial differential equations.

3.7. Fractional Variational Calculus in Economics

In mathematical economics, theorems on the existence of extreme values of certain parameters are proved, the properties of equilibrium points and equilibrium growth trajectories are actively studied. The existence of optimal solutions for fractional differential equations should be considered for economic processes with memory and non-locality.

Methods of the fractional calculus of variations are actively developing [248,249]. However, at the present time, none of the variational problems, which are well known in economics, has been generalized to the case of processes with memory using fractional calculus.

In the variation approach, there are some problems that restrict the possibilities of its application. One of the problems associated with the property of integration in parts, which actually turns the left-second fractional derivative into a right-sided derivative. As a result, we will obtain equations in which, in addition to being dependent on the past, there is a dependence on the future, that is, the principle of causality is violated.

We assume that this problem cannot be solved within the framework of using the principle of stationarity of the holonomic functional (action). It is necessary to use non-holonomic functionals. We can also consider non-holonomic constraints with fractional derivatives of non-integer orders [250]. We can also consider variations of non-integer order [251] and fractional variational derivatives [252].

Another problem is the mathematical interpretation and the economic (and physical) interpretations of extreme values. The non-holonomic constraints and variations of fractional orders should also have a correct economic (and physical) interpretation.

However, we emphasize that for the economics, finding the optimality and stability of the solution is very important.

3.8. Fractional Differential Games in Economics

Models of differential games in which derivatives of non-integer orders are used and, thereby, the power-fading memory is taken into account were proposed in the works of Arkadiy A. Chikriy (Arkadii Chikrii), Ivan I. Matychyn and Alexander G. Chentsov [253–257] (see also [258–260]), which are clearly not related to economy. Note that the construction of models of economic behavior, using differential games with power memory, instead of games with full memory, currently remains an open question. The construction of such models requires further research on economic behavior within the framework of game theory. The basis for such constructions can be the methods and results described in [253–260].

3.9. Economic Data and Fractional Calculus in Economic Modelling

We note the importance of using fractional calculus in computer simulations and modeling of real economic data, including data related to both macroeconomics and microeconomics.

The first works that can be attributed to the mathematical economics stage/approach are works published in 2014–2016 by Inés Tejado, Duarte Valério, Nuno Valério, [214–216]. An application of fractional calculus for modeling the national economies in the framework of the fractional generalizations of the Gross domestic product (GDP) model, which are described by the fractional differential equations are used, were considered by Inés Tejado, Duarte Valério, Nuno Valério, Pedro Pires [214–220] in 2014–2019, and by Dahui Luo, JinRong Wang, Michal Feckan in 2018 in the paper [221]. The fractional differential equation used in the fractional GDP model was obtained by replacing first-order derivatives with fractional derivatives. Therefore, this model requires theoretical justification and consistent derivivation.

To describe the real economic processes in the framework of fractional dynamic models, it is necessary to combine theoretical constructions and computer modeling.

3.10. Big Data

It is obvious that Big Data that describes behavior of peoples and other economic agents should contain information that can be considered as "Traces of People's Memory". It would be strange if these Big Data neglected memory, since people have memory if they don't suffer from amnesia. We can assume that economic modeling in the era of Big Data will describe the memory effects in microeconomics and macroeconomics. The Big Data will give us a possibility to take into account the effects of memory and non-locality in those economic and financial processes in which they were not even suspected.

3.11. Fractional Econometrics

Economic theory is a branch of economics that employs mathematical models and abstractions of economic processes and objects to rationalize, explain and predict economic phenomena.

One of the main goals of economic theory and mathematical economics is to explain the processes and phenomena in economy and make predictions. To achieve this goal, within the framework of economic theory and mathematical economics, new notions, concepts, tools and methods should be developed for describing and interpreting economic processes with memory and non-locality. Obviously, it is impossible to explain an economy with memory without having adequate concepts.

Economic theory and mathematical economics are branches of economics in which the creation of concepts and theoretical (primarily mathematical) models of phenomena and their comparison with reality is used as the main method of understanding economy. Economic theory is a separate way of studying economy, although its content is naturally formed taking into account the observations of economy. The methodology of economic theory consists in constructing main economic concepts; in formulating (in mathematical language) the principles and laws of economics connecting these concepts; in explaining observable economic phenomena and effects by using the formulated concepts and laws; in predicting new phenomena that may be discovered.

Mathematical economics, when viewed in a narrow sense as a branch of mathematics, is reduced only to the study of the properties of economic models at the mathematical level of rigor. In this approach, mathematical economics is often denied in the choice of economic concepts, interpretation and comparison of models with economic reality. For fractional mathematical economics, to describe processes with memory this view is erroneous. Obviously, it is impossible to explain economic processes with memory without having adequate concepts, since many standard concepts are not applicable.

Now the economics is undergoing a new revolution, "Memory revolution". A mathematic tool in the revolution is a new mathematics (fractional calculus), which was not previously used in mathematical economics. As a result, the present stage is a stage of the formation of new concepts and methods. In this stage, the mathematical economics cannot be isolated from the process of formation of new concepts and methods. Non-standard properties of fractional operators should be reflected in new economic concepts that take into account memory effects. Economic theory and mathematical economics can explain and predict processes with memory in real economy only if they create a solid foundation of new adequate economic concepts and principles.

To explain and predict the processes and phenomena with memory in economy, we must have a good instrument for conducting observations and their adequate description. This instrument is econometrics, or rather fractional econometrics. Econometrics is a link that connects economic theory and mathematical economics with the phenomena and processes in real economy.

Econometrics mainly based on statistics for formulating and testing models and hypotheses about economic processes or estimating parameters for them. Theoretical econometrics considers the statistical properties of assessments and tests, while applied econometrics deals with the use of econometric methods for evaluating economic models. Theoretical econometrics develops tools and methods, and also studies the properties of econometric methods. Applied econometrics uses theoretical econometrics and economic data to evaluate economic theories, develop econometric models, analyzing economic dynamics, and forecasting.

Fractional econometrics is based on statistics of long-memory processes [29–32]. Currently, fractional econometrics methods are actually related to ARFIMA models and the well-known Grunwald–Letnikov fractional differences in the form of the Granger–Joyeux–Hosking fractional differencing and integrating.

Fractional econometrics can reach new opportunities in the development of new econometric methods and their use in describing economic reality by applying methods of modern fractional calculus, various types of fractional finite differences, differential and integral operators of non-integer order.

As a result, we can state that the main goals of fractional economics such as explain the economy and to make predictions for processes with memory, and correctly describe economic events, data, processes, and to give adequate predictions, we should have fractional econometrics.

One of the main goals of fractional mathematical economics and economic theory is to explain the processes and phenomena with memory in economy and make predictions. However, to explain the economic processes with memory, it is necessary to understand what memory is and how to describe it. Note that a clear understanding of the memory does not even exist within the framework of fractional calculus approach.

3.12. Development Concept of Memory

Further development of the concept of memory for economic processes in the framework of fractional calculus is of great importance. It should be emphasized that not all types of fractional derivatives and integrals of non-integer order can describe processes with memory. The concept of memory itself for economic processes is discussed in [29–35], and [39,40,110–117]. One of the possible criteria of memory proposed in the work [116]. Let us give some comments about memory concept.

From mathematical point of view, economic models may be classified as stochastic or deterministic and as discrete or continuous. For simplification, let us consider the deterministic approach with continuous time. In this case, memory can be defined as a property of the process, when there exists at least one endogenous variable $Y(t)$, and an associated exogenous (or endogenous) variable $X(t)$, such that the variable $Y(t)$ at the time $t > t_0$ depends on the history of the change of $X(\tau)$ on the interval $\tau \in (t_0, t)$. However, not all such dependencies are due to the memory effect.

To describe processes with memory, this dependence of one variable on another should satisfy the causality principle. For economic and physical processes with memory, the causality can be described by the Kramers–Kronig relations [116].

An important property of memory is described by the principle of memory fading that was proposed by Ludwig Boltzmann in 1874 and 1876. Then, it was significantly developed by Vito Volterra in 1928 and 1930. The principle of memory fading states that the increasing of the time interval leads to a decrease in the corresponding contribution to the variable $Y(t)$.

Note that in physics the concept of fading memory assumes a set of stronger restrictions on memory. For example, it is often assumed that the memory is described by functions, which tends to zero monotonically with increasing the time variable. In this form, the principle of fading memory assumes that it is less probable to expect strengthening of the memory with respect to the more distant events. However, in some economic processes, it should be taken into account that the economic agents may remember sharp and significant changes of the exogenous variable $X(\tau)$, despite the fact that these changes were a more distant past compared to weaker changes in the near past. For this reason, in economics we can use memory functions that are not monotonic decrease.

For a simple case, we can consider the dependence in the form

$$Y(t) = \int_{t_0}^{t} M(t,\tau) X(\tau) d\tau,$$

where the kernel $M(t,\tau)$ of this integral operator is called the memory function (or the linear response function). Obviously, the derivative of the integer orders of some variable can be considered as an associated variable $X(\tau)$. We also can consider integer-order derivatives of $Y(t)$ as endogenous variables.

It is obvious that not every kernels $M(t,\tau)$ can be used to describe the memory in the economic processes. Possible restrictions on the memory function are discussed in paper [112,113].

In this paper [112,113], we describe some general restrictions that can be imposed on the structure and properties of memory. In addition, to the causality principle [116], these restrictions include the following three principles:

- The principle of fading memory;
- The principle of memory homogeneity on time (the principle of non-aging memory);
- The principle of memory reversibility (the principle of memory recovery).

Mathematically, the principle of non-aging memory means that the memory function has a property $M(t,\tau) = M(t-\tau)$. In this case, the integral operator can be described by the convolution $Y(t) = (M * X)(t)$, [112,113].

The principle of memory reversibility is connected with the principle of duality of accelerator with memory and multiplier with memory, which is proposed in [123,124]. In general, fractional calculus, which was proposed in [239,240] and based on the use of differential-convolution operators, the principle of memory reversibility means that the general operators should have a right inverse (a kind of a fractional integral).

Note that the Kober and Erdelyi–Kober fractional operators, which are interpreted in [112,113] as operators that describe memory with generalized power-law fading, really are integer-order operators with continuously distributed scaling or dilation (see [241] and Section 9 in [228]), and therefore, these operators cannot describe the memory.

Note that time delay, which is sometimes interpreted as a complete (perfect, ideal) memory [112, 113], cannot describe memory. In economics and electrodynamics, processes with time delay (lag) are not referred to as processes with memory and time delay is not interpreted as a memory. The interpretation of the time delay, which is usually called a lag in economics, as some kind of memory seems to be incorrect for the following reasons.

From economic and physical points of view, the time delay is caused by finite speeds of processes, i.e., the change of one variable does not lead to instant changes of another variable. Therefore, the time delay cannot be considered as memory in processes. This fact is well-known in physics as the retarded potential of an electromagnetic field, when a change in the electromagnetic field at the observation point is delayed with respect to the change in the sources of the field located at another point. The processes of propagation of the electromagnetic field in a vacuum are not interpreted in physics as presence of memory in these processes.

From a mathematical point of view, the kernels of integral operators for distributed time delay (lag) and fading memory are distinguished by the fact that the normalization condition holds for the time delay case. Note that the probability distribution functions as kernels, which are usually called the weighting function in economics, are actively used for macroeconomic models with distributed delay time. Equivalent differential equations of integer orders in economics are usually used instead of equations with integro-differential operators, in which the weighting function in the kernels. It is known that under certain conditions, equations with continuously distributed lag are equivalent to differential equations with standard derivatives of integer orders. Mathematically, this means that processes with time delay can be described by equations containing only a finite number of derivatives of integer orders. The integer-order derivatives of functions are determined by the properties of these functions in small neighborhood of the considered point. As a result, differential equations of integer orders cannot describe a memory. To describe processes with fading memory and distributed time delay, we should use the distributed lag fractional calculus [228], (see also [185–187]).

As a result, within the framework of fractional calculus, it is necessary to distinguish between fractional operators that describe distributed time delay and distributed scaling from operators describing memory, and the combination of memory with these phenomena. However, there are open questions about what types of memory we can describe by using fractional calculus (for example, see [116,117]), and in what directions the concept of memory for economic processes will develop.

4. Conclusions

In this brief historical description, an attempt was made to draw a sketch picture of the development of fractional calculus applications in economics, the birth of a new direction in mathematical economics, a new revolution in economic theory. Due to brevity and schematics, this picture obviously cannot reflect the fullness and complexity of the development of a fractional mathematical economics. As a result, it was possible that some directions and approaches, results and works close in the described history were missed. One can hope that the written short history will be perceived with understanding and will be supplemented in the future with new works on the history of the use of fractional calculus in the economics.

We can hope that the further development of the use of fractional calculus to describe economic phenomena and processes will take an important place with modern mathematical economics and economic theory. Generally speaking, it is strange to neglect memory in the economics, since the most important actors are people with memory.

References

1. Samko, S.G.; Kilbas, A.A.; Marichev, O.I. *Fractional Integrals and Derivatives Theory and Applications*; Gordon and Breach: New York, NY, USA, 1993; 1006p, ISBN 9782881248641.
2. Kiryakova, V. *Generalized Fractional Calculus and Applications*; Longman and John Wiley: New York, NY, USA, 1994; 360p, ISBN 9780582219779.
3. Podlubny, I. *Fractional Differential Equations*; Academic Press: San Diego, CA, USA, 1998; 340p.
4. Kilbas, A.A.; Srivastava, H.M.; Trujillo, J.J. *Theory and Applications of Fractional Differential Equations*; Elsevier: Amsterdam, The Netherlands, 2006; 540p.
5. Diethelm, K. *The Analysis of Fractional Differential Equations: An Application-Oriented Exposition Using Differential Operators of Caputo Type*; Springer: Berlin, Germany, 2010; 247p.
6. Letnikov, A.V. On the historical development of the theory of differentiation with arbitrary index. *Math. Collect.* **1868**, *3*, 85–112. (In Russian)
7. Ross, B. A brief history and exposition of the fundamental theory of fractional calculus. In *Fractional Calculus and Its Applications. Proceedings of the International Conference Held at the University of New Haven, June 1974*; Series: Lecture Notes in Mathematics; Springer: Berlin/Heidelberg, Germany, 1975; Volume 457, pp. 1–36. [CrossRef]
8. Ross, B. The development of fractional calculus 1695–1900. *Hist. Math.* **1977**, *4*, 75–89. [CrossRef]
9. Ross, B. Fractional Calculus. *Math. Mag.* **1977**, *50*, 115–122. [CrossRef]
10. Kiryakova, V. A brief story about the operators of the generalized fractional calculus. *Fract. Calc. Appl. Anal.* **2008**, *11*, 203–220.
11. Tenreiro Machado, J.; Kiryakova, V.; Mainardi, F. Recent history of fractional calculus. *Commun. Nonlinear Sci. Numer. Simul.* **2011**, *16*, 1140–1153. [CrossRef]
12. Tenreiro Machado, J.A.; Galhano, A.M.; Trujillo, J.J. Science metrics on fractional calculus development since 1966. *Fract. Calc. Appl. Anal.* **2013**, *16*, 479–500. [CrossRef]
13. Tenreiro Machado, J.A.; Galhano, A.M.; Trujillo, J.J. On development of fractional calculus during the last fifty years. *Scientometrics* **2014**, *98*, 577–582. [CrossRef]
14. Valerio, D.; Machado, J.; Kiryakova, V. Some pioneers of the applications of fractional calculus. *Fract. Calc. Appl. Anal.* **2014**, *17*, 552–578. [CrossRef]
15. Tenreiro Machado, J.A.; Kiryakova, V. The chronicles of fractional calculus. *Fract. Calc. Appl. Anal.* **2017**, *20*, 307–336. [CrossRef]
16. Tarasov, V.E. No violation of the Leibniz rule. No fractional derivative. *Commun. Nonlinear Sci. Numer. Simul.* **2013**, *18*, 2945–2948. [CrossRef]
17. Ortigueira, M.D.; Tenreiro Machado, J.A. What is a fractional derivative? *J. Comput. Phys.* **2015**, *293*, 4–13. [CrossRef]

18. Tarasov, V.E. On chain rule for fractional derivatives. *Commun. Nonlinear Sci. Numer. Simul.* **2016**, *30*, 1–4. [CrossRef]
19. Tarasov, V.E. Leibniz rule and fractional derivatives of power functions. *J. Comput. Nonlinear Dyn.* **2016**, *11*, 31014. [CrossRef]
20. Tarasov, V.E. No nonlocality. No fractional derivative. *Commun. Nonlinear Sci. Numer. Simul.* **2018**, *62*, 157–163. [CrossRef]
21. Sayevand, K.; Tenreiro Machado, J.; Baleanu, D. A new glance on the Leibniz rule for fractional derivatives. *Commun. Nonlinear Sci. Numer. Simul.* **2018**, *62*, 244–249. [CrossRef]
22. Granger, C.W.J. *The Typical Spectral Shape of an Economic Variable*; Technical Report No. 11; Department of Statistics, Stanford University: Stanford, CA, USA, 1964; 21p, Available online: https://statistics.stanford.edu/sites/default/files/PAR%20NSF%2011.pdf (accessed on 29 May 2019).
23. Granger, C.W.J. The typical spectral shape of an economic variable. *Econometrica* **1966**, *34*, 150–161. [CrossRef]
24. Granger, C.W.J. *Essays in Econometrics: Collected Papers of Clive W.J. Granger. Volume I: Spectral Analysis, Seasonality, Nonlinearity, Methodology, and Forecasting*; Ghysels, E., Swanson, N.R., Watson, M.W., Eds.; Cambridge University Press: Cambridge, NY, USA, 2001; 523p.
25. Granger, C.W.J. *Essays in Econometrics: Collected Papers of Clive W.J. Granger. Volume II: Causality, Integration and Cointegration, and Long Memory*; Ghysels, E., Swanson, N.R., Watson, M.W., Eds.; Cambridge University Press: Cambridge, NY, USA, 2001; 398p.
26. Granger, C.W.J.; Joyeux, R. An introduction to long memory time series models and fractional differencing. *J. Time Ser. Anal.* **1980**, *1*, 15–39. [CrossRef]
27. NobelPrize.org. *The Sveriges Riksbank Prize in Economic Sciences in Memory of Alfred Nobel 2003*; Press Release; Nobel Media AB: Stockholm, Sweden, 2019; Available online: https://www.nobelprize.org/prizes/economic-sciences/2003/summary/ (accessed on 29 May 2019).
28. Hosking, J.R.M. Fractional differencing. *Biometrika* **1981**, *68*, 165–176. [CrossRef]
29. Beran, J. *Statistics for Long-Memory Processes*; Capman and Hall: New York, NY, USA, 1994; 315p, ISBN 0-412-04901-5.
30. Palma, W. *Long-Memory Time Series: Theory and Methods*; Wiley-InterScience: Hoboken, NJ, USA, 2007; 304p, ISBN 978-0-470-11402-5.
31. Beran, J.; Feng, Y.; Ghosh, S.; Kulik, R. *Long-Memory Processes: Probabilistic Properties and Statistical Methods*; Springer: Berlin/Heidelberg, Germany; New York, NY, USA, 2013; 884p. [CrossRef]
32. Robinson, P.M. (Ed.) *Time Series with Long Memory*; Series: Advanced Texts in Econometrics; Oxford University Press: Oxford, UK, 2003; 392p, ISBN 978-0199257300.
33. Teyssiere, G.; Kirman, A.P. (Eds.) *Long Memory in Economics*; Springer: Berlin/Heidelberg, Germany, 2007; 390p.
34. Tschernig, R. *Wechselkurse, Unsicherheit und Long Memory*; Physica-Verlag: Heidelberg, Germany, 1994; 232p, (In German). ISBN 978-3-7908-0753-0. [CrossRef]
35. Baillie, R.N. Long memory processes and fractional integration in econometrics. *J. Econom.* **1996**, *73*, 5–59. [CrossRef]
36. Parke, W.R. What is fractional integration? *Rev. Econ. Stat.* **1999**, *81*, 632–638. [CrossRef]
37. Banerjee, A.; Urga, G. Modelling structural breaks, long memory and stock market volatility: An overview. *J. Econom.* **2005**, *129*, 1–34. [CrossRef]
38. Gil-Alana, L.A.; Hualde, J. Fractional Integration and Cointegration: An Overview and an Empirical Application. In *Palgrave Handbook of Econometrics. Volume 2: Applied Econometrics*; Mills, T.C., Patterson, K., Eds.; Springer: Berlin, Germany, 2009; pp. 434–469.
39. Tarasov, V.E.; Tarasova, V.V. Long and short memory in economics: Fractional-order difference and differentiation. *IRA-Int. J. Manag. Soc. Sci.* **2016**, *5*, 327–334. [CrossRef]
40. Tarasova, V.V.; Tarasov, V.E. Comments on the article «Long and short memory in economics: Fractional-order difference and differentiation». *Probl. Mod. Sci. Educ.* **2017**, *31*, 26–28. [CrossRef]
41. Kolmogoroff, A.N. Wiener Spirals and some other interesting curves in Gilbert's room. (Wienersche Spiralen und einige andere interessante Kurven im Hilbertschen Raum, cr (Doklady). *Acad. Sci. Urss* **1940**, *26*, 115–118. (In German)
42. Rogers, L.C.G. Arbitrage with fractional Brownian motion. *Math. Financ.* **1997**, *7*, 95–105. Available online: http://www.skokholm.co.uk/wp-content/uploads/2013/02/fbm.pdf (accessed on 29 May 2019). [CrossRef]

43. Duncan, T.E.; Hu, Y.; Pasik-Duncan, B. Stochastic calculus for fractional Brownian motion. I. Theory. *Siam J. Control Optim.* **2000**, *38*, 582–612. [CrossRef]
44. Tudor, C.; Viens, F. Statistical aspects of the fractional stochastic calculus. *Ann. Stat.* **2007**, *35*, 1183–1212. Available online: https://projecteuclid.org/download/pdfview_1/euclid.aos/1185304003 (accessed on 29 May 2019). [CrossRef]
45. Mishura, Y.S. *Stochastic Calculus for Fractional Brownian Motion and Related Processes*; Lecture Notes in Mathematics; Springer: Berlin/Heidelberg, Germany, 2008; 393p, ISBN 978-3540758723. [CrossRef]
46. Black, F.; Scholes, M.S. The pricing of options and corporate liabilities. *J. Polit. Econ.* **1973**, *81*, 637–654. Available online: https://www.cs.princeton.edu/courses/archive/fall09/cos323/papers/black_scholes73.pdf (accessed on 29 May 2019). [CrossRef]
47. NobelPrize.org. *The Sveriges Riksbank Prize in Economic Sciences in Memory of Alfred Nobel 1997*; Press Release; Nobel Media AB: Stockholm, Sweden, 2019; Available online: https://www.nobelprize.org/prizes/economic-sciences/1997/press-release (accessed on 29 May 2019).
48. Wyss, W. The fractional Black–Scholes equation. *Fract. Calc. Appl. Anal.* **2000**, *3*, 51–61.
49. Cartea, A.; Meyer-Brandis, T. How duration between trades of underlying securities affects option prices. *Rev. Financ.* **2010**, *14*, 749–785. [CrossRef]
50. Cartea, A. Derivatives pricing with marked point processes using tick-by-tick data. *Quant. Financ.* **2013**, *13*, 111–123. [CrossRef]
51. Akrami, M.H.; Erjaee, G.H. Examples of analytical solutions by means of Mittag-Leffler function of fractional Black-Scholes option pricing equation. *Fract. Calc. Appl. Anal.* **2015**, *18*, 38–47. [CrossRef]
52. Muniandy, S.V.; Lim, S.C. Modeling of locally self-similar processes using multifractional Brownian motion of Riemann-Liouville type. *Phys. Rev. E* **2001**, *63*, 7. [CrossRef] [PubMed]
53. Muniandy, S.V.; Lim, S.C.; Murugan, R. Inhomogeneous scaling behaviors in Malaysian foreign currency exchange rates. *Phys. A Stat. Mech. Appl.* **2001**, *301*, 407–428. [CrossRef]
54. Kluppelberg, C.; Kuhn, C. Fractional Brownian motion as a weak limit of Poisson shot noise processes—with applications to finance. *Stoch. Process. Appl.* **2004**, *113*, 333–351. [CrossRef]
55. Thao, T.H. An approximate approach to fractional analysis for finance. *Nonlinear Anal. Real World Appl.* **2006**, *7*, 124–132. [CrossRef]
56. Cartea, A.; Del-Castillo-Negrete, D. Fractional diffusion models of option prices in markets with jumps. *Phys. A Stat. Mech. Appl.* **2007**, *374*, 749–763. [CrossRef]
57. Li, M.; Lim, S.C.; Hu, B.J.; Feng, H. Towards describing multi-fractality of traffic using local Hurst function. In Proceedings of the 7th International Conference on Computational Science (ICCS 2007: Computational Science), Beijing, China, 27–30 May 2007; Lecture Notes in Computer Science. Springer: Berlin/Heidelberg, Germany, 2007; Volume 4488, pp. 1012–1020. [CrossRef]
58. Blackledge, J. Application of the fractal market hypothesis for modelling macroeconomic time series. *Isast Trans. Electron. Signal. Process* **2008**, *2*, 89–110. [CrossRef]
59. Mendes, R.V. A fractional calculus interpretation of the fractional volatility model. *Nonlinear Dyn.* **2009**, *55*, 395–399. [CrossRef]
60. Kuroda, K.; Murai, J. Long memory in finance and fractional Brownian motion. *Prog. Theor. Phys. Suppl.* **2009**, *179*, 26–37. [CrossRef]
61. Marom, O.; Momoniat, E. A comparison of numerical solutions of fractional diffusion models in finance. *Nonlinear Anal. Real World Appl.* **2009**, *10*, 3435–3442. [CrossRef]
62. Blackledge, J. Application of the fractional diffusion equation for predicting market behavior. *Int. J. Appl. Math.* **2010**, *40*, 130–158. [CrossRef]
63. Tenreiro Machado, J.; Duarte, F.B.; Duarte, G.M. Fractional dynamics in financial indices. *Int. J. Bifurc. Chaos* **2012**, *22*, 12. [CrossRef]
64. Jiang, Y.; Wang, X.; Wang, Y. On a stochastic heat equation with first order fractional noises and applications to finance. *J. Math. Anal. Appl.* **2012**, *396*, 656–669. [CrossRef]
65. Dung, N.T. Fractional stochastic differential equations with applications to finance. *J. Math. Anal. Appl.* **2013**, *397*, 334–348. [CrossRef]
66. Zeng, C.; Chen, Y.Q.; Yang, Q. Almost sure and moment stability properties of fractional order Black-Scholes model. *Fract. Calc. Appl. Anal.* **2013**, *16*, 317–331. [CrossRef]

67. Rostek, S.; Schobel, R. A note on the use of fractional Brownian motion for financial modeling. *Econ. Model.* **2013**, *30*, 30–35. [CrossRef]
68. Kerss, A.; Leonenko, N.; Sikorskii, A. Fractional Skellam processes with applications to finance. *Fract. Calc. Appl. Anal.* **2014**, *17*, 532–551. [CrossRef]
69. Kleinerta, H.; Korbel, J. Option pricing beyond Black-Scholes based on double-fractional diffusion. *Phys. A Stat. Mech. Its Appl.* **2016**, *449*, 200–214. [CrossRef]
70. Korbel, J.; Luchko, Y. Modeling of financial processes with a space-time fractional diffusion equation of varying order. *Fract. Calc. Appl. Anal.* **2016**, *19*, 1414–1433. [CrossRef]
71. Aguilar, J.P.; Coste, C.G. Non-Gaussian analytic option pricing: A closed formula for the Levy-stable model. *arXiv* **2016**, arXiv:1609.00987. Available online: https://ssrn.com/abstract=2828673 (accessed on 29 May 2019). [CrossRef]
72. Rostek, S. *Option Pricing in Fractional Brownian Markets*; Springer: Berlin/Heidelberg, Germany, 2009. [CrossRef]
73. Fallahgoul, H.A.; Focardi, S.M.; Fabozzi, F.J. *Fractional Calculus and Fractional Processes with Applications to Financial Economics, Theory and Application*; Academic Press: London, UK, 2016; 118p, ISBN 9780128042489.
74. Scalas, E.; Gorenflo, R.; Mainardi, F. Fractional calculus and continuous-time finance. *Phys. A Stat. Mech. Its Appl.* **2000**, *284*, 376–384. [CrossRef]
75. Mainardi, F.; Raberto, M.; Gorenflo, R.; Scalas, E. Fractional calculus and continuous-time finance II: The waiting-time distribution. *Phys. A Stat. Mech. Appl.* **2000**, *287*, 468–481. [CrossRef]
76. Gorenflo, R.; Mainardi, F.; Raberto, M.; Scalas, E. Fractional diffusion in finance: Basic theory. In Proceedings of the MDEF2000—Workshop "Modelli Dinamici in Economia e Finanza", Urbino, Italy, 28–30 September 2000; Available online: http://www.mdef.it/fileadmin/user_upload/mdef/meetings/MDEF2000/MainardiMDEF.pdf (accessed on 29 May 2019).
77. Gorenflo, R.; Mainardi, F.; Scalas, E.; Raberto, M. Fractional calculus and continuous-time finance III: The diffusion limit. In *Mathematical Finance*; Kohlmann, A., Tang, S., Eds.; Birkhäuser: Basel, Switzerland, 2001; pp. 171–180. [CrossRef]
78. Raberto, M.; Scalas, E.; Mainardi, F. Waiting-times and returns in high-frequency financial data: An empirical study. *Phys. A Stat. Mech. Its Appl.* **2002**, *314*, 749–755. [CrossRef]
79. Scalas, E.; Gorenflo, R.; Luckock, H.; Mainardi, F.; Mantelli, M.; Raberto, M. Anomalous waiting times in high-frequency financial data. *Quant. Financ.* **2004**, *4*, 695–702. [CrossRef]
80. Scalas, E. The application of continuous-time random walks in finance and economics. *Phys. A Stat. Mech. Its Appl.* **2006**, *362*, 225–239. [CrossRef]
81. Meerschaert, M.M.; Scalas, E. Coupled continuous time random walks in finance. *Phys. A Stat. Mech. Its Appl.* **2006**, *370*, 114–118. [CrossRef]
82. Laskin, N. Fractional market dynamics. *Phys. A Stat. Mech. Its Appl.* **2000**, *287*, 482–492. [CrossRef]
83. West, B.J.; Picozzi, S. Fractional Langevin model of memory in financial time series. *Phys. Rev. E* **2002**, *65*, 37106. [CrossRef] [PubMed]
84. Picozzi, S.; West, B.J. Fractional Langevin model of memory in financial markets. *Phys. Rev. E* **2002**, *66*, 12. [CrossRef] [PubMed]
85. Scalas, E. Five years of continuous-time random walks in econophysics. In *The Complex Networks of Economic Interactions*; Lecture Notes in Economics and Mathematical Systems; Springer: Berlin, Germany, 2006; Volume 567, pp. 3–16. [CrossRef]
86. Tarasov, V.E.; Tarasova, V.V. Time-dependent fractional dynamics with memory in quantum and economic physics. *Ann. Phys.* **2017**, *383*, 579–599. [CrossRef]
87. Chen, W.C. Nonlinear dynamics and chaos in a fractional-order financial system. *Chaos Solitons Fract.* **2008**, *36*, 1305–1314. [CrossRef]
88. Chen, W.C. Dynamics and control of a financial system with time-delayed feedbacks. *Chaos Solitons Fract.* **2008**, *37*, 1198–1207. [CrossRef]
89. Abd-Elouahab, M.S.; Hamri, N.-E.; Wang, J. Chaos control of a fractional-order financial system. *Math. Probl. Eng.* **2010**, *2010*, 18. [CrossRef]
90. Chen, L.; Chai, Y.; Wu, R. Control and synchronization of fractional-order financial system based on linear control. *Discret. Dyn. Nat. Soc.* **2011**, *2011*, 21. [CrossRef]

91. Wang, Z.; Huang, X.; Shi, G. Analysis of nonlinear dynamics and chaos in a fractional order financial system with time delay. *Comput. Math. Appl.* **2011**, *62*, 1531–1539. [CrossRef]
92. Pan, I.; Korre, A.; Das, S.; Durucan, S. Chaos suppression in a fractional order financial system using intelligent regrouping PSO based fractional fuzzy control policy in the presence of fractional Gaussian noise. *Nonlinear Dyn.* **2012**, *70*, 2445–2461. [CrossRef]
93. Ma, S.; Xu, Y.; Yue, W. Numerical solutions of a variable order fractional financial system. *J. Appl. Math.* **2012**, *2012*, 14. [CrossRef]
94. Danca, M.F.; Garrappa, R.; Tang, W.K.S.; Chen, G. Sustaining stable dynamics of a fractional-order chaotic financial system by parameter switching. *Comput. Math. Appl.* **2013**, *66*, 702–716. [CrossRef]
95. Xu, Y.; He, Z. Synchronization of variable-order fractional financial system via active control method. *Cent. Eur. J. Phys.* **2013**, *11*, 824–835. [CrossRef]
96. Yue, Y.; He, L.; Liu, G. Modeling and application of a new nonlinear fractional financial model. *J. Appl. Math.* **2013**, *2013*, 9. [CrossRef]
97. Jajarmi, A.; Hajipour, M.; Baleanu, D. New aspects of the adaptive synchronization and hyperchaos suppression of a financial model. *Chaos Solitons Fract.* **2017**, *99*, 285–296. [CrossRef]
98. Hajipour, A.; Hajipour, M.; Baleanu, D. On the adaptive sliding mode controller for a hyperchaotic fractional-order financial system. *Phys. A Stat. Mech. Its Appl.* **2018**, *497*, 139–153. [CrossRef]
99. Tacha, O.I.; Munoz-Pacheco, J.M.; Zambrano-Serrano, E.; Stouboulos, I.N.; Pham, V.-T. Determining the chaotic behavior in a fractional-order finance system with negative parameters. *Nonlinear Dyn.* **2018**, *94*, 1303–1317. [CrossRef]
100. Dadras, S.; Momeni, H.R. Control of a fractional-order economical system via sliding mode. *Phys. A Stat. Mech. Its Appl.* **2010**, *389*, 2434–2442. [CrossRef]
101. Wang, Z.; Huang, X.; Shen, H. Control of an uncertain fractional order economic system via adaptive sliding mode. *Neurocomputing* **2012**, *83*, 83–88. [CrossRef]
102. Baskonus, H.M.; Mekkaoui, T.; Hammouch, Z.; Bulut, H. Active control of a chaotic fractional order economic system. *Entropy* **2015**, *17*, 5771–5783. [CrossRef]
103. He, L.; Yi, L.; Tang, P. Numerical scheme and dynamic analysis for variable-order fractional van der Pol model of nonlinear economic cycle. *Adv. Differ. Equ.* **2016**, *2016*, 195. [CrossRef]
104. David, S.A.; Tenreiro Machado, J.A.; Quintino, D.D.; Balthazar, J.M. Partial chaos suppression in a fractional order macroeconomic model. *Math. Comput. Simul.* **2016**, *122*, 55–68. [CrossRef]
105. David, S.A.; Fischer, C.; Tenreiro Machado, J.A. Fractional electronic circuit simulation of a nonlinear macroeconomic model. *AEU Int. J. Electron. Commun.* **2018**, *84*, 210–220. [CrossRef]
106. Skovranek, T.; Podlubny, I.; Petras, I. Modeling of the national economies in state-space: A fractional calculus approach. *Econ. Model.* **2012**, *29*, 1322–1327. [CrossRef]
107. Tenreiro Machado, J.A.; Mata, M.E. A fractional perspective to the bond graph modelling of world economies. *Nonlinear Dyn.* **2015**, *80*, 1839–1852. [CrossRef]
108. Tenreiro Machado, J.A.; Mata, M.E. Pseudo phase plane and fractional calculus modeling of western global economic downturn. *Commun. Nonlinear Sci. Numer. Simul.* **2015**, *22*, 396–406. [CrossRef]
109. Tenreiro Machado, J.A.; Mata, M.E.; Lopes, A.M. Fractional state space analysis of economic systems. *Entropy* **2015**, *17*, 5402–5421. [CrossRef]
110. Tarasova, V.V.; Tarasov, V.E. Criteria hereditarity of economic process and memory effect. *Young Sci.* **2016**, *14*, 396–399. (In Russian). Available online: https://elibrary.ru/item.asp?id=26389117 (accessed on 29 May 2019).
111. Tarasova, V.V.; Tarasov, V.E. Economic indicators: Ambiguity and memory effects. *Econ. Manag. Law* **2016**, *3*, 3–5. (In Russian). Available online: https://istina.msu.ru/media/publications/article/925/f43/26341086/EUP2016.pdf (accessed on 29 May 2019).
112. Tarasova, V.V.; Tarasov, V.E. Concept of dynamic memory in economics. *Commun. Nonlinear Sci. Numer. Simul.* **2018**, *55*, 127–145. [CrossRef]
113. Tarasova, V.V.; Tarasov, V.E. Notion of dynamic memory in economic theory. *J. Econ. Entrep.* **2017**, *6*, 868–880. (In Russian). Available online: https://elibrary.ru/item.asp?id=29679697 (accessed on 29 May 2019).
114. Tarasova, V.V.; Tarasov, V.E. Long-term and short-term memory in discrete economic models. *Compet. A Glob. World Econ. Sci. Technol.* **2017**, *7*, 155–160. (In Russian). Available online: https://elibrary.ru/item.asp?id=29901818 (accessed on 29 May 2019).

115. Tarasova, V.V.; Tarasov, V.E. Comments to the article "Long-term and short-term memory in discrete economic models". *Probl. Sci.* **2017**, *8*, 12–13. Available online: https://elibrary.ru/item.asp?id=29862856 (accessed on 29 May 2019).
116. Tarasov, V.E.; Tarasova, V.V. Criterion of existence of power-law memory for economic processes. *Entropy* **2018**, *20*, 414. [CrossRef]
117. Tarasov, V.E. Generalized memory: Fractional calculus approach. *Fractal Fract.* **2018**, *2*, 23. [CrossRef]
118. Tarasova, V.V.; Tarasov, V.E. Marginal utility for economic processes with memory. *Alm. Mod. Sci. Educ.* **2016**, *7*, 108–113. (In Russian). Available online: http://www.gramota.net/materials/1/2016/7/28.html (accessed on 29 May 2019).
119. Tarasova, V.V.; Tarasov, V.E. Economic indicator that generalizes average and marginal values. *J. Econ. Entrep.* **2016**, *11*, 817–823. (In Russian). Available online: https://elibrary.ru/item.asp?id=27340824 (accessed on 29 May 2019).
120. Tarasova, V.V.; Tarasov, V.E. Marginal values of non-integer order in economic analysis. *Azimuth Sci. Res. Econ. Manag.* **2016**, *3*, 197–201. (In Russian). Available online: https://elibrary.ru/item.asp?id=27198798 (accessed on 29 May 2019).
121. Tarasova, V.V.; Tarasov, V.E. Economic interpretation of fractional derivatives. *Prog. Fract. Differ. Appl.* **2017**, *3*, 1–7. [CrossRef]
122. Tarasova, V.V.; Tarasov, V.E. Microeconomic meaning of derivatives of non-integer order. *Sci. Educ. Today* **2017**, *8*, 32–39. (In Russian). Available online: https://elibrary.ru/item.asp?id=29870013 (accessed on 29 May 2019).
123. Tarasova, V.V.; Tarasov, V.E. A generalization of concepts of accelerator and multiplier to take into account memory effects in macroeconomics. *J. Econ. Entrep.* **2016**, *10*, 1121–1129. (In Russian). Available online: https://elibrary.ru/item.asp?id=27211611 (accessed on 29 May 2019).
124. Tarasov, V.E.; Tarasova, V.V. Accelerator and multiplier for macroeconomic processes with memory. *IRA Int. J. Manag. Soc. Sci.* **2017**, *9*, 86–125. [CrossRef]
125. Tarasova, V.V.; Tarasov, V.E. Exact discretization of economic accelerator and multiplier with memory. *Fractal Fract.* **2017**, *1*, 6. [CrossRef]
126. Tarasova, V.V.; Tarasov, V.E. Exact discretization of economic accelerators and multipliers with memory. *J. Econ. Entrep.* **2017**, *7*, 1063–1069. (In Russian). Available online: https://elibrary.ru/item.asp?id=29774025 (accessed on 29 May 2019).
127. Tarasova, V.V.; Tarasov, V.E. Accelerators in macroeconomics: A comparison of discrete and continuous approaches. *Sci. J.* **2017**, *8*, 4–14. (In Russian). Available online: https://elibrary.ru/item.asp?id=30561974 (accessed on 29 May 2019). [CrossRef]
128. Tarasova, V.V.; Tarasov, V.E. Accelerators in macroeconomics: Comparison of discrete and continuous approaches. *Am. J. Econ. Bus. Adm.* **2017**, *9*, 47–55. [CrossRef]
129. Tarasov, V.E. Exact discretization by Fourier transforms. *Commun. Nonlinear Sci. Numer. Simul.* **2016**, *37*, 31–61. [CrossRef]
130. Tarasova, V.V.; Tarasov, V.E. Economic accelerator with memory: Discrete time approach. *Probl. Mod. Sci. Educ.* **2016**, *36*, 37–42. [CrossRef]
131. Tarasova, V.V.; Tarasov, V.E. Discrete accelerator with memory in macroeconomics. *Economics* **2017**, *8*, 32–40. (In Russian). Available online: https://elibrary.ru/item.asp?id=29944864 or https://economic-theory.com/blizhajshij-nomer/matematicheskie-i-instrumentalnye/385-discrete-accelerato.html (accessed on 29 May 2019).
132. Tarasova, V.V.; Tarasov, V.E. Elasticity for economic processes with memory: Fractional differential calculus approach. *Fract. Differ. Calc.* **2016**, *6*, 219–232. [CrossRef]
133. Tarasova, V.V.; Tarasov, V.E. Price elasticity of demand with memory. *Econ. Sociol. Law* **2016**, *4*, 98–106. (In Russian). Available online: https://elibrary.ru/item.asp?id=26093967& (accessed on 29 May 2019).
134. Tarasova, V.V.; Tarasov, V.E. Elasticity of OTC cash turnover of currency market of Russian Federation. *Actual Probl. Humanit. Nat. Sci.* **2016**, *7*, 207–215. (In Russian). Available online: https://publikacia.net/archive/uploads/pages/2016_7_1/49.pdf (accessed on 29 May 2019).
135. Tarasova, V.V.; Tarasov, V.E. On applicability of point elasticity of demand on price to exchange trading on US dollar. *Sci. Perspect.* **2016**, *6*, 6–11. (In Russian). Available online: https://elibrary.ru/item.asp?id=26344263 or http://naupers.ru/6archive.html or https://docplayer.ru/55299569-O-primenimosti-tochechnoy-elastichnosti-sprosa-po-cene-dlya-birzhevyh-torgov-po-dollaru-ssha.html (accessed on 29 May 2019).

136. Tarasova, V.V.; Tarasov, V.E. Non-local measures of risk aversion in the economic process. *Econ. Theory Pract.* **2016**, *44*, 54–58. (In Russian). Available online: https://elibrary.ru/item.asp?id=27541974 or http://econ.kubsu.ru/images/4_2016.pdf (accessed on 29 May 2019).
137. Tarasova, V.V.; Tarasov, V.E. Risk aversion for investors with memory: Hereditary generalizations of Arrow-Pratt measure. *Financ. J.* **2017**, *2*, 46–63. (In Russian). Available online: https://elibrary.ru/item.asp?id=28966889 or http://www.nifi.ru/images/FILES/Journal/Archive/2017/2/statii_2/fm_2017_2_05 (accessed on 29 May 2019).
138. Tarasova, V.V.; Tarasov, V.E. Deterministic factor analysis: Methods of integro-differentiation of non-integral order. *Actual Probl. Econ. Law* **2016**, *10*, 77–87. (In Russian) [CrossRef]
139. Tarasova, V.V.; Tarasov, V.E. Fractional deterministic factor analysis of economic processes with memory and nonlocality. In *Chaotic, Fractional, and Complex Dynamics: New Insights and Perspectives*; Edelman, M., Macau, E., Sanjuan, M.A.F., Eds.; Springer International Publishing: Berlin, Germany, 2018; pp. 173–189. ISBN 978-3-319-68109-2. [CrossRef]
140. Harrod, R. An Essay in dynamic theory. *Econ. J.* **1939**, *49*, 14–33. [CrossRef]
141. Harrod, R. *Towards a Dynamic Economics*; Macmillan: London, UK, 1948.
142. Harrod, R. *Economic Dynamics*; Macmillan: London, UK, 1973; ISBN 978-0-333-14247-9.
143. Domar, E.D. Capital expansion, rate of growth and employment. *Econometrica* **1946**, *14*, 137–147. [CrossRef]
144. Domar, E.D. Expansion and employment. *Am. Econ. Rev.* **1947**, *37*, 34–55.
145. Keynes, J.M. *The General Theory of Employment, Interest and Money*; Macmillan: London, UK, 1936.
146. Keynes, J.M. *The General Theory of Employment, Interest and Money: With the Economic Consequences of the Peace*, Series: Classics of World Literature; Wordsworth Editions ed; Ware: Hertfordshire, UK, 2017; 576p, ISBN 978-1840227475.
147. Keynes, J.M. *The General Theory of Employment, Interest and Money: With the Economic Consequences of the Peace*; Palgrave Macmillan: London, UK, 2018; 438p. [CrossRef]
148. Keynes, J.M.; Johnson, E.; Moggridge, D.; Robinson, A. *The Collected Writings of John Maynard Keynes*, Reprint Edition ed; Cambridge University Press: Cambridge, UK, 2013; 15126p, ISBN 978-1107677722.
149. Leontief, W.W. *The Structure of the American Economy 1919–1939: An Empirical Application of Equilibrium Analysis*, 2nd ed.; Oxford University Press: New York, NY, USA, 1951; 282p.
150. Leontief, W.W. *Input–Output Economics*, 2nd ed.; Oxford University Press: New York, NY, USA, 1986.
151. Phillips, A.W. Stabilisation policy in a closed economy. *Econ. J.* **1954**, *64*, 290–323. [CrossRef]
152. Phillips, A.W. *A. W. H. Phillips Collected Works in Contemporary Perspective*; Leeson, R., Ed.; Cambridge University Press: Cambridge, UK, 2000; 515p, ISBN 9780521571357.
153. Allen, R.G.D. *Mathematical Economics*; Macmillan: London, UK, 1956; 812p.
154. Allen, R.G.D. *Mathematical Economics*, 2nd ed.; Macmillan: London, UK, 1960; 812p, ISBN 978-1-349-81547-0. [CrossRef]
155. Allen, R.G.D. *Macro-Economic Theory. A Mathematical Treatment*; Palgrave Macmillan: London, UK, 1967; 420p, ISBN 978-1-349-81541-8. [CrossRef]
156. Allen, R.G.D. *Macro-Economic Theory. A Mathematical Treatment*; Macmillan: London, UK, 1968; 420p, ISBN 978-033304112.
157. Solow, R.M. A contribution to the theory of economic growth. *Q. J. Econ.* **1956**, *70*, 65–94. Available online: http://piketty.pse.ens.fr/files/Solow1956.pdf (accessed on 29 May 2019). [CrossRef]
158. Solow, R.M. Neoclassical growth theory. *Handb. Macroecon.* **1999**, *1*, 637–667. [CrossRef]
159. Swan, T.W. Economic growth and capital accumulation. *Econ. Rec.* **1956**, *32*, 334–361. [CrossRef]
160. Kaldor, N. A model of the trade cycle. *Econ. J.* **1940**, *50*, 78–92. [CrossRef]
161. Kaldor, N. Capital accumulation and economic growth. In *The Theory of Capital*; Hague, D.C., Ed.; Palgrave Macmillan: London, UK, 1961; pp. 177–222. Available online: http://www.masterhdfs.org/masterHDFS/wp-content/uploads/2014/05/Kaldor_1961.pdf (accessed on 29 May 2019).
162. Chang, W.W.; Smyth, D.J. The existence and persistence of cycles in a nonlinear model: Kaldor's 1940 model re-examined. *Rev. Econ. Stud.* **1971**, *38*, 37–44. [CrossRef]
163. Kalecki, M. A macrodynamic theory of business cycles. *Econometrica* **1935**, *3*, 327–344. Available online: https://archive.org/details/Kalecki1935.AMacrodynamicTheoryOfBusinessCycles/page/n1 (accessed on 29 May 2019). [CrossRef]

164. Lancaster, K. *Mathematical Economics*; The Macmillan Company: New York, NY, USA, 1968; ISBN 978-0023221316. (Revised edition, Dover Publications: Mineola, NY, USA, 2011; 448p, ISBN 978-0486653914).
165. Romer, D. *Advanced Macroeconomics*, 4th ed.; McGrow-Hill: New York, NY, USA, 2012; 716p, ISBN 978-0-07-351137-5.
166. Nicholson, W.; Snyder, C. *Microeconomic Theory. Basic Principles and Extensions*, 11th ed.; South-Western, Cengage Learning: Masson, OH, USA, 2012; 758p, ISBN 978-111-1-52553-8.
167. Varian, H. *Microeconomic Analysis*, 3rd ed.; W.W. Norton: New York, NY, USA, 1992; 548p, ISBN 0-393-95735-7.
168. Tarasova, V.V.; Tarasov, V.E. Fractional dynamics of natural growth and memory effect in economics. *Eur. Res.* **2016**, *12*, 30–37. [CrossRef]
169. Tarasova, V.V.; Tarasov, V.E. Economic model of natural growth with dynamic memory. *Actual Probl. Humanit. Nat. Sci.* **2017**, *4*, 51–58. (In Russian). Available online: https://elibrary.ru/item.asp?id=28855511 or https://publikacia.net/archive/uploads/pages/2017_4_2/15.pdf (accessed on 29 May 2019).
170. Tarasova, V.V.; Tarasov, V.E. Model of economic growth with constant rate and dynamic memory. *Econ. Sociol. Law* **2017**, *8*, 18–24. (In Russian). Available online: https://elibrary.ru/item.asp?id=29938971 (accessed on 29 May 2019).
171. Tarasova, V.V.; Tarasov, V.E. Economic growth model with constant pace and dynamic memory. *Probl. Mod. Sci. Educ.* **2017**, *2*, 40–45. [CrossRef]
172. Tarasova, V.V.; Tarasov, V.E. Hereditary generalization of Harrod-Domar model and memory effects. *J. Econ. Entrep.* **2016**, *10*, 72–78. (In Russian). Available online: https://elibrary.ru/item.asp?id=27220550 (accessed on 29 May 2019).
173. Tarasova, V.V.; Tarasov, V.E. Memory effects in hereditary Harrod-Domar model. *Probl. Mod. Sci. Educ.* **2016**, *32*, 38–44. (In Russian). Available online: https://elibrary.ru/item.asp?id=27253247 (accessed on 29 May 2019). [CrossRef]
174. Tarasova, V.V.; Tarasov, V.E. Macroeconomic models with dynamic memory. *J. Econ. Entrep.* **2017**, *3*, 26–35. (In Russian). Available online: https://elibrary.ru/item.asp?id=29078471 (accessed on 29 May 2019).
175. Tarasova, V.V.; Tarasov, V.E. Macroeconomic models with dynamic memory: Fractional calculus approach. *Appl. Math. Comput.* **2018**, *338*, 466–486. [CrossRef]
176. Tarasov, V.E. Economic models with power-law memory. In *Handbook of Fractional Calculus with Applications. Volume 8: Applications in Engineering, Life and Social Sciences, Part B*; Baleanu, D., Lopes, A.M., Tenreiro Machado, J.A., Eds.; De Gruyter: Berlin, Germany; Boston, MA, USA, 2019; pp. 1–32. ISBN 978-3-11-057092. [CrossRef]
177. Tarasova, V.V.; Tarasov, V.E. Keynesian model of economic growth with memory. *Econ. Manag. Probl. Solut.* **2016**, *10*, 21–29. (In Russian). Available online: https://elibrary.ru/item.asp?id=27542599 (accessed on 29 May 2019).
178. Tarasova, V.V.; Tarasov, V.E. Memory effects in hereditary Keynes model. *Probl. Mod. Sci. Educ.* **2016**, *38*, 56–61. (In Russian). Available online: https://cyberleninka.ru/article/n/effekty-pamyati-v-ereditarnoy-modeli-keynsa (accessed on 29 May 2019). [CrossRef]
179. Tarasova, V.V.; Tarasov, V.E. Influence of memory effects on world economics and business. *Azimuth Sci. Res. Econ. Manag.* **2016**, *5*, 369–372. (In Russian). Available online: https://cyberleninka.ru/article/n/vliyanie-effektov-pamyati-na-mirovuyu-ekonomiku-i-biznes (accessed on 29 May 2019).
180. Tarasova, V.V.; Tarasov, V.E. Dynamic intersectoral models with memory that generalize Leontief model. *J. Econ. Entrep.* **2017**, *2*, 913–924. (In Russian). Available online: https://elibrary.ru/item.asp?id=28791089 (accessed on 29 May 2019).
181. Tarasova, V.V.; Tarasov, V.E. Dynamic intersectoral models with power-law memory. *Commun. Nonlinear Sci. Numer. Simul.* **2018**, *54*, 100–117. [CrossRef]
182. Tarasova, V.V.; Tarasov, V.E. Chronological exponent for processes with memory and dynamic intersectoral economic models. *Sci. Educ. Today* **2017**, *4*, 29–39. (In Russian). Available online: https://cyberleninka.ru/article/n/hronologicheskaya-eksponenta-dlya-protsessov-s-pamyatyu-i-dinamicheskie-mezhotraslevye-modeli-ekonomiki (accessed on 29 May 2019).
183. Tarasova, V.V.; Tarasov, V.E. Logistic map with memory from economic model. *Chaos Solitons Fract.* **2017**, *95*, 84–91. [CrossRef]
184. Tarasov, V.E.; Tarasova, V.V. Logistic equation with continuously distributed lag and application in economics. *Nonlinear Dyn.* **2019**. Submitted.

185. Tarasov, V.E.; Tarasova, V.V. Phillips model with exponentially distributed lag and power-law memory. *Comput. Appl. Math.* **2019**, *38*, 13. [CrossRef]
186. Tarasov, V.E.; Tarasova, V.V. Harrod-Domar growth model with memory and distributed lag. *Axioms* **2019**, *8*, 9. [CrossRef]
187. Tarasov, V.E.; Tarasova, V.V. Dynamic Keynesian model of economic growth with memory and lag. *Mathematics* **2019**, *7*, 178. [CrossRef]
188. Tarasova, V.V.; Tarasov, V.E. Productivity with fatigue and long memory: Fractional calculus approach. *Int. J. Appl. Comput. Math.* **2019**, *5*, 16. [CrossRef]
189. Tarsasov, V.E. Rules for fractional-dynamic generalizations: Difficulties of constructing fractional dynamic models. *Mathematics* **2019**. (Special Issue "Mathematical Economics: Application of Fractional Calculus". Submitted).
190. Rehman, H.U.; Darus, M.; Salah, J. A note on Caputo's derivative operator interpretation in economy. *J. Appl. Math.* **2018**, *2018*, 7. [CrossRef]
191. Caputo, M. The memory function of the reactivity of investments caused by step of the prime rate. *Econ. Politica* **2005**, *22*, 365–379. Available online: https://www.rivisteweb.it/doi/10.1428/21175 (accessed on 29 May 2019). [CrossRef]
192. Caputo, M. Planning output dynamics with memory. *Econ. Politica* **2009**, *26*, 79–97. Available online: https://www.rivisteweb.it/doi/10.1428/29093 (accessed on 29 May 2019). [CrossRef]
193. Caputo, M. The memory response of populations and markets to extreme events. *Econ. Politica* **2012**, *29*, 261–282. Available online: https://www.rivisteweb.it/doi/10.1428/37632 (accessed on 29 May 2019). [CrossRef]
194. Caputo, M. The memory response of the populations to extreme events. In *Atti dell'Accademia delle Scienze di Ferrara*; Volume 88, Anno Accademico 188, 2010–2011; Accademia delle Scienze di Ferrara: Ferrara, Italy, 2012; pp. 225–240. 433p, ISBN 88-7400-041-3.
195. Caputo, M. Memory oscillator for modeling socio-economic oscillatory responses to extreme events. *Econ. Politica* **2013**, *30*, 221–239. Available online: https://www.rivisteweb.it/doi/10.1428/74241 (accessed on 29 May 2019). [CrossRef]
196. Caputo, M. The convergence of economic developments. *In Stud. Nonlinear Dyn. Econom.* **2012**, *16*, 23. [CrossRef]
197. Caputo, M. The evolution and homogeneity of EU economies (with an econometric approach). *Meccanica* **2014**, *49*, 2237–2246. [CrossRef]
198. Caputo, M. *The role of memory in modeling social and economic cycles of extreme events. Chapter 11 in A Handbook of Alternative Theories of Public Economics*; Forte, F., Mudambi, R., Navarra, P.M., Eds.; Edward Elgar Publishing: Cheltenham, UK, 2014; pp. 245–259. 576p, ISBN 9781781004715. Available online: https://books.google.ru/books?hl=ru&lr=&id=bekyAwAAQBAJ&oi=fnd&pg=PA245&ots=4pzWJ8won7&sig=BKAM1zBH1dezS9CD78TOKK8wK8o&redir_esc=y#v=onepage&q&f=false (accessed on 29 May 2019).
199. Caputo, M.; Kolari, J. An analytical model of the Fisher equation with memory functions. *Altern. Perspect. Financ. Account.* **2001**, *1*, 1–14.
200. Caputo, M.; Di Giorgio, G. Monetary Policy, Memory and Output Dynamics. In *Monetary Policy and Institutions*; Di Giorgio, G., Neri, F., Eds.; LUISS University Press: Rome, Italy, 2006; pp. 165–176.
201. Nakhushev, A.M. Loaded equations of mathematical economics. Reports of the Adyghe (Circassian). *Int. Acad. Sci.* **2010**, *12*, 91–97. Available online: https://elibrary.ru/item.asp?id=16950586 (accessed on 29 May 2019).
202. Nakhushev, A.M. Section 4.6. Loaded equations of mathematical economics. In *Loaded equations and their application*; Nakhushev, A.M., Ed.; Nauka: Moscow, Russia, 2012; pp. 145–153. 232p.
203. Kalazhokov, K.K. Some classes of dynamic models of productive and economic systems with "memory". *News Kabard. -Balkar. Sci. Cent. Russ. Acad. Sci.* **2012**, *4*, 26–34.
204. Nakhusheva, Z.A. On a one-sector macroeconomic model of long-term prognosis. *News Kabard. -Balkar. Sci. Cent. Russ. Acad. Sci.* **2012**, *4*, 35–38.
205. Samuta, V.V.; Strelova, V.A.; Parovik, R.I. Nonlocal Solow model of neoclassical economic growth. *Bull. Krasec. Phys. Math. Sci.* **2012**, *2*, 37–41. Available online: http://mi.mathnet.ru/eng/vkam72 (accessed on 29 May 2019). [CrossRef]

206. Shpilko, Y.E.; Solomko, A.A.; Parovik, R.I. Parametrization Samuelson equation model for Evans fixing, equilibrium price of the same product market. *Bull. Krasec. Phys. Math. Sci.* **2012**, *2*, 33–36. Available online: http://mi.mathnet.ru/eng/vkam71 (accessed on 29 May 2019). [CrossRef]
207. Makarov, D.V. On a dynamic hereditarity system that simulates the economic cycle. *Bull. Krasec. Phys. Math. Sci.* **2016**, *2*, 55–61. Available online: http://mi.mathnet.ru/eng/vkam132 (accessed on 29 May 2019). [CrossRef]
208. Chu, S.Y.; Shane, C. Using the hybrid Phillips curve with memory to forecast US inflation. *Stud. Nonlinear Dyn. Econom.* **2017**, *21*, 20160088. [CrossRef]
209. Pakhira, R.; Ghosh, U.; Sarkar, S. Study of memory effects in an inventory model using fractional calculus. *Appl. Math. Sci.* **2018**, *12*, 797–824. Available online: http://www.m-hikari.com/ams/ams-2018/ams-17-20-2018/p/ghoshAMS17-20-2018.pdf (accessed on 29 May 2019). [CrossRef]
210. Pakhira, R.; Ghosh, U.; Sarkar, S. Application of memory effects in an inventory model with linear demand and no shortage. *Int. J. Res. Advent Technol.* **2018**, *6*, 1853–1871. Available online: http://www.ijrat.org/downloads/Vol-6/august-2018/paperID-68201804.pdf (accessed on 29 May 2019).
211. Pakhira, R.; Ghosh, U.; Sarkar, S. Study of memory effect in an inventory model with linear demand and salvage value. *Int. J. Appl. Eng. Res.* **2018**, *13*, 14741–14751. Available online: https://www.ripublication.com/ijaer18/ijaerv13n20_40.pdf (accessed on 29 May 2019).
212. Pakhira, R.; Ghosh, U.; Sarkar, S. Study of memory effect in an inventory model with linear demand and shortage. *Int. J. Math. Sci. Comput.* **2019**, *5*, 54–70. [CrossRef]
213. Pakhira, R.; Ghosh, U.; Sarkar, S. Study of memory effect in an inventory model with quadratic type demand rate and salvage value. *Appl. Math. Sci.* **2019**, *13*, 209–223. Available online: http://www.m-hikari.com/ams/ams-2019/ams-5-8-2019/p/pakhiraAMS5-8-2019.pdf (accessed on 29 May 2019). [CrossRef]
214. Tejado, I.; Valerio, D.; Valerio, N. Fractional calculus in economic growth modeling. The Portuguese case. In Proceedings of the Conference: 2014 International Conference on Fractional Differentiation and its Applications (FDA'14), Catania, Italy, 23–25 June 2014; ISBN 978-1-4799-2591-9. [CrossRef]
215. Tejado, I.; Valerio, D.; Valerio, N. Fractional calculus in economic growth modelling. The Spanish case. In *CONTROLO'2014—Proceedings of the 11th Portuguese Conference on Automatic Control*; Moreira, A.P., Matos, A., Veiga, G., Eds.; Lecture Notes in Electrical Engineering; Springer International Publishing: Cham, Switzerland, 2015; Volume 321, pp. 449–458.
216. Tejado, I.; Valerio, D.; Perez, E.; Valerio, N. Fractional calculus in economic growth modelling: The economies of France and Italy. In Proceedings of the International Conference on Fractional Differentiation and its Applications, Novi Sad, Serbia, 18–20 July 2016; Spasic, D.T., Grahovac, N., Zigic, M., Rapaic, M., Atanackovic, T.M., Eds.; University of Novi Sad: Novi Sad, Serbia, 2016; pp. 113–123.
217. Tejado, I.; Valerio, D.; Perez, E.; Valerio, N. Fractional calculus in economic growth modelling: The Spanish and Portuguese cases. *Int. J. Dyn. Control* **2017**, *5*, 208–222. [CrossRef]
218. Tejado, I.; Perez, E.; Valerio, D. Economic growth in the European Union modelled with fractional derivatives: First results. *Bull. Pol. Acad. Sci. Tech. Sci.* **2018**, *66*, 455–465. [CrossRef]
219. Tejado, I.; Perez, E.; Valerio, D. Fractional calculus in economic growth modelling of the group of seven. *Ssrn Electron. J.* **2018**, *22*, 139–157. [CrossRef]
220. Tejado, I.; Perez, E.; Valerio, D. Fractional calculus in economic growth modelling of the group of seven. *Fract. Calc. Appl. Anal.* **2019**, *22*, 139–157. [CrossRef]
221. Luo, D.; Wang, J.R.; Feckan, M. Applying fractional calculus to analyze economic growth modelling. *J. Appl. Math. Stat. Inform.* **2018**, *14*, 25–36. [CrossRef]
222. Tarasov, V.E. Self-organization with memory. *Commun. Nonlinear Sci. Numer. Simul.* **2019**, *72*, 240–271. [CrossRef]
223. Zhang, W.-B. *Synergetic Economics. Time and Change in Nonlinear Economics*; Springer: Berlin/Heidelberg, Germany, 1991; 246p, ISBN 978-3-642-75911-6.
224. Koblo, R.B. *The Visible Hand: Synergetic Microfoundation of Macroeconomic Dynamics*; Springer: Berlin/Heidelberg, Germany, 1991; 131p, ISBN 978-3-540-54595-8.
225. Stanley, H.E.; Amaral, L.A.N.; Buldyrev, S.V.; Gopikrishnan, P.; Plerou, V.; Salinger, M.A. Self-organized complexity in economics and finance. *Proc. Natl. Acad. Sci. United States Am.* **2002**, *99* (Suppl. S1), 2561–2565. [CrossRef] [PubMed]

226. Caputo, M.; Fabrizio, M. A new definition of fractional derivative without singular kernel. *Prog. Fract. Differ. Appl.* **2015**, *1*, 73–85. [CrossRef]
227. Caputo, M.; Fabrizio, M. Applications of new time and spatial fractional derivatives with exponential kernels. *Prog. Fract. Differ. Appl.* **2016**, *2*, 1–11. [CrossRef]
228. Tarasov, V.E.; Tarasova, S.S. Fractional and integer derivatives with continuously distributed lag. *Commun. Nonlinear Sci. Numer. Simul.* **2019**, *70*, 125–169. [CrossRef]
229. Caputo, M. Mean fractional-order-derivatives differential equations and filters. *Ann. Dell'universita Di Ferrara* **1995**, *41*, 73–84. [CrossRef]
230. Bagley, R.L.; Torvik, P.J. On the existence of the order domain and the solution of distributed order equations—Part I. *Int. J. Appl. Math.* **2000**, *2*, 865–882.
231. Bagley, R.L.; Torvik, P.J. On the existence of the order domain and the solution of distributed order equations—Part II. *Int. J. Appl. Math.* **2000**, *2*, 965–987.
232. Caputo, M. Distributed order differential equations modelling dielectric induction and diffusion. *Fract. Calc. Appl. Anal.* **2001**, *4*, 421–442.
233. Lorenzo, C.F.; Hartley, T.T. Variable order and distributed order fractional operators. *Nonlinear Dyn.* **2002**, *29*, 57–98. [CrossRef]
234. Jiao, Z.; Chen, Y.Q.; Podlubny, I. *Distributed-Order Dynamic Systems: Stability, Simulation, Applications and Perspectives*; Springer: London, UK, 2012; 90p.
235. Nakhushev, A.M. On the positivity of continuous and discrete differentiation and integration operators that are very important in fractional calculus and in the theory of equations of mixed type. *Differ. Equ.* **1998**, *34*, 103–112. Available online: http://mi.mathnet.ru/eng/de9635 (accessed on 29 May 2019).
236. Nakhushev, A.M. *Fractional Calculus and its Application*; Fizmatlit: Moscow, Russia, 2003; 272p, ISBN 5-9221-0440-3. (In Russian)
237. Pskhu, A.V. On the theory of the continual integro-differentiation operator. *Differ. Equ.* **2004**, *40*, 128–136. [CrossRef]
238. Pskhu, A.V. *Partial Differential Equations of Fractional Order*; Nauka: Moscow, Russia, 2005; 199p, ISBN 5-02-033721-8. (In Russian)
239. Kochubei, A.N. General fractional calculus, evolution equations, and renewal processes. *Integral Equ. Oper. Theory* **2011**, *71*, 583–600. [CrossRef]
240. Kochubei, A.N. General fractional calculus. Chapter 5. In *Handbook of Fractional Calculus with Applications*; Kochubei, A., Luchko, Y., Tenreiro Machado, J.A., Eds.; De Gruyter: Berlin, Germany; Boston, MA, USA, 2019; pp. 111–126. [CrossRef]
241. Tarasov, V.E.; Tarasova, S.S. Probabilistic interpretation of Kober fractional integral of non-integer order. *Prog. Fract. Differ. Appl.* **2019**, *5*, 1–5. [CrossRef]
242. Kochubei, A.N. Distributed order calculus and equations of ultraslow diffusion. *J. Math. Anal. Appl.* **2008**, *340*, 252–281. [CrossRef]
243. Sin, C.-S. Well-posedness of general Caputo-type fractional differential equations. *Fract. Calc. Appl. Anal.* **2018**, *21*, 819–832. [CrossRef]
244. Kochubei, A.N.; Kondratiev, Y. Fractional kinetic hierarchies and intermittency. Kinetic and Related Models. *Am. Inst. Math. Sci.* **2017**, *10*, 725–740. [CrossRef]
245. Kochubei, A.N.; Kondratiev, Y. Growth equation of the general fractional calculus. *Mathematics* **2019**. (Special Issue "Mathematical Economics: Application of Fractional Calculus" edited by V.E. Tarasov. Submitted).
246. Achdou, Y.; Buera, F.J.; Lasry, J.-M.; Lions, P.-L.; Moll, B. Partial differential equation models in macroeconomics. *Philos. Trans. R. Soc. A Math. Phys. Eng. Sci.* **2014**, *372*, 201303977. [CrossRef]
247. Burger, M.; Caffarelli, L.; Markowich, P.A. Partial differential equation models in the socio-economic sciences. *Philos. Trans. R. Soc. A Math. Phys. Eng. Sci.* **2014**, *372*, 20130406. Available online: https://royalsocietypublishing.org/doi/pdf/10.1098/rsta.2013.0406 (accessed on 29 May 2019). [CrossRef]
248. Malinowska, A.B.; Odzijewicz, T.; Torres, D.F.M. *Advanced Methods in the Fractional Calculus of Variations*; Springer: Heidelberg, Germany; New York, NY, USA, 2015; 135p.
249. Almeida, R.; Tavares, D.; Torres, D.F.M. *The Variable-Order Fractional Calculus of Variations*; Springer: Heidelberg, Germany; New York, NY, USA, 2019; 124p.
250. Tarasov, V.E.; Zaslavsky, G.M. Nonholonomic constraints with fractional derivatives. *J. Phys. A* **2006**, *39*, 9797–9815. [CrossRef]

251. Tarasov, V.E. Fractional Stability. *ArXiv* **2007**, arXiv:0711.2117. Available online: https://arxiv.org/pdf/0711.2117.pdf (accessed on 29 May 2019).
252. Tarasov, V.E. Fractional-order variational derivative. *Int. J. Appl. Math.* **2014**, *27*, 491–518. [CrossRef]
253. Chikrii, A.A. Game dynamic problems for systems with fractional derivatives. In *Pareto Optimality, Game Theory and Equilibria*; Chinchuluun, A., Pardalos, P.M., Migdalas, A., Pitsoulis, L., Eds.; Springer: New York, NY, USA, 2008; Volume 17, pp. 349–386.
254. Chikrii, A.A.; Matychyn, I.I. Game problems for fractional-order linear systems. *Proc. Steklov Inst. Math.* **2010**, *268*, 54–70. (In Russian). Available online: http://mi.mathnet.ru/eng/timm419 (accessed on 29 May 2019). [CrossRef]
255. Chikriy, A.A.; Chentsov, A.G.; Matychyn, I.I. Differential games of the fractional order with separated dynamics. *J. Autom. Inf. Sci.* **2009**, *41*, 17–27. [CrossRef]
256. Chikrii, A.A.; Matychyn, I.I. Riemann–Liouville, Caputo, and sequential fractional derivatives in differential games. In *Advances in Dynamic Games*; Breton, M., Szajowski, K., Eds.; Springer Science Business Media: Berlin, Germany, 2011; pp. 61–81.
257. Chikrii, A.A.; Matychyn, I.I. On linear conflict-controlled processes with fractional derivatives. *Work. Inst. Math. Mech. Ural Branch Russ. Acad. Sci.* **2011**, *17*, 256–270. (In Russian). Available online: http://mi.mathnet.ru/eng/timm711 (accessed on 29 May 2019).
258. Matychyn, I.I.; Chikriy, A.A.; Onyshchenko, V.V. Conflict-controlled processes involving fractional differential equations with impulses. *Math. Balk.* **2012**, *26*, 159–168. [CrossRef]
259. Matychyn, I.I.; Onyshchenko, V.V. Differential games of fractional order with impulse effect. *J. Autom. Inf. Sci.* **2015**, *47*, 43–53. [CrossRef]
260. Zhukovskiy, V.J.; Chikriy, A.A. On discrete conflict-controlled processes described by Grunvald-Letnikov fractional systems. *J. Autom. Inf. Sci.* **2015**, *47*, 24–34. [CrossRef]

2

A Deep Neural Network Algorithm for Semilinear Elliptic PDEs with Applications in Insurance Mathematics

Stefan Kremsner [1,*], **Alexander Steinicke** [2] **and Michaela Szölgyenyi** [3]

1 Department of Mathematics, University of Graz, Heinrichstraße 36, 8010 Graz, Austria
2 Department of Mathematics and Information Technology, Montanuniversitaet Leoben, Peter Tunner-Straße 25/I, 8700 Leoben, Austria; alexander.steinicke@unileoben.ac.at
3 Department of Statistics, University of Klagenfurt, Universitätsstraße 65-67, 9020 Klagenfurt, Austria; michaela.szoelgyenyi@aau.at
* Correspondence: stefan.kremsner@uni-graz.at

Abstract: In insurance mathematics, optimal control problems over an infinite time horizon arise when computing risk measures. An example of such a risk measure is the expected discounted future dividend payments. In models which take multiple economic factors into account, this problem is high-dimensional. The solutions to such control problems correspond to solutions of deterministic semilinear (degenerate) elliptic partial differential equations. In the present paper we propose a novel deep neural network algorithm for solving such partial differential equations in high dimensions in order to be able to compute the proposed risk measure in a complex high-dimensional economic environment. The method is based on the correspondence of elliptic partial differential equations to backward stochastic differential equations with unbounded random terminal time. In particular, backward stochastic differential equations—which can be identified with solutions of elliptic partial differential equations—are approximated by means of deep neural networks.

Keywords: backward stochastic differential equations; semilinear elliptic partial differential equations; stochastic optimal control; unbounded random terminal time; machine learning; deep neural networks

MSC: 60H35; 65N75; 68T07

---

1. Introduction

Classical optimal control problems in insurance mathematics include finding risk measures like the probability of ruin or the expected discounted future dividend payments. Mathematically, these are problems over a potentially infinite time horizon, ending at an unbounded random terminal time—the time of ruin of the insurance company. In recent models which take multiple economic factors into account, the problems are high dimensional. For computing these risk measures, optimal control problems need to be solved numerically. A standard method for solving control problems is to derive the associated Hamilton–Jacobi–Bellman (HJB) equation—a semilinear (sometimes integro) partial differential equation (PDE)—and show that its (numerical) solution also solves the original control problem. In the case of infinite time horizon problems, these HJB equations are (degenerate) elliptic. *In this paper we propose a novel deep neural network algorithm for semilinear (degenerate) elliptic PDEs associated to infinite time horizon control problems in high dimensions.*

We apply this method to solve the dividend maximization problem in insurance mathematics. This problem originates in the seminal work by De Finetti (1957), who introduced expected discounted future dividend payments as a valuation principle for a homogeneous insurance portfolio. This constitutes an alternative risk measure to the (even more) classical probability of ruin. Classical results on the dividend maximization problem are Asmussen and Taksar (1997); Jeanblanc-Picqué and Shiryaev (1995); Radner and Shepp (1996); Shreve et al. (1984). Overviews can be found in Albrecher and Thonhauser (2009); Avanzi (2009); for an introduction to optimization problems in insurance we refer to Azcue and Muler (2014); Schmidli (2008). Recent models for the surplus of an insurance company allow for changes in the underlying economy. Such models have been studied, e.g., in Jiang and Pistorius (2012); Leobacher et al. (2014); Sotomayor and Cadenillas (2011); Zhu and Chen (2013); Szölgyenyi (2013, 2016); Reppen et al. (2020). In Leobacher et al. (2014); Szölgyenyi (2013, 2016) hidden Markov models for the underlying economic environment were proposed that allow for taking (multiple) exogenous, even not directly observable, economic factors into account. While these authors study the dividend maximization problem from a theoretical perspective, we are interested in *computing* the risk measure. However, classical numerical methods fail when the problem becomes high-dimensional, that is for example when exogenous economic factors are taken into account. In this paper we propose a novel deep neural network algorithm to solve high-dimensional problems. As an application we use it to solve the dividend maximization problem in the model from Szölgyenyi (2016) in high dimensions numerically.

Classical algorithms for solving semilinear (degenerate) elliptic PDEs like finite difference or finite element methods suffer from the so-called curse of dimensionality—the computational complexity for solving the discretized equation grows exponentially in the dimension. In high-dimensions (say > 10) one has to resort to costly quadrature methods such as multilevel-Monte Carlo or the quasi-Monte Carlo-based method presented in Kritzer et al. (2019). In recent years, deep neural network (DNN) algorithms for high-dimensional PDEs have been studied extensively. Prominent examples are Han et al. (2017, 2018), where semilinear parabolic PDEs are associated with backward stochastic differential equations (BSDEs) through the (nonlinear) Feynman-Kac formula and a DNN algorithm is proposed that solves these PDEs by solving the associated BSDEs. In the literature there exists a variety of DNN approaches for solving PDEs, in particular (degenerate) parabolic ones. Great literature overviews are given, e.g., in Beck et al. (2020); Grohs et al. (2019a), out of which we list some contributions here: (Beck et al. 2018, 2019b, 2019c; Becker et al. 2019a, 2019b; Berg and Nyström 2018; Chan-Wai-Nam et al. 2019; Chen and Wan 2020; Dockhorn 2019; E and Yu 2018; Farahmand et al. 2017; Fujii et al. 2019; Goudenège et al. 2019; Han and Long 2020; Han et al. 2020; Henry-Labordère 2017; Huré et al. 2019; Jacquier and Oumgari 2019; Long et al. 2018; Lu et al. 2019; Lye et al. 2020; Magill et al. 2018; Pham et al. 2019; Raissi 2018; Sirignano and Spiliopoulos 2018).

While mathematical finance control problems (e.g., investment problems) are studied over relatively short time horizons, leading to (degenerate) parabolic PDEs, in insurance mathematics they are often considered over the whole lifetime of the insurance company, leading to (degenerate) elliptic PDEs. For elliptic PDEs, a multilevel Picard iteration algorithm is studied in Beck et al. (2020), a derivative-free method using Brownian walkers without explicit calculation of the derivatives of the neural network is studied in Han et al. (2020), and a walk-on-the-sphere algorithm is introduced in Grohs and Herrmann (2020) for the Poisson equation, where the existence of DNNs that are able to approximate the solution to certain elliptic PDEs is shown.

In the present article we propose a novel DNN algorithm for a large class of semilinear (degenerate) elliptic PDEs. For this, we adopt the approach from Han et al. (2018) for (degenerate) parabolic PDEs. The difference here is that we use the correspondence between the PDEs we seek to solve and BSDEs with random terminal time. This correspondence was first presented in Pardoux (1998), and elaborated afterwards, e.g., in Briand and Hu (1998); Briand and Confortola (2008); Darling and Pardoux (1997); Pardoux (1999); Royer (2004).

As these results are not as standard as the BSDE correspondence to parabolic PDEs, we summarize the theory in Section 2 for the convenience of the reader. In Section 3 we present the DNN algorithm, and test it in Sections 4.1 and 4.2. In Section 4.3 we present the model from Szölgyenyi (2016) in which we seek to solve the dividend maximization problem and hence to compute the risk measure. That this method works also in high dimensions is demonstrated at the end of Section 4.3, where numerical results are presented.

The method presented here can be applied to many other high-dimensional semilinear (degenerate) elliptic PDE problems in insurance mathematics, such as the calculation of ruin probabilities, but we emphasize that its application possibilities are not limited to insurance problems.

2. BSDEs Associated with Elliptic PDEs

This section contains a short survey on scalar backward stochastic differential equations with random terminal times and on how they are related to a certain type of semilinear elliptic partial differential equations.

2.1. BSDEs with Random Terminal Times

Let $(\Omega, \mathcal{F}, \mathbb{P}, (\mathcal{F}_t)_{t\in[0,\infty)})$ be a filtered probability space satisfying the usual conditions and let $W = (W_t)_{t\in[0,\infty)}$ be a d-dimensional standard Brownian motion on it. We assume that $(\mathcal{F}_t)_{t\in[0,\infty)}$ is equal to the augmented natural filtration generated by W. For all real valued row or column vectors x, let $|x|$ denote their Euclidean norm. We need the following notations and definitions for BSDEs.

Definition 1. *A BSDE with random terminal time is a triple (τ, ξ, f), where*

- *the terminal time $\tau\colon \Omega \to [0,\infty]$ is an $(\mathcal{F}_t)_{t\in[0,\infty)}$-stopping time,*
- *the generator $\mathrm{f}\colon \Omega \times [0,\infty) \times \mathbb{R} \times \mathbb{R}^{1\times d} \to \mathbb{R}$ is a process which satisfies that for all $(y,z) \in \mathbb{R} \times \mathbb{R}^{1\times d}$, the process $t \mapsto \mathrm{f}(t,y,z)$ is progressively measurable,*
- *the terminal condition $\xi\colon \Omega \to \mathbb{R}$ is an $\mathcal{F}_\tau$-measurable random variable with $\xi = 0$ on $\{\tau = \infty\}$.*

Definition 2. *A solution to the BSDE (τ, ξ, f) is a pair of progressively measurable processes $(Y, Z) = ((Y_t)_{t\in[0,\infty)}, (Z_t)_{t\in[0,\infty)})$ with values in $\mathbb{R} \times \mathbb{R}^{1\times d}$, where*

- *Y is continuous $\mathbb{P}$-a.s. and for all $T \in (0,\infty)$, the trajectories $t \mapsto Z_t$ belong to $L^2([0,T], \mathbb{R}^{1\times d})$, and $t \mapsto \mathrm{f}(t, Y_t, Z_t)$ is in $L^1([0,T])$,*
- *for all $T \in (0,\infty)$ and all $t \in [0,T]$ it holds a.s. that*

$$Y_t = Y_T + \int_{t\wedge\tau}^{T\wedge\tau} \mathrm{f}(s, Y_s, Z_s)ds - \int_{t\wedge\tau}^{T\wedge\tau} Z_s dW_s, \tag{1}$$

- *$Y_t = \xi$ and $Z_t = 0$ on $\{t \geq \tau\}$.*

Results on existence of solutions of BSDEs with random terminal time can be found in Pardoux' seminal article Pardoux (1998) (see (Pardoux 1998, Theorem 3.2)), in Briand and Confortola (2008) for generators with quadratic growth (see (Briand and Confortola 2008, Theorem 3.3)), and, e.g., in Briand and Hu (1998); Briand et al. (2003); Darling and Pardoux (1997); Pardoux (1999); Royer (2004); many of them cover multidimensional state spaces for the Y-process.

Optimal control problems which can be treated using a BSDE setting have for example been studied in (Briand and Confortola 2008, Section 6). For this they consider generators of the forward-backward form

$$\mathrm{f}(t,y,z) = F(X_t, y, z) = \inf\{g(X_t, u) + zr(X_t, u)\colon u \in \mathcal{U}\} - \lambda y, \tag{2}$$

where X is a forward diffusion (see also the notation in the following subsection), $\mathcal{U}$ is a Banach space, r is a Hilbert space-valued function (in their setting z takes values in the according dual space) with linear growth, g a real valued function with quadratic growth in u, and $\lambda \in (0,\infty)$. In the sequel we focus on generators of forward-backward form.

2.2. Semilinear Elliptic PDEs and BSDEs with Random Terminal Time

In this subsection we recall the connection between semilinear elliptic PDEs and BSDEs with random (and possibly infinite) terminal time. The relationship between the theories is based on a nonlinear extension of the Feynman-Kac formula, see (Pardoux 1998, Section 4).

We define the *forward process* X as the stochastic process satisfying a.s.,

$$X_t = x + \int_0^t \mu(X_s)ds + \int_0^t \sigma(X_s)dW_s, \quad t \in [0,\infty), \tag{3}$$

where $x \in \mathbb{R}^d$ and $\mu\colon \mathbb{R}^d \to \mathbb{R}^d$ and $\sigma\colon \mathbb{R}^d \to \mathbb{R}^{d\times d}$ are globally Lipschitz functions.

In this paper we consider the following class of PDEs.

Definition 3.

- *A semilinear (degenerate) elliptic PDE on the whole $\mathbb{R}^d$ is of the form*

$$\mathcal{L}u + F(\cdot, u, (\nabla u)\sigma) = 0, \tag{4}$$

where the differential operator $\mathcal{L}$ acting on $C^2(\mathbb{R}^d)$ is given by

$$\mathcal{L} := \frac{1}{2}\sum_{i,j=1}^{d} (\sigma\sigma^\top)_{i,j}(x)\frac{\partial^2}{\partial x_i \partial x_j} + \sum_{i=1}^{d} \mu_i(x)\frac{\partial}{\partial x_i}, \tag{5}$$

and $F\colon \mathbb{R}^d \times \mathbb{R} \times \mathbb{R}^{1\times d} \to \mathbb{R}$ is such that the process $(t,y,z) \mapsto F(X_t,y,z)$ is a generator of a BSDE in the sense of Definition 1.

- *We say that a function u satisfies Equation (4) with Dirichlet boundary conditions on the open, bounded domain $G \subseteq \mathbb{R}^d$, if*

$$\begin{aligned} &\mathcal{L}u + F(\cdot, u, (\nabla u)\sigma) = 0, \quad x \in G, \\ &u(x) = g(x), \quad x \in \partial G, \end{aligned} \tag{6}$$

where $g\colon \mathbb{R}^d \to \mathbb{R}$ is a bounded, continuous function.

Definition 4.

1. *A BSDE associated to the PDE (4) on the whole $\mathbb{R}^d$ is given by the triplet (τ, ξ, f), where $\tau \equiv \infty$, $\xi = 0$, $\mathrm{f}(t,y,z) = F(X_t,y,z)$, X is as in (3), and the solution satisfies a.s. for all $T \in (0,\infty)$ that*

$$Y_t = Y_T + \int_t^T F(X_s,Y_s,Z_s)ds - \int_t^T Z_s dW_s, \quad t \in [0,T]. \tag{7}$$

2. *A BSDE associated to the PDE (6) with Dirichlet boundary conditions is given by the triplet $(\tau, g(X_\tau), \mathrm{f})$, where $\tau = \inf\{t \in [0,\infty)\colon X_t \notin \overline{G}\}$, $\mathrm{f}(t,y,z) = F(X_t,y,z)$, X is as in (3), and the solution satisfies a.s. for all $T \in (0,\infty)$ that*

$$\begin{aligned} &Y_t = Y_T + \int_{t\wedge\tau}^{T\wedge\tau} F(X_s,Y_s,Z_s)ds - \int_{t\wedge\tau}^{T\wedge\tau} Z_s dW_s, \quad t \in [0,T], \\ &Y_t = g(X_\tau),\ Z_t = 0, \quad t \geq \tau. \end{aligned} \tag{8}$$

In order to keep the notation simple, we do not highlight the dependence of X, Y, Z on x.

For later use we also introduce the following notion of solutions of PDEs, which we will use later.

Definition 5.

- *A function $u \in C(\mathbb{R}^d)$ is called viscosity subsolution of* (4), *if for all $\varphi \in C^2(\mathbb{R}^d)$ and all points $x \in \mathbb{R}^d$ where $u - \varphi$ has a local maximum,*

$$\mathcal{L}\varphi(x) + F(x, u(x), (\nabla\varphi(x))\sigma(x)) \geq 0.$$

- *A function $u \in C(\mathbb{R}^d)$ is called viscosity supersolution of* (4), *if for all $\varphi \in C^2(\mathbb{R}^d)$ and all points $x \in \mathbb{R}^d$ where $u - \varphi$ has a local minimum,*

$$\mathcal{L}\varphi(x) + F(x, u(x), (\nabla\varphi(x))\sigma(x)) \leq 0.$$

- *A function $u \in C(\mathbb{R}^d)$ is called viscosity solution of* (4), *if it is a viscosity sub- and supersolution.*

A similar definition of viscosity solutions can be given for the case of Dirichlet boundary conditions (6), see Pardoux (1998).

For later use, note that (8) can be rewritten in forward form as

$$\begin{aligned} Y_t &= Y_0 - \int_0^t F(X_s, Y_s, Z_s)ds + \int_0^t Z_s dW_s, \quad t \in [0, \tau), \\ Y_t &= g(X_\tau),\ Z_t = 0, \quad t \geq \tau. \end{aligned} \tag{9}$$

The following theorems link the semilinear elliptic PDEs (4) and (6) to the associated BSDEs.

Theorem 1 ((Pardoux 1998, Theorem 4.1)). *Let $(t, y, z) \mapsto F(X_t, y, z)$ meet the assumptions of (Pardoux 1998, Theorem 3.2) and let $u \in C^2(\mathbb{R}^d)$ satisfy*

$$\mathbb{E}\left[\int_0^\infty e^{\lambda t} |((\nabla u)\sigma)(X_t)|^2 dt\right] < \infty$$

with λ as in (Pardoux 1998, Theorem 3.2). If u is a classical solution of the PDE (4), *then*

$$Y_t = u(X_t), \quad Z_t = ((\nabla u)\sigma)(X_t)$$

solve the BSDE (7). *An equivalent statement can be established for the system with boundary conditions* (6) *and Equation* (8), *see Pardoux (1998).*

Note that for all $x \in \mathbb{R}^d$, Y and Z are stochastic processes adapted to $(\mathcal{F}_t)_{t \in [0,\infty)}$. Therefore, Y_0, Z_0 are $\mathcal{F}_0$-measurable and hence a.s. deterministic. For us, the connection between PDEs and BSDEs is of relevance because of the converse result, where $x \mapsto Y_0$ delivers a solution to the respective PDE.

Theorem 2 ((Pardoux 1998, Theorem 4.3)). *Assume that for some $K, K', p \in (0, \infty)$, $\gamma \in (-\infty, 0)$ the function F satisfies for all x, y, y', z, z',*

(i) $|F(x, y, z)| \leq K'(1 + |x|^p + |y| + |z|)$,
(ii) $\langle y - y', F(x, y, z) - F(x, y', z)\rangle \leq \gamma |y - y'|^2$,
(iii) $|F(x, y, z) - F(x, y, z')| \leq K|z - z'|$.

Then (Pardoux 1998, Theorem 3.2) can be applied to the generator $(t, y, z) \mapsto F(X_t, y, z)$, showing that the function u given by $u(x) = Y_0$ is a viscosity solution to (4), *where Y is the first component of the unique solution to* (7) *in the class of solutions from (Pardoux 1998, Theorem 3.2).*

The case of the Dirichlet problem requires additional assumptions on the domain G and the exit time τ from (8). We refer to (Pardoux 1998, Theorem 4.3). A corresponding result for BSDEs with quadratic generator is (Briand and Confortola 2008, Theorem 5.2).

To conclude, the correspondence between PDE (6) and BSDE (8) is given by $Y_t = u(X_t)$, $Z_t = ((\nabla u)\sigma)(X_t)$, $\xi = g(X_\tau)$. For tackling elliptic PDEs which are degenerate (as it is the case for our insurance mathematics example) we need to take the relationship a little further in order to escape the not so convenient structure of the Z-process. We factor $\mathcal{Z}\sigma(X) = Z$ for cases where this equation is solvable for $\mathcal{Z}$ (σ needs not necessarily be invertible) and define $f(x,y,\zeta) := F(x,y,\zeta\sigma(x))$[1], giving the correspondence $Y_t = u(X_t)$, $\mathcal{Z}_t = \nabla u(X_t)$, $\xi = g(X_\tau)$. This relationship motivates us to solve semilinear degenerate elliptic PDEs by solving the corresponding BSDEs forward in time (cf. (9))

$$Y_t = Y_0 - \int_0^t f(X_s, Y_s, \mathcal{Z}_s)ds + \int_0^t \mathcal{Z}_s\sigma(X_s)dW_s, \quad t \in [0, \tau)$$

for Y_0 by approximating the paths of $\mathcal{Z} = \nabla u(X)$ by a DNN, see Section 3. Doing so, we obtain an estimate of a solution value $u(x)$ for a given $x \in \mathbb{R}^d$.

3. Algorithm

The idea of the proposed algorithm is inspired by Han et al. (2018), where the authors use the correspondence between BSDEs and semilinear parabolic PDEs to construct a DNN algorithm for solving the latter. In the same spirit, we construct a DNN algorithm based on the correspondence to BSDEs with random terminal time for solving semilinear elliptic PDEs.

The details of the algorithm are described in three steps of increasing specificity. First we explain the DNN algorithm mathematically. This is done below. Second, Algorithm 1 at the end of this section provides a pseudocode. Third, our program code is provided on Github[2] under a creative commons license. The algorithm is implemented in a generic manner so that it can be reused for other elliptic PDE problems.

The goal of the algorithm is to calculate solution values $u(x)$ of the semilinear (degenerate) elliptic PDE of interest. For the construction of the algorithm we use the correspondence to a BSDE with random terminal time. Recall from Section 2 that such a BSDE is given by a triplet $(\tau, g(X_\tau), f)$ that can be determined from the given PDE and by

$$X_t = x + \int_0^t \mu(X_s)ds + \int_0^t \sigma(X_s)dW_s \tag{10}$$

and

$$Y_t = Y_0 - \int_0^t f(X_s, Y_s, \mathcal{Z}_s)ds + \int_0^t \mathcal{Z}_s\sigma(X_s)dW_s. \tag{11}$$

Furthermore, recall that we have identified $Y_t = u(X_t)$, where u is the solution of the PDE we are interested in.

The first step for calculating u is to approximate (10) up to the stopping time τ. To make this computationally feasible, we choose T large and stop at $\tau \wedge T$, hence at T at the latest. Now let $0 = t_0 < t_1 < \cdots < t_N = T$, $\Delta t_n = t_{n+1} - t_n$. We simulate M paths $\omega_1, \ldots, \omega_M$ of the Brownian motion W. With this we approximate the forward process using the Euler–Maruyama scheme, that is $X_0 = x$ and

$$X_{t_{n+1}} \approx X_{t_n} + \mu(X_{t_n})\Delta t_n + \sigma(X_{t_n})\Delta W_n. \tag{12}$$

In the next step we compute $\mathcal{Z}$. For all t_n, $\mathcal{Z}_{t_n} = \nabla u(X_{t_n})$ are approximated by DNNs, each mapping G to $\mathbb{R}^d$. As noted above, the implementation of this (and all other steps) is provided.

---

1 Since $\mathcal{Z}\sigma(X) = Z$ is solvable for $\mathcal{Z}$, f is well-defined.
2 https://github.com/stefankremsner/elliptic-pdes.

Now, we initialize $u(x)$ and use the above approximations to compute the solution to the BSDE forward in time by approximating (11):

$$\begin{aligned} u(X_{t_{n+1}}) \approx u(X_{t_n}) - \mathbb{1}_{(0,\tau)}(t_n) f\left(X_{t_n}, u(X_{t_n}), \nabla u(X_{t_n})\right) \Delta t_n \\ + \mathbb{1}_{(0,\tau)}(t_n) \nabla u(X_{t_n}) \sigma(X_{t_n}) \Delta W_n. \end{aligned} \tag{13}$$

Note that due to this construction, indirectly $u(X_{t_{n+1}})$ is also approximated by a DNN as a combination of DNNs.

For the training of the involved DNNs, we compare $u(X_{\tau\wedge T})$ with the terminal value ξ. This defines the loss function for the training:

$$\frac{1}{M}\sum_{k=1}^{M} |u(X_{\tau\wedge T}(\omega_k)) - \xi(\omega_k)|^2.$$

After a certain number of training epochs the loss function is minimized and we obtain an approximate solution value $u(x)$ of the PDE.

Remark 1. *Several approximation errors arise in the proposed algorithm:*

1. *the approximation error of the Euler–Maruyama method, which is used for sampling the forward equation,*
2. *the error of approximating the expected loss,*
3. *the error of cutting off the potentially unbounded random terminal time at time T,*
4. *the approximation error of the deep neural network model for approximating $\mathcal{Z}_{t_n}$ for each t_n.*

It is well known that for any continuous function we can find DNNs that approximate the function arbitrarily well, see Hornik (1991); Hornik et al. (1989). This is, however, not sufficient to make any statement about the approximation quality. Results on convergence rates are required. Though this question is already studied in the literature (see, e.g., Beck et al. 2019a, 2020; Berner et al. 2020; Elbrächter et al. 2018; Gonon et al. 2019; Grohs et al. 2018, 2019a, 2019b; Hutzenthaler et al. 2018, 2020a, 2020b; Jentzen et al. 2018; Kutyniok et al. 2019; Reisinger and Zhang 2019), results on convergence rates for given constructions are yet scarce and hence many questions remain open while the number of proposed DNN algorithms grows.

We close this section with some comments on the implementation.

Remark 2.

- *All DNNs are initialized with random numbers.*
- *For each value of x we average $u(x)$ over 5 independent runs. The estimator for $u(x)$ is calculated as the mean value of $u(x)$ in the last 3 network training epochs of each run, sampled according to the validation size (see below).*
- *We choose a nonequidistant time grid in order to get a higher resolution for earlier (and hence probably closer to the stopping time) time points.*
- *We use* tanh *as activation function.*
- *We compute $u(x)$ simultaneously for 8 values of x by using parallel computing.*

Algorithm 1 Elliptic PDE Solver for a BSDE (f, ξ) with stopping time τ

Require: number of training epochs E, maximal time T, step-size Δt, number of timesteps N, number of sample paths M, number of hidden layer neurons dim, initial (random) starting values $(\theta_0^{(u)}, \theta_0^{(\zeta)})$

function TRAINABLEVARIABLES(dim, θ) ▷ see Pytorch or Tensorflow
    return a trainable variable with dimension $1 \times$ dim initialized by θ.
end function
function SUBNETWORK(x) ▷ allowing x to be a tensor containing M rows (samples)
    return a trainable DNN, evaluated at x.
end function
for $i = 0, \ldots, N$ **do**
    $t_i = \text{timesteps}(i)$ ▷ Initialize nonequidistant timesteps
end for
for $j = 1, \ldots, M$ **do**
    Sample Brownian motion trajectory $\left(w_{t_i}^{(j)}\right)_{0 \le i \le N}$
    Sample path from forward process $\left(x_{t_i}^{(j)}\right)_{0 \le i \le N}$
    calculate stopping time $\tau^{(j)}$
    calculate terminal value $\xi^{(j)}$
    set $x_t^{(j)} = x_{\tau^{(j)}}^{(j)}$ for all $t > \tau^{(j)}$
end for
$u_0 = $ TRAINABLEVARIABLES$(1, \theta_0^{(u)})$ ▷ Initialize u
$\nabla u_0 = $ TRAINABLEVARIABLES$(d, \theta_0^{(\zeta)})$ ▷ Initialize $\mathcal{Z}$
for $j = 1, \ldots, M$ **do**
    $u^{(j)} = u_0$
    $\nabla u^{(j)} = \nabla u_0$
end for
for $e = 1, \ldots, E$ **do**
    for $i = 1, \ldots, N-1$ **do**
        for $j = 1, \ldots, M$ **do**
            $u^{(j)} = u^{(j)} - f(x_{t_i}^{(j)}, u^{(j)}, \nabla u^{(j)})(t_{i+1} - t_i) + \nabla u^{(j)} \sigma(x_{t_i}^{(j)})(w_{t_{i+1}}^{(j)} - w_{t_i}^{(j)})$
            if $t_{i+1} > \tau^{(j)}$ **then** break
            end if
        end for
        $\nabla u = $ SUBNETWORK$(x_{t_{i+1}})$
    end for
    update all trainable variables and the subnetwork's weights according to the loss function

$$\frac{1}{M} \sum_{j=1}^{M} (u^{(j)} - \xi^{(j)})^2$$

end for
    return $(u_0, \nabla u_0)$

4. Examples

In this section we apply the proposed algorithm to three examples. The first one serves as a validity check, the second one as an academic example with a nonlinearity. Finally, we apply the algorithm to solve the dividend maximization problem under incomplete information.

4.1. The Poisson Equation

The first example we study is the Poisson equation—a linear PDE.

Let $r \in (0,\infty)$, $G = \left\{x \in \mathbb{R}^d \colon |x| < r\right\}$, $\partial G = \left\{x \in \mathbb{R}^d \colon |x| = r\right\}$, $b \in \mathbb{R}$, and

$$\begin{aligned} \Delta u(x) &= -b, \quad x \in G, \\ u(x) &= 0, \quad x \in \partial G. \end{aligned} \tag{14}$$

Solving (14) is equivalent to solving the BSDE with

$$\begin{aligned} dX_t &= \sqrt{2} dW_t, & X_0 &= x, \\ f(x,y,\zeta) &= b, & \xi &= 0, \end{aligned}$$

up to the stopping time $\tau = \inf\{t \in [0,T] \colon |x| > r\}$.

To obtain a reference solution for this linear BSDE we use an analytic formula for the expectation of τ, see (Øksendal 2003, Example 7.4.2, p. 121). This yields

$$u(x) = \frac{b}{2d}\left(r^2 - |x|^2\right).$$

4.1.1. Numerical Results

We compute $u(x)$ on the $\mathbb{R}^2$ and the $\mathbb{R}^{100}$ for 15 different values of x. Figure 1 shows the approximate solution of u obtained by the DNN algorithm on the diagonal points $\{(x,\ldots,x) \in \mathbb{R}^d \colon x \in [-r,r]\}$ (in blue) and the analytical reference solution (in green). Table 1 contains the parameters we use.

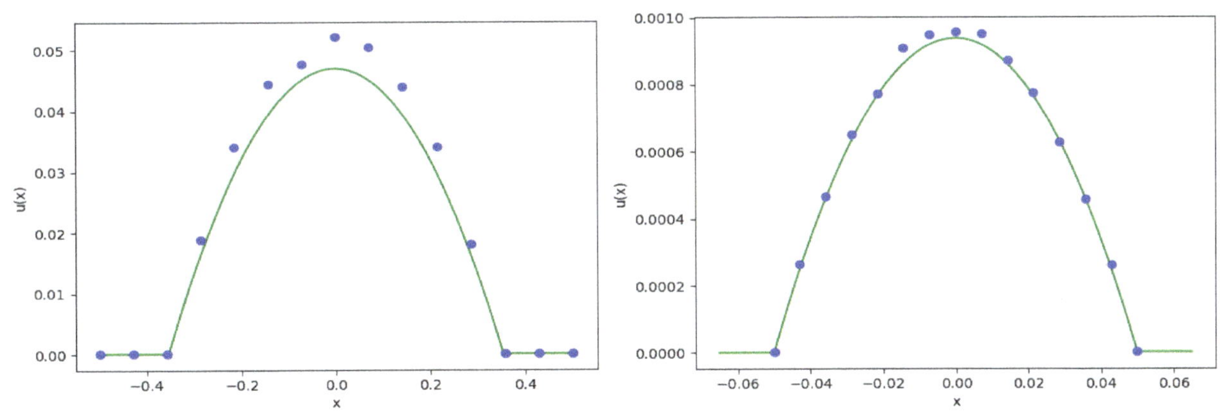

Figure 1. Approximate solution (blue) and reference solution (green) for the Poisson equation on the $\mathbb{R}^2$ (**left**) and on the $\mathbb{R}^{100}$ (**right**).

Table 1. Parameters for the Poisson equation.

d	r	b	N	T	E	M	Validation Size	Time per Eight Points[3]
2	0.5	0.75	500	0.5	200	64	256	119.17 s
100	0.5	0.75	500	0.01	200	64	256	613.86 s

Note that as the expected value of τ decreases linearly in d, we adapt the cut off time T for $d = 100$ accordingly.

4.2. *Quadratic Gradient*

The second example is a semilinear PDE with a quadratic gradient term.

Let $r \in (0, \infty)$, $G = \{x \in \mathbb{R}^d \colon |x| < r\}$, and $\partial G = \{x \in \mathbb{R}^d \colon |x| = r\}$. We consider the PDE

$$\begin{aligned} \Delta u(x) + |\nabla u(x)|^2 &= 2e^{-u(x)}, \quad x \in G, \\ u(x) &= \log\left(\frac{r^2+1}{d}\right), \quad x \in \partial G. \end{aligned} \tag{15}$$

corresponding to the BSDE

$$dX_t = \sqrt{2} dW_t, \qquad X_0 = x, \tag{16}$$

$$f(x,y,\zeta) = |\zeta|^2 - 2e^{-y}, \qquad \xi = \log\left(\frac{|r|^2+1}{d}\right). \tag{17}$$

In addition, for this example we have an analytic reference solution given by

$$u(x) = \log\left(\frac{|x|^2+1}{d}\right).$$

4.2.1. Numerical Results

As in the previous example we compute $u(x)$ for 15 different values of x on the $\mathbb{R}^2$ and the $\mathbb{R}^{100}$. Figure 2 shows the approximate solution of u obtained by the DNN algorithm on the diagonal points $\{(x, \ldots, x) \in \mathbb{R}^d \colon x \in [-r, r]\}$ (in blue) and the analytical reference solution (in green). Table 2 contains the parameters we use.

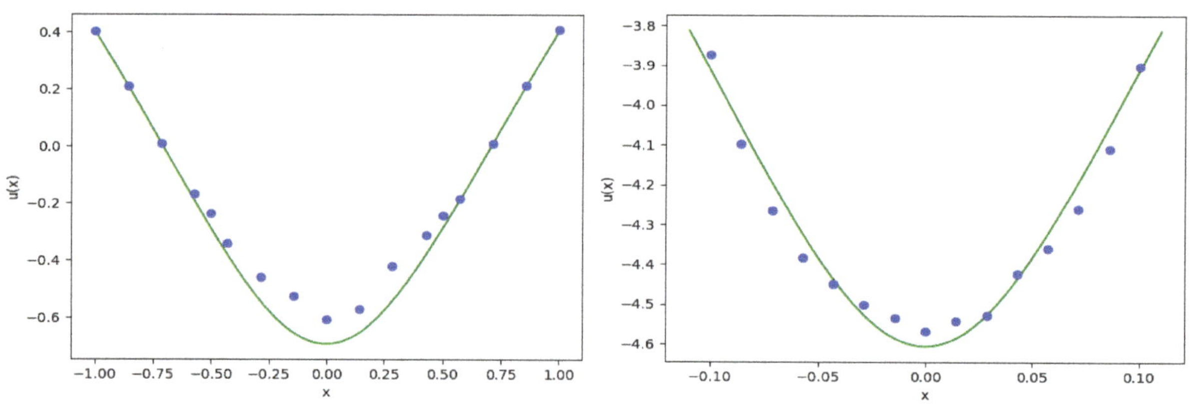

Figure 2. Approximate solution (blue) and reference solution (green) for the equation with quadratic gradient on the $\mathbb{R}^2$ (**left**) and on the $\mathbb{R}^{100}$ (**right**).

---

[3] The numerical examples were run on a Lenovo Thinkpad notebook with an Intel Core i7 processor (2.6 GHz) and 16 GB memory, without CUDA.

Table 2. Parameters for the equation with quadratic gradient.

d	r	N	T	E	M	Validation Size	Time per Eight Points
2	1	100	5	500	64	256	204.58 s
100	1	100	0.1	500	64	256	321.13 s

While classical numerical methods for PDEs would be a much better choice in the case $d = 2$, their application would not be feasible in the case $d = 100$.

4.3. Dividend Maximization

The goal of this paper is to show how to use the proposed DNN algorithm to solve high-dimensional control problems that arise in insurance mathematics. We finally arrived at the point where we are ready to do so.

Our example comes from Szölgyenyi (2016), where the author studies De Finetti's dividend maximization problem in a setup with incomplete information about the current state of the market. The hidden market-state process determines the trend of the surplus process of the insurance company and is modeled as a d-state Markov chain. Using stochastic filtering, in Szölgyenyi (2016) they achieve to transform the one-dimensional problem under incomplete information to a d-dimensional problem under complete information. The cost is $(d-1)$ additional dimensions in the state space. We state the problem under complete information using different notation than in Szölgyenyi (2016) in order to avoid ambiguities.

The probability that the Markov chain modeling the market-state is in state $i \in \{1, \ldots, d-1\}$ is given by

$$\pi_i(t) = x_i + \int_0^t \left(q_{d,i} + \sum_{j=1}^{d-1} (q_{j,i} - q_{d,i}) \pi_j(s) \right) ds + \int_0^t \pi_i(s) \frac{a_i - \nu_s}{\rho} \, dB_s, \tag{18}$$

where

$$\nu_t = a_d + \sum_{j=1}^{d-1} (a_j - a_d) \pi_j(t), \tag{19}$$

$x_i \in (0,1)$, B is a one-dimensional Brownian motion, $a_1, \ldots, a_d \in \mathbb{R}$ are the values of the surplus trend in the respective market-states of the hidden Markov chain, and $(q_{i,j})_{i,j \in \{1,\ldots,d\}} \in \mathbb{R}^{d \times d}$ denotes the intensity matrix of the chain.

Let $(\ell_t)_{t \in [0,\infty)}$ be the dividend rate process. The surplus of the insurance company is given by

$$\widetilde{X}_t^d = x_d + \int_0^t (\nu_s - \ell_s) \, ds + \rho B_t, \quad t \in [0, \infty), \tag{20}$$

where $x_d, \rho \in (0, \infty)$. For later use we define also the dividend free surplus

$$X_t^d = x_d + \int_0^t \nu_s \, ds + \rho B_t, \quad t \in [0, \infty). \tag{21}$$

The processes (18) and (20) form the d-dimensional state process underlying the optimal control problem we aim to solve.

The goal of the insurance company is to determine its value by maximizing the discounted dividends payments until the time of ruin $\eta = \inf\{t \in (0, \infty] \colon \widetilde{X}_t^d < 0\}$, that is it seeks to find

$$u(x_1, \ldots, x_d) = \sup_{(\ell_t)_{t \in [0,\infty)} \in A} \mathbb{E}_{x_1, \ldots, x_d} \left[\int_0^\eta e^{-\delta t} \ell_t \, dt \right], \tag{22}$$

where $\delta \in (0,\infty)$ is a discount rate, A is the set of admissible controls, and $\mathbb{E}_{x_1,\ldots,x_d}[\cdot]$ denotes the expectation under the initial conditions $\pi_i(0) = x_i$ for $i \in \{1,\ldots,d-1\}$ and $\widetilde{X}_0^d = x_d$. Admissible controls are $(\mathcal{F}_t^{X^d})_{t\geq 0}$-progressively measurable, $[0,K]$-valued for $K \in (0,\infty)$ and fulfill $\ell_t \equiv 0$ for $t > \eta$, cf. Szölgyenyi (2016).

In order to tackle the problem, we solve the corresponding Hamilton–Jacobi–Bellmann (HJB) equation[4] from Szölgyenyi (2016),

$$(\mathcal{L}-\delta)u + \sup_{\ell\in[0,K]} (\ell(1-u_{x_d})) = 0, \tag{23}$$

where $\mathcal{L}$ is the second order degenerate elliptic operator

$$\begin{aligned}\mathcal{L}u = a_d u_{x_d} + \sum_{i=1}^{d-1}\Bigg((a_i-a_d)x_i u_{x_d} + \left(q_{di} + \sum_{j=1}^{d-1}(q_{ji}-q_{di})x_i\right)u_{x_i} + x_i\,(a_i-\nu)\,u_{x_d x_i}\\ + \frac{1}{2}\sum_{j=1}^{d-1}\left(\left(x_i\frac{a_i-\nu}{\rho}\right)\left(x_j\frac{a_j-\nu}{\rho}\right)u_{x_i x_j}\right)\Bigg) + \frac{1}{2}\rho^2 u_{x_d x_d}.\end{aligned}$$

The supremum in (23) is attained at

$$\ell = \begin{cases} K, & u_{x_d} \leq 1 \\ 0, & u_{x_d} > 1. \end{cases}$$

Plugging this into (23) we end up with a d-dimensional semilinear degenerate elliptic PDE:

$$(\mathcal{L}-\delta)u + K(1-u_{x_d})\mathbb{1}_{\{u_{x_d}\leq 1\}} = 0. \tag{24}$$

The boundary conditions in x_d direction are given by

$$u(x_1,\ldots,x_d) = \begin{cases} K/\delta, & x_d \to \infty \\ 0, & x_d = 0. \end{cases}$$

No boundary conditions are required for the other variables, cf. Szölgyenyi (2016).

In (Szölgyenyi 2016, Corollary 3.6) it is proven that the unique viscosity solution to (24) solves the optimal control problem (22). Hence, we can indeed solve the control problem by solving the HJB equation.

For the numerical approximation we cut off x_d at $r \in (0,\infty)$. Hence, $G = \left\{x \in \mathbb{R}^d : 0 < x_d < r\right\}$ and $\partial G = \left\{x \in \mathbb{R}^d : x_d \in \{0,r\}\right\}$.

For the convenience of the reader we derive the BSDE corresponding to (24). The forward equation is given by

$$dX_t = (d\pi_1(t),\ldots,d\pi_{d-1}(t),dX_t^d)^\top, \qquad X_0 = x,$$

that is

$$dX_t = \mu(X_t)dt + \sigma(X_t)dW_t, \qquad X_0 = x,$$

4 For abbreviation we use u_{x_d} for $\frac{\partial u}{\partial x_d}$ etc.

where $W = (B, W^2, \dots, W^d)^\top$, $x = (x_1, \dots, x_d)^\top$, and

$$\mu(x) = \left(q_{d,1} + \sum_{j=1}^{d-1}(q_{j,1} - q_{d,1})x_j, \dots, q_{d,d-1} + \sum_{j=1}^{d-1}(q_{j,d-1} - q_{d,d-1})x_{d-1}, a_d + \sum_{j=1}^{d-1}(a_j - a_d)x_j\right)^\top,$$

$$\sigma(x) = \begin{pmatrix} x_1 \frac{a_1 - a_d + \sum_{j=1}^{d-1}(a_j - a_d)x_j}{\rho} & 0 & \dots & 0 \\ \dots & 0 & \dots & 0 \\ x_{d-1}\frac{a_{d-1} - a_d + \sum_{j=1}^{d-1}(a_j - a_d)x_j}{\rho} & 0 & \dots & 0 \\ \rho & 0 & \dots & 0 \end{pmatrix}.$$

We claim that the BSDE associated to (24) is given in forward form by

$$\begin{aligned} u(X_t) = u(x) &- \int_0^t [K(1 - u_{x_d}(X_s))\mathbb{1}_{\{u_{x_d}(X_s) \le 1\}} - \delta u(X_s)]dt \\ &+ \int_0^t \nabla u(X_s)\sigma(X_s)dW_s. \end{aligned} \tag{25}$$

Applying Itô's formula to $u(X)$ yields

$$u(X_t) = u(x) + \int_0^t \mathcal{L}u(X_s)dt + \int_0^t \nabla u(X_s)\sigma(X_s)dW_s. \tag{26}$$

Combining (25) and (26) gives

$$\begin{aligned} u(x) - \int_0^t [K(1 - u_{x_d}(X_s))\mathbb{1}_{\{u_{x_d}(X_s) \le 1\}} - \delta u(X_s)]dt + \int_0^t \nabla u(X_s)\sigma(X_s)dW_s \\ = u(x) + \int_0^t \mathcal{L}u(X_s)dt + \int_0^t \nabla u(X_s)\sigma(X_s)dW_s. \end{aligned}$$

Canceling terms verifies (in a heuristic manner) (24).

Hence, the corresponding BSDE has the parameters

$$f(x, y, \zeta) = K(1 - \zeta_d)\mathbb{1}_{\{\zeta_d \le 1\}} - \delta y \tag{27}$$

and

$$\xi = \begin{cases} K/\delta, & X_\tau^d = r, \\ 0, & X_\tau^d = 0, \end{cases}$$

if $\tau < \infty$.

4.3.1. Numerical Results

As for this example we have no analytic reference solution at hand, we use the solution from Szölgyenyi (2016) for the case $d = 2$, which was obtained by a finite difference method and policy iteration. Then we show that the DNN algorithm also provides an approximation in high dimensions in reasonable computation time.

As in the previous examples we compute $u(x)$ on the $\mathbb{R}^2$ and on the $\mathbb{R}^{100}$ for 15 different values of x. Figure 3 shows the approximate solution of the HJB equation and hence the value of the insurance company obtained by the DNN algorithm (in blue) and the reference solution from Szölgyenyi (2016) (in green) for the case $d = 2$. For $d = 100$ we have no reference solution at hand. Figure 4 shows the loss for a fixed value of x in the case $d = 100$. Tables 3 and 4 contain the parameters we use.

Table 3. Parameters for the dividend problem.

d	r	K	δ	ρ	a_i	N	T	E	M	Validation Size	Time per Eight Points
2	5	1.8	0.5	1	$\left(2-\frac{i}{d}\right)$	100	5	500	64	256	317.42 s
100	5	1.8	0.5	1	$\left(2-\frac{i}{d}\right)$	100	5	500	64	256	613.15 s

Table 4. Intensity matrix values for the dividend problem.

Case	$i=j$ Even	$i=j$ Odd	$i=j+1$ Even	$i=j+1\geq 3$ Odd	$i=1, j=d$	Otherwise
$q_{i,j}$	-0.5	-0.25	0.5	0.25	0.25	0

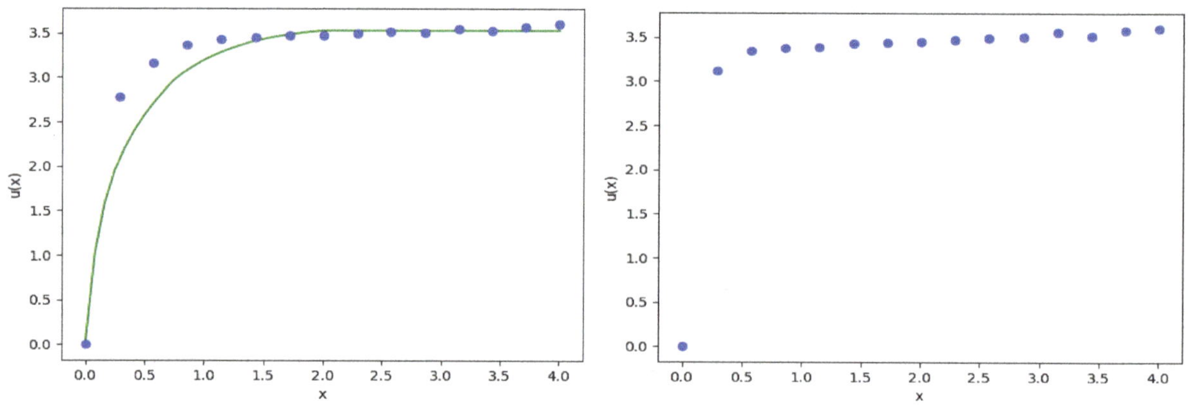

Figure 3. Approximate solution (blue) and reference solution (green) for the dividend problem on the $\mathbb{R}^2$ for fixed $\pi_1 = \pi_2 = 0.5$ (**left**) and on the $\mathbb{R}^{100}$ for fixed $\pi_1 = \cdots = \pi_{100} = 0.01$ (**right**, without reference solution).

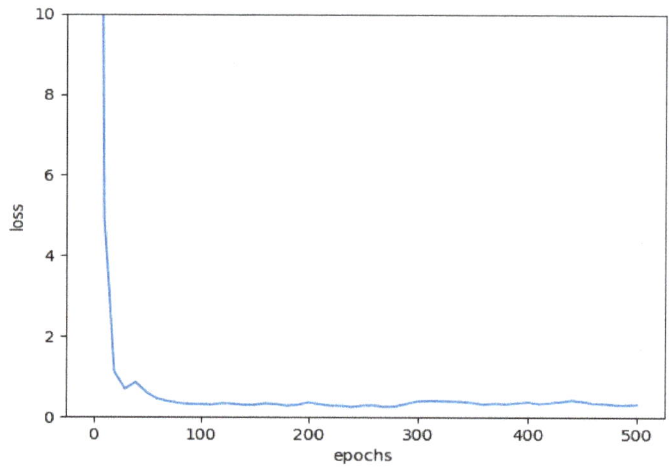

Figure 4. Interpolated loss for the case $d = 100$.

5. Conclusions

The goal of this paper was to compute the risk measure given by the expected discounted future dividend payments in a complex high-dimensional economic environment. This demonstrates the effectiveness of using DNN algorithms for solving some high-dimensional PDE problems in insurance mathematics that cannot be solved by classical methods. In the literature the focus so far was on parabolic PDE problems; however, in insurance mathematics we often face problems up to an unbounded random terminal time, e.g., the time of ruin of the insurance company, leading to (degenerate) elliptic problems.

Hence, we have proposed a novel deep neural network algorithm for a large class of semilinear (degenerate) elliptic PDEs associated to infinite time horizon control problems in high dimensions. The method extends the DNN algorithm proposed by Han, Jetzen, and E Han et al. (2018), which was developed for parabolic PDEs, to the case of (degenerate) elliptic semilinear PDEs. We have attacked the problem inspired by a series of results by Pardoux Pardoux (1998).

Of course, in low dimensions one would not use the proposed DNN algorithm—classical methods are more efficient. However, recent models are frequently high dimensional, in which case classical methods fail due to the curse of dimensionality. Then the DNN algorithm presented here can be applied to compute the desired quantity.

We emphasize that the method presented here can also be applied to many other high-dimensional semilinear (degenerate) elliptic PDE problems in insurance mathematics and beyond.

An implementation of the algorithm is provided on Github[5] under a creative commons license.

Author Contributions: Writing–original draft, S.K., A.S. and M.S. All authors have read and agreed to the published version of the manuscript.

Acknowledgments: The authors thank Gunther Leobacher for discussions and suggestions that improved the paper.

References

1. Albrecher, Hansjörg, and Stefan Thonhauser. 2009. Optimality results for dividend problems in insurance. *RACSAM Revista de la Real Academia de Ciencias Exactas, Fisicas y Naturales. Serie A. Matematicas* 103: 295–320. [CrossRef]
2. Asmussen, Søren, and Michael Taksar. 1997. Controlled diffusion models for optimal dividend pay-out. *Insurance: Mathematics and Economics* 20: 1–15. [CrossRef]
3. Avanzi, Benjamin. 2009. Strategies for dividend distribution: A review. *North American Actuarial Journal* 13: 217–51. [CrossRef]
4. Azcue, Pablo, and Nora Muler. 2014. *Stochastic Optimization in Insurance—A Dynamic Programming Approach.*
5. Springer Briefs in Quantitative Finance. New York, Heidelberg, Dordrecht and London: Springer.
6. Beck, Christian, Sebastian Becker, Philipp Grohs, Nor Jaafari, and Arnulf Jentzen. 2018. Solving stochastic differential equations and Kolmogorov equations by means of deep learning. *arXiv* arXiv:1806.00421.
7. Beck, Christian, Fabian Hornung, Martin Hutzenthaler, Arnulf Jentzen, and Thomas Kruse. 2019a. Overcoming the curse of dimensionality in the numerical approximation of Allen-Cahn partial differential equations via truncated full-history recursive multilevel Picard approximations. *arXiv* arXiv:1907.06729.
8. Beck, Christian, Sebastian Becker, Patrick Cheridito, Arnulf Jentzen, and Ariel Neufeld. 2019b. Deep splitting method for parabolic PDEs. *arXiv* arXiv:1907.03452.
9. Beck, Christian, Weinan E, and Arnulf Jentzen. 2019c. Machine learning approximation algorithms for high-dimensional fully nonlinear partial differential equations and second-order backward stochastic differential equations. *Journal of Nonlinear Science* 29: 1563–619. [CrossRef]
10. Beck, Christian, Lukas Gonon, and Arnulf Jentzen. 2020. Overcoming the curse of dimensionality in the numerical approximation of high-dimensional semilinear elliptic partial differential equations. *arXiv* arXiv:2003.00596. Becker, Sebastian, Patrick Cheridito, and Arnulf Jentzen. 2019a. Deep optimal stopping. *Journal of Machine Learning Research* 20: 74.
11. Becker, Sebastian, Patrick Cheridito, Arnulf Jentzen, and Timo Welti. 2019b. Solving high-dimensional optimal stopping problems using deep learning. *arXiv* arXiv:1908.01602.

[5] https://github.com/stefankremsner/elliptic-pdes.

12. Berg, Jens, and Kaj Nyström. 2018. A unified deep artificial neural network approach to partial differential equations in complex geometries. *Neurocomputing* 317: 28–41. [CrossRef]
13. Berner, Julius, Philipp Grohs, and Arnulf Jentzen. 2020. Analysis of the generalization error: Empirical risk minimization over deep artificial neural networks overcomes the curse of dimensionality in the numerical approximation of Black–Scholes partial differential equations. *SIAM Journal on Mathematics of Data Science* 3: 631–57. [CrossRef]
14. Briand, Philippe, and Ying Hu. 1998. Stability of BSDEs with random terminal time and homogenization of semi-linear elliptic PDEs. *Journal of Functional Analysis* 155: 455–94. [CrossRef]
15. Briand, Philippe, Bernard Delyon, Ying Hu, Étienne Pardoux, and Lucretiu Stoica. 2003. *Lp* solutions of backward stochastic differential equations. *Stochastic Processes and their Applications* 108: 109–29. [CrossRef]
16. Briand, Philippe, and Fulvia Confortola. 2008. Quadratic BSDEs with random terminal time and elliptic PDEs in infinite dimension. *Electronic Journal of Probability* 13: 1529–61.
17. Chan-Wai-Nam, Quentin, Joseph Mikael, and Xavier Warin. 2019. Machine learning for semi linear PDEs. *Journal of Scientific Computing* 79: 1667–712. [CrossRef]
18. Chen, Yangang, and Justin W. L. Wan. 2020. Deep neural network framework based on backward stochastic differential equations for pricing and hedging american options in high dimensions. *Quantitative Finance* 1–23. [CrossRef]
19. Darling, Richard W. R., and Étienne Pardoux. 1997. Backwards SDE with random terminal time and applications to semilinear elliptic PDE. *The Annals of Probability* 25: 1135–59. [CrossRef]
20. De Finetti, Bruno. 1957. Su un'impostazione alternativa della teoria collettiva del rischio. *Transactions of the XVth International Congress of Actuaries* 2: 433–43.
21. Dockhorn, Tim. 2019. A discussion on solving partial differential equations using neural networks. *arXiv* arXiv:1904.07200.
22. E, Weinan, and Bing Yu. 2018. The deep Ritz method: A deep learning-based numerical algorithm for solving variational problems. *Communications in Mathematics and Statistics* 6: 1–12. [CrossRef]
23. Elbrächter, Dennis, Philipp Grohs, Arnulf Jentzen, and Christoph Schwab. 2018. DNN expression rate analysis of high-dimensional PDEs: Application to option pricing. *arXiv* arXiv:1809.07669.
24. Farahmand, Amir-Massoud, Saleh Nabi, and Daniel Nikovski. 2017. Deep reinforcement learning for partial differential equation control. Paper presented at 2017 American Control Conference (ACC), Seattle, WA, USA, May 24–26. pp. 3120–27.
25. Fujii, Masaaki, Akihiko Takahashi, and Masayuki Takahashi. 2019. Asymptotic expansion as prior knowledge in deep learning method for high dimensional BSDEs. *Asia-Pacific Financial Markets* 26: 391–408. [CrossRef]
26. Gonon, Lukas, Philipp Grohs, Arnulf Jentzen, David Kofler, and David Šiška. 2019. Uniform error estimates for artificial neural network approximations. *arXiv* arXiv:1911.09647.
27. Goudenège, Ludovic, Andrea Molent, and Antonino Zanette. 2019. Machine learning for pricing American options in high dimension. *arXiv* arXiv:1903.11275.
28. Grohs, Philipp, Fabian Hornung, Arnulf Jentzen, and Philippe Von Wurstemberger. 2018. A proof that artificial neural networks overcome the curse of dimensionality in the numerical approximation of Black-Scholes partial differential equations. *arXiv* arXiv:1809.02362.
29. Grohs, Philipp, Arnulf Jentzen, and Diyora Salimova. 2019a. Deep neural network approximations for Monte Carlo algorithms. *arXiv* arXiv:1908.10828.
30. Grohs, Philipp, Fabian Hornung, Arnulf Jentzen, and Philipp Zimmermann. 2019b. Space-time error estimates for deep neural network approximations for differential equations. *arXiv* arXiv:1908.03833.
31. Grohs, Philipp, and Lukas Herrmann. 2020. Deep neural network approximation for high-dimensional elliptic PDEs with boundary conditions. *arXiv* arXiv:2007.05384.
32. Han, Jiequn, Arnulf Jentzen, and Weinan E. 2017. Deep learning-based numerical methods for high-dimensional parabolic partial differential equations and backward stochastic differential equations. *Communications in Mathematics and Statistics* 5: 349–80.
33. Han, Jiequn, Arnulf Jentzen, and Weinan E. 2018. Solving high-dimensional partial differential equations using deep learning. *Proceedings of the National Academy of Sciences* 115: 8505–10. [CrossRef]

34. Han, Jiequn, and Jihao Long. 2020. Convergence of the deep BSDE method for coupled FBSDEs. *Probability, Uncertainty and Quantitative Risk* 5: 1–33. [CrossRef]

35. Han, Jihun, Mihai Nica, and Adam Stinchcombe. 2020. A derivative-free method for solving elliptic partial differential equations with deep neural networks. *Journal of Computational Physics* 419: 109672. [CrossRef]

36. Henry-Labordère, Pierre. 2017. Deep primal-dual algorithm for BSDEs: Applications of machine learning to CVA and IM. *SSRN Electronic Journal*. [CrossRef]

37. Hornik, Kurt. 1991. Approximation capabilities of multilayer feedforward networks. *Neural Networks* 4: 251–57. [CrossRef]

38. Hornik, Kurt, Maxwell Stinchcombe, and Halbert White. 1989. Multilayer feedforward networks are universal approximators. *Neural Networks* 2: 359–66. [CrossRef]

39. Huré, Côme, Huyên Pham, and Xavier Warin. 2019. Some machine learning schemes for high-dimensional nonlinear PDEs. *arXiv* arXiv:1902.01599.

40. Hutzenthaler, Martin, Arnulf Jentzen, Thomas Kruse, Tuan Anh Nguyen, and Philippe von Wurstemberger. 2018. Overcoming the curse of dimensionality in the numerical approximation of semilinear parabolic partial differential equations. *arXiv* arXiv:1807.01212.

41. Hutzenthaler, Martin, Arnulf Jentzen, and Philippe von Wurstemberger. 2020a. Overcoming the curse of dimensionality in the approximative pricing of financial derivatives with default risks. *Electronic Journal of Probability* 25: 73. [CrossRef]

42. Hutzenthaler, Martin, Arnulf Jentzen, Thomas Kruse, and Tuan Anh Nguyen. 2020b. A proof that rectified deep neural networks overcome the curse of dimensionality in the numerical approximation of semilinear heat equations. *SN Partial Differential Equations and Applications* 1: 1–34. [CrossRef]

43. Jacquier, Antoine Jack, and Mugad Oumgari. 2019. Deep PPDEs for rough local stochastic volatility. *arXiv* arXiv:1906.02551.

44. Jeanblanc-Picqué, Monique, and Albert Nikolaevich Shiryaev. 1995. Optimization of the flow of dividends. *Russian Mathematical Surveys* 50: 257–77. [CrossRef]

45. Jentzen, Arnulf, Diyora Salimova, and Timo Welti. 2018. A proof that deep artificial neural networks overcome the curse of dimensionality in the numerical approximation of Kolmogorov partial differential equations with constant diffusion and nonlinear drift coefficients. *arXiv* arXiv:1809.07321.

46. Jiang, Zhengjun, and Martijn Pistorius. 2012. Optimal dividend distribution under markov regime switching. *Finance and Stochastics* 16: 449–76. [CrossRef]

47. Kritzer, Peter, Gunther Leobacher, Michaela Szölgyenyi, and Stefan Thonhauser. 2019. Approximation methods for piecewise deterministic markov processes and their costs. *Scandinavian Actuarial Journal* 2019: 308–35. [CrossRef] [PubMed]

48. Kutyniok, Gitta, Philipp Petersen, Mones Raslan, and Reinhold Schneider. 2019. A theoretical analysis of deep neural networks and parametric PDEs. *arXiv* arXiv:1904.00377.

49. Leobacher, Gunther, Michaela Szölgyenyi, and Stefan Thonhauser. 2014. Bayesian dividend optimization and finite time ruin probabilities. *Stochastic Models* 30: 216–49. [CrossRef]

50. Long, Zichao, Yiping Lu, Xianzhong Ma, and Bin Dong. 2018. PDE-Net: Learning PDEs from Data. Paper presented at 35th International Conference on Machine Learning, Stockholm, Sweden, July 10–15. pp. 3208–16.

51. Lu, Lu, Xuhui Meng, Zhiping Mao, and George Karniadakis. 2019. DeepXDE: A deep learning library for solving differential equations. *arXiv* arXiv:1907.04502.

52. Lye, Kjetil O, Siddhartha Mishra, and Deep Ray. 2020. Deep learning observables in computational fluid dynamics. *Journal of Computational Physics* 410: 109339. [CrossRef]

53. Magill, Martin, Faisal Qureshi, and Hendrick de Haan. 2018. Neural networks trained to solve differential equations learn general representations. *Advances in Neural Information Processing Systems* 31: 4071–81.

54. Øksendal, Bernt. 2003. *Stochastic Differential Equations*. Berlin: Springer.

55. Pardoux, Étienne. 1998. Backward stochastic differential equations and viscosity solutions of systems of semilinear parabolic and elliptic PDEs of second order. In *Stochastic Analysis and Related Topics VI*. Berlin: Springer, pp. 79–127.

56. Pardoux, Étienne. 1999. BSDEs, weak convergence and homogenization of semilinear PDEs. In *Nonlinear Analysis, Differential Equations and Control*. Berlin: Springer, pp. 503–49.
57. Pham, Huyen, Xavier Warin, and Maximilien Germain. 2019. Neural networks-based backward scheme for fully nonlinear PDEs. *arXiv* arXiv:1908.00412.
58. Radner, Roy, and Larry Shepp. 1996. Risk vs. profit potential: A model for corporate strategy. *Journal of Economic Dynamics and Control* 20: 1373–93. [CrossRef]
59. Raissi, Maziar. 2018. Deep hidden physics models: Deep learning of nonlinear partial differential equations. *The Journal of Machine Learning Research* 19: 932–55.
60. Reisinger, Christoph, and Yufei Zhang. 2019. Rectified deep neural networks overcome the curse of dimensionality for nonsmooth value functions in zero-sum games of nonlinear stiff systems. *arXiv* arXiv:1903.06652.
61. Reppen, A Max, Jean-Charles Rochet, and H Mete Soner. 2020. Optimal dividend policies with random profitability. *Mathematical Finance* 30: 228–59. [CrossRef]
62. Royer, Manuela. 2004. BSDEs with a random terminal time driven by a monotone generator and their links with PDEs. *Stochastics and Stochastic Reports* 76: 281–307. [CrossRef]
63. Schmidli, Hanspeter. 2008. *Stochastic Control in Insurance*. Probability and its Applications. London: Springer.
64. Shreve, Steven E., John P. Lehoczky, and Donald P. Gaver. 1984. Optimal consumption for general diffusions with absorbing and reflecting barriers. *SIAM Journal on Control and Optimization* 22: 55–75. [CrossRef]
65. Sirignano, Justin, and Konstantinos Spiliopoulos. 2018. DGM: A deep learning algorithm for solving partial differential equations. *Journal of Computational Physics* 375: 1339–64. [CrossRef]
66. Sotomayor, Luz R., and Abel Cadenillas. 2011. Classical and singular stochastic control for the optimal dividend policy when there is regime switching. *Insurance: Mathematics and Economics* 48: 344–54. [CrossRef]
67. Szölgyenyi, Michaela. 2013. Bayesian dividend maximization: A jump diffusion model. In *Handelingen Contactforum Actuarial and Financial Mathematics Conference, Interplay between Finance and Insurance, February 7–8*. Brussel: Koninklijke Vlaamse Academie van België voor Wetenschappen en Kunsten, pp. 77–82. Szölgyenyi, Michaela. 2016. Dividend maximization in a hidden Markov switching model. *Statistics & Risk Modeling* 32: 143–58.
68. Zhu, Jinxia, and Feng Chen. 2013. Dividend optimization for regime-switching general diffusions. *Insurance: Mathematics and Economics* 53: 439–56. [CrossRef]

3

Algorithmic Foundations of Economic and Mathematical Modeling of Network Logistics Processes

Sergey Yevgenievich Barykin [1], Irina Vasilievna Kapustina [1], Sergey Mikhailovich Sergeev [1] and Vladimir Konstantinovich Yadykin [2,*]

[1] Graduate School of Service and Trade, Peter the Great St. Petersburg Polytechnic University, 195251 St. Petersburg, Russia; sbe@list.ru (S.Y.B.); ivk65@list.ru (I.V.K.); sergeev2@yandex.ru (S.M.S.)
[2] Laboratory «Advanced Production Technologies» of the National Technological Initiative Center, Peter the Great St. Petersburg Polytechnic University, 195251 St. Petersburg, Russia
* Correspondence: v.yadikin@mail.ru

Abstract: Nowadays, digitizing the data stream is enabling the evolution of logistics processes. The data-driven network logistics processes are evaluated by leading economic indicators. The purpose of this study is to further develop the algorithmic foundations of economic and mathematical modeling of logistics networks based on advanced technologies that the digitalization process provides. Methods of mathematical modeling of flows of various resources in logistic networks, the structure of which is presented in the form of a graph, are used in the work. The economic benefit lies in the implementation of the planning concept based on leading indicators. As a result, using a set of formalisms, a mathematical model has been developed, which will make it possible to search for optimal solutions based on the criterion of economic efficiency. The results obtained will find application not only in transport problems. Network logistics includes the transportation of liquid and gaseous materials through pipelines, energy through electrical networks. A universal mathematical model will allow the results to be applied in many industries and economic activities when it is required to make economically sound decisions based on a stream of digital data coming in real time.

Keywords: logistics network; smart supply chains; digital logistics; simulation model

1. Introduction

The problem of cost-effective organization of logistics activities for a long time was solved using relatively simple techniques, the basis of which was a set of economic indicators obtained during the reporting period. Since such indicators are classified as lagging, the efforts of the developers were aimed at creating better software applications for managers of logistics services of enterprises. Over the past decade, technologies have become widely available, as well as equipment that can fundamentally change the approach to managing the processes of moving goods and cargo. This includes the possibility of machine-readable information exchange on goods and cargoes between machines, mobile computing devices, tracking systems, cloud solutions that coordinate in real time the activities of all participants in the supply chain. At the same time, the structure of relations between participants in this segment of the economy has become more complex. This is caused by the processes of consolidation into commercial structures, which leads to an increasing complexity of management of such business objects, as well as a manifold increase in the time and money spent on ensuring the material flows of goods and cargo necessary to maintain a competitive business.

To solve such voluminous problems, the use of scientifically grounded mathematical models is required. This approach will allow using the digital footprint of processes in the logistics network and developing an algorithmic basis for a whole line of software tools for better management of the logistics industry.

The research gap could be identified as the dynamics of discrete and continuous flows of material resources has not been mathematically described yet. This was due to the fact that there were no widespread and available technologies for machine-to-machine information exchange, especially in digital form. In addition, the existing mathematical apparatus for describing such processes by systems of partial differential equations was mainly in demand in problems of mathematical physics. In the presented article, the authors outlined the results of research that will combine the achievements of mathematical theory with the capabilities of modern digital technologies in the field of logistics. The advantage of the presented model is also the invariance of the description of network logistics processes. This model reflects the entire spectrum of flows of material resources from discrete to continuous.

Taking into account the importance of the issue of the stability of solutions depending on the unevenness of flows in network logistics processes we could consider such a task possible in linear models or by imposing a number of restrictions and assumptions. In general, the study of stability was not the task of our study. For linear cases, there are well-developed techniques, substantiated by a number of practical examples. For the problem considered in our article, the issue of the stability in network logistics processes regarding the economic indicators of such activities is the subject of further deep research and is limited to the specific practical application of the developed mathematical model. Thus, we have presented a general concept.

The authors set a goal to apply the methods of mathematical modeling based on the use of equations describing the dynamics of both discrete and continuous flows of data. In our case, such characteristics as cargo volumes and the current time are interrelated. Therefore, we apply complex mathematical partial differential equations that will allow us to describe models for realizing the full potential of digitalization of the network logistics processes. Currently, the ability to use a digital data as arguments to a mathematical model in real time has appeared due to machine-to-machine communication technologies.

2. Review the Status of the Problem

Since the necessary digital technologies and equipment have become available to a wide range of participants in the logistics business relatively recently, research in the direction of their application is being developed only now, mainly in countries leading intensive. commercial activities. Digital business models go against economic and operational principles which guide companies in all industries [1]. Likewise, high-performance companies have invested a large share of their digital capital into new digital business compared to competitors [2]. Indeed, the concept "digital" is widely seen as an updated term for defining what Information technology (IT) or digital marketing does. However, a wider, more holistic view of what digital actually stands for should be applied. In the opinion of the authors, one should agree with the consulting firm McKinsey that a digital rethinking of activities makes it possible to benefit from a structural process, combining search, development, realization, and risk reduction of its digital investments [3], as well as to look at digital broadcasting as a practically instantaneous, free, and perfect opportunity to connect people, devices, and physical objects in any place with the purpose to increase the efficiency of commercial activities in cooperation with various partners [4–10].

With the development of markets, client expectations are growing, and companies react to the increased expectations with new value propositions which consumers were previously unaware of and in such a way that it contradicts the generally accepted view of business [7]. Such companies as Apple, Tencent, and Google erase traditional industry definitions, spanning categories of goods and client segments. Owners of such hyperscale platforms enjoy huge operational benefits from the automation of processes, algorithms, and network effects, created by interactions of hundreds of millions, billions or more users, clients, and devices.

Schotanus, F. and Telgen, J. developed a typology for purchasing groups consisting five main forms of cooperative purchasing on the basis of two distinguishing dimensions: the influence by all members on the group activities and the number of different group activities [11]. Those five forms of cooperative purchasing are as follows: piggy-backing groups (informal purchasing groups), third-party groups (long term cooperation), lead buying groups (outsourcing purchasing), project groups (an intensive form of cooperative purchasing), and programme groups (regularly meeting of the management teams of the cooperating organizations). The work [12] considered the case of Poland in respect with the business model to inter-entity cooperation within purchasing groups in the renewable energy industry improving its profitability. The research [13] indicates the complexity of the inter-organizational dynamics, not only from a dyadic perspective (purchasing group and its members), but as well from a member-to-member perspective. We could agree that different types of cooperation should be taken into account.

Transshipment points are shown at the center of a traditional logistics network, with a linear structure with multiple ways available to communicate with other suppliers and customers (Figure 1). This figure illustrates the existing information and material flows. Double-headed arrows indicate opportunities for mutual exchange between participants in logistics activities.

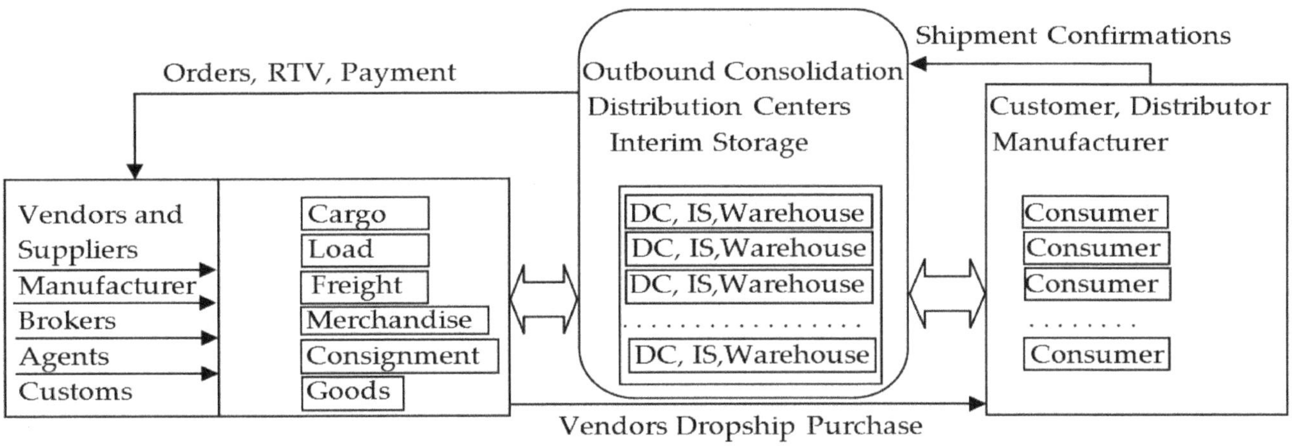

Figure 1. Schematic diagram of a traditional logistics network (DC—distribution center; RTV—return to vendor; IS—interim storage).

The research gap regards the shift of the paradigm which leads to a reformation of the concept of supply chains by creating connections between links traditionally not connected (from the static sequence of members of the supply chain) into a system of members interacting with each other—digital logistics network (Figure 2).

This scheme is not just a development of the traditional model of interaction but has a number of fundamental differences. The study of these differences provides the possibility of applying the theoretical results obtained in this article. This primarily refers to real-time information flows. This factor makes it possible to apply the algorithms developed below to optimize the logistics process. It is also taken into account that the management of the logistics system is carried out on the basis of advanced planning calculated on the host computer. Previously, such an organization of the process could not be achieved in a traditional logistics network due to the lack of both machine-to-machine interaction technologies and the development of global high-speed mobile Internet channels.

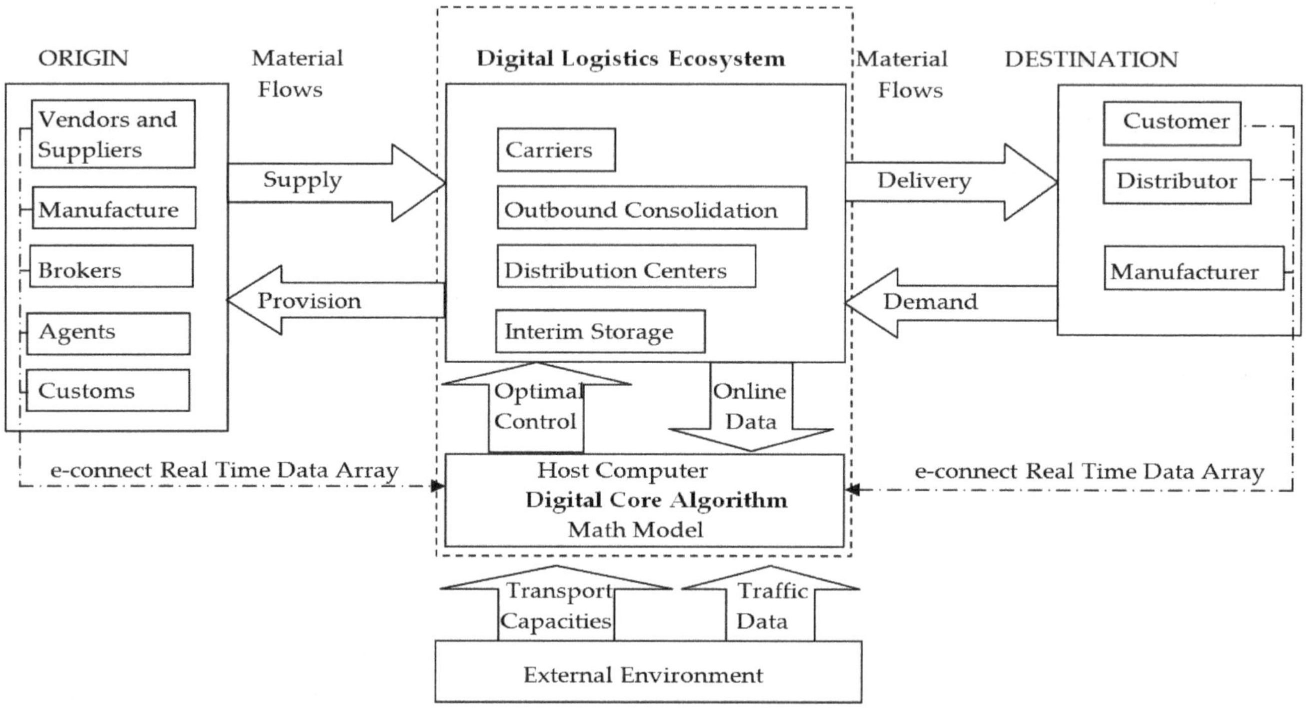

Figure 2. Model of digital logistics processes.

3. Literature Review

Network effects become the key differentiator and driver of value creation since the value of a good or a service increases as more supply-side partners augment the service and more products and services become digital and connected [14]. Digital business strategy is different from traditional IT strategy in the sense that it is much more than a cross-functional strategy, and it transcends traditional functional areas (such as marketing, procurement, logistics, operations, or others). Three main technologies are tended to change supply chain business processes: robotic process automation (RPA), artificial intelligence (AI)/machine learning (ML), and blockchain [15]. The formation and development of digital logistics platforms [16] is determined by market demands. Dynamically developing consumer demand and intercontinental expansion of network trading structures encourage companies to invest heavily in the development of new technologies. First of all, the direction of machine-to-machine interaction, Internet of things (IoT), and cloud solutions XaaS (Anything as a Service) is being developed. The need for Big Data technologies stems from the fact that the ever-growing complexity of the supply chain continues to pose a major obstacle for supply chain companies. Applying up-to-date technology to specific parts of the supply chain alone cannot reach its full potential if the company is unable to share data and use data to solve problems.

The paper [17] covers the difference between computer simulation and emulation while considering the designing of logistics systems with using computer modelling. A simulation model helps to uncover functional dependencies of logistics system, both technical and construction problems effecting on logistics route. Computer emulation aims to test the company control systems by various loadings of the logistic model system and find technical and construction problems effecting on logistics route.

It can be shown that there is currently a paradigm shift from the traditional view of a supply chain to a network-centric concept, initially proposed by the company Deloitte in 2019 [18]. A traditional supply chain is a linear structure with discrete development of the process of design, planning, flow source, production, delivery, and after-sales service.

The particularity of modern logistics is found in its role as the common denominator. In this concept, a variety of sources such as suppliers, producers, customs flows use a single network of sea and air routes. Until now, the coordination of the participants in the logistics process has been difficult. This is primarily due to the fact that there were no information exchange technologies, and mobile communications were poorly developed [19]. The lack of available technical means, such as tablets with geolocation, smartphones with GPS trackers among transport workers, drivers, and forwarders, was especially affected. Hence followed another important factor such as the absence of a coordination server and, accordingly, algorithms for managing the interaction of participants in the logistics process scattered and moving across a large territory. Work is carried out without consideration of real traffic, as a result causing traffic jams on the roads and lines at border crossings. Further, significant is the loss of time waiting for unloading at intermediate warehouses and temporary storage areas. Transportation is not coordinated with cargo parameters, with significant demurrage and detention, as well as problems of reverse logistics and the influence of seasonal changes in the flow densities [20–24].

A hybrid scheme that combines a simulation model and a mathematical programming model was proposed by [25] for designing logistic networks for co-firing biomass, specifically switchgrass, in conventional coal-fired power plants. Sustainable logistics business models extending was considered regarding 1PL (First-party logistics) to 5PL (Fifth-party logistics) scheme and related sustainable logistics practices [26]. This research [27] focusses on special issues of using a monitoring system for integrating sensor location and quality data into transport processes in automotive supply chains. Both the environmental influence parameters and the potential effects of sensor-based quality data for supply chain performance were considered by the researchers. The reliability of complex emergency logistics networks is investigated in the work [28]. It could be agreed that the reliability of the logistics network is significantly important to reducing environmental and public health losses in post-accident emergency rescues. The interactive development of the logistics and manufacturing industries in view of the interdependence of Manufacturing and Logistics Industries in China studied in [29].

When developing a method for solving the problem of constructing an economic and mathematical model of logistics processes, an analysis of the literature and approaches of a number of authors in similar situations was carried out [30–33] with both new circumstances and peculiarities of the global business consolidation trend being taken into account. The emergence of logistics networks of complex topology, the allocation of a segment of third party logistics, the need to support emergent stock levels concentrated in the transportation nodes can be formalized using mathematical modeling methods, which take into account various aspects of interaction of financial and data flows [34], and with consideration of the specifics of developing digital ecosystems [16,35–39]. These network-like objects can easily be associated with the geometric graph used in mathematics. The edges of the graph are an element of linear interaction taking place in the nodes of the graph (or at its vertices). This concept of formation is established in systems of logistics, supply, interim storage, and processing of flows of goods, raw materials, and other cargo. The on-going processes developing over time allow a mathematical description to be developed using dynamic models, linked to a geometric graph.

The works [40–42] show that in this approach to operating a logistics network, the formalized processes on the graph edges are ratios reflecting the patterns of current activities. The concept of internal nodes is formalized with principles of interactions of contiguous continuums. The correspondence of real suppliers and consumers to boundary nodes is achieved using boundary conditions as well as the boundaries denoted in mathematics to reflect the features of a specific object of commercial activity. An overview of literature [43,44] shows that the section of mathematics dedicated to solving boundary value problems in a class of differential equations regarding distributed parameters realized on a graph of varying topology can serve as the basis for researching the dynamics of economic processes on networks of arbitrary configuration [45]. The paper [46] describes the solvability of hyperbolic systems with distributed parameters on the graph in the weak formulation. The common characteristic when examining such mathematical models is to assign them to a class of boundary or boundary value problems. This meets all the requirements for solving equations describing systems with parameters distributed on a graph.

4. Methodology

Techniques such as linear programming or network planning are well known. Their use is justified in deterministic problems of distribution and planning. The modern market environment shows a high degree of uncertainty, which forces us to look for new ways to solve the problem of efficient logistics organization.

A significant breakthrough was the available technologies of machine-to-machine interaction, mobile high-speed data transmission networks along all significant routes, and unlimited access to geolocation. These and other devices provide a data stream containing a complete set of information about the nature of the goods, its movement, expiration dates, conditions of detention, and other important information. To develop control algorithms, we need to formally represent where these data will enter in the form of arguments of a mathematical model.

In the digital concept, data exchange happens not only between those involved in commercial activities but also with consideration of the expected loading of terminals on the near horizon. Likewise, the algorithm of the management server takes into account traffic in real time and possibilities of consolidated transport pools. At the same time, data processing and management decision making is done on the planning horizon using mathematical optimization methods [34]. The modern logistics system includes a very large number of participants in trading activities. This includes manufacturers, suppliers, intermediate distribution centers, customers, and their own warehouses. The most common type of topology today is star. This is due to the fact that over 80% of trade is consolidated in retail chains. This type of business has a centralized system of management and distribution of goods and cargo flows. It should be noted that each spoke of a star topology in a paradigm of logistics networks (spoke–hub distribution paradigm) represents a chain of hundreds or thousands of intermediate nodes, partners of the logistics network. Figure 3 shows the structure of interaction in a linear form as a set of information and material flows in the spoke of the star topology.

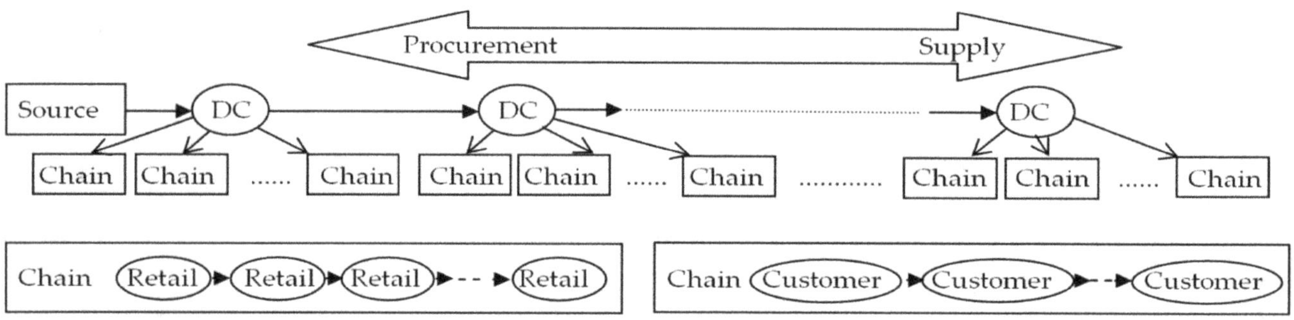

Figure 3. Individual spokes of a star topology within supply chains.

Analysis and exchange of information between all members of a logistics network is carried out based on a digital logistics grid, built on data acquisition technology with sensors and real-time transmission by way of mobile communication aiming to conduct a subsequent analysis and digital technology exchange data. The work [47] considers the mechanism for setting up a supply chain based on economic–mathematical models with optimization, artificial intelligence, and analytics.

It shows that the process of setting up a digital chain (DC) network involves reacting to interruptions on the fourth day by adapting the logistics configuration of the supply chain using optimization with the purpose to continue operating in the best way possible. The developed model makes it possible to analyze the market and react in a timely manner to client demands in terms of the dynamic development of a logistics network and not statically, as is the case with the linear structure of traditional supply chains.

5. Main Formalisms

The symbol $\Im$—is introduced for the bounded compact graph of arbitrary topology (Figure 4).

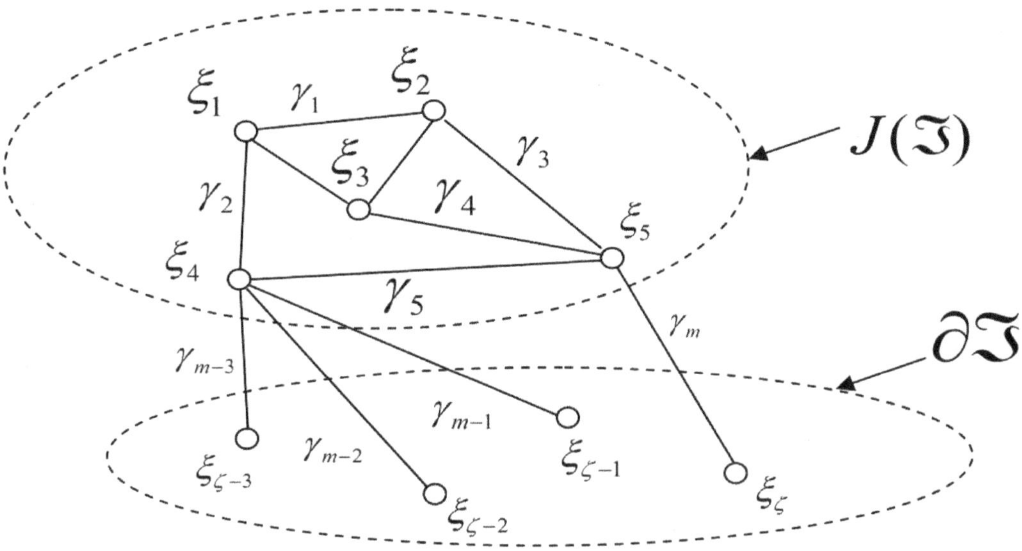

Figure 4. Graph $\mathfrak{I}$.

Next, the edges of this graph are denoted as γ_k. For the nodes of the graph, the symbol ξ_ζ is introduced. The number is identified with the symbols k, ζ, independent for the nodes and m edges; a number of boundary nodes are denoted as A $[\mathfrak{I}]$; a number of internal nodes are $J(\mathfrak{I})$. Every γ_k is an oriented edge. Furthermore, each γ_k is parameterized by segment. The indicated properties for parameterizing and orientation depend on the topology of the network, which is formalized with a graph. In practice, the most popular types are star, chain, and arbitrary [45,46].

The first example is that of star topology (Figure 5).

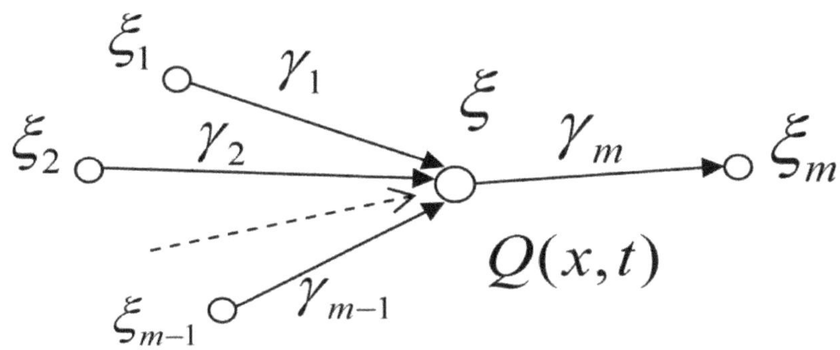

Figure 5. The star topology graph Γ.

The manifold Γ—is denoted as the geometric graph Γ—which reflects the given type of network interaction. The edges are denoted as γ_k $(k = \overline{1,m})$ and the central node as ξ; For each of the edges γ_k $(k = \overline{1,m-1})$ there is a parameterization by segment $[0, \pi/2]$. Next, γ_m is parameterized by segment $[\pi/2, \pi]$. Given orientation on γ_k $(k = \overline{1,m-1})$—towards ξ; on γ_m—away from ξ; condition $x \in \gamma_k$ is introduced in order for each point x on γ_k to have a corresponding numeric value x: $0 \le x \le \pi/2$ or $\pi/2 \le x \le \pi$ ($x = \pi/2 \in \gamma_k$. Where k for all $(k = \overline{1,m})$ is fixed and proves that x belongs to center ξ).

Function $f(x)$ on the graph is scalar. $\mathfrak{I}$ is displayed as $f : \mathfrak{I} \to \mathbb{R}$; the symbol $f(x)_\gamma$ denotes the restriction of the scalar $f(x)$ to γ.

The symbol $C(\mathfrak{I})$ is introduced for a set of functions which are continuous on the graph $\mathfrak{I}$. Likewise, $C[\mathfrak{I}]$ denotes a set of piecewise continuous functions. Here it is necessary to satisfy the conditions: the functions on the graph edges are continuous, in ξ the limits can vary. $C^2[\mathfrak{I}]$ denotes a set of twice continuously differentiable functions meeting the condition that the derivatives up to the second order belong to the set $C[\mathfrak{I}]$. Here, they are one-sided differentiable at the ends of the edges.

A linear differential equation on the edge is considered on a curve with an arbitrary combination of the initial and boundary derivatives of the function in the node where conditions of agreement exist. A group of differential equations [46,47] on edges γ_k of graph $\Im$, such as:

$$\frac{d}{dx}\left(a(x)_{\gamma_k}\frac{d}{dx}u(x)_{\gamma_k}\right)+b(x)_{\gamma_k}u(x)_{\gamma_k}=f(x)_{\gamma_k} \tag{1}$$

with transmission conditions of in internal nodes of the graph with consideration of orientation and parameterization on the graph $\Im$:

$$\sum_{\gamma} a(\alpha)_{\gamma}\frac{d}{dx}u(\alpha)_{\gamma}=0. \tag{2}$$

is a differential equation on the graph. In this case $a(x)_{\gamma_k}, a(x)_{\gamma_k}, b(x)_{\gamma_k}$ are the functions [48,49] defined for each γ_k in the process. Given the above, the summation is carried out along the edges γ adjacent to α.

Conditions (2) can be set by other ratios. In boundary nodes belonging to the boundary edges $\widetilde{\gamma}$ of the graph $\Im$, boundary conditions such as the following are given

$$u\,\big|_{\partial\Im}=0 \tag{3}$$

or

$$a(\beta)_{\widetilde{\gamma}}\frac{d}{dx}u(\beta)_{\widetilde{\gamma}}+hu(\beta)_{\widetilde{\gamma}}=0. \tag{4}$$

The set of linear differential equations given above on edges (1) and the boundary conditions (3) or (4) in boundary nodes which are supplemented with agreement conditions in internal nodes (2) as a whole allow the boundary value problem to be formulated on the graph. In this case h, β are the parameters [50] defined in the process.

Boundary value problems in a class of equations with partial derivatives are formulated similarly to problems (1)–(4), adding to them initial conditions.

6. Results

Mathematical models could be used for the optimization of the processes occurring in the network logistics structures. Commercial activities involve objects for whose formalization differential equations with partial derivatives are involved. Belonging to these, first and foremost, are systems with distributed parameters. These problems occur in a wide range of applications, in particular, movement on networks, logistics, distribution.

Mathematical models of these objects make it possible to solve important issues occurring when examining the dynamics of a process (primal problems) and the parameters of the network (inverse problems).

The distribution of the volume of goods over a segment of the commercial network of length L is described by the function $Q(x,t)$, $x \in [0,L]$, $t \in [0,T]$ [48–50] obeys the mass transfer equation [51]:

$$\frac{\partial}{\partial t}Q(x,t)=\frac{\partial^2}{\partial x^2}Q(x,t)-q(x)Q(x,t) \tag{5}$$

everywhere in the area $(0,L)\times(0,T)$, excluding a set of changes in transfer parameters. This is the semi-discrete set $\left\{(x,t):\ x=k\frac{L}{m},\ t\in(0,T)\right\}$, $k=\overline{1,m-1}$, where the variable x takes discrete values, in which for any $t\in(0,T)$ intensity of distribution of the commodity volume $Q(x,t)$ remains continuous, i.e., $Q(x,t)_{x=k\frac{L}{m}+0}=Q(x,t)_{x=k\frac{L}{m}-0}$, and the flow of commodity volume, which is reflected in this mathematical model by the quantity per unit of time $\frac{\partial}{\partial x}Q(x,t)$ (here the effect of loading/unloading is taken into account), undergoes jumps with the indicator α_k, $k=\overline{1,m-1}$, i.e., $\frac{\partial}{\partial x}Q(x,t)_{x=k\frac{L}{m}+0}-\frac{\partial}{\partial x}Q(x,t)_{x=k\frac{L}{m}-0}=\alpha_k Q(x,t)_{x=k\frac{L}{m}}$. Thus, the distribution of commodity volume over a fragment of a commercial network is due to the property of matching (conjugation) at certain points (nodes) of the commercial network:

$$\begin{aligned} &Q(x,t)_{x=k\frac{L}{m}+0} = Q(x,t)_{x=k\frac{L}{m}-0}, \\ &\tfrac{\partial}{\partial x}Q(x,t)_{x=k\frac{L}{m}+0} - \tfrac{\partial}{\partial x}Q(x,t)_{x=k\frac{L}{m}-0} = \alpha_k Q(x,t)_{x=k\frac{L}{m}}, \end{aligned} \tag{6}$$

here $k = \overline{1, m-1}$. Relationships (2) describe the situation when the conditions of movement at certain points (nodes) affect the flow rate through these points, while taking into account the phenomenon of a jump in flows proportional to the distribution of the commodity volume at the indicated points.

For the mathematical description and construction of a mathematical model of the transfer (diffusion) process in commercial networks, functions with a spatial variable varying on the graph are used. In this case, the considered simplest graph is the area of variation of the spatial variable x.

The symbol Γ is introduced for the graph in question. Its edges are likewise formalized as γ_k $(k = \overline{1,m})$. The indices of the nodes ξ_k $(k = \overline{0,m})$ are introduced. The orientation of the edges γ_k is accepted for each ξ_k. The edges are parameterized using $[(k-1)L/m, kL/m](k = \overline{1,m})$. For the internal nodes looked at in this topology of the mass ξ_k $(k = \overline{1, m-1})$, the identification kL/m $(k = \overline{1, m-1})$ is introduced. To take into account the border nodes of the network under consideration, we assign numbers to each of them as follows: $\{\xi_0,\ \xi_m - 0,\ \mathrm{L}\}$. Aiming to describe the flow process in the considered network and its distribution: $Q(x,t)$, $(x,t) \in \Gamma \times [0,T]$, the following ratio can be written:

$$\frac{\partial}{\partial t}Q(x,t)_{\gamma_k} = \frac{\partial^2}{\partial x^2}Q(x,t)_{\gamma_k} - q(x)_{\gamma_k}Q(x,t)_{\gamma_k} \tag{7}$$

Next, the ratios for the considered γ_k $(k = \overline{1,m})$ are written out in the following form when accounting for the parameterization introduced above:

$$\begin{aligned} &Q(x,t)_{x=k\frac{L}{m}\in\gamma_k} = Q(x,t)_{x=k\frac{L}{m}\in\gamma_{k+1}}, \\ &\tfrac{\partial}{\partial x}Q(x,t)_{x=k\frac{L}{m}\in\gamma_k} - \tfrac{\partial}{\partial x}Q(x,t)_{x=k\frac{L}{m}\in\gamma_{k+1}} = \alpha_k Q(x,t)_{x=k\frac{L}{m}\in\gamma_{k+1}}, \end{aligned} \tag{8}$$

This is, accordingly, carried out for all ξ_k $(k = \overline{1, m-1})$. For values $(k = \overline{1, m-1})$ since Equations (3) and (5) are carried out, after transformations it gives:

$$\begin{aligned} &Q(x,t)_{x=k\frac{L}{m}\in\gamma_k} = Q(x,t)_{x=k\frac{L}{m}\in\gamma_{k+1}}, \\ &\tfrac{\partial}{\partial x}Q(x,t)_{x=k\frac{L}{m}\in\gamma_k} - \tfrac{\partial}{\partial x}Q(x,t)_{x=k\frac{L}{m}\in\gamma_{k+1}} = C_k \tfrac{\partial}{\partial t}Q(x,t)_{x=k\frac{L}{m}\in\gamma_{k+1}}, \end{aligned} \tag{9}$$

Thus, the set of Equations (4) and (6) allow the transfer processes to be mathematically modeled. The topology of the corresponding network is then formalized by the graph Γ.

For a strictly mathematical description and solution of the problem, the initial conditions need to be given:

$$Q(x,t)_{t=0} = \varphi(x) \tag{10}$$

as well as the corresponding boundaries of the form:

$$\begin{aligned} &\tfrac{\partial}{\partial x}Q(x,t)_{x=0\in\gamma_1} - hQ(x,t)_{x=0\in\gamma_1} = \mu(t), \\ &\tfrac{\partial}{\partial x}Q(x,t)_{x=L\in\gamma_m} + HQ(x,t)_{x=L\in\gamma_m} = \nu(t), \end{aligned} \tag{11}$$

which completely determines the boundary value problem along with (4) and (6) on the graph $\Gamma \times [0,T]$.

In this case $q(x)$, $\varphi(x)$, $\mu(t)$, $\nu(t)$—are the functions defined in the process. The corresponding constants are fixed in the set α_k $(k = \overline{1, m-1})$, h, H. In this way, in the network modeled on the graph Γ in the corresponding area of values $C(\Gamma) \cap C^2[\Gamma]$, the classical Sturm–Liouville theory is formulated, dual boundary, defined by the ratios (4)–(7), or in the symbols (4), (5), (7) and (8) and denoting the variable as y:

$$-y''_{\gamma k}+q(x)_{\gamma_k}y_{\gamma_k}=\lambda y_{\gamma_k}\ (k=\overline{1,m}), \tag{12}$$

in the set γ_k $(k=\overline{1,m})$, here the problem is parameterized by a set of equations:

$$y'(kL/2)_{\gamma_{k+1}}-y'(kL/2)_{\gamma_k}=y(kL/2)_{\gamma_k} \tag{13}$$

or

$$-y'(kL/2)_{\gamma_{k+1}}+y'(kL/2)_{\gamma_k}=\lambda y(kL/2)_{\gamma_k}), \tag{14}$$

by defined nodes ξ_k $(k=1,\overline{m-1})$.

For the spectral parameter λ the corresponding boundary conditions are presented as

$$y'(0)_{\gamma_1}-hy(0)_{\gamma_1}=0, \tag{15}$$

$$y'(L)_{\gamma_m}+Hy(L)_{\gamma_m}=0 \tag{16}$$

A system of differential equations on the star topology Γ will be the set of ratios (8), (9) (or (8), (10)).

The solution to the boundary value problem (4)–(7) on $\Gamma\times[0,T]$ is methodologically possible by a series expansion using an orthonormal system of eigenfunctions $\{y_n(x)\}_{n\geq 0}$ which reflect the Sturm–Liouville theory (8), (9), (11) and (12) (or (8), (10)–(12)):

$$Q(x,t)=\sum_{n=0}^{\infty}Q_n(t)y_n(x),\ Q_n(t)=\int_{\Gamma}Q(x,t)y_n(x)dx. \tag{17}$$

The function $Q_n(t)$ is differentiated according to the variable t. Next, using the ratios (8), (9) $Q_n(t)$ t, and possibly (8), (10) on the topology in question, reflected by Γ, the integrals dependent on $\frac{\partial}{\partial t}Q(x,t)$ are calculated. As a result it can be written out as

$$\begin{aligned}\dot{Q}_n(t)&=\sum_{k=1}^{m}\int_{(k-1)\frac{L}{m}}^{k\frac{L}{m}}\left(\frac{\partial^2}{\partial x^2}Q(x,t)-q(x)Q(x,t)\right)y_n(x)dx_{\gamma_k}=\\&=\sum_{k=1}^{m}\left(\frac{\partial}{\partial x}Q(x,t)y_n(x)-Q(x,t)y'_n(x)\right)_{(k-)1\frac{L}{m}\ \gamma_k}^{k\frac{L}{m}}-\\&-\lambda_n\sum_{k=1}^{m}\int_{(k-)1\frac{L}{m}}^{k\frac{L}{m}}Q(x,t)y_n(x)dx_{\gamma_k},\end{aligned}$$

considering that

$$\int_{\Gamma}p(x)dx=\sum_{k=1}^{m}\int_{\gamma_k}p(x)dx$$

Applying for $Q(x,t)$ the initial and boundary value (7) and (8), respectively, and for $y_n(x)$ the Equations (8) and (9) as for the eigenfunctions, combining with (11), (12) boundary conditions necessary for the certainty of the problem (11) and (12), the desired expression for $Q_n(t)$ can be obtained by completing $(n\geq 0)$:

$$\dot{Q}_n(t)=-\lambda_nQ_n(t)+z_n(t), \tag{18}$$

where

$$\begin{aligned}z_n(t)&=\frac{\partial}{\partial x}Q\,(L,t)y_n(L)-Q\,(L,t)y'_n(L))-\\&-\left(\frac{\partial}{\partial x}Q\,(0,t)y_n(0)-Q\,(0,t)y'_n(0)\right)_{\gamma_k}=\\&=v(t)y_n(L)_{\gamma_L}-\mu_k(t)y_n(0)_{\gamma_1};\end{aligned}$$

In this arrangement, for (14) the initial conditions are achieved by expanding $\varphi(x)$ using a set of eigenfunctions $\{y_n(x)\}_{n\geq 0}$:

$$\varphi(x) = \sum_{n=0}^{\infty} \varphi_n y_n(x),\ \varphi_n = \int_{\Gamma} \varphi(x) y_n(x) dx.$$

The solution $Q_n(t)$ of Equation (14) with consideration of the initial conditions is written in the form:

$$Q_n(t) = \varphi_n e^{-\lambda_n t} + \int_0^t e^{-\lambda_n (t-\tau) z_n(\tau)} d\tau,$$

The solution $Q(x,t)$ of the boundary value problem (4)–(7) on $\Gamma \times [0,T]$ is of the form:

$$Q(x,t) = \sum_{n=0}^{\infty} \varphi_n e^{-\lambda_n t} y_n(x) + \sum_{n=0}^{\infty} \int_0^t e^{-\lambda_n (t-\tau) z_n(\tau)} d\tau y_n(x).$$

An important effect of this approach to solving the problem of modeling flows in a network presented as a graph is the possibility of applying the result $Q(x,t)$ as a sequence for searching for a solution to problems of modal control. This is relevant for practical cases of control that changes the eigenvalues of a boundary value problem or the mode for achieving the set goals.

We should take into account the concept for optimization under uncertainty: recoverable robustness being considered in a specific literature. A solution is recovery robust if it can be recovered by limited means in all likely scenarios [52–55]. These serious works show the application of linear programming methods in the field of transport problems and investigate the stability of solutions to random perturbations of parameters. This issue is very important for modelling of the network logistics processes. Our research aims to apply mathematical modeling of logistics processes in dynamics; that is, to relate volumes and movement in time.

7. Conclusions

The presented results of mathematical modeling of flows on networks were obtained as a result of the development of the problem of creating the algorithmic foundations of the core of a digital logistics platform. Modern technologies for the exchange of information in digital form are capable of providing real-time data flow on the location of transport, route of travel, the nature of the cargo, including expire date, storage, and transportation conditions. This information constitutes the information flow. In addition, knowing the entire set of possible routes, transfer points, intermediate storage warehouses and distribution centers, one can formalize them using mathematical graph theory. Using this information as arguments of a mathematical model, it becomes possible to calculate the material flows of goods and cargo. Thus, a tool appears for predicting the entire logistics process and solving the main problem of finding the most economically profitable options for organizing logistics. The criteria of economic efficiency should combine the balance between the costs of transporting goods and cargo, the time spent on performing the entire range of logistics services from the point of receiving the cargo to its transfer to the consumer, and the level of utilization of the capacities of the consolidated transport pool. If, when working with goods with a short expire date or components according to "Just in time" supply programs, delivery time becomes more important, then for FMCG (fast moving consumer goods) goods, costs are more important. Since distribution centers and intermediate warehouses are part of the logistics network structure, optimization will expand the use of modern warehouse technologies such as pick-by-line, cross docking and others. It will also increase cost efficiency by expanding the use of the Quant, Minimum Order Quantity. For the end consumer, the profitability also increases in terms of interaction with logistics outsourcing, since the possible losses from Out-Of-Stock Sales will decrease, as well as the freezing of working capital due to the Over Stock factor.

First of all, the obtained results are in demand by operators of the third party logistics segment. This is due to the global trend of separating logistics into a separate industry, which allows manufacturing and trading companies to focus on their core competencies. Since there are a large number of software add-ons for solving problems formalized by mathematical models, including those from the field of scientifically based search for optimal solutions by mathematical methods, the obtained algorithms will allow creating cross-platform applications for supporting managerial decisions of managers of logistics services. Implementation of applications in cloud servers will enable online interaction with freight forwarders and transport directly in the process of moving, regardless of their location. As a result, it is possible to combine the activities of all participants within a single digital logistics platform.

8. Points for Scientific Discussion

In his famous article, Christensen considered the determinants of open modes of innovation associated with the industrial dynamics of an industry segment undergoing a process of radical technological innovation [56] unraveling the Open Innovation concept which was initially studied by Chesbrough from the company-level perspective (in contrary to the closed innovation old model) and illustrated with cases of large American companies such as IBM (International Business Machines Corporation), Intel, Lucent, and Xerox.

The open innovation engineering model including both open-innovation engineering channels and determining ways of operating the channels through conceptual experiments are considered by JinHyo Joseph Yun [57]. In this work the important research question is investigated regarding the open innovation channels and its operating as a knowledge funnel to conquer the growth limit of capitalism in the fourth industrial revolution. Open innovation engineering channels mean open source computing, theory of solving inventive problem (TRIZ), open supply chain management (SCM), system dynamics, mechanism design or big data. This scientific research could be treated as a fundamental theory for our consideration.

Our approach for describing a process in a node is not the unique one. Much depends both on the specific commercial situation in the network and on the capabilities of mathematical tools in the mathematical analysis of the obtained problems. It is very important to note: an arbitrary network (graph) is the union of a finite number of the simplest networks (the simplest graphs) and star networks (star graphs). Hence, it follows that the mathematical description of transfer processes on an arbitrary network (graph) is a combination of those on the simplest and stellar networks (graphs). The development of a number of particular cases of application of the obtained mathematical model is of interest. For example, it is known that intermediate storage and operations at distribution centers constitute a significant part of the total time of movement of goods from producer to consumer. At the same time, it is necessary to compare various technologies, such as, for example, cross-docking, pick-by-line, as well as the throughput of the nodes of the logistics network. Separately, we can consider the case of routes containing cross-border movement, which is often not the only one, since the existence of customs procedures requires separate consideration in the model. It is also necessary to assess the possibility of using mathematical modeling in conditions of market uncertainty. In this case, part of the arguments awakens to be described by distribution functions, part by interval data. In our opinion, it is possible to use queueing theory, which will allow us to formalize the uncertainty of the flow described by Poisson distribution using Erlang solution. So, to solve the problems of planning logistics activities for a longtime horizon, it is necessary to take into account the seasonality factor of both demand and the use of modes of transport. This can be formalized by the expansion of demand in the Fourier series, and the variable structure of the mathematical graph.

We describe a mathematical apparatus for modeling flows in logistics networks, and not only the movement of discrete, but also continuous flows (for example, not only containers and other containers, but also liquid substances such as hydrocarbons). Specific examples of calculations can be the object of promising research in the field of practical application in various areas of industry and transport.

As far as the limitations of the proposed approach are concerned the issues of the reliability of the network logistics processes remains outside the framework of the study and such a simulation model could be a subject for future research. The practical significance of the developed mathematical model is not limited to the logistics of movement of goods and cargoes by various modes of transport (road, rail, sea, and air). The above formalisms are also suitable for describing the processes of moving liquid cargo. This is relevant today for managing flows in oil pipelines, since their structure is also networked with pumping and distribution stations at the nodes. Moreover, the obtained equations can be used to study the processes in network gas transmission systems with complex topology. This is a topic for further investigation.

Author Contributions: All the authors contributed substantially to the entire work reported. I.V.K. has performed project administration and supervision, S.M.S. has prepared both a conceptualization and data curation as well as formal analysis, V.K.Y. contributed to the literature review, S.Y.B. has particularly developed the methodology with editing of manuscript. All authors have read and agree to the published version of the manuscript.

Acknowledgments: The authors would like to thank the four anonymous referees for their very useful suggestions.

References

1. Bughin, J.; Catlin, T.; LaBerge, L. *A Winning Operating Model for Digital Strategy*; McKinsey Digital, McKinsey & Company: New York, NY, USA, 23 January 2019; Available online: https://www.mckinsey.com/business-functions/mckinsey-digital/our-insights/a-winning-operating-model-for-digital-strategy (accessed on 12 December 2020).
2. Bughin, J.; Catlin, T.; LaBerge, L. *The Drumbeat of Digital: How Winning Teams Play*; McKinsey Digital, McKinsey & Company: New York, NY, USA, 27 June 2019; Available online:https://www.mckinsey.com/business-functions/digital-mckinsey/our-insights/the-drumbeat-of-digital-how-winning-teams-play?cid=other-eml-alt-mcq-mck&hlkid=6b36b3176deb4fbbb500a7f87ff58af7&hctky=10306162&hdpid=b371d6c7-b2b9-4b71-84ae-73189c6806e0 (accessed on 12 December 2020).
3. Bughin, J.; LaBerge, L.; Mellbye, A. *The Case for Digital Reinvention*; McKinsey Digital, McKinsey & Company: New York, NY, USA, 9 February 2017; pp. 26–41. Available online: https://www.mckinsey.com/business-functions/mckinsey-digital/our-insights/the-case-for-digital-reinvention (accessed on 12 December 2020).
4. Catlin, T.; Scanlan, J.; Willmott, P. *Raising Your Digital Quotient*; McKinsey & Company: New York, NY, USA, 1 June 2015. Available online: https://www.mckinsey.com/business-functions/strategy-and-corporate-finance/our-insights/raising-your-digital-quotient (accessed on 12 December 2020).
5. Catlin, T.; LaBerge, L.; Varney, S. *Digital Strategy: The Four Fights You Have to Win*; McKinsey Digital, McKinsey & Company: New York, NY, USA, 18 October 2018; pp. 78–89. Available online: https://www.mckinsey.com/business-functions/mckinsey-digital/our-insights/digital-strategy-the-four-fights-you-have-to-win (accessed on 12 December 2020).
6. Chin, J.K.; Hagstroem, M.; Rifai, A.; Khaled, L. *Advanced Analytics: Nine Insights from the C-Suite*; McKinsey & Company: New York, NY, USA, 5 July 2017; pp. 1–10. Available online: https://www.mckinsey.com/business-functions/mckinsey-analytics/our-insights/advanced-analytics-nine-insights-from-the-c-suite (accessed on 12 December 2020).
7. Dawson, A.; Hirt, M.; Scanlan, J. *The Economic Essentials of Digital Strategy*; McKinsey & Company: New York, NY, USA, 15 March 2016; pp. 30–44. Available online: https://www.mckinsey.com/business-functions/strategy-and-corporate-finance/our-insights/the-economic-essentials-of-digital-strategy (accessed on 12 December 2020).

8. de la Boutetière, H.; Montagner, A.; Reich, A. *Unlocking Success in Digital Transformations*; McKinsey & Company: New York, NY, USA, 29 October 2018; pp. 1–14. Available online: https://www.mckinsey.com/business-functions/organization/our-insights/unlocking-success-in-digital-transformations?_lrsc=6f6e9270-299b-43f6-8909-12da4c085403&source=SNS-13040&utm_source=linkedin&utm_medium=elevate (accessed on 12 December 2020).
9. Koeleman, J.; Ribeirinho, M.J.; Rockhill, D.; Sjödin, E.; Strube, G. *Decoding Digital Transformation in Construction*; McKinsey & Company: New York, NY, USA, 20 August 2019; Available online: https://www.mckinsey.com/industries/capital-projects-and-infrastructure/our-insights/decoding-digital-transformation-in-construction (accessed on 12 December 2020).
10. Johnson, R.; Moore, S.; Petriwsky, K.; Rice, C.; John, C.; Sand, D. *Digital McKinsey: Insights of Winning in Digital Ecosystems*; McKinsey Digital, McKinsey & Company: New York, NY, USA, 9 January 2018; pp. 5–25. Available online: https://www.mckinsey.com/~{}/media/McKinsey/Business%20Functions/McKinsey%20Digital/Our%20Insights/Digital%20McKinsey%20Insights%20Number%203/Digital-McKinsey-Insights-Issue-3-revised.pdf (accessed on 12 December 2020).
11. Schotanus, F.; Telgen, J. Developing a typology of organisational forms of cooperative purchasing. *J. Purch. Supply Manag.* **2007**, *13*, 53–68. [CrossRef]
12. Zimon, G.; Sobolewski, M.; Lew, G. An influence of group purchasing organizations on financial security of SMEs operating in the renewable energy sector-case for Poland. *Energies* **2020**, *13*, 2926. [CrossRef]
13. Nollet, J.; Beaulieu, M.; Fabbe-Costes, N. The impact of performance measurement on purchasing group dynamics: The Canadian experience. *J. Purch. Supply Manag.* **2017**, *23*, 17–27. [CrossRef]
14. Bharadwaj, A.; El, O.A.; Pavlou, P.A.; Venkatraman, N. Digital Business Strategy: Toward a Next Generation of Insights. *MIS Q.* **2013**, *37*, 471–482. [CrossRef]
15. Hartley, J.L.; Sawaya, W.J. Tortoise, not the hare: Digital transformation of supply chain business processes. *Bus. Horiz.* **2019**, *62*, 707–715. [CrossRef]
16. Rožman, N.; Vrabič, R.; Corn, M.; Požrl, T.; Diaci, J. Distributed logistics platform based on blockchain and IoT. *Procedia CIRP* **2019**, *81*, 826–831. [CrossRef]
17. Bučková, M.; Skokan, R.; Fusko, M.; Hodoň, R. Designing of logistics systems with using of computer simulation and emulation. *Transp. Res. Procedia* **2019**, *40*, 978–985. [CrossRef]
18. Burke, R.; Mussomeli, A.; Laaper, S.; Hartigan, M.; Sniderman, B. The Smart Factory. The Smart Factory Responsive, Adaptive, Connected Manufacturing. 2017. Available online: http://media.daimler.com/marsMediaSite/en/instance/ko.xhtml?oid=9905147 (accessed on 12 December 2020).
19. Borovkov, A.; Ryabov, Y. Digital twins: Definition, approaches and methods of development. In *Digital Transformation of Economy and Industry. Works of the X Research-to-Practice Conference with Foreign Participation*; Babkin, A.V., Ed.; Peter the Great St. Petersburg Polytechnic University: St. Petersburg, Russia, 20–22 June 2019; pp. 234–245.
20. Barykin, S.Y.; Bochkarev, A.A.; Kalinina, O.V.; Yadykin, V.K. Concept for a Supply Chain Digital Twin. *Int. J. Math. Eng. Manag. Sci.* **2020**, *5*, 1498–1515. [CrossRef]
21. Kalinina, O.; Alekseeva, L.; Varlamova, D.; Barykin, S.; Kapustina, I. Logistic approach to intellectual property. *E3S Web Conf.* **2019**, *110*, 02103. [CrossRef]
22. Kalinina, O.; Kapustina, I.; Barykin, S.; Balchik, E.; Sedyakina, A. Development of a combined approach of innovative and traditional scenarios of the company's strategy. In Proceedings of the 33rd International Business Information Management Association Conference, IBIMA 2019: Education Excellence and Innovation Management through Vision 2020, Granada, Spain, 10–11 April 2019.
23. Kalinina, O.; Kapustina, I.; Burova, A.; Firsova, S.; Barykin, S.; Sedyakina, A. Financial logistics theory as innovative approach to management. In Proceedings of the 33rd International Business Information Management Association Conference, IBIMA 2019: Education Excellence and Innovation Management through Vision 2020, Granada, Spain, 10–11 April 2019.
24. Schislyaeva, E.; Saychenko, O.; Barykin, S.; Kapustina, I. International Energy Strategies Projects of Magnetic Levitation Transport. In *Advances in Intelligent Systems and Computing*; Springer: Berlin/Heidelberg, Germany, 2019.
25. Aranguren, M.F.; Castillo-Villar, K.K.; Aboytes-Ojeda, M.; Giacomoni, M.H. Simulation-optimization approach for the logistics network design of biomass co-firing with coal at power plants. *Sustainability* **2018**, *10*, 4299. [CrossRef]

26. Gruchmann, T.; Melkonyan, A.; Krumme, K. Logistics Business Transformation for Sustainability: Assessing the Role of the Lead Sustainability Service Provider (6PL). *Logistics* **2018**, *2*, 25. [CrossRef]
27. Teucke, M.; Broda, E.; Börold, A.; Freitag, M. Using Sensor-Based Quality Data in Automotive Supply Chains. *Machines* **2018**, *6*, 53. [CrossRef]
28. Wang, W.; Huang, L.; Liang, X. On the Simulation-Based Reliability of Complex Emergency Logistics Networks in Post-Accident Rescues. *Int. J. Environ. Res. Public Health* **2018**, *15*, 79. [CrossRef] [PubMed]
29. Jiang, P.; Hu, Y.-C.; Yen, G.-F.; Jiang, H.; Chiu, Y.-J. Using a Novel Grey DANP Model to Identify Interactions between Manufacturing and Logistics Industries in China. *Sustainability* **2018**, *10*, 3456. [CrossRef]
30. Kukushkin, S.A.; Osipov, A.V.; Osipova, E.V. Mechanism of molecule migration of carbon and silicon monoxides in silicon carbide crystal. *Mater. Phys. Mech.* **2019**, *42*, 178–182. [CrossRef]
31. Poltavtseva, M.A. High-performance NIDS Architecture for Enterprise Networking. In Proceedings of the 2019 IEEE International Black Sea Conference on Communications and Networking (BlackSeaCom), Sochi, Russia, 3–6 June 2019; pp. 1–3.
32. Sheinerman, A.G.; Castro, R.H.R.; Gutkin, M.Y. A model for direct and inverse Hall-Petch relation for nanocrystalline ceramics. *Mater. Lett.* **2020**, *260*, 126886. [CrossRef]
33. Vorobyov, S.; Perlovsky, L.; Yadykin, V. Reasoning and learning in a digital economy. Technological challenges of the modern age. *IOP Conf. Ser. Mater. Sci. Eng.* **2019**, *497*, 012038. [CrossRef]
34. Barykin, S.; Gazul, S.; Kiyaev, V.; Kalinina, O.; Yadykin, V. Forming Ontologies and Dynamically Configurable Infrastructures at the Stage of Transition to Digital Economy Based on Logistics. *Adv. Intell. Syst. Comput.* **2020**, *1116*, 844–852. [CrossRef]
35. Angrish, A.; Craver, B.; Hasan, M.; Starly, B. A Case Study for Blockchain in Manufacturing: "fabRec": A Prototype for Peer-to-Peer Network of Manufacturing Nodes. *Procedia Manuf.* **2018**, *26*, 1180–1192. [CrossRef]
36. Evdokimov, I.V.; Tsarev, R.Y.; Yamskikh, T.N.; Pupkov, A.N. Using PERT and Gantt charts for planning software projects on the basis of distributed digital ecosystems. *J. Phys. Conf. Ser.* **2018**, *1074*, 012127. [CrossRef]
37. Kayikci, Y. Sustainability impact of digitization in logistics. *Procedia Manuf.* **2019**, *21*, 782–789. [CrossRef]
38. Scherbakov, V.; Silkina, G. Logistics of smart supply chains. In Proceedings of the International Conference on Digital Technologies in Logistics and Infrastructure, St. Petersburg, Russia, 4–5 April 2019; pp. 66–71.
39. Schniederjans, D.G.; Curado, C.; Khalajhedayati, M. Supply chain digitisation trends: An integration of knowledge management. *Int. J. Prod. Econ.* **2020**, *220*, 107439. [CrossRef]
40. Borisoglebskaya, L.N.; Provotorov, V.V.; Sergeev, S.M.; Kosinov, E.S. Mathematical aspects of optimal control of transference processes in spatial networks. *IOP Conf. Ser. Mater. Sci. Eng.* **2019**, *537*, 042025. [CrossRef]
41. Borisoglebskaya, L.N.; Provotorova, E.N.; Sergeev, S.M.; Khudyakov, A.P. Automated storage and retrieval system for Industry 4.0 concept. *IOP Conf. Ser. Mater. Sci. Eng.* **2019**, *537*, 032036. [CrossRef]
42. Krasnov, S.; Sergeev, S.; Titov, A.; Zotova, Y. Modelling of digital communication surfaces for products and services promotion. *IOP Conf. Ser. Mater. Sci. Eng.* **2019**, *497*, 012032. [CrossRef]
43. Krasnov, S.; Sergeev, S.; Zotova, E.; Grashchenko, N. Algorithm of optimal management for the efficient use of energy resources. *E3S Web Conf.* **2019**, *110*, 02052. [CrossRef]
44. Pilipenko, O.V.; Provotorova, E.N.; Sergeev, S.M.; Rodionov, O.V. Automation engineering of adaptive industrial warehouse. *J. Phys. Conf. Ser.* **2019**, *1399*, 044045. [CrossRef]
45. Podvalny, S.L.; Podvalny, E.S.; Provotorov, V.V. The Controllability of Parabolic Systems with Delay and Distributed Parameters on the Graph. *Procedia Comput. Sci.* **2017**, *103*, 324–330. [CrossRef]
46. Provotorov, V.V.; Sergeev, S.M.; Part, A.A. Solvability of hyperbolic systems with distributed parameters on the graph in the weak formulation. *Vestn. Sankt Peterbg. Univ. Prikl. Mat. Inform. Protsessy Upr.* **2019**, *15*, 107–117. [CrossRef]
47. AnyLogistix. Supply Chain Digital Twins. Definition, the Problems They Solve, and How to Develop Them. 2020. Available online: https://www.anylogistix.com/supply-chain-digital-twins/ (accessed on 12 December 2020).
48. Provotorov, V.V.; Ryazhskikh, V.I.; Gnilitskaya, Y.A. Unique weak solvability of a nonlinear initial boundary value problem with distributed parameters in a netlike domain. *Vestn. Sankt Peterbg. Univ. Prikl. Mat. Inform. Protsessy Upr.* **2017**, *13*, 264–277. [CrossRef]
49. Tyurin, I.S. Math-Net Ru All Russian mathematical portal. *Uspekhi. Mat. Nauk.* **2010**, *65*, 201–202.

50. Zhabko, A.P.; Shindyapin, A.I.; Provotorov, V.V. Stability of weak solutions of parabolic systems with distributed parameters on the graph. *Vestn. Sankt Peterbg. Univ. Prikl. Mat. Inform. Protsessy Upr.* **2019**, *15*, 457–471. [CrossRef]
51. Balaban, O.R. Approximation of evolutionary differential systems with distributed parameters on the network and moment methods. *Modeling Optim. Inf. Technol.* **2019**, *7*. [CrossRef]
52. Liebchen, C.; Lübbecke, M.; Möhring, R.; Stiller, S. *The Concept of Recoverable Robustness, Linear Programming Recovery, and Railway Applications BT-Robust and Online Large-Scale Optimization: Models and Techniques for Transportation Systems*; Ahuja, R.K., Möhring, R.H., Zaroliagis, C.D., Eds.; Springer: Berlin/Heidelberg, Germany, 2009; pp. 1–27. ISBN 978-3-642-05465-5.
53. Hatefi, S.M.; Jolai, F. Robust and reliable forward-reverse logistics network design under demand uncertainty and facility disruptions. *Appl. Math. Model.* **2014**, *38*, 2630–2647. [CrossRef]
54. Iris, Ç.; Lam, J.S.L. Recoverable robustness in weekly berth and quay crane planning. *Transp. Res. Part B Methodol.* **2019**, *122*, 365–389. [CrossRef]
55. Polinder, G.J.; Breugem, T.; Dollevoet, T.; Maróti, G. An adjustable robust optimization approach for periodic timetabling. *Transp. Res. Part B Methodol.* **2019**, *128*, 50–68. [CrossRef]
56. Christensen, J.F.; Olesen, M.H.; Kjær, J.S. The industrial dynamics of Open Innovation—Evidence from the transformation of consumer electronics. *Res. Policy* **2005**, *34*, 1533–1549. [CrossRef]
57. Yun, J.J.; Kim, D.; Yan, M.R. Open innovation engineering—preliminary study on new entrance of technology to market. *Electronics* **2020**, *9*, 791. [CrossRef]

4

Macroeconomic Shocks and Changing Dynamics of the U.S. REITs Sector

Rangan Gupta [1], Zhihui Lv [2,*] and Wing-Keung Wong [3,4,5]

[1] Department of Economics, University of Pretoria, Pretoria 0002, South Africa; rangan.gupta@up.ac.za
[2] KLASMOE & School of Mathematics and Statistics, Northeast Normal University, Changchun 130024, China
[3] Department of Finance, Fintech Center, and Big Data Research Center, Asia University, Taichung 41354, Taiwan; wong@asia.edu.tw
[4] Department of Medical Research, China Medical University Hospital, Taichung 40402, Taiwan
[5] Department of Economics and Finance, The Hang Seng University of Hong Kong, Shatin 999077, Hong Kong, China
* Correspondence: luzh694@nenu.edu.cn

Abstract: Unlike the existing literature, which primarily studies the impact of only monetary policy shocks on real estate investment trusts (REITs), this paper develops a change-point vector autoregressive (VAR) model and then analyzes, for the first time, regime-specific impact of demand, supply, monetary policy, and spread yield shocks, identified using sign-restrictions, on US REITs returns. The model first isolates four major macroeconomic regimes in the US since the 1970s and discloses important changes to the statistical properties of REITs returns and its responses to the identified shocks. A variance decomposition analysis revealed aggregate supply shocks to have dominated in the early part of the sample period, and monetary policy and spread shocks at the end. Our results imply that ignoring other possible shocks in the model is likely to lead to incorrect inferences, and over-reliance on (conventional) monetary policy in correcting for possible bubbles in the REITs sector, which it will fail to rectify, given the importance of other shocks driving the REITs sector.

Keywords: change-point VAR model; macroeconomic shocks; US REITs sector

---

1. Introduction

The rapid decline in real estate prices, following a prolonged boom, is commonly associated as the main underlying reason for the global economic and financial crisis of 2008 to 2009 [1,2]. Naturally, understanding what macroeconomic and financial shocks drives the real estate market is of paramount importance, especially for a policymaker aiming to avoid future catastrophic effects observed under the 'Great Recession'. While there exists a large number of studies that have analyzed the role of both conventional and unconventional (in the wake of the zero lower bound (ZLB) scenario) monetary policy [3–8], and more recently, fiscal policy shocks on real estate markets [9,10], and the feedback from it in shaping policy decisions, there is dearth of studies that have analyzed the role of aggregate demand, aggregate supply, and bond yield spread shocks on real estate markets. The only exception to this is the recent paper by Plakandaras et al. [11], where the authors study the effect of macroeconomic shocks in the determination of house prices in the US and the UK by employing time-varying parameter vector autoregressive (TVP-VAR) models covering the historical annual periods of 1830 to 2016 and 1845 to 2016, respectively. From the examination of the impulse responses of house prices on macroeconomic shocks, Plakandaras et al. [11], found that technology shocks dominate in the U.S. real estate market, while their effect is unimportant in the U.K, where, monetary policy shocks drives most of the house price evolution.

Against this backdrop, realizing that housing markets are regional in nature, with tremendous heterogeneity in terms of their response to (monetary) policy shocks [12–14], we analyze the role of various macroeconomic shocks in driving the Real Estate Investment Trusts (REITs) prices of the US, which tends to be homogenous across the country, being based on a broad single index. For our purpose, unlike Plakandaras et al. [11], we use higher-frequency (monthly) data covering the more recent period 1972:12 of 2016:12. The use of monthly data allows us to identify the shocks in a relatively cleaner manner [15,16], based on a change-point vector autoregressive (VAR) model that allows for different regimes throughout the sample period and identifies a variety of shocks (supply, demand, monetary policy, and the spread between long- and short-run maturities), derived from the theoretical reactions of an innovative general equilibrium model developed by Liu et al. [17]. This approach enables the VAR model to endogenously identify changes to the structure of the real estate market, as widely discussed in Simo-Kengne et al. [18], as well as variations to the properties of exogenous shocks during the sample period. We prefer to use this approach over the complete TVP-VAR framework used by Plakandaras et al. [11], as we want to explicitly identify regimes over our high-frequency data, rather than assuming that each point in time is a separate regime, as done in TVP-VARs—which is, perhaps, more appropriate at lower frequency data (like quarterly and annual). It is important to note that the spread shock is important for us, since the time period of our analysis involves the period of ZLB and hence, that of unconventional monetary policy, which in turn involved compression in the long-term yield spread (Beginning in the summer of 2007, money markets around the world experienced sustained periods of dysfunction with sharply higher short-term interest rates for commercial paper and interbank borrowing. This intense liquidity squeeze led the Federal Reserve (Fed) to substantially lower its Federal funds rate (FFR) and act as the liquidity provider of last resort to supply funds to banks and the broader financial system via its Term Auction Facility (TAF). The FFR, the Fed's traditional policy instrument, reached its effective ZLB in December 2008, and the Fed faced the challenge of how to further ease the stance of monetary policy as the economic outlook deteriorated. While the FFR had reached its effective ZLB, large-scale asset purchases (LSAPs), which reduced the supply of riskier long term assets and increased the supply of safer liquid assets (bank reserve), causing the spread to decline.). To the best of our knowledge, this is the first attempt to analyze the role of various macroeconomic and financial shocks over and above the monetary policy shock, in driving the REITs prices based on a change-point VAR. In this regard, it must be mentioned that the role of macroeconomic news surprises, along with monetary policy surprises for real estate markets have been recently studied by Marfatia et al. [19] and Nyakabawo et al. [20], based on single-equation approaches. However, these studies do not make an attempt to identify these shocks in a structural fashion based on a VAR model, and hence, cannot track the impact of these shocks over time, but just its correlation with the real estate returns (and volatility).

To summarize, given the importance of the real estate sector in the recent financial crisis, it is important to study the role of macroeconomic shocks driving the sector. However, existing studies have primarily concentrated on the role of monetary policy shocks and, in this regard, we deviate from the current literature by developing a change-point VAR model and then analyzing, for the first time, regime-specific impact of demand, supply, monetary policy, and spread yield shocks, identified using sign-restrictions, on US REITs returns. As indicated, based on our analysis over the monthly period of 1972:12 to 2016:12, aggregate supply shocks have dominated in the early part of the sample period, and monetary policy and spread shocks at the end. Our results imply that ignoring other possible shocks in the model is likely to lead to incorrect inferences, and over-reliance on (conventional) monetary policy in correcting for possible bubbles in the REITs sector, which it will fail to rectify, given the importance of other shocks driving the REITs sector. The remainder of the paper is organized as follows: Section 2 presents the data and the methodology, with Section 3 discussing the results, and Section 4 concluding the paper.

2. Data and Methodology

2.1. Sign Restrictions and Data

In this model, according to Kapetanios et al. [21] and Liu et al. [17], we investigated the four structural shocks: The monetary policy shock, the spread shock, the demand shock, and the supply shock and six variables: The short-term nominal interest rate (I_t), the REITs returns (R_t), the unemployment rate (U_t), the money holdings (M_t), the price inflation (π_t), and the interest rate spread S_t. We imposed the sign restrictions on the first period reaction of the VAR model and set the nominal interest rate such that it did not react to shocks during the financials crisis. The sign restrictions are presented in Table 1.

Table 1. Sign restrictions.

Shock\Variables	I_t	R_t	U_t	M_t	π_t	S_t
Monetary policy shock	≥	≤	≥	≤	≤	≤
Spread shock	≤	≥	≥	≥	≤	≤
Demand shock	≥	≥	≤	≤	≥	≥
Supply shock	≥	≥	≤	?	≤	≤

Note: The sign '≥' denotes a positive response, the sign '≤' denotes a negative response, and '?' denotes an uncertain response that the sign can either be positive or negative, decided by the calibration of the model.

To derive the sign restrictions to impose on the change-point VAR model, we used the results derived from the New Keynesian Dynamic Stochastic General Equilibrium (NKDSGE) model of Liu et al. [17] to determine how each variable reacts to shocks. In the aftermath of a positive monetary policy shock, the real money holdings fall due to the higher cost of holding money. The increase in the nominal interest rate leads to a rise in the demand for short-term bonds that generates a fall in real activity and REITs prices and a rise in unemployment. The fall in output generates an increase in the long-run nominal interest rate, which is lower than the increase in the short-run interest rate, and hence the spread between long- and short-run interest rates falls. A positive interest rate spread shock increases the long-run interest rate, which generates a fall in consumption and output, as implied by the demand for long-term bonds. The contraction in output induces REITs prices to fall and unemployment to rise. The fall in output generates a reduction in inflation, as implied by the Phillips curve, whose effect is to induce a fall in the short-run interest rate (through the Taylor rule), which causes real money holdings to increase since the money demand is negatively related to the short-run nominal interest rate. The direct effect of the demand shock is to increase real activity and REITs prices with unemployment falling, since this shock actually increases the marginal utility of consumption for any given level of consumption, which in turn also increases the long-term nominal interest rate sharply due to the demand for long-term bond. The rise in output growth generates an increase in inflation, whose effect is to increase the short-term nominal interest rate, causing real money holdings to fall. The spread increases, since the increase in the long-term interest rate is stronger than the corresponding short-term interest rate increase. Finally, the aggregate supply shock produces an increase (decrease) in output (inflation), which results in increases in REITs prices and a decrease in unemployment. Output growth rises sharply and, therefore, induces the central bank to raise the short-term nominal interest rate, which generates a fall in the interest rate spread, and possibly also real money balances, with the final effect on the latter uncertain due to the positive income effect.

We collected data for the effective FFR, 10-Year Treasury bond yield at constant maturity, civilian unemployment rate, consumer price index (CPI), M2 definition of the money supply, and the monthly total returns index for the FTSE Nareit U.S. ALL REITs. The ALL REITs index is a market capitalization-weighted index that includes all tax-qualified REITs listed on the New York Stock Exchange, the American Stock Exchange, or the NASDAQ National Market List. We took data from the FRED database of the Federal Reserve Bank of St. Louis for all variables, barring the REITs index, which, in turn, was obtained from www.reit.com. Our sample covers the monthly period from 1972:12 to

2016:12, with the starting date driven by data availability at the time of writing this paper. We note that the end date is in line with one year from the end of the unconventional monetary policy regime, given that it is widely-believed that monetary policy takes over a year to affect the macroeconomic variables. In addition, the end date is also aligned with tapering of policies aimed towards stimulating the real estate market directly. The unemployment rate, CPI, and M2 were seasonally adjusted. The interest rate spread is defined as the 10-year yield minus the FFR. We used the 12-month percentage change to compute inflation, the growth rate of M2, and the growth rate of REITs prices.

2.2. Change-Point VAR Model

The model used in this paper is based on the change-point VAR model developed by Chib [22,23]. The detailed description is as follows:

$$Z_t = C_s + \sum_{j=1}^{K} B_s Z_{t-j} + \theta_s^{\frac{1}{2}} \varepsilon_t \tag{1}$$

where B_s and θ_s are the autoregressive coefficients depended on the regime and reduced form variance covariance matrices, the state variable s is modeled as a discrete time and follow an M state Markov chain with the transition probability matrix, and the transition probability matrix specifies s to be either stay at the current value or switch to the next higher value, but not allow to switch back to past regimes. The restricted transition probabilities matrix P is a diagonal matrix with the diagonal elements

$$p_{ij} = p(S_t = j \middle| S_{t-1} = i) \tag{2}$$

where

$$p_{ij} > 0 \; if \; j = i + 1 \text{ or } i = j$$
$$p_{MM} = 1$$
$$p_{ij} = 0 \text{ otherwise.}$$

And in this paper, according to Liu et al. [17], it is suitable for us to set $M = 3$. The readers can refer to Chib [22,23] and Liu et al. [17] for more details. Thus, the restricted transition probability matrix is denoted by

$$\widetilde{P} = \begin{pmatrix} p_{11} & 0 & 0 & 0 \\ 1-p_{11} & p_{22} & 0 & 0 \\ 0 & 1-p_{22} & p_{33} & 0 \\ 0 & 0 & 1-p_{33} & 1 \end{pmatrix} \tag{3}$$

2.3. Setting Dummy Observations

Based on the literature [17,24–26], we constructed the following matrices of dummy observations:

$$Y_D = \begin{pmatrix} \frac{diag(\gamma_1\sigma_1 \cdots \gamma_N\sigma_N)}{\tau} \\ 0_{N\times(P-1)\times N} \\ \cdots \\ diag(\sigma_1 \cdots \sigma_N) \\ \cdots \\ 0_{1\times N} \end{pmatrix} \text{ and } X_D = \begin{pmatrix} \frac{J_P \otimes diag(\gamma_1\sigma_1 \cdots \gamma_N\sigma_N)}{\tau} & 0_{NP\times 1} \\ 0_{N\times NP} & 0_{N\times 1} \\ \cdots & \cdots \\ 0_{1\times NP} & c \end{pmatrix} \tag{4}$$

where the matrix J_P stands for $diag(1, 2, \cdots, P)$, $\tau = 0.03$, and $c = 1$ standing for the tightness of the prior on the VAR coefficients and the constant terms, respectively [25]. We obtain the estimates of both σ_i and γ_i from the AR(1) model via Ordinary Least Squares (OLS) for $i = 1, 2, \cdots, N$, where σ_i stands for the standard deviation of the residual and γ_i is the estimate of the AR(1) coefficient.

2.4. Priors for VARs

We assume the priors of the coefficients to follow a normal distribution and the covariances to follow an inverted Wishart distribution, with the first M regimes assumed to follow a Normal Inverse Wishart prior [27,28]. The traditional approach is to assume that the priors of the coefficients follow the Multivariate Gaussian distribution with the vector zero mean and the covariance matrix with $diag(1000, 1000, \cdots, 1000)$. Howevwe, in this paper, to be consistent with the unconventional monetary policy regime and to ensure the lagged coefficients on the non-dependent variables in the interest rate equation are close to zero, we imposed the prior of the coefficients in this period to follow Multivariate Gaussian distribution with zero mean. In addition, the covariance matrix with the diagonal elements corresponding to the coefficients of interest in the interest rate equation was set to the value of 1×10^{-12}, and the remaining diagonal elements were set to be 1000, and other elements were set to zero.

2.5. Priors for the Transition Probability

We assume the priors for the nonzero elements of the transition matrix p_{ij} follow the Dirichlet distribution, namely $p^0_{ij} = D(u_{ij})$, where $D(\cdot)$ denotes the Dirichlet distribution and

$$u_{ij} = \begin{cases} 10\ i = j \\ 1\ i \neq j \end{cases} \tag{5}$$

In this model setting, one could easily show that the posterior distribution follows the Dirichlet distribution:

$$p_{ij} = D(u_{ij} + \pi_{ij}) \tag{6}$$

where π_{ij} denotes the times of regime i that is followed by regime j.

In addition, we tool the sample by using the Gibbs sampling algorithm, estimate the change-point VAR model with the 200,000 replications, and deleted the first 195,000 replications so that the remaining replications became more random. Readers can refer to Chib [22,23], Kim and Nelson [29] and Liu et al. [17] for more details.

3. Empirical Results

Figure 1 shows the estimated probability of the four regimes, with them corresponding to the periods of June 1973 to January 1985, February 1985 to January 2009, February 2009 to May 2013, and June 2013 to December 2016. The VAR model was estimated based on six lags, as suggested by the Bayesian Information Criterion (BIC), and hence the first regime starts from June, 1972. The estimate for the first breakpoint is consistent with financial liberalization in the US, with the second one corresponding to the end of the global financial crisis, and the third one with the 'tapering' of the unconventional monetary policies.

To tie these breakpoints to changing macroeconomic dynamics, Figure 2 plots some key reduced form summary statistics from the change-point VAR. The top panel of Figure 2 presents the persistence of each of the endogenous variables in the change-point VAR for each regime. The FFR, bond yield spread, and M2 growth performed very similarly throughout the sample period. These variables increased from regime 1 to regime 2 and decreased during regime 3, and then increased in regime 4. Moreover, the unemployment rate showed a similar trend in the first three regimes. The persistence of inflation and REITs return changed over all four regimes, and during the financial crisis, the persistence of inflation reached its lowest value, while the persistence of REITs returns reached its highest value.

The second panel of Figure 2 shows the diagonal elements of the error covariance matrix in each regime. We observed that the volatility of the reduced-form errors declined for all the time series, with a different extent from regime 1 to regime 2. Furthermore, during the last two regimes covering the financial crisis and unconventional monetary policies due to the ZLB, the volatility of the reduced-form errors increased for all the variables, except for the bond yield spread and the FFR.

The last panel of Figure 2 shows the unconditional volatility of each variable in each regime. The volatility of the bond yield spread, and CPI inflation were extremely similar throughout the whole sample period. In general, all the plots were consistent to the second panel, except the behavior of the CPI inflation in regime 3.

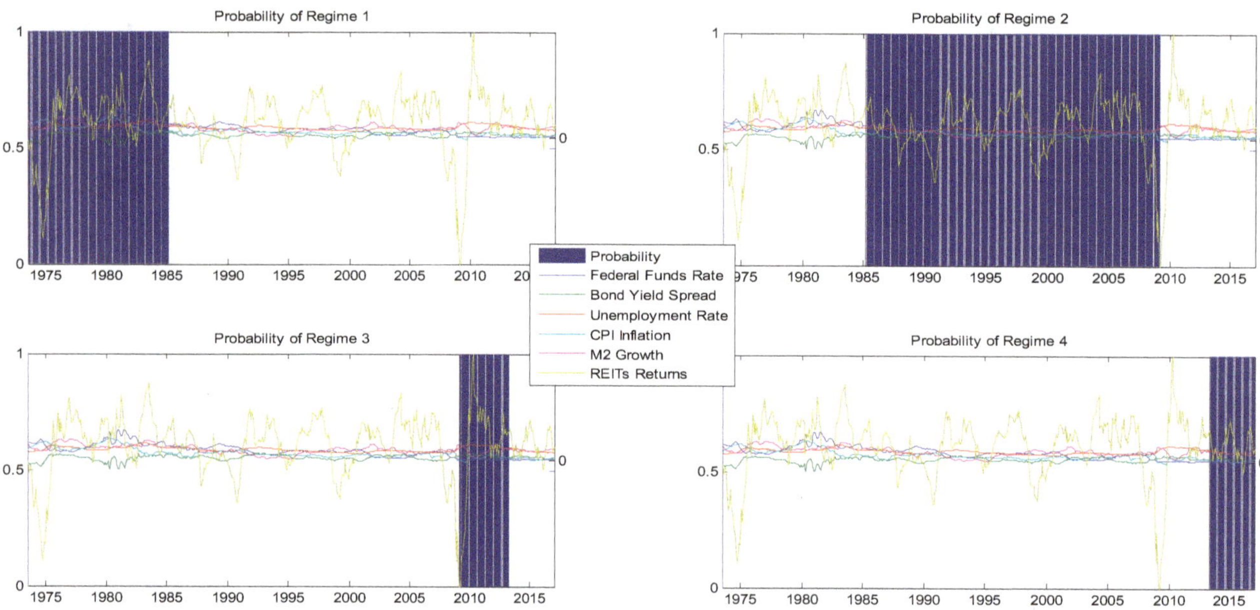

Figure 1. The estimated probability of each regime. Notes: The four regimes correspond to the periods June 1973 to January 1985, February 1985 to January 2009, February 2009 to May 2013, and June 2013 to December 2016.

The empirical framework is well-suited to investigate changes in macroeconomic dynamics across the sample horizon, since the change-point VAR model allows the coefficients in the model to vary across regimes. Figures 3–6 plot the impulse response functions (IRFs) of the six endogenous variables to a one-standard-deviation shock for the four identified shocks across the four regimes. We obtained the median and 68% confidence bands based on 5000 retained Gibbs replications. Since our focus is the REITs returns, we concentrate on discussing the effect of the various shocks on this variable. The effects on the other variables for the four shocks were similar to those obtained by Liu et al. [17], and the reader can refer to that paper for a more detailed discussion.

Figure 3 presents the responses of the variables to a contractionary monetary policy shock (i.e., an increase in the nominal interest rate). For the third regime, this shock was absent since the nominal interest rate was set at approximately zero, corresponding to the ZLB scenario. The size of the negative impact was quite similar in regimes 1 and 2, though it was relatively stronger under regime 1, with the effect being significant for about a year. The recovery was faster in regime 1 relative to regime 2, though the effect in the former regime increased again from three-years onwards. However, the strongest negative effect was observed in regime 4, with the effect being significant for over one and half years. This strong impact is probably an indication of the recovery that took place in the US real estate sector, and the economy in general, post the 'Great Recession'. In all cases, however, the effect on REITs returns was negative over the entire horizons of the 50 months considered.

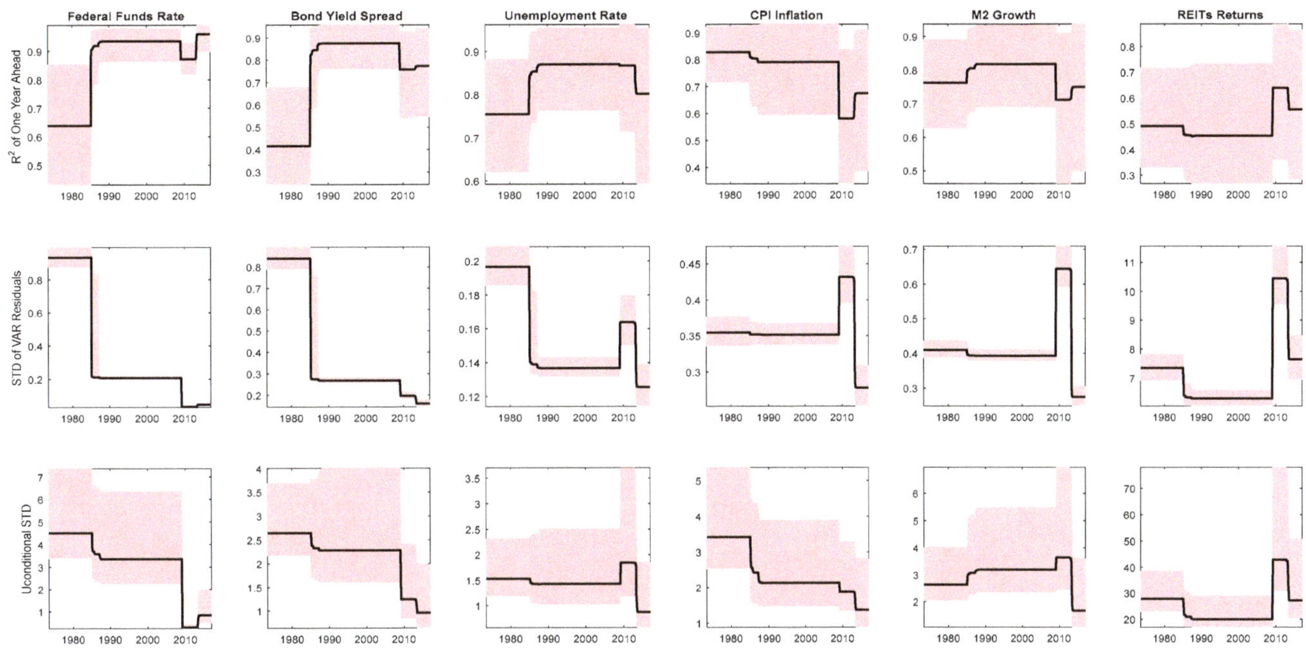

Figure 2. Regime dependent summary statistics; Note: See Notes to Figure 1.

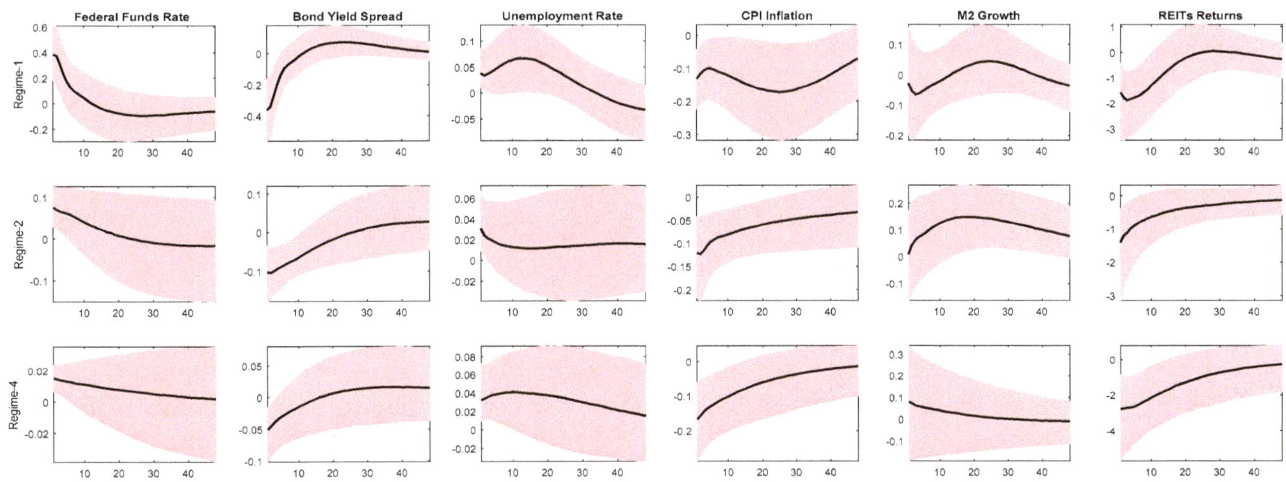

Figure 3. Impulse response functions to a contractionary monetary policy shock; Note: See Notes to Figure 1.

Next, Figure 4 presents the responses of the variables to a negative interest rate spread shock. To implement the analysis, we made it so that the short-term interest rate was exogenous to the spread shock in the third regime. Unsurprisingly, the positive impact on REITs returns tended to increase both in magnitude and length of the periods for which the effect was significant as we move from regimes 1 to 4. These results highlight the enhanced role of unconventional monetary policies in the third and fourth regimes aiming to reduce borrowing costs, as well as attempts made to directly stimulate the real estate sector, especially in the last identified sub-sample.

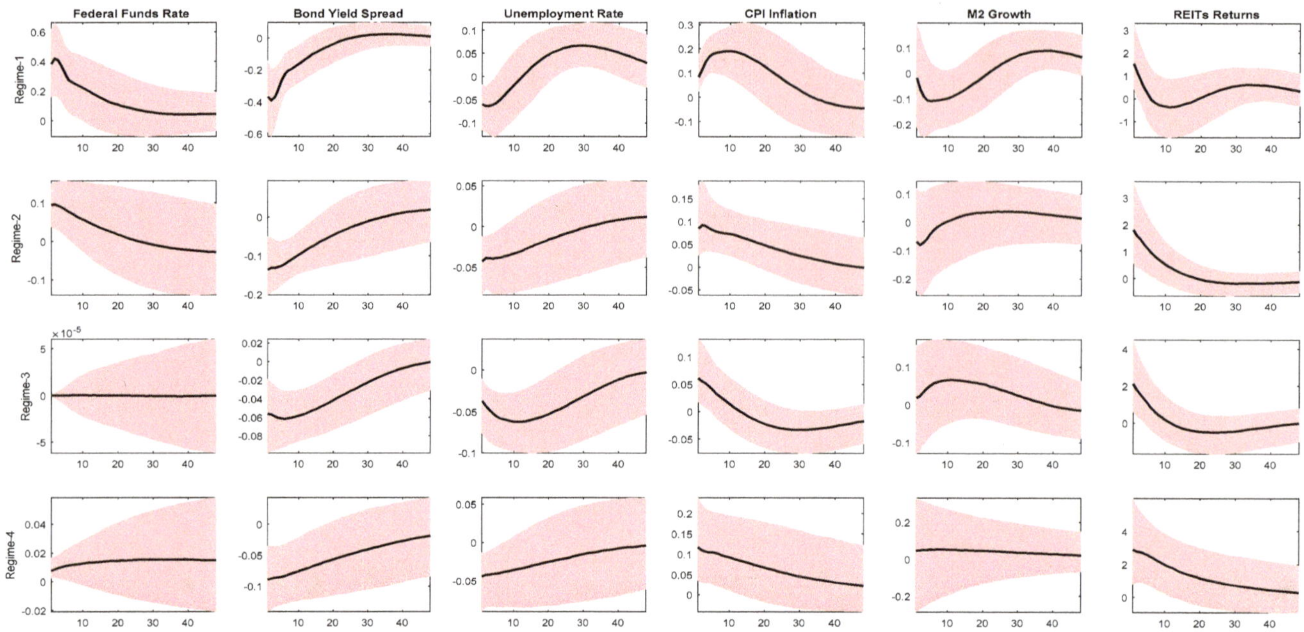

Figure 4. Impulse response functions to a negative interest rate spread shock; Note: See Notes to Figure 1.

Figure 5 presents the responses of the variables to an expansionary demand shock. The positive impact of REITs returns continued to increase in magnitude over the regimes, with the statistical significance also lasting for a longer number of horizons, especially in the last regime (where the effect was significant for over a year). While in Figure 6, we can see that the aggregate supply shock tended to positively affect the REITs returns, with the strongest effects observed in regimes 1, 3, and 4, with the effect declining during regime 2, with the effect being statistically longest-lasting (for over a year) in regime 3, i.e., right after the depth of financial crisis.

In summary, looking across all these impulse responses suggests that the transmission mechanism of the different shocks on REITs returns changed across the four regimes. To understand the extent to which movements of REITs returns can be explained by each shock and how the contribution of shocks changed across regimes, Figure 7 highlights the forecast error variance decompositions of the six endogenous variables for each of the four shocks. Concentrating on REITs returns, we observed that, the policy shock played an important role in the last regime (compared to the first two regimes), explaining over 30% of the variation in REITs returns. The spread shock was found to have quite a strong impact on regimes 2 and 4, with it explaining over 30% of the fluctuations in the real estate returns. Demand shocks explain about 14% and 8% of the variations in REITs returns in regimes 3 and 1, respectively. But the importance of the aggregate supply shocks stand out in regimes 1 and 2, with it explaining over 50% and 40% of the variations in regimes 1 and 2, and over 20% and 10% of the fluctuations of the REITs returns in regimes 3 and 4, respectively. The importance of the supply shocks is in line with Plakandaras et al. [11]. Overall, while supply shocks have been shown to be important in the early part of the sample, the spread and monetary shocks seem to dominate towards the end of the sample period under consideration.

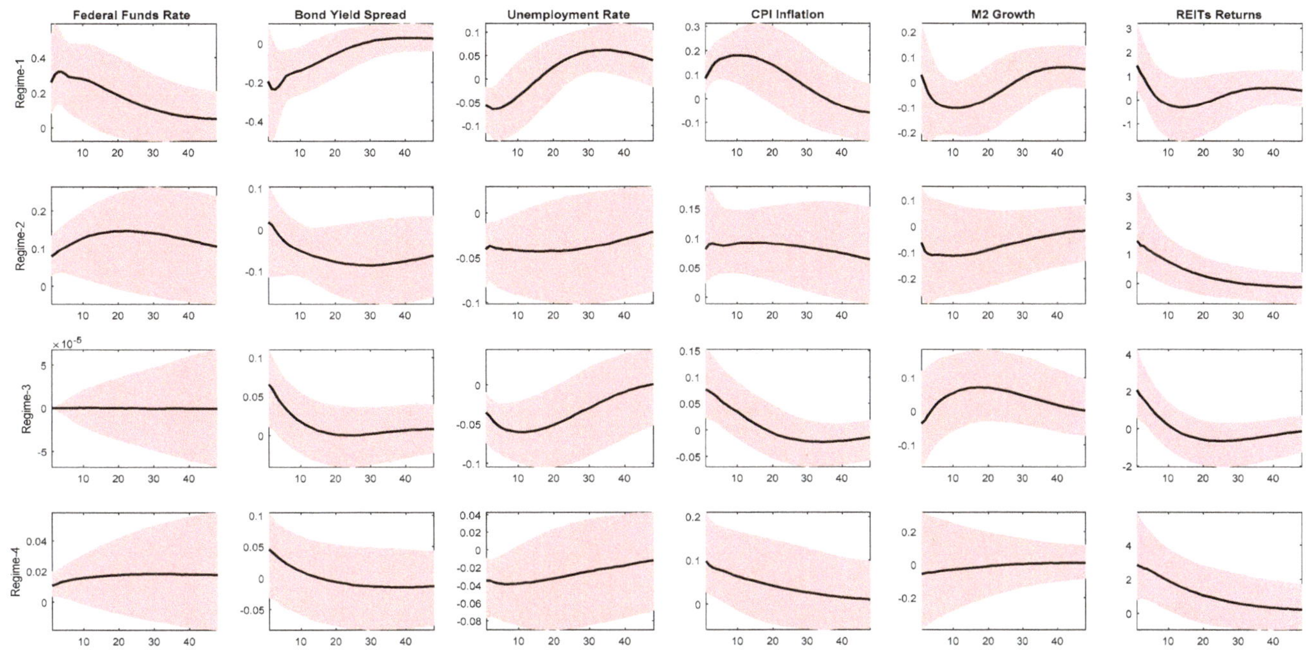

Figure 5. Impulse response functions to an expansionary demand shock; Note: See Notes to Figure 1.

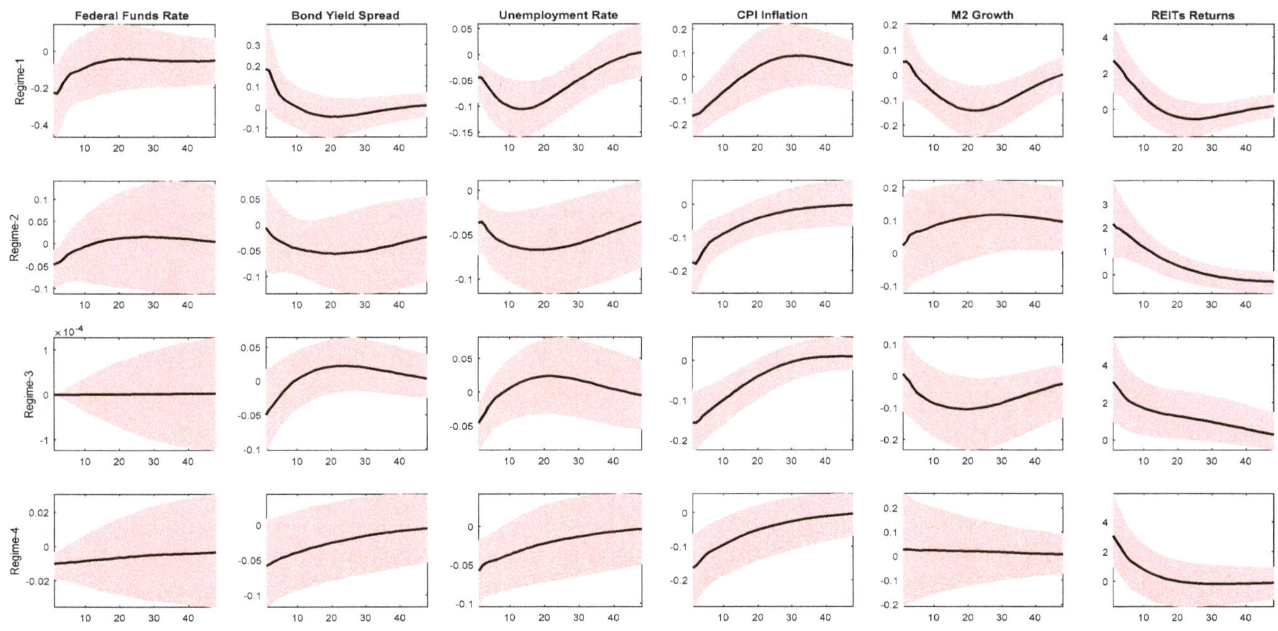

Figure 6. Impulse response functions to an expansionary supply shock; Notes: See Notes to Figure 1.

These results tend to suggest the importance of technical progress, i.e., the aggregate supply shocks, post-World War II in the US, which in turn led to a growth in productivity and hence output growth. This output growth is likely to have been driven by the consistently booming real estate market, until the collapse in 2007. The importance of the monetary policy and the spread shock in the last two regimes, basically coincided with the post-crisis period, where various measures of unconventional monetary policies were undertaken to boost the housing market and the overall macroeconomy. Our analysis thus indicates that while the role of monetary policy is important in driving the real estate sector of the US, it is also necessary to identify the role of other shocks, so that researchers do not overemphasize the role of monetary policy shocks.

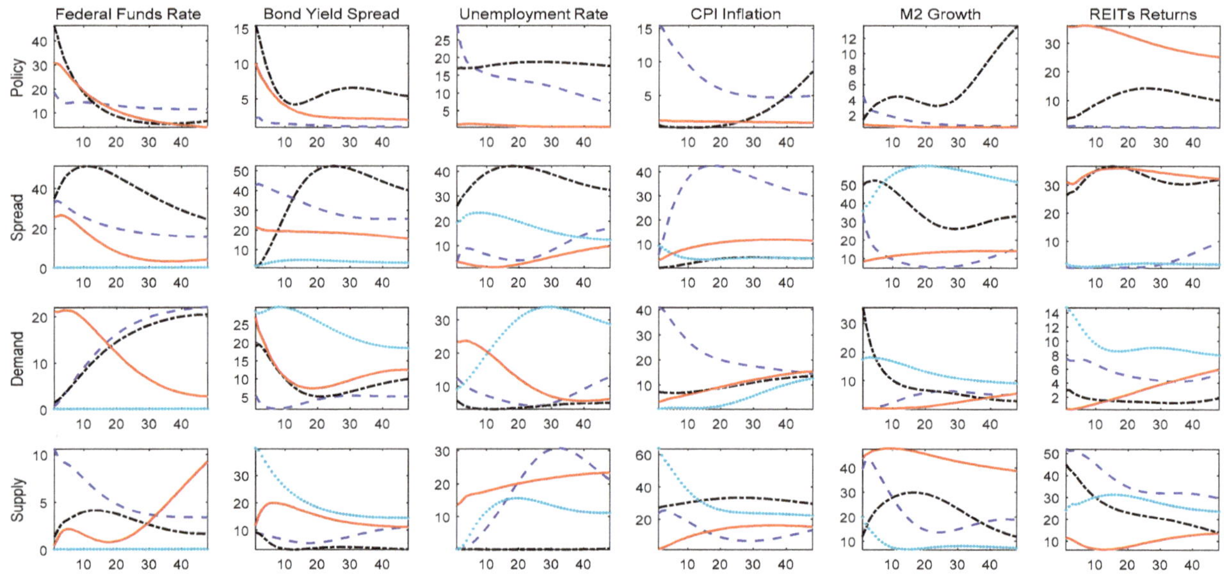

Figure 7. Forecast error variance decomposition; Notes: The four regimes correspond to the periods June 1973 to January 1985 (dashed blue line), February 1985 to January 2009 (dashed-dotted black line), February 2009 to May 2013 (dotted cyan line), and June 2013 to December 2016 (solid red line).

4. Conclusions

Given the importance of the real estate sector in causing the recent financial crisis, this paper uses a flexible change-point VAR model to analyze the regime-specific impact of various macroeconomic and financial shocks, identified based on sign-restrictions, on the US REITs returns. We deviate from the existing literature, which merely analyzes the role of monetary policy shocks on the US REITs sector and ignores the possible influence and importance of other shocks. The empirical model identifies three break points (four regimes) over the monthly sample period from 1972:12 to 2016:12. The third regime, coincides with the crisis period. The analysis discloses a range of important changes in the statistical and dynamic properties of REITs returns over the sample period. Statistical properties, such as persistence and volatility of fluctuations in REITs returns and the volatility of the reduced-form errors are found to have changed throughout the different regimes, with the crisis period being characterized by higher volatility. In addition, although quantitative changes are recorded throughout the whole period, supply, monetary policy, and spread shocks generate movements in REITs returns at the early and last parts of the sample period under consideration, respectively.

Hence, while the role of monetary policy is important in driving the real estate sector of the US, it is also necessary to identify the role of other shocks, in particular aggregate supply shocks to capture the role of productivity on the real estate sector, so that researchers do not overemphasize the role of monetary policy shocks. As we show, monetary policy shocks are only dominant in terms of moving the REITs sector post the recent financial crisis, in the wake of wide-array of unconventional monetary policy measures. This result also tends to suggest that, compared to productivity shocks, the role of monetary policy was minimal in heating up the US real estate market [30] before its collapse that led to the 'Great Recession'. Hence, loose monetary policy cannot be blamed for the real estate market bubble alone, though it is indeed true that post the financial liberalization in the US, the importance of monetary policy in affecting the real estate sector did increase [14].

From a policy perspective, our results have important implications. The relatively weaker role of conventional monetary policy, in affecting the REITs sector, tends to suggest that if there are bubbles in the US REITs sector, the Federal Reserve will not be successful in preventing it from bursting. In other words, besides the limited role of monetary policy on the REITs sector, the fact that interest rates are a blunt instrument to prick a bubble resulting in unintended collateral damage, the main policy message from our analysis is that the Federal Reserve should focus on stabilizing inflation and the output gap only—an observation in line with Bernanke and Gertler [31,32].

One limitation of this study is that we consider the overall REITs sector of the US. However, REITs data is available in a sector-specific manner involving equities and mortgages, which in turn could be affected differently from these shocks compared to the overall market. These possible dissimilarities could be studied as part of future research. Moreover, we ignore the role of fiscal policies in the paper, which also played an important role in the US macroeconomy, especially during the ZLB. In addition, our current study can be extended by analyzing REITs markets of other developed countries or regions like the UK, Euro Area, and Japan, which also faced a ZLB situation. Finally, our approach can also be applied to study the possible heterogenous impact of these shocks across the regional housing markets of the US.

Author Contributions: Conceptualization, R.G.; Formal analysis, R.G., Z.L. and W.-K.W.; Methodology, R.G. and W.-K.W.; Software, Z.L.; Writing—original draft, R.G., Z.L. and W.-K.W.

Acknowledgments: We would like to thank three anonymous referees for many helpful comments. However, any remaining errors are solely ours. The third author would like to thank Robert B. Miller and Howard E. Thompson for their continuous guidance and encouragement. This research has been supported by Northeast Normal University, The Education University of Hong Kong, Asia University, China Medical University Hospital, The Hang Seng University of Hong Kong, the Research Grants Council of Hong Kong (Project Number 12500915), and Ministry of Science and Technology (MOST, Project Numbers 106-2410-H-468-002 and 107-2410-H-468-002-MY3), Taiwan.

References

1. Nyakabawo, W.V.; Miller, S.M.; Balcilar, M.; Das, S.; Gupta, R. Temporal Causality between House Prices and Output in the U.S.: A Bootstrap Rolling-window Approach. *N. Am. J. Econ. Financ.* **2015**, *33*, 55–73. [CrossRef]
2. Emirmahmutoglu, F.; Balcilar, M.; Apergis, N.; Simo-Kengne, B.D.; Chang, T.; Gupta, R. Causal Relationship between Asset Prices and Output in the US: Evidence from State-Level Panel Granger Causality Test. *Reg. Stud.* **2016**, *50*, 1728–1741. [CrossRef]
3. Claus, E.; Claus, I.; Krippner, L. *Asset Markets and Monetary Policy Shocks at the Zero LOWER Bound*; Discussion Paper No. DP2014/03; Reserve Bank of New Zealand: Wellington, New Zealand, 2014.
4. Claus, E.; Claus, I.; Krippner, L. Monetary policy spillovers across the Pacific when interest rates are at the zero lower bound. *Asian Econ. Pap.* **2016**, *15*, 1–27. [CrossRef]
5. Rahal, C. Housing Markets and Unconventional Monetary Policy. *J. Hous. Econ.* **2016**, *32*, 67–80. [CrossRef]
6. Simo-Kengne, B.D.; Miller, S.M.; Gupta, R.; Balcilar, M. Evolution of the Monetary Transmission Mechanism in the US: The Role of Asset Returns. *J. Real Estate Financ. Econ.* **2016**, *52*, 226–243. [CrossRef]
7. Gupta, R.; Marfatia, H.A. The Impact of Unconventional Monetary Policy Shocks in the US on Emerging Market REITs: A Qual VAR Approach. *J. Real Estate Lit.* **2018**, *26*, 175–188.
8. Huber, F.; Punzi, M.T. International Housing Markets, Unconventional Monetary Policy and the Zero Lower Bound. *Macroecon. Dyn.* **2018**. [CrossRef]
9. El Montasser, G.; Gupta, R.; Jooste, C.; Miller, S.M. The Time-Series Linkages between US Fiscal Poliy and Asset Prices. *Public Financ. Rev.* **2019**, forthcoming.
10. Gupta, R.; Lau, C.K.M.; Miller, S.M.; Wohar, M.E. U.S. Fiscal Policy and Asset Prices: The Role of Partisan Conflict. *Int. Rev. Financ.* **2018**. [CrossRef]
11. Plakandaras, V.; Gupta, R.; Katrakilidis, C.; Wohar, M.E. Time-Varying Role of Macroeconomic Shocks on House Prices in the US and UK: Evidence from Over 150 Years of Data. *Empir. Econ.* **2018**. [CrossRef]
12. Gupta, R.; Kabundi, A. The effect of monetary policy on house price inflation: A factor augmented vector autoregression (FAVAR) approach. *J. Econ. Stud.* **2010**, *37*, 616–626. [CrossRef]
13. Gupta, R.; Jurgilas, M.; Kabundi, A.; Miller, S.M. Monetary Policy and Housing Sector Dynamics in a Large-Scale Bayesian Vector Autoregressive Model. *Int. J. Strateg. Prop. Manag.* **2012**, *16*, 1–20. [CrossRef]
14. Gupta, R.; Miller, S.M.; Van Wyk, D. Financial Market Liberalization, Monetary Policy, and Housing Price Dynamics. *Int. Bus. Econ. Res.* **2012**, *11*, 69–82. [CrossRef]

15. Nakamura, E.; Steinsson, J. High Frequency Identification of Monetary Non-Neutrality: The Information Effect. *Quart. J. Econ.* **2018**, *133*, 1283–1330. [CrossRef]
16. Nakamura, E.; Steinsson, J. Identification in Macroeconomics. *J. Econ. Perspect.* **2018**, *32*, 59–86. [CrossRef]
17. Liu, P.; Mumtaz, H.; Theodoridis, K.; Zanetti, F. Changing macroeconomic dynamics at the zero lower bound. *J. Bus. Econ. Stat.* **2017**. [CrossRef]
18. Simo-Kengne, B.D.; Miller, S.; Gupta, R.; Aye, C. Time-varying effects of housing and stock returns on U.S. consumption. *J. Real Estate Financ. Econ.* **2015**, *50*, 339–354. [CrossRef]
19. Marfatia, H.A.; Gupta, R.; Cakan, E. The International REITs Time Varying Response to the U.S. Monetary Policy and Macroeconomic Surprises. *N. Am. J. Econ. Financ.* **2017**, *42*, 640–653. [CrossRef]
20. Nyakabawo, W.; Gupta, R.; Marfatia, H.A. High Frequency Impact of Monetary Policy and Macroeconomic Surprises on US MSAs, Aggregate US Housing Returns and Asymmetric Volatility. *Adv. Decis. Sci.* **2018**, *22*, 2–26.
21. Kapetanios, G.; Mumtaz, H.; Stevens, I.; Theodoridis, K. Assessing the economy-wide effects of quantitative easing. *Econ. J.* **2012**, *122*, 316–347. [CrossRef]
22. Chib, S. Calculating posterior distributions and modal estimates in Markov mixture models. *J. Econom.* **1996**, *75*, 79–97. [CrossRef]
23. Chib, S. Estimation and comparison of multiple change-point models. *J. Econom.* **1998**, *86*, 221–241. [CrossRef]
24. Doan, T.; Litterman, R.; Sims, C. Forecasting and conditional projection using realistic prior distributions. *Econ. Rev.* **1984**, *3*, 1–100. [CrossRef]
25. Sims, C.A.; Zha, T. Bayesian methods for dynamic multivariate models. *Int. Econ. Rev.* **1998**, *39*, 949–968. [CrossRef]
26. Giannone, D.; Lenza, M.; Primiceri, G.E. Prior selection for vector autoregressions. *Rev. Econ. Stat.* **2015**, *97*, 436–451. [CrossRef]
27. Kadiyala, K.R.; Karlsson, S. Numerical methods for estimation and inference in Bayesian VAR models. *J. Appl. Econom.* **1997**, *12*, 99–132. [CrossRef]
28. Canova, F. *Methods for Applied Macroeconomic Research*; Princeton University Press: Princeton, NJ, USA, 2011.
29. Kim, C.J.; Nelson, C.R. *State-Space Models with Regime Switching: Classical and Gibbs-Sampling Approaches with Applications*; MIT Press: Cambridge, MA, USA, 1999.
30. Del Negro, M.; Otrok, C. Monetary policy and the house price boom across U.S. states. *J. Monet. Econ.* **2007**, *54*, 1962–1985. [CrossRef]
31. Bernanke, B.S.; Gertler, M. Monetary Policy and Asset Price Volatility. In *New Challenges for Monetary Policy*; Federal Reserve Bank of Kansas City: Kansas City, MO, USA, 1999; pp. 77–128.
32. Bernanke, B.S.; Gertler, M. Should Central Banks Respond to Movements in Asset Prices? *Am. Econ. Rev.* **2001**, *91*, 253–257. [CrossRef]

5

The Impact of Market Condition and Policy Change on the Sustainability of Intra-Industry Information Diffusion

Chi Dong [1], Hooi Hooi Lean [2,*], Zamri Ahmad [3] and Wing-Keung Wong [4,5,6]

1 School of Economics, Hebei University, Baoding 071002, China; dongchi30@163.com
2 Economics Program, School of Social Sciences, Universiti Sains Malaysia, Penang 11800, Malaysia
3 School of Management, Universiti Sains Malaysia, Penang 11800, Malaysia; zahmad@usm.my
4 Department of Finance, Fintech Center, and Big Data Research Center, Asia University, Taichung City 41354, Taiwan; wong@asia.edu.tw
5 Department of Medical Research, China Medical University Hospital, Taichung 40402, Taiwan
6 Department of Economics and Finance, Hang Seng University of Hong Kong, Shatin 999077, Hong Kong
* Correspondence: hooilean@usm.my

Abstract: Through an investigation into seven major industries in China's stock market from 2002 to 2013, this study focuses on two main external determinants: market condition and policy change on intra-industry information diffusion. We employ both time-series and panel Vector Auto-regression (VAR) methods on a sample data of 1175 firms for the analysis. The investigation reveals that market conditions and policy changes affect the process of intra-industry information diffusion in China. The speed of intra-industry information diffusion in a down-market state is slower than an upmarket, especially when the evidence is more significant in the longer horizon of the market condition. Policy changes, especially the split-share structure reform, impede the process of intra-industry information diffusion. The investigation outcome also reveals that there is an increasing delay in intra-industry information diffusion over time in China's stock market after 2005. However, because of the decreasing information volatility of intra-industry information diffusion, policy changes are useful to a certain extent.

Keywords: market condition; policy change; information diffusion; intra-industry; China

1. Introduction

Under the Efficient Market Hypothesis (EMH), information diffuses without any delay in a complete and frictionless market. However, ever since the seminal work of Lo and MacKinlay [1], researchers increasingly discover that information gradually diffuses in the realistic market. From research views to research methods, an abundance of researchers continually explore the study of gradual information diffusion [2–7]. Many past studies contribute internal determinants, such as the firm's characteristics in the process of information diffusion [8–10].

Additionally, external factors that could affect the process of information diffusion have also been explored. Two potential external determinants that can affect information diffusion are market condition and policy change. Certain literatures focus on market condition to explore information diffusion. For example, McQueen et al. [11] and Chang et al. [12] suggest that, by reason of small stocks' lagged response in up market, gradual information diffusion is more significant in up market rather than down market. In contrary to McQueen et al. [11], Hameed and Kusnadi [3] claim that the speed of information diffusion is supposed to be slower when the market falls. Chen & Rhee [13] suggest that both short sale and market conditions could affect the speed of information diffusion.

They argue that the speeds of information diffusion are similar in the both up and down markets. Therefore, the market condition that can delay the diffusion of information seems be controversial.

Another external determinant is policy change. As an important setting in a market environment, policy change has significant impact on the financial market from various aspects and the influence on information diffusion is just a sub-fraction. It is the process of gradual discovery. Any policy change is not always smooth and successful and the market environment and institutional arrangement can be responsible for the speed of information diffusion. Merton [14] recognizes the importance of institutional constraints in the information achievement and diffusion procedure. In recent years, the impact of policy changes on financial markets has become one of the more recent research hotspots. Theoretically and empirically, the importance of a variety of policies and environmental changes on the process of information diffusion is explored by several researchers. Lin & Swanson [15] argue that policy changes in China could influence the China segmented stock market more. They suggest that the policy changes alleviate barriers of information diffusion. In addition, Bae et al. [16] argue that the policy of liberalization of stock market produces more information on the efficiency of stock prices for emerging markets. They discover that foreign investors can facilitate the diffusion of global market information into stock prices. On the other hand, Mori [17] investigates how policy and environmental changes in the Real Estate Investment The trust market could affect the process of information diffusion in the United States (U.S.) market. He discovers that changes of the process of information diffusion depend on both different government policies and changes of firm size.

On the other hand, most of the previous studies investigate the process of information diffusion based on the whole market and, by narrowing the research scope, a few researches have also examined information diffusion that relates to industries such as customer-supplier and upstream-downstream industries [5,6,18]. However, researches rarely focus on firms within an industry to investigate the process of information diffusion. Cen et al. [19] report that industry-wide information is first incorporated into the stock prices of industry leaders who are more liquid and have high level of analyst coverage, and then the information gradually distributes to other industry followers. Importantly, Hou [4] particularly examines the intra-industry information diffusion. He argues that gradual information diffusion mainly exists in intra-industry rather than cross-industry or outside-industry. Haque [20] further support the hypotheses of Hou [4] with data in Australia. However, they only focus on the internal impact factors of intra-industry information diffusion. External determinants of intra-industry information diffusion have not been adequately touched on in their researches.

By including the market conditions and policy changes, this study stresses the roles of external determinants on intra-industry information diffusion in China's stock market. To the best of our knowledge, this study is the first of its kind, which focuses on the intra-industry to investigate the process of information diffusion with views of market conditions and policy changes. The research not only focuses on individual industries, but it also processes a major investigation of intra-industry. The findings of this research contribute to the pool of existing literature in several ways. First, as an external determinant, how market conditions affect information diffusion in the stock market is still controversial. Moreover, the research scope focuses on intra-industry. This study is the first attempt to explore the impact of market condition on information diffusion with focus on intra-industry.

Second, as the largest emerging market, China's stock market has unique microstructures and institutional arrangement, which are different with most developed markets. Due to the relatively shorter development period, China's stock market suffers from market immaturity and investors irrationality. With the specific conditions in China, the study focuses on whether and how policy changes influence the process of intra-industry information diffusion. Institutional frictions are accountable for producing the delay in the process of information diffusion. Thus, comprehending the process of information diffusion is very important for policy considerations. Institutional reforms in China's stock market have been implemented for many years since the establishment of the market. However, the effectiveness of the changes in policy is still in dispute. Whether policy reforms are effective in China stock market? Whether China government can professionally regular and controls the market? How to smooth the process of information diffusion and increase informativeness of stock price? How do investors make use of information? These problems always puzzle government authorities and investors. Therefore, revolving around intra-industry information diffusion, further systematic investigation and exploration are necessary. Policy considerations and market mechanisms in China should keep pace with the times, which could, in turn, ensure that stock prices develop more effectively and informatively. Based on the most important policy changes, i.e., the split-share structure reform in 2005 and lifting short-sale constraints in 2010, this study is the first to investigate the impact of policy change on intra-industry information diffusion. Consequently, this study provides several evidences to help the government authorities in smoothing the process of intra-industry information diffusion and augmenting the market efficiency.

Third, the study focuses on China's stock market. As the biggest emerging market, research on China's stock market is a significant reference for investigation into other emerging markets. Most researches about information diffusion in China concentrate on the whole market [7,21] or segmented markets, such as A-share and B-share [15,22]. As far as we know, no literature focuses on intra-industry to investigate information diffusion in China's stock market. Based on the main intra-industry analysis, the study fills the gap.

The organization of the paper is stated, as follows: Section 2 discusses policy changes in China's stock market; Section 3 shows the data and main methods, whereas the impact of market condition on intra-industry information diffusion is examined in Section 4; Section 5 presents the impact of policy changes on the process of intra-industry information diffusion; and, the conclusion and discussion are described in Section 6.

2. Policy Changes in China's Stock Market

Since the reform and opening in 1978, China has experienced a fast transformation from the planned economy to market economy at the national level. Over the past three decades, China has gone through impressive economic growth and turned into the world's second largest economy. It became a member of the World Trade Organization (WTO) that is recognized as one of the BRICs (Brazil Russia India China) by international investment banks (Goldman Sachs) in 2001. Due to its fast economic development and enormous growth opportunities in China, as an indispensable part of the Chinese economy, China's stock market increasingly attracts domestic and foreign investors' attention. As an emerging market, China's stock market has the second largest trading volume, as well as the second largest market capitalization of $6.4 trillion in 2014 [23], only after the U.S. China's stock market became one of the most active markets based on the number of listed companies, the total trading volume, the market capitalization, participation of foreign investors, and the unique categorization of stocks. Therefore, a considerable amount of investment interests and academic attention around the world concentrate on China's stock market.

Notwithstanding its fast development and emerging importance, China's stock market may suffer from market irrationality and excessive fluctuation. Therefore, China's government has to continuously regulate and control the market, as well as stabilize its stock prices. However, the regulation effects are always met with skepticism. For the last ten years, among all of the policies, two policies are the most significant and they show the greatest impact to China's stock market. First, the split-share structure reform that happened in 2005. Based on the tradability, the stocks of listed companies can be put into two major classes: tradable stocks and non-tradable stocks. More specifically, non-tradable stocks belong to all levels of government or government-controlled financial institutions. Wu [24] argues that the issuance of non-tradable stocks increases the inefficiency of China's stock market. For example, less tradable stocks can bring about a decrease in liquidity and they are convenient to the practice of insider information trading.

On the other hand, tradable stocks can be freely traded by individual, as well as institutional investors. All companies have non-tradable shares in varying proportions. Before 2005, non-tradable shares contain about two-thirds of the total number of outstanding shares. An excess of non-tradable shares in the stock market bring out several problems for further development of the market. In April 2005, the China Securities Regulatory Commission (CSRC) initiated the reform of non-tradable shares, i.e., the split-share structure reform, trying to transfer all non-tradable shares into tradable shares. The central focus of the split-share structure reform is that holders of non-tradable shares are obliged to compensate the holders of tradable shares in order to obtain the liquidity rights for the option to sell their shares in the future [25]. The potential impact of the split-share structure reform has been discussed by a few empirical literatures. Li et al. [26] suggest that the split-share structure reform might be the most powerful policy reform of China's stock market in recent years. Beltratti et al. [25] discuss that this reform lays down the conditions for essential future changes in ownership, liquidity, and corporate governance in China. However, Carpenter et al. [27] suggest that the split-share structure reform has only little direct immediate impact on the structure of China's stock market in the short term.

The second important policy is lifting short-sale constraints. Before 2010, there were strict short-sale constraints in China's stock market. Under short-sale constraints, due to the ban of law, investors are unable to freely short-sell stocks that they do not hold. Theoretically, short-sale constraints could affect the process of information diffusion. Diamond and Verrecchia [28] maintain that short-sale constraints could delay new information that is to be incorporated into stock prices. Negative information also has difficulties in incorporating stock price and diffusing slowly. In order to improve the process of China's financial market marketization, as well as acting on international convention, CSRC finally abolished the short-sale constraints of China's stock market in February 2010. Therefore, after 2010, after short-sale constraints disappeared, market transactions might have further development room. Chang et al. [29] report that Chinese investors seemed to be unfamiliar with the short-sale mechanism and it is deemed that many of them choose to keep away from short-sales. However, Zhao et al. [30] argue that permitting short-sales could decrease market volatility and provide more suitable stock return allocation in China's stock market. As a result, China's stock market provides appropriate areas to investigate the process of information diffusion with or without short-sale constraints.

3. Data and Methodology

3.1. Data

China's stock market was established in the early 1990s, and in the initial ten years, stock prices fluctuated excessively. CSRC is obliged to continuously introduce policies to stabilize the market. For the purpose of obtaining a relatively stable period of China's stock market, we exclude the initial years since its establishment. Hence, the study period will be from January 2002 to December 2013.

It also focuses on the investigation of intra-industry in China's stock market, because the number of industry is relatively larger. There are 38 industries in China's stock market in the present. However, the number of firms within the industry varies in different industries. Some have more than 100 firms, while some industries only have a few. Sufficient research data is necessary to support the research objectives of this study. The industry that had the number of firms greater than 80 is chosen. (Hou [4] chooses the industry in the U.S. market with the number of firms that are greater than 80. This is a better reference. Not only that, the number of firms in each portfolio should be enough for analysis. Examining information diffusion within an industry in the Australian market, Haque [20] chooses industries that have five to 26 firms. Thus, the number of firms in each portfolio is only two to seven. Due to a smaller firm number, it is difficult to not suspect the validity of the results. Consequently, we chose the industry where the number of firms is greater.) However, the number of firms constantly changes every year. Therefore, to be more specific, we chose the industry with more than 80 firms in 2013. In addition, major industries in China also required selection to guarantee the comprehensiveness of the study. Consequently, we chose the industry with a number of firms greater than 80 and consider this to be a major industry in China. As a result, we chose seven industries and 1175 firms to be the sample in this study. Table 1 shows the number of firms in the sample industries.

Table 1. Number of Firms in Sample Industries.

Industry	Number of Firms
Automobiles parts	127
Construction and materials	202
Food producers	95
Electronic equipment	126
Industrial engineering	230
Industrial metals and mining	234
Pharmaceuticals and biotechnology	161

In order to avoid the considerable bias that is connected with nonsynchronous trading and some microstructure effects at the daily level, weekly returns rather than daily returns are employed in our paper. In addition, seasonal patterns might affect weekly autocorrelations of stock returns [31]. Hou [4] argues that, based on five trading days, if Friday is close, then the autocorrelations of the corresponding weekly return should be higher. On the other hand, if Tuesday is closed, then the autocorrelations of the corresponding weekly return should be smaller. Thus, if Wednesday is closed, then the autocorrelations of the corresponding weekly return should be in between. Using this finding, we estimate the weekly returns from Wednesday close to the subsequent Wednesday close. If the following Wednesday is not a trading day, it will be extended to the next trading day. This method of calculating weekly returns is commonly used in the literature, see, for example, Hameed and Kusnadi [3], and Hou [4]. Nevertheless, Chordia and Swaminathan [10] and Haque [20] employ both the weekly data and daily data to run the Vector Auto-regression (VAR) model. They find that the result of weekly data and the result of daily data are similar.

3.2. Descriptive Statistics

In order to avoid the impact of non-synchronous trading and microstructure effects, many studies use weekly and size-based portfolio data [3,4]. Following the same scenario, the empirical investigation is processed on a weekly and size-based portfolio return.

The size portfolios within the industry are formed, ranking all the firms based on their market capitalization i.e., total capital in the December of each year. The firms are divided into three portfolios: bottom 30%, middle 40%, and top 30%. Portfolio S denotes the smallest 30% firms and portfolio B includes the largest 30% firms. The equal-weighted portfolio weekly returns for each size-ranked portfolio are estimated. R_B and R_S are the weekly returns of the biggest and smallest size portfolios, respectively. Before the empirical analysis is presented, necessary descriptive statistics are essential. More specific descriptive statistics are stated in Table 2:

Table 2 displays the descriptive statistics for the largest and smallest 30% size portfolios of all sample industries from 2002 to 2013. There are 626 weekly returns in each industry-size portfolio. The average weekly returns of the smallest 30% firms are obviously greater than the average weekly returns of the largest 30% firms. Therefore, small firms usually obtain a higher average return, which is consistent with previous studies on size premium [32–35]. Moreover, the standard deviation of the smallest 30% firms' return is always greater than the standard deviation of the largest 30% firms' return. These results imply that the small firm poses higher risk with regards to higher returns. Kurtosis in each portfolio is greater than three, while the skewness in each portfolio is closed to zero. Furthermore, the unit root test is generally employed to examine the stationary of the time-series data. As shown in Table 2, the Augmented Dickey-Fuller (ADF) and Phillips-Perron (PP) tests reject the null hypothesis at 1% level in all industries, which exhibited that the data has no root unit. The results displayed in these returns are stationary.

Table 3 describes the results from the first through fourth order autocorrelations and cross-autocorrelations of the largest 30% firms and the smallest 30% firms in each industry. The first-order autocorrelation coefficient declines as we move from the smallest firms to the largest.

The longer it lags, from two to four weeks, the autocorrelation functions decline faster. Second, for most industries, the correlation coefficient between the returns on the lagged largest 30% firms and the current smallest 30% firms is greater than the correlation coefficient between returns on the lagged smallest 30% firms and the current largest 30% firms. Table 3 also shows that the cross-autocorrelations decay in most industries, as more lags come. Therefore, the cross-autocorrelations show that the big firms' lagged returns provide predictive ability for smaller firms' current returns. Consequently, the lead-lag effect between the big and small firms is evidently displayed within the industry. Furthermore, these asymmetric cross-autocorrelations are consistent with the hypothesis of gradual information diffusion: when new information comes, small firms react more slowly than big firms.

Table 2. Descriptive Statistics for the weekly return of Intra-industry Portfolios.

Industry Portfolio	Mean	Std	Median	Max	Min	Kurtosis	Skewness	ADF Test	PP Test
Auto-big	0.0005	0.048	−0.0005	0.1580	−0.1866	4.2936	−0.0812	−14.969 ***	−25.490 ***
Auto-small	0.00056	0.051	0.0026	0.1481	−0.2524	5.0236	−0.5042	−23.492 ***	−23.614 ***
Cons-big	0.0002	0.047	0.0006	0.1523	−0.2028	4.5305	−0.2174	−15.479 ***	−25.159 ***
Cons-small	0.0009	0.052	0.0048	0.1601	−0.3004	5.5341	−0.5967	−24.146 ***	−24.158 ***
Elec-big	0.0003	0.047	0.0015	0.1822	−0.1893	4.2391	−0.1793	−25.130 ***	−25.129 ***
Elec-small	0.0014	0.051	0.0056	0.1535	−0.2241	4.9526	−0.4652	−24.822 ***	−24.823 ***
Food-big	0.0006	0.046	0.0024	0.1414	−0.2388	4.5246	−0.1952	−24.630 ***	−24.630 ***
Food-small	0.0009	0.049	0.0036	0.1931	0.2543	5.4559	−0.4885	−24.121 ***	−24.172 ***
Engi-big	0.0001	0.049	6.82E-05	0.1608	−0.1982	4.2426	−0.0678	−24.940 ***	−24.947 ***
Engi-small	0.0012	0.051	0.0040	0.1498	−0.2764	5.4045	-0.5923	−24.221 ***	−24.279 ***
Meta-big	−0.0006	0.049	−0.0024	0.1793	−0.1796	4.4632	−0.0823	−15.329 ***	−24.292 ***
Meta-small	0.0010	0.051	0.0034	0.1380	−0.2672	4.8873	−0.4950	−14.906 ***	−23.702 ***
Phar-big	0.0014	0.042	0.0040	0.1656	−0.1710	4.7004	−0.0728	−15.413 ***	−25.626 ***
Phar-small	0.0017	0.049	0.0039	0.1497	−0.2486	5.2476	−0.5787	−15.234 ***	−24.081 ***

Notes: Auto-big and Auto-small refer to the largest 30% size portfolio and the smallest 30% size portfolio in Automobiles parts industry, respectively. Similarly, Cons-big and Cons-small, Elec-big and Elec-small, Food-big and Food-big, Engi-big and Engi-small, Meta-big and Meta-small, and Phar-big and Phar-small refer to the largest 30% size portfolio and the smallest 30% size portfolio in Construction and materials industry, Electronic equipment industry, Food producer industry, Industrial engineering industry, Industrial metals and mining industry, andPharmaceuticals and biotechnology industry, correspondingly. N denotes the average number of firms in each portfolio from 2002 to 2013. Finally, ***, **, and * denote the significance at the 1, 5, and 10 % levels, respectively.

Table 3. Autocorrelation Matrices.

Industry Portfolio	$\rho_0(j,B)$	$\rho_0(j,S)$	$\rho_1(j,B)$	$\rho_1(j,S)$	$\rho_2(j,B)$	$\rho_2(j,S)$	$\rho_3(j,B)$	$\rho_3(j,S)$	$\rho_4(j,B)$	$\rho_4(j,S)$
Auto-big	1	0.814	−0.029	−0.082	0.163	0.053	0.065	−0.049	−0.038	−0.013
Auto-small	0.913	1	0.083	0.034	−0.045	0.074	0.057	0.060	0.017	−0.049
Cons-big	1	0.831	−0.022	−0.062	0.134	0.045	0.071	−0.034	−0.083	0.010
Cons-small	0.974	1	0.086	0.016	−0.044	0.069	0.041	0.054	−0.011	−0.089
Elec-big	1	0.869	−0.023	−0.026	0.113	−0.001	−0.002	−0.032	−0.123	−0.043
Elec-small	0.988	1	0.032	−0.015	−0.002	0.093	0.040	0.034	0.045	−0.051
Food-big	1	0.876	−0.003	−0.037	0.095	0.009	0.061	−0.006	−0.103	0.010
Food-small	0.977	1	0.035	0.022	−0.002	0.075	0.021	0.067	−0.135	−0.096
Engi-big	1	0.854	−0.016	−0.069	0.116	0.034	0.091	−0.004	−0.113	−0.014
Engi-small	0.911	1	0.047	0.003	−0.025	0.090	0.008	0.050	0.023	−0.063
Meta-big	1	0.819	0.020	−0.049	0.122	0.042	0.058	−0.033	−0.091	−0.022
Meta-small	0.863	1	0.064	0.037	−0.014	0.129	0.027	0.055	0.022	−0.084
Phar-big	1	0.753	−0.039	−0.076	0.148	0.035	0.053	−0.003	−0.097	−0.016
Phar-small	0.991	1	0.083	0.018	−0.029	0.116	0.003	0.020	0.005	−0.058

Notes: $\rho_m(j,k)$, m = 0 to 4, j = B or S, and k = B or S, is correlation coefficient. B and S refer to the largest 30% size portfolio and the smallest 30% size portfolio, respectively. $\rho_m(j,k)$ refers to the mth order correlation coefficient between returns on the largest 30% size portfolio and the smallest 30% size portfolio. For example, ρ1(S, B) denotes the correlation between week t return on the smallest 30% size portfolio and week t−1 return on the largest 30% size portfolio. ρ2 (B, S) represents the correlation between week t return on the largest 30% size portfolio and week t−2 return on the smallest 30% size portfolio. On the other hand, $\rho_m(j,k)$ also displays autocorrelation of portfolios' return. For instance, ρ1 (B, B) refers to the first-order autocorrelation of the largest 30% size portfolio. ρ4 (S, S) means the fourth-order autocorrelation of the smallest 30% size portfolio.

3.3. Vector Auto-regression (VAR)

According to the hypothesis of time-varying expected returns, the cross-autocorrelations between the big firms' lagged returns and the small firms' current returns are caused by a combination of small firms' high autocorrelations and a high contemporaneous correlation between the big and small firms [31,36] Moreover, the contemporaneous correlation coefficients between the small and the big firms are always greater than 0.7 in all sample industries. These results imply that high contemporaneous correlation also appear between the small and big firms. Thus, vector-autoregressive regression (VAR) tests are employed to control the autocorrelations of small firms and the contemporaneous correlation between big and small firms. Brennan et al. [8] first employ the VAR model to investigate the process of intra-industry information diffusion. They conclude that, when there is only lagged impact rather than contemporaneous impact among variables, it is suitable to set up the VAR procedure. They further propose that error term actually implies contemporaneous impact. Chordia and Swaminathan [10] state that the VAR model not only prove whether big firms' lagged returns lead small firms' current returns, but more importantly, it could provide a kind of measure about the speed of information diffusion. The corresponding VAR model for each respective industry is described in the following equations:

$$\mathrm{R_{S,t}} = a_0 + \sum_{k=1}^{K} a_k R_{S,t-k} + \sum_{k=1}^{K} b_k R_{B,t-k} + u_t \tag{1}$$

$$\mathrm{R_{B,t}} = c_0 + \sum_{k=1}^{K} c_k R_{S,t-k} + \sum_{k=1}^{K} d_k R_{B,t-k} + v_t \tag{2}$$

Furthermore, by combining all the sample firms, regardless of the industry, a panel VAR model to process the entire investigation of intra-industry is also built:

$$\mathrm{R_{S,i(t)}} = a_{i,0} + \sum_{k=1}^{K} a_k R_{S,i(t-k)} + \sum_{k=1}^{K} b_k R_{B,i(t-k)} + u_{i,t} \tag{3}$$

$$\mathrm{R_{B,i(t)}} = c_{i,0} + \sum_{k=1}^{K} c_k R_{S,i(t-k)} + \sum_{k=1}^{K} d_k R_{B,i(t-k)} + v_{i,t} \tag{4}$$

In Equations (1) and (2), $\mathrm{R_{S,t}}$ and $\mathrm{R_{S,t\text{-}k}}$ are the equal-weighted weekly returns on the smallest 30% portfolio at period t and period t-k, while $\mathrm{R_{B,t}}$ and $\mathrm{R_{B,t\text{-}k}}$ present the equal-weighted weekly return on the largest 30% portfolio at period t and period t-k. (We obtain similar results using value-weighted weekly returns, results are available upon request.) On the other hand, in Equations (3) and (4), $\mathrm{R_{S,i}}$(t) and $\mathrm{R_{S,i}}$(t-k) are the equal-weighted weekly returns on the smallest 30% portfolio at period t and period t-k in industry i, while $\mathrm{R_{B,i}}$(t) and $\mathrm{R_{B,i}}$(t-k) present the equal-weighted weekly return on the largest 30% portfolio at period t and period t-k in industry i. Moreover, in Equations (1) and (3), a_k and b_k are the coefficients of the lagged returns of $\mathrm{R_S}$ and $\mathrm{R_B}$, respectively. In Equations (2) and (4), $\mathrm{c_k}$ and $\mathrm{d_k}$ are the coefficients of lagged returns of $\mathrm{R_S}$ and $\mathrm{R_B}$, respectively. a_0 and c_0 ($a_{i,0}$ and $\mathrm{c}_{i,0}$) are the constant terms, correspondingly. Finally, u_t and v_t ($u_{i,t}$ and $\mathrm{v}_{i,t}$) are the error terms, respectively.

In the above time-series and panel VAR settings, $\sum_{k=1}^{K} a_K$ and $\sum_{k=1}^{K} d_K$ denote the degree of the autocorrelations of small and big firms, respectively. $\sum_{k=1}^{K} b_K$ and $\sum_{k=1}^{K} c_K$ refer to the impact of lagged big firms' returns on current small firms' returns, as well as the impact of lagged small firms' returns on current big firms' returns correspondingly. If there is lead-lag relation between the big and small firms, which is generated by gradual information diffusion, the sum of coefficients $\sum_{k=1}^{K} b_K \geq 0$ is expected. Furthermore, according to Brennan et al. [8], we could employ the cross-equation test for null hypothesis: $\sum_{k=1}^{K} b_K = \sum_{k=1}^{K} c_K$ to check whether one portfolio's lagged return can predict another portfolio's current return. If the lead-lag relation is driven by a gradual diffusion of information from big firms to small firms, we expect $\sum_{k=1}^{K} b_K > \sum_{k=1}^{K} c_K$. (We estimate the VAR for the full sample period and find the impact of lagged big firms' returns on current small firms' returns is significantly greater than the impact of lagged small firms' returns on current big firms' returns. The results suggest the existence of the significantly gradual intra-industry information diffusion in China's stock market, by means of a significant intra-industry lead-lag relationship between big stocks' lagged returns and small stocks' current returns. The empirical results are available upon request.) Additionally, we also exclude the effect of cross-industry information diffusion in this study. The gradual information diffusion between big and small firms only appears within the industry, rather than across the different industries. (We confirm the gradual information diffusion actually is intra-industry information diffusion.)

4. Market Conditions and Intra-Industry Information Diffusion

To explore the impact of market conditions, they are categorized as up or down, depending on whether the previous market return is positive or negative. According to Hameed and Kusnadi [3], the period definition of market conditions might affect the impact of market condition on cross-autocorrelations. There is no theoretical guide on period definitions regarding up and down markets, as it depends on the research objectives and sample markets. Some studies employ longer period definitions of market conditions. For example, both Cooper et al. [33] and Wu [24] employ 36-month market returns as the definition of market conditions in order to examine momentum strategy in the U.S. and China markets. However, some of the studies use shorter period definitions of market conditions. For instance, in examining the lead lag effect in the Warsaw's stock market, Gębka [37] defines market conditions using daily market return. In the U.S. and six Asia markets, McQueen et al. [11] and Chang et al. [12] employ a month's market return as the proxy of up and down markets to examine the cross-autocorrelation of stock returns.

Therefore, we employ four weeks to be the shorter horizon of the market condition. On the other hand, to comprehensively investigate the impact of market conditions on the process of intra-industry information diffusion, longer period definitions of market conditions should also be considered. Meanwhile, due to excessive volatility in China's stock market, periods that are too long have difficulties reflecting the fluctuations in market returns. Therefore, we employ 26 weeks to be the longer horizon of market condition in this study. (Hameed and Kusnadi [3] examine information diffusion and market conditions in the Japan market using both shorter and longer period definitions. They define the previous four or 26 weeks to determine market conditions.) As a result, by employing shorter and longer standards of period definitions, we define the previous four and 26 weeks to respectively establish the market conditions. (We obtain similar results using other period definitions, such as the previous 12 weeks, to determine market conditions; the results are available upon request.)

Consequently, if the previous four-week or 26-week market return is positive, the market condition can be confirmed as the up market state, or otherwise the down market state. Our main objective is to investigate the impact of market conditions on intra-industry information diffusion. To test this objective, two dummy variables, i.e., $\mathrm{D}_{\mathrm{up,t\text{-}k}}$ and $\mathrm{D}_{\mathrm{down,t\text{-}k}}$, are added into the original VAR model. Particularly, the new conditional VAR model is stated in the following equations:

$$\mathrm{R}_{\mathrm{S,t}} = a_0 + \sum_{k=1}^{K} a_{k,up} R_{s,t-k} \cdot D_{up,t-k} + \sum_{k=1}^{K} b_{k,up} R_{B,t-k} \cdot D_{up,t-k} + \sum_{k=1}^{K} a_{k,down} R_{s,t-k} \cdot D_{down,t-k} + \sum_{k=1}^{K} b_{k,down} R_{B,t-k} \cdot D_{down,t-k} + u_t \quad (5)$$

$$\mathrm{R}_{\mathrm{B,t}} = a_0 + \sum_{k=1}^{K} c_{k,up} R_{s,t-k} \cdot D_{up,t-k} + \sum_{k=1}^{K} d_{k,up} R_{B,t-k} \cdot D_{up,t-k} + \sum_{k=1}^{K} c_{k,down} R_{s,t-k} \cdot D_{down,t-k} + \sum_{k=1}^{K} d_{k,down} R_{B,t-k} \cdot D_{down,t-k} + v_t \quad (6)$$

In Equations (5) and (6), $D_{up,t\text{-}k}$ and $D_{down,t\text{-}k}$ are dummy variables, which correspondingly reflect the up and down markets conditions at period t-k. $D_{up,t\text{-}k}$ equals one if the market condition becomes up and zero otherwise. In a similar way, $D_{down,t\text{-}k}$ equals one if the market state is down and zero otherwise. The reason that two dummy variables are set is to achieve the VAR investigations independently of the up and down conditions. For example, we examine whether big firms react faster than smaller firms to acquire common information in the down market state by employing a cross-equation test of null hypothesis: $\sum_{k=1}^{K} b_{K,down} = \sum_{k=1}^{K} c_{K,down}$. On the other hand, in an up market condition, we examine whether big firms react faster than smaller firms to acquire common information by using a cross-equation test of null hypothesis: $\sum_{k=1}^{K} b_{K,up} = \sum_{k=1}^{K} c_{K,up}$.

In Equation (5), $a_{k,\,up}$ and $b_{k,\,up}$ are the coefficients of the lagged returns of R_S and R_B in a up market state, respectively. $a_{k,\,down}$ and $b_{k,\,down}$ are the coefficients of the lagged returns of R_S and R_B in down market state correspondingly. Similarly, in Equation (6), $c_{k,\,up}$ and $d_{k,\,up}$ are, respectively, the coefficients of the lagged returns of R_S and R_B in up market state, while $c_{k,\,down}$ and $d_{k,\,down}$ are the coefficients of the lagged returns of R_S and R_B in a down market state.

With regards to the smaller firms' current returns, $\sum_{k=1}^{K} b_{K,up}$ and $\sum_{k=1}^{K} b_{K,down}$ reflect the impact of the big firms' lagged returns in an up market state and the impact of the big firms' lagged returns in a down market state. Greater coefficients show more striking cross-autocorrelations between the big firms' lagged returns and the smaller firms' current returns, which suggest that the more significant lead-lag relation between big and small firms. As the lead-lag relation reflects slow diffusion of information from big to small firms, the more significant lead-lag effect suggests a slower diffusion of information. (Most studies argue that slow diffusion of common information is a primary cause of the lead-lag effect. Thus, the stronger lead-lag effect suggests slower diffusion of information [1,4,8–10].) Therefore, in order to estimate the speed of intra-industry information diffusion in different market conditions, we compare $\sum_{k=1}^{K} b_{K,down}$ and $\sum_{k=1}^{K} b_{K,up}$. If $\sum_{k=1}^{K} b_{K,down} > \sum_{k=1}^{K} c_{K,up}$, intra-industry information diffusion is slower in a down market state, and vice versa.

4.1. *Shorter Horizon of Market Conditions*

Based on the seven sample industries, we first employ the previous four-week market returns to be the shorter horizon of market conditions. The time-series empirical results of the seven industries are stated in Table 4:

In Panel A of Table 4, in regards to the small firms' current returns, "Big-up" is the sum of coefficients of the lagged big firms' returns in an up market state, reflecting the impact of the big firms' lagged returns in an up market state. On the contrary, "Big-down" denotes the sum of coefficients of lagged big firms' returns in a down market state, revealing the impact of the big firms' lagged returns. It is found that the "Big-down" is greater than the "Big-up" in all industries (except the electronic equipment industry and the industrial engineering industry that are not significant). It shows that the impact of the big firms' lagged returns in a down market state is greater than the impact of the big firms' lagged returns in the up market state. Furthermore, the cross-equation test is more significant in the down market in four of the industries. These results display the more significant lead-lag effect in down market state, which suggest that slower information diffusion appears in the down market state than the up market state. The results also suggest that there are more obstacles in the process of intra-industry information diffusion when market condition becomes a down market state. Furthermore, to process an entire investigation of intra-industry, a conditional panel VAR is employed by including all firms. Panel B of Table 4 displays the conditional panel VAR in a shorter horizon.

Table 4. Conditional Vector Auto-regression (VAR) in Shorter Horizon of Market condition.

Industry		Conditional Vector Auto-Regression				
		Small-up	Big-up	Small-down	Big-down	Cross-Equation Tests
Panel A: The time-series Conditional VAR						
Automobiles parts	R_S	−0.111	0.582 ***	−0.614 ***	0.654 ***	Up:
		(0.315)	(7.218)	(6.164)	(6.273)	0.652
	R_B	−0.410 **	0.735 ***	−0.666 ***	0.629 ***	Down:
		(5.473)	(13.527)	(8.850)	(7.048)	27.446 ***
Construction and materials	R_S	−0.376	0.748 ***	−0.728**	0.750 ***	Up:
		(2.254)	(6.986)	(6.175)	(7.013)	15.393 ***
	R_B	−0.364	0.628 **	−0.693 **	0.68 5**	Down:
		(2.474)	(5.710)	(6.548)	(5.822)	22.096 ***
Electronic equipment	R_S	0.065	0.189	−0.286	0.305	Up:
		(0.059)	(0.386)	(0.651)	(0.682)	1.126
	R_B	−0.134	0.240	−0.120	0.043	Down:
		(0.289)	(0.709)	(0.131)	(0.015)	1.324
Food producers	R_S	−0.413	0.616 **	−0.610 **	0.774 ***	Up:
		(2.455)	(4.233)	(5.165)	(6.821)	11.302 ***
	R_B	−0.391	0.498 *	−0.615 **	0.734 ***	Down:
		(2.570)	(3.226)	(6.144)	(7.168)	21.958 ***
Industrial engineering	R_S	0.052	0.236	−0.264	0.269	Up:
		(0.069)	(1.066)	(0.876)	(1.141)	2.415
	R_B	−0.119	0.379 *	−0.241	0.221	Down:
		(0.397)	(2.983)	(0.792)	(0.690)	3.766 *
Industrial metals and mining	R_S	0.148	0.214 *	−0.257	0.318 *	Up:
		(0.545)	(2.810)	(1.293)	(2.773)	1.668
	R_B	−0.061	0.309 *	−0.196 *	0.189 *	Down:
		(−0.061)	(2.842)	(3.487)	(2.922)	4.374 **
Pharmaceuticals and biotechnology	R_S	0.405 *	0.198 *	−0.404	0.521 *	Up:
		(3.574)	(2.746)	(2.380)	(3.006)	1.661
	R_B	0.147	0.072	−0.499 **	0.500 **	Down:
		(0.661)	(0.102)	(5.108)	(3.886)	11.532 ***
Panel B: The Panel Conditional VAR						
All sample industries	$R_{S,i}$	0.028	0.296 ***	−0.389 ***	0.420 ***	Up:
		(0.12)	(10.03)	(14.61)	(15.35)	23.70 ***
	$R_{B,i}$	−0.159 **	0.397 ***	−0.359 ***	0.328 ***	Down:
		(4.33)	(20.66)	(14.21)	(10.69)	52.74 ***

Notes: R_S is the equal-weighted weekly return on the smallest 30% portfolio, while R_B presents the equal-weighted weekly return on the largest 30% portfolio. $R_{S,i}(t)$ and $R_{B,i}(t)$ are the equal-weighted weekly return on the portfolio of the smallest and the largest 30% firms at period t in industry i, correspondingly. Small-up indicates the sum of coefficients of lagged small firms' returns in up market. Small-down show the sum of coefficients of lagged small firms' returns in down market. Small-up indicates the sum of coefficients of lagged small firms' returns in up market. Small-down show the sum of coefficients of lagged small firms' returns in down market. On the other hand, Big-up indicates the sum of coefficients of lagged big firms' returns in up market, while Big-down denotes the sum of coefficients of lagged big firms' returns in down market. F-statistics are reported in parentheses. Furthermore, in cross-equation tests, Up is the F-statistic for the null hypothesis in up market i.e., $\sum_{k=1}^{4} b_{K,up} = \sum_{k=1}^{4} c_{K,up}$. Down is F-statistic for the null hypothesis in down market i.e., $\sum_{k=1}^{4} b_{K,down} = \sum_{k=1}^{4} c_{K,down}$. Finally, ***, **, and * denote significance at the 1, 5, and 10% levels, respectively. Both AIC and HQIC information criterions support the four-lag to be adaptive order criteria. Thus, four-lag is used in the VAR model. (The result is similar with the view of Hou [4]. He claims that the lag order should be one or four because it is reasonable to assume that small firms will react to information within a month's time.)

Regarding the small firms' current returns, "Big-up" is 0.296 and "Big-down" equals 0.420. Both are significant at the 1% level. It shows that the impact of the big firms' lagged returns in the down market state is greater than the impact of the big firms' lagged returns in the up market state. These results display the more significant lead-lag effect in the down market state, which suggest that slower information diffusion appears in down market state. Therefore, the results of the conditional panel VAR also support that the intra-industry information diffusion from big firms to small firms becomes slower in down market state than the up market state. (The results of value weighted portfolios are consistent. The results are available upon request.)

The results are consistent with Hameed and Kusnadi's study [3], which claims that the speed of information diffusion becomes faster in the up market condition rather than the down market condition. On the other hand, Hong et al. [38], Doukas and McKnight [39], and Yalçın [40] argue that bad news diffuses slower in the market. When the market is turning downward, increasingly bad information is full of the market. However, firms react slower to bad news, especially the smaller ones. Negative information diffuses more slowly from big firms to small firms in a down market. Therefore, the gradual intra-industry information diffusion is more significant when the market goes down. Additionally, from another aspect, as the market continually declines, pessimistic sentiment is full of the market. Thus, investors ultimately lose investment confidence and they take less notice of the stocks. Da et al. [41,42] discuss that less investors' attention generates slower information diffusion. Consequently, slower information diffusion appears more easily in the down market.

4.2. Longer Horizon of Market Conditions

As a robustness check, a longer horizon of market condition (previous 26-week market return) is also employed to explore the impact of market conditions on intra-industry information diffusion. The empirical results of seven industries are shown in Table 5:

Table 5. Conditional VAR in Longer Horizon of Market condition.

Industry		Conditional Vector Auto-Regression				
		Small-up	Big-up	Small-down	Big-down	Cross-Equation Tests
		Panel A: The time-series Conditional VAR				
Automobiles parts	R_S	−0.043 (0.050)	0.386 * (3.400)	−0.637 *** (7.482)	0.815 *** (11.269)	Up: 11.996 ***
	R_B	−0.339 * (3.526)	0.539 *** (7.498)	−0.698 *** (10.152)	0.803 *** (12.342)	Down: 38.835 ***
Construction and materials	R_S	−0.246 (0.943)	0.521 * (3.667)	−0.770 *** (7.426)	0.919 *** (8.935)	Up: 7.906 ***
	R_B	−0.244 (1.080)	0.430 * (2.902)	−0.753 *** (8.281)	0.846 *** (8.826)	Down: 29.572 ***
Electronic equipment	R_S	0.068 (0.067)	0.069 (0.056)	−0.276 (0.577)	0.398 (1.071)	Up: 0.320
	R_B	−0.096 (0.156)	0.109 (0.159)	−0.138 (0.165)	0.140 (0.150)	Down: 1.943
Food producers	R_S	−0.246 (0.943)	0.521 * (3.667)	−0.767 *** (7.426)	0.919 *** (8.935)	Up: 7.907 ***
	R_B	−0.244 (1.079)	0.430 * (2.902)	−0.753 *** (8.281)	0.846 *** (8.826)	Down: 29.901 ***
Industrial engineering	R_S	0.225 (1.368)	0.018 (0.008)	−0.581** (4.203)	0.701** (5.839)	Up: 0.110
	R_B	0.049 (0.069)	0.093 (0.229)	−0.529 * (3.739)	0.613 ** (4.798)	Down: 12.902 ***
Industrial metals and mining	R_S	0.264 (1.643)	0.029 * (3.020)	−0.341 * (2.515)	0.490 ** (4.300)	Up: 0.272
	R_B	−0.078 (0.152)	0.120 (0.360)	−0.299 (2.003)	0.358 * (2.798)	Down: 11.146 ***
Pharmaceuticals and biotechnology	R_S	0.400 * (3.565)	0.217** (4.689)	−0.318 * (1.978)	0.486 ** (4.393)	Up: 1.074
	R_B	0.054 (0.090)	0.136 (0.380)	−0.297 (1.928)	0.362 * (2.868)	Down: 7.246 ***
		Panel B: The Panel Conditional VAR				
All sample industries	$R_{S,i}(t)$	0.143 (0.145)	0.097 (1.20)	−0.493 *** (24.63)	0.626 *** (34.62)	Up: 2.52
	$R_{B,i}(t)$	−0.044 ** (4.33)	0.201 *** (20.66)	−0.465 *** (25.00)	0.528 *** (28.07)	Down: 105.11 ***

Notes: The settings of coefficients are same to Table 4.

Consistent with the analysis of the four-week horizon of market condition, the time-series empirical results show that market conditions affect intra-industry information diffusion under the investigation of a longer horizon of market condition. The results also suggest that the gradual intra-industry information diffusion is more significant in the down market state than the up market state.

As stated in Panel B, in regards to the small firms' current returns, "Big-down" is much bigger and significant than the "Big-up". It shows that the impact of the big firms' lagged returns in a down market state is greater than the impact of the big firms' lagged returns in an up market state. Moreover, we find that the cross-equation test ($F = 105.11$) is significant only in a down market state. These results display the more significant lead-lag effect in down market state as compared to the up market state, which suggest that slower information diffusion appears in down market state. Therefore, the results of the conditional panel VAR also suggest that information diffusion from big firms to small firms becomes slower in the down market condition than the up market condition under the analysis of a longer horizon of market condition.

When compared to Table 4, the results of a longer horizon of market condition are more significant than the results of a shorter horizon of market condition. These results also suggest that when the market turned downwards for a longer period, the speed of intra-industry information diffusion develops more slowly. As the longer bearish market exists, investors become gloomier and their investment sentiment becomes lower. Hence, many investors might lose investment interest on stocks. Consequently, when the market falls off for a longer period, less investors' attention is brought into the market. Thus, when compared to a shorter horizon down market condition, information diffuses more slowly in a longer horizon down market condition.

5. Policy Change and Intra-Industry Information Diffusion

5.1. *Examining the Impact of Policy Changes*

There are two most important policy changes in China: the split-share structure reform in 2005 and lifting the short-sale constraints in 2010. These significant times in policy changes have generated two break points. The full study period is divided into three sub-periods: January 2002–February 2005, March 2005–January 2010, and February 2010–December 2013. The first sub-period mainly shows the situation of China's stock market before the split-share structure reform and the lifting of the short-sale constraints. What happens in China's stock market after the split-share structure reform is displayed in the second sub-period. Meanwhile, the second sub-period also shows the situation of China's stock market with the short-sale constraints. After lifting the short-sale constraints and the split-share structure reform, the situation is presented in the last sub-period.

Therefore, in order to examine the impact of policy changes from 2002 to 2013 on intra-industry information diffusion over time, the VAR procedure is continuously employed to estimate the lead-lag effect between the big and small firms. Three dummy variables, i.e., D_{p1}, D_{p2}, and D_{p3}, are added into the original VAR model. Hence, the new conditional VAR model is stated in the underlying equations:

$$R_{S,t} = a_0 + \sum_{k=1}^{K} a_{k,p1} R_{s,t-k} \cdot D_{p1,t-k} + \sum_{k=1}^{K} b_{k,p1} R_{B,t-k} \cdot D_{p1,t-k} + \sum_{k=1}^{K} a_{k,p2} R_{s,t-k} \cdot D_{p2,t-k} + \sum_{k=1}^{K} b_{k,p2} R_{B,t-k} \cdot D_{p2,t-k} + \sum_{k=1}^{K} a_{k,p3} R_{s,t-k} \cdot D_{p3,t-k} + \sum_{k=1}^{K} b_{k,p3} R_{B,t-k} \cdot D_{p3,t-k} + u_t \quad (7)$$

$$R_{B,t} = a_0 + \sum_{k=1}^{K} c_{k,p1} R_{s,t-k} \cdot D_{p1,t-k} + \sum_{k=1}^{K} d_{k,p1} R_{B,t-k} \cdot D_{p1,t-k} + \sum_{k=1}^{K} c_{k,p2} R_{s,t-k} \cdot D_{p2,t-k} + \sum_{k=1}^{K} d_{k,p2} R_{B,t-k} \cdot D_{p2,t-k} + \sum_{k=1}^{K} c_{k,p3} R_{s,t-k} \cdot D_{p3,t-k} + \sum_{k=1}^{K} d_{k,p3} R_{B,t-k} \cdot D_{p3,t-k} + v_t \quad (8)$$

In Equations (7) and (8), $D_{p1,\, t\text{-}k}$, $D_{p2,\, t\text{-}k}$, and $D_{p3,\, t\text{-}k}$ are dummy variables, which respectively reflect the three sub-periods at period t-k. $D_{p1,\, t\text{-}k}$ equals one if the market is in the first sub-period (January 2002–February 2005) and zero otherwise. In a similar way, $D_{p2,\, t\text{-}k}$ equals one if the market is in the second sub-period (March 2005–January 2010) and is zero otherwise. $D_{p3,\, t\text{-}k}$ equals one if the market is in the third sub-period (February 2010–December 2013) and zero, or else. The purpose for setting the three dummy variables is to identify the VAR analysis separately for the different sub-periods. For example, the study examines whether big firms react faster than the smaller firms to common information in the first sub-period by employing a cross-equation test for null hypothesis: $\sum_{k=1}^{k} b_{K,p1} = \sum_{k=1}^{k} c_{K,p1}$. Similarly, a cross-equation test for the null hypothesis is used in the second (third) sub-period: $\sum_{k=1}^{k} b_{K,p2} = \sum_{k=1}^{k} c_{K,p2}$. ($\sum_{k=1}^{k} b_{K,p3} = \sum_{k=1}^{k} c_{K,p3}$.).

In Equation (7), $a_{k,p1}$ and $b_{k,p1}$ ($a_{k,p2}$ and $b_{k,p2}$; $a_{k,p3}$ and $b_{k,p3}$) are the coefficients of the lagged returns of R_S and R_B, in the first (second; third) sub-period, correspondingly. Similarly, in Equation (8), $c_{k,p1}$ and $d_{k,p1}$ ($c_{k,p2}$ and $d_{k,p2}$; $c_{k,p3}$ and $d_{k,p3}$) are, respectively, the coefficients of the lagged returns of R_S and R_B in the first (second; third) sub-period.

In this conditional VAR setting, significances of coefficients are similar with the original VAR model. With regards to the smaller firms' current returns, $\sum_{k=1}^{K} b_{K,p1}$, $\sum_{k=1}^{K} b_{K,p2}$, and $\sum_{k=1}^{K} b_{K,p3}$ correspondingly reflect the impact of the big firms' lagged returns in the first, second, and third sub-periods. A greater coefficient shows more impact of the big firms' lagged returns on the small firms' current returns, which suggest a more prominent lead-lag relation between the bigger and smaller firms. Thus, a greater coefficient reflects slower diffusion of information from big firms to the smaller ones in this sub-period. By comparing $\sum_{k=1}^{K} b_{K,p1}$, $\sum_{k=1}^{K} b_{K,p2}$, and $\sum_{k=1}^{K} b_{K,p3}$, an estimation of the impact of policy changes on intra-industry information diffusion in different sub-periods is made.

Based on Panel A of Table 6, there is no strong statistical evidence to discover the relatively consistent intra-industry information diffusion in the second and third sub-periods. Most coefficients are insignificant or marginal significant in either one sub-period only (except the automobile parts industry and the construction and materials industry). Additionally, the cross-equation tests are also unable to show consistent results among the industries (except the automobile parts industry and the construction and materials industry). Due to these inconsistent results among the industries, we further employ panel data analysis by including all firms. Panel B of Table 6 displays the results of the panel data.

Based on Panel B, among the three coefficients in the small firms' current returns, "Big-P_3" is the biggest and "Big-P_2" is in the middle, whereas "Big-P_1" is the smallest. These results suggest that the intra-industry lead-lag effect becomes stronger over time. Therefore, intra-industry information diffusion from big firms to smaller firms becomes slower from the first sub-period to the third sub-period. The policy changes impede intra-industry information diffusion. More delay is brought into intra-industry information diffusion along with the policy changes.

Next, as for the robustness test, we separately employ the conditional panel VAR to analyze intra-industry information diffusion in each sub-period. The empirical results are described in Table 7.

With regards to the smaller firms' current returns, the sum of coefficients of big firms' lagged returns is correspondingly 0.069, 0.277, and 0.438 in the three sub-periods, respectively. They increase over time and are only statistically significant in the latter two sub-periods. Therefore, the impact of the big firms' lagged returns on the smaller firms' current returns becomes bigger over time. The results suggest that the lead-lag effect between the big firms and smaller firms becomes stronger over time. Thus, intra-industry information diffusion from big firms to small firms becomes slower over time. As a result, the policy changes influence the intra-industry information diffusion, which suggests that more delay is brought into the process of intra-industry information diffusion over time.

Table 6. Conditional VAR for Policy Changes.

Industry		Three Sub-Pperiods						Cross-Equation Tests		
		Small-P_1	Big-P_1	Small-P_2	Big-P_2	Small-P_3	Big-P_3	Test-P_1	Test-P_2	Test-P_3
Panel A: The time-series Conditional VAR										
Automobiles parts	R_S	−0.468	0.373	−0.241	0.523 **	−0.377	0.636 *			
		(1.664)	(0.767)	(1.598)	(6.565)	(1.345)	(3.582)	1.710	29.071 ***	10.754 ***
	R_B	−0.184	0.250	−0.578 ***	0.755 ***	−0.466	0.519 *			
		(0.293)	(0.390)	(10.473)	(15.450)	(2.344)	(2.712)			
Construction and materials	R_S	−0.693	0.575	−0.345	0.563 **	−0.644 *	0.830 **			
		(1.653)	(0.663)	(1.771)	(4.126)	(2.953)	(5.142)	2.035	12.580 ***	16.689 ***
	R_B	−0.433	0.295	−0.420 *	0.592**	−0.665 *	0.673 **			
		(0.753)	(0.204)	(3.078)	(5.335)	(3.673)	(3.951)			
Electronic equipment	R_S	0.425	0.717	−0.153	0.371	−0.368	0.477			
		(0.817)	(2.190)	(0.344)	(1.723)	(0.373)	(0.544)	4.191 **	4.920 **	0.907
	R_B	0.275	−0.662	−0.256	0.336	−0.139	0.152			
		(0.392)	(2.131)	(1.111)	(1.616)	(0.060)	(0.063)			
Food roducers	R_S	−0.480	0.215	0.030	0.148	−0.004	0.027			
		(0.797)	(0.180)	(0.011)	(0.237)	(0.068)	(0.003)	2.535	0.051	0.007
	R_B	−0.592	0.383	0.079	0.030	0.066	−0.017			
		(1.364)	(0.642)	(0.090)	(0.011)	(0.026)	(0.001)			
Industrial engineering	R_S	−0.489	0.261	0.110	0.062	−0.502	0.690 *			
		(0.820)	(0.187)	(0.355)	(0.108)	(1.594)	(2.897)	2.028	0.193	8.073 *
	R_B	−0.597	0.366	−0.021	0.175	−0.462	0.507			
		(1.334)	(0.403)	(0.014)	(0.927)	(1.467)	(1.699)			
Industrial metals and mining	R_S	−0.397	0.146	0.144	0.082	−0.358	0.580 *			
		(1.682)	(0.203)	(0.541)	(0.159)	(1.171)	(2.880)	2.199	0.066	8.731 ***
	R_B	−0.335	0.161	0.029	0.120	−0.430	0.481			
		(1.258)	(0.258)	(0.023)	(0.354)	(1.172)	(2.077)			
Pharmaceuticals and biotechnology	R_S	−0.500	0.262	−0.023	0.307	0.404	0.406			
		(0.708)	(0.141)	(0.014)	(1.605)	(1.526)	(1.188)	0.911	5.175**	2.577
	R_B	−0.404	0.252	−0.244	0.455 **	0.192	0.245			
		(0.640)	(0.181)	(2.158)	(4.905)	(0.478)	(0.600)			
Panel B: The Panel Conditional VAR										
All sample industries	$R_{S,i}(t)$	−0.353**	0.112	−0.048	0.267 ***	−0.262*	0.421 ***			
		(5.07)	(0.41)	(0.38)	(9.64)	(3.62)	(8.47)	4.84**	30.25 ***	35.05 ***
	$R_{B,i}(t)$	−0.272*	0.077	−0.206 ***	0.352 ***	−0.303**	0.343**			
		(3.43)	(0.23)	(7.72)	(19.12)	(5.52)	(6.45)			

Notes: R_S and R_B are the equal-weighted weekly return on the smallest and the largest 30% firms, correspondingly. $R_{S,i}(t)$ and $R_{B,i}(t)$ are the equal-weighted weekly return on the portfolio of the smallest and the largest 30% firms at period t in industry i, correspondingly. Small-P_1 and Big-P_1 respectively indicate the sum of coefficients of lagged small firms' returns and the sum of coefficients of lagged big firms' returns in the first sub-period. Similarly, Small-P_2 and Big-P_2, respectively, refer to the sum of coefficients of lagged small firms' returns and lagged big firms' returns in the second sub-period. Small-P_3 and Big-P_3 respectively refer to the sum of coefficients of lagged small firms' returns and lagged big firms' returns in the third sub-period. F-statistics are reported in parentheses. Test-P_1 is F-statistics for cross-equation tests for the null hypothesis in the first sub-period i.e., $\sum_{k=1}^{4} bk,_{P1} = \sum_{k=1}^{4} ck,_{P1}$., Test-$P_2$ and Test-P_3 are also corresponding F-statistics in the second sub-period and the third sub-period. Finally, ***, **, and * denote significance at the 1, 5, and 10 % levels, respectively. Both AIC and HQIC information criterions support the four-lag to be adaptive order criteria. Thus, four-lag is used in the VAR model.

Additionally, by observing the "Big-P_1", "Big-P_2", and "Big-P_3" in Table 6 and the sum of coefficients of big firms' lagged returns in Table 7, it is discovered that the sum of coefficients of big firms' lagged return decreasingly increase over time, i.e., the growth rate of the sum of coefficients decreases from sub-period 1 to sub-period 2 and from sub-period 2 to sub-period 3. It is found that the first policy change, i.e., the split-share structure reform, has more impact on intra-industry information diffusion than the lifting of short-sale constraints. The empirical results show that the split-share structure reform actually impedes the process of intra-industry information diffusion. However, most people think that the reforms help to improve market efficiency. Do the reforms improve market efficiency? As the most powerful policy reform of China stock market in recent years, the potential impacts of the split share structure reform have been discussed by a few empirical researches. However, effectiveness of the split share structure reform is still in dispute. For example, Chen et al. [13] argue that the split share structure reform improves the liquidity of the market and increases the market efficiency. Yet, Beltratti et al. [25] discover this reform had no impact on the ownership structure of firms in their research. They argue that only some small stocks and historically neglected stocks are partially beneficial from this reform. Additionally, Carpenter et al. [27] suggest that the split share structure reform has little direct immediate impact on the structure of the China stock market in the short term.

Table 7. Separate Panel VAR in Three Sub-periods.

	Sub-period1: Jan 2002–Feb 2005		
			Cross-equation tests
	$\Sigma_{K=1}^{4} R_{S,i}(t-k)$	$\Sigma_{K=1}^{4} R_{B,i}(t-k)$	$\sum_{k=1}^{4} b_k = \sum_{k=1}^{4} c_k$
$R_{S,i}(t)$	−0.454 *** (16.99)	0.069 (0.33)	11.86 ***
$R_{B,i}(t)$	−0.347 *** (12.46)	0.058 (0.29)	
	Sub-period2: Mar 2005–Jan 2010		
			Cross-equation tests
	$\Sigma_{K=1}^{4} R_{S,i}(t-k)$	$\Sigma_{K=1}^{4} R_{B,i}(t-k)$	$\sum_{k=1}^{4} b_k = \sum_{k=1}^{4} c_k$
$R_{S,i}(t)$	−0.070 (0.47)	0.277 ** (6.27)	20.75 ***
$R_{B,i}(t)$	−0.227 ** (5.71)	0.359 *** (12.16)	
	Sub-period3: Feb 2010–Dec 2013		
			Cross-equation tests
	$\Sigma_{K=1}^{4} R_{S,i}(t-k)$	$\Sigma_{K=1}^{4} R_{B,i}(t-k)$	$\sum_{k=1}^{4} b_k = \sum_{k=1}^{4} c_k$
$R_{S,i}(t)$	−0.282 *** (6.84)	0.438 *** (15.01)	43.02 ***
$R_{B,i}(t)$	−0.304 *** (8.38)	0.340 *** (9.55)	

Notes: $R_{S,i}(t)$ and $R_{B,i}(t)$ are the equal-weighted weekly return on the smallest and the largest 30% firms at period t in industry i, correspondingly. $R_{S,i}(t-k)$ and $R_{B,i}(t-k)$, respectively, are the equal-weighted weekly return on the smallest and the largest 30% firms at period t-k in industry i. Cross-equation test denotes F-statistic for the cross-equation null hypothesis: $\sum_{k=1}^{4} bk = \sum_{k=1}^{4} ck$. Finally, ***, **, and * denote significance at the 1, 5, and 10 % levels, respectively. Both AIC and HQIC information criterions support the four-lag to be adaptive order criteria.

5.2. Additional Tests on the Impact of Policy Changes

5.2.1. The Time-series Change of Lead-lag Effects among Three Sub-periods

In the previous analysis, the impact of policy changes on intra-industry information diffusion is examined by considering the impact of lagged big firms' returns on the current smaller firms' returns and vice versa. Contrary to the previous section and following Mori [17], the effect of small firms leading to big firms is subsequently excluded. Only the lead-lag effect from big firms to small firms is exhibited. The lead-lag effect is estimated in a one-lag panel VAR that is based on the weekly returns of the same equal-weighted size portfolios with a quarterly window. More specifically, the one-lag panel VAR is stated in the following equations:

$$R_{S,i(t)} = a_{i,0} + a_1 R_{S,i(t-1)} + b_1 R_{B,i(t-1)} + u_{i,t} \tag{9}$$

$$R_{B,i(t)} = c_{i,0} + c_1 R_{S,i(t-1)} + d_1 R_{B,i(t-1)} + v_{i,t} \tag{10}$$

In Equations (9) and (10), $R_{S,i}(t)$ and $R_{S,i}(t-1)$ are the weekly returns of the smallest 30% portfolio at period t and period t-1, respectively, in industry i, while $R_{B,i}(t)$ and $R_{B,i}(t-1)$ present the weekly returns of the largest 30% portfolio at period t and period t-1 in industry i.

According to Mori [17], the time-series lead-lag effect could be evaluated by acquiring the difference between b_1 in Equation (9) and c_1 in Equation (10), which examines the size of the lead-lag effect from big firms to smaller firms. Although Mori [17] only investigates the Real Estate Investment Trust market in the U.S., this method is a better reference for our underlying analysis. Furthermore, b_1 actually implies the effect that big firms lead small firms, while c_1 suggests the effect that small firms lead big firms. Therefore, (b_1-c_1) evaluates the lead-lag effect from big firms to small firms, while control for the reverse lead-lag effect from small firms to big firms. If big firms actually could lead small firms, then b_1 should be greater than c_1 and (b_1-c_1) should be greater than zero. It presents a distinct lead-lag effect between big and small firms, which reflects that the delayed degree of information diffusion is stronger from big firms to smaller firms. Additionally, if (b_1-c_1) is less than zero, it implies that, instead of the lead-lag effect from big firms to small firms, the reverse lead-lag effect from small firms to big firms appears.

Table 8 shows the mean and standard deviation of (b_1-c_1) in each three sub-periods. First, the mean becomes bigger over time. It suggests that the lead-lag effects develop stronger from the first sub-period to the last sub-period. Second, the F-statistic for mean difference among three sub-periods is significant at the 1% level. Thus, intra-industry information diffusion is also dissimilar in different sub-periods. Based on the above two viewpoints, the delay of intra-industry information diffusion from big stocks to small stocks becomes greater over time, which imply that policy changes impede intra-industry information diffusion. These results support our results in the previous section.

Table 8. Mean compare and variance compare among Three Sub-periods.

Sub-Period	Mean	Std	Comparison Sub-Period	Mean Difference
Sub-period 1	−0.313	1.669	Sub-period 2	−0.711**
			Sub-period 3	−1.009**
Sub-period 2	0.398	1.562	Sub-period 1	0.711**
			Sub-period 3	−0.298
Sub-period 3	0.696	1.517	Sub-period 1	1.009**
			Sub-period 2	0.298
F-test	12.459 ***	2.658*		

Notes: Mean denotes mean of (b_1-c_1) in the sub-period. Std refers to standard deviation of (b_1-c_1) in the sub-period. F-test refers to F-statistics for mean compare and variance compare among three sub-periods. ***, **, and * denote significance at the 1, 5, and 10% levels, respectively. Mean Difference denotes the difference of mean between sub-periods.

On the other hand, the standard deviations of (b_1-c_1) show a downtrend over time. Moreover, the F-statistic for standard deviation difference among the three sub-periods is significant at the 10% level, which suggests that the difference of standard deviation exists among the three sub-periods. The results show that the volatility of lead-lag effects decrease over time, which suggests that the fluctuation amplitude of information diffusion reduces over time. Consequently, these results support the information volatility of China's stock market declines, along with its policy changes. With the policy changes, the information environment and transparency of market improve over time. Informational efficiency and transparency are brought into the Chinese stock market.

Table 8 also exhibits multiple comparisons of the mean among the three sub-periods. However, the difference of mean between sub-period 1 and sub-period 2, as well as the difference of mean between sub-period 1 and sub-period 3 are significant. The demarcation of the sub-period 1 depends on the first policy change, i.e., the split-share structure reform. Consequently, the impact of the split-share structure reform on the information diffusion has been relatively substantial. On the other hand, the difference of mean between sub-period 3 and sub-period 2 is insignificant. The demarcation of sub-period 3 depends on the second policy change, i.e., lifting of the short-sale constraints. Therefore, lifting short-sale constraints has less impact on information diffusion. As a result, the impact of the split-share structure reform in 2005 is more significant to intra-industry information diffusion in China, which generates more friction of intra-industry information diffusion.

5.2.2. Potential Reasons on the Lead-lag Changes

With the intention of investigating the potential reasons of increasing delay of intra-industry information diffusion over time, further analysis is stated in Table 9:

Table 9. Comparison of Market Situations among Three Sub-periods.

Variables	Mean	Std	Max	Min	F-Test	
Sub-period 1: Jan 2002–Feb 2005					Mean	Variance
Market-return	−0.029	0.106	0.152	−0.218	1.529	12.206 ***
Market-capitalization	41032	4867	50417	31590	41.792 ***	72.619 ***
Market-trading volume	414	179	682	137	31.087 ***	34.727 ***
Proportion-institutional	0.0056	8.64E-05	0.0057	0.0055	48.305 ***	62.510 ***
Proportion-individual	0.9943	8.64E-05	0.9945	0.9943	48.305 ***	62.510 ***
Sub-period 2: Mar 2005–Jan 2010						
Market-return	0.056	0.221	0.425	-0.416		
Market-capitalization	151824	87563	327140	32430		
Market-trading volume	2552	1334	4454	506		
Proportion-institutional	0.0052	0.0059	0.0059	0.0046		
Proportion-individual	0.9947	0.00042	0.9954	0.9941		
Sub-period 3: Feb 2010–Dec 2013						
Market-return	−0.026	0.101	0.101	−0.260		
Market-capitalization	233433	22013	277662	195138		
Market- trading volume	3226	956	5015	1961		
Proportion- institutional	0.0046	4.58E-05	0.0047	0.0045		
Proportion-individual	0.9953	4.58E-05	0.9954	0.9953		

Notes: Degree-lead lag is (b_1–c_1). F-test refers to F-statistics for mean compare and variance compare among three sub-periods. Finally, ***, **, and * refer to significance at the 1, 5, and 10% levels, respectively.

Table 9 describes the comparison of the different market situations among three sub-periods in China's stock market. As shown, market capitalization and market trading volume grow over time, which suggest the booming development of China's stock market. However, as opposed to the general uptrend of the proportions of individual investors, the proportion of institutional investors remarkably declines, especially after the split-share structure reform in 2005. This result is not consistent with many developed markets. An advanced market eventually needs more institutional investors. However, with the expansion of China's stock market, the proportion of institutional investors is not rising, while the proportion of individual investors is on the rise.

Due to the lack of information processing capacity and channel, most Chinese individual investors tend to follow institutional investors who possess superiority in information acquisition [43,44]. Hence, information generally diffuses from institutional investors to individual investors in China's stock market [45,46]. Reduced institutional investors might make the information diffusion more gradual between institutional investors and individual investors. As a result, the increasing proportion of individual investors and the decreasing proportion of institutional investors could potentially cause the delay of intra-industry information diffusion over time in China.

6. Conclusions

This paper investigates the impact of market conditions and policy changes on intra-industry information diffusion in China. Different with previous studies [4–6,18], the study focuses on intra-industry to investigate the process of information diffusion with view of both market conditions and policy changes. Moreover, according to specific conditions in China, different from previous studies [7,21], as far as we know, this paper is the first paper studying the impact of market conditions and policy changes on intra-industry information diffusion in China.

The main findings are: first, the market conditions significantly affect the process of intra-industry information diffusion. The speed of intra-industry information diffusion in the down market condition is slower than in the up market condition. Conversely, when the market is turning upward, the speed of intra-industry information diffusion develops faster. Second, the impact of a longer horizon of market condition is more significant than the shorter horizon. In other words, when the market turns downward for a longer period, the speed of intra-industry information diffusion develops more slowly. These findings are consistent with the gradual-information diffusion theory of Hong et al. [38]. They suggest that, when the market falls off, the market is full of negative information and negative information diffuses more slowly across the market. Market frictions are responsible for the gradual diffusion of information. Moreover, the impact of market frictions is usually more prominent when bad news arrives (for example, the short sale constraint will delay the incorporation of negative information into stock prices [28]).

This finding provides some trading strategies for investors. When good common information comes to some big firms, based on the principle of gradual information diffusion, investors usually choose small firms from the whole market. However, it is suggested that investors should choose high quality small firms from the same industry, rather than the whole market. Investors should take long positions in these stocks as early as possible and then wait for potential abnormal profit. When the market falls off, investors should slow these investments. Alternatively, investors might accelerate investment behaviors as the market turns upward.

Third, the policy change also has an effect on intra-industry information diffusion. Especially, we find that the split-share structure reform actually impedes the process of intra-industry information diffusion. These findings are consistent with previous theories, such as Merton [14], Lin and Swanson [15], and Mori [17], which mean some external institutional restrictions, such as policy changes, could significantly affect the process of information intra-industry information diffusion. The intra-industry information diffusion from big firms to small firms becomes slower along with policy changes. These results show that due to the policy changes in China, more delay is brought into the process of intra-industry information diffusion over time. Therefore, policy changes impede intra-industry information diffusion.

Fourth, there is a continuously decreasing information volatility of intra-industry information diffusion in China's stock market. Along with the policy changes in China's stock market, the information environment and transparency of market are improved over time. Fifth, the impact of the split-share structure reform in 2005 is more significant to the intra-industry information diffusion of China's stock market, which generates more friction regarding intra-industry information diffusion.

Finally, this paper provides policy implications to policy considerations and market mechanisms. The impact of policy changes on information diffusion is one of the impacts of policy changes on financial market. Based on the split share structure reform and lifting short sale constraints, this paper suggests that these policy changes in China stock market impede the process of intra-industry information diffusion and they seem ineffective in some degree. Institutional frictions are accountable for producing the delay in the process of information diffusion. Thus, comprehending the process of information diffusion is very significant for policy considerations. Institutional reforms in China's stock market have been implemented for many years since the establishment of the market. However, the effectiveness of the policy changes is still in dispute. Policy considerations and market mechanisms in China should keep pace with the times, which could, in turn, facilitate that stock prices to develop more effectively and informatively. Nevertheless, policy considerations, especially in China, seldom consider the effectiveness and informativeness of stock prices, as well as the principle of gradual information diffusion when policies are formulated. Therefore, smoothing the process of intra-industry information diffusion and augmenting the market efficiency should be included into policy-making in the future.

Author Contributions: C.D., H.H.L. and Z.A. conceived and designed the experiments; C.D. and H.H.L. analyzed the data; W.-K.W. contributed materials/analysis tools; all authors wrote the paper.

Acknowledgments: The authors are grateful to the Editor and anonymous referees for constructive comments and suggestions that led to a significant improvement of an early manuscript. This research has been supported by Hebei University, Universiti Sains Malaysia, Asia University, China Medical University Hospital, The Hang Seng University of Hong Kong, Research Grants Council (RGC) of Hong Kong (project number 12500915 and UGC/IDS14/15), and Ministry of Science and Technology (MOST, Project Numbers 106-2410-H-468-002 and 107-2410-H-468-002-MY3), Taiwan. The fourth author would like to thank Robert B. Miller and Howard E. Thompson for their continuous guidance and encouragement.

References

1. Lo, A.W.; MacKinlay, A.C. When are contrarian profits due to stock market overreaction? *Rev. Financ. Stud.* **1990**, *3*, 175–205. [CrossRef]
2. Chen, N.F.; Kan, R.; Miller, M.H. Are the Discounts on Closed-End Funds a Sentiment Index? *J. Financ.* **1993**, *48*, 795–800. [CrossRef]
3. Hameed, A.; Kusnadi, Y. Stock Return Cross-Autocorrelations and Market Conditions in Japan. *J. Bus.* **2006**, *79*, 3029–3056. [CrossRef]
4. Hou, K. Industry information diffusion and the lead-lag effect in stock returns. *Rev. Financ. Stud.* **2007**, *20*, 1113–1138. [CrossRef]
5. Cohen, L.; Frazzini, A. Economic links and predictable returns. *J. Financ.* **2008**, *63*, 1977–2011. [CrossRef]
6. Menzly, L.; Ozbas, O. Market Segmentation and Cross-predictability of Returns. *J. Financ.* **2010**, *65*, 1555–1580. [CrossRef]
7. Zhang, Y.; Song, W.; Shen, D.; Zhang, W. Market reaction to internet news: Information diffusion and price pressure. *Econ. Model.* **2016**, *56*, 43–49. [CrossRef]
8. Brennan, M.J.; Jegadeesh, N.; Swaminathan, B. Investment analysis and the adjustment of stock prices to common information. *Rev. Financ. Stud.* **1993**, *6*, 799–824. [CrossRef]
9. Badrinath, S.G.; Kale, J.R.; Noe, T.H. Of shepherds, sheep, and the cross-autocorrelations in equity returns. *Rev. Financ. Stud.* **1995**, *8*, 401–430. [CrossRef]
10. Chordia, T.; Swaminathan, B. Trading volume and cross-autocorrelations in stock returns. *J. Financ.* **2000**, *55*, 913–935. [CrossRef]
11. McQueen, G.; Pinegar, M.; Thorley, S. Delayed reaction to good news and the cross-autocorrelation of portfolio returns. *J. Financ.* **1996**, *51*, 889–919. [CrossRef]
12. Chang, E.C.; McQueen, G.R.; Pinegar, J.M. Cross-autocorrelation in Asian stock markets. *Pac. Basin Financ. J.* **1999**, *7*, 471–493. [CrossRef]
13. Chen, C.X.; Rhee, S.G. Short sales and speed of price adjustment: Evidence from the Hong Kong stock market. *J. Bank. Financ.* **2010**, *34*, 471–483. [CrossRef]
14. Merton, R.C. A simple model of capital market equilibrium with incomplete information. *J. Financ.* **1987**, *42*, 483–510. [CrossRef]
15. Lin, A.Y.; Swanson, P.E. The effect of China's reform policies on stock market information transmission. *Q. J. Financ. Account.* **2008**, *47*, 49–76.
16. Bae, K.-H.; Ozoguz, A.; Tan, H.; Wirjanto, T.S.D. foreigners facilitate information transmission in emerging markets? *J. Financ. Econ.* **2012**, *105*, 209–227. [CrossRef]
17. Mori, M. Information Diffusion in the US Real Estate Investment Trust Market. *J. Real Estate Financ. Econ.* **2015**, *51*, 190–214. [CrossRef]
18. Hong, H.; Torous, W.; Valkanov, R.D. Do industries lead stock markets? *J. Financ. Econ.* **2007**, *83*, 367–396. [CrossRef]
19. Cen, L.; Chan, K.; Dasgupta, S.; Gao, N. When the Tail Wags the Dog: Industry Leaders, Limited Attention, and Spurious Cross-Industry Information Diffusion. *Manag. Sci.* **2013**, *59*, 2566–2585. [CrossRef]
20. Haque, T. Lead–Lag Effects in Australian Industry Portfolios. *Asia-Pac. Financ. Mark.* **2011**, *18*, 267–290. [CrossRef]
21. Wang, C.; Xie, L. Information diffusion and overreaction: Evidence from the Chinese stock market. *Emerg. Mark. Financ. Trade* **2010**, *46*, 80–100. [CrossRef]
22. Sjöö, B.; Zhang, J. Market segmentation and information diffusion in China's stock markets. *J. Multinatl. Financ. Manag.* **2000**, *10*, 421–438. [CrossRef]

23. China Statistics Press. *Chinese Securities Registration and Settlement Statistical Yearbook*; China Statistics Press: Beijing, China, 2015.
24. Wu, Y. The Momentum Premium under the Influence of Information Uncertainty—Evidence from the Chinese Stock Market. Ph.D. Thesis, University of Southampton, Southampton, UK, 2012.
25. Beltratti, A.; Bortolotti, B.; Caccavaio, M. The stock market reaction to the 2005 split share structure reform in China. *Pac. Basin Financ. J.* **2012**, *20*, 543–560. [CrossRef]
26. Li, K.; Wang, T.; Cheung, Y.-L.; Jiang, P. Privatization and risk sharing: Evidence from the split share structure reform in China. *Rev. Financ. Stud.* **2011**, *24*, 2499–2525. [CrossRef]
27. Carpenter, J.N.; Lu, F.; Whitelaw, R.F. *The Real Value of China's Stock Market*; NBER Working Paper No. 20957; NBER: Cambridge, MA, USA, 2015.
28. Diamond, D.W.; Verrecchia, R.E. Constraints on short-selling and asset price adjustment to private information. *J. Financ. Econ.* **1987**, *18*, 277–311. [CrossRef]
29. Chang, E.C.; Luo, Y.; Ren, J. Short-selling, margin-trading, and price efficiency: Evidence from the Chinese market. *J. Bank. Financ.* **2014**, *48*, 411–424. [CrossRef]
30. Zhao, Z.; Li, S.; Xiong, H. Short sale constraints, disperse pessimistic beliefs and market efficiency—Evidence from the Chinese stock market. *Econ. Model.* **2014**, *42*, 333–342. [CrossRef]
31. Boudoukh, J.; Richardson, M.P.; Whitelaw, R.F. A tale of three schools: Insights on autocorrelations of short-horizon stock returns. *Rev. Financ. Stud.* **1994**, *7*, 539–573. [CrossRef]
32. Banz, R.W. The relationship between return and market value of common stocks. *J. Financ. Econ.* **1981**, *9*, 3–18. [CrossRef]
33. Cooper, M.J.; Gutierrez, R.C.; Hameed, A. Market states and momentum. *J. Financ.* **2004**, *59*, 1345–1365. [CrossRef]
34. Fama, E.F.; French, K.R. Size, value, and momentum in international stock returns. *J. Financ. Econ.* **2012**, *105*, 457–472. [CrossRef]
35. Fama, E.F.; French, K.R. A five-factor asset pricing model. *J. Financ. Econ.* **2015**, *116*, 1–22. [CrossRef]
36. Conrad, J.; Kaul, G. Time-variation in expected returns. *J. Bus.* **1988**, *61*, 409–425. [CrossRef]
37. Gębka, B. Volume-and size-related lead–lag effects in stock returns and volatility: An empirical investigation of the Warsaw Stock Exchange. *Int. Rev. Financ. Anal.* **2008**, *17*, 134–155. [CrossRef]
38. Hong, H.; Lim, T.; Stein, J.C. Bad news travels slowly: Size, analyst coverage, and the profitability of momentum strategies. *J. Financ.* **2000**, *55*, 265–295. [CrossRef]
39. Doukas, J.A.; McKnight, P.J. European momentum strategies, information diffusion, and investor conservatism. *Eur. Financ. Manag.* **2005**, *11*, 313–338. [CrossRef]
40. Yalçın, A. Gradual information diffusion and contrarian strategies. *Q. Rev. Econ. Financ.* **2008**, *48*, 579–604. [CrossRef]
41. Da, Z.; Engelberg, J.; Gao, P. In search of attention. *J. Financ.* **2011**, *66*, 1461–1499. [CrossRef]
42. Da, Z.; Engelberg, J.; Gao, P. The sum of all fears investor sentiment and asset prices. *Rev. Financ. Stud.* **2015**, *28*, 1–32. [CrossRef]
43. Kang, J.; Liu, M.-H.; Ni, S.X. Contrarian and momentum strategies in the China stock market: 1993–2000. *Pac. Basin Financ. J.* **2002**, *10*, 243–265. [CrossRef]
44. Kim, K.A.; Nofsinger, J.R. Behavioral finance in Asia. *Pac. Basin Financ. J.* **2008**, *16*, 1–7. [CrossRef]
45. Tan, L.; Chiang, T.C.; Mason, J.R.; Nelling, E. Herding behavior in Chinese stock markets: An examination of A and B shares. *Pac. Basin Financ. J.* **2008**, *16*, 61–77. [CrossRef]
46. Piotroski, J.D.; Wong, T. Institutions and information environment of Chinese listed firms. In *Capitalizing China*; Fan, J.F., Morck, R., Eds.; University of Chicago Press: Chicago, IL, USA, 2012.

6

Organizational Climate and Work Style: The Missing Links for Sustainability of Leadership and Satisfied Employees

Massoud Moslehpour [1,2], Purevdulam Altantsetseg [3], Weiming Mou [4] and Wing-Keung Wong [5,6,7,*]

1 Department of Business Administration, Asia University, Taichung 41354, Taiwan; writetodrm@gmail.com
2 Department of Business Administration, Saigon Institute of Technology, District 12, HCMC 70000, Vietnam
3 Law School, Mongolian National University, Ulaanbaatar 16060-0012, Mongolia; pvrevdulam@gmail.com
4 College of Economics and Management, Changzhou Institute of Technology, Changzhou 213022, China; muwm@czu.cn
5 Department of Finance, Fintech Center, and Big Data Research Center, Asia University, Taichung 41354, Taiwan
6 Department of Medical Research, China Medical University Hospital, Taichung 40402, Taiwan
7 Department of Economics and Finance, Hang Seng University of Hong Kong, Shatin, Hong Kong 999077, China
* Correspondence: wong@asia.edu.tw

Abstract: People try to find the role of government in today's modern society. Citizens of any country look forward to benefit from government services. Although the government implements laws and policies in all areas of society, people only know about it through government's services. We describe a good government's service of organization, department, unit, and division that has an appropriate human strategy. **Purpose:** Purpose of this study is to investigate which factors have been missing that connects and maintains the sustainability between the leadership style and employees' satisfaction in the government sector of Mongolia. More specifically, the purpose of the study is to investigate the missing link between leadership style and job satisfaction among Mongolian public sector employees. This study reiterates the mediating role of organizational climate (OC) and work style (WS) in a new proposed model. **Methodology:** The questionnaire is designed by a synthesis of existing constructs in current relevant literature. The research sample consisted of 143 officers who work in the primary and middle units of the territory and administration of Mongolia. Factor analysis, a reliability test, a collinearity test, and correlation analyses confirm the validity and reliability of the model. Multiple regression analysis, using Structural Equation Modeling (SEM), tests the hypotheses of the study. The sample of this study is chosen from the public organization. Mongolia is a developing country. This country needs good public leaders who can serve citizens. This study will be extended further. In addition, Mongolia really needs sufficient studies. **Practical implications:** This study has several important implications for studies related to organizational behavior and job satisfaction. Furthermore, the implications of these findings are beneficial to organizations aimed at improving policies and practices related to organizational behavior and human resource management. Regulators and supervisors of private or public organizations aiming to increase the level of their employees' job satisfaction will also benefit from the findings. Therefore, this study's new proposed model can be the basis of fundamental research to build a better human resource policy. Although the leadership style is an influential factor for job satisfaction, this study identifies the mediating missing links between the leadership style and employees' job satisfaction. **Findings:** The findings of this research indicate that the organizational climate and work style complement and fully mediate the relationship between leadership style and job satisfaction. An appropriate leadership style is most effective when it matches the organizational climate as well as employees' work style. Furthermore, a suitable organizational climate will increase the level of job satisfaction.

If the work style of employees is respected and taken into consideration, the leadership style can find its way into job satisfaction. **Originality/value:** This study is the first to understand the motivators of job satisfaction in the government sector of Mongolia. This study suggests valuable findings for executive officers who are junior and primary unit's officers of the register sector of government in Mongolia. The findings of this study help managers and executives in their effort develop and implement successful human resource strategies.

Keywords: job satisfaction (JS); work style (WS); leadership style (LS); organizational climate (OC); register office; Mongolia

JEL Classification: D23; J01; J24; J28; J45; J53; J81; M12

---

1. Introduction

In Mongolia, it is more likely for the job seekers to pursue employment in government sectors such as a register office than in private companies. Young graduates encouraged by their parents are urged to become a civil servant and to seek a position in the government. Although satisfaction with the organizations is one of the most crucial factors in the sustainability of private companies [1], it does not seem to be the same situation in public sector organizations. Often, a low level of job satisfaction is observed in public sector organizations. Buchanan [2] and Lachman [3] concluded that employees in the public sector are less satisfied with their work than private companies' employees do. Employees who work in primary units of government or in provinces are less satisfied with their leader/supervisors. Efficient leadership and management style can help increase employee satisfaction [4].

While the public sector organization has been receiving increasing attention in the last two decades, little research focuses specifically on the job satisfaction of the registration organization [5]. In this sector, there is still a lack of performance appraisal, employee job satisfaction, workload balance, and a healthy subordinate-supervisory relationship. The registration organization in Mongolia, especially the primary administrative units and provinces, is less technologically resourced largely due to a vertical organizational structure and underpaid employees. The organizational climate seems to depend also on the particular characteristics of the work environment [4,6–8]. Employees should realize the positive organizational importance and they should create it for success.

Job satisfaction literature has been studied in private sector organizations. Recent empirical studies have looked at service industries and service firms [9]. To our knowledge, there are almost no empirical studies exploring the employees' job satisfaction in the Mongolian public organization in the government register sector. Our study includes registrars, inspector, and administrative staff of the Mongolian register organization. In this sector, there are no contemporary studies of registrars' job satisfaction. None of the previous studies looked at the influence leadership style on job satisfaction through the organizational climate and work style. The current study is an attempt to address this gap in the literature. We hypothesized that the leadership style with the presence of the organizational climate and work style has no direct effect on job satisfaction. However, the leadership style through the organizational climate and work style will have an indirect effect on employees' job satisfaction. In this study, we aim to investigate how the leadership style through meditating factors, synchronously and asynchronously, influence job satisfaction of registration organization employees. The organizational climate and work style are synchronous mediators since they work in parallel to influence the relationship between leadership style and job satisfaction. The organizational climate and work style also mediate the relationship between leadership style and job satisfaction synchronously as they work in series. Figure 1 depicts visually the synchronous and asynchronous influences of the mediators.

2. Literature Review and Hypotheses Development

This section reviews motivator factors used in this paper including work style, leadership style, and organizational climate studies relevant to job satisfaction. In addition, the relationship among the variables leading to the development of the hypotheses is discussed.

2.1. Leadership Style (LS)

Leadership is one of the main factors for success [10] in any kind of group activities. The leadership style inspires people with a specific vision to work, helps clarify some concrete goals, and motivates and helps employees communicate well within their team. Wilkinson and Wagner [11] show that the leaders' significant support influences employees' attitude. According to Drucker [12], the style of leadership is an engine of effective organization and it is based on the interaction between leader and employees in the workplace. Furthermore, Edgar and Geare [13] argue that the workers-leader relationship is a key factor that influences workers' satisfaction in their workplace. In this regard, the leader represents his/her employees and lets employees assess their leader.

Alola, Avci, and Ozturen [14] study the effect of leadership style on job satisfaction in the Nigerian tourist industry. The results show that the leadership style affects hotel employees' job satisfaction. Transformational Leadership emphasizes an increasing work commitment, job satisfaction, and well-being of the employees [15,16]. Authentic Leadership depends on the organizational context and an individual's positive psychological attitude. This type of leadership determines self-awareness and self-regulated positive behaviors of both leaders and employees. Entrepreneurial leadership converges and directs the group members' performances toward the attainment of organizational objectives that involves identifying and implementing entrepreneurial opportunities [17]. The following sections discuss and define the variables of this study.

2.2. Organizational Climate (OC)

According to McGregor [18], the organizational climate is defined as how employees perceive organizations' internal functions like decision-making and rule-setting in the workplace. It can also be defined as a set of behaviors that describe an organization [19]. An organizational climate can be specific for each organization. It may make an organization different from other organizations and influence employees' work behavior in the organization. The organizational climate can also leave a perception in the employees' mind towards the management of their working unit [20]. It is related to employees' perceptions on their own and other colleagues' effectiveness in job and task implementation. In organizations that are public or private where employees' perception of their organizational climate is more egoistic and less ethical, employees are more prone to corruption [21].

Griffin [22] suggests that the climate generally refers to direct perceptions of the work environment. Organizations need a positive climate in their workplace to boost employee motivation and raise the opportunity that employees will implement adequate efforts doing their tasks. Therefore, a positive climate encourages employees' productivity and decreases turnover. Thus, it is vital for business success. Chang, Wu, and Liu [23] collected data from 34 human resources managers and 354 employees working in the Chinese manufacturing and service industries. Their results demonstrate that work style and workplace events influence employees' job satisfaction. A three-year study (2007, 2009, 2010) of 5656, 6274, and 5841 public employees facilitated by the Ministry of Labor and Social Security of Spain indicates that the organizational climate is among the top five influential factors of job satisfaction among the employees [24].

According to Jung, Chow, and Wu [25] and Jung and Ali [26], the organizational climate is one of the most important characteristics of a great and comfortable workplace. Therefore, if a leader can create a great workplace, it will increase employees' productivity. Several studies [27–29] point out the positive impact of leadership style on the organizational climate. There is, however, a lack of research with the Mongolian population and specifically Mongolian government employees. Therefore, in this paper, we follow the previous study's suggestions to make the following hypothesis for LS and OC for Mongolian register office employees.

H1. *LS has a positive association with OC.*

2.3. Work Style (WS)

There are several definitions of work styles proposed by researchers. Mihut [30] suggests that the work style is the combination of professional, organizational, political, and moral qualities expressed in daily professional activities of individuals. Dawis and Lofquist [31] define work styles as an employee's originally conceived working attributes. These traits are generally established in childhood through experimentation, which crystallized in adulthood and declined due to the aging process. Subsequently, an individual might possess the appropriate skills and abilities to meet the demands of the job. However, if the work style is ineffectively communicated or perceived, the job environment satisfies neither the employer nor the employee. Work styles, thus, have an impact for job satisfaction [31,32]

Niculiţă [33] has observed the relationship between work style and organizational climate in the scope of Romanian employees. He found that there are several factors in an organizational climate that can influence some specific work style factors such as a positive interpersonal relationship, a positive motivation, an effective and efficient management in an organization, and organizational support. Therefore, the organization climate has a significant impact on work style. In this paper, we follow his suggestion to make the following hypothesis for OC and WS for Mongolian register office employees.

H2. *OC has a positive association with WS.*

2.4. Job Satisfaction (JS)

In organizational behavior studies, there are numerous definitions of job satisfaction. Locke [34] defines employee's satisfaction to be the positive emotional state stemming from the evaluation of a person's experience associated with the job. According to Spector [35], job satisfaction is the degree to which one likes his or her job. However, Brief's [36] job satisfaction represents an attitude towards the job. Mathieu and Zajac [37] and Hirschfeld, Field, and Bedeian [38] define the term to be the result of some factors that affect the quality of individuals' working life. On the other hand, Altuntas and Baykal [39] state that job satisfaction is of interest to employers. Job satisfaction continues to be studied since it is considered to be a desirable outcome of employment [39]. This study is based on previous findings and the notion introduced by Durst and DeSantis [40] that employee's satisfaction is important in public sector employees who are often perceived as unhappy workers. Their low morale may be associated with low productivity.

Job satisfaction is an important factor in an organization that the absence of it can lead to team's lethargy and a lack of enthusiasm so that it may reduce organizational commitment. If there is a lack in job satisfaction, it may cause some good employees to quit their jobs [41].

Many studies have observed the positive relationship between work style and job satisfaction. For example, Dawis and Lofquist [31] shows that work style positively influences job satisfaction. They found that, even though employees have the appropriate skills and abilities to meet the demands of their jobs and their work style is ineffectively expressed, their manager would not be fully satisfied with their performance. Thereby, it is necessary for employees to have a decent work style in order to make their manager/leader satisfied with their performance. Empirical studies by Arbuckle et al. [42], Chang et al. [43], Chuang et al. [44], Harley et al. [45], Harmon et al. [46], and Young et al. [47] show that a high-performance work system has been connected with higher employee satisfaction. Fan et al. [48] indicated that the high level of adoption would increase job satisfaction. Based on the information above, in this paper, we follow previous studies' suggestions to make the following hypothesis for OC and WS for the Mongolian register office employees.

H3. *WS has a positive association with JS.*

2.5. Mediators between Leadership Style and Job Satisfaction

The relationship between leadership style and job satisfaction is one of the most critical factors for success in an organization [49,50]. Several studies have looked at this relationship and established the significant influence of leadership style on job satisfaction [49,51–53]. Some studies went beyond and looked at the intermediary influence of the organizational climate [54]. Jung and Ali [26] look at the influence of organizational climate as the moderator between corporate social responsibility and job satisfaction.

Leadership style and the organizational climate have been reported to positively and significantly influence employee satisfaction [55]. Priyankara et al. [56] reported on employees of textile and apparel manufacturing factories in Sri Lanka. Their findings indicate that the organizational climate is the partial mediator between leader's support and employee behavior. Experimental evidence from the Alola, Avci, and Ozturen [14] study in Nigeria shows that work style mediates the relationship between leadership style and job satisfaction. In this paper, based on the previous findings, we made the following hypothesis for LS and JS with OC and WS as mediators for Mongolian register office employees.

H4. *OC mediates the relationship between LS and JS.*

H5. *WS mediates the relationship between LS and JS.*

H6. *OC and WS are serial multiple mediators between LS and JS.*

2.6. Mediator between Leadership Style and Work Style

Leaders have their own leadership style towards their employees while each employee also has their individual work style [33]. Work style is the accumulation of personalized work-related experiences. Different definitions of work style result in typologies with different theoretical or applied values. For example, Scherpereel and Bowers [57] have designed several workshops that aim to help create work teams based on heterogeneity and complementarity. In their approach, work style during teamwork consists of four different classifications: doers, expressive, amiable, and analytics works. These work styles together have strong correlation with leadership style. Work style in the organization depends on leadership style [33]. Leaders have their own leadership style to lead their employees. In addition, the style of work offered in different organizations may not be the same [58–60]. Sarros et al. [61] examined the relationship between leader's behavior (transactional and transformational styles) and aspects of an organization's structure (i.e., centralization, formalization dimensions). In this paper, we hypothesize that organizational culture is the mediator that has not been studied previously. The following hypothesis for LS and WS with OC as the mediator for Mongolian register employees.

H7. *OC mediates the relationship between LS and WS.*

2.7. Mediator between Organizational Climate and Job Satisfaction

Many studies have observed a positive relationship between the organizational climate and job satisfaction. For example, Chen and Spector [62], Brockner [63], and De Cremer [64] have shown that negative leader-employee interactions have a negative influence on the employees' satisfaction, which results in signs of stress and unwillingness to go to work. Tsai [65], Hashemi and Sadeqi [41], Ángel Calderón Molina et al. [66], and Ahmad et al. [67] predict that the organizational climate has a significant effect on job satisfaction. In this paper, we introduce work style as a

mediator. The organizational climate is also related to employee corruption [21]. We mentioned that organizational climate influences work style. We also established that work style has a positive association with job satisfaction. Based on previous research findings, we make the following hypothesis for OC and JS with WS as the mediator for Mongolian register employees.
H8. *WS mediates the relationship between OC and JS.*

3. Research Methodology

3.1. Sample Selection and Instrumentation

This paper uses a convenient sampling technique in which we select the registration sector of Mongolian government units accessible via postal mail or email. Data is gathered from 143 employees who are working in primary and middle units of administration in the Mongolian registration offices. The survey questionnaires of this paper are fundamentally built by the features that are chosen based on the considerations of the research framework, definitions of the variables, and literature reviews. Most of the items of the instrument are based on questions used in previous research. Some questions are used in their original form while others are slightly modified to address the specific nature of this study. In the design of a questionnaire for our survey, a complex construct is used in order to enrich both the meaning and multi-dimensionality.

3.2. Data Analysis Procedure

Structured and unstructured observations are used in this study. After collecting some information relevant to the Mongolian government's structure and administration, sample data is collected from the registration organization's primary and middle units of the Mongolian government. Second, the interview method is used in this study before the sample is collected. The data is collected from leaders/supervisor of government employees of the register office of Mongolia. Questions are based on theoretical and previous empirical studies and the result of the observation and interviews. Method of analysis of the sample is a quantitative method. Based on the proposed research model, the quantitative model is the best suitable method to draw conclusions utilizing techniques that emphasize the validity and the reliability.

3.3. Theoretical Framework and Hypotheses

The framework below shows the study hypotheses, which examines the interrelationships between examination variables. The framework hypothesizes that leadership style (LS), the organizational climate (OC), and work style (WS) influences job satisfaction (JS). The model depicted in Figure 1 suggests that job satisfaction (JS) is the endogenous variable, which is influenced by leadership style (LS) as an exogenous variable. Moreover, the effect of LS on JS is mediated by the organizational climate (OC) and work style (WS) or $\eta = f(\xi 1, \xi 2, \xi 3)$. Where η is job satisfaction (JS), $\xi 1$ will be leadership style (LS), $\xi 2$ will be the organizational climate (OC), and $\xi 3$ will be the work style (WS). OC and WS are not only the endogenous variables but also the mediators for η. Therefore, job satisfaction is a dependent variable (DV) that is influenced by the independent variables' leadership style (LS) and the mediating variables' organizational climate (OC) and work style (WS). The equation is visualized in Figure 1.

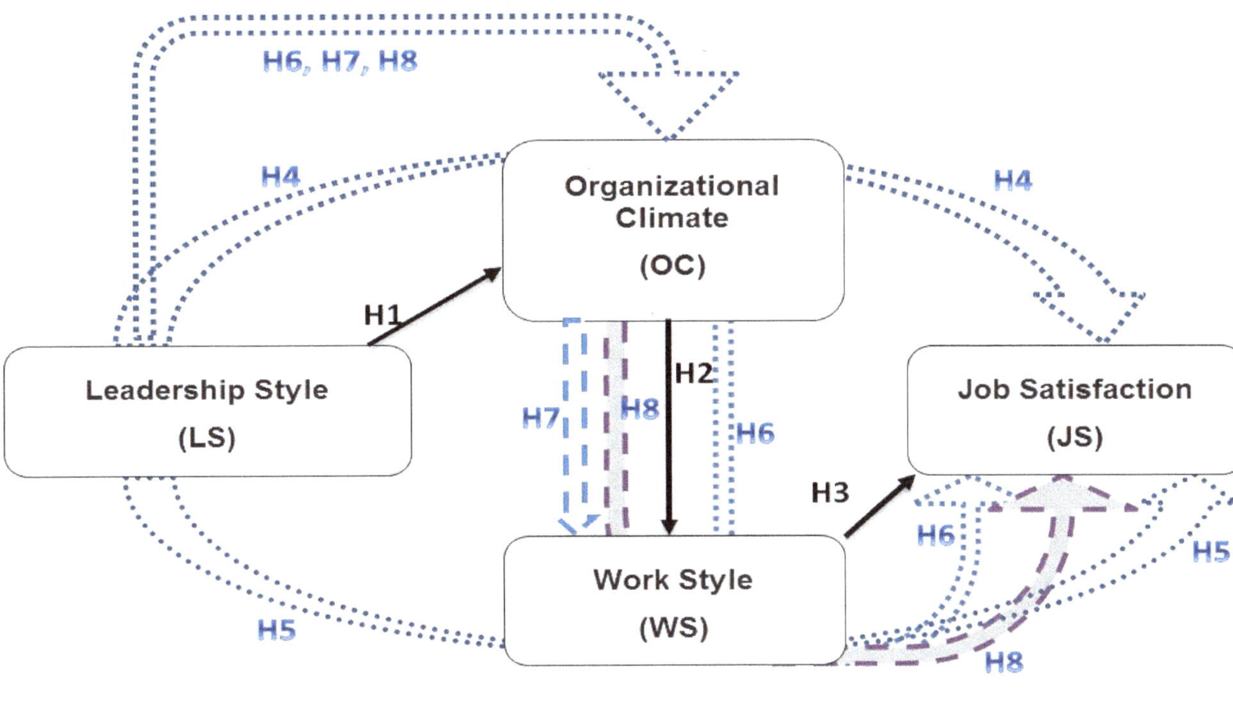

Figure 1. Research framework.

4. Results and Findings

A total of 200 questionnaires were distributed to employees of the register organization and 143 questionnaires were collected for this study. This paper studied a case and illustrated the demographics of respondents.

4.1. Demographic Characteristics

Eight major categories are computed to identify all the characteristics of the participants of this study. Demographics have shown that 23.1% of the respondents are male and 76.9% of the respondents are female. The profile of respondents exhibited the frequency and percentage of age dispersion, which was divided into five categories. The majority of the respondents are aged between 25–34 years old (44.8%), which is followed by respondents aged 35–44 years old (37.1%), 45-to-55 years olds (15.4%), and employees aged under 24 are 4 (2.8%). In terms of the occupation, most of the respondents are lawyers (58 = 40.6%). There are also other occupation types (47 = 32.9%) and economists (26 = 18.2%). These are related to the gender category. The highest percentage of respondents have a Bachelor's degree (74.8%), which is followed by a Master's degree (24.5%), and a Ph.D. and up is composed of only 0.7%. Work duration in the register office is grouped into four categories. Most of the respondents have 0–5 years of experience (61 = 42.7%), which is followed by 6–10 years (55 = 38.5%), 11–15 years (21 = 14.7%) and then 16 years and more (6 = 4.2%). The salary is divided into four categories: 46.9% of respondents have a salary with less than $300 USD per month, which is followed by $301–500 USD (39.9%), $501–500 USD (12.6%), and respondents with a salary range of more than $701 USD (0.7%). From other descriptive statistics, most of the respondents are living in an apartment (68 = 47.6%), which is followed by a private house (33 = 23.1%), a rental (30 = 21%), and respondents who live in a Mongolian traditional house (12 = 8.4%). Final demographic information is working hours per day, which is partitioned into three measurements: 84 (58.7%) of respondents work 9–12 h, which is followed by 53 (37.1%) respondents who work 8 h in a day, and then 6 people responded that they work 13 h and up. This occupied only 4.2% of all respondents for this research.

4.2. Test of Reliability and Validity

Exploratory factor analysis (EFA) is an important tool for organizational researchers. It can be useful for refining measures, evaluating construct validity, and testing hypotheses. The general suggestion that, in order to get a good model, factorability of the Kaiser-Meyer-Olkin Measure of sampling adequacy (KMO) must be greater than 0.6, communality values must be greater than 0.5, eigenvalues must be greater than 1, and factor loadings should be at least 0.5 or higher [68].

From Table 1, all factor loadings are found to be higher than 0.5. KMO is 0.915, which is higher than 0.6. Thus, the validity of the instrument for this study passed the Bartlett's Test of Sphericity. All factors have an Eigenvalue of 1 or greater. As shown in Table 1, reliability coefficient of each factor as well as the whole instrument is higher than the acceptable level of ($\alpha \geq 0.7$). All factor loadings are above 0.7. In short, the results shown in Table 1 indicate that all factors are valid and reliable. Thus, we can further conduct additional statistical analysis, which is discussed in the next subsections.

Table 1. Factor Analysis, Instrument Validity, and Reliability.

Variables	Items	M	SD	% of Variance	Loadings		Cronbach's Alpha
					EFA	CFA	
Leadership Style (LS)	LS1	2.97	0.996	23.536	0.842	0.848	0.847
	LS2	3.07	1.066		0.869	0.923	
	LS3	3.16	1.018		0.855	0.913	
	LS4	2.83	0.957		0.527	0.550	
Organizational Climate (OC)	OC1	3.38	0.925	18.365	0.830	0.808	0.839
	OC2	3.10	0.894		0.768	0.792	
	OC3	3.39	0.839		0.755	0.799	
	OC4	3.24	0.864		0.79	0.847	
Work style (WS)	WS1	2.95	0.891	16.334	0.662	0.837	0.899
	WS2	2.94	0.882		0.673	0.836	
	WS3	3.06	0.753		0.679	0.872	
	WS4	2.89	1.101		0.759	0.744	
	WS5	2.94	0.925		0.641	0.769	
Job satisfaction (JS)	JS3	3.55	1.787	7.252	0.631	0.663	0.718
	JS4	3.35	0.944		0.894	0.882	
Instrument Total	KMO			0.915			0.921
	p-value			0.000			

Note: Item details are as follows: LS1: Stability and sustainability of my current job. LS2: The supervisor-subordinate relationship in registration (civil) office. LS3: The professional ability of my supervisor in registration (civil) office. LS4: My current working condition in the registration (civil) office. OC1: The relationship between co-workers in my organization (registration office). OC2: Having a professional status if I continue working in this organization. OC3: My success and outcome is from my current work. OC4: The way my co-workers get along with each other. WS1: The freedom to use my own judgment. WS2: A chance to do something for my coworkers. WS3: A chance to do different things from time to time. WS4: The chances for advancement at my current job. WS5: Encouragement and praise from my supervisor for my good job performance. JS3: I'm satisfied with the contents of my job in general. JS4: I'm satisfied about the workload in general.

4.3. Confirmatory Factor Analysis (CFA)

After conducting EFA, researchers use CFA. According to the CFA, variables WS2, WS5, and LS4 are removed to get a better fit for the model. Consequently, goodness of fit of each model is evaluated and compared with the suggested criteria by the ratio of chi-square to degrees of freedom (χ^2/df), goodness-of-fit index (GFI), the adjusted goodness-of-fit index (AGFI), the root mean square error of approximation (RMSEA), and the comparative fit index (CFI). The measurement model of CFA in this model shows the fit index for the structural model, which indicated a good fit ($\chi^2/\text{df} = 1.342$), RMSEA = 0.049, NFI = 0.895, CFI = 0.970, GFI = 0.903). Based on these statistics, the CFA model is accepted and the model is fit.

4.4. Composite Reliability, Convergent, and Discriminant Validity

Composite Reliability (CR), Convergent Validity, and Discriminant Validity are the extent to which indicators of a specific variable 'converge' or share a high proportion of variance in common. Convergent Validity includes two items: Composite Reliability (CR) and Average Variance Extracted (AVE). CR is a measure of reliability and internal consistency based on the square of the total of factor loadings for a construct [69]. AVE is a summary measure of convergence among a set of items representing a variable [70]. It is the average percent of variation explained among the items [69]. Anderson and Gerbing [69] suggest that the CR should be greater than 0.7 and Fornell and Larcker [70] suggest AVE to be at least 0.5. Table 2 summarizes the results of validity and reliability. The results provide the evidence supporting the reliability and validity of the indicators of the research model [71].

Table 2. Test of composite reliability, convergent validity, and discriminant validity.

	CR	AVE	MSV	Max r	JS	WS	LS	OC
JS	0.753	0.609	0.417	0.646	**0.780**			
WS	0.907	0.661	0.648	0.805	0.646	**0.813**		
LS	0.890	0.677	0.437	0.661	0.372	0.612	**0.823**	
OC	0.885	0.659	0.648	0.805	0.576	0.805	0.661	**0.812**

Note: CR > 0.7, AVE > 0.5, MSV < AVE, $\sqrt{AVE}$ > Max r, $\sqrt{AVE}$ is bold face diagonal.

4.5. Test of Hypotheses and Mediations

This study employs Structural Equation Modeling in order to test our proposed model and all the formulated hypotheses, which was discussed in Section 3. The results of the model fit for the structural model include the following values: $\chi^2/df = 1.113$ ($p > 0.05$), RMSEA = 0.028, NFI = 0.919, TLI = 0.989, CFI = 0.991, and GFI = 0.923. Table 3 recapitulates the results of hypotheses testing. Based on the results, three hypotheses are accepted (H1, H2, H3).

Table 3. Results of the hypotheses (standardized regression weights).

Hypothesis	Paths	Estimate	Statement of Hypothesis	Results
H1	LS → OC	0.622 ***	LS has a positive association with OC	Supported
H2	OC → WS	0. 812 ***	OC has a positive association with WS	Supported
H3	WS → JS	0.665 *	WS has a positive association with JS	Supported

* $p < 0.05$, *** $p < 0.001$.

Table 4 exhibits the result of the mediation hypotheses for the research model of this study. The results of mediation analysis, using 5000 resampling bootstrapping, support all mediation hypotheses (H4~H8) [72,73]. The following sections present meticulous discussion of the results shown in Tables 3 and 4.

Table 4. Results of the mediation hypotheses (standardized regression weights).

	Path	Indirect (ab)	Direct (c′)	Total (c)	Mediation
H4	LS → OC → JS	0.363 ***	0.016 (NS)	0.379 **	Supported
H5	LS → WS → JS	0.414 ***	0.035 (NS)	0.449 **	Supported
H6	LS → (OC & WS) → JS (Double Mediation)	0.378 ***	0.012 (NS)	0.390 *	Supported
H7	LS → OC → WS	0.475 ***	0.130 (NS)	0.605 **	Supported
H8	OC → WS → JS	0.441 *	0.128 (NS)	0.569 **	Supported

* $p < 0.05$, ** $p < 0.01$, *** $p < 0.001$.

5. Discussion and Managerial Implications

5.1. The Influence of Leadership Style (LS) on the Organizational Climate (OC)

Our findings exhibited in Table 3 accept H1 and conclude that LS has a positive association with OC. This important finding exhibits the positive and strong influence of LS on OC for register office employees in Mongolia. According to Jung et al. [25], a good organizational climate means a comfortable workplace. The leaders and managers of the organization create a content office. Consequently, the positive relationship between OC and LS is of utmost importance. Therefore, an effective leadership style can improve the organizational climate and, therefore, develop the organization's morale and upturn employee effectiveness.

This finding is also consistent with prior scholars' findings [27] emphasizing more support for the model with the Mongolian public register sector. The result shows strong ($\beta = 0.622$) and significant ($p < 0.001$) influence of leadership style on the organizational climate of the register sector. Therefore, H1 is accepted.

5.2. The Influence of Leadership Style (LS) on Job Satisfaction (JS) (Single Mediation of Organizational Climate and Mediation of Work Style)

H2 states that LS influences JS and hypothesizes that LS has a positive association with JS. The results of SEM analyses, however, indicate that, for the given model, the leadership style does not influence job satisfaction directly. H2 is, therefore, rejected. This result may not be consistent with some of the previous findings [49,52,53]. However, the previous studies did not take into consideration the mediation influences of the organizational climate (OC) and work style (WS). The proposed model of this study leads to a new discovery regarding the mediation of OC and WS (Table 4) as single separate mediators. Therefore, H4 and H5 are supported.

5.3. The Influence of the Leadership Style on Job Satisfaction (Serial Mediations of Organizational Climate and Work Style)

Hayes [74] illustrates serial multiple mediations with data from research conducted by Tal-Or et al. [75]. We showed that OC and WS as separate single mediators fully mediate the relationship between LS and JS. Furthermore, based on Hayes [74], we tested the serial multiple mediations of OC and WS. The result indicated full double mediation of OC and WS for the relationship between LS and JS (Table 4). Therefore, H6 is supported. This finding underscores the importance of OC and WS as the mediator between LS and JS.

5.4. The Influence of Leadership Style on Work Style and the Mediation of the Organizational Climate

H3 proposes that LS has a significant influence on OC. The structural model of this study rejects this hypothesis. Therefore, H3 is rejected. Furthermore, H10 states that OC is the mediator between LS and WS. The result of SEM analyses using the bootstrapping technique indicates that, for the given model, even though LS does not have a direct influence on WS, OC fully mediates the relationship between LS and WS. Therefore, H7 accepted.

5.5. The Influence of Organizational Climate (OC) on Work Style (WS)

H4 hypothesizes that OC has a positive association with WS. Niculiţă [33] indicates that "organizational climate factors such as positive motivation, positive interpersonal relationships, efficient management, and organizational support have proven to deliver positive influence on specific work style factors" (p. 1042). The results of current path analyses, which are shown in Table 3, indicate that OC significantly and positively influence WS ($\beta = 0.812$ and $p < 0.001$). H2 is, therefore, supported.

5.6. The influence of Organizational Climate (OC) on Job Satisfaction (JS) and the Mediation of Work Style (WS)

H5 hypothesizes that OC has a positive association with JS. Several previous studies [41,65,66] have obtained the positive and significant relationship between the organizational climate and job satisfaction. However, the results of the path analyses indicate (Table 3) that, with the presence of work style, there is no significant influence of OC on JS. H5 is, therefore, rejected.

The finding, however, leads to another more important discovery regarding the mediation effect of work style, which was proposed by the new model (Table 4). WS fully mediates the influence of OC on JS. Thus, H11 is accepted. A good organizational climate requires a fair and clear policy, clear information, and an effective leader. Although the finding is not consistent with previous studies regarding the direct effect of OC on JS, this study introduces the significant mediating role of WS.

5.7. The Influence of Work Style (WS) on Job Satisfaction (JS)

H6 states that WS has a positive association with JS. Many studies [31,43–48,76] have acquired the positive and significant relationship between work style and job satisfaction. The result of this study ($\beta = 0.665$, $p < 0.001$) is consistent with a previous study and, consequently, H3 is accepted.

5.8. Discussion

In recent years, numerous scholars have been studying the relationship between employees' job satisfaction (JS) and respective factors such as leadership style (LS), organizational climate (OC), and work style (WS). However, very few papers have considered the above issue in the public sector. In addition, previous studies only found a direct and positive effect on employees' job satisfaction (JS) but ignored the mediating effects. This is one of the most important issues for human resource management because this could help improve employees' job satisfaction if we know its relationship with LS, OC, and WS. Our goal is to identify the factors influencing employees' job satisfaction. Furthermore, this study proposes a new model not only to test the direct effects but also the mediating effects on employees' job satisfaction. Thus, this paper bridges the gap of the literature to study the issue using Mongolian register office employees.

Previous studies have shown the importance of LS on JS and employee turnover. The proposed model of this study illustrates the importance of OC and WS in the relationship between the LS and JS. Leadership is one of the main factors for success in any kind of group activities. The workers-leader relationship is a key factor that influences workers' satisfaction in the workplace. However, what about employees' perceptions about organizational features like decision-making and rule setting in the workplace? The organizational climate is specific for each group and one leadership style will not fit all climates. Leaders need to rely on a positive climate in their workplace to enhance employee motivation and satisfaction. The proposed model of this study gives strong evidence for the important role of the organizational climate in order to increase job satisfaction.

Likewise, the harmony and accord of individual's professional activities and moral qualities are essential to one's satisfaction in life and work. Working style is stable and trait-like attributes of an employee. An individual's work style is developed in childhood through experimentation and reinforcement and then crystallized in adulthood. Leaders should pay attention to an individual's work style to develop sustainable and higher job satisfaction. The direct effect of LS on JS was studied. However, the results of this study introduce the intermediary role of WS on JS. Thus, when LS is combined with OC, WS will result in sustainable and higher JS.

Providing the right leadership is the key element in employee job satisfaction. However, the leaders should also take into consideration the organizational climate as well as employees' work style. In organizations with skillful employees and a good leadership style, a proper organizational climate and consideration for employees' work style would further influence job satisfaction and can improve employee retention.

Findings of this study contribute to research on job satisfaction by delineating several combinations of antecedents that influence employees' job satisfaction in order to register the organization of Mongolia. For employees, working in public sector organizations may require effort to improve his/her moral and attention for the advancement of high productivity. Nevertheless, working in a positive organizational climate and identifying with a suitable leadership style can improve job satisfaction in register offices. Thus, when officers of the register office create a positive organizational climate through positive interaction as well as an appropriate leadership style to match employees' work style, employees' job satisfaction will be high. Leadership style will help job satisfaction, but sustainability of job satisfaction relies on the organizational climate and the work style of employees. When leaders of an organization implement employee's work style into their leadership style, job satisfaction increases. The suitable organizational climate will also influence employees' work style. The combination of the organizational climate and work style implemented properly into the leadership style would improve the sustainability of the job satisfaction level.

5.9. *Managerial Implications*

The results of current research show that respective factors are important to study employees' job satisfaction. Managers can use the results to improve planning of the human resource strategy and implement their leadership style more effectively. The results also suggested that not only effective leadership style is required in this sector. The mediating role of the organizational climate and work style should not be ignored. Furthermore, by using the proposed research model, this research can be expanded to other public sector organizations employees' job satisfaction.

A good understanding of the mediating role of work style and organizational climate would improve the influence of leadership style on job satisfaction. Our research provides guidance for Mongolian public office managers who wonder what they should do to improve job satisfaction. The findings of this study will be utilized for the managerial practice and improvement of human resource policy.

6. Conclusions

This study bases itself on the traditional variables relating to job satisfaction with the new model to suggest mediating variables that can help sustain employees' satisfaction. Furthermore, Mongolia as one of the emerging economies seldom has been the topic of various studies. Findings of this study paves the road to research on job satisfaction by outlining traditional antecedents that influence employees' job satisfaction and integrating them into a new model. This is the first study to investigate the relationship between leadership style and job satisfaction with Mongolian public sector employees. The main emphasis of this paper is to show the importance of the mediators. The findings of this study reconfirm the previous studies' outcomes that are associated with the positive influence of leadership style on the organizational climate. Likewise, the positive and significant influence of organizational climate on work style is tested and confirmed. Furthermore, we established and reconfirmed the positive significant influence of work style on job satisfaction.

The first three hypotheses were to show and reconfirm the external validity of the study. The next five hypotheses introduced in this model bring new discoveries and reiterate the importance of work style and organizational climate as the mediating variables. The role of the mediating variables is to improve sustainability of the relationship between leadership style and job satisfaction. The organizational climate is a significant mediator that fully binds and helps sustain the relationship between leadership style and job satisfaction. The same is true for work style. The organizational climate and work style combination, as the mediators helping the sustainability of the relationship between leadership style and job satisfaction, is also tested and the results show strong significant full mediation. The organizational climate fully mediates the relationship between leadership style and work style. Therefore, leaders can create a more sustainable work style by improving the organization's climate. This study signposts the importance of work style in sustaining the relationship between the organizational climate and job satisfaction. The organizational climate can sustainably influence employees' job satisfaction if the work style of each individual employee is respected and taken into account.

This paper studies sustainability of leadership and satisfied employees for the organizational climate and work style. An extension of our paper could study sustainability of leadership and satisfied employees for other variables. Further research could also study sustainability for other issues. For example, extending Mou et al. [77] and others to study the sustainability for enterprise supply chains, extend Li et al. [78] and others to study the sustainability of portfolio selection, extend Tsendsuren et al. [79] and others to study the sustainability of life insurance, extend Wong, et al. [80] to study the sustainability of warrant markets, extend Liao and Wong [81], Liao et al. [82], Purevdulam et al. [83], Moslehpour et al. [71] to study the sustainability of e-shopping, extend Pham et al. [84] to study the sustainability of outsourcing business, and extend Moslehpour et al. [85,86] to study the sustainability of marketing. This study is limited to public employees of the Mongolian public sector in Ulaanbaatar. However, the capital of Ulaanbaatar has 9 districts and 152 primary units of registration office. Future studies need to study the private sector employees in Mongolia and look at the differences if there are any.

The Government of Mongolia, as one of the emerging economies of the world, strives to implement appropriate human resource strategy to satisfy and retain government employees. There is an inevitable need for the sustainability of leadership and satisfied employees. Mongolian government organizations can benefit from empirical studies to implement a good human resource strategy. This study provides an opportunity to establish the fundamental basis by providing the grounds for future studies in this area. In practice, leaders and supervisors should pay attention to which factors are the most important and influential in the current transitional situation of Mongolia. Especially, as discussed in this study, factors such as organizational climate and work style are essential for the sustainability of the path between leadership style and employee satisfaction. Therefore, they must focus on human research management in theory and practice.

Author Contributions: In this paper, M.M. initiated the ideas and formulated the problems. P.A. performed the experiments, conducted the analysis, and wrote the first draft. W.M. contributed some useful materials to our paper. W.-K.W. assisted M.M. and P.A. in the detailed planning, conceiving and designing the experiments, and writing the entire paper.

References

1. Uslu, T. Innovation culture and strategic human resource management in public and private sector within the framework of employee ownership. *Procedia-Soc. Behav. Sci.* **2015**, *195*, 1463–1470. [CrossRef]
2. Buchanan, B. Government managers, business executives, and organizational commitment. *Public Adm. Rev.* **1974**, 339–347. [CrossRef]
3. Lachman, R. Public and private sector differences: CEOs' perceptions of their role environments. *Acad. Manag. J.* **1985**, *28*, 671–680.
4. Marques, I.; Willis, S.C.; Schafheutle, E.I.; Hassell, K. Development of an instrument to measure organisational culture in community pharmacies in Great Britain. *J. Health Organ. Manag.* **2018**, *32*, 176–189. [CrossRef] [PubMed]
5. Chang, S.; Jia, L.; Takeuchi, R.; Cai, Y. Do high-commitment work systems affect creativity? A multilevel combinational approach to employee creativity. *J. Appl. Psychol.* **2014**, *99*, 665. [CrossRef]
6. Cumbey, D.A.; Alexander, J.W. The relationship of job satisfaction with organizational variables in public health nursing. *J. Nurs. Adm.* **1998**, *28*, 39–46. [CrossRef]
7. Gumusluoglu, L.; Ilsev, A. Transformational leadership, creativity, and organizational innovation. *J. Bus. Res.* **2009**, *62*, 461–473. [CrossRef]

8. Tovey, E.J.; Adams, A.E. The changing nature of nurses' job satisfaction: An exploration of sources of satisfaction in the 1990s. *J. Adv. Nurs.* **1999**, *30*, 150–158. [CrossRef]
9. Singh, H.; Saufi, R.A.; Tasnim, R.; Hussin, M. The relationship between employee job satisfaction, perceived customer satisfaction, service quality, and profitability in luxury hotels in Kuala Lumpur. *Prabandhan Indian J. Manag.* **2017**, *10*, 26–39. [CrossRef]
10. Dansereau, F., Jr.; Graen, G.; Haga, W.J. A vertical dyad linkage approach to leadership within formal organizations: A longitudinal investigation of the role making process. *Organ. Behav. Hum. Perform.* **1975**, *13*, 46–78. [CrossRef]
11. Wilkinson, A.D.; Wagner, R.M. Supervisory Leadership Styles and State Vocational Rehabilitation Counselor Job Satisfaction and Productivity. *Rehabil. Couns. Bull.* **1993**, *37*, 15–24.
12. Drucker, P. *Geleceğin Toplumunda Yönetim, (Çev. Zaman, M.)*; Hayat Yayıncılık: Stanbul, Turkey, 2003.
13. Edgar, F.; Geare, A. HRM practice and employee attitudes: Different measures–different results. *Pers. Rev.* **2005**, *34*, 534–549. [CrossRef]
14. Alola, U.; Avci, T.; Ozturen, A. Organization Sustainability through Human Resource Capital: The Impacts of Supervisor Incivility and Self-Efficacy. *Sustainability* **2018**, *10*, 2610. [CrossRef]
15. Sofarelli, D.; Brown, D. The need for nursing leadership in uncertain times. *J. Nurs. Manag.* **1998**, *6*, 201–207. [CrossRef] [PubMed]
16. Thyer, G.L. Dare to be different: Transformational leadership may hold the key to reducing the nursing shortage. *J. Nurs. Manag.* **2003**, *11*, 73–79. [CrossRef]
17. Renko, M.; El Tarabishy, A.; Carsrud, A.L.; Brännback, M. Understanding and measuring entrepreneurial leadership style. *J. Small Bus. Manag.* **2015**, *53*, 54–74. [CrossRef]
18. McGregor, D. *The Human Side of Enterprise*; McGraw-Hill Book Company: New York, NY, USA, 1960.
19. Forehand, G.A.; Von Haller, G. Environmental variation in studies of organizational behavior. *Psychol. Bull.* **1964**, *62*, 361. [CrossRef]
20. Burke, W.W.; Litwin, G.H. A causal model of organizational performance and change. *J. Manag.* **1992**, *18*, 523–545. [CrossRef]
21. Gorsira, M.; Steg, L.; Denkers, A.; Huisman, W. Corruption in organizations: Ethical climate and individual motives. *Adm. Sci.* **2018**, *8*, 4. [CrossRef]
22. Griffin, M.L. Job satisfaction among detention officers: Assessing the relative contribution of organizational climate variables. *J. Crim. Justice* **2001**, *29*, 219–232. [CrossRef]
23. Chang, P.-C.; Wu, T.; Liu, C.-L. Do High-Performance Work Systems Really Satisfy Employees? Evidence from China. *Sustainability* **2018**, *10*, 3360. [CrossRef]
24. Sánchez Sellero, M.C.; Sánchez Sellero, P. Factores Determinantes de la Satisfacción Laboral en España antes y Durante la Crisis de 2008. *OmniaScience* **2016**, *12*, 1192–1220.
25. Jung, D.I.; Chow, C.; Wu, A. The role of transformational leadership in enhancing organizational innovation: Hypotheses and some preliminary findings. *Leadersh. Q.* **2003**, *14*, 525–544. [CrossRef]
26. Jung, H.-J.; Ali, M. Corporate Social Responsibility, Organizational Justice and Positive Employee Attitudes: In the Context of Korean Employment Relations. *Sustainability* **2017**, *9*, 1992. [CrossRef]
27. Ekvall, G.; Ryhammar, L. Leadership style, social climate and organizational outcomes: A study of a Swedish University College. *Creat. Innov. Manag.* **1998**, *7*, 126–130. [CrossRef]
28. Kao, R.-H. The relationship between work characteristics and change-oriented organizational citizenship behavior: A multi-level study on transformational leadership and organizational climate in immigration workers. *Pers. Rev.* **2017**, *46*, 1890–1914. [CrossRef]
29. Maamari, B.E.; Majdalani, J.F. Emotional intelligence, leadership style and organizational climate. *Int. J. Organ. Anal.* **2017**, *25*, 327–345. [CrossRef]
30. Mihuț, I. *Self-Management and Creativity*; Dacia: Cluj-Napoca, Romania, 1989.
31. Dawis, R.V.; Lofquist, L.H. *A Psychological Theory of Work Adjustment: An Individual Differences Model and Its Application*; University of Minnesota: Minneapolis, MN, USA, 1984.
32. Dawis, R.V. The Minnesota Theory of Work Adjustment. In *Career Development and Counseling: Putting Theory and Research to Work*; Brown, S.D., Lent, R.W., Eds.; John Wiley & Sons Inc.: Hoboken, NJ, USA, 2005.
33. Niculiţă, Z. The relationship between work style and organizational climate for Romanian employees. *Procedia Econ. Financ.* **2015**, *32*, 1042–1049. [CrossRef]

34. Locke, E.A.; Dunnette, M.D. Handbook of industrial and organizational psychology. *Nat. Causes Job Satisf.* **1976**, 1297–1349.
35. Spector, P.E. Measurement of human service staff satisfaction: Development of the Job Satisfaction Survey. *Am. J. Community Psychol.* **1985**, *13*, 693–713. [CrossRef]
36. Brief, A.P. *Attitudes in and around Organizations*; Sage: Newcastle upon Tyne, UK, 1998; Volume 9.
37. Mathieu, J.E.; Zajac, D.M. A review and meta-analysis of the antecedents, correlates, and consequences of organizational commitment. *Psychol. Bull.* **1990**, *108*, 171. [CrossRef]
38. Hirschfeld, R.R.; Feild, H.S.; Bedeian, A.G. Work Alienation as an Individual-Difference Construct for Predicting Workplace Adjustment: A Test in Two Samples 1. *J. Appl. Soc. Psychol.* **2000**, *30*, 1880–1902. [CrossRef]
39. Altuntas, S.; Baykal, U. Relationship between nurses' organizational trust levels and their organizational citizenship behaviors. *J. Nurs. Sch.* **2010**, *42*, 186–194. [CrossRef] [PubMed]
40. Durst, S.L.; DeSantis, V.S. The determinants of job satisfaction among federal, state, and local government employees. *State Local Gov. Rev.* **1997**, *29*, 7–16. [CrossRef]
41. Hashemi, J.; Sadeqi, D. The relationship between job satisfaction and organizational climate: A case study of government departments in Divandarreh. *World Sci. News* **2016**, *45*, 373–383.
42. Arbuckle, M.R.; DeGolia, S.G.; Esposito, K.; Miller, D.A.; Weinberg, M.; Brenner, A.M. Associate residency training directors in psychiatry: Demographics, professional activities, and job satisfaction. *Acad. Psychiatry* **2012**, *36*, 391–394. [CrossRef]
43. Chang, W.Y.; Ma, J.C.; Chiu, H.T.; Lin, K.C.; Lee, P.H. Job satisfaction and perceptions of quality of patient care, collaboration and teamwork in acute care hospitals. *J. Adv. Nurs.* **2009**, *65*, 1946–1955. [CrossRef]
44. Chuang, E.; Dill, J.; Morgan, J.C.; Konrad, T.R. A configurational approach to the relationship between high-performance work practices and frontline health care worker outcomes. *Health Serv. Res.* **2012**, *47*, 1460–1481. [CrossRef]
45. Harley, B.; Allen, B.C.; Sargent, L.D. High performance work systems and employee experience of work in the service sector: The case of aged care. *Br. J. Ind. Relat.* **2007**, *45*, 607–633. [CrossRef]
46. Harmon, J.; Scotti, D.J.; Behson, S.; Farias, G. Effects of high-involvement work systems on employee satisfaction and service costs in veterans healthcare. *J. Healthc. Manag.* **2003**, *48*, 393. [CrossRef]
47. Young, S.; Bartram, T.; Stanton, P.; Leggat, S.G. High performance work systems and employee well-being: A two stage study of a rural Australian hospital. *J. Health Organ. Manag.* **2010**, *24*, 182–199. [CrossRef] [PubMed]
48. Fan, D.; Cui, L.; Zhang, M.M.; Zhu, C.J.; Härtel, C.E.; Nyland, C. Influence of high performance work systems on employee subjective well-being and job burnout: Empirical evidence from the Chinese healthcare sector. *Int. J. Hum. Resour. Manag.* **2014**, *25*, 931–950. [CrossRef]
49. Lok, P.; Crawford, J. The effect of organisational culture and leadership style on job satisfaction and organisational commitment: A cross-national comparison. *J. Manag. Dev.* **2004**, *23*, 321–338. [CrossRef]
50. McColl-Kennedy, J.R.; Anderson, R.D. Subordinate–manager gender combination and perceived leadership style influence on emotions, self-esteem and organizational commitment. *J. Bus. Res.* **2005**, *58*, 115–125. [CrossRef]
51. Afshinpour, S. Leadership Styles and Employee Satisfaction: A Correlation Study. *Int. Lett. Soc. Humanist. Sci. ILSHS* **2014**, *16*, 156–169.
52. Alonderiene, R.; Majauskaite, M. Leadership style and job satisfaction in higher education institutions. *Int. J. Educ. Manag.* **2016**, *30*, 140–164. [CrossRef]
53. Babalola, S.S. The effect of leadership style, job satisfaction and employee-supervisor relationship on job performance and organizational commitment. *J. Appl. Bus. Res.* **2016**, *32*, 935. [CrossRef]
54. Brimhall, K.C.; Mor Barak, M.E.; Hurlburt, M.; McArdle, J.J.; Palinkas, L.; Henwood, B. Increasing workplace inclusion: The promise of leader-member exchange. *Hum. Serv. Organ. Manag. Leadersh. Gov.* **2017**, *41*, 222–239. [CrossRef]
55. Wu, X.; Yin, W.; Wu, C.; Luo, X. The Spillover Effects on Employees' Life of Construction Enterprises' Safety Climate. *Sustainability* **2017**, *9*, 2060. [CrossRef]
56. Priyankara, H.P.R.; Luo, F.; Saeed, A.; Nubuor, S.A.; Jayasuriya, M.P.F. How Does Leader's Support for Environment Promote Organizational Citizenship Behaviour for Environment? A Multi-Theory Perspective. *Sustainability* **2018**, *10*, 271. [CrossRef]

57. Scherpereel, C.M.; Bowers, M.Y. Using critical problem based learning factors in an integrated undergraduate business curriculum: A business course success. In Proceedings of the Annual ABSEL Conference on Developments in Business Simulation and Experiential Learning, 2014. Available online: https://www.google.com.hk/url?sa=t&rct=j&q=&esrc=s&source=web&cd=1&cad=rja&uact=8&ved=2ahUKEwix0Z_Z6pvfAhVWEnAKHZiLDwsQFjAAegQIChAC&url=https%3A%2F%2Fjournals.tdl.org%2Fabsel%2Findex.php%2Fabsel%2Farticle%2Fdownload%2F493%2F462&usg=AOvVaw25wZ8bk2j9WgjwY1l_iki- (accessed on 12 December 2018).
58. Borges, N.J.; Savickas, S. Work style preferences among medical specialties. *J. Vocat. Behav.* **2014**, *84*, 303–306. [CrossRef]
59. Holloway, J.C. The guided tour a sociological approach. *Ann. Tour. Res.* **1981**, *8*, 377–402. [CrossRef]
60. Wang, K.-C.; Jao, P.-C.; Chan, H.-C.; Chung, C.-H. Group package tour leader's intrinsic risks. *Ann. Tour. Res.* **2010**, *37*, 154–179. [CrossRef]
61. Sarros, J.C.; Tanewski, G.A.; Winter, R.P.; Santora, J.C.; Densten, I.L. Work alienation and organizational leadership. *Br. J. Manag.* **2002**, *13*, 285–304. [CrossRef]
62. Chen, P.Y.; Spector, P.E. Negative affectivity as the underlying cause of correlations between stressors and strains. *J. Appl. Psychol.* **1991**, *76*, 398. [CrossRef] [PubMed]
63. Brockner, J. *Self-Esteem at Work: Research, Theory, and Practice*; Lexington Books/DC Heath and Com: Lexington, MA, USA, 1988.
64. De Cremer, D. Why inconsistent leadership is regarded as procedurally unfair: The importance of social self-esteem concerns. *Eur. J. Soc. Psychol.* **2003**, *33*, 535–550. [CrossRef]
65. Tsai, C.-L. The organizational climate and employees' job satisfaction in the Terminal Operation Context of Kaohsiung Port. *Asian J. Ship Log* **2014**, *30*, 373–392. [CrossRef]
66. Ángel Calderón Molina, M.; Manuel Hurtado González, J.; Palacios Florencio, B.; Luis Galán González, J. Does the balanced scorecard adoption enhance the levels of organizational climate, employees' commitment, job satisfaction and job dedication? *Manag. Decis.* **2014**, *52*, 983–1010. [CrossRef]
67. Ahmad, K.Z.B.; Jasimuddin, S.M.; Kee, W.L. Organizational climate and job satisfaction: Do employees' personalities matter? *Manag. Decis.* **2018**, *56*, 421–440. [CrossRef]
68. Tabachnick, B.G.; Fidell, L.S. Principal components and factor analysis. *Using Multivar. Stat.* **2001**, *4*, 582–633.
69. Anderson, J.C.; Gerbing, D.W. Structural equation modeling in practice: A review and recommended two-step approach. *Psychol. Bull.* **1988**, *103*, 411. [CrossRef]
70. Fornell, C.; Larcker, D.F. Structural equation models with unobservable variables and measurement error: Algebra and statistics. *J. Mark. Res.* **1981**, 382–388. [CrossRef]
71. Moslehpour, M.; Pham, V.K.; Wong, W.-K.; Bilgiçli, İ. e-Purchase Intention of Taiwanese Consumers: Sustainable Mediation of Perceived Usefulness and Perceived Ease of Use. *Sustainability* **2018**, *10*, 234. [CrossRef]
72. Bollen, K.A.; Stine, R. Direct and indirect effects: Classical and bootstrap estimates of variability. *Sociol. Methodol.* **1990**, 115–140. [CrossRef]
73. Shrout, P.E.; Bolger, N. Mediation in experimental and nonexperimental studies: New procedures and recommendations. *Psychol. Methods* **2002**, *7*, 422. [CrossRef] [PubMed]
74. Hayes, A.F. *Introduction to Mediation, Moderation, and Conditional Process Analysis: A Regression-Based Approach*; The Guilford Press: New York, NY, USA, 2013.
75. Tal-Or, N.; Cohen, J.; Tsfati, Y.; Gunther, A.C. Testing causal direction in the influence of presumed media influence. *Commun. Res.* **2010**, *37*, 801–824. [CrossRef]
76. Weinberg, D.B.; Avgar, A.C.; Sugrue, N.M.; Cooney-Miner, D. The importance of a high-performance work environment in hospitals. *Health Serv. Res.* **2013**, *48*, 319–332. [CrossRef] [PubMed]
77. Mou, W.; Wong, W.-K.; McAleer, M. Financial credit risk evaluation based on core enterprise supply chains. *Sustainability* **2018**, *10*, 3699. [CrossRef]
78. Li, Z.; Li, X.; Hui, Y.; Wong, W.-K. Maslow Portfolio Selection for Individuals with Low Financial Sustainability. *Sustainability* **2018**, *10*, 1128. [CrossRef]
79. Tsendsuren, S.; Li, C.-S.; Peng, S.-C.; Wong, W.-K. The Effects of Health Status on Life Insurance Holdings in 16 European Countries. *Sustainability* **2018**, *10*, 3454. [CrossRef]
80. Wong, W.-K.; Lean, H.; McAleer, M.; Tsai, F.-T. Why Are Warrant Markets Sustained in Taiwan but Not in China? *Sustainability* **2018**, *10*, 3748. [CrossRef]

81. Liao, Z.; Wong, W.-K. The determinants of customer interactions with internet-enabled e-banking services. *J. Oper. Res. Soc.* **2008**, *59*, 1201–1210. [CrossRef]
82. Liao, Z.; Shi, X.; Wong, W.-K. Consumer perceptions of the smartcard in retailing: An empirical study. *J. Int. Consum. Mark.* **2012**, *24*, 252–262. [CrossRef]
83. Altantsetseg, P.; Chen, K.C.; Chang, M.L. Male and female leaders' entrepreneurial leadership: A comparative study of Mongolia, Taiwan and Thailand on leader-member exchange. *J. Adm. Bus. Stud.* **2017**, *3*, 144–152.
84. Pham, V.; Wong, W.; Moslehpour, M.; Musyoki, D. Simultaneous Adaptation of AHP and Fuzzy AHP to Evaluate Outsourcing Service in East and Southeast Asia. *J. Test. Eval.* **2018**, *48*. [CrossRef]
85. Moslehpour, M.; Wong, W.-K.; Pham, K.V.; Aulia, C.K. Repurchase intention of Korean beauty products among Taiwanese consumers. *Asia Pac. J. Mark. Logist.* **2017**, *29*, 569–588. [CrossRef]
86. Moslehpour, M.; Wong, W.-K.; Lin, Y.H.; Nguyen, T.L.H. Top purchase intention priorities of Vietnamese low cost carrier passengers: Expectations and satisfaction. *Eurasian Bus. Rev.* **2018**, *8*, 371–389. [CrossRef]

7

Does Herding Bias Drive the Firm Value? Evidence from the Chinese Equity Market

Sayyed Sadaqat Hussain Shah [1], Muhammad Asif Khan [2,3,*], Natanya Meyer [4], Daniel F. Meyer [5] and Judit Oláh [6]

1 Department of Commerce and Finance, Faculty of Arts and Social Sciences, Government College University Lahore, Lahore 54000, Pakistan; shah.sadaqat@gmail.com
2 School of Economics and Management, Yanshan University, 438, Hebei Avenue, Qinhuangdao City 066004, China
3 Department of Commerce, Faculty of Management Sciences, University of Kotli, Village Kurti, City Kotli, Azad Jammu and Kashmir 11100, Pakistan
4 WorkWell Research Unit, North-West University, Faculty of Economic and Management Sciences, School of Management, Vanderbijlpark 1900, South Africa; Natanya.Meyer@nwu.ac.za
5 TRADE Research Entity, North-West University, Faculty of Economic and Management Sciences, Vanderbijlpark 1900, South Africa; Daniel.Meyer@nwu.ac.za
6 University of Debrecen, Faculty of Economics and Business, Institute of Applied Informatics and Logistics, 4032 Debrecen, Hungary; olah.judit@econ.unideb.hu
* Correspondence: khanasif82@hotmail.com

Abstract: Equity markets play a pivotal role in the sustainability of developing countries, such as China. The literature on the detection of herding biases is confined to the aggregate level (firms, sector/industry and market). The present study adds to the behavioral finance literature by addressing the surprisingly unnoticed phenomena of the behavioral impact of herding bias on firm value (FV) at the firm level, using the sample of A-Shares listed firms at the Shanghai and Shenzhen Stock Exchanges (SSE and SZSE) under panel fixed effect specification. Initially, we detect the existence of investors and managers herding (IHR and MHR) biases at firm-level, and later, we examine their impact (distinct and interactive) upon the FV. The empirical results document the presence of IHR and MHR bias at market, sector and firm-level in both equity markets, which potentially drive the FV, while the impact is more pronounced during the extreme trading period. The findings are robust under different time intervals, and industry classification, therefore, offers useful policy implications to understand the behavioral dynamics of investors and managers.

Keywords: Investor herding bias; manager herding bias; firm value; Shanghai stock exchange; Shenzhen stock exchange

---

1. Introduction

The stock market trading dilemma is the cumulative reflections of investors' behavior [1]. Investors exhibit behavioral irregularities (biases) which potentially influence market efficiency [2,3]. Among these biases, herding bias is the most prominent, which is associated with the trading behavior of financial markets' participants [4,5]. It has become a subject of widespread interest in the recent decade [6–8]. Herding refers to the situation wherein rational people start behaving irrationally by imitating the judgments of others while making decisions [3]. Herding theories posit that market participants prefer to follow the financial experts in their trading patterns instead of their own source of information [9].The study of [10] believes that the herding of investors is one of the major risk factors that is typically ignored by statistical approaches.

In the past decade, the study of herding documents this diverse behavioral pattern across the globe. In the context of the U.S. markets, Christie and Huang [5] report the absence of herding bias, even during extreme market movements. Conversely, Choi and Sias [11] point out the presence of a strong institutional industry herding bias. Likewise, Wang and Zhang [12] investigate the impact of individual investor trading on the firm value (FV) at the New York Stock Exchange (NYSE), and find the positive impact of investor trading on FV. European evidence [13] illustrates the presence of herding bias in the "during crises" period. Also, Walter and Moritz Weber [14] identify the herding bias of mutual fund managers in Germany during extreme market movements. Chinese, Taiwanese and South Korean stock markets also reveal herding behavior [15–18]. In the Chinese equity market, Demirer and Kutan [19] empirically analyze the behavior of return dispersions during periods of unusually large upward and downward changes in the market index of both the SSE and SZSE, and conclude that the Chinese Market is free from herding bias, and a similar approach is used by Demirer et al. [20]. Conversely, Tan et al. [21] explore the evidence of herding bias at the SSE and the SZSE, the A-share and B-share markets. They also report the existence of herding bias in both rising and falling market conditions, specifically more pronounced in the A-shares of the Shanghai Market during rising market conditions. Bo et al. [22] witness the investment herding bias among the corporate board, directors, and CEOs of non-financial firms from 1999 to 2004, and the consequent positive and significant impact on the FV. Similarly, another group of studies [23–25] report the mixed results of herding bias at the SSE and SZSE.

The above-mentioned studies highlight herding bias in two ways: First, the evidence of investors herding at market, industry/sector and firm-level during the extreme market conditions [17,19]; Second, the evidence of an investment-herding bias of the corporate manager [14] and their impact on the FV [22]. For the best of our knowledge, there is not a single study which explains the individual and interactive impact of investor and manager herding (IHR and MHR) biases on the FV. So, motivated by the recent studies [6,12,22] that manager and investor demonstrate herding bias in their investment decision, this study empirically investigates the following questions:

1. Whether the investor herding bias exists at market-, sectors- and firm-level Chinese equity markets?
2. Do managers of the firm also exhibit herding bias in Chinese equity markets?
3. What is the individual and interactive impact of investors' and managers' herding bias on the FV?

The Chinese Financial Equity Market is important to be analyzed as it has an influence on integrated markets [26], while in China there is a need to strengthen the financial resources for sustainable development and poverty reduction [27]. Based on the literature and the questions stated above, this study adds to the existing literature in the following ways: Firstly, it hypothesizes the presence of herding bias in the Chinese equity markets at the market and industry/sector level, in line with [8,15,19,28], and later it extends the phenomena at the firm level, which is a unique addition to the behavioral finance literature. Importantly, the market and sector level herding is insufficient to explain the investor's behavior associated to the firm, as Demirer and Zhang [17] find that the firm characteristics, their size and the past return has a significant effect on the herding behavior of the investor. Secondly, to the best of our knowledge, this is the first study that examines the impact of IHR and MHR on the FV. Finally, another most interesting contribution is in the form of the interactive impact of both IHR and MHR on the FV, which provides insights into understanding how both stakeholders jointly influence the FV.

Overall results demonstrate that: (i) Herding behavior exists at market-, sector- and firm-level at the SSE and SZSE, and a non-linear and significant relationship exists between stock return and cross-sectional absolute deviation (CSAD), which seems to be more pronounced in herding bias at all levels at the SZSE. The CSAD model explains 95% and 99% herding bias at the market level, 26% and 32% at sectors level, and 10% and 12% at the firm level at SSE and SZSE, respectively. While an absolute investment deviation model detects 51% and 54% of managers herding bias at SSE and SZSE, respectively.

The empirical results also suggest that IHR and MHR affect the FV significantly during the extreme trading period (2014 to 2015), at both stock exchanges, while the interaction of IHR and MHR reveals the same at the SZSE in 2013. Importantly, the results are robust under different time intervals and industry classification.

The rest of this study is arranged as follows: Section 2 describes a brief literature and hypotheses development. Section 3 explains the methodological approach, including variable definitions, data sources and the sample period. Section 4 states the empirical results and discussion, while the final section concludes the study along with policy recommendations.

2. Literature Review and Hypothesis Development

Prior literature finds a diverse herding bias among participants in various stock markets. Empirical evidence on U.S. and Europeans investors and managers exhibits the presence of herding bias among mutual fund managers [29], analysts recommendation [30] and pension fund managers [31]. The aggregate effect of herding behavior is more prevalent in international markets, especially in emerging markets. Chang et al. [15] find significant evidence of herding bias in Taiwan and South Korea, alimited bias in Japan, and no bias in the U.S. and Hong Kong.

Later on, the Bueno [32] document herding bias in both theA-shares and B-shares of theChinese Stock Market. Furthermore, empirical analysis of herding on eighteen international markets by Chiang and Zheng [33] show the existence of herding in seven Asian and six advanced markets, whereas thenonexistence of herding behavior among both Latin American and U.S. markets, except during a crises period. Recent studies of Balcilar et al. [34] and Zheng et al. [35] also document herding behavior in the Gulf Arab and Asian markets. In Pakistan, the study of Javed et al. [36] and Javaira and Hassan [37] found no evidence of herding behavior in KSE 100 index companies at the Karachi Stock Exchange (KSE) for the period of 2002 to 2014. Whereas, the study of Yousaf et al. [38] on investor herding behavior in the Pakistan Stock Market during 2004 to 2014 reports the existence of herding behavior in the market, particularly in 2005 to 2008. Likewise, the empirical work of Shah et al. [28] for 2004 to 2013 also supports the significant evidence of herding behavior in this Pakistan Stock Market, specifically during the extreme market movements. Additionally, they found more than 50% of sectors at the PSX exhibit herding behavior during the upward market movements.

Demirer and Kutan [19] examine the presence of herd formation in Chinese markets using both individual firm and sector level data. They analyze the behavior of return dispersions during periods of unusually large upward and downward changes in the market index. They also distinguish sample data between the Shanghai and Shenzhen stock exchanges at the sector-level. Their findings show that herding bias does not exist in Chinese markets. However, comparing return dispersions for upside and downside movements of the market, these return dispersions during extreme downside movements of the market are much lower than those for upside movements, indicating that stock returns behave more similarly during down markets. Munkh-Ulzii et al. [39] find the presence of significant herding behavior in Chinese and Taiwan stock markets. Tan et al. [21] explore herding behavior in dual-listed Chinese A-share and B-share stocks. They find evidence of herding within both the Shanghai and Shenzhen A-share markets that are dominated by domestic individual investors, and also within both B-share markets, in which foreign institutional investors are the main participants.

Herding occurs in both rising and falling market conditions. Herding behavior by A-share investors in the Shanghai Market is more pronounced under conditions of rising markets, high trading volumeand high volatility, while no asymmetry is apparent in the B-share market. Lee et al. [24] document the effect of institutional herding on future stock returns in the China A-share Market at both the market and industry level from 2003 to 2012. Using a unique institutional holding database, they test the herding effect at different time horizons. The results suggest that institutional herding has a significantly positive effect on future excess returns for A shares in the short, medium and long periods of time. In the China A-share market, institutional herding is more significant on the buy-side than the sell-side due to short sell restrictions.

At the industry level, manufacturing and construction sectors experience an institutional herding effect at all time horizons. The financial industry is found to present a significant institutional effect only in the long term.

The institutional herding has a positive and significant impact on the medium-term and long-term excess stock returns in the rest of ten sectors. Yao et al. [25] report the existence and prevalence of investor herding behavior in a segmented market setting, the Chinese A and B stock markets. The results indicate that investors exhibit different levels of herding behavior, in particular, herding strongly exists in the B-share markets. They also find that across markets, herding behavior is more prevalent at industry-level, is stronger for the largest and smallest stocks, and is stronger for growth stocks relative to value stocks. Herding behavior is also more pronounced under conditions of declining markets. Over the sample period which we are examining, herding behavior diminishes over time. The results provide some indication to the effectiveness of regulatory reforms in China aimed at improving information efficiency and market integration.

Lao and Singh [23] investigated herding behavior in the Chinese and Indian stock markets. Their results support that although both the Indian and Chinese stock markets are considered inefficient with low information disclosure standards, the Chinese Market exhibits herding behavior greater than the herding behavior in the Indian Market. Nevertheless, in both markets, herding behavior finds itself stronger in large market movements. Asymmetry investigation discovered that the Chinese Stock Market has the most profound herding behavior when the market is low and trading volume is high. Instead, in the Indian Market, herding behavior is observed when the market is high. In the Indian Market, herding behavior also had no association with trading volume. The reasons for herd behavior existing in the Chinese Stock Market, in both up and down states, are analyst forecast, short-term investor horizon, and inclusion of risk in decision making [40].

Although herding mentioned in the above studies contributesmuch to a better understanding of investor behavior at the SSE and SZSE, their aggregate results are confined at market and sector level, which also explains the mixed results, existence and nonexistence, of herding bias over time. Thus, consistent with the prior literature, we postulate the first hypothesis to test whether herding bias exists at the SSE and the SZSE during the sample period 2008 to 2017.

Hypothes (H1). *Stock prices show significant herding behavior at the market and sector level.*

Investors usually invest in those stocks with which they are familiar. Study of Huberman [41] considers the leading example of this phenomena. He explores the higher attention of employees in buying the security of those firms for which they work or are informed about from their peers. Ha [42] examined the impact of herding on the stock performance, and documentsthe very strong impact of herding on the stock returns and stock returns affect book to the market value of firms [43]. Also, Van Nieuwerburgh and Veldkamp [44] found the investors trending in home stock are much higher than the foreign stocks, while careful policy actions are needed to prevent malpractices [45]. Gebka and Wohar [46] document stronger irrationality behavior among the investors particularly in the Consumer Services, Oil and Gas and Basic Materials industries in the international equity markets. Following these examples, it can be figured that investors mostly invest in familiar stocks and industries preferably in the national stock market. Focusing on individual stock information for a specific industry may help to explore the herd behavior better rather than at the aggregate industry or market level. To address the answer to this question, we postulate the second hypothesis as below:

Hypothes (H2). *Stock prices show significant herding behavior at the firm level in the Chinese stock market.*

Detection of herding at any level is not enough to explain the behavior of investors toward the specific firm. Investors usually consider the FV while making their investment decision. The market value of stock reacts on the price momentum based upon the frequency of the investors' trade. Therefore, investors' trading patterns show many behavior irregularities and biases which affect the firm's performance. Among these biases, herding bias is the main behavioral bias [4], which significantly affects the firm's performance [6,8,22]. Wang and Zhang [12] elaborate on the positive impact of investor trading on the FV.

Also, Hilliard and Zhang [47] find the weaker size and price to book value effect on the herding behavior of the Chinese Stock Market relative to U.S. markets over the period of 1999 to 2012. Our study differs uniquely from the prior studies, and tries to capture the impact of the herding bias of investors, at the individual firm, on the FV listed as A-share at the SSE and SZSE. To examine such a relationship, we construct the following hypothesis.

Hypothes (H3). *Ceteris paribus, IHR bias has a positive impact on the FV.H3: Ceteris paribus, IHR bias has a positive impact on the FV.*

Effects of herding are not bounded to the investors only. Firms' managers also exhibit herding behavior in their financial decisions. Theories on herding behavior in standard literature assume that the information set upon which corporate managers are making investment decisions is truly perfect, and informative under a mature market system that guarantees a transparent corporate reporting system, mature laws and regulations, strong shareholders' protection and effective corporate governance mechanisms. Under such circumstances, the manager should make investment decisions based on the information set relevant to the firm. In contrast, Prendergast and Stole [48] discuss the herding intention of the managers who make investment decisions over time.Demirer and Zhang [17] find that small firms with a high level of herding significantly underperform from those small firms that experience low herding. They observe no significant interactions between book-to-market and market beta with herding. Chen and Demirer [8] point those industries that experience a high level of herding yield higher subsequent returns, regardless of their past performance.

Theories on herding find firms' managers usually follow their peers in investment decisions, instead of relying on their own source of information [9]. Garber [4] elaborates herding behavior as the most prominent bias in the psychology of judgment. In the recent past, the studies on manager investment herding behavior present the diverse behavioral pattern across the world. Fong et al. [49] demonstrate four general theories, classified into twoparts: Thefirst part belongs to intentional herding, and the second for unintentional herding. The authors state why managers may engage in herding behavior in their investment decisions as such: (1) Firm managers are subject to reputational risk when they behave differently from the crowd. Thus they may ignore private information to trade with the herd. (2) Managers may infer the private information of rival managers (perceived on their prior trades), resulting in the formation of informational cascades. (3) Managers may also receive similar private information because they also examine the same priced factors which caused them to arrive at similar conclusions regarding individual stocks. (4) Managers may exhibit similar aversions to stocks showing characteristics, such as low liquidity or low analyst coverage.

In the U.S. and European markets, herding behavior among managers of different industries is different. Choi and Sias [11] document strong institutional herding in U.S. corporations. Also, Walter and Moritz Weber [14] pinpoint the herding behavior of mutual fund managers in Germany. TheSouth Korea, Taiwanand China markets also exhibit herding behavior [15,16]. Many scholars examine the relationship between managerial career concerns and herding. Devenow and Welch [50] analytically illustrate herd behavior in making corporate investment decisions. In light of the above literature, we postulate hypothesis 4:

Hypothes (H4). *MHR bias has a positive impact on FV.*

Firm financial performance is considered the most important indicator for investors and managers for the evaluation of their financial decisions. It has broad implications for investments, capital allocation and market efficiency of the business. Alabass [6] and Bo et al. [22] demonstrate a positive and significant impact of MHR bias on the FV. Theprevious two hypotheses, H3 and H4, are constructed to test the

IHR and MHR bias individually. Perhaps it might be more logical to test the combined effect of herding bias to explore the magnitude of firm financial performance during the trading period. To investigate the combined effect of IHR and MHR bias on the FV, we test the following hypothesis:

Hypothes (H5). *Interaction of the IHR and MHR has a positive influence on FV.*

3. Methodological Approach

3.1. Data Source and Study Period

In this study, data are compiled from two data series of China Stock Market & Accounting Research (CSMAR). Firstly, we collect stock-based data, e.g., closing price, trading volume for individual stocks, sector/industry indices and market indices from stock market series during the sample period of 2008 through 2017. Secondly, we collect firm-level data, e.g., market to book value (MB), cash flow (CF), firm leverage (FL), firm growth (FG) and firm size (FS) from the annual audited financial statement. Initially, we consider all the firms listed with Shanghai and Shenzhen Stock Exchanges (SSE and SZSE) during the stated period. Later the data constraint problem limits our sample to 664 and 379 from 41 and 67 sectors at the SSE and SZSE, respectively.

These sub-sections initially describe the detection mechanisms of investors herding (IHR) and managers herding (MHR) biases market, sector and firm-level, and later explain the fixed effect specification used to examine the impact of IHR and MHR on firm value (FV).

3.2. Investors Herding

Since there is no direct measure of herding in financial markets, in financial literature different proxies are used to capture it indirectly at different time spans. Accordingly, the herding behavior can be summarized in two ways. [17] first employs the asymmetric trading orders of buying and selling the security in the market, which shows herding behavior on the buying side or the selling side, e.g., if the buyer orders are more than the selling order, then it is identified as herd in buying, otherwise herd in selling. This strand of the literature explains herding behavior at the investors level [31]. Whereas, the later detects the herding behavior using a regression approach based on an asset-pricing model which links the cross-sectional deviation of security returns to the extreme movements of industry returns and market return. Usually, this approach captures herding behavior at the market/industry level. Mostly, the herding literature falls into the second approach (market and sector level), because in this way an appropriate sample of market participants can be analyzed at different time spans. This approach follows two common methodologies for herding bias. First is CSSD, and the second is Cross Sectional Absolute Deviation (CSAD). CSSD, initially proposed by Christie and Huang [5], calculates the cross-sectional deviation of stock returns as:

$$\mathrm{CSSD}_t = \sqrt{\frac{\sum_{i=1}^{n}(r_{i,t} - r_{m,t})^2}{n_t - 1}} \tag{1}$$

Where n denotes the number of listed firms in the portfolio, $r_{i,t}$ is security i return at time t, and $r_{m,t}$ explains the equally-weighted returns of the portfolio at deviations. Christie and Huang [5] suggest that herding exists if the stock return dispersion by CSSD is significantly lower. Later on, Chang et al. [15] generalize the method for the herding behavior by adding the phenomena of CSAD, which is built on CAPM, for all market conditions. Our study is also based on the CSAD approach [15] for the detection of herd bias among the market participants, which is calculated as:

$$\mathrm{CSAD}_t = \frac{1}{N}\sum_{i=1}^{N}\left|R_{i,t} - R_{m,t}\right| \tag{2}$$

Chang et al. [15] suggest that there should be a linear correlation of CSAD with the absolute value of the security. However, when herd bias occurs, investor trades follow the same market direction, and individual security returns tend to cluster around the overall market return. Thus, the linear relation turns to a nonlinear one.

Under the following situation, the negative and significant nonlinear relationship between CSAD and stock market return illustrates the presence of herding. Hence, the CSAD model for exploring herding behavior is constructed as follows:

$$CSAD_{m,t} = \alpha_0 + \gamma_1 |R_{m,t}| + \gamma_2 R^2_{m,t} + \varepsilon_t \tag{3}$$

Where negative and significant $\gamma 2$ shows the presence of herding bias. As our study also focuses on industry level and firm-level herding, we transform the above model, as below:

$$CSAD_{Ind,t} = \frac{1}{N}\sum_{i=1}^{N} |R_{i,t} - R_{ind,t}| \tag{4}$$

$$CSAD_{ind,t} = \alpha_0 + \gamma_1 |R_{ind\_m,t}| + \gamma_2 R^2_{ind\_m,t} + \varepsilon_t \tag{5}$$

In Equation (4), the $CSAD_{ind,t}$ is calculated based on N, the wholenumber of firms' security returns within the industry. For the calculation of $CSAD_{ind,t}$, we use the average industry return ($R_{ind,t}$) for each of theindustry in the markets, along with the individual stock return ($R_{i,t}$) listed in the same industry.

In Equation (5), $R_{ind\_m,t} = R_{ind,t} - E(R_{ind,t})$, where $E(R_{ind,t})$ is the expected industry return which is based on CAPM, and calculated as $E(R_{ind,t}) = \alpha + \beta R_{m,t}$.

$$CSAD_{firm,t} = \frac{1}{n}\sum_{i}^{n} |R_{i,t} - R_{ind,t}| \tag{6}$$

$$CSAD_{firm,t} = \alpha_0 + \gamma_1 |R_{firm\_ind,t}| + \gamma_2 R^2_{firm\_ind} + \varepsilon_t \tag{7}$$

In Equation (6), we extend the model and calculate $CSAD_{firm\_ind,t}$ of all firms' security returns within the sectors, based on n numbers of observations. Moreover, in Equation (7), we replace return of firm in the industry at time t instead of the return of industry at time t in the Equation (5), where $R_{firm\_ind,t} = R_{firm\_ind,t} - E(R_{firm\_ind,t})$, as expected firm return in the sector based on $E(R_{firm\_ind,t}) = \alpha + \beta R_{ind,t}$. We calculate stock returns of market, industry and firm as $R = \log(P_t / P_{t-1})$, where Pt denotes the recent price of stock and P_{t-1} is the last price of the stock. For consideration of handling the outliers, we trim the return data at the 99th percentile. The specification of this model is consistent with [25]. On the basis of $\gamma 2$ of the ($CSAD_{firm\_ind,t}$) model, we construct our index investor herding bias (IHR) of each firm from each sector and assign dummy values 1, if $\gamma 2$ of ($CSAD_{firm\_ind,t}$) model is negative and significant and 0 otherwise.

3.3. *Managers Herding*

We use an absolute investment deviation ratio model as a proxy of MHR bias as suggested by Alabass [6] andBo et al. [22]. In the investment ratio model, herding exists if managers of firm i follow the investment decisions of their peers. In normal practice, it is impossible to consider that managers observe the contemporaneous investment decisions of other firms while making their own investment decisions. Perhapsit is more logical to presume that firms' managers are aware of the average investment value of other firms, listed in the same industry, in recent years. Managers often consider the last year industry average investment value as a reference for their investment decisions, therefore, the proxy for investment herding is defined as:

$$MHR_t = \left\| \left|\frac{I}{K_{i,t}}\right| - \left|\overline{\frac{I}{K_{-i,t-1}}}\right| \right\| \quad (8)$$

Which is the absolute deviation of the investment ratios; the ratio of investment to the capital stock of firm *i* at the time *t*, and the average investment ratio of other firms in the same sectors, excluding firm *i* at time year (t-1). While computing the investment ratio $(I/K)_{i,t}$, we first sort the data by sectors, followed by sorting within sectors for the measurement of the average investment ratio $\overline{(I/K)}_{-i,t-1}$ of other firms in the same sectors. Following Bo et al. [22] we also calculate net investment I, such as the net changes in fixed assets (FA) of the firm i.e., ($I=\Delta FA$) and capital stock at the beginning of the period, $K_{i,t}$ by the total assets (TA) of a firm. A smaller investment deviation suggests herding, the managers of firm *i* make a similar investment decision to the other firms listed in the same industry. Therefore, based on a smaller investment deviation of the model as a proxy of manager herding, we construct a new index for MHR, and assign adummy value of 1 if herding exists, otherwise 0.

3.4. Herding and Firm Value

To examine the effect of IHR, MHR on FV, the theoretical association between these variables can functionally be expressed as:

$$FV_t = f(IHR_t,\ MHR_t,\ CF_t, FL_t,\ FS_t, FG_t) \quad (9)$$

We transformed Equation (1) into mathematical expression:

$$FV_t = \beta_0 + \beta_1 IHR_t + \beta_2 MHR_t + \beta_3 CF_t + \beta_4 FL_t + \beta_5 FS_t + \beta_6 FG_t + \gamma + \mu + \epsilon \quad (10)$$

In the above Equation, FV_t denotes FV as the dependent variable, and is measured by the market to book value (MB) [22,51–53]. IHR_t and MHR_t show investors and managers herding as independent variables, and this is measured by the methodologies of Chang et al. [15], and Bo et al. [22]. Whereas, CF_t for cash flow to assets, FL_t for firm leverage,FS_t for firm size and FG_t are control variables as suggested by bothChen and Lin [54] and Bo et al. [22]. γ and μ are used for industry and years fixed effects, whereas ϵ explains the error terms of the model. Table 1 presents the detailed information of all variables.

Table 1. Explanation of Variables.

Variable Type	Name	Proxy	Explanation
Dependent variable	FV_t	MB	Market value of assets/book value of assets
Independent variable	Investor herding (IHR)	Cross-sectional absolute deviation	Market, sector and firm-level bias exists if $\gamma 2$ of CSAD has a significantly negative value. Dummy 1 is assigned when bias exists, otherwise it is 0
	Manager herding (MHR)	Investment to capital ratio	Bias exists if an absolute deviation of investment ratio would be minimum. Dummy 1 is assigned when bias exists, otherwise 0
Control variable	Cash flow to assets (CF)t	Cash flow at time t	Cash flow to assets ratio
	Firm leverage (FL)t	Firm leverage at time t	Total debt to equity ratio
	Firm size (FS)t	Firm size at time t	Natural log of total assets
	Firm growth (FG)t	Firm growth at time t	Natural log of sales

Source: Authors' own research, 2019.

4. Empirical Results and Discussion

Table 2 presents the descriptive analysis of the firm's financial data at the SSE and SZSE for the period of 2008 to 2017, in terms of mean, minimum and maximum values, and standard deviation of the FV, Tobin's Q—Ahmad et al. [55] and control variables such as cash flow (CF), firm leverage (FL), firm size (FS), and firm growth (FG). Column (1) and (6) report the mean values of FV, i.e., 1.88 and 2.136 with the standard deviation of 1.92 and 1.94, and the minimum to maximum range, 0.188 to 11.967 and 0 to 0.49, at the SSE and SZSE, respectively. While the rest of the columns explain the description of the control variables, where FS has a relatively higher mean value with lower deviation, and CF has a relatively least average value with least deviation among the firms of two stock exchanges.

Table 2. Descriptive Statistics at the Shanghai and Shenzhen Stock Exchanges (SSE and SZSE) (2008–2017).

Variable	SSE					SZSE				
	(1)	(2)	(3)	(4)	(5)	(6)	(7)	(8)	(9)	(10)
	FV	CF	FL	FS	FG	FV	CF	FL	FS	FG
Mean	1.88	0.099	1.586	22.28	0.971	2.136	0.1	1.319	21.94	0.841
Std.Dev.	1.926	0.099	1.776	1.365	0.645	1.949	0.1	1.492	1.269	0.594
Min	0.188	0	−1.953	19.22	0.246	0.188	0	−1.953	19.22	0.246
Max	11.967	0.49	10.845	25.88	2.203	11.967	0.49	10.85	25.88	2.203
Obs	6640	6640	6640	6640	6640	3790	3790	3790	3790	3790

Source: Authors' own research, 2019.

The pairwise correlation results of Table 3 haveno evidence of multicollinearityamong variables of SSE and SZSE for the period of 2008 to 2017. All variables are significantly related to each other, except the CF in SZSE, which has a positive and insignificant relation with FG.

Table 3. Correlation matrix at SSE and SZSE (2008–2017).

Variables SSE/SZE	FV	CF	FL	FS	FG
FV	1	0.131 *	−0.162 *	−0.490 *	−0.335 *
CF	0.050 *	1	−0.138 *	−0.033 *	0.004
FL	−0.130 *	−0.128 *	1	0.191 *	0.159 *
FS	−0.528 *	−0.025 *	0.145 *	1	0.678 *
FG	−0.392 *	0.043 *	0.138 *	0.707 *	1

Note: * shows significance at the 0.05 level. The lower part of principal diagonal "1" explains correlation matrix for SSE and upper part present matrix for SZSE.Source: Authors' own research, 2019.

4.1. *Herding at Equity Markets*

This section presents the empirical results of herding bias at a market level between two stock markets, i.e., the SSE and the SZSE by using the CSAD model [15,28]. Therefore, a negative and significant γ_2 (CSAD model coefficient) exhibits evidence of herding behavior.

Table 4 exhibits the evidence of herding behavior by CSAD model in A-shares of SSE and SZSE during the sample period starting from 2008 to 2017. In Table 4, negative and significant γ_2 with coefficients (−1.146) and (−1.741), and t-values (−2.08) and (−4.49), present the evidence of a herding bias in the SSE and SZSE, respectively, during the said sample period. Furthermore, this herding bias is seeming more prevalent in the A- Shares of SZSE, at a 99% level of confidence, which are consistent with the literature [16,19].

Table 4. Level A-Share Herding Bias at SSE and SZSE (2008–2017).

$CSAD_{m,t}$	A	γ_1	γ_2	Adjusted R^2
SSE	0.013 ***	0.197 ***	−1.146 **	0.037
	(24.3)	(4.94)	(−2.08)	
SZSE	0.013 ***	0.209 ***	−1.741 ***	0.067
	(27.74)	(7.27)	(−4.49)	

Source: Authors' own research, 2019; Note: *,**,*** denote test statistics significant at 10%, 5%, and1% respectively, while t-value in parenthesis.

4.2. IHR Bias at Industry/Sector Level

Tables 5 and 6 incorporate the evidence of industry/sector level herding bias by CSAD model (5) in the A-shares of the SSE and SZSE. The results in Table 5 indicate herding bias among 11 sectors out of 41—these sectors are agriculture, food manufacturing, leather, fur, feathers and footwear production, petroleum processing, coking and nuclear fuel processing, metal products industry, housing construction, warehousing industry, other financial industry, health and comprehensive industry(γ_2 is negative and significant). Table 6 attributes investors' herding bias among 22 sectors out of 67 at the SZSE. These sectors include animal husbandry, forestry and fishery services, the agricultural and food processing industries, food manufacturing, the wood processing industry, culture and entertainment products manufacturing, the rubber and plastic products industry, non-ferrous metal smelting and rolling processing industry, instrumentation manufacturing, handling and transportation agency, internet and related services, ecological protection and environmental management, news and publishing, comprehensive, the wholesale industry, retail industry, air transport industry, catering, monetary financial services, the real estate industry, and media operations. While, 30/41 and 45/67 sectors at SSE and SZSE, respectively, are free from the herding, γ_2 ($CSAD_{int,t}$ model, coefficient) is negative/positive and insignificant. Our findings are supported by prior literature [16,19,28].

Table 5. Industry Herding Bias at the SSE (2008–2017).

Sectors	Name	A	t-stat	γ_1	t-stat	γ_2	t-stat	Adjusted R^2
1	A01	0.010 ***	(19.21)	0.346 ***	(9.27)	−2.649 ***	(−5.49)	0.065
2	A02	0.007 ***	(21.76)	0.088 ***	(7.99)	−0.050	(−1.49)	0.055
3	A03	0.008 ***	(22.29)	−0.125 ***	(−7.65)	2.662 ***	(20.98)	0.232
4	A04	0.011 ***	(29.95)	−0.036 **	(−2.24)	−2.273 ***	(18.44)	0.244
5	A05	0.009 ***	(16.27)	−0.015	(−0.60)	3.234 ***	(20.85)	0.316
6	B07	0.010 ***	(21.21)	0.119 ***	(3.95)	2.223 ***	(6.23)	0.164
7	B08	0.012 ***	(19.94)	0.019	(0.51)	2.340 ***	(5.26)	0.081
8	B09	0.013 ***	(44.92)	0.061 ***	(4.71)	2.484 ***	(62.95)	0.756
9	B11	0.010 ***	(22.72)	0.026	(1.46)	2.120 ***	(26.37)	0.409
10	C13	0.014 ***	(25.88)	−0.012	(−0.33)	2.808 ***	(6.56)	0.096
11	C14	0.013 ***	(28.46)	0.128 ***	(8.73)	−0.067 ***	(−6.36)	0.072
12	C15	0.014 ***	(58.48)	0.078 ***	(7.86)	1.798 ***	(77.08)	0.839
13	C18	0.016 ***	(49.71)	−0.265 ***	(−18.02)	6.179 ***	(57.24)	0.636
14	C19	0.006 ***	(6.60)	0.415 ***	(7.01)	−4.284 ***	(−6.56)	0.158
15	C20	0.007 ***	(5.48)	0.329 ***	(3.44)	−2.354	(−1.37)	0.216
16	C21	0.011 ***	(9.92)	0.033	(0.53)	6.484 ***	(18.51)	0.835
17	C22	0.013 ***	(10.43)	−0.144	(−1.19)	16.392 ***	(6.88)	0.425
18	C23	0.007 ***	(7.91)	0.146 *	(1.81)	0.752	(0.41)	0.197
19	C24	0.008 ***	(10.51)	0.463 ***	(6.83)	5.617 ***	(16.35)	0.933
20	C25	−0.002	(−0.47)	1.138 ***	(3.50)	−12.514 ***	(−3.01)	0.389
21	C28	0.006 ***	(6.75)	0.309 ***	(3.08)	0.328	(0.12)	0.270
22	C29	0.008 ***	(9.11)	−0.006	(−0.05)	24.212 ***	(5.16)	0.412
23	C32	0.009 ***	(8.78)	0.293 ***	(3.66)	1.232	(0.68)	0.306
24	C33	0.007 ***	(9.34)	0.101	(1.25)	−6.916 ***	(2.89)	0.349
25	C38	0.006 ***	(6.92)	0.201 **	(2.52)	2.854	(1.63)	0.370

Table 5. *Cont.*

26	C40	0.011 ***	(13.11)	0.085	(1.22)	7.396 ***	(4.02)	0.429
27	E47	0.012 ***	(7.46)	−0.062	(−0.44)	−10.440 ***	(4.64)	0.311
28	G53	0.008 ***	(6.80)	0.198	(1.55)	3.351	(0.94)	0.177
29	G58	0.006 ***	(6.56)	0.350 ***	(2.84)	4.851	(1.55)	0.293
30	G59	0.005 ***	(5.61)	0.140	(1.39)	−5.289 **	(2.53)	0.292
31	I63	0.100 **	(6.25)	−1.182	(−1.73)	1.770	(0.25)	0.999
32	I64	0.011 ***	(7.28)	−0.187	(−1.38)	9.974 ***	(5.95)	0.406
33	J66	0.008 ***	(5.05)	0.336 ***	(3.02)	−1.149	(−0.76)	0.175
34	J68	0.009 ***	(7.55)	0.374 ***	(3.95)	−0.938	(−0.74)	0.217
35	J69	0.003 ***	(4.32)	0.310 ***	(5.30)	−3.294 ***	(−4.54)	0.118
36	M74	0.010 ***	(8.93)	−0.126 ***	(−2.71)	3.313 ***	(17.83)	0.779
37	N77	0.006 ***	(5.75)	0.139 **	(2.01)	−0.364	(−0.35)	0.072
38	Q83	0.009 ***	(4.58)	0.487 ***	(4.53)	−5.222 ***	(−4.11)	0.172
39	R85	0.007 ***	(5.03)	0.358 ***	(3.51)	−3.016	(−1.50)	0.174
40	R86	0.009 ***	(7.15)	0.073	(0.89)	0.153	(0.13)	0.062
41	S90	0.007 ***	(15.05)	0.406 ***	(14.59)	−3.765 ***	(−11.00)	0.140

Note: *,**,*** denote test statistics significant at 10%, 5%, and 1% respectively, while p-value in parenthesis.

Table 6. Industry Herding Bias at the SZSE (2008–2017).

Sectors	Codes	α	t-stat	γ_1	t-stat	γ_2	t-stat	Adjusted R^2
1	A01	0.013 ***	(21.15)	−0.017	(−0.44)	3.557 ***	(8.00)	0.120
2	A02	0.013 ***	(28.11)	−0.169 ***	(−7.39)	5.350 ***	(26.80)	0.374
3	A03	0.014 ***	(24.27)	−0.194 ***	(−5.47)	−6.004 ***	(14.77)	0.194
4	A03	0.015 ***	(25.95)	−0.165 ***	(−5.66)	5.456 ***	(23.82)	0.289
5	A04	0.009 ***	(19.35)	0.146 ***	(7.11)	−2.294 ***	(22.28)	0.498
6	A05	0.009 ***	(20.66)	0.135 ***	(4.75)	0.230	(0.65)	0.101
7	B06	0.010 ***	(17.58)	0.027	(1.17)	2.850 ***	(27.75)	0.583
8	B07	0.009 ***	(19.74)	0.135 ***	(5.14)	0.277	(0.92)	0.128
9	B08	0.015 ***	(41.11)	−0.133 ***	(−8.95)	3.841 ***	(36.06)	0.442
10	B09	0.010 ***	(15.89)	0.290 ***	(11.50)	−1.766 ***	(17.41)	0.483
11	B11	0.013 ***	(24.06)	0.265 ***	(7.45)	−2.010 ***	(−4.28)	0.048
12	C14	0.017 ***	(38.17)	−0.288 ***	(−13.19)	7.423 ***	(37.20)	0.456
13	C15	0.014 ***	(50.29)	0.085 ***	(7.26)	1.605 ***	(60.64)	0.772
14	C17	0.016 ***	(38.32)	−0.241 ***	(−9.64)	5.937 ***	(18.97)	0.220
15	C18	0.017 ***	(36.88)	−0.346 ***	(−13.27)	−8.768 ***	(32.78)	0.393
16	C19	0.010 ***	(13.17)	0.132 ***	(4.24)	2.445 ***	(21.73)	0.479
17	C20	0.008 ***	(18.64)	0.240 ***	(15.52)	0.580 ***	(16.69)	0.400
18	C21	0.015 ***	(28.16)	−0.267 ***	(−9.97)	7.089 ***	(31.99)	0.480
19	C22	0.014 ***	(37.79)	0.026 *	(1.80)	−2.708 ***	(41.56)	0.562
20	C23	0.009 ***	(20.55)	0.242 ***	(14.25)	0.872 ***	(18.47)	0.401
21	C24	0.012 ***	(27.95)	−0.025	(−1.49)	2.415 ***	(28.15)	0.362
22	C25	0.011 ***	(23.42)	0.203 ***	(6.53)	−1.012 **	(−2.50)	0.079
23	C26	0.012 ***	(27.52)	0.228 ***	(8.48)	−1.950 ***	(−5.50)	0.083
24	C27	0.016 ***	(57.70)	−0.169 ***	(−15.23)	4.517 ***	(57.08)	0.648
25	C28	0.013 ***	(35.34)	0.035 ***	(2.60)	1.768 ***	(28.25)	0.404
26	C29	0.016 ***	(30.98)	−0.201 ***	(−6.22)	−5.631 ***	(13.92)	0.160
27	C30	0.013 ***	(26.21)	0.173 ***	(5.33)	−0.262	(−0.62)	0.074
28	C31	0.012 ***	(42.43)	−0.054 ***	(−4.68)	2.733 ***	(48.69)	0.599
29	C32	0.017 ***	(37.33)	−0.364 ***	(−14.36)	−6.702 ***	(23.14)	0.231
30	C33	0.016 ***	(45.67)	−0.229 ***	(−14.99)	4.988 ***	(37.94)	0.445
31	C34	0.015 ***	(31.98)	−0.048 *	(−1.70)	2.687 ***	(7.53)	0.101
32	C35	0.013 ***	(24.94)	0.238 ***	(7.44)	−1.675 ***	(−3.93)	0.074
33	C36	0.017 ***	(43.78)	−0.336 ***	(−16.74)	6.796 ***	(31.09)	0.353
34	C37	0.013 ***	(24.17)	0.145 ***	(4.22)	0.892 **	(2.02)	0.098
35	C38	0.016 ***	(9.08)	−0.065	(−0.78)	1.643	(1.34)	0.120
36	C39	0.015 ***	(9.63)	−0.016	(−0.23)	0.795	(0.83)	0.093
37	C40	0.005 ***	(2.80)	0.385 ***	(3.56)	−3.662 ***	(−2.88)	0.115
38	C41	0.012 ***	(8.48)	−0.132 **	(−2.41)	3.585 ***	(14.31)	0.734
39	D44	0.009 ***	(23.58)	0.277 ***	(11.66)	−1.954 ***	(−6.31)	0.150

Table 6. *Cont.*

40	D45	0.012 ***	(27.78)	−0.234 ***	(−10.49)	5.519 ***	(29.77)	0.380
41	E47	0.011 ***	(25.96)	−0.086 ***	(−4.64)	−3.734 ***	(29.33)	0.379
42	E48	0.018 ***	(41.11)	−0.343 ***	(−15.49)	7.722 ***	(35.95)	0.420
43	E50	0.011 ***	(22.07)	0.059 ***	(2.69)	3.498 ***	(29.80)	0.511
44	F51	0.011 ***	(25.41)	0.172 ***	(6.33)	−0.717 **	(−2.02)	0.112
45	F52	0.009 ***	(22.78)	0.295 ***	(10.41)	−1.831 ***	(−4.77)	0.145
46	G54	0.012 ***	(31.35)	−0.210 ***	(−9.14)	5.300 ***	(20.95)	0.262
47	G55	0.015 ***	(32.84)	−0.340 ***	(−13.52)	7.214 ***	(28.44)	0.329
48	G56	0.003 ***	(9.47)	0.402 ***	(16.24)	−3.627 ***	(−11.78)	0.142
49	G58	0.009 ***	(20.42)	0.099 ***	(5.15)	2.301 ***	(27.36)	0.515
50	G59	0.014 ***	(26.77)	−0.279 ***	(−10.23)	8.040 ***	(41.49)	0.702
51	H61	0.009 ***	(20.28)	0.122 ***	(4.39)	0.056	(0.17)	0.117
52	H62	0.009 ***	(21.74)	0.038 **	(2.48)	−1.786 ***	(35.00)	0.533
53	I63	0.017 ***	(29.84)	−0.160 ***	(−5.32)	5.971 ***	(20.80)	0.268
54	I64	0.017 ***	(27.86)	−0.302 ***	(−8.57)	−8.097 ***	(19.40)	0.277
55	I65	0.016 ***	(32.24)	−0.159 ***	(−5.34)	4.849 ***	(13.62)	0.159
56	J66	0.006 ***	(14.54)	0.069 ***	(3.78)	−2.773 ***	(25.33)	0.468
57	J67	0.008 ***	(17.71)	0.013	(0.44)	1.683 ***	(4.85)	0.086
58	K70	0.008 ***	(22.90)	0.230 ***	(12.03)	−1.877 ***	(−7.54)	0.231
59	L72	0.012 ***	(23.34)	0.195 ***	(5.55)	0.220	(0.48)	0.093
60	M73	0.009 ***	(11.10)	−0.031	(−0.86)	3.165 ***	(17.90)	0.553
61	M74	0.014 ***	(27.28)	−0.166 ***	(−7.08)	5.986 ***	(32.69)	0.458
62	N77	0.007 ***	(11.05)	0.370 ***	(14.80)	0.428 ***	(5.72)	0.332
63	Q83	0.009 ***	(16.25)	0.089 ***	(4.55)	1.820 ***	(32.97)	0.730
64	R85	0.012 ***	(19.27)	−0.048 *	(−1.96)	2.732 ***	(24.70)	0.472
65	R86	0.006 ***	(7.92)	0.484 ***	(19.38)	−0.284 ***	(−5.14)	0.279
66	R87	0.006 ***	(4.56)	0.165 ***	(2.88)	1.690 ***	(9.42)	0.803
67	S90	0.008 ***	(20.87)	0.036 **	(2.42)	2.183 ***	(30.38)	0.456

Note: *,**,*** denote test statistics significant at 10%, 5%, and 1% respectively, while p-value in parenthesis.

4.3. Firm-Level Herding Bias

4.3.1. IHR Bias

Table 7 reports the dummies oftheIHR index among 667 and 379 traded firms of SSE and SZSE, respectively, and favors the hypothesis 2 [28,38,56]. The proportion of holding IHR, dummy 1, among traded firms varies with respect to time and more variation in IHR seems at SZSE, i.e., minimum 7% to maximum 13% during the sample periods.

Table 7. Investors Herding (IHR) index at the SSE and SZSE (2008–2017).

Year	SSE		SZSE	
	Total of 664 A-shares		Total of 379 A-shares	
	1	0	1	0
2008	56	608	51	328
2009	63	601	39	340
2010	66	598	25	354
2011	62	602	46	333
2012	60	604	49	330
2013	56	608	47	332
2014	59	605	45	334
2015	64	600	47	332
2016	63	601	32	347
2017	58	606	58	339

Source: Authors' own research, 2019.

4.3.2. MHR Bias

Table 8 demonstrates that the managers of A-shares listed firms at the SZSE appear more likely to follow their peers in their investment decisions. The average proportion of existence MHR, dummy 1, is 34% and 35%, varies from 31% to 38% and 31% to 39% at the SSE and SZSE, respectively. Minimum ratio of holding MHR appears in 2008 and 2010, while the maximum evidence of MHR looks at 2016 and 2012 at the SSE and SZSE, respectively. Table 8 provides a snapshot of IHR and MHR indices among listed firms of the SSE and SZSE for the said sample period.

Table 8. Managers herding (MHR) Index at the SSE and SZSE (2008–2017).

Year	(SSE)		(SZSE)	
	Total of 664 A-shares		Total of 379 A-shares	
	1	0	1	0
2008	209	455	135	244
2009	230	434	143	236
2010	229	435	118	261
2011	218	446	135	244
2012	235	429	146	233
2013	210	454	135	244
2014	230	434	140	239
2015	234	430	130	249
2016	242	422	124	255
2017	220	444	122	257

Source: Authors' own research, 2019.

Bars in Figure 1 explain the increase, decrease and non-monotonic relation between IHR and MHR. At the SSE, both the IHR and MHR both increase in 2008, 2014 and 2015, decreases in 2011, 2013 and 2017. Likewise, both the IHR and MHR at the SZSE both increase in 2008, 2011 2012, and decrease in 2010, 2013 and 2016, the rest of the years show a different trend between IHR and MHR.

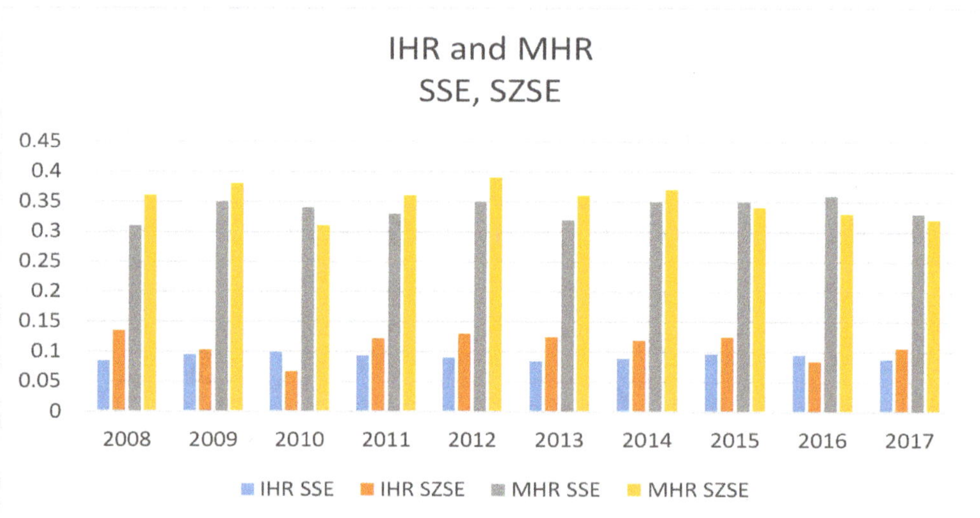

Figure 1. IHR and MHR percentages associated with listed firms of 664-SSE and 379-SZSE. Source: Authors' own research, 2019.

Figure 2 explains the versatile trading behavior of Chinese investors during the sample periods. In this figure, the period of 2013 to 2017 seems to be a highly volatile period of both of the markets where the trading index has divergent experiences.

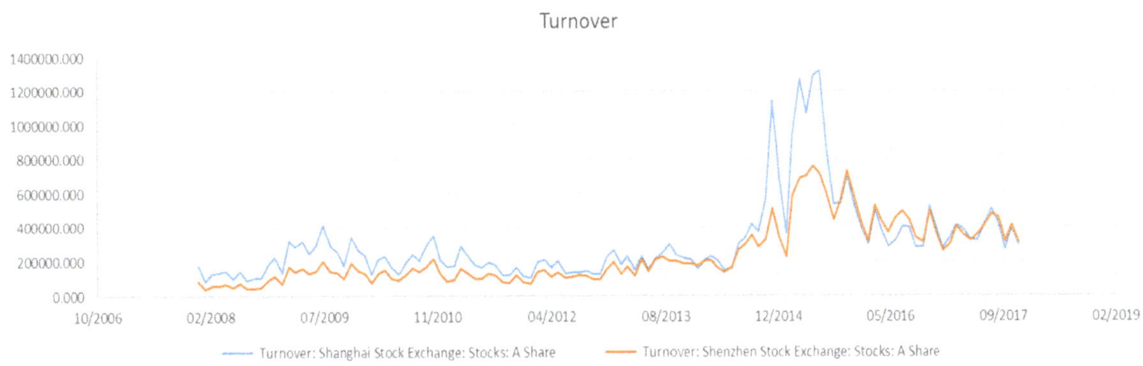

Figure 2. Turnover of A-Shares at SSE and SZSE: Source; CEIC Data. Source: Authors' own research, 2019.

4.4. Herding Bias and Firm Value

Impact of IHR and MHR on FV is analyzed through multivariate regression with respect to hypotheses 3 to 5. In Table 9, Table 10, Table 11, Table 12, we use the market to book value as the proxy of FV, which is explained in Table 1.The Hausman test guides us to use the fixed effect regression analysis, which assumes a rejection of the random effect hypothesis under a significant p-value. Hence, we reject the null hypothesis, the random effect is appropriate. Using the following Equations (11)–(13), fixed-effect regression analysis with industries and time dummies reports result in Table 9, Table 10, Table 11, Table 12.

$$FV_t = \beta_0 + \beta_1 IHR_t + \beta_2 CF_t + \beta_3 FS_t + \beta_4 FL_t + \beta_5 FG_t + \gamma + \mu + \epsilon \quad (11)$$

$$FV_t = \beta_0 + \beta_1 MHR_t + \beta_2 CF_t + \beta_3 FS_t + \beta_4 FL_t + \beta_5 FG_t + \gamma + \mu + \epsilon \quad (12)$$

$$FV_t = \beta_0 + \beta_1 IHR_t + \beta_2 MHR_t + \beta_3 IHR_t{*}MHR_t + \beta_4 CF_t + \beta_5 FS_t + \beta_6 FL_t + \beta_7 FG_t + \gamma + \mu + \epsilon \quad (13)$$

Table 9, a fixed effect regression model with year and industry dummies illustrates the impact of IHR, MHR and their interaction (IHR*MHR) on FV at the listed firms of the SSE and SZSE under the full sample period. The results support the third hypothesis in both of the markets, which implies that IHR positively drives the FV ceteris paribus. Whereas, the fourth and fifth hypotheses based on MHR hold true at the SZSE, where MHR and interaction demonstrate the positive impact on the FV. Overall findings document the influence of herding bias upon the FV, which gains support by prior literature [6,12,22]. However, the strength of relation exists insignificant during the sample period. To further diagnose the intensity of the said relation, we revisit the sample and select the extreme trading period of A-shares in line with the related literature [16,28], based upon the turnover of shares at the SSE and the SZSE. Table 10 presents the result of IHR, MHR and their interaction on the FV from 2013 to 2017, a highly divergent period, shown in Figure 2 of A-shares trading at the SSE and SZSE.

The results in Table 10 reveal that herding bias derives the FV at the SSE and SZSE. It explains that FV at the SSE is adversely affected by the MHR at the 5% level of significance with t-value (2.03). Whereas, at the SZSE, herding bias positively derives the FV, and this impact seems to be more profound by the IHR, i.e., 10% significance with a t-value (1.68). Further, CF significantly increases among those firms that are positively influenced by the interaction of IHR and MHR, while FG is positively and significantly caused by negative interaction of herding biases. On the other hand, FS shows the negative and significant impact on the FV regardless of the magnitude of interaction. FL explains the positive impact on FV among the listed firms of both the markets. Results of control variables are consistent with prior literature [57,58]. The results support the third and fifth hypotheses of the study only at the SZSE, and contradict all hypotheses at the SSE. The reason for controverting findings from the prior literature, specifically at the SSE, might be due to the high and sharp shift in trading behavior from boom to slump. To capture the impact of this relation at a specific time interval, we divide the subsample into annual and bi-annual periods, based on a sharp, shifty, yearly edge turnover of A-shares.

Table 9. MHR, and firm value (FV) (2008–2017).

VARIABLES	SSE			SZSE		
	(1)	(2)	(3)	(4)	(5)	(6)
	MB	MB	MB	MB	MB	MB
IHR	0.033			0.072		
	(0.49)			(0.86)		
MHR		−0.063			0.032	
		(−1.52)			(0.57)	
IHR*MHR			−0.166			0.059
			(−1.19)			(0.33)
CF	0.459 **	0.459 **	0.463 **	1.362 ***	1.355 ***	1.359 ***
	(2.26)	(2.26)	(2.28)	(5.03)	(5.01)	(5.02)
FL	−0.030 ***	−0.030 **	−0.030 **	−0.036 *	−0.036 *	−0.037 *
	(−2.59)	(−2.55)	(−2.54)	(−1.94)	(−1.93)	(−1.95)
FG	−0.035 *	−0.034 *	−0.034 *	0.031	0.031	0.031
	(−1.88)	(−1.82)	(−1.82)	(1.16)	(1.16)	(1.15)
FS	−0.672 ***	−0.672 ***	−0.672 ***	−0.708 ***	−0.709 ***	−0.709 ***
	(−30.44)	(−30.41)	(−30.42)	(−23.81)	(−23.80)	(−23.81)
Constant	17.185 ***	17.172 ***	17.162 ***	17.063 ***	17.062 ***	17.071 ***
	(42.83)	(42.80)	(42.76)	(28.15)	(28.14)	(28.14)
Observations	6640	6640	6640	3790	3790	3790
R-squared	0.354	0.355	0.355	0.329	0.329	0.330
Adj. R^2	0.346	0.347	0.347	0.318	0.318	0.318
F-Stat	43.91	43.95	42.92	29.05	29.04	28.15
Year Effect	Yes	Yes	Yes	Yes	Yes	Yes
Ind. Effect	Yes	Yes	Yes	Yes	Yes	Yes

Note: *,**,*** denote test statistics significant at 10%, 5%, and 1%, respectively,while the p-value is in parentheses. Where MB = FV measured market to book value of assets, IHR = investor herding, MHR = managers herding, CF = cash flow, FL= firm leverage, FG = firm growth, FS = firm size.Source: Authors' own research, 2019.

Table 10. MHR, and FV (2013–2017).

VARIABLES	SSE			SZSE		
	(1)	(2)	(3)	(4)	(5)	(6)
	MB	MB	MB	MB	MB	MB
IHR	−0.028			0.127 *		
	(−0.16)			(1.68)		
MHR		−0.218 **			−0.059	
		(−2.03)			(−0.65)	
IHR*MHR			−0.196			0.136
			(−0.53)			(0.46)
CF	0.516	0.526	0.528	1.160 ***	1.161 ***	1.177 ***
	(0.98)	(1.00)	(1.01)	(2.69)	(2.69)	(2.72)
FL	0.042	0.045	0.045	0.028	0.028	0.027
	(1.40)	(1.48)	(1.50)	(0.92)	(0.92)	(0.91)
FG	0.089 *	0.092 *	0.093 *	−0.023	−0.020	−0.022
	(1.81)	(1.88)	(1.89)	(−0.52)	(−0.47)	(−0.50)
FS	−0.965 ***	−0.963 ***	−0.964 ***	−0.712 ***	−0.710 ***	−0.711 ***
	(−16.68)	(−16.66)	(−16.66)	(−15.12)	(−15.04)	(−15.06)
Constant	20.731 ***	20.664 ***	20.655 ***	18.233 ***	18.158 ***	18.210 ***
	(19.95)	(19.89)	(19.87)	(19.14)	(19.06)	(19.08)
Observations	3320	3320	3320	1895	1895	1895
R-squared	0.200	0.201	0.201	0.323	0.323	0.323
Adj. R^2	0.181	0.182	0.181	0.302	0.301	0.301
F-Stat	10.52	10.59	10.32	15.10	15.08	14.59
Year Effect	Yes	Yes	Yes	Yes	Yes	Yes
Ind. Effect	Yes	Yes	Yes	Yes	Yes	Yes

Note: *,**,*** denote test statistics significant at 10%, 5%, and 1%, respectively, while their p-value is in parentheses. Where MB = FV measured market to book value of assets, IHR = investor herding, MHR = managers herding, CF = cash flow, FL = firm leverage, FG = firm growth, FS = firm size.Source: Authors' own research, 2019.

4.4.1. IHR, MHR, and FFP During Economic Shocks

Table 11 reports the impact of IHR and MHR on FV during the economic shocks, as an exogenous factor, we divide the sub-sample into four intervals, i.e., 2013, 2014–2015, 2016, 2017, annually and bi-annually based on the turnover trend shown inFigure 2. Among these four intervals, second interval, 2014–2015, is bi-annual, as this period contains the versatile trading behavior, bottom-peak-bottom, of the index. Thefirst interval 2013 is in a less volatile period of A-shares at both the markets. During this year, IHR negatively influences the FV, while MHR positively influenced the FV at the SSE and SZSE, respectively. The interaction term explains the positive relation with FV, and this relation seems 10% significant at the SZSE. The second interval 2014–2015 shows the extreme trading behavior of A-shares at both the market where the SSE seems more volatile relative to the SZSE. Over this period, IHR exhibits a positive and significant effect on the FV, while MHR significantly and negatively influences the FV. Apparently, FV at SSE seems to be more sensitive towards the IHR, whereas, at the SZSE, IHR and MHR both significantly drive the FV with a 90% level of confidence. The interaction term explains that in the extreme trading period, IHR and MHR negatively influenced the FV.

The results in 2016, the immediate year after the highest and the lowest market index in 2015, capture the effects of the aftershocks. Market movement over this year quarterly moves up and down and explains the negative impact of IHR and MHR on the FV at both markets. The interaction term explains the mixed results at both the SSE and SZSE, respectively.

The last interval (2017), is relatively low volatile, compared with second and third interval, which explains the negative and positive impact of IHR and its interaction term on FV at the SSE and SZSE, respectively. However, MHR clarifies a negative and positive impact on FV at the SSE and SZSE.

Theoverall finding over the four intervals demonstrates that IHR and MHR strongly appears, and interactively negatively derives the FV during the extreme market movements. Whereas, in the low volatile period, the significance disappears, and the negative interactive effect on the FV at SSE continues as aftereffects. We also capture the impact of herding bias during the said sample in the group of industries listed at the SSE and SZSE. For this purpose, we rearrange our sample based on the group A-industry classification cited in the CSMAR database. Table 12 describes the results of industries and market wise relation of herding bias with FV.

Table 11. IHR, MHRand FV during economic shocks.

VARIABLES	2013		2014–2015		2016		2017	
	(1)	(3)	(3)	(3)	(3)	(4)	(5)	(6)
	SSE	SSE	SSE	SZSE	SSE	SZSE	SSE	SZSE
	MB	MB	MB	MB	MB	MB	MB	MB
IHR	−0.301	−0.233	0.360 ***	0.327 **	−0.159	−0.198	−0.097	0.344
	(−1.30)	(−0.90)	(2.78)	(2.41)	(−0.70)	(−0.68)	(−0.44)	(1.24)
MHR	0.031	0.217	−0.143 *	−0.201 **	−0.048	−0.074	0.142	0.269
	(0.22)	(1.21)	(−1.73)	(−2.26)	(−0.34)	(−0.42)	(1.07)	(1.46)
IHR*MHR	0.240	0.921 *	−0.135	−0.188	−0.124	0.003	−0.220	0.748
	(0.47)	(1.65)	(−0.49)	(−0.65)	(−0.27)	(0.00)	(−0.41)	(1.21)
Observations	1707	1422	1707	1422	1707	1422	1707	1422
Year Effect	Yes	Yes	Yes	Yes	Yes	Yes	Yes	Yes
Ind. Effect	Yes	Yes	Yes	Yes	Yes	Yes	Yes	Yes

t-statistics in parentheses; *** $p < 0.01$, ** $p < 0.05$, * $p < 0.1$; Source: Authors' own research, 2019.

4.4.2. Group A-Industry Classification

Table 12 presents the relation of herding bias on the FV at the SSE and SZSE among six groups of industries (Group A-industry classification). Empirical results show that IHR positively and significantly derives the FV at the SZSE in the industry group. While MHR explains the negative and significant impact on the FV under the same industry head. However, the interaction term of IHR and

MHR exhibits positive impact on FV at the SSE and SZSE, respectively. Likewise, MHR also has a positive significant effect on FV between the Business and Financial sector at the SZSE. The significant impact of MHR on FV at the SZSE is relatively more pronounced than the SSE. IHR and MHR among other sectors explain the mixed on the FV.

Table 12. Interactive impact of IHR and MHR on FV among Industry Group A.

Groups	SSE			SZSE			SSE		SZSE	
	(1)	(2)	(3)	(4)	(5)	(6)	(7)	(8)	(9)	(10)
	IHR	MHR	IHR * MHR	IHR	MHR	IHR * MHR	Adj. R^2	F-Stat	Adj. R^2	F-Stat
Comprehensive	−0.276 (−0.60)			−1.148 (−1.59)			0.388	17.98	0.615	16.67
		−0.145 (−0.44)			−0.152 (−0.25)		0.387	17.93	0.594	15.32
			−1.298 (−1.18)			0.817 (0.40)	0.386	13.04	0.600	11.49
Utilities	−0.143 (−0.49)			−0.704 (−1.37)			0.294	40.39	0.222	19.48
		0.158 (0.95)			−0.003 (−0.01)		0.295	40.58	0.212	18.99
			−0.597 (−0.98)			−1.472 (−1.19)	0.293	29.11	0.218	16.95
Business	0.264 (1.24)			0.213 (0.43)			0.391	47.06	0.008	12.06
		0.014 (0.11)			0.512 * (1.95)		0.388	46.55	0.103	11.89
			−0.352 (−0.77)			0.781 (0.37)	0.388	33.57	0.100	11.72
Financial	−0.013 (−0.02)			−1.008 (−0.64)			0.508	10.10	0.306	12.23
		0.828 (1.57)			1.594 * (1.87)		0.538	11.22	0.479	13.56
			−0.157 (−0.12)			−0.170 (−0.43)	0.514	7.63	0.628	14.93
Industry	0.030 (0.22)			0.297 ** (2.27)			0.258	137.16	0.260	112.18
		−0.149 * (−1.79)			0.023 (0.26)		0.260	138.01	0.258	110.80
			0.128 (0.45)			0.228 (0.80)	0.259	98.53	0.260	80.18
Real estate	0.051 (0.23)			−0.034 (−0.06)			0.331	35.53	0.321	16.59
		−0.004 (−0.04)			−0.125 (−0.33)		0.331	35.52	0.323	16.62
			−0.517 (−1.07)			1.899 (1.63)	0.329	25.48	0.331	15.16

t-statistics in parentheses *** $p < 0.01$, ** $p < 0.05$, * $p < 0.1$; Source: Authors' own research, 2019.

5. Conclusions

The literature on herding biases is confined to detection at the aggregate firms, sector/industry, and market level. The study adds to the behavioral finance literature by addressing the surprisingly unnoticed phenomena of the behavioral impact of herding bias on FV at the firm level, using the sample of 1,043 A-Shares listed firms at the SSE and SZSE under fixed effect specification. Initially, we detect the existence of IHR and MHR biases at firm-level applying a CSAD model [15,35] and an investment model of firms' investment absolute deviation approach [6,22]. After such detection, we deploy the panel fixed-effect model with industry and years dummies to investigate the effect of: (1) IHR on FV, (2) MHR on FV and (3) interaction of IHR, and MHR on the FV respectively.

The empirical results document the presence of IHR and MHR bias at market, sector and firm-level in both equity markets, which potentially drive the FV, while the impact is more pronounced during the extreme trading period i.e., 2014 to 2015. The findings are robust under different time intervals and industry classification, and therefore, offers useful policy implications to understand the behavioral dynamics of investors and managers.

Given the vital role of finance in economic sustainability, the study adds invaluable inputs for policy formulation [59,60], specifically, the findings appear to be important for potential investors, as the firm-level financial information is more relevant to their decision, rather relying on an index. Specifically, we infer that the negative interaction of IHR with MHR results in a bullish trend to the stock markets, while the bearish trend is explained by the positive interaction of IHR and MHR. The probability of a market crash may become higher in those circumstances when both negative IHR and MHR interact with each other and cause the FV to decline. Furthermore, this study infersthat at the SSE, if IHR and MHR shift from insignificance to positive significance, it might be the signal of a sudden boom in the market. Whereas, at the SZSE, this suggests that when a positive and significant impact of IHR disappears with the negative impact of MHR, this might be the reason for the sudden decline in trading activity, and vice versa. Thus, the study facilitates to understand the herding biases associated with the investment decisions of investors and managers and their impact on the FV that help corporate stakeholders, financial analysts and stock market regulators to devise their strategic and regulatory policies accordingly.

Author Contributions: S.S.H.S., M.A.K., and J.O. conceived and designed the experiment; S.S.H.S. analyzed the data; N.M., contributed analysis tool, and S.S.H.S., M.A.K., and D.F.M. wrote the paper.

References

1. Foucault, T.; Sraer, D.; Thesmar, D.J. Individual investors and volatility. *J. Finance* **2011**, *66*, 1369–1406. [CrossRef]
2. Barber, B.M.; Odean, T. Trading is hazardous to your wealth: The common stock investment performance of individual investors. *J. Finance* **2000**, *55*, 773–806. [CrossRef]
3. Kumar, S.; Goyal, N. Behavioural biases in investment decision making–a systematic literature review. *Qual. Res. Financ. Mark.* **2015**, *7*, 88–108. [CrossRef]
4. Garber, P.M. *Famous first bubbles: The fundamentals of early manias*; The mit Press: London, UK, 2001.
5. Christie, W.G.; Huang, R.D. Following the pied piper: Do individual returns herd around the market? *Financ. Anal. J.* **1995**, *51*, 31–37. [CrossRef]
6. Alabass, H.S.H.H. The Impact Of Corporate Investment Behaviour On The Corporate Performance. Available online: https://www.abacademies.org/articles/the-impact-of-corporate-investment-behaviour-on-the-corporate-performance-evidence-from-an-emerging-market-7800.html (accessed on 20 July 2019).
7. Blasco, N.; Corredor, P.; Ferreruela, S. Herding, Volatility, and Market Stress in the Spanish Stock Market. In *Handbook of Investors' Behavior During Financial Crises*; Economou, F., Gavriilidis, K., Gregoriuo, N.G., Kallinterakis, V., Eds.; Elsevier: Amsterdam, The Netherlands, 2017; pp. 151–168.
8. Chen, C.D.; Demirer, R. The profitability of herding: Evidence from Taiwan. *Manage. Financ.* **2018**, *44*, 919–934. [CrossRef]
9. Bikhchandani, S.; Hirshleifer, D.; Welch, I. A theory of fads, fashion, custom, and cultural change as informational cascades. *J. Polit. Econ.* **1992**, *100*, 992–1026. [CrossRef]
10. Krkoska, E.; Schenk-Hoppé, K.R. Herding in Smart-Beta Investment Products. *J. Risk Financ. Manage.* **2019**, *12*, 47. [CrossRef]
11. Choi, N.; Sias, R.W. Institutional industry herding. *J. Financ. Econ.* **2009**, *94*, 469–491. [CrossRef]
12. Wang, Q.; Zhang, J. Does individual investor trading impact firm valuation? *J. Corp. Finan.* **2015**, *35*, 120–135. [CrossRef]

13. Mobarek, A.; Mollah, S.; Keasey, K. A cross-country analysis of herd behavior in Europe. *J. Int. Financ. Mark. I.* **2014**, *32*, 107–127. [CrossRef]
14. Walter, A.; Moritz Weber, F. Herding in the German Mutual Fund Industry. *Eur. Financ. Manag.* **2006**, *12*, 375–406. [CrossRef]
15. Chang, E.C.; Cheng, J.W.; Khorana, A. An examination of herd behavior in equity markets: An international perspective. *J. Bank. Financ.* **2000**, *24*, 1651–1679. [CrossRef]
16. Chiang, T.C.; Li, J.; Tan, L. Empirical investigation of herding behavior in Chinese stock markets: Evidence from quantile regression analysis. *Global Finance J.* **2010**, *21*, 111–124. [CrossRef]
17. Demirer, R.; Zhang, H. Do firm characteristics matter in explaining the herding effect on returns? *Rev. Financ. Econ.* **2019**, *37*, 256–271. [CrossRef]
18. Zhang, F.; Li, M.; Zhang, M. Chinese Financial Market Investors Attitudes toward Corporate Social Responsibility: Evidence from Mergers and Acquisitions. *Sustainability* **2019**, *11*, 2615. [CrossRef]
19. Demirer, R.; Kutan, A.M. Does herding behavior exist in Chinese stock markets? *J. Int. Financ. Mark. I.* **2006**, *16*, 123–142. [CrossRef]
20. Demirer, R.; Gupta, R.; Lv, Z.; Wong, W.-K. Equity Return Dispersion and Stock Market Volatility: Evidence from Multivariate Linear and Nonlinear Causality Tests. *Sustainability* **2019**, *11*, 351. [CrossRef]
21. Tan, L.; Chiang, T.C.; Mason, J.R.; Nelling, E. Herding behavior in Chinese stock markets: An examination of A and B shares. *Pac.-Basin Financ. J.* **2008**, *16*, 61–77. [CrossRef]
22. Bo, H.; Li, T.; Sun, Y. Board attributes and herding in corporate investment: Evidence from Chinese-listed firms. *Eur. J. Finance* **2013**, *22*, 432–462. [CrossRef]
23. Lao, P.; Singh, H. Herding behaviour in the Chinese and Indian stock markets. *J. Asian Econ.* **2011**, *22*, 495–506. [CrossRef]
24. Lee, C.C.; Chen, M.P.; Hsieh, K.M. Industry herding and market states: Evidence from Chinese stock markets. *Quant. Financ.* **2013**, *13*, 1091–1113. [CrossRef]
25. Yao, J.; Ma, C.; He, W.P. Investor herding behaviour of Chinese stock market. *Int. Rev. Econ. Finance.* **2014**, *29*, 12–39. [CrossRef]
26. Cheng, A.W.W.; Chow, N.S.C.; Chui, D.K.H.; Wong, W.K. The Three Musketeers Relationships between Hong Kong, Shanghai and Shenzhen Before and After Shanghai–Hong Kong Stock Connect. *Sustainability* **2019**, *11*, 3845. [CrossRef]
27. Cho, C.H.; Yang, L.J.; Chu, Y.P.; Yang, H.Y. Renewable Energy and Renewable R&D in EU Countries: A Cointegration Analysis. 2013. Available online: http://www.ajsc.leena-luna.co.jp/AJSCPDFs/Vol.2(1)/AJSC2013(2.1-02).pdf (accessed on 20 February 2019).
28. Shah, M.U.D.; Shah, A.; Khan, S.U. Herding behavior in the Pakistan stock exchange: Some new insights. *Res. Int. Business Finance* **2017**, *42*, 865–873. [CrossRef]
29. Grinblatt, M.; Titman, S.; Wermers, R. Momentum investment strategies, portfolio performance, and herding: A study of mutual fund behavior. *Am. Econ. Rev.* **1995**, *85*, 1088–1105. Available online: https://www.jstor.org/stable/2950976?seq=1#page_scan_tab_contents (accessed on 20 July 2019).
30. Welch, I. Herding Among Security Analysts. *J. Financ. Econ.* **2005**, *58*, 369–396. [CrossRef]
31. Lakonishok, J.; Schleifer, A.; Vishny, R. *Do Institutional Investors Destabilize Share Prices? Evidence on Herding and Feedback Trading*; National Bureau of Economic Research Inc.: Cambridge, MA, USA, 1991.
32. Bueno, P.B. *Social Risks in Aquaculture*; Bondad-Reantaso, M.G., Arthur, J.R., Subasinghe, R.P., Eds.; FAO: Rome, Italy, 2008; pp. 209–228.
33. Chiang, T.C.; Zheng, D. An empirical analysis of herd behavior in global stock markets. *J. Bank. Financ.* **2010**, *34*, 1911–1921. [CrossRef]
34. Balcilar, M.; Demirer, R.; Hammoudeh, S. Investor herds and regime-switching: Evidence from Gulf Arab stock markets. *J. Int. Financ. Mark. I.* **2013**, 295–321. [CrossRef]
35. Zheng, D.; Li, H.; Chiang, T.C. Herding within industries: Evidence from Asian stock markets. *Int. Rev. Econ. Financ.* **2017**, *51*, 487–509. [CrossRef]
36. Javed, T.; Zafar, N.; Hafeez, B. Herding behavior in Karachi stock exchange. *Int. J. Manag. Sci. Bus. Res.* **2011**, *2*, 19–28. [CrossRef]
37. Javaira, Z.; Hassan, A. An examination of herding behavior in Pakistani stock market. *Int. J. Emerg. Mark.* **2015**, *10*, 474–490. [CrossRef]

38. Yousaf, I.; Ali, S.; Shah, S.Z.A. Herding behavior in Ramadan and financial crises: The case of the Pakistani stock market. *Financ. Innov.* **2018**, *4*, 1–16. [CrossRef]
39. Munkh-Ulzii, B.; McAleer, M.; Moslehpour, M.; Wong, W.K. Confucius and herding behaviour in the stock markets in China and Taiwan. *Sustainability* **2018**, *10*, 4413. [CrossRef]
40. Chong, T.T.L.; Liu, X.; Zhu, C. What explains herd behavior in the Chinese stock market? *J. Behav. Finance* **2017**, *18*, 448–456. [CrossRef]
41. Huberman, G. Familiarity Breeds Investment. *Rev. Financ. Stud.* **2005**, *4*, 659–680. Available online: https://ideas.repec.org/a/oup/rfinst/v14y2001i3p659-80.html (accessed on 20 July 2019).
42. Ha, T.V. Price limit regulation and herd behavior in the Vietnamese stock market. 2007. Available online: https://www.researchgate.net/profile/Tran_Ha4/publication/242124528_Price_limit_regulation_and_herd_behavior_in_the_Vietnamese_stock_market/links/5419c8d30cf2218008bfa031.pdf (accessed on 20 July 2019).
43. Fama, E.F.; French, K.R. The cross-section of expected stock returns. *J. Finance* **1992**, *47*, 427–465. [CrossRef]
44. Van Nieuwerburgh, S.; Veldkamp, L. Information immobility and the home bias puzzle. *J. Finance* **2009**, *64*, 1187–1215. [CrossRef]
45. Sadaf, R.; Oláh, J.; Popp, J.; Máté, D. An investigation of the influence of the worldwide governance and competitiveness on accounting fraud cases: A cross-country perspective. *Sustainability* **2018**, *10*, 588. [CrossRef]
46. Gebka, B.; Wohar, M.E. Causality between trading volume and returns: Evidence from quantile regressions. *I. R. E. F.* **2013**, *27*, 144–159. [CrossRef]
47. Hilliard, J.; Zhang, H. Size and price-to-book effects: Evidence from the Chinese stock markets. *Pac.-Basin Financ. J.* **2015**, *32*, 40–55. [CrossRef]
48. Prendergast, C.; Stole, L. Impetuous youngsters and jaded old-timers: Acquiring a reputation for learning. *J. Political Econ.* **1996**, *104*, 1105–1134. Available online: https://www.journals.uchicago.edu/doi/pdfplus/10.1086/262055 (accessed on 20 July 2019). [CrossRef]
49. Fong, K.; Gallagher, D.R.; Gardner, P.; Swan, P.L. A closer examination of investment manager herding behavior. Sydney, AU. 2004; Unpublished manuscript.
50. Devenow, A.; Welch, I. Rational herding in financial economics. *Eur. Econ. Rev.* **1996**, *40*, 603–615. [CrossRef]
51. Malmendier, U.; Tate, G. CEO overconfidence and corporate investment. *J. Finance* **2005**, *60*, 2661–2700. [CrossRef]
52. Demsetz, H.; Villalonga, B. Ownership structure and corporate performance. *J. Corp. Financ.* **2001**, *7*, 209–233. [CrossRef]
53. Chung, K.H.; Pruitt, S.W. A Simple Approximation of Tobin's q. *Financ. Manage.* **1994**, *23*, 70–74. [CrossRef]
54. Chen, I.J.; Lin, S.H. Will Managerial Optimism Affect the Investment Efficiency of a Firm? *Proc. Econ. Financ.* **2012**, *2*, 73–80. [CrossRef]
55. Ahmad, I.; Oláh, J.; Popp, J.; Máté, D. Does business group affiliation matter for superior performance? Evidence from Pakistan. *Sustainability* **2018**, *10*, 3060. [CrossRef]
56. Javed, H.; Bagh, T.; Razzaq, S. Herding Effects, Over Confidence, Availability Bias and Representativeness as Behavioral Determinants of Perceived Investment Performance: An Empirical Evidence from Pakistan Stock Exchange (PSX). *J. Glob. Econ.* **2017**, *6*, 2. [CrossRef]
57. Fosu, S.; Danso, A.; Ahmad, W.; Coffie, W. Information asymmetry, leverage and firm value: Do crisis and growth matter? *I. R. F. A.* **2016**, *46*, 140–150. [CrossRef]
58. Ni, Y.; Huang, P.; Chiang, P.; Liao, Y. Cash flow statements and firm value: Evidence from Taiwan. *Q. Rev. Econ. Finance* **2019**, *71*, 280–290. [CrossRef]
59. Khan, M.A.; Kong, D.; Xiang, J.; Zhang, J. Impact of Institutional Quality on Financial Development: Cross-Country Evidence based on Emerging and Growth-Leading Economies. *Emerg. Mark. Financ. Trade* **2019**, 1–17. [CrossRef]
60. Khan, M.A.; Khan, M.A.; Abdulahi, M.E.; Liaqat, I.; Shah, S.S.H. Institutional quality and financial development: The United States perspective. *J. Multinatl. Financ. Manag.* **2019**, *49*, 67–80. [CrossRef]

8

An Event Study Analysis of Political Events, Disasters and Accidents for Chinese Tourists to Taiwan

Chia-Lin Chang [1,2,3], Shu-Han Hsu [1] and Michael McAleer [3,4,5,6,7,*]

1 Department of Applied Economics, National Chung Hsing University, Taichung 402, Taiwan; changchialin@email.nchu.edu.tw (C.-L.C.); h31944@gmail.com (S.-H.H.)
2 Department of Finance, National Chung Hsing University, Taichung 402, Taiwan
3 Department of Finance, Asia University, Taichung 41354, Taiwan
4 Discipline of Business Analytics, University of Sydney Business School, Sydney 2006, Australia
5 Econometric Institute, Erasmus School of Economics, Erasmus University Rotterdam, 3000 Rotterdam, The Netherlands
6 Department of Economic Analysis and ICAE, Complutense University of Madrid, 28040 Madrid, Spain
7 Institute of Advanced Sciences, Yokohama National University, Yokohama 240-8501, Japan
* Correspondence: michael.mcaleer@gmail.com

Abstract: The number of Chinese tourists visiting Taiwan has been closely related to the political relationship across the Taiwan Strait. The occurrence of political events and disasters or accidents have had, and will continue to have, a huge impact on the Taiwan tourism market. To date, there has been relatively little empirical research conducted on this issue. Tourists are characterized as being involved in one of three types of tourism: group tourism (group-type), individual tourism (individual-type), and medical cosmetology (medical-type). We use the fundamental equation in tourism finance to examine the correlation that exists between the rate of change in the number of tourists and the rate of return on tourism. Second, we use the event study method to observe whether the numbers of tourists have changed abnormally before and after the occurrence of major events on both sides of the Strait. Three different types of conditional variance models, namely, the Generalized Autoregressive Conditional Heteroscedasticity, GARCH (1,1), Glosten, Jagannathan and Runkle, GJR (1,1) and Exponential GARCH, EGARCH (1,1), are used to estimate the abnormal rate of change in the number of tourists. The empirical results concerning the major events affecting the changes in the numbers of tourists from China to Taiwan are economically significant, and confirm the types of tourists that are most likely to be affected by such major events.

Keywords: event study; abnormal rate of change; Chinese tourists; OLS; GARCH; GJR; EGARCH; tourism finance

JEL: G14; C22; C52; C58

---

1. Introduction

According to statistics compiled by Taiwan's Tourism Bureau under its Ministry of Transportation and Communications for the year 2016, international visitors to Taiwan mostly came from five regions, namely, China and Hong Kong (including Macao), Japan, South Korea, Malaysia, and Singapore. However, from 2010 onwards, with the relaxation of the Cross-Strait tourism policy, the number of tourists to Taiwan from China markedly increased, reaching 3.43 million by the end of 2015, accounting for 45.80% of the total number of international visitors to Taiwan. The number of Chinese tourists in 2016, nevertheless, appears to have exhibited a significantly downward trend (see Figure 1).

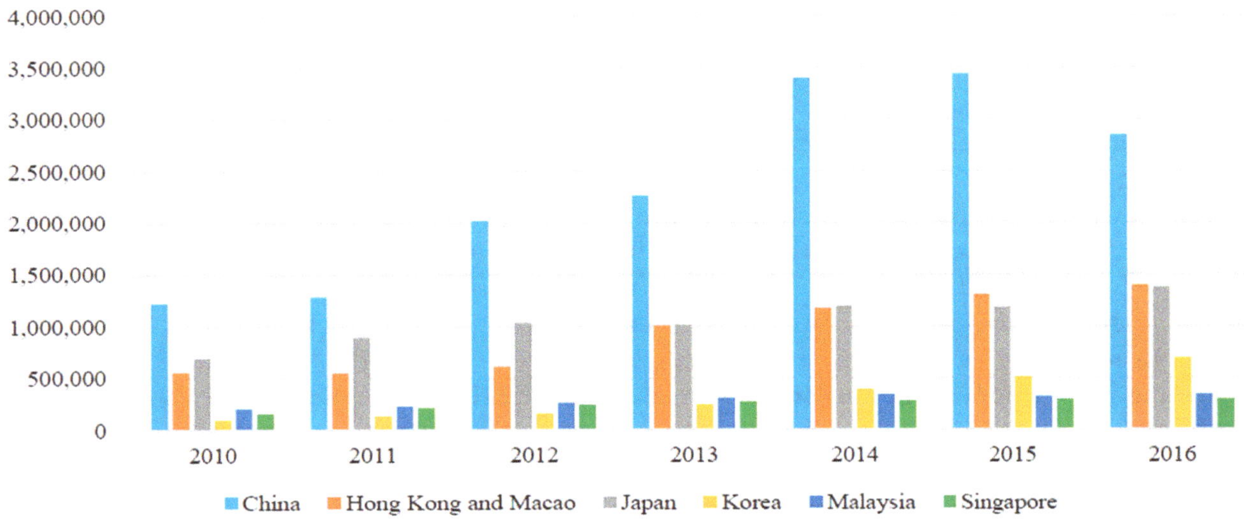

Figure 1. Top five international tourist arrivals to Taiwan, 2010–2016. Sources: Taiwan Tourism Bureau (2017).

The number of Chinese tourists coming to Taiwan has been very closely related to the political relationship across the Taiwan Strait. Beginning in 1949, when the Chinese Communist Party announced the establishment of the People's Republic of China, and the Republic of China relocated to Taiwan, a period of mutual confrontation and division between the two sides ensued, and both sides held fast to the principle of there being only one China. In 1987, after Taiwan announced the lifting of martial law, citizens of Taiwan were allowed to travel to China to visit relatives.

On 1 January 2001, Taiwan piloted its "Three Small Links" policy, whereby mainland Chinese were allowed to apply to visit the offshore islands of Kinmen and Matsu for sightseeing, and passengers on both sides of the Taiwan Strait could travel to and from these islands. On 1 January 2002, mainland Chinese who had gone overseas to study, or who had acquired permanent residence in another foreign country, were allowed to visit Taiwan. On 1 May 2002, mainland Chinese who were allowed to travel on business trips abroad were permitted to visit Taiwan, but they needed to pass through a third country before entering Taiwan.

With the Kuomintang President Ma Ying-Jeou's substantial relaxation of restrictions on Cross-Straits tourism in 2008, group-type tourism by Chinese to visit Taiwan was allowed. On 22 June 2011, the restrictions were further relaxed to allow individual-type travel to Taiwan by Chinese citizens. So far, Taiwan has allowed people in 47 cities in China to apply for individual-type travel to Taiwan, subject to a maximum number of 6000 applications per day. On 1 January 2012, Taiwan relaxed the restrictions on medical-type tourism, so that Chinese citizens could travel to Taiwan for health checks and/or for cosmetic treatments.

In the increasingly competitive tourism market, the willingness of Chinese tourists to travel in Taiwan has not only been affected by the relaxation of tourism policies across the Taiwan Strait, but also by the complicated and close Cross-Straits political relationship and concerns over tourism safety in Taiwan. The occurrence of political events and disasters or accidents have had, and will continue to have, a huge impact on the Taiwan tourism market, although so far, there has been relatively little empirical research conducted on this issue.

For this reason, this paper uses Chinese tourists as the major focus of its analysis to examine whether or not major events that have taken place on both sides of the Strait in the past three years have given rise to abnormal changes in the number of visitors to Taiwan. Moreover, the paper compares the reactions of the group-type, individual-type, and medical-type tourists to these major events.

The important events are divided into political events and disasters/accidents, and tourists are characterized as being involved in one of three types of tourism: group tourism (group-type), individual tourism (individual-type), and medical cosmetology (medical-type). First, we use McAleer's [1] fundamental equation in tourism finance to examine the correlation that exists between the rate of change in the number of tourists, and the rate of return on tourism. Second, we use the event study method to observe whether the numbers of tourists have changed abnormally before and after the occurrence of major events on both sides of the Strait.

With regard to the estimation method used to calculate the abnormal changes in the numbers of tourists, in addition to using the Ordinary Least squares (OLS) method that is most commonly used in the historical literature, we also consider the rate of change in the number of tourists and the time-varying variance in the residuals. To this end, we use three different types of conditional variance models, namely Generalized Autoregressive Conditional Heteroscedasticity, GARCH (1,1), Glosten, Jagannathan and Runkle, GJR (1,1) and Exponential GARCH, EGARCH (1,1), to estimate the abnormal rate of change in the number of tourists. In this way, we intend to obtain a more accurate estimate of the abnormal rate of change in the number of tourists.

The empirical results concerning the major events affecting the changes in the numbers of tourists from China to Taiwan are economically significant, and they confirm which types of tourists are more likely to be affected by such major events. These results can serve as a valuable reference to the Taiwan government, and to public and private policy-makers as they formulate new economic and financial tourism policies in the future.

The remainder of the paper is organized as follows. In Section 2, the background and literature are reviewed. In Section 3, the empirical models are presented. The data and variables are described in Section 4. In Section 5, the empirical results are analyzed. Some concluding comments are given in Section 6.

2. Background and Literature

It can be difficult to assess the demand for events in tourist destinations. In the following section, we break down the major events of both a political nature, as well as disasters and accidents, to focus our attention on windows in time that are easier to analyze on an individual basis.

2.1. Identifying the Cross-Strait Events in 2014–2016

Changes in Cross-Straits political stances and the environment may bring about abnormal changes in the numbers of tourists visiting Taiwan. The political orientation has always been an important event that has plagued the authorities on both sides, especially with the constant strengthening of the subjective consciousness of the Taiwanese and the united consciousness of the mainland Chinese, which has led to an extremely sensitive relationship between the two. After the Kuomintang's presidential candidate Ma Ying-Jeou took office in 2008, the "1992 Consensus, according to which both sides recognize that there is only one China, but have different opinions on what that means" (The "1992 Consensus, where both sides recognize only one China, but have different opinions", developed through the mutual non-recognition of sovereignty, mutual non-denial of each other's jurisdiction, and reciprocity and mutual benefit), was used in the institutionalized consultations between the two sides, in the hope that peaceful and stable development between the two could be maintained.

However, in 2016 there was a switch in the ruling party in Taiwan, with the election of the Democratic Progressive Party's candidate, Tsai Ing-Wen, as the Republic of China's 14th President. While it was still hoped that the peaceful and stable development of the two sides of the Straits would be maintained, in her inaugural presidential speech, President Tsai did not mention the one-China principle, thereby causing China to feel dissatisfied, and the Cross-Straits political relationship was once again affected.

A summary of the important political events that occurred on the two sides of the Taiwan Strait over the 2014–2016 period is provided below. These are also presented in Table 1.

18 March 2014–10 April 2014–The Sunflower Youth Movement: The social movement that resulted in the occupation of the Taiwan legislature by students was mainly in response to the opposition to the Kuomintang's forced passing of the review by the committee on the Cross-Straits Agreement on Trade in Services. This led to the formation of a social movement that resulted in the occupation of the Legislative Yuan by Taiwanese students and various civic groups. This event attracted the attention of people from all walks of life, and also impacted the implementation of various Cross-Straits agreements.

Table 1. Literature review of event studies.

Disaster and Accident Events		
Mazzocchi and Montini (2001)	26 September 1997	Magnitude 5.9 earthquake in Umbria (Italy)
Tao (2014)	20 April 2013	Magnitude 7.0 earthquake in Lushan (China)
Chen et al. (2007)	22 April 2003	SARS (Severe Acute Respiratory Syndrome) in Taiwan
Political Events		
Johnson et al. (2015)	4 March 2010	Travel Promotion Act of 2000
Economic Events		
Nicolau (2002)	1997–1999	New hotel openings announcement in Spain
Szutowski and Bednarska (2014)		Innovation announcement from tourism enterprises in Poland
International Competitions		
Dick and Wang (2010)	1988–2014	The Olympic Games announcement
Ogawa (2017)	9 September 2013	Tokyo 2020 Summer Olympic Games announcement

29 November 2014—Taiwan's nine-in-one local elections: These were the largest local elections for public officials in Taiwan's political history. The Kuomintang (KMT) won six seats (compared to the 15 seats it held before the election), while the Democratic Progressive Party (DPP) won 13 seats (compared to the six seats it held before the election), and independent candidates won three seats. The KMT (the ruling party) suffered an unprecedented defeat, and former president Ma Ying-jeou resigned as chairman of the KMT. This election outcome had a short-term impact on Cross-Straits relations.

7 November 2015—Ma-Xi Summit: The top leaders of Taiwan and China met at the Shangri-La Hotel in Singapore for the first time since the two sides of the Taiwan Strait became politically separated in 1949. Although the two sides did not sign an agreement or issue a joint statement, the meeting nevertheless constituted a major breakthrough in Cross-Straits relations.

16 January 2016—Taiwan's 14th presidential election and Taiwan's ninth legislative election: In Taiwan's third political party rotation, with Tsai Ing-wen being elected as Taiwan's 14th President, the DPP took charge of the executive administration and controlled over half the seats in the Legislative Yuan, a symbol of the Democratic Progressive Party being totally in power.

20 May 2016—Taiwan 14th Presidential inauguration: At her inauguration ceremony as Taiwan's 14th President, while Tsai Ing-wen advocated the maintenance of goodwill and peace across the Taiwan Strait, she did not clearly express the one-China principle, which again caused China to feel dissatisfied, thereby leading to a stalemate in Cross-Strait relations. As rumors that Chinese officials were setting limits on the numbers of Chinese tourists that would be allowed to visit Taiwan continued to spread, the willingness of Chinese tourists to visit Taiwan was indirectly affected.

18 September 2016—Taiwan mayors visit China: This was a visit by the mayors of eight counties and cities in Taiwan to Beijing to support the cooperation and exchange event to promote "China's eight measures to benefit Taiwan".

In addition to unavoidable natural disasters, tourism safety is also one of the factors that affects tourists' decisions regarding whether or not to visit a country or region. According to the Ministry of Transportation and Communications of the Republic of China, since 2008 when Taiwan relaxed restrictions to allow Chinese tourists to fly directly to and from Taiwan, 90 Chinese tourists have been killed and 390 injured in Taiwan. The following is a list of the major accidents on the two sides of the Strait between 2014 and 2016.

31 July 2014—The Kaohsiung Petrochemical gas explosion: This caused serious damage to a number of important roads in Kaohsiung, and resulted in 32 deaths and 321 people injured.

4 September 2014—Taiwan's "gutter oil" scandal: Illegal use by manufacturers of inferior-quality oil products: Taiwan's food safety issues caught the attention of the Chinese government. By immediately going through "Cross-Strait food safety agreement" channels, a comprehensive survey of food products imported into Taiwan has been conducted to maintain food safety.

6 February 2016—Kaohsiung's magnitude 6.6 Meinong earthquake: This resulted in 117 deaths and 551 people injured. The Yongkang District of Tainan suffered the most serious casualties (a total of 115 deaths), with the collapse of a large residential building. In addition, the frequency of the aftershocks following the incident resulted in increased uncertainty regarding the safety of tourists.

1 July 2016—95th Anniversary of the founding of the Communist Party of China: In commemoration of this special day, in the morning of that day, as the Taiwan Navy was conducting training operations, it accidentally fired a Hsiung Feng series 3 anti-ship missile, which resulted in the captain of a Kaohsiung fishing boat being killed and three of his crew members injured. The Taiwan government stressed that this unfortunate incident was due to negligence on the part of staff, and not political factors. This event added to the tensions between the two sides.

During the period 2014–2016, there were two major accidents involving transportation, the first being the crash of TransAsia Airways Flight No. 235 that took place on 4 February 2015; the plane came down in Taipei City, plunging into the Keelung River and killing 43 people, of whom 28 were Chinese tourists. The second major incident took place on 19 July 2016, when a tour bus, in which a tour group from Liaoning in China was travelling, struck a roadside guardrail on the way to Taoyuan Airport and immediately burst into flames, leaving a total of 26 dead.

In summary, over the 2014–2016 period, there were six important political events and disasters/accidents that occurred in Taiwan and China. These important events during 2014–2016 are listed chronologically in Figure 2.

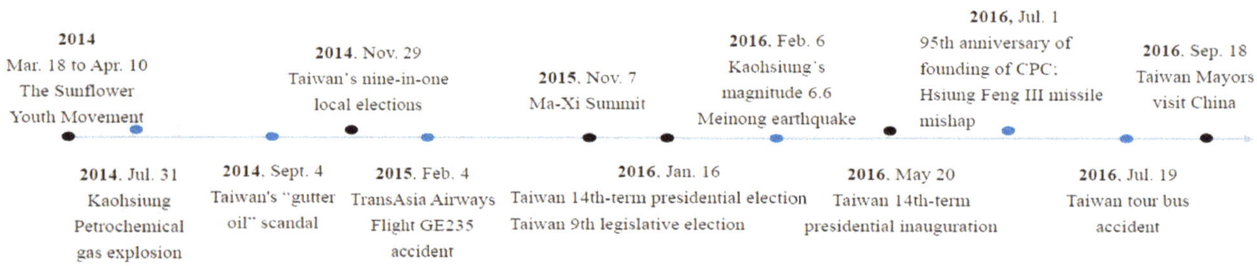

Figure 2. Major Cross-Strait events, 2014–2016.

2.2. Literature Review of Event Studies

The event study method dates back to 1933, when Dolley [2] studied the impact of stock segmentation on stock prices. The approach was subsequently widely used in the fields of economics, finance, and accounting (Ball and Brown [3]; Fama et al. [4]; Fama [5]; Boehmer et al. [6]; MacKinlay [7]; Binder [8]; Corrado [9]). The event study method has also been used in tourism research. A summary of the literature on the application of the event study approach to tourism-related issues is provided below.

Mazzocchi and Montini [10] examined the impact of the 26 September 1997 magnitude 5.9 earthquake on the flow of tourists in the Umbria region of central Italy using the event study approach. They used data covering the period January 1988–July 1998, with a particular focus on the months in which visits by tourists stopped, in order to analyze the impact of the earthquake on tourists' total number of visits. In estimation, OLS was used to estimate the average number of visits by tourists, and Patell's [11] standardized residual test was applied to estimate any abnormal changes in the number of these visits. The empirical results showed that the earthquake had a significant abnormal impact on the numbers of visits by both local tourists and foreign tourists. The number of visits by local tourists decreased by more than that for foreign tourists. In a comparison of local tourists with foreign tourists in terms of the economic losses brought about by the earthquake, for domestic tourists, the economic losses were also greater than for foreign tourists, amounting to as much as US$ 5.19 million.

Tao [12] used the event study method to study the economic impact on China's stock market of the magnitude-7.0 earthquake that occurred on 20 April 2013 in Lushan, Sichuan Province, China. The daily trading data for the China stock market included the Shanghai Composite Index, the Shenzhen Component Index, and the CSI 300 Index. Using data covering the period 20 April 2012–19 April 2013, Tao analyzed the impact of the Lushan earthquake on stock market returns. He used OLS to estimate the expected average abnormal returns, and the t-statistic to inspect the abnormal returns. The empirical results showed that the Lushan earthquake did not significantly impact the stock returns of the Shanghai Composite Index, the Shenzhen Component Index, or the CSI 300 Index. Tao attributed the reason for this to the fact that the region where the earthquake struck was not developed, and hence the impact on the economic benefits was not significant.

Nicolau [13] used the event study method to examine the impact of a hotel's announcement that it was opening for business on the stock price returns in the hotel industry. The stock prices and IBEX-35 index daily trading data for 42 newly-opened hotels listed on the Spanish Stock Exchange located in Madrid from 1997–1999 were analyzed. The GARCH(1,1) model was used to estimate the average abnormal stock returns, and Boehmer et al.'s [6] standardized cross-sectional method and Corrado's [14] non-parametric test were used to test the abnormal returns resulting from the changes in stocks. The empirical results showed that the hotel's announcement that it was opening for business had a significantly positive impact on the hotel's stock price on the day, in 61.9% of the cases.

Chen et al. [15] used the event study approach to examine the impact of the outbreak of SARS (Severe Acute Respiratory Syndrome) on the stock prices of publicly-traded hotel stock. Using the period 2 May 2002–7 April 2003 for estimation, attention was particularly focused on the 10 days and 20 days prior to and after the event date of 22 April 2003. The study used OLS, GARCH(1,1), GJR(1,1) and EGARCH(1,1) to estimate the accumulated average abnormal returns. The empirical results showed that the outbreak of the SARS epidemic after the Taiwan hotel stock price compensation had a significantly negative impact on hotel stock price returns in Taiwan.

Dick and Wang [16] used the event study method to examine the impact of announcements made by the International Olympic Committee (IOC), on which cities would host the games, on the major stock index returns of the winning and losing countries. Data covering the period 1988–2014 in relation to 15 announcements as to which countries would host future Olympic Games were used in the event study. OLS was applied to estimate the cumulative average abnormal returns, and the t-statistic was used to inspect the abnormal returns. The empirical results showed that the announcements regarding the cities that had been selected to host the Olympic Games indicated that the cumulative average abnormal returns of the stock indexes in those countries in which the cities that had placed first in the selection process had increased by about 2%, while the stock index returns of those countries that were ranked last were not significantly affected. Announcements regarding the selection as to which cities would host the Winter Olympics also did not have a significant impact on the respective countries' stock returns.

Ogawa [17] used the event study approach to analyze the impact of large-scale sporting activities on the yields of Japanese Real Estate Investment Trusts (J-REITs). Data were used for a total of 41 J-REITs quoted on the Tokyo Stock Exchange with 18 July 2013–8 September 2013 as the estimation period (there being 37 trading days after holidays were excluded), and 9 September 2013 was regarded as the event date. OLS was used to estimate the average abnormal returns, and the t-statistic was used to examine the abnormal returns. The empirical results showed that Japan's winning the bid to be selected to host the 2020 Olympic Games had both a positive and significant impact on the overall returns to real estate stocks, and the effect on J-REITs, with a particular emphasis on hotels in terms of average abnormal returns, was relatively large.

Szutowski and Bednarska [18] applied the event study method to examine the impact of tourism business announcements on stock market value. Stock price data obtained from the Warsaw Stock Exchange (WSE) and 34 innovative news reports and seven innovative types in the last six years were used in conducting the analysis. The estimation period was set to cover 250 days before the event, and the event period was established as covering 10 days before and 10 days after the announcement. OLS was used to estimate the cumulative average abnormal returns, and the Szyszka [19] J-statistic was used to check the abnormal returns. The empirical results showed that the impact of the innovative announcements by the tourism businesses on the stock market abnormal returns was 0.63%, and the cumulative average abnormal returns reached 2% during the five days before and 5 days after the announcement was made.

Johnson et al. [20] used the event study method to examine the impact of the Travel Promotion Act (TPA) of 2000 on stock price returns. They used data obtained from the Center for Research in Security Prices (CRSP), and for Real Estate Investment Trusts (REITs) in performing their analysis. With the estimation period covering 255 trading days in which the event date fell (4 March 2010), and an event period (which covered the day of the event, the day before the event and the day after the event), they used OLS to estimate the cumulative average abnormal returns and the z-statistic to test the cumulative average abnormal returns. The empirical results showed that the US Travel Promotion Act had a significant positive impact on the hotel industry's stock price returns. In addition, the large hotel chains were found to benefit more as a result of the TPA than smaller hotel chains.

In summary, when used in research related to tourism issues, the event study method has mainly been used to examine the impact of changes in the tourism environment on financial markets. The scope of the events considered includes the tourism natural environment (disaster and accident events), tourism cultural environment (political events, economic events, and international competitions), and tourism resources. These studies are classified according to different events, as shown in Table 1. Furthermore, the results of the studies has indicated that the changes in the tourism environment have a significant impact on both the number of tourist arrivals to a country, as well as its stock market returns. We have not found such connections in other studies.

3. Models

3.1. *Defining the Event Study's Period*

An event refers to new relevant information, which through its impact on stock prices determines whether it is a major event or not. Moreover, an event study as a form of empirical research is commonly used to investigate the impact of specific events in terms of abnormal returns in financial markets (MacKinlay [7], Binder [8], Corrado [9]). This method is derived from Fama's [5] efficient markets hypothesis (EMH), which posits that any financially-related information will immediately be reflected in stock prices.

The event study method is used to establish the difference between the counterfactual price that is not affected by the information, and the actual price, in order to estimate the price effect arising from the event (McWilliams and Siegel [21], Binder [8]). This paper uses the event study method to estimate the impact of Cross-Straits political and disaster-related incidents on Chinese tourists travelling to Taiwan.

When using the event study method, it is necessary to determine the event and the date on which the event first occurred (t_0), as well as the part of the estimation period that was not affected by the event ($T = t_2 - t_1 + 1$), and the event period ($W = t_4 - t_3 + 1$). The event study method does not have a set standard in terms of the period between the estimation period and the event period. From a review of the literature, it can be found that where the daily data are used, the estimation period tends to be in the range of 100 days to 300 days, while the event period is between 2 days and 121 days.

The events considered in this study include both political events and disaster-related incidents. The estimation period for political events ranges from 110 days prior to the date of the event, to 11 days before it ($t_1 = -110$ to $t_2 = -11$), and the event period ranges from 10 days before the political event to 20 days after it ($t_3 = -10$ to $t_4 = 20$). The estimation period for disaster-related incidents ranges from 100 days prior to the event to one day before it ($t_1 = -100$ to $t_2 = -1$), and the event period ranges from the date of the event to 30 days after it ($t_3 = 0$ to $t_4 = 30$). Regardless of whether the events are political or disaster-related, the estimation period is always 100 days, and the event period is 31 days, so that the period under observation covers a total of 131 days.

3.2. Fundamental Tourism Finance Equation and Tourism Financial Returns

McAleer [1] developed the fundamental tourism finance equation to connect the growth in the number of tourists and the returns on the associated tourism financial asset. The fundamental equation is used to derive the relationship between the change rate of tourist arrivals and the financial (tourism) returns, which is explained below.

Consider Equation (1), where total daily tourist expenditure, y_t, is equal to the daily total number of tourist arrivals, x_t, times the daily average expenditure by tourists, z_t, which is given by:

$$y_t = x_t \times z_t \tag{1}$$

It is argued in McAleer [1] that there is little evidence to suggest that the average daily expenditure by tourists, z_t , changes on a daily basis, so that z_t can be replaced by a constant, c, and Equation (1) can be replaced by:

$$y_t = c \times x_t$$

from which it follows that:

$$\Delta y_t = c \times \Delta x_t. \tag{2}$$

where Δ is the first difference operator. In Equation (2), Δy_t is the change in total daily tourism expenditure, and Δx_t is the change in the net daily tourist arrivals, where the net daily tourist arrivals is the total number of daily tourist arrivals minus the daily tourist departures.

Using the lagged version of Equation (1) to divide the left-hand side of Equation (2) by y_{t-1} and the right-hand side of Equation (3) by x_{t-1}, gives:

$$\frac{\Delta Y_t}{Y_{t-1}} = \frac{\Delta X_t}{X_{t-1}} \tag{3}$$

in which Equation (3) leads to the fundamental equation in tourism finance. This equation relates the growth in total daily tourism expenditure, or alternatively, the daily returns on total tourism, $\Delta y_t / y_{t-1}$, to the net daily tourist arrivals divided by the previous day's total number of tourists, $\Delta x_t / x_{t-1}$.

Equation (3) is the fundamental tourism finance equation, which shows that the changes in daily returns on total tourism are approximately equal to the net change rate in daily tourist arrivals. Therefore, we use the change rate of tourist arrivals to be the change rate of the total daily Chinese tourism expenditure for purpose of analysis.

The change rate of tourist arrivals, R_t, is given as the first difference in log arrivals, and multiplied by 100, as follows:

$$R_t = \ln(A_t / A_{t-1}) \times 100 \tag{4}$$

where A_t and A_{t-1} are the daily tourist arrivals for the time periods t and $t-1$, respectively.

3.3. Estimating the Expected Rate of Change in Tourist Arrivals

The market model of Sharpe [22], one of several risk-adjusted returns models, is used to estimate the expected rate of change in the number of Chinese tourists to Taiwan (MacKinlay [7]).

In order to estimate the expected rate of change in the number of Chinese tourists, this paper uses OLS and three frequently applied conditional volatility models, namely, GARCH (1,1), GJR (1,1), and

EGARCH (1,1), to evaluate the abnormal returns from significant events. The methods of estimation cover the standard OLS approach, whereby the conditional volatilities are constant, and the three most widely used methods, when the conditional volatilities vary dynamically over time.

3.3.1. OLS

$$\begin{gathered} R_t = \phi_1 + \phi_2 R_{mt} + \varepsilon_t,\ t \in T = [t_1, t_2] \\ E(\varepsilon_t) = 0 \\ var(\varepsilon_t) = \sigma_\varepsilon^2 \end{gathered} \tag{5}$$

where R_t is the rate of change in the number of tourists; $t = [t_1, t_2]$ refers to different time points within the estimation period; R_{mt} is the rate of change in the number of tourists in the market; ε_{it} is the error term, where $\varepsilon_t \sim N(0, \sigma_\varepsilon^2)$; ϕ_1 and ϕ_2 are regression coefficients, where ϕ_1 is the intercept, and ϕ_2 is systematic risk, referring to the sensitivity of the rate of change in the number of visits by Chinese tourists as compared to the rate of change in the number of visits by foreign tourists as a whole; T is the length (or number of periods) in the estimation period, where $T = t_2 - t_1 + 1$.

However, the classical regression model assumes that the variance of the regression error term is a fixed constant, but time series data are mostly characterized by time-varying heteroscedasticity. If OLS is used to estimate the expected rate of change in the number of Chinese tourists visiting Taiwan, the estimation is likely to be biased. To resolve this problem, Engle [23] proposed the Auto-Regressive Conditional Heteroskedasticity (ARCH) model to compensate for the changes in the time series data due to the changes in the time points, as well as for the volatility clustering and heavy tails. Given below are the regression equations for three univariate conditional volatility models that are used to estimate the expected rate of change in the number of Chinese tourists. For a more detailed derivation, the interested reader may refer to McAleer [24] and Chang et al. [25].

3.3.2. GARCH

Bollerslev [26] generalized the Auto-Regressive Conditional Heteroskedasticity (ARCH) model, and proposed the Generalized Auto-Regressive Conditional Heteroskedasticity (GARCH) model. At the same time, the concepts of the Auto-Regressive (AR) model and the Moving-Average (MA) model were used in the estimation of the conditional variance. The model uses GARCH(1,1) to construct the regression equation and conditional mean equation, as follows:

$$R_t = \phi_1 + \phi_2 R_{mt} + \varepsilon_t,\ t \in T = [t_1, t_2] \tag{6}$$

$$\begin{gathered} \varepsilon_t = \theta_t \varepsilon_{t-1} + \eta_t \\ \theta_t \sim iid(0, \alpha); \eta_t \sim iid(0, \omega) \\ \eta_t = \varepsilon_t / \sqrt{h_t} \end{gathered} \tag{7}$$

$$h_t = E(\varepsilon_{t-1}^2 | I_{t-1}) = \omega + \alpha \varepsilon_{t-1}^2 + \beta h_{t-1} \tag{8}$$

where $\varepsilon_t | I_{t-1} \sim N(0, h_t)$, and I_{t-1} is the information set in period $t-1$. The mean of the conditional distribution of the error terms is zero, the variance is h_t, and η_t is the standardized residual. In accordance with Engle's [23] ARCH(1) model, Tsay [27] obtained the ARCH(1,1) conditional variance equation as shown in Equation (8), with $\beta = 0$.

As Equation (8) shows, h_t is the conditional volatility, α is the impact of short-term persistence in the ARCH effect, and $(\alpha + \beta)$ is the impact of long-term persistence in the GARCH effect. According to McAleer [24], $\omega > 0$, $\alpha > 0$ and $\beta \in [-1, 1]$ in Equation (8), in order to satisfy the sufficient condition that $h_t > 0$. Moreover, from Equation (7), it can be seen that $\omega > 0$ and $\alpha > 0$. When the condition that $\alpha + \beta < 1$ is satisfied, this means that the quasi-maximum likelihood estimates (QMLE) of the parameters in Equation (8) satisfy the sufficient conditions for consistency and asymptotic normality (see Ling and McAleer [28]).

3.3.3. GJR

GARCH is unable to capture the asymmetric effect in financial time series data. In order to capture such asymmetry, Glosten et al. [29] proposed the Threshold or asymmetric GARCH (or GJR) model, using an indexed random variable ($I(\varepsilon_{t-1})$) to represent different conditions inside and outside the threshold variance values, so that the conditional variation value can exhibit two different phenomena. The regression equation for GJR(1,1) is as follows:

$$R_t = \phi_1 + \phi_2 R_{mt} + \varepsilon_t,\ t \in T = [t_1, t_2] \tag{9}$$

$$\begin{gathered} \varepsilon_t = \theta_t \varepsilon_{t-1} + \psi_t I(\varepsilon_{t-1}) + \eta_t \\ \theta_t \sim iid(0,\alpha);\ \psi_t \sim iid(0,\gamma);\ \eta_t \sim iid(0,\omega) \\ I(\varepsilon_{t-1}) = 1\ when\ \varepsilon_{t-1} < 0 \\ I(\varepsilon_{t-1}) = 0\ when\ \varepsilon_{t-1} \geq 0 \\ \eta_t = \varepsilon_t / \sqrt{h_t} \end{gathered} \tag{10}$$

$$h_t = E\left(\varepsilon_{t-1}^2 | I_{t-1}\right) = \omega + \alpha\varepsilon_{t-1}^2 + \gamma I(\varepsilon_{t-1}\Big) + \beta h_{t-1} \tag{11}$$

where γ is the asymmetry parameter; when $\gamma > 0$, there is an asymmetric effect inherent within the time series data. $\alpha + \gamma/2$ is the short-term impact persistence, and $\alpha + \beta + \gamma/2$ is the long-term impact persistence. As the GARCH model is nested inside the GJR model, with the exception of the asymmetry parameter (γ), the coefficients of the two models are explained in the same way. A sufficient condition for the QMLE of the parameters in GJR(1,1) to be consistent and asymptotically normal is $\alpha + \beta + \gamma/2 < 0$ (see Ling and McAleer [28]).

3.3.4. EGARCH

Nelson [30] proposed the Exponential GARCH (EGARCH) model, in which the conditional variance equation is set as a logarithmic function. The EGARCH model can capture the asymmetric effect in the time series data. The EGARCH(1,1) regression equation may be expressed as follows (for a detailed derivation, see McAleer and Hafner [31]):

$$R_t = \phi_1 + \phi_2 R_{mt} + \varepsilon_t,\ t \in T = [t_1, t_2] \tag{12}$$

$$\begin{gathered} \varepsilon_t = \theta_t \sqrt{|\eta_{t-1}|} + \psi_t \sqrt{\eta_{t-1}} + \eta_t \\ \theta_t \sim iid(0,\alpha);\ \psi_t \sim iid(0,\gamma);\ \eta_t \sim iid(0,\omega) \end{gathered} \tag{13}$$

$\sqrt{\eta_{t-1}}$ is a complex-valued function of η_{t-1}.

$$\begin{gathered} \eta_t = \varepsilon_t / \sqrt{h_t} \\ h_t = E(\varepsilon_{t-1}^2 | I_{t-1}) = \omega + \alpha|\eta_{t-1}| + \gamma\eta_{t-1} + \beta h_{t-1} \end{gathered} \tag{14}$$

$$logh_t = E(\varepsilon_{t-1}^2 | I_{t-1}) = \omega + \alpha|\eta_{t-1}| + \gamma\eta_{t-1} + \beta h_{t-1} \tag{15}$$

$logh_t = \log(1 + (h_{t-1} - 1)) \approx h_{t-1} - 1$ is an approximation used to replace h_t in Equation (14).

3.4. *Calculating the Cumulative Abnormal Change Rate*

By using the OLS, GARCH(1,1), GJR(1,1), and EGARCH(1,1) regression equations mentioned above, we can estimate the regression coefficients $\hat{\phi}_1$ and $\hat{\phi}_2$, respectively, and $\hat{\phi}_1$ and $\hat{\phi}_2$ can be brought into the events period data, in order to forecast the rate of change in the number of Chinese tourists visiting Taiwan, as shown in Equation (16) (see McAleer and Hafner [31]):

$$ER_E = \hat{\phi}_1 + \hat{\phi}_2 \cdot R_{mE},\ E \in W = [t_3, t_4] \tag{16}$$

where ER_E is the rate of change in the number of Chinese tourists visiting Taiwan in period E within the event period, R_{mE} is the rate of change in the total number of tourists visiting Taiwan in period E within the event period, and W is the length of the event period (the number of periods), where $W = t_4 - t_3 + 1$.

The formula used to calculate the abnormal rate of change in the number of Chinese tourists visiting Taiwan is as follows:

$$AR_E = R_E - ER_E,\ E \in W = [t_3, t_4] \tag{17}$$

where AR_E is the abnormal rate of change in the number of Chinese tourists visiting Taiwan in period E within the event period, R_E is the rate of change in the number of Chinese tourists actually visiting Taiwan in period E within the event period, and ER_E is the rate of change in the number of Chinese tourists that are expected to visit Taiwan in period E within the event period.

The cumulative abnormal change rate (CAR) is the cumulative abnormal rate of change in the number of tourists between any two periods within the event period. The formula is as follows:

$$\mathrm{CAR}(\tau_1, \tau_2) = \sum_{E=\tau_1}^{\tau_2} AR_E,\ [\tau_1, \tau_2] \in W = [t_3, t_4] \tag{18}$$

where $\mathrm{CAR}(\tau_1, \tau_2)$ is the abnormal rate of change in the cumulative number of Chinese tourists from period τ_1 to τ_2 during the event period, and AR_E is the abnormal rate of change in the number of Chinese tourists in period E in the event period. $[\tau_1, \tau_2]$ represents a total of m periods, from periods τ_1 to τ_2 during the event period, where $m = \tau_2 - \tau_1 + 1$, and $t_4 \geq \tau_2 \geq \tau_1 \geq t_3$.

3.5. Testing the Cumulative Abnormal Change Rate

The traditional method (Brown and Warner [32]) and the standardized-residual method (Patell [11]) are used to test the cumulative abnormal change rate in terms of the number of tourists. The null (H_0) and alternative hypotheses (H_1) are as follows:

$$\begin{aligned} H_0 &: CAR(\tau_1, \tau_2) = 0 \\ H_1 &: CAR(\tau_1, \tau_2) \neq 0 \end{aligned} \tag{19}$$

The traditional method (hereafter TM) uses the residual variance in the estimation period to simulate the residual variance in the event period. This test assumes that the residual variance in the estimation period is equal to that in the event period. The event will not cause the event-induced variance in the abnormal returns to change in the event period. Moreover, the abnormal returns in the estimation period and the event period will not lead to structural change, indicating that the parameters estimated by the equation for the expected returns in the estimation period will not change in the event period. The test statistic for the cumulative abnormal change rate in terms of the number of tourists is as shown in the following equation:

$$t^{\mathrm{TM}} = \frac{CAR(\tau_1, \tau_2)}{\sqrt{Var(CAR(\tau_1, \tau_2))}} = \frac{\sum_{E=\tau_1}^{\tau_2} \left(\frac{AR_E}{\sqrt{m}} \right)}{\hat{S}_i} \tag{20}$$

where $CAR(\tau_1, \tau_2)$ is the abnormal change rate in the cumulative number of tourists from period $\tau_1$toτ_2 in the event period; $Var(CAR(\tau_1, \tau_2))$ is the variance of the abnormal change rate in the cumulative number of Chinese tourists from period $\tau_1$toτ_2 in the event period; AR_E refers to the abnormal returns of the Chinese tourists in period E in the event period; $\hat{S}$ is the standardized error of the residual for Chinese tourists in the estimation period, that is:

$$\hat{S} = \sqrt{\frac{\sum_{t=t_1}^{t_2} \left(\hat{\varepsilon}_t - \sum_{t=t_1}^{T} \frac{\hat{\varepsilon}_t}{T} \right)^2}{T-1}}$$

$\hat{\varepsilon}_t$ is the residual for Chinese tourists in period t in the estimation period, that is, $\hat{\varepsilon}_t = R_t - E(\hat{R}_t)$, where T is the length of the estimation period (the number of periods), and $T = t_2 - t_1 + 1$; and m is the length of the estimation period from period $\tau_1$toτ_2 in the event period (the number of periods), where $m = \tau_2 - \tau_1 + 1$.

The standardized-residual method (hereafter SRM) standardizes the abnormal change rate in the number of Chinese tourists, resulting in the distribution of the abnormal change rate in the number of each type of tourist being a unit-normal distribution, thereby ensuring that the abnormal change rate for the cumulative number of tourists is normally distributed. The test statistic for the abnormal change rate in the cumulative number of tourists is as shown in the following equation:

$$t^{\text{SRM}} = \frac{\text{SCAR}(\tau_1, \tau_2)}{\sqrt{Var(\text{SCAR}(\tau_1, \tau_2))}} = \frac{\sum_{E=\tau_1}^{\tau_2}\left(\frac{SAR_E}{\sqrt{m}}\right)}{\left[\frac{T-2}{T-4}\right]^{\frac{1}{2}}} \tag{21}$$

where $\text{SC}AR(\tau_1, \tau_2)$ is the abnormal rate of change in the standardized cumulative number of Chinese tourists from period $\tau_1$toτ_2 in the event period; $\text{Var}(\text{SC}AR\tau_1, \tau_2)$ is the variance of the abnormal rate of change in the standardized cumulative number of Chinese tourists from period $\tau_1$toτ_2 in the event period; SAR_E is the abnormal rate of change in the standardized cumulative number of Chinese tourists from period $\tau_1$toτ_2 in the event period. The formula used to calculate SAR_E is as follows:

$$SAR_E = \frac{AR_E}{\hat{S}\sqrt{1 + \frac{1}{T} + \frac{\left(R_{mE} - \overline{R}_{mT}\right)^2}{\sum_{t=t_1}^{t_2}\left(R_{mt} - \overline{R}_{mT}\right)^2}}} \tag{22}$$

where $\hat{S}$ is the standard deviation of the residuals for the Chinese tourists in the estimation period, as give above, $\hat{\varepsilon}_t$ is the residual for the Chinese tourists in period t in the estimation period, that is, $\hat{\varepsilon}_t = R_t - E(\hat{R}_t)$; R_{mE} is the rate of change in the total number of international travelers visiting Taiwan in period E in the event period; R_{mt} is the rate of change in the total number of international travelers visiting Taiwan in period t in the estimation period; $\overline{R}_{mT}$ is the mean of the rate of change in the total number of international travelers visiting Taiwan in period T in the estimation period, that is, $\overline{R}_{mT} = \frac{1}{T}\sum_{t=t_1}^{t_2} R_{mt}$; T is the length of the estimation period (number of periods), that is, $T = t_2 - t_1 + 1$. In addition, because of the differences in the data, which lead to the observed values of T in each sample period being likely to be different, the expected value of SAR_E is equal to zero, and the variance is $(T-2)/(T-4)$. Therefore, the standardized cumulative abnormal rate of change is $\text{SC}AR(\tau_1, \tau_2) = \sum_{E=\tau_1}^{\tau_2} SAR_E$. Moreover, the variance of the standardized cumulative abnormal change rate in the number of tourists is $Var(\text{SC}AR(\tau_1, \tau_2)) = m\left(\frac{T-2}{T-4}\right)$, where m is the length of that part of the event period from period $\tau_1$toτ_2 (number of periods), that is, $m = \tau_2 - \tau_1 + 1$.

In summary, the paper uses the traditional method and the standardized residual method to test the cumulative abnormal rate of change in the number of tourists in the event period. If the test statistic rejects the null hypothesis (H_0), this indicates that abnormal change arising from the event is present.

4. Data and Variables

The data set comprises daily tourist arrivals from the world and China to Taiwan for the period 1 January 2014 to 31 October 2016, giving 1035 observations that are obtained from the National Immigration Agency of Taiwan (Taiwan Tourism Bureau, Statistic Data, Retrieved 17 June 2017 from http://admin.taiwan.net.tw/ (in Chinese).

The data were collected by the National Immigration Agency of Taiwan. The original data source comprises daily tourist arrivals from the world and China to Taiwan for the period from 1 January 2014 to 31 October 2016, giving 1035 observations. Based on the original data source from the National

Immigration Agency of Taiwan, we can disaggregate three types of Chinese tourists to Taiwan, namely Group-type, Individual-type, and Medical-type.

We have selected several of the most important political events, and disaster and accident events, based on public news that highlighted the important events at the time. Given the limitations in obtaining data from the National Immigration Agency in Taiwan, we focus on three different types of Chinese visitors: (1) Group type, (2) Individual type, and (3) Medical type. Figure 3 presents the trend for international tourists and for the three types of Chinese tourists to Taiwan.

The paper examines the effect of six political events and six disaster and accident events on the change rate of Chinese tourist arrivals to Taiwan, using an event study approach. The explanations of each major Cross-Strait event and sample period are given below. Table 2 presents the time period corresponding to each event.

Table 2. Major cross-strait events and sample periods.

	Notation	Event	Event Date T = 0	Sample Period	
				Estimation Period $[t_1, t_2]$	Event Period $[t_3, t_4]$
Political events	Case I	The Sunflower Youth Movement	18 March 2014	2 January 2014–17 March 2014	18 March 2014–17 April 2014
	Case II	Taiwan's nine-in-one local elections	29 November 2014	11 August 2014–18 November 2014	19 November 2014–19 December 2014
	Case III	Ma-Xi Summit	7 November 2015	20 July 2015–27 October 2015	28 October 2015–27 November 2015
	Case IV	Taiwan 14th-term presidential election and Taiwan ninth legislative election	16 January 2016	28 September 2015–5 January 2016	6 January 2016–5 February 2016
	Case V	Taiwan 14th-term presidential inauguration	20 May 2016	31 January 2016–9 May 2016	10 May 2016–9 June 2016
	Case VI	Taiwan mayors visit China	18 September 2016	31 May 2016–7 September 2016	8 September 2016–8 October 2016
Disaster and accident events	Case VII	The Kaohsiung Petrochemical gas explosion	31 July 2014	22 April 2014–30 July 2014	31 July 2014–30 August 2014
	Case VIII	Taiwan's "gutter oil" scandal	4 September 2014	27 May 2014–3 September 2014	4 September 2014–4 October 2014
	Case IX	TransAsia Airways Flight GE235 accident	4 February 2015	27 October 2014–3 February 2015	4 February 2015–6 March 2015
	Case X	Kaohsiung's magnitude 6.6 Meinong earthquake	6 February 2016	29 October 2015–5 February 2016	6 February 2016–7 March 2016
	Case XI	95th anniversary of the founding of the Communist Party of China (CPC) and the Hsiung Feng III missile mishap	1 July 2016	23 March 2016–30 June 2016	1 July 2016–31 July 2016
	Case XII	Taiwan tour bus accident	19 July 2016	10 April 2016–18 July 2016	19 July 2016–18 August 2016

(1) Political Events

Case I: The Sunflower Youth Movement

Event date (t = 0): 18 March 2014

Estimation period: 2 January 2014–17 March 2014 (75 days)

Event period ($\tau_1 = 0, \tau_2 = 30$): 18 March 2014–17 April 2014 (31 days)

Case II: Taiwan's nine-in-one local elections

Event date (t = 0): 29 November 2014

Estimation period: 8 November 2014–18 November 2014 (100 days)

Event period ($\tau_1 = -10,\ \tau_2 = 20$): 19 November 2014–19 December 2014 (31 days)

Case III: Ma-Xi Summit

Event date (t = 0): 7 November 2015

Estimation period: 20 July 2015–27 October 2015 (100 days)
Event period ($\tau_1 = -10,\ \tau_2 = 20$): 28 October 2015–27 November 2015 (31 days)

Case IV: Taiwan 14th presidential election and Taiwan ninth legislative election
Event date (t = 0): 16 January 2016
Estimation period: 28 September 2015–5 January 2016 (100 days)
Event period ($\tau_1 = -10,\ \tau_2 = 20$): 6 January 2016–5 February 2016 (31 days)

Case V: Taiwan 14th Presidential inauguration
Event date (t = 0): 20 May 2016
Estimation period: 31 January 2016–9 May 2016 (100 days)
Event period ($\tau_1 = -10,\ \tau_2 = 20$): 10 May 2016–9 June 2016 (31 days)

Case VI: Taiwan mayors visit China
Event date (t = 0): 18 September 2016
Estimation period: 31 May 2016–7 September 2016 (100 days)
Event period ($\tau_1 = -10,\ \tau_2 = 20$): 8 September 2016–8 October 2016 (31 days)

(2) Disaster and Accident Events

Case VII: The Kaohsiung Petrochemical gas explosion
Event date (t = 0): 31 July 2014
Estimation period: 22 April 2014–30 July 2014 (100 days)
Event period ($\tau_1 = 0, \tau_2 = 30$): 31 July 2014–30 August 2014 (31 days)

Case VIII: Taiwan's "gutter oil" scandal
Event date (t = 0): 4 September 2014
Estimation period: 27 May 2014–3 September 2014 (100 days)
Event period ($\tau_1 = 0, \tau_2 = 30$): 4 September 2014–4 October 2014 (31 days)

Case IX: TransAsia Airways Flight GE235 accident
Event date (t = 0): 4 February 2015
Estimation period: 27 October 2014–3 February 2015 (100 days)
Event period ($\tau_1 = 0, \tau_2 = 30$): 4 February 2015–6 March 2015 (31 days)

Case X: Kaohsiung's magnitude 6.6 Meinong earthquake
Event date (t = 0): 6 February 2016
Estimation period: 29 October 2015–5 February 2016 (100 days)
Event period ($\tau_1 = 0, \tau_2 = 30$): 6 February 2016–7 March 2016 (31 days)

Case XI: 95th anniversary of the founding of the Communist Party of China and the Hsiung Feng III missile mishap
Event date (t = 0): 1 July 2016
Estimation period: 23 March 2016–30 June 2016 (100 days)
Event period ($\tau_1 = 0, \tau_2 = 30$): 1 July 2016–31 July 2016 (31 days)

Case XII: Taiwan tour bus accident
Event date (t = 0): 19 July 2016
Estimation period: 10 April 2016–18 July 2016 (100 days)
Event period ($\tau_1 = 0, \tau_2 = 30$): 19 July 2016–18 August 2016 (31 days)

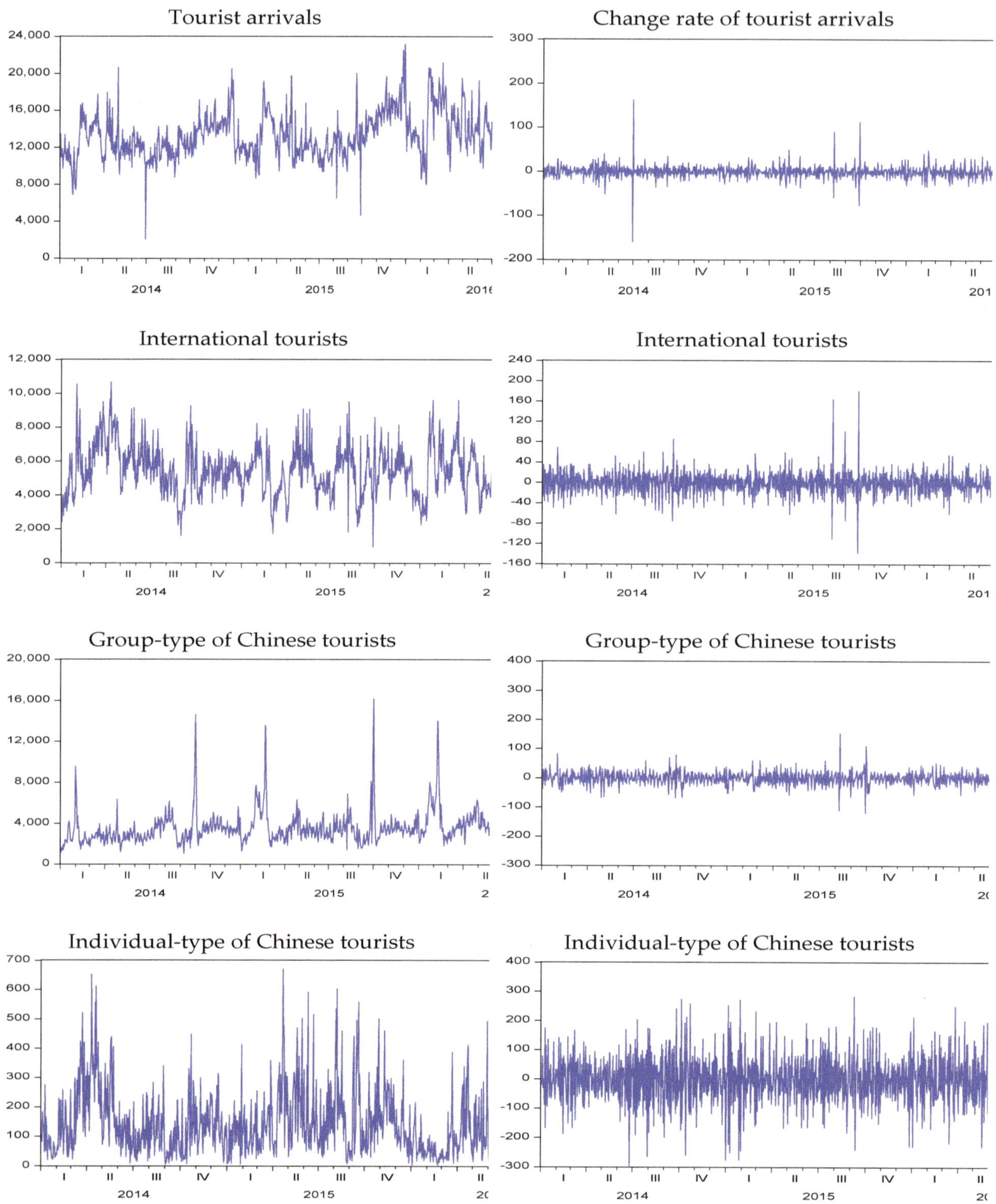

Medical-type of Chinese tourists Medical-type of Chinese tourists

Figure 3. Daily tourist arrivals to Taiwan, 1/1/2014–31/10/2016

5. Empirical Results

As discussed previously, in this section we use the OLS, GARCH (1,1), GJR (1,1), and EGARCH (1,1) models to estimate the expected number of tourists during the event periods, and we use the difference between the expected number of tourists and the actual number of tourists to calculate the average abnormal rate of change and cumulative abnormal rate of change. We extend the analysis to use the traditional method (Brown and Warner [32]) and the standardized residual method (Patell [11]) to determine whether there are abnormal changes in the cumulative numbers of Chinese tourists visiting Taiwan, due to the occurrence of each event in Table 3. For the detailed results of the estimation by OLS, GARCH, GJR, and EGARCH, refer to Tables A1–A48 (in Appendix A). The trend for the cumulative rate of change in the number of tourists is given in Figure 4.

The empirical results can and do differ according to the different political events, and different disasters and accident events, as well as with the different methods of estimation. In order to provide a comprehensive analysis of each type of event, as estimated by alternative methods, a detailed analysis of each combination is required.

The Augmented Dickey–Fuller (ADF) and Phillips–Perron (PP) tests are used to determine whether the data for the rate of change in the number of tourists are stationary. As shown in Table 4, the series for the rate of change in the number of Chinese tourists visiting Taiwan is stationary. The empirical results regarding the tests that were carried out to determine whether the returns to Chinese tourists visiting Taiwan are abnormally affected by the political and disaster-related events are listed sequentially.

Table 3. Results for cumulative abnormal change rate of Chinese tourist arrivals.

		Political Events							
Event	**Types**	**OLS**		**GARCH(1,1)**		**GJR(1,1)**		**EGARCH(1,1)**	
		TM	**SRM**	**TM**	**SRM**	**TM**	**SRM**	**TM**	**SRM**
Case I	Group								
	Individual								
	Medical								
Case II	Group								
	Individual								
	Medical								
Case III	Group								
	Individual								
	Medical								
Case IV	Group	+	+	+	+	+	+	+	+
	Individual	+	+	+	+				
	Medical								
Case V	Group	-	-						
	Individual								
	Medical								
Case VI	Group	+	+	+	+				
	Individual	+	+	+	+	+	+	+	+
	Medical	-	-						
		Disaster and Accident Events							
Event	**Types**	**OLS**		**GARCH(1,1)**		**GJR(1,1)**		**EGARCH(1,1)**	
		TM	**SRM**	**TM**	**SRM**	**TM**	**SRM**	**TM**	**SRM**
Case VII	Group	-	-	-	-	-	-		
	Individual	-	-	-	-	-	-	-	-
	Medical	+	+	+	+	+	+		
Case VIII	Group	+	+	+	+	+	+	+	+
	Individual	+	+	+	+	+	+	+	+
	Medical	+	+						

Table 3. *Cont.*

Disaster and Accident Events									
Event	**Types**	**OLS**		**GARCH(1,1)**		**GJR(1,1)**		**EGARCH(1,1)**	
		TM	**SRM**	**TM**	**SRM**	**TM**	**SRM**	**TM**	**SRM**
Case IX	Group	-	-	-	-	-	-	-	-
	Individual	-	-	-	-	-	-	-	-
	Medical	-	-	-	-				
Case X	Group								
	Individual	-	-	-	-	-	-		
	Medical	-	-			-	-		
Case XI	Group								
	Individual								
	Medical								
Case XII	Group								
	Individual								
	Medical								

Notes: (1) Traditional method (TM) is the traditional method proposed by Brown and Warner [32]. (2) SRM is the standardized-residual method proposed by Pattel [11]. (3) - and + denote that the cumulative change rate of Chinese tourist arrivals are negative abnormal and positive abnormal, respectively.

Table 4. Unit root tests.

Variables		**Augmented Dickey-Fuller (ADF) Test**		
		No Trend and Intercept	**With Intercept**	**With Trend and Intercept**
International tourists		−20.34 *	−20.34 *	−20.33 *
Chinese tourists	Group-type	−14.90 *	−14.90 *	−14.90 *
	Individual-type	−15.24 *	−15.23 *	−15.24 *
	Medical-type	−19.54 *	−19.53 *	−19.52 *
Variables		**PP test**		
		No Trend and Intercept	**With Intercept**	**With Trend and Intercept**
International tourists		−151.73 *	−151.95 *	−151.94 *
Chinese tourists	Group-type	−111.90 *	−112.66 *	−124.12 *
	Individual-type	−79.35 *	−79.27 *	−80.91 *
	Medical-type	−284.46 *	−307.89 *	−377.68 *

Note: * denotes significant at the 1% level.

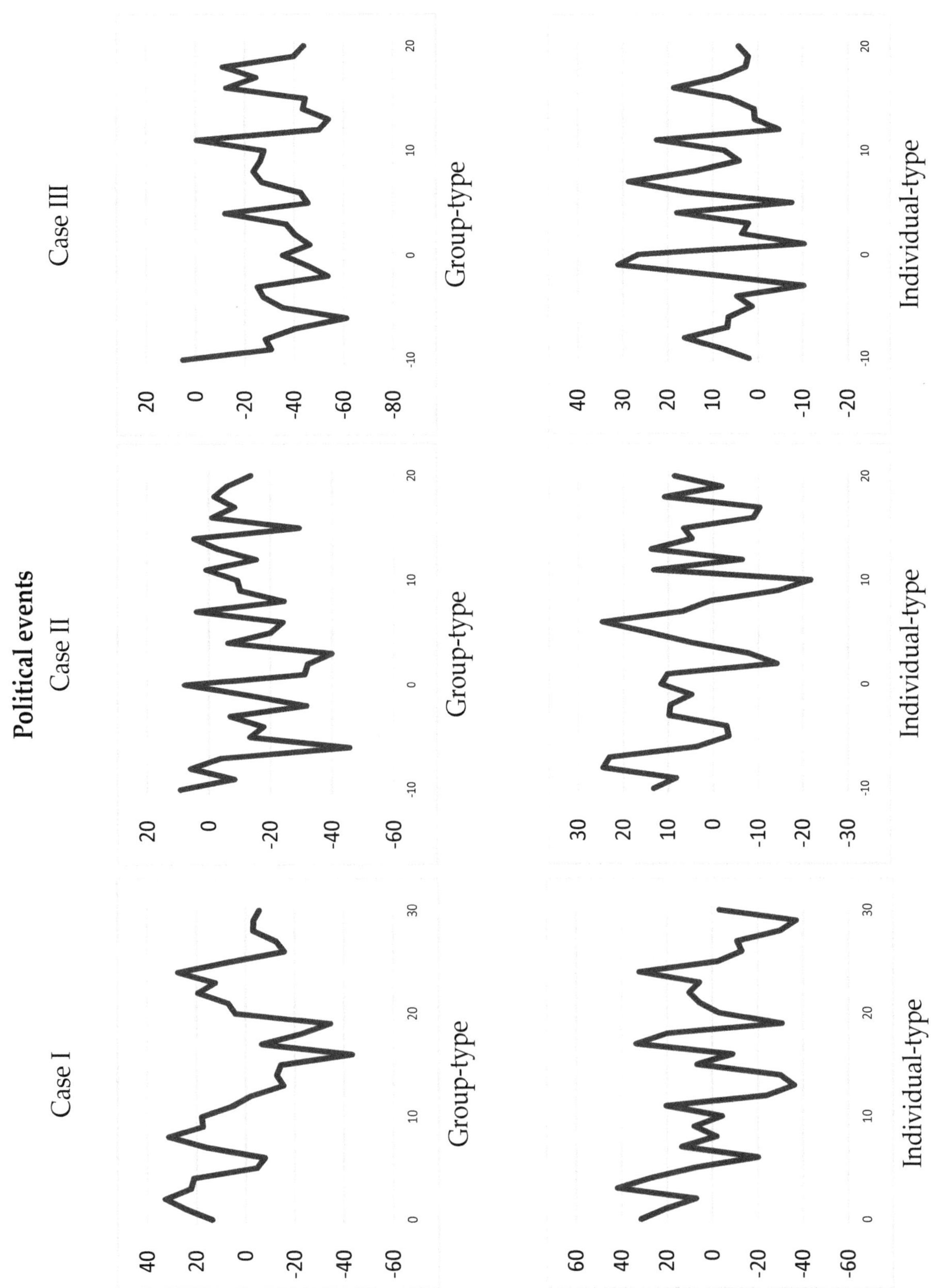

Figure 4. *Cont.*

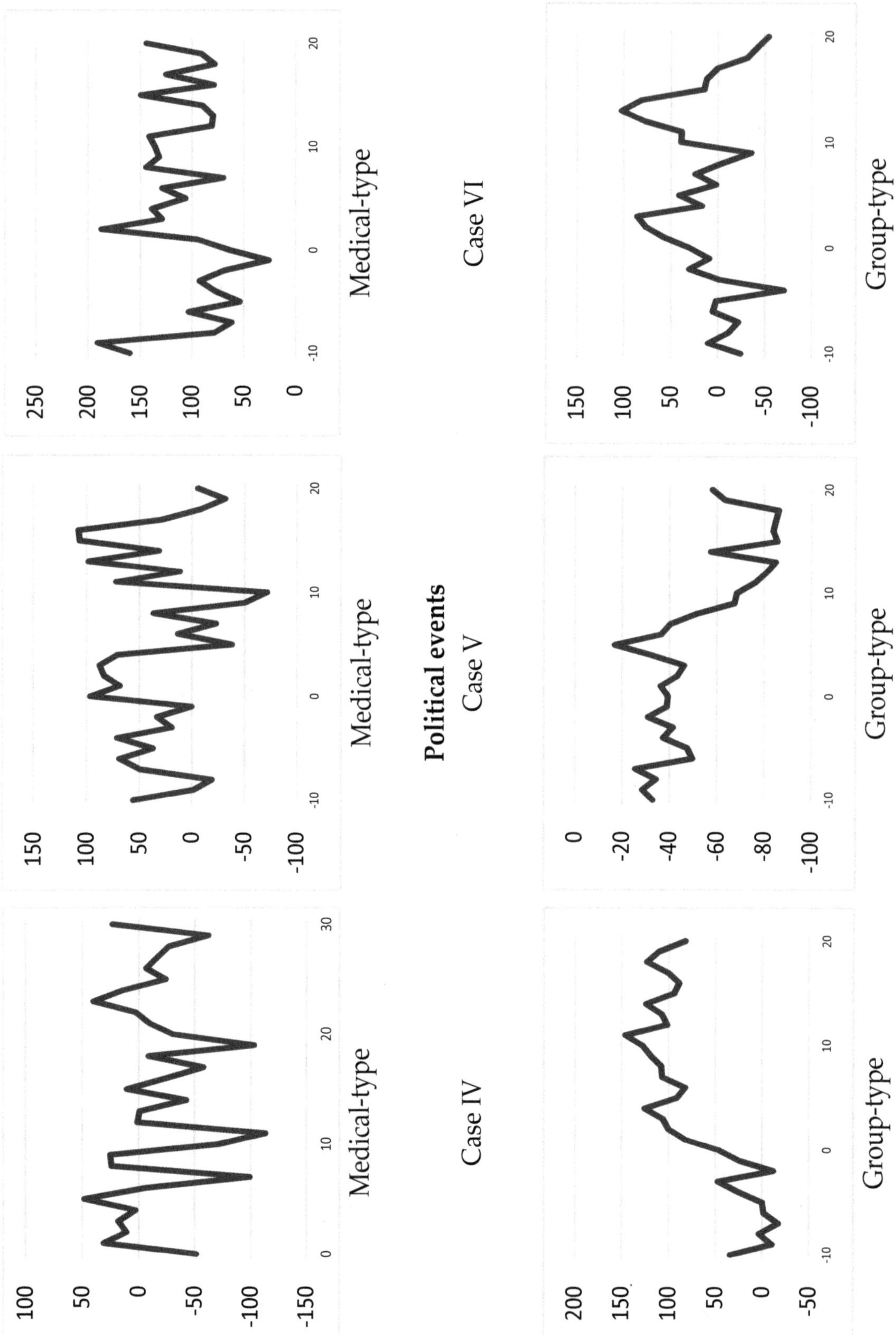

Figure 4. *Cont.*

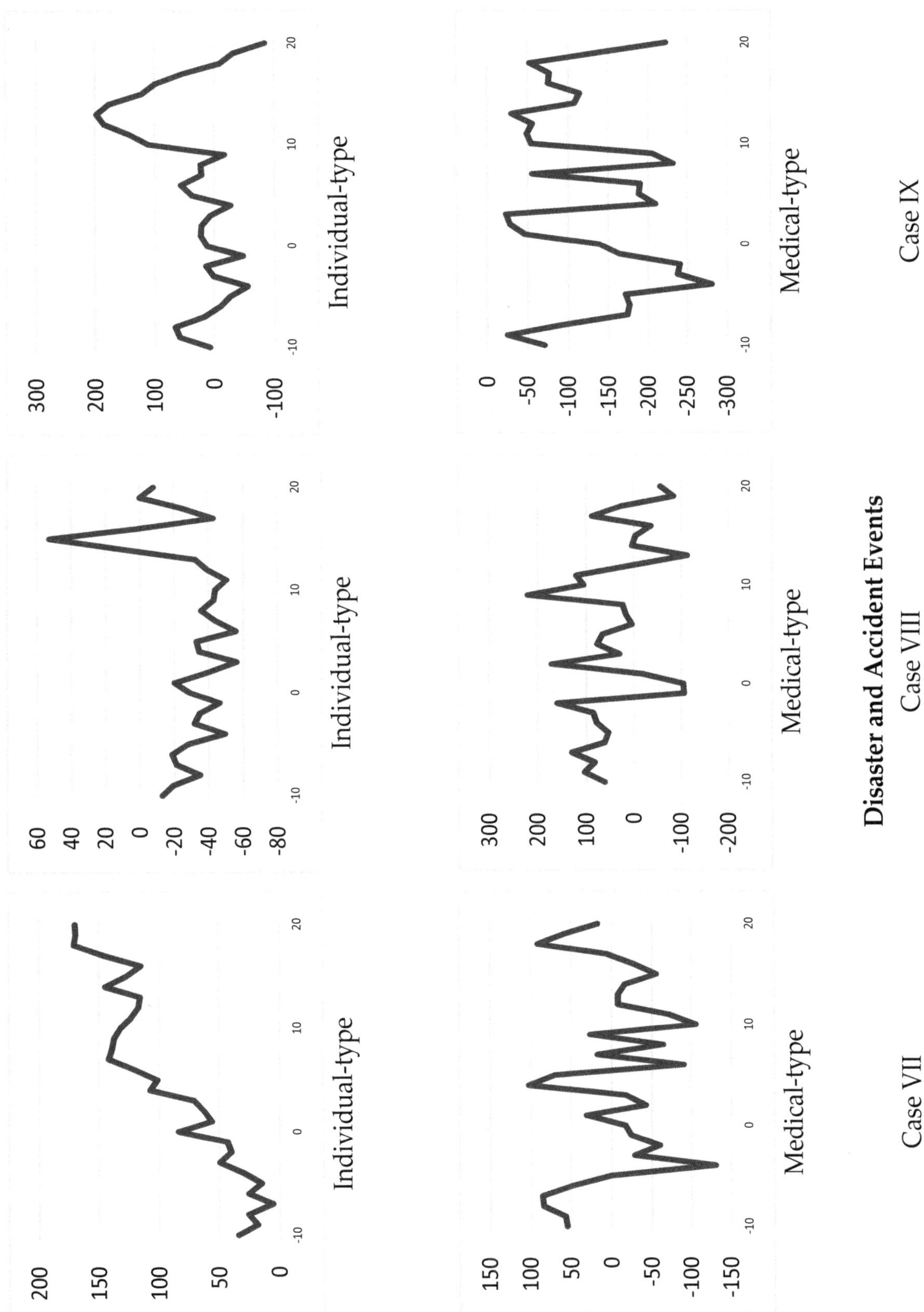

Figure 4. *Cont.*

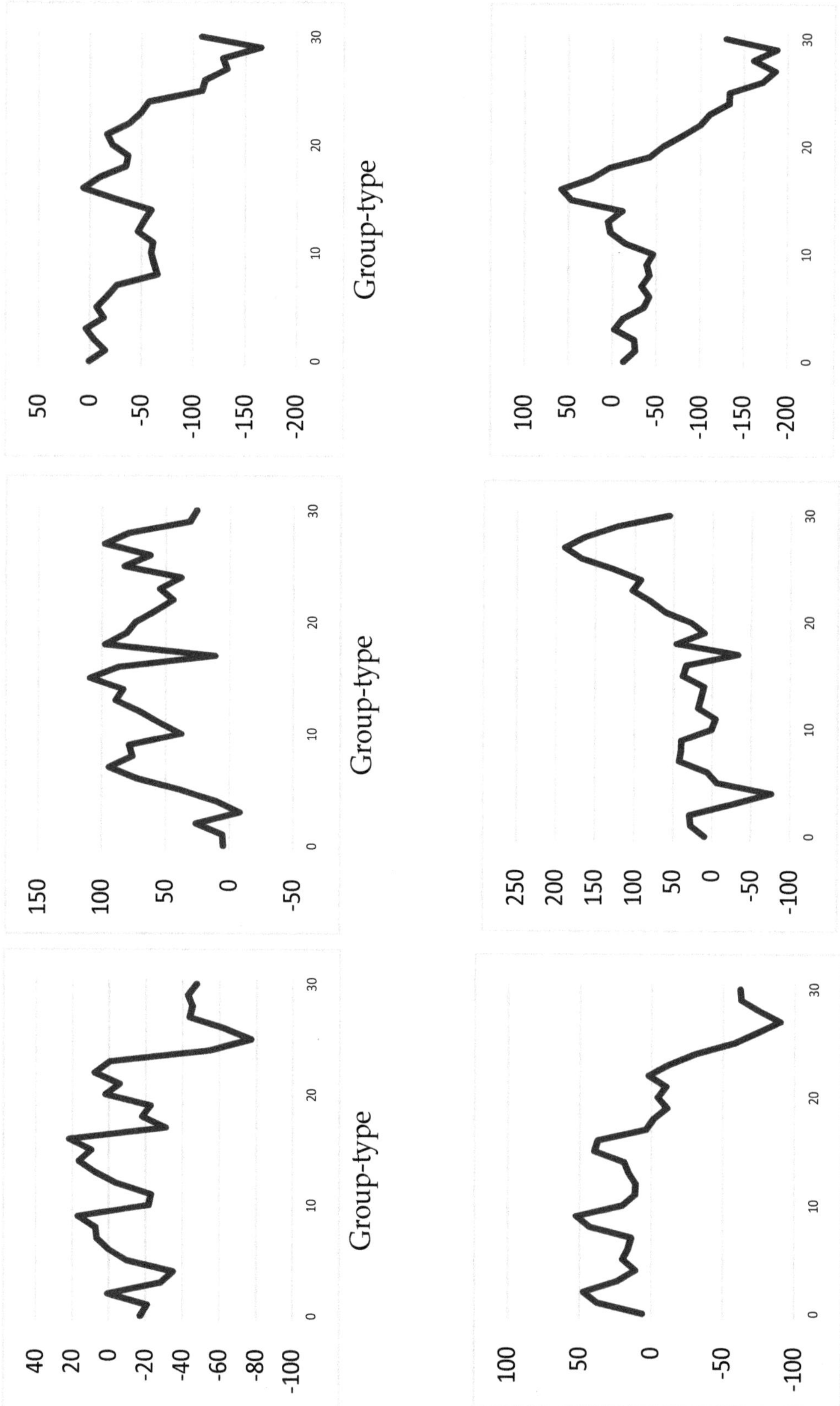

Figure 4. *Cont.*

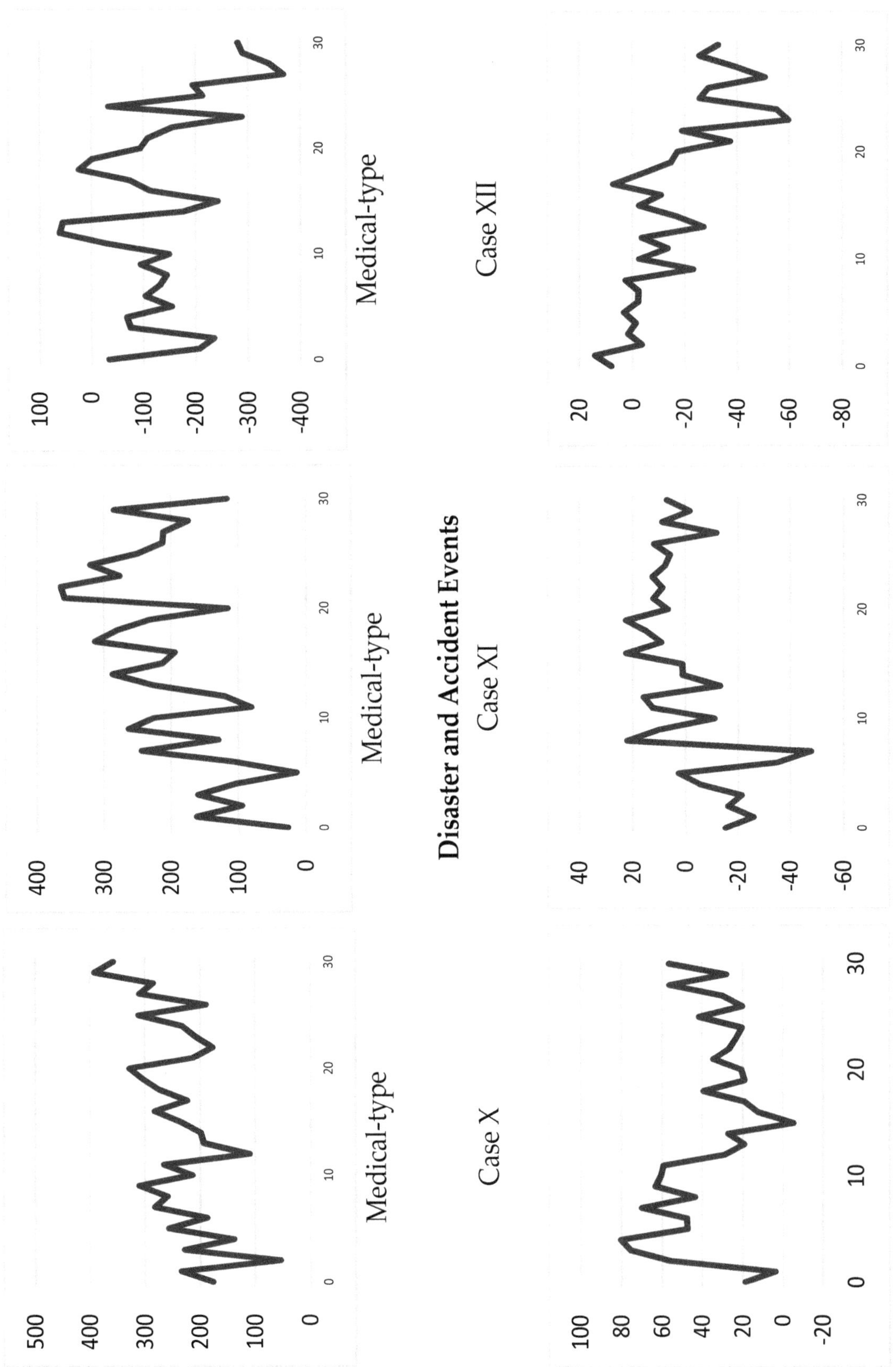

Figure 4. *Cont.*

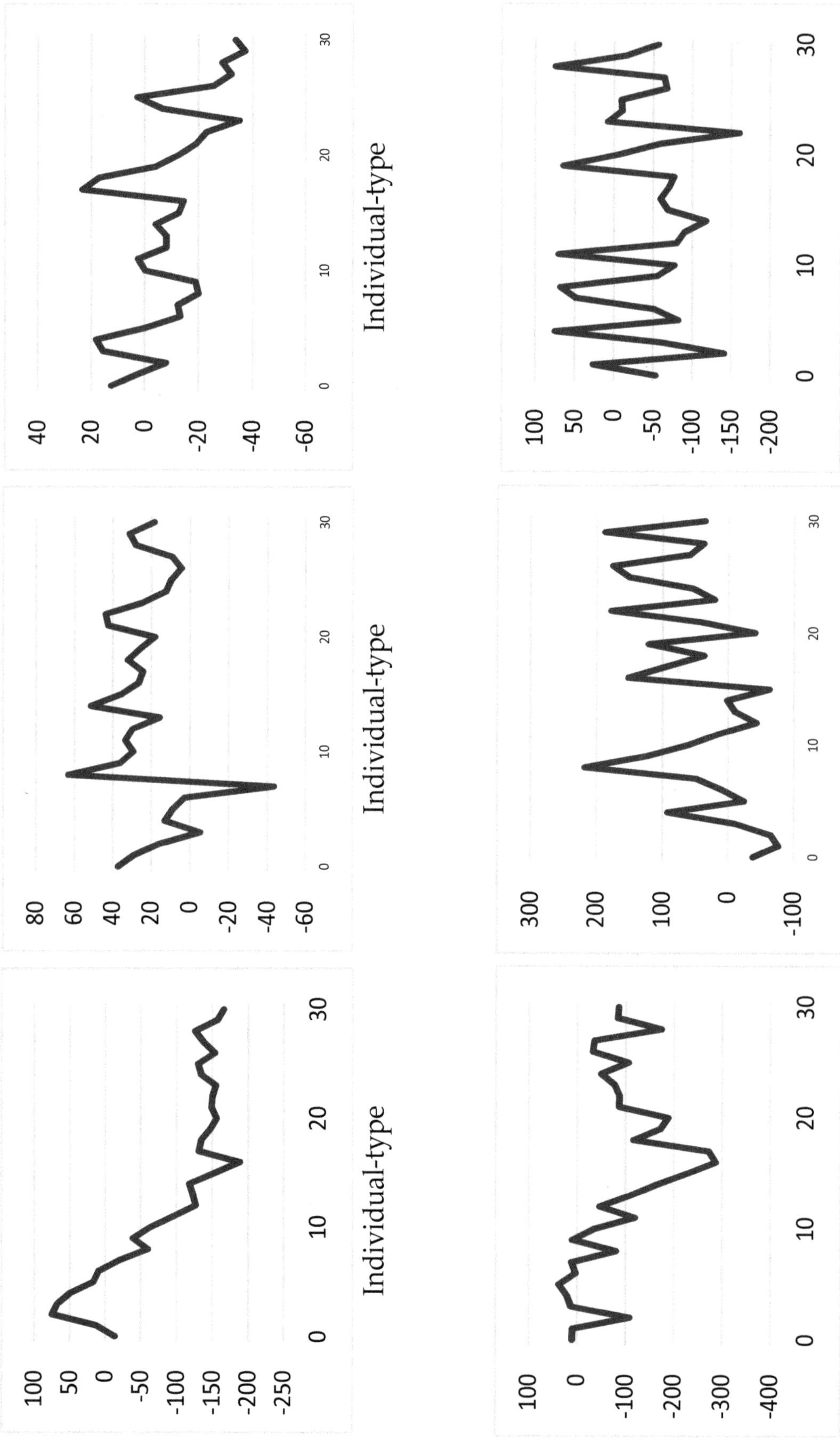

Figure 4. Cumulative abnormal change rate of Chinese tourist arrivals to Taiwan.

5.1. Empirical Results for Political Events

(1) Case I: The Sunflower Youth Movement

Although the Sunflower movement, which resulted in students and civic groups occupying Taiwan's Legislative Yuan for half a month, raised concerns from people in all walks of life and impacted the implementation of various Cross-Strait agreements, the empirical results did not reveal any significant changes in the number of each group of Chinese tourists visiting Taiwan. For the detailed results of the model parameter estimation, see Tables A1–A4.

The cumulative abnormal change rate (CAR) for three types of Chinese tourist arrivals to Taiwan are given according to four estimation methods, namely OLS, GARCH, GJR, and EGARCH. The empirical results are consistent in that there are no significant factors for any group of Chinese tourist arrivals to Taiwan, regardless of whether the traditional or standardized-residual method is used.

(2) Case II: Taiwan's nine-in-one local elections

Taiwan's nine-in-one local elections that were held in 2014 resulted in the Kuomintang (KMT) suffering an unprecedented defeat; as a consequence, the former President Ma Ying-jeou resigned as chairman of the KMT party. Although there was much public concern as to what impact the election results might have on future Cross-Straits relationship, the two sides continued to maintain friendly and interactive relations. The empirical results do not show that there was a significant abnormal change in the number of each group of Chinese tourists visiting Taiwan. For the detailed results of the parameter estimation, see Tables A5–A8.

The CAR for three types of Chinese tourist arrivals to Taiwan are given according to four estimation methods. The empirical results are consistent, in that there are no significant factors for any group of Chinese tourist arrivals to Taiwan, regardless of whether the traditional or standardized-residual method is used.

(3) Case III: Ma-Xi Summit

For the first time since the political separation in 1949 between the two sides of the Taiwan Strait, the top leaders of Taiwan and China met in Singapore. Although the meeting symbolized a major breakthrough in Cross-Strait relations, the two sides did not sign an agreement or issue a joint statement. For this reason, the empirical results did not exhibit a significant abnormal change in the number of each group of Chinese tourists visiting Taiwan. See Tables A9–A12 for the detailed results of the model estimation.

The CAR for three types of Chinese tourist arrivals to Taiwan are given according to four estimation methods. As in Cases I and II, the empirical results are consistent in that there are no significant factors for any group of Chinese tourist arrivals to Taiwan, regardless of whether the traditional or standardized-residual method is used.

(4) Case IV: Taiwan 14th Presidential election and Taiwan ninth legislative election

President Tsai Ing-wen's speech on 4 June 2015, prior to the presidential election and the 12 December 2015 subsequent political statements made on 22 December 2015, stated that the status quo would be maintained in the Cross-Strait relationship, and that good Cross-Strait interactions and goodwill would also continue. The results for all models show that there was a significant abnormal increase in the number of Group-type tourists from China after the event took place, and the results of OLS and GARCH (1,1) estimation indicate that the number of Individual-type tourists from China also increased abnormally after the event. The Medical-type tourists from China did not, however, experience any abnormal changes. These results show that the number of both Group-type and Individual-type tourists increased abnormally (with + effects) after the Taiwan 14th Presidential election and the Taiwan ninth legislative election. However, Medical-type tourists do not seem to have been affected by this event. See Tables A13–A16 for the detailed results of the model estimation.

These empirical results are important as they show that CAR varies according to the type of Chinese tourists, as well as the method of estimation, and whether the traditional or standardized-residual method is used.

(5) Case V: Taiwan 14th Presidential inauguration

OLS estimates showed that the number of Group-type tourists significantly and abnormally declined following the incident, but the numbers of Individual-type and Medical-type tourists did not experience any abnormal changes. As President Tsai Ing-wen did not mention the 1992 Consensus in her inaugural address, the Chinese government expressed dissatisfaction and Cross-Strait relations stalled, affecting interactions between the two sides. It was rumored that the Chinese government had decided to limit the numbers of Group-type tourists visiting Taiwan. The empirical results confirm the above statements. However, the numbers of Individual-type tourists visiting Taiwan did not decline abnormally. Since the quality of Taiwan's medical treatment is high and its cost is low, the numbers of Medical-type tourists, who mainly come to Taiwan for medical check-ups or cosmetic treatments, were not affected by the political events. See Tables A17–A20 for the detailed results of the model estimation.

The CAR for three types of Chinese tourist arrivals to Taiwan are given, according to four estimation methods. As in Cases I, II, and III, the empirical results are consistent in that there are no significant factors for any groups of Chinese tourist arrivals to Taiwan, regardless of whether the traditional or standardized-residual method is used, with the sole exception being OLS for the Group-type tourists, with decreasing CAR (with − effects). It is worth noting that there are no dynamic effects from estimating conditional volatility.

(6) Case VI: Taiwan mayors visit China

The OLS and GARCH (1,1) estimates reveal that Group-type tourists experienced a significant abnormal increase following this event. The results of the four models all showed that the numbers of Individual-type tourists increased significantly after the event. Only the OLS estimates indicated that Medical-type tourists experienced a significant abnormal increase prior to the event's occurrence. These results show that the visit by the mayors of eight counties and cities in Taiwan to Beijing, to support the cooperation and exchange event to promote "China's eight measures to benefit Taiwan", had a relatively more significant impact on Individual-type tourists. For the detailed results of the model estimation, see Tables A21–A24.

These results show that the numbers of both Group-type and Individual-type tourists increased abnormally (with + effects) after the Taiwan mayors visited China, for two and four methods of estimation, respectively. However, Medical-type tourists had a decreasing CAR (with − effects) for OLS, but not for the three time-varying conditional volatility models.

These empirical results are important as they show that CAR varies according to the type of Chinese tourists, as well as according to the method of estimation.

5.2. Empirical Results for Disaster and Accident Events

(1) Case VII: The Kaohsiung Petrochemical gas explosion

The results of the OLS, GARCH (1,1), and GJR (1,1) estimates showed that the numbers of Group-type tourists experienced a significant abnormal decrease following the occurrence of the event. The results of all four models revealed that Individual-type tourists also declined significantly. However, the results of the OLS, GARCH (1,1), and GJR (1,1) estimates showed that the numbers of Medical-type tourists significantly increased. According to the above results, the Kaohsiung Petrochemical gas explosion event had a relatively large impact on Group-type and Individual-type tourists, but it did not affect the Medical-type tourists who came to Taiwan for medical treatment. See Tables A25–A28 for the detailed results of model estimation.

These results show that the number of both Group-type and Individual-type tourists decreased abnormally (with − effects), for three and four methods of estimation, respectively. However, Medical-type tourists had an increasing CAR (with + effects) for three methods of estimation.

These empirical results are important as they show that CAR varies according to the type of Chinese tourists, as well as with the method of estimation.

(2) Case VIII: Taiwan's "gutter oil" scandal

The results of the four different kinds of models show that the numbers of Group-type and Individual-type tourists experienced significant abnormal increases following the event, but that the numbers of Medical-type tourists only increased significantly when OLS was used. As the time when the contaminated cooking oil scandal occurred in Taiwan was simultaneous to the Chinese national holidays (1 October 2014–7 October 2014), there was no impact on the willingness of Chinese tourists to visit Taiwan. On the contrary, due to the long holiday, the number of each group of Chinese visitors to Taiwan during that period was actually higher than expected, and therefore they exhibited abnormal increases. See Tables A29–A32 for the detailed results of model estimation.

These results show that the number of Group-type, Individual-type, and Medical-type tourists increased abnormally (with + effects), for four, four, and one methods of estimation, respectively. Only Medical-type tourists showed no dynamic effects from time-varying conditional volatility.

These empirical results are important as they show that CAR varies consistently and positively for all three types of Chinese tourists, as well as for the method of estimation.

(3) Case IX: TransAsia Airways Flight GE235 accident

The estimates of the four models showed that there was a significant abnormal decline in the numbers of Group-type and Individual-type tourists following the event, but only the results of OLS and GARCH (1,1) indicated that the numbers of Medical-type tourists declined significantly. From these results, it can be inferred that the crash of TransAsia Airways Flight 235 impacted the willingness of each group of Chinese tourists to visit Taiwan, due to their concerns over flight safety. The detailed results of the model estimates are given in Tables A33–A36.

These results are the polar opposite of Case VIII in that the numbers of Group-type, Individual-type, and Medical-type tourists were decreased abnormally (with − effects), for four, four, and two methods of estimation, respectively.

These empirical results are important as they show that CAR varies consistently and negatively for all three types of Chinese tourists, as well as for the method of estimation.

(4) Case X: Kaohsiung's magnitude 6.6 Meinong earthquake

While the number of Group-type tourists was not abnormally changed, the results of the OLS, GARCH (1,1) and GJR (1,1) estimates showed that the number of Individual-type tourists was significantly and abnormally reduced after the event occurred, as was the number of Medical-type tourists from the results of OLS and GJR (1,1). As the 6.6 magnitude Meinong, Kaohsiung earthquake struck at the same time as the Chinese Lunar New Year holiday (7 February 2016–13 February 2016), and the area where it happened was not a tourist attraction, Group-type tourists were not affected. However, after the Chinese New Year holiday, the numbers of Individual-type and Medical-type tourists declined significantly. See Tables A37–A40 for the detailed results of model estimation.

These results show that the number of Individual-type and Medical-type tourists decreased abnormally (with − effects), for three and one methods of estimation, respectively. Only Group-type tourists showed no significant constant or dynamic effects of time-varying conditional volatility.

These empirical results are important as they show that CAR varies consistently and negatively for two types of Chinese tourists, as well as with the method of estimation.

(5) Case XI: 95th anniversary of the founding of the Communist Party of China and the Hsiung Feng III missile mishap

The results for the four models all show that the numbers of Group-type, Individual-type, and Medical-type tourists were not affected by this accident. The Taiwan government issued a statement immediately after the mishap to point out that the incident occurred due to negligence in personnel training, and not because of political factors. It was for this reason that the willingness of each group of Chinese tourists to visit Taiwan from the mainland was not affected. See Tables A41–A44 for the detailed results of the model estimation.

As in Cases I, II, and III, the empirical results are consistent in that there are no significant factors for any group of Chinese tourist arrivals to Taiwan, regardless of the method of estimation, and whether the traditional or standardized-residual method is used.

(6) Case XII: Taiwan tour bus accident

The results for all four models showed that the numbers of Group-type, Individual-type, and Medical type tourists from China were not affected by this accident. From the empirical results, it can be seen that the tour bus accident that resulted in the deaths of tourists from Liaoning, China was due to human factors, and that the likelihood of such an incident recurring was low. In addition, the accident victims were part of a tour bus tour group, and the unfortunate event had no effect on Individual-type tourists who made their own arrangements regarding their itinerary and transportation. See Tables A45–A48 for the detailed results of the model estimation.

As in Cases I, II, III, and XI, the empirical results are consistent in that there are no significant factors for any group of Chinese tourist arrivals to Taiwan, regardless of the method of estimation, and whether the traditional or standardized-residual method is used.

6. Conclusions

The Cross-Strait relationship has long been a major focus of attention among the general public, not only in Taiwan and China, but also throughout the entire Asia–Pacific region, having become one of the more important issues of concern to the global community. The different official political stances on the two sides of the Taiwan Strait have indirectly affected private sector exchanges. Since 2008, when President Ma Ying-jeou relaxed the Cross-Strait policy, mainland Chinese have been allowed to apply to travel to Taiwan as Group-type tourists, without having to transit through a third country. With the relaxation of the conditions for Cross-Strait tourism, increasing numbers of Chinese tourists have been attracted to visit Taiwan. From 2010 onwards, Chinese tourists have accounted for the largest proportion of international tourists visiting Taiwan (though both China and Taiwan sometimes regard such tourism as domestic).

In 2016, Taiwan's 14th President Tsai Ing-wen's Cross-Strait policy was unable to satisfy the expectations for one China, which led to a gradual stalemate in Cross-Strait relations. Rumors circulated that the Chinese government had limited the number of Chinese tourists that could visit Taiwan. The data also indicated that the number of Chinese tourists visiting Taiwan was also exhibiting a clear downward trend. In addition to political factors, Taiwan's tourism environment in relation to facilities and safety considerations was also affecting the willingness of Chinese tourists to visit Taiwan.

Previous studies have rarely examined the impact of political and disaster-related events on tourism demand from China to Taiwan. In this research, an approach that has frequently been applied in financial studies, namely the event study methodology, was adopted to analyze the effects of changes in the number of three types of Chinese tourists to Taiwan caused by political events, and by disaster and accident events.

The purpose of this study was to demonstrate a potential application of the event study method to tourism data, which could be applied to analyze the impact of such detailed information on tourism. This research has used data on the numbers of Chinese tourists visiting Taiwan over the period

1 January 2014–31 October 2016 to examine the impact of Cross-Strait political events, and disaster and accident events, on the numbers of Chinese tourists visiting Taiwan during the period 2014–2016.

Major political events and increased uncertainty regarding the Cross-Strait relationship have affected the numbers of Chinese tourists visiting Taiwan. The empirical results of this paper show that President Tsai Ing-wen's lack of a specific mention of the "1992 Consensus" Cross-Strait policy resulted in an abnormal reduction in the number of Group-type Chinese tourists visiting Taiwan, an outcome that confirms the rumors that the Chinese government has limited the numbers of its citizens that can visit Taiwan.

The visit by eight of Taiwan's county and city mayors to Beijing, China, and the ensuing agreement between the two sides to jointly promote the "Eight measures to benefit Taiwan" in Taiwan and China through exchange and cooperation, resulted in the numbers of both Group-type and Individual-type tourists increasing abnormally. This paper confirms that political events have had relatively little impact on the numbers of Medical-type tourists visiting Taiwan, mainly because Medical-type tourists come to Taiwan for health checks or cosmetic treatments, and are thereby not generally affected by political events.

Given the restrictions in obtaining (daily) data from the National Immigration Agency in Taiwan, the data used in the paper focused on daily Chinese and international tourist arrivals data from 1 January 2014 to 31 October 2016.

Overall, we have focused on two major issues that affect Chinese tourists to travel to Taiwan, namely political events, and disaster and accident events. Based on the data sources, we can verify the impacts from different political events, and disaster and accident events, for three types of Chinese tourists to Taiwan, four methods of estimation, and the traditional and standardized-residual methods.

From the results of the disaster-related event research, it has been found that the impact of disasters and accidents on the number of Chinese tourists visiting Taiwan mainly depends on the level of an incident's impact. For example, the Kaohsiung Petrochemical gas explosion resulted in a significant abnormal reduction in the numbers of Group-type and Individual-type Chinese tourists visiting Taiwan.

The TransAsia Airways Flight 235 crash incident directly affected the tourists' concerns over travel safety and hence their willingness to travel, so that the numbers of each type of tourist exhibited a significant abnormal reduction. The accidental firing of a missile by the Taiwan Navy and the accident involving a Chinese tour group travelling on a tour bus did not affect the numbers of Chinese tourists visiting Taiwan.

In the cases where the events occurred on a national holiday, there was not an abnormal change in the number of Chinese tourists visiting Taiwan. If the incident took place during the Chinese New Year holiday, while it did not affect the numbers of Group-type tourists; after the holidays were over, the numbers of Individual-type and Medical-type tourists did in fact experience a significant abnormal reduction.

Based on the above empirical results, we estimated the impacts from different political events, and disaster and accident events, for three types of Chinese tourists to Taiwan. For political events, Group-type tourists are the most sensitive to the impact of Cross-Strait political events, but Individual-type and Medical-type tourists are seemingly not affected by political events.

In the past, in order to attract Chinese tourists to visit Taiwan, Taiwan businesses adopted low-cost group price competition as their business model. This not only undermined the quality of tourism in Taiwan, but also gave rise to bad money driving out good money, with the exclusion of international travelers with high spending power who would otherwise have been willing to visit Taiwan.

For disaster-related events, different levels of an incident generate different effects on the rate of change in the numbers of different types of Chinese tourists to Taiwan. These empirical results should serve as a valuable reference to the Taiwan Government, as well as to public and private policy-makers, as they formulate new economic and financial tourism policies and strategies for the future.

Therefore, in the future, tourism businesses in Taiwan should enhance their own competitiveness, and extricate themselves from the vicious cycle of price competition. The Taiwan government should also actively promote a unique style of tourism, establish tourism groups with specific purposes, and create a friendly and safe tourism environment. It should also enhance the quality of tourism in Taiwan, strengthen the depth of tourism, attract tourists with high spending power, and create new sources of tourism revenue.

Future research would also use additional data from leading tourism source countries to Taiwan, such as Hong Kong and Macao, Japan, South Korea, Singapore, Malaysia, and USA. This would enable a greater understanding of the effects of tourism demand to Taiwan caused by major events. Additionally, further research would also examine the effects of further information and factors that affect tourism demand movements.

Author Contributions: Conceptualization, C.-L.C.; Data curation, S.-H.H.; Formal analysis, C.-L.C. and M.M.; Funding acquisition, C.-L.C. and M.M.; Investigation, C.-L.C., S.-H.H. and M.M.; Methodology, M.M.; Project administration, C.-L.C.; Software, S.-H.H.; Supervision, C.-L.C. and M.M.; Validation, S.-H.H.; Writing—original draft, C.-L.C. and S.-H.H.; Writing—review & editing, M.M.

Acknowledgments: The authors are most grateful to three reviewers for very helpful comments and suggestions. For financial support, the first author wishes to thank the Ministry of Science and Technology (MOST), Taiwan, and the third author acknowledges the Australian Research Council and the Ministry of Science and Technology (MOST), Taiwan.

Appendix A.

Table A1. Case I: OLS—Cumulative abnormal change rate of Chinese tourist arrivals.

Event Period $[\tau_1, \tau_2]$	Group-Type			Individual-Type			Medical-Type		
	CAR	t-Value		CAR	t-Value		CAR	t-Value	
		TM	SRM		TM	SRM		TM	SRM
[0, 0]	13.66	0.54	0.53	31.44	0.84	0.82	−51.38	−0.69	−0.67
[0, 1]	24.20	0.96	0.94	20.65	0.55	0.54	30.91	0.41	0.40
[0, 2]	32.79	1.31	1.27	7.25	0.19	0.19	10.87	0.15	0.14
[0, 3]	22.26	0.89	0.85	41.95	1.13	1.08	17.94	0.24	0.23
[0, 4]	21.08	0.84	0.82	26.77	0.72	0.70	2.82	0.04	0.04
[0, 5]	−4.61	−0.18	−0.18	7.26	0.20	0.19	47.95	0.64	0.62
[0, 6]	−7.84	−0.31	−0.31	−19.91	−0.53	−0.52	−5.90	−0.08	−0.08
[0, 7]	15.89	0.63	0.62	13.55	0.36	0.36	−99.14	−1.33	−1.30
[0, 8]	31.35	1.25	1.22	−1.80	−0.05	−0.05	24.10	0.32	0.31
[0, 9]	17.39	0.69	0.68	8.08	0.22	0.21	25.03	0.34	0.33
[0, 10]	17.85	0.71	0.70	−4.17	−0.11	−0.11	−71.81	−0.96	−0.94
[0, 11]	5.54	0.22	0.22	20.30	0.55	0.53	−113.08	−1.51	−1.48
[0, 12]	−2.25	−0.09	−0.09	−23.66	−0.64	−0.62	1.11	0.01	0.01
[0, 13]	−15.50	−0.62	−0.60	−36.02	−0.97	−0.94	−0.83	−0.01	−0.01
[0, 14]	−12.78	−0.51	−0.50	−29.60	−0.80	−0.78	−42.67	−0.57	−0.56
[0, 15]	−14.42	−0.57	−0.56	6.77	0.18	0.18	10.41	0.14	0.14
[0, 16]	−43.32	−1.73	−1.67	−8.64	−0.23	−0.22	−25.34	−0.34	−0.33
[0, 17]	−6.60	−0.26	−0.26	33.69	0.90	0.88	−57.86	−0.77	−0.76
[0, 18]	−22.73	−0.91	−0.89	20.09	0.54	0.53	−9.03	−0.12	−0.12
[0, 19]	−34.47	−1.37	−1.34	−30.43	−0.82	−0.80	−103.00	−1.38	−1.34
[0, 20]	4.05	0.16	0.16	−3.21	−0.09	−0.08	−30.57	−0.41	−0.40
[0, 21]	7.00	0.28	0.27	5.70	0.15	0.15	−9.71	−0.13	−0.13
[0, 22]	19.26	0.77	0.75	10.29	0.28	0.27	2.34	0.03	0.03
[0, 23]	12.32	0.49	0.47	5.85	0.16	0.15	39.83	0.53	0.51
[0, 24]	27.48	1.10	1.07	32.14	0.86	0.84	14.09	0.19	0.18
[0, 25]	6.59	0.26	0.26	−2.22	−0.06	−0.06	−24.09	−0.32	−0.32

Table A1. *Cont.*

Event Period $[\tau_1, \tau_2]$	Group-Type			Individual-Type			Medical-Type		
	CAR	t-Value		CAR	t-Value		CAR	t-Value	
		TM	SRM		TM	SRM		TM	SRM
[0, 26]	−15.79	−0.63	−0.62	−12.66	−0.34	−0.33	−6.66	−0.09	−0.09
[0, 27]	−12.56	−0.50	−0.49	−10.79	−0.29	−0.28	−16.85	−0.23	−0.22
[0, 28]	−3.24	−0.13	−0.12	−29.64	−0.80	−0.77	−27.12	−0.36	−0.35
[0, 29]	−3.31	−0.13	−0.13	−36.86	−0.99	−0.97	−62.19	−0.83	−0.81
[0, 30]	−5.63	−0.22	−0.22	−3.13	−0.08	−0.08	23.12	0.31	0.30

Table A2. Case I: GARCH(1,1)—Cumulative abnormal change rate of Chinese tourist arrivals.

Event Period $[\tau_1, \tau_2]$	Group-Type			Individual-Type			Medical-Type		
	CAR	t-Value		CAR	t-Value		CAR	t-Value	
		TM	SRM		TM	SRM		TM	SRM
[0, 0]	13.86	0.43	0.41	32.38	0.48	0.47	−52.80	−0.63	−0.61
[0, 1]	24.51	0.75	0.73	21.25	0.32	0.31	28.30	0.34	0.33
[0, 2]	33.25	1.02	0.99	8.14	0.12	0.12	6.97	0.08	0.08
[0, 3]	22.78	0.70	0.67	42.01	0.62	0.60	12.97	0.15	0.15
[0, 4]	22.07	0.68	0.66	31.31	0.46	0.45	−4.29	−0.05	−0.05
[0, 5]	−3.54	−0.11	−0.11	11.15	0.17	0.16	39.73	0.47	0.46
[0, 6]	−6.51	−0.20	−0.20	−14.39	−0.21	−0.21	−15.70	−0.19	−0.18
[0, 7]	17.47	0.54	0.52	20.64	0.31	0.30	−110.49	−1.31	−1.28
[0, 8]	33.05	1.01	0.99	5.12	0.08	0.07	11.54	0.14	0.13
[0, 9]	19.28	0.59	0.58	15.87	0.24	0.23	11.06	0.13	0.13
[0, 10]	20.06	0.62	0.60	6.11	0.09	0.09	−87.52	−1.04	−1.02
[0, 11]	8.01	0.25	0.24	32.09	0.48	0.47	−130.34	−1.55	−1.51
[0, 12]	0.48	0.01	0.01	−10.02	−0.15	−0.15	−17.76	−0.21	−0.21
[0, 13]	−12.56	−0.39	−0.38	−21.48	−0.32	−0.31	−21.12	−0.25	−0.24
[0, 14]	−9.71	−0.30	−0.29	−15.10	−0.22	−0.22	−64.20	−0.76	−0.74
[0, 15]	−11.15	−0.34	−0.33	22.22	0.33	0.32	−12.55	−0.15	−0.15
[0, 16]	−39.71	−1.22	−1.18	9.53	0.14	0.14	−50.09	−0.59	−0.57
[0, 17]	−2.98	−0.09	−0.09	50.43	0.75	0.73	−83.56	−0.99	−0.97
[0, 18]	−18.95	−0.58	−0.57	37.12	0.55	0.54	−36.03	−0.43	−0.42
[0, 19]	−30.45	−0.93	−0.91	−11.88	−0.18	−0.17	−131.55	−1.56	−1.52
[0, 20]	8.06	0.25	0.24	13.51	0.20	0.20	−59.99	−0.71	−0.70
[0, 21]	11.15	0.34	0.33	22.56	0.34	0.33	−40.39	−0.48	−0.47
[0, 22]	23.55	0.72	0.71	27.39	0.41	0.40	−29.63	−0.35	−0.34
[0, 23]	16.50	0.51	0.48	19.92	0.30	0.28	7.24	0.09	0.08
[0, 24]	32.11	0.99	0.96	50.31	0.75	0.73	−20.58	−0.24	−0.24
[0, 25]	11.44	0.35	0.34	17.12	0.25	0.25	−60.24	−0.71	−0.70
[0, 26]	−10.77	−0.33	−0.32	7.30	0.11	0.11	−44.17	−0.52	−0.51
[0, 27]	−7.32	−0.22	−0.22	10.33	0.15	0.15	−55.83	−0.66	−0.65
[0, 28]	1.90	0.06	0.06	−11.43	−0.17	−0.16	−66.76	−0.79	−0.76
[0, 29]	2.36	0.07	0.07	−13.68	−0.20	−0.20	−104.07	−1.23	−1.21
[0, 30]	0.02	0.00	0.00	18.24	0.27	0.26	−19.63	−0.23	−0.23

Table A3. Case I: GJR(1,1)—Cumulative abnormal change rate of Chinese tourist arrivals.

Event Period $[\tau_1, \tau_2]$	Group-Type			Individual-Type			Medical-Type		
	CAR	t-Value		CAR	t-Value		CAR	t-Value	
		TM	SRM		TM	SRM		TM	SRM
[0, 0]	10.16	0.11	0.11	32.28	0.67	0.65	−51.27	−0.14	−0.14
[0, 1]	18.30	0.20	0.20	21.38	0.44	0.43	22.53	0.06	0.06
[0, 2]	23.95	0.27	0.26	8.34	0.17	0.17	−1.76	0.00	0.00
[0, 3]	11.44	0.13	0.12	42.56	0.88	0.84	−6.54	−0.02	−0.02
[0, 4]	3.70	0.04	0.04	30.86	0.64	0.62	2.30	0.01	0.01
[0, 5]	−24.12	−0.27	−0.26	11.01	0.23	0.22	36.81	0.10	0.10
[0, 6]	−31.46	−0.35	−0.34	−14.80	−0.31	−0.30	−12.22	−0.03	−0.03
[0, 7]	−11.76	−0.13	−0.13	19.97	0.41	0.40	−101.12	−0.28	−0.27
[0, 8]	1.15	0.01	0.01	4.64	0.10	0.09	14.76	0.04	0.04
[0, 9]	−16.25	−0.18	−0.18	15.31	0.32	0.31	15.32	0.04	0.04
[0, 10]	−20.65	−0.23	−0.23	5.06	0.10	0.10	−70.88	−0.19	−0.19
[0, 11]	−36.94	−0.41	−0.40	30.80	0.64	0.62	−108.24	−0.30	−0.29
[0, 12]	−49.03	−0.55	−0.53	−11.64	−0.24	−0.23	12.23	0.03	0.03
[0, 13]	−65.75	−0.73	−0.72	−23.19	−0.48	−0.47	10.16	0.03	0.03
[0, 14]	−65.68	−0.73	−0.72	−16.66	−0.34	−0.34	−38.18	−0.10	−0.10
[0, 15]	−70.83	−0.79	−0.77	20.56	0.42	0.41	15.06	0.04	0.04
[0, 16]	−104.78	−1.17	−1.13	7.32	0.15	0.15	−8.55	−0.02	−0.02
[0, 17]	−69.52	−0.78	−0.76	48.73	1.01	0.98	−56.89	−0.16	−0.15
[0, 18]	−88.58	−0.99	−0.97	35.49	0.73	0.72	−12.39	−0.03	−0.03
[0, 19]	−104.34	−1.17	−1.14	−13.76	−0.28	−0.28	−102.32	−0.28	−0.27
[0, 20]	−66.91	−0.75	−0.73	12.25	0.25	0.25	−48.49	−0.13	−0.13
[0, 21]	−66.78	−0.75	−0.73	21.40	0.44	0.43	−32.87	−0.09	−0.09
[0, 22]	−57.42	−0.64	−0.63	26.31	0.54	0.53	−25.48	−0.07	−0.07
[0, 23]	−64.43	−0.72	−0.69	19.75	0.41	0.39	−14.64	−0.04	−0.04
[0, 24]	−55.51	−0.62	−0.61	49.25	1.02	0.99	−18.94	−0.05	−0.05
[0, 25]	−80.10	−0.89	−0.87	15.89	0.33	0.32	−55.45	−0.15	−0.15
[0, 26]	−105.72	−1.18	−1.15	6.07	0.13	0.12	−40.01	−0.11	−0.11
[0, 27]	−106.17	−1.19	−1.16	8.94	0.18	0.18	−48.68	−0.13	−0.13
[0, 28]	−97.03	−1.08	−1.04	−11.93	−0.25	−0.24	−84.80	−0.23	−0.22
[0, 29]	−104.08	−1.16	−1.14	−15.31	−0.32	−0.31	−92.51	−0.25	−0.25
[0, 30]	−107.54	−1.20	−1.17	17.21	0.36	0.35	−25.61	−0.07	−0.07

Table A4. Case I: EGARCH(1,1)—Cumulative abnormal change rate of Chinese tourist arrivals.

Event Period $[\tau_1, \tau_2]$	Group-Type			Individual-Type			Medical-Type		
	CAR	t-Value		CAR	t-Value		CAR	t-Value	
		TM	SRM		TM	SRM		TM	SRM
[0, 0]	8.92	0.08	0.08	33.31	0.82	0.80	−51.76	−0.68	−0.67
[0, 1]	15.58	0.14	0.13	19.85	0.49	0.48	32.95	0.44	0.42
[0, 2]	19.87	0.18	0.17	6.01	0.15	0.14	13.97	0.18	0.18
[0, 3]	5.78	0.05	0.05	36.27	0.90	0.86	24.56	0.32	0.31
[0, 4]	−2.51	−0.02	−0.02	35.57	0.88	0.86	1.25	0.02	0.02
[0, 5]	−31.87	−0.28	−0.28	12.27	0.30	0.30	49.51	0.65	0.64
[0, 6]	−40.31	−0.36	−0.35	−10.54	−0.26	−0.25	−6.28	−0.08	−0.08
[0, 7]	−21.73	−0.19	−0.19	27.03	0.67	0.65	−101.28	−1.34	−1.31
[0, 8]	−10.27	−0.09	−0.09	9.61	0.24	0.23	24.02	0.32	0.31
[0, 9]	−28.92	−0.26	−0.25	21.11	0.52	0.51	24.73	0.33	0.32
[0, 10]	−34.25	−0.30	−0.30	16.29	0.40	0.39	−75.95	−1.00	−0.98
[0, 11]	−51.67	−0.46	−0.45	44.65	1.11	1.08	−118.85	−1.57	−1.54
[0, 12]	−64.81	−0.58	−0.56	5.82	0.14	0.14	−7.06	−0.09	−0.09
[0, 13]	−82.77	−0.73	−0.72	−4.79	−0.12	−0.12	−9.31	−0.12	−0.12
[0, 14]	−84.13	−0.75	−0.73	0.01	0.00	0.00	−49.38	−0.65	−0.64
[0, 15]	−90.52	−0.80	−0.78	38.28	0.95	0.92	3.30	0.04	0.04
[0, 16]	−125.35	−1.11	−1.07	31.11	0.77	0.74	−36.77	−0.49	−0.47
[0, 17]	−91.79	−0.81	−0.80	66.88	1.66	1.62	−64.45	−0.85	−0.83
[0, 18]	−112.21	−1.00	−0.97	52.82	1.31	1.28	−14.55	−0.19	−0.19
[0, 19]	−129.09	−1.15	−1.12	6.24	0.15	0.15	−110.20	−1.46	−1.42
[0, 20]	−93.44	−0.83	−0.81	25.45	0.63	0.62	−32.02	−0.42	−0.41
[0, 21]	−94.70	−0.84	−0.82	33.40	0.83	0.81	−9.79	−0.13	−0.13
[0, 22]	−86.71	−0.77	−0.75	37.35	0.92	0.90	3.43	0.05	0.04
[0, 23]	−95.73	−0.85	−0.81	20.62	0.51	0.49	49.32	0.65	0.62
[0, 24]	−87.43	−0.78	−0.76	60.07	1.49	1.45	16.19	0.21	0.21
[0, 25]	−113.20	−1.00	−0.98	28.41	0.70	0.69	−22.88	−0.30	−0.30
[0, 26]	−140.12	−1.24	−1.22	18.73	0.46	0.45	−5.15	−0.07	−0.07
[0, 27]	−141.77	−1.26	−1.23	23.23	0.57	0.56	−16.19	−0.21	−0.21
[0, 28]	−134.61	−1.19	−1.15	−7.48	−0.19	−0.18	−18.34	−0.24	−0.23
[0, 29]	−142.12	−1.26	−1.23	1.58	0.04	0.04	−62.72	−0.83	−0.81
[0, 30]	−147.34	−1.31	−1.27	27.39	0.68	0.66	28.28	0.37	0.36

Table A5. Case II: OLS—Cumulative abnormal change rate of Chinese tourist arrivals.

Event Period $[\tau_1, \tau_2]$	Group-Type			Individual-Type			Medical-Type		
	CAR	t-Value		CAR	t-Value		CAR	t-Value	
		TM	SRM		TM	SRM		TM	SRM
[−10, −10]	9.27	0.33	0.33	13.21	0.31	0.31	55.70	0.61	0.60
[−10, −9]	−8.31	−0.30	−0.29	8.25	0.20	0.19	−1.36	−0.01	−0.01
[−10, −8]	5.94	0.21	0.21	24.61	0.58	0.56	−19.03	−0.21	−0.20
[−10, −7]	−4.03	−0.15	−0.14	23.11	0.55	0.52	49.90	0.55	0.52
[−10, −6]	−45.58	−1.64	−1.60	3.64	0.09	0.08	68.84	0.75	0.73
[−10, −5]	−13.37	−0.48	−0.47	−3.39	−0.08	−0.08	37.01	0.41	0.40
[−10, −4]	−17.77	−0.64	−0.63	−2.93	−0.07	−0.07	70.98	0.78	0.76
[−10, −3]	−6.93	−0.25	−0.25	9.78	0.23	0.23	18.99	0.21	0.20
[−10, −2]	−31.69	−1.14	−1.11	9.55	0.23	0.22	33.19	0.36	0.35
[−10, −1]	−12.91	−0.47	−0.46	4.84	0.11	0.11	0.24	0.00	0.00
[−10, 0]	7.89	0.28	0.28	11.58	0.27	0.27	96.21	1.05	1.04
[−10, 1]	−31.06	−1.12	−1.10	10.14	0.24	0.23	68.48	0.75	0.73
[−10, 2]	−32.15	−1.16	−1.13	−14.08	−0.33	−0.33	83.34	0.91	0.89
[−10, 3]	−39.89	−1.44	−1.41	−7.76	−0.18	−0.18	87.41	0.96	0.94
[−10, 4]	−6.31	−0.23	−0.22	4.91	0.12	0.11	70.98	0.78	0.76
[−10, 5]	−20.15	−0.73	−0.71	14.34	0.34	0.33	−38.17	−0.42	−0.41
[−10, 6]	−24.07	−0.87	−0.85	24.75	0.59	0.57	13.04	0.14	0.14
[−10, 7]	3.94	0.14	0.14	6.93	0.16	0.16	−23.09	−0.25	−0.25
[−10, 8]	−24.44	−0.88	−0.85	0.71	0.02	0.02	36.32	0.40	0.39
[−10, 9]	−10.19	−0.37	−0.36	−14.26	−0.34	−0.33	−49.92	−0.55	−0.53
[−10, 10]	−9.20	−0.33	−0.33	−21.61	−0.51	−0.50	−71.42	−0.78	−0.77
[−10, 11]	0.84	0.03	0.03	13.20	0.31	0.30	71.94	0.79	0.77
[−10, 12]	−15.34	−0.55	−0.54	−6.32	−0.15	−0.15	11.52	0.13	0.12
[−10, 13]	−2.99	−0.11	−0.11	13.75	0.33	0.32	97.96	1.07	1.05
[−10, 14]	4.71	0.17	0.16	4.77	0.11	0.11	31.61	0.35	0.34
[−10, 15]	−29.35	−1.06	−1.03	6.56	0.16	0.15	106.55	1.17	1.14
[−10, 16]	−1.09	−0.04	−0.04	−8.82	−0.21	−0.20	107.58	1.18	1.15
[−10, 17]	−8.37	−0.30	−0.30	−10.22	−0.24	−0.24	28.71	0.31	0.31
[−10, 18]	−1.84	−0.07	−0.07	10.77	0.26	0.25	−8.52	−0.09	−0.09
[−10, 19]	−6.10	−0.22	−0.21	−1.86	−0.04	−0.04	−31.73	−0.35	−0.34
[−10, 20]	−13.63	−0.49	−0.48	8.57	0.20	0.20	−5.68	−0.06	−0.06

Table A6. Case II: GARCH(1,1)—Cumulative abnormal change rate of Chinese tourist arrivals.

Event Period $[\tau_1, \tau_2]$	Group-Type			Individual-Type			Medical-Type		
	CAR	t-Value		CAR	t-Value		CAR	t-Value	
		TM	SRM		TM	SRM		TM	SRM
[−10, −10]	7.18	0.10	0.09	15.05	0.23	0.22	54.85	0.57	0.56
[−10, −9]	−11.39	−0.15	−0.15	14.63	0.22	0.21	0.88	0.01	0.01
[−10, −8]	1.16	0.02	0.01	33.80	0.51	0.49	−16.22	−0.17	−0.16
[−10, −7]	−10.63	−0.14	−0.14	34.81	0.52	0.50	52.84	0.55	0.52
[−10, −6]	−56.08	−0.75	−0.73	12.68	0.19	0.19	64.35	0.67	0.65
[−10, −5]	−27.90	−0.37	−0.37	2.70	0.04	0.04	24.68	0.26	0.25
[−10, −4]	−33.95	−0.46	−0.45	6.08	0.09	0.09	59.37	0.62	0.60
[−10, −3]	−25.76	−0.35	−0.34	19.26	0.29	0.28	4.53	0.05	0.05
[−10, −2]	−51.80	−0.70	−0.68	22.85	0.34	0.33	20.77	0.22	0.21
[−10, −1]	−36.09	−0.48	−0.48	17.56	0.26	0.26	−16.56	−0.17	−0.17
[−10, 0]	−18.01	−0.24	−0.24	24.60	0.37	0.36	76.32	0.79	0.78
[−10, 1]	−58.56	−0.79	−0.77	26.20	0.39	0.39	49.50	0.51	0.50
[−10, 2]	−61.72	−0.83	−0.81	3.84	0.06	0.06	63.51	0.66	0.64
[−10, 3]	−72.27	−0.97	−0.95	10.25	0.15	0.15	64.18	0.67	0.65
[−10, 4]	−40.38	−0.54	−0.53	25.73	0.39	0.38	48.32	0.50	0.49
[−10, 5]	−57.24	−0.77	−0.75	34.69	0.52	0.51	−65.06	−0.68	−0.66
[−10, 6]	−62.82	−0.84	−0.82	48.00	0.72	0.70	−13.15	−0.14	−0.13
[−10, 7]	−37.12	−0.50	−0.49	31.45	0.47	0.46	−50.95	−0.53	−0.52
[−10, 8]	−67.31	−0.90	−0.88	27.79	0.42	0.41	8.65	0.09	0.09
[−10, 9]	−55.76	−0.75	−0.73	13.16	0.20	0.19	−80.63	−0.84	−0.82
[−10, 10]	−58.21	−0.78	−0.77	4.30	0.06	0.06	−107.88	−1.12	−1.10
[−10, 11]	−49.28	−0.66	−0.64	43.35	0.65	0.63	38.15	0.40	0.39
[−10, 12]	−67.78	−0.91	−0.89	25.12	0.38	0.37	−23.94	−0.25	−0.24
[−10, 13]	−58.35	−0.78	−0.77	44.96	0.68	0.66	58.63	0.61	0.60
[−10, 14]	−52.26	−0.70	−0.68	39.00	0.59	0.57	−6.84	−0.07	−0.07
[−10, 15]	−88.82	−1.19	−1.16	41.60	0.62	0.61	65.75	0.68	0.66
[−10, 16]	−63.36	−0.85	−0.83	26.33	0.40	0.39	63.39	0.66	0.64
[−10, 17]	−74.02	−0.99	−0.98	23.57	0.35	0.35	−21.01	−0.22	−0.21
[−10, 18]	−69.29	−0.93	−0.91	47.11	0.71	0.69	−58.05	−0.60	−0.59
[−10, 19]	−74.96	−1.01	−0.98	38.00	0.57	0.56	−79.65	−0.83	−0.81
[−10, 20]	−84.46	−1.13	−1.10	50.54	0.76	0.74	−54.07	−0.56	−0.54

Table A7. Case II: GJR(1,1)—Cumulative abnormal change rate of Chinese tourist arrivals.

Event Period $[\tau_1, \tau_2]$	Group-Type			Individual-Type			Medical-Type		
	CAR	t-Value		CAR	t-Value		CAR	t-Value	
		TM	SRM		TM	SRM		TM	SRM
[−10, −10]	10.33	0.30	0.29	13.35	0.31	0.30	66.30	0.23	0.23
[−10, −9]	−4.86	−0.14	−0.13	8.74	0.20	0.20	28.97	0.10	0.10
[−10, −8]	10.93	0.31	0.30	25.31	0.59	0.56	25.18	0.09	0.09
[−10, −7]	2.35	0.07	0.06	24.01	0.56	0.53	106.97	0.38	0.36
[−10, −6]	−40.33	−1.15	−1.12	4.31	0.10	0.10	121.23	0.43	0.42
[−10, −5]	−9.40	−0.27	−0.26	−2.99	−0.07	−0.07	83.80	0.30	0.29
[−10, −4]	−12.21	−0.35	−0.34	−2.31	−0.05	−0.05	132.01	0.47	0.46
[−10, −3]	−0.97	−0.03	−0.03	10.42	0.24	0.24	85.97	0.30	0.30
[−10, −2]	−23.70	−0.68	−0.66	10.50	0.24	0.24	117.45	0.41	0.40
[−10, −1]	−5.04	−0.14	−0.14	5.72	0.13	0.13	86.91	0.31	0.30
[−10, 0]	16.07	0.46	0.45	12.47	0.29	0.28	188.27	0.66	0.65
[−10, 1]	−21.22	−0.61	−0.59	11.26	0.26	0.25	175.21	0.62	0.60
[−10, 2]	−21.24	−0.61	−0.59	−12.82	−0.30	−0.29	200.69	0.71	0.69
[−10, 3]	−28.77	−0.82	−0.81	−6.50	−0.15	−0.15	209.42	0.74	0.72
[−10, 4]	6.35	0.18	0.18	6.37	0.15	0.14	206.88	0.73	0.71
[−10, 5]	−7.56	−0.22	−0.21	15.75	0.36	0.36	100.49	0.35	0.35
[−10, 6]	−9.89	−0.28	−0.28	26.38	0.61	0.59	165.88	0.59	0.57
[−10, 7]	18.91	0.54	0.53	8.65	0.20	0.19	138.43	0.49	0.48
[−10, 8]	−8.06	−0.23	−0.22	2.63	0.06	0.06	210.85	0.74	0.72
[−10, 9]	6.52	0.19	0.18	−12.33	−0.29	−0.28	130.13	0.46	0.45
[−10, 10]	6.94	0.20	0.19	−19.83	−0.46	−0.45	107.86	0.38	0.37
[−10, 11]	19.22	0.55	0.53	15.32	0.35	0.34	269.96	0.95	0.93
[−10, 12]	3.83	0.11	0.11	−4.11	−0.09	−0.09	218.24	0.77	0.75
[−10, 13]	16.24	0.46	0.45	15.92	0.37	0.36	308.27	1.09	1.06
[−10, 14]	25.58	0.73	0.71	7.17	0.17	0.16	256.52	0.90	0.88
[−10, 15]	−7.92	−0.23	−0.22	9.01	0.21	0.20	338.58	1.19	1.16
[−10, 16]	20.56	0.59	0.57	−6.37	−0.15	−0.14	344.31	1.21	1.19
[−10, 17]	12.78	0.37	0.36	−7.90	−0.18	−0.18	265.18	0.94	0.92
[−10, 18]	20.72	0.59	0.58	13.28	0.31	0.30	240.96	0.85	0.83
[−10, 19]	18.35	0.52	0.51	0.93	0.02	0.02	234.04	0.83	0.80
[−10, 20]	12.02	0.34	0.33	11.52	0.27	0.26	271.57	0.96	0.93

Table A8. Case II: EGARCH(1,1)—Cumulative abnormal change rate of Chinese tourist arrivals.

Event Period $[\tau_1, \tau_2]$	Group-Type			Individual-Type			Medical-Type		
	CAR	t-Value		CAR	t-Value		CAR	t-Value	
		TM	SRM		TM	SRM		TM	SRM
[−10, −10]	8.66	0.23	0.23	12.69	0.32	0.32	61.71	0.30	0.29
[−10, −9]	−8.69	−0.23	−0.23	7.15	0.18	0.18	10.45	0.05	0.05
[−10, −8]	5.25	0.14	0.14	22.97	0.58	0.56	−1.29	−0.01	−0.01
[−10, −7]	−5.13	−0.14	−0.13	20.95	0.53	0.51	73.61	0.35	0.34
[−10, −6]	−48.66	−1.31	−1.28	1.06	0.03	0.03	98.91	0.47	0.46
[−10, −5]	−18.54	−0.50	−0.49	−6.39	−0.16	−0.16	73.45	0.35	0.35
[−10, −4]	−23.21	−0.63	−0.61	−6.47	−0.16	−0.16	113.35	0.54	0.53
[−10, −3]	−13.40	−0.36	−0.35	5.76	0.15	0.14	67.48	0.32	0.32
[−10, −2]	−38.16	−1.03	−1.00	4.97	0.13	0.12	87.54	0.42	0.41
[−10, −1]	−20.73	−0.56	−0.55	−0.20	−0.01	−0.01	60.79	0.29	0.29
[−10, 0]	−1.02	−0.03	−0.03	6.05	0.15	0.15	162.89	0.78	0.77
[−10, 1]	−40.20	−1.08	−1.06	4.06	0.10	0.10	141.08	0.68	0.66
[−10, 2]	−41.89	−1.13	−1.10	−20.67	−0.52	−0.51	161.94	0.78	0.76
[−10, 3]	−50.78	−1.37	−1.34	−14.82	−0.38	−0.37	172.16	0.83	0.81
[−10, 4]	−17.50	−0.47	−0.46	−2.70	−0.07	−0.07	161.66	0.77	0.76
[−10, 5]	−32.67	−0.88	−0.86	6.27	0.16	0.16	58.70	0.28	0.28
[−10, 6]	−36.87	−0.99	−0.97	16.14	0.41	0.40	115.84	0.56	0.54
[−10, 7]	−9.63	−0.26	−0.25	−2.19	−0.06	−0.05	85.77	0.41	0.40
[−10, 8]	−38.40	−1.03	−1.00	−8.94	−0.23	−0.22	151.14	0.72	0.70
[−10, 9]	−25.23	−0.68	−0.66	−24.40	−0.62	−0.60	71.02	0.34	0.33
[−10, 10]	−25.87	−0.70	−0.68	−32.19	−0.82	−0.80	55.79	0.27	0.26
[−10, 11]	−15.70	−0.42	−0.41	2.05	0.05	0.05	204.98	0.98	0.96
[−10, 12]	−32.66	−0.88	−0.86	−17.97	−0.46	−0.44	150.61	0.72	0.70
[−10, 13]	−21.55	−0.58	−0.57	1.62	0.04	0.04	243.22	1.17	1.14
[−10, 14]	−14.10	−0.38	−0.37	−7.90	−0.20	−0.19	182.79	0.88	0.85
[−10, 15]	−49.08	−1.32	−1.29	−6.60	−0.17	−0.16	263.82	1.26	1.23
[−10, 16]	−21.96	−0.59	−0.58	−22.46	−0.57	−0.56	270.99	1.30	1.27
[−10, 17]	−30.83	−0.83	−0.82	−24.31	−0.62	−0.61	198.39	0.95	0.94
[−10, 18]	−24.69	−0.66	−0.65	−3.85	−0.10	−0.10	167.11	0.80	0.79
[−10, 19]	−29.04	−0.78	−0.76	−17.04	−0.43	−0.42	149.78	0.72	0.70
[−10, 20]	−37.09	−1.00	−0.97	−7.12	−0.18	−0.18	181.82	0.87	0.85

Table A9. Case III: OLS—Cumulative abnormal change rate of Chinese tourist arrivals.

Event Period $[\tau_1, \tau_2]$	Group-Type			Individual-Type			Medical-Type		
	CAR	t-Value		CAR	t-Value		CAR	t-Value	
		TM	SRM		TM	SRM		TM	SRM
[−10, −10]	5.16	0.19	0.19	2.09	0.05	0.05	160.17	1.79	1.75
[−10, −9]	−30.70	−1.14	−1.12	8.41	0.20	0.20	190.49	2.13	2.09
[−10, −8]	−28.43	−1.06	−1.04	16.27	0.39	0.38	78.31	0.87	0.86
[−10, −7]	−40.46	−1.51	−1.47	6.80	0.16	0.16	61.67	0.69	0.67
[−10, −6]	−61.14	−2.28	−2.24	6.58	0.16	0.16	102.99	1.15	1.13
[−10, −5]	−35.51	−1.32	−1.30	1.40	0.03	0.03	53.78	0.60	0.59
[−10, −4]	−27.64	−1.03	−1.01	4.72	0.11	0.11	77.14	0.86	0.85
[−10, −3]	−25.18	−0.94	−0.91	−10.21	−0.25	−0.24	92.73	1.04	1.01
[−10, −2]	−53.66	−2.00	−1.95	9.42	0.23	0.22	69.13	0.77	0.75
[−10, −1]	−45.53	−1.70	−1.65	31.06	0.75	0.73	26.10	0.29	0.28
[−10, 0]	−35.49	−1.32	−1.29	26.53	0.64	0.62	63.90	0.71	0.70
[−10, 1]	−46.41	−1.73	−1.69	−10.25	−0.25	−0.24	94.44	1.05	1.03
[−10, 2]	−40.34	−1.50	−1.47	3.59	0.09	0.08	186.93	2.09	2.04
[−10, 3]	−36.82	−1.37	−1.35	2.18	0.05	0.05	128.85	1.44	1.41
[−10, 4]	−12.10	−0.45	−0.44	17.94	0.43	0.42	138.84	1.55	1.52
[−10, 5]	−45.64	−1.70	−1.65	−7.53	−0.18	−0.18	106.35	1.19	1.15
[−10, 6]	−42.65	−1.59	−1.55	15.72	0.38	0.37	128.75	1.44	1.40
[−10, 7]	−26.97	−1.01	−0.98	28.67	0.69	0.67	69.94	0.78	0.76
[−10, 8]	−23.51	−0.88	−0.85	13.84	0.33	0.32	144.21	1.61	1.57
[−10, 9]	−26.28	−0.98	−0.96	4.25	0.10	0.10	131.81	1.47	1.44
[−10, 10]	−27.82	−1.04	−1.01	7.61	0.18	0.18	135.79	1.52	1.48
[−10, 11]	−0.64	−0.02	−0.02	22.39	0.54	0.52	141.20	1.58	1.54
[−10, 12]	−50.16	−1.87	−1.81	−4.61	−0.11	−0.11	80.84	0.90	0.87
[−10, 13]	−53.98	−2.01	−1.93	0.73	0.02	0.02	79.65	0.89	0.85
[−10, 14]	−43.62	−1.63	−1.55	0.96	0.02	0.02	89.81	1.00	0.96
[−10, 15]	−44.63	−1.66	−1.62	6.23	0.15	0.15	149.34	1.67	1.62
[−10, 16]	−12.59	−0.47	−0.46	18.62	0.45	0.44	78.99	0.88	0.86
[−10, 17]	−24.56	−0.92	−0.90	8.40	0.20	0.20	124.89	1.39	1.37
[−10, 18]	−11.21	−0.42	−0.41	2.78	0.07	0.07	78.18	0.87	0.85
[−10, 19]	−39.86	−1.49	−1.44	2.22	0.05	0.05	90.85	1.01	0.99
[−10, 20]	−43.98	−1.64	−1.58	4.30	0.10	0.10	143.90	1.61	1.55

Table A10. Case III: GARCH(1,1)—Cumulative abnormal change rate of Chinese tourist arrivals.

Event Period $[\tau_1, \tau_2]$	Group-Type			Individual-Type			Medical-Type		
	CAR	t-Value		CAR	t-Value		CAR	t-Value	
		TM	SRM		TM	SRM		TM	SRM
[−10, −10]	5.33	0.10	0.10	2.16	0.05	0.05	149.85	0.48	0.47
[−10 ,−9]	−32.51	−0.63	−0.62	8.28	0.20	0.20	170.02	0.55	0.54
[−10, −8]	−30.78	−0.60	−0.58	16.13	0.39	0.38	47.57	0.15	0.15
[−10, −7]	−43.16	−0.84	−0.82	6.66	0.16	0.16	20.65	0.07	0.06
[−10, −6]	−66.74	−1.29	−1.27	6.13	0.15	0.15	51.91	0.17	0.16
[−10, −5]	−42.96	−0.83	−0.82	0.78	0.02	0.02	−7.45	−0.02	−0.02
[−10, −4]	−36.58	−0.71	−0.70	3.96	0.10	0.09	5.73	0.02	0.02
[−10, −3]	−32.74	−0.63	−0.62	−10.75	−0.26	−0.25	10.88	0.04	0.03
[−10, −2]	−63.10	−1.22	−1.19	8.69	0.21	0.21	−22.87	−0.07	−0.07
[−10, −1]	−55.94	−1.08	−1.05	30.26	0.73	0.71	−76.13	−0.25	−0.24
[−10, 0]	−48.00	−0.93	−0.91	25.52	0.62	0.60	−48.45	−0.16	−0.15
[−10, 1]	−59.88	−1.16	−1.13	−11.33	−0.27	−0.27	−28.15	−0.09	−0.09
[−10, 2]	−55.45	−1.08	−1.05	2.36	0.06	0.06	54.18	0.17	0.17
[−10, 3]	−53.77	−1.04	−1.02	0.78	0.02	0.02	−14.06	−0.05	−0.04
[−10, 4]	−30.76	−0.60	−0.59	16.37	0.40	0.39	−14.23	−0.05	−0.05
[−10, 5]	−63.64	−1.23	−1.20	−8.97	−0.22	−0.21	−57.09	−0.18	−0.18
[−10, 6]	−62.77	−1.22	−1.19	14.07	0.34	0.33	−44.82	−0.14	−0.14
[−10, 7]	−48.16	−0.93	−0.91	26.93	0.65	0.64	−113.85	−0.37	−0.36
[−10, 8]	−45.88	−0.89	−0.87	12.01	0.29	0.28	−49.79	−0.16	−0.16
[−10, 9]	−51.23	−0.99	−0.97	2.15	0.05	0.05	−72.27	−0.23	−0.23
[−10, 10]	−53.40	−1.04	−1.01	5.48	0.13	0.13	−78.55	−0.25	−0.25
[−10, 11]	−27.11	−0.53	−0.51	20.20	0.49	0.48	−83.38	−0.27	−0.26
[−10, 12]	−77.08	−1.49	−1.45	−6.80	−0.16	−0.16	−154.02	−0.50	−0.48
[−10, 13]	−81.48	−1.58	−1.52	−1.49	−0.04	−0.03	−165.47	−0.53	−0.51
[−10, 14]	−71.64	−1.39	−1.32	−1.27	−0.03	−0.03	−165.58	−0.53	−0.51
[−10, 15]	−76.29	−1.48	−1.44	3.60	0.09	0.08	−116.05	−0.37	−0.36
[−10, 16]	−46.62	−0.90	−0.89	15.75	0.38	0.37	−196.50	−0.63	−0.62
[−10, 17]	−59.84	−1.16	−1.14	5.43	0.13	0.13	−160.80	−0.52	−0.51
[−10, 18]	−47.05	−0.91	−0.89	−0.22	−0.01	−0.01	−217.78	−0.70	−0.69
[−10, 19]	−76.59	−1.48	−1.44	−0.84	−0.02	−0.02	−215.34	−0.70	−0.68
[−10, 20]	−81.07	−1.57	−1.51	1.25	0.03	0.03	−172.57	−0.56	−0.54

Table A11. Case III: GJR(1,1)—Cumulative abnormal change rate of Chinese tourist arrivals.

Event Period $[\tau_1, \tau_2]$	Group-Type			Individual-Type			Medical-Type		
	CAR	t-Value		CAR	t-Value		CAR	t-Value	
		TM	SRM		TM	SRM		TM	SRM
[−10, −10]	7.11	0.24	0.23	−0.34	−0.01	−0.01	157.94	1.49	1.46
[−10, −9]	−28.60	−0.96	−0.95	4.67	0.08	0.08	186.43	1.75	1.72
[−10, −8]	−24.97	−0.84	−0.82	10.46	0.17	0.17	72.15	0.68	0.67
[−10, −7]	−35.49	−1.19	−1.16	−1.17	−0.02	−0.02	53.38	0.50	0.49
[−10, −6]	−56.78	−1.91	−1.88	−2.23	−0.04	−0.04	93.04	0.88	0.86
[−10, −5]	−30.89	−1.04	−1.02	−8.79	−0.15	−0.14	41.98	0.39	0.39
[−10, −4]	−22.45	−0.76	−0.74	−7.04	−0.12	−0.11	63.42	0.60	0.59
[−10, −3]	−17.04	−0.57	−0.56	−25.03	−0.42	−0.40	76.55	0.72	0.70
[−10, −2]	−45.28	−1.52	−1.49	−6.77	−0.11	−0.11	51.10	0.48	0.47
[−10, −1]	−36.15	−1.22	−1.18	13.03	0.22	0.21	6.05	0.06	0.06
[−10, 0]	−26.06	−0.88	−0.86	7.25	0.12	0.12	42.05	0.40	0.39
[−10, 1]	−35.97	−1.21	−1.18	−31.37	−0.52	−0.51	70.57	0.66	0.65
[−10, 2]	−29.46	−0.99	−0.97	−19.02	−0.32	−0.31	161.17	1.52	1.48
[−10, 3]	−25.67	−0.86	−0.85	−21.82	−0.36	−0.35	101.23	0.95	0.93
[−10, 4]	−0.57	−0.02	−0.02	−7.51	−0.12	−0.12	109.35	1.03	1.01
[−10, 5]	−31.75	−1.07	−1.04	−35.67	−0.59	−0.57	74.53	0.70	0.68
[−10, 6]	−28.73	−0.97	−0.94	−13.65	−0.23	−0.22	95.13	0.90	0.87
[−10, 7]	−12.13	−0.41	−0.40	−2.50	−0.04	−0.04	34.32	0.32	0.31
[−10, 8]	−7.85	−0.26	−0.26	−19.06	−0.32	−0.31	106.61	1.00	0.98
[−10, 9]	−10.96	−0.37	−0.36	−29.65	−0.49	−0.48	92.50	0.87	0.85
[−10, 10]	−11.22	−0.38	−0.37	−28.31	−0.47	−0.46	94.40	0.89	0.87
[−10, 11]	17.03	0.57	0.56	−15.41	−0.26	−0.25	97.77	0.92	0.90
[−10, 12]	−31.07	−1.05	−1.01	−44.51	−0.74	−0.71	35.29	0.33	0.32
[−10, 13]	−33.57	−1.13	−1.09	−41.21	−0.68	−0.66	32.02	0.30	0.29
[−10, 14]	−21.83	−0.73	−0.70	−43.06	−0.71	−0.68	40.07	0.38	0.36
[−10, 15]	−24.07	−0.81	−0.79	−38.25	−0.63	−0.62	98.08	0.92	0.90
[−10, 16]	7.80	0.26	0.26	−26.96	−0.45	−0.44	25.99	0.24	0.24
[−10, 17]	−3.40	−0.11	−0.11	−38.87	−0.65	−0.63	69.92	0.66	0.64
[−10, 18]	11.29	0.38	0.37	−46.55	−0.77	−0.75	21.11	0.20	0.19
[−10, 19]	−16.30	−0.55	−0.53	−48.99	−0.81	−0.79	31.75	0.30	0.29
[−10, 20]	−18.91	−0.64	−0.61	−49.06	−0.81	−0.78	82.67	0.78	0.75

Table A12. Case III: EGARCH(1,1)—Cumulative abnormal change rate of Chinese tourist arrivals.

Event Period $[\tau_1, \tau_2]$	Group-Type			Individual-Type			Medical-Type		
	CAR	t-Value		CAR	t-Value		CAR	t-Value	
		TM	SRM		TM	SRM		TM	SRM
[−10, −10]	8.83	0.28	0.28	0.79	0.02	0.02	160.50	1.50	1.47
[−10, −9]	−29.20	−0.94	−0.92	5.95	0.12	0.11	193.68	1.81	1.78
[−10, −8]	−25.17	−0.81	−0.79	12.55	0.25	0.24	82.66	0.77	0.76
[−10, −7]	−34.93	−1.12	−1.10	1.81	0.04	0.03	66.96	0.63	0.61
[−10, −6]	−60.25	−1.94	−1.90	0.49	0.01	0.01	112.23	1.05	1.03
[−10, −5]	−36.43	−1.17	−1.15	−5.85	−0.11	−0.11	65.74	0.61	0.60
[−10, −4]	−29.38	−0.95	−0.93	−3.73	−0.07	−0.07	91.39	0.85	0.84
[−10, −3]	−19.98	−0.64	−0.62	−20.04	−0.39	−0.38	105.87	0.99	0.96
[−10, −2]	−50.35	−1.62	−1.58	−1.58	−0.03	−0.03	85.02	0.80	0.78
[−10, −1]	−41.63	−1.34	−1.30	18.83	0.37	0.36	43.66	0.41	0.40
[−10, 0]	−34.07	−1.10	−1.07	13.15	0.26	0.25	84.48	0.79	0.77
[−10, 1]	−44.36	−1.43	−1.39	−24.85	−0.49	−0.47	116.67	1.09	1.06
[−10, 2]	−39.54	−1.27	−1.24	−12.20	−0.24	−0.23	211.63	1.98	1.93
[−10, 3]	−37.78	−1.22	−1.19	−14.77	−0.29	−0.28	156.24	1.46	1.43
[−10, 4]	−14.50	−0.47	−0.46	−0.19	0.00	0.00	168.79	1.58	1.55
[−10, 5]	−43.05	−1.39	−1.34	−27.00	−0.53	−0.51	136.05	1.27	1.23
[−10, 6]	−42.59	−1.37	−1.34	−4.90	−0.10	−0.09	161.48	1.51	1.47
[−10, 7]	−26.58	−0.86	−0.83	6.83	0.13	0.13	104.45	0.98	0.95
[−10, 8]	−23.11	−0.74	−0.72	−9.21	−0.18	−0.18	180.65	1.69	1.64
[−10, 9]	−29.67	−0.96	−0.94	−19.92	−0.39	−0.38	171.83	1.61	1.57
[−10, 10]	−29.69	−0.96	−0.93	−17.81	−0.35	−0.34	177.08	1.66	1.62
[−10, 11]	−1.70	−0.05	−0.05	−4.26	−0.08	−0.08	184.05	1.72	1.68
[−10, 12]	−49.26	−1.59	−1.53	−32.52	−0.64	−0.61	124.76	1.17	1.13
[−10, 13]	−51.44	−1.66	−1.59	−28.44	−0.56	−0.53	124.78	1.17	1.12
[−10, 14]	−39.25	−1.26	−1.20	−29.47	−0.58	−0.55	136.07	1.27	1.21
[−10, 15]	−46.92	−1.51	−1.47	−25.25	−0.49	−0.48	200.43	1.87	1.82
[−10, 16]	−18.11	−0.58	−0.57	−13.99	−0.27	−0.27	133.43	1.25	1.22
[−10, 17]	−30.24	−0.97	−0.95	−25.41	−0.50	−0.49	181.33	1.70	1.66
[−10, 18]	−15.20	−0.49	−0.48	−32.29	−0.63	−0.61	135.80	1.27	1.24
[−10, 19]	−43.04	−1.39	−1.35	−34.09	−0.67	−0.65	150.05	1.40	1.36
[−10, 20]	−44.94	−1.45	−1.39	−33.27	−0.65	−0.63	204.05	1.91	1.84

Table A13. Case IV: OLS—Cumulative abnormal change rate of Chinese tourist arrivals.

Event Period $[\tau_1, \tau_2]$	Group-Type			Individual-Type			Medical-Type		
	CAR	t-Value		CAR	t-Value		CAR	t-Value	
		TM	SRM		TM	SRM		TM	SRM
[−10, −10]	34.16	1.54	1.52	34.15	0.91	0.90	54.99	0.78	0.77
[−10 ,−9]	−10.42	−0.47	−0.46	18.30	0.49	0.48	57.01	0.81	0.80
[−10, −8]	3.44	0.16	0.15	25.86	0.69	0.68	83.84	1.19	1.17
[−10, −7]	−17.28	−0.78	−0.77	5.60	0.15	0.15	85.41	1.21	1.19
[−10, −6]	−1.56	−0.07	−0.07	25.75	0.69	0.67	48.79	0.69	0.68
[−10, −5]	0.02	0.00	0.00	14.94	0.40	0.39	0.91	0.01	0.01
[−10, −4]	25.15	1.14	1.12	29.92	0.80	0.78	−130.89	−1.85	−1.82
[−10, −3]	47.40	2.14	2.11	49.47	1.32	1.30	−28.62	−0.41	−0.40
[−10, −2]	−12.05	−0.54	−0.53	40.07	1.07	1.05	−60.18	−0.85	−0.84
[−10, −1]	24.56	1.11	1.09	43.11	1.15	1.13	−24.37	−0.35	−0.34
[−10, 0]	46.52	2.10	2.07	83.99	2.24	2.20	−17.14	−0.24	−0.24
[−10, 1]	81.60	3.69 *	3.63 *	56.07	1.49	1.47	31.27	0.44	0.44
[−10, 2]	99.79	4.51 **	4.44 **	62.56	1.67	1.64	−42.54	−0.60	−0.59
[−10, 3]	106.06	4.79 **	4.71 **	70.71	1.88	1.85	−17.11	−0.24	−0.24
[−10, 4]	125.32	5.66 **	5.58 **	107.40	2.86	2.82	102.25	1.45	1.43
[−10, 5]	91.15	4.12 *	4.05 *	101.34	2.70	2.65	70.06	0.99	0.98
[−10, 6]	82.22	3.72 *	3.66 *	120.37	3.21 *	3.16 *	−90.69	−1.28	−1.27
[−10, 7]	106.70	4.82 **	4.75 **	141.77	3.78 *	3.72 *	17.59	0.25	0.25
[−10, 8]	107.43	4.86 **	4.78 **	138.98	3.70 *	3.65 *	−64.56	−0.91	−0.90
[−10, 9]	118.65	5.36 **	5.28 **	137.37	3.66 *	3.60 *	26.75	0.38	0.37
[−10, 10]	127.78	5.78 **	5.68 **	132.07	3.52 *	3.46 *	−106.14	−1.50	−1.48
[−10, 11]	145.84	6.59 **	6.49 **	123.24	3.28 *	3.23 *	−71.55	−1.01	−1.00
[−10, 12]	101.45	4.59 **	4.51 **	116.94	3.12 *	3.06 *	−8.19	−0.12	−0.11
[−10, 13]	107.00	4.84 **	4.76 **	115.69	3.08 *	3.03 *	−8.08	−0.11	−0.11
[−10, 14]	124.09	5.61 **	5.52 **	144.69	3.85 *	3.79 *	−16.41	−0.23	−0.23
[−10, 15]	94.22	4.26 *	4.19 *	127.17	3.39 *	3.34 *	−55.82	−0.79	−0.78
[−10, 16]	88.80	4.01 *	3.95 *	114.97	3.06 *	3.02 *	−27.97	−0.40	−0.39
[−10, 17]	100.93	4.56 **	4.44 **	145.31	3.87 *	3.76 *	5.77	0.08	0.08
[−10, 18]	123.14	5.56 **	5.48 *	170.81	4.55 **	4.48 **	90.92	1.29	1.27
[−10, 19]	110.07	4.97 **	4.89 *	169.21	4.51 **	4.44 **	58.15	0.82	0.81
[−10, 20]	82.15	3.71 *	3.65 *	169.72	4.52 **	4.45 **	17.53	0.25	0.24

Note: ** and * denote significance at the 5% and 10% levels, respectively.

Table A14. Case IV: GARCH(1,1)—Cumulative abnormal change rate of Chinese tourist arrivals.

Event Period $[\tau_1, \tau_2]$	Group-Type			Individual-Type			Medical-Type		
	CAR	t-Value		CAR	t-Value		CAR	t-Value	
		TM	SRM		TM	SRM		TM	SRM
[−10, −10]	31.30	1.21	1.19	32.32	1.09	1.08	54.44	0.76	0.75
[−10, −9]	−9.14	−0.35	−0.35	17.20	0.58	0.57	57.47	0.80	0.79
[−10, −8]	9.99	0.39	0.38	25.89	0.88	0.86	85.57	1.20	1.18
[−10, −7]	−1.56	−0.06	−0.06	8.20	0.28	0.27	89.26	1.25	1.23
[−10, −6]	1.68	0.06	0.06	23.00	0.78	0.76	49.95	0.70	0.68
[−10, −5]	−0.57	−0.02	−0.02	10.01	0.34	0.33	1.30	0.02	0.02
[−10, −4]	17.97	0.69	0.68	21.79	0.74	0.72	−131.88	−1.84	−1.81
[−10, −3]	37.93	1.47	1.44	39.72	1.34	1.32	−30.03	−0.42	−0.41
[−10, −2]	−11.83	−0.46	−0.45	33.06	1.12	1.10	−59.34	−0.83	−0.82
[−10, −1]	20.21	0.78	0.77	33.66	1.14	1.12	−24.46	−0.34	−0.34
[−10, 0]	46.18	1.78	1.76	75.21	2.54	2.51	−16.25	−0.23	−0.22
[−10, 1]	84.72	3.27 *	3.22 *	47.78	1.62	1.59	33.02	0.46	0.45
[−10, 2]	101.58	3.93 *	3.87 *	52.99	1.79	1.77	−41.01	−0.57	−0.56
[−10, 3]	101.68	3.93 *	3.86 *	58.09	1.97	1.93	−16.87	−0.24	−0.23
[−10, 4]	122.97	4.75 **	4.68 **	94.75	3.21 *	3.16 *	103.04	1.44	1.42
[−10, 5]	96.84	3.74 *	3.68 *	90.84	3.07 *	3.02 *	72.72	1.02	1.00
[−10, 6]	85.91	3.32 *	3.27 *	108.34	3.67 *	3.61 *	−88.38	−1.24	−1.22
[−10, 7]	107.62	4.16 *	4.09 *	127.94	4.33 *	4.26 *	19.37	0.27	0.27
[−10, 8]	108.40	4.19 *	4.12 *	124.39	4.21 *	4.14 *	−62.69	−0.88	−0.86
[−10, 9]	120.44	4.65 **	4.58 **	122.30	4.14 *	4.07 *	28.90	0.40	0.40
[−10, 10]	124.09	4.79 **	4.72 **	114.20	3.86 *	3.80 *	−105.13	−1.47	−1.45
[−10, 11]	139.54	5.39 **	5.31 **	103.63	3.51 *	3.45 *	−71.03	−0.99	−0.98
[−10, 12]	103.87	4.01 *	3.94 *	99.73	3.37 *	3.32 *	−5.64	−0.08	−0.08
[−10, 13]	104.47	4.04 *	3.97 *	95.89	3.24 *	3.19 *	−6.55	−0.09	−0.09
[−10, 14]	117.73	4.55 **	4.48 **	122.69	4.15 *	4.09 *	−15.64	−0.22	−0.22
[−10, 15]	85.30	3.30 *	3.25 *	103.46	3.50 *	3.45 *	−55.53	−0.78	−0.76
[−10, 16]	82.36	3.18 *	3.13 *	91.37	3.09 *	3.04 *	−27.05	−0.38	−0.37
[−10, 17]	74.54	2.88	2.80	113.63	3.84 *	3.74 *	2.33	0.03	0.03
[−10, 18]	94.14	3.64 *	3.58 *	137.40	4.65 **	4.58 **	86.99	1.22	1.20
[−10, 19]	87.01	3.36 *	3.31 *	137.18	4.64 **	4.57 **	55.63	0.78	0.77
[−10, 20]	65.04	2.51	2.47	139.08	4.71 **	4.63 **	16.43	0.23	0.23

Note: ** and * denote significance at the 5% and 10% levels, respectively.

Table A15. Case IV: GJR(1,1)—Cumulative abnormal change rate of Chinese tourist arrivals.

Event Period $[\tau_1, \tau_2]$	Group-Type			Individual-Type			Medical-Type		
	CAR	t-Value		CAR	t-Value		CAR	t-Value	
		TM	SRM		TM	SRM		TM	SRM
[−10, −10]	31.65	1.02	1.01	29.23	0.43	0.42	61.21	0.28	0.27
[−10, −9]	−8.44	−0.27	−0.27	12.57	0.18	0.18	71.19	0.32	0.32
[−10, −8]	11.02	0.36	0.35	19.97	0.29	0.29	106.27	0.48	0.47
[−10, −7]	−0.19	−0.01	−0.01	1.85	0.03	0.03	117.05	0.53	0.52
[−10, −6]	3.42	0.11	0.11	11.44	0.17	0.16	84.26	0.38	0.37
[−10, −5]	1.52	0.05	0.05	−4.86	−0.07	−0.07	42.35	0.19	0.19
[−10, −4]	20.42	0.66	0.65	3.01	0.04	0.04	−84.15	−0.38	−0.37
[−10, −3]	40.73	1.32	1.30	17.98	0.26	0.26	24.48	0.11	0.11
[−10, −2]	−8.70	−0.28	−0.28	11.01	0.16	0.16	2.27	0.01	0.01
[−10, −1]	23.70	0.77	0.76	8.14	0.12	0.12	43.87	0.20	0.19
[−10, 0]	50.01	1.62	1.59	48.12	0.71	0.69	59.03	0.27	0.26
[−10, 1]	88.90	2.88	2.83	18.99	0.28	0.27	115.24	0.52	0.51
[−10, 2]	106.11	3.44 *	3.38 *	21.45	0.31	0.31	48.02	0.22	0.21
[−10, 3]	106.56	3.45 *	3.39 *	22.74	0.33	0.33	78.85	0.36	0.35
[−10, 4]	128.20	4.15 *	4.09 *	57.38	0.84	0.83	205.65	0.93	0.91
[−10, 5]	102.41	3.32 *	3.26 *	52.80	0.77	0.76	182.39	0.82	0.81
[−10, 6]	91.83	2.97 *	2.93 *	67.40	0.99	0.97	28.08	0.13	0.12
[−10, 7]	113.89	3.69 *	3.63 *	83.94	1.23	1.21	142.60	0.64	0.63
[−10, 8]	115.02	3.72 *	3.67 *	77.93	1.14	1.13	67.39	0.30	0.30
[−10, 9]	127.40	4.12 *	4.06 *	73.57	1.08	1.06	165.84	0.75	0.74
[−10, 10]	131.41	4.25 *	4.18 *	61.80	0.91	0.89	38.51	0.17	0.17
[−10, 11]	147.21	4.77 **	4.69 **	48.20	0.71	0.70	79.39	0.36	0.35
[−10, 12]	111.88	3.62 *	3.56 *	43.78	0.64	0.63	151.85	0.68	0.67
[−10, 13]	112.83	3.65 *	3.59 *	36.39	0.53	0.53	157.66	0.71	0.70
[−10, 14]	126.44	4.09 *	4.03 *	59.88	0.88	0.86	155.31	0.70	0.69
[−10, 15]	94.37	3.06 *	3.01 *	37.63	0.55	0.54	122.20	0.55	0.54
[−10, 16]	91.78	2.97 *	2.93 *	23.63	0.35	0.34	157.60	0.71	0.70
[−10, 17]	84.33	2.73	2.66	39.03	0.57	0.56	193.29	0.87	0.85
[−10, 18]	104.28	3.38 *	3.32 *	59.76	0.88	0.86	284.73	1.28	1.26
[−10, 19]	97.49	3.16 *	3.11 *	58.40	0.86	0.84	260.37	1.17	1.15
[−10, 20]	75.86	2.46	2.42	59.15	0.87	0.85	228.17	1.03	1.01

Note: ** and * denote significance at the 5% and 10% levels, respectively.

Table A16. Case IV: EGARCH(1,1)—Cumulative abnormal change rate of Chinese tourist arrivals.

Event Period $[\tau_1, \tau_2]$	Group-Type			Individual-Type			Medical-Type		
	CAR	t-Value		CAR	t-Value		CAR	t-Value	
		TM	SRM		TM	SRM		TM	SRM
[−10, −10]	32.49	0.84	0.82	29.71	0.46	0.46	66.87	0.18	0.17
[−10, −9]	−7.68	−0.20	−0.19	12.84	0.20	0.20	82.37	0.22	0.21
[−10, −8]	11.57	0.30	0.29	19.93	0.31	0.31	122.95	0.32	0.32
[−10, −7]	−0.38	−0.01	−0.01	1.11	0.02	0.02	139.15	0.37	0.36
[−10, −6]	5.33	0.14	0.13	12.11	0.19	0.18	112.21	0.30	0.29
[−10, −5]	4.40	0.11	0.11	−3.61	−0.06	−0.06	75.99	0.20	0.20
[−10, −4]	24.63	0.63	0.62	5.10	0.08	0.08	−44.78	−0.12	−0.12
[−10, −3]	45.71	1.18	1.16	20.49	0.32	0.31	69.50	0.18	0.18
[−10, −2]	−4.52	−0.12	−0.11	12.77	0.20	0.20	52.70	0.14	0.14
[−10, −1]	28.94	0.75	0.73	10.54	0.16	0.16	100.00	0.26	0.26
[−10, 0]	55.19	1.42	1.40	50.33	0.78	0.77	120.68	0.32	0.31
[−10, 1]	94.09	2.42	2.39	21.06	0.33	0.32	182.42	0.48	0.47
[−10, 2]	111.95	2.88	2.84	23.85	0.37	0.37	120.84	0.32	0.31
[−10, 3]	113.67	2.93 *	2.88	25.94	0.40	0.40	157.39	0.41	0.41
[−10, 4]	135.52	3.49 *	3.44 *	60.58	0.94	0.93	289.75	0.76	0.75
[−10, 5]	109.14	2.81	2.76	55.41	0.86	0.85	271.93	0.72	0.70
[−10, 6]	99.28	2.56	2.52	70.41	1.10	1.08	123.27	0.32	0.32
[−10, 7]	122.17	3.15 *	3.10 *	87.41	1.36	1.34	243.45	0.64	0.63
[−10, 8]	123.77	3.19 *	3.14 *	81.60	1.27	1.25	173.84	0.46	0.45
[−10, 9]	136.51	3.52 *	3.46 *	77.35	1.20	1.19	277.88	0.73	0.72
[−10, 10]	141.70	3.65 *	3.59 *	66.33	1.03	1.02	156.27	0.41	0.41
[−10, 11]	158.32	4.08 *	4.01 *	53.18	0.83	0.82	202.81	0.53	0.53
[−10, 12]	122.30	3.15 *	3.10 *	48.10	0.75	0.74	280.69	0.74	0.73
[−10, 13]	124.38	3.20 *	3.15 *	41.39	0.64	0.63	292.21	0.77	0.76
[−10, 14]	138.96	3.58 *	3.52 *	65.46	1.02	1.00	295.54	0.78	0.77
[−10, 15]	107.68	2.77	2.73	43.65	0.68	0.67	268.08	0.71	0.70
[−10, 16]	105.23	2.71	2.67	29.61	0.46	0.45	309.03	0.81	0.80
[−10, 17]	100.86	2.60	2.53	47.15	0.73	0.71	350.74	0.92	0.90
[−10, 18]	121.62	3.13 *	3.08 *	68.33	1.06	1.05	447.83	1.18	1.16
[−10, 19]	114.52	2.95 *	2.90 *	66.59	1.04	1.02	428.95	1.13	1.11
[−10, 20]	92.58	2.38	2.35	66.97	1.04	1.03	402.24	1.06	1.04

Note: * denotes significance at the 10% level.

Table A17. Case V: OLS—Cumulative abnormal change rate of Chinese tourist arrivals.

Event Period $[\tau_1, \tau_2]$	Group-Type			Individual-Type			Medical-Type		
	CAR	t-Value		CAR	t-Value		CAR	t-Value	
		TM	SRM		TM	SRM		TM	SRM
[−10, −10]	−32.96	−1.36	−1.33	−12.93	−0.32	−0.31	61.37	0.62	0.61
[−10, −9]	−28.58	−1.18	−1.13	−19.31	−0.47	−0.46	103.52	1.04	1.01
[−10, −8]	−34.42	−1.42	−1.39	−34.99	−0.86	−0.84	82.38	0.83	0.82
[−10, −7]	−25.58	−1.05	−1.03	−21.17	−0.52	−0.51	129.40	1.31	1.28
[−10, −6]	−49.76	−2.05	−2.00	−18.73	−0.46	−0.45	61.36	0.62	0.60
[−10, −5]	−47.51	−1.96	−1.93	−27.98	−0.68	−0.67	53.56	0.54	0.53
[−10, −4]	−37.33	−1.54	−1.51	−49.55	−1.21	−1.19	78.26	0.79	0.78
[−10, −3]	−41.53	−1.71	−1.68	−31.87	−0.78	−0.77	85.57	0.86	0.85
[−10, −2]	−30.93	−1.27	−1.25	−34.90	−0.85	−0.84	159.54	1.61	1.58
[−10, −1]	−38.94	−1.60	−1.55	−46.41	−1.14	−1.10	−106.69	−1.08	−1.04
[−10, 0]	−39.42	−1.62	−1.58	−29.24	−0.72	−0.70	−105.01	−1.06	−1.03
[−10, 1]	−36.34	−1.50	−1.47	−20.13	−0.49	−0.48	−17.77	−0.18	−0.18
[−10, 2]	−43.42	−1.79	−1.76	−39.64	−0.97	−0.96	170.96	1.72	1.70
[−10, 3]	−46.19	−1.90	−1.87	−56.16	−1.38	−1.35	29.96	0.30	0.30
[−10, 4]	−32.28	−1.33	−1.30	−34.72	−0.85	−0.83	77.10	0.78	0.76
[−10, 5]	−16.99	−0.70	−0.68	−32.96	−0.81	−0.79	66.08	0.67	0.65
[−10, 6]	−36.57	−1.50	−1.48	−55.84	−1.37	−1.35	3.99	0.04	0.04
[−10, 7]	−40.35	−1.66	−1.63	−44.23	−1.08	−1.07	16.75	0.17	0.17
[−10, 8]	−51.49	−2.12	−2.09	−35.77	−0.88	−0.86	23.60	0.24	0.23
[−10, 9]	−67.44	−2.78	−2.73	−43.04	−1.05	−1.04	220.30	2.22	2.19
[−10, 10]	−68.55	−2.82	−2.78	−43.96	−1.08	−1.06	105.48	1.06	1.05
[−10, 11]	−76.15	−3.13 *	−3.08 *	−50.54	−1.24	−1.22	120.17	1.21	1.19
[−10, 12]	−81.02	−3.33 *	−3.28 *	−39.36	−0.96	−0.95	4.94	0.05	0.05
[−10, 13]	−84.93	−3.49 *	−3.43 *	−32.21	−0.79	−0.77	−113.75	−1.15	−1.13
[−10, 14]	−57.46	−2.36	−2.26	10.51	0.26	0.25	3.50	0.04	0.03
[−10, 15]	−85.57	−3.52 *	−3.42 *	52.75	1.29	1.25	−3.43	−0.03	−0.03
[−10, 16]	−83.87	−3.45 *	−3.37 *	1.17	0.03	0.03	−36.17	−0.36	−0.36
[−10, 17]	−84.93	−3.49 *	−3.42 *	−42.91	−1.05	−1.03	87.49	0.88	0.86
[−10, 18]	−86.15	−3.55 *	−3.49 *	−24.12	−0.59	−0.58	26.67	0.27	0.26
[−10, 19]	−63.30	−2.60	−2.56	−0.24	−0.01	−0.01	−84.63	−0.85	−0.84
[−10, 20]	−58.10	−2.39	−2.34	−8.00	−0.20	−0.19	−56.51	−0.57	−0.56

Note: * denotes significance at the 10% level.

Table A18. Case V: GARCH(1,1)—Cumulative abnormal change rate of Chinese tourist arrivals.

Event Period $[\tau_1, \tau_2]$	Group-Type			Individual-Type			Medical-Type		
	CAR	t-Value		CAR	t-Value		CAR	t-Value	
		TM	SRM		TM	SRM		TM	SRM
[−10, −10]	−32.40	−1.07	−1.05	−14.71	−0.29	−0.29	62.53	0.57	0.55
[−10, −9]	−26.94	−0.89	−0.86	−20.83	−0.42	−0.40	90.48	0.82	0.79
[−10, −8]	−32.15	−1.06	−1.04	−38.02	−0.76	−0.75	68.39	0.62	0.61
[−10, −7]	−22.46	−0.74	−0.73	−24.82	−0.49	−0.49	107.86	0.97	0.96
[−10, −6]	−46.17	−1.52	−1.48	−24.58	−0.49	−0.48	44.04	0.40	0.39
[−10, −5]	−43.22	−1.42	−1.40	−35.06	−0.70	−0.69	33.29	0.30	0.30
[−10, −4]	−32.33	−1.07	−1.05	−57.83	−1.15	−1.14	54.64	0.49	0.49
[−10, −3]	−35.86	−1.18	−1.16	−41.52	−0.83	−0.81	60.03	0.54	0.53
[−10, −2]	−24.43	−0.81	−0.79	−45.29	−0.90	−0.89	127.28	1.15	1.13
[−10, −1]	−31.38	−1.03	−1.00	−56.59	−1.13	−1.09	−152.70	−1.38	−1.33
[−10, 0]	−31.43	−1.04	−1.01	−41.73	−0.83	−0.81	−145.95	−1.32	−1.28
[−10, 1]	−27.72	−0.91	−0.90	−34.15	−0.68	−0.67	−59.50	−0.54	−0.53
[−10, 2]	−34.10	−1.12	−1.11	−54.90	−1.09	−1.08	126.28	1.14	1.12
[−10, 3]	−36.18	−1.19	−1.17	−72.73	−1.45	−1.43	−17.11	−0.15	−0.15
[−10, 4]	−21.72	−0.72	−0.70	−53.07	−1.06	−1.04	31.14	0.28	0.28
[−10, 5]	−5.53	−0.18	−0.18	−51.78	−1.03	−1.01	11.37	0.10	0.10
[−10, 6]	−24.33	−0.80	−0.79	−75.59	−1.51	−1.48	−56.00	−0.51	−0.50
[−10, 7]	−27.35	−0.90	−0.89	−64.98	−1.30	−1.28	−47.93	−0.43	−0.43
[−10, 8]	−37.83	−1.25	−1.23	−57.93	−1.15	−1.14	−42.76	−0.39	−0.38
[−10, 9]	−53.09	−1.75	−1.72	−66.45	−1.32	−1.30	151.09	1.37	1.34
[−10, 10]	−53.48	−1.76	−1.74	−68.55	−1.37	−1.35	32.85	0.30	0.29
[−10, 11]	−60.29	−1.99	−1.96	−76.02	−1.52	−1.49	41.99	0.38	0.37
[−10, 12]	−64.41	−2.12	−2.09	−65.83	−1.31	−1.29	−78.00	−0.70	−0.69
[−10, 13]	−67.75	−2.23	−2.19	−60.50	−1.21	−1.18	−195.37	−1.77	−1.73
[−10, 14]	−39.14	−1.29	−1.23	−17.27	−0.34	−0.33	−94.16	−0.85	−0.81
[−10, 15]	−66.85	−2.20	−2.14	22.58	0.45	0.44	−95.37	−0.86	−0.84
[−10, 16]	−64.64	−2.13	−2.08	−31.02	−0.62	−0.60	−125.22	−1.13	−1.11
[−10, 17]	−65.19	−2.15	−2.10	−77.12	−1.54	−1.50	1.41	0.01	0.01
[−10, 18]	−65.72	−2.17	−2.13	−59.58	−1.19	−1.17	−62.30	−0.56	−0.55
[−10, 19]	−42.09	−1.39	−1.37	−36.61	−0.73	−0.72	−179.05	−1.62	−1.59
[−10, 20]	−36.01	−1.19	−1.16	−44.92	−0.90	−0.88	−159.05	−1.44	−1.41

Table A19. Case V: GJR(1,1)—Cumulative abnormal change rate of Chinese tourist arrivals.

Event Period $[\tau_1, \tau_2]$	Group-Type			Individual-Type			Medical-Type		
	CAR	t-Value		CAR	t-Value		CAR	t-Value	
		TM	SRM		TM	SRM		TM	SRM
[−10, −10]	−34.20	−0.62	−0.61	−14.18	−0.35	−0.35	73.79	0.25	0.25
[−10, −9]	−32.38	−0.59	−0.56	−16.97	−0.42	−0.41	113.70	0.39	0.38
[−10, −8]	−39.65	−0.72	−0.71	−33.24	−0.83	−0.81	102.96	0.35	0.35
[−10, −7]	−32.81	−0.59	−0.58	−17.93	−0.45	−0.44	154.09	0.53	0.52
[−10, −6]	−57.97	−1.05	−1.02	−17.71	−0.44	−0.43	101.39	0.35	0.34
[−10, −5]	−57.31	−1.04	−1.02	−26.91	−0.67	−0.66	102.09	0.35	0.34
[−10, −4]	−48.76	−0.88	−0.87	−48.32	−1.20	−1.18	134.90	0.46	0.46
[−10, −3]	−54.47	−0.98	−0.97	−30.92	−0.77	−0.76	151.69	0.52	0.51
[−10, −2]	−45.79	−0.83	−0.81	−32.72	−0.81	−0.80	230.56	0.79	0.78
[−10, −1]	−56.32	−1.02	−0.98	−40.78	−1.01	−0.98	−37.48	−0.13	−0.12
[−10, 0]	−57.71	−1.04	−1.01	−26.10	−0.65	−0.63	−19.65	−0.07	−0.07
[−10, 1]	−56.05	−1.01	−1.00	−17.63	−0.44	−0.43	78.15	0.27	0.26
[−10, 2]	−64.72	−1.17	−1.15	−37.10	−0.92	−0.91	275.38	0.94	0.93
[−10, 3]	−69.04	−1.25	−1.23	−53.76	−1.34	−1.32	143.41	0.49	0.48
[−10, 4]	−56.39	−1.02	−1.00	−33.56	−0.83	−0.82	202.92	0.70	0.68
[−10, 5]	−43.19	−0.78	−0.76	−29.92	−0.74	−0.73	194.86	0.67	0.65
[−10, 6]	−64.57	−1.17	−1.15	−52.02	−1.29	−1.27	139.04	0.48	0.47
[−10, 7]	−70.09	−1.27	−1.25	−39.82	−0.99	−0.97	158.64	0.54	0.54
[−10, 8]	−82.72	−1.50	−1.47	−31.72	−0.79	−0.78	175.20	0.60	0.59
[−10, 9]	−100.26	−1.81	−1.78	−38.97	−0.97	−0.95	380.49	1.31	1.29
[−10, 10]	−103.00	−1.86	−1.83	−39.71	−0.99	−0.97	273.72	0.94	0.92
[−10, 11]	−112.42	−2.03	−2.00	−45.43	−1.13	−1.11	294.42	1.01	0.99
[−10, 12]	−119.05	−2.15	−2.12	−33.63	−0.84	−0.82	185.96	0.64	0.63
[−10, 13]	−124.19	−2.24	−2.20	−27.79	−0.69	−0.68	79.84	0.27	0.27
[−10, 14]	−99.44	−1.80	−1.72	19.10	0.47	0.45	193.09	0.66	0.63
[−10, 15]	−128.41	−2.32	−2.25	58.65	1.46	1.41	202.93	0.70	0.68
[−10, 16]	−127.80	−2.31	−2.26	5.27	0.13	0.13	184.26	0.63	0.62
[−10, 17]	−129.95	−2.35	−2.30	−40.63	−1.01	−0.99	322.07	1.11	1.08
[−10, 18]	−132.77	−2.40	−2.36	−21.82	−0.54	−0.53	269.81	0.93	0.91
[−10, 19]	−111.73	−2.02	−1.99	2.88	0.07	0.07	164.61	0.56	0.56
[−10, 20]	−108.56	−1.96	−1.92	−3.20	−0.08	−0.08	196.30	0.67	0.66

Table A20. Case V: EGARCH(1,1)—Cumulative abnormal change rate of Chinese tourist arrivals.

Event Period $[\tau_1, \tau_2]$	Group-Type			Individual-Type			Medical-Type		
	CAR	t-Value		CAR	t-Value		CAR	t-Value	
		TM	SRM		TM	SRM		TM	SRM
[−10, −10]	−34.56	−0.46	−0.45	−14.24	−0.34	−0.34	74.59	0.24	0.23
[−10, −9]	−34.31	−0.46	−0.44	−16.37	−0.40	−0.38	115.61	0.37	0.35
[−10, −8]	−42.11	−0.56	−0.56	−32.60	−0.79	−0.78	105.72	0.33	0.33
[−10, −7]	−36.31	−0.49	−0.48	−16.94	−0.41	−0.40	157.82	0.50	0.49
[−10, −6]	−61.59	−0.83	−0.80	−16.91	−0.41	−0.40	105.86	0.33	0.33
[−10, −5]	−61.62	−0.83	−0.81	−25.99	−0.63	−0.62	107.45	0.34	0.33
[−10, −4]	−53.78	−0.72	−0.71	−47.24	−1.14	−1.13	141.15	0.45	0.44
[−10, −3]	−60.10	−0.81	−0.79	−29.75	−0.72	−0.71	158.80	0.50	0.49
[−10, −2]	−52.40	−0.70	−0.69	−31.25	−0.76	−0.74	238.63	0.76	0.74
[−10, −1]	−64.46	−0.86	−0.83	−38.67	−0.94	−0.90	−28.30	−0.09	−0.09
[−10, 0]	−65.90	−0.88	−0.86	−24.23	−0.59	−0.57	−9.75	−0.03	−0.03
[−10, 1]	−64.75	−0.87	−0.85	−15.72	−0.38	−0.37	88.89	0.28	0.28
[−10, 2]	−74.11	−0.99	−0.98	−35.06	−0.85	−0.84	287.00	0.91	0.89
[−10, 3]	−79.07	−1.06	−1.04	−51.60	−1.25	−1.23	155.91	0.49	0.49
[−10, 4]	−66.77	−0.90	−0.88	−31.46	−0.76	−0.75	216.22	0.68	0.67
[−10, 5]	−54.72	−0.73	−0.72	−27.42	−0.66	−0.65	209.16	0.66	0.65
[−10, 6]	−76.97	−1.03	−1.02	−49.28	−1.19	−1.18	154.27	0.49	0.48
[−10, 7]	−83.31	−1.12	−1.10	−36.87	−0.89	−0.88	174.79	0.55	0.54
[−10, 8]	−96.52	−1.29	−1.27	−28.69	−0.70	−0.68	192.21	0.61	0.60
[−10, 9]	−114.74	−1.54	−1.52	−35.81	−0.87	−0.85	398.38	1.26	1.24
[−10, 10]	−118.20	−1.59	−1.56	−36.39	−0.88	−0.87	292.50	0.93	0.91
[−10, 11]	−128.51	−1.72	−1.70	−41.85	−1.01	−1.00	314.15	0.99	0.98
[−10, 12]	−135.96	−1.82	−1.79	−29.84	−0.72	−0.71	206.61	0.65	0.64
[−10, 13]	−141.45	−1.90	−1.86	−24.06	−0.58	−0.57	101.28	0.32	0.31
[−10, 14]	−118.41	−1.59	−1.52	23.57	0.57	0.55	215.68	0.68	0.65
[−10, 15]	−147.38	−1.98	−1.92	62.85	1.52	1.48	226.24	0.72	0.69
[−10, 16]	−146.99	−1.97	−1.93	9.33	0.23	0.22	208.33	0.66	0.64
[−10, 17]	−149.36	−2.00	−1.96	−36.71	−0.89	−0.87	346.90	1.10	1.07
[−10, 18]	−152.86	−2.05	−2.02	−17.76	−0.43	−0.42	295.52	0.94	0.92
[−10, 19]	−132.70	−1.78	−1.75	7.19	0.17	0.17	191.26	0.61	0.60
[−10, 20]	−130.63	−1.75	−1.72	1.48	0.04	0.04	223.94	0.71	0.69

Table A21. Case VI: OLS—Cumulative abnormal change rate of Chinese tourist arrivals.

Event Period $[\tau_1, \tau_2]$	Group-Type			Individual-Type			Medical-Type		
	CAR	t-Value		CAR	t-Value		CAR	t-Value	
		TM	SRM		TM	SRM		TM	SRM
[−10, −10]	−24.32	−0.81	−0.80	7.76	0.30	0.29	−70.72	−0.86	−0.85
[−10, −9]	10.40	0.35	0.34	58.26	2.25	2.21	−25.18	−0.31	−0.30
[−10, −8]	−11.30	−0.38	−0.37	65.74	2.53	2.47	−92.40	−1.12	−1.10
[−10, −7]	−21.85	−0.73	−0.72	17.20	0.66	0.65	−173.94	−2.12	−2.08
[−10, −6]	5.36	0.18	0.18	−9.47	−0.36	−0.36	−176.40	−2.15	−2.11
[−10, −5]	1.89	0.06	0.06	−25.76	−0.99	−0.98	−171.38	−2.09	−2.05
[−10, −4]	−70.65	−2.36	−2.33	−55.13	−2.13	−2.09	−280.66	−3.42*	−3.36*
[−10, −3]	−1.99	−0.07	−0.06	1.47	0.06	0.05	−237.28	−2.89	−2.78
[−10, −2]	30.52	1.02	1.00	14.08	0.54	0.53	−240.59	−2.93*	−2.87
[−10, −1]	9.21	0.31	0.30	−47.44	−1.83	−1.80	−164.63	−2.00	−1.97
[−10, 0]	30.07	1.01	0.98	12.36	0.48	0.47	−138.47	−1.69	−1.65
[−10, 1]	57.50	1.92	1.89	22.56	0.87	0.86	−47.02	−0.57	−0.56
[−10, 2]	76.82	2.57	2.53	21.41	0.83	0.81	−28.55	−0.35	−0.34
[−10, 3]	85.86	2.87	2.81	6.47	0.25	0.24	−23.41	−0.28	−0.28
[−10, 4]	16.91	0.57	0.53	−26.98	−1.04	−0.98	−209.17	−2.55	−2.41
[−10, 5]	41.20	1.38	1.36	37.75	1.46	1.43	−188.17	−2.29	−2.26
[−10, 6]	1.79	0.06	0.06	55.76	2.15	2.12	−189.74	−2.31	−2.27
[−10, 7]	24.03	0.80	0.79	21.28	0.82	0.81	−55.95	−0.68	−0.67
[−10, 8]	−4.04	−0.14	−0.13	22.59	0.87	0.86	−231.67	−2.82	−2.78
[−10, 9]	−35.66	−1.19	−0.72	−16.96	−0.65	−0.40	−205.18	−2.50	−1.51
[−10, 10]	38.92	1.30	1.25	110.78	4.27 *	4.10 *	−54.61	−0.66	−0.64
[−10, 11]	38.62	1.29	1.25	142.38	5.49 **	5.32 **	−49.38	−0.60	−0.58
[−10, 12]	77.89	2.60	2.55	184.77	7.12 **	6.96 **	−56.23	−0.68	−0.67
[−10, 13]	102.38	3.42 *	3.34 *	197.50	7.61 **	7.43 **	−30.23	−0.37	−0.36
[−10, 14]	81.26	2.72	2.66	176.59	6.81 **	6.67 **	−107.71	−1.31	−1.29
[−10, 15]	14.57	0.49	0.48	121.64	4.69 **	4.61 **	−114.08	−1.39	−1.37
[−10, 16]	12.02	0.40	0.40	98.97	3.81 *	3.76 *	−75.79	−0.92	−0.91
[−10, 17]	0.16	0.01	0.01	52.26	2.01	1.98	−77.20	−0.94	−0.93
[−10, 18]	−31.51	−1.05	−1.03	−9.70	−0.37	−0.37	−52.78	−0.64	−0.63
[−10, 19]	−42.43	−1.42	−1.37	−31.32	−1.21	−1.16	−136.38	−1.66	−1.60
[−10, 20]	−54.12	−1.81	−1.71	−84.43	−3.25	−3.08	−222.72	−2.71	−2.56

Note: ** and * denote significance at the 5% and 10% levels, respectively.

Table A22. Case VI: GARCH(1,1)—Cumulative abnormal change rate of Chinese tourist arrivals.

Event Period $[\tau_1, \tau_2]$	Group-Type			Individual-Type			Medical-Type		
	CAR	t-Value		CAR	t-Value		CAR	t-Value	
		TM	SRM		TM	SRM		TM	SRM
[−10,−10]	−24.57	−0.78	−0.77	10.83	0.24	0.24	−66.73	−0.51	−0.50
[−10,−9]	9.91	0.31	0.31	62.18	1.39	1.36	−17.66	−0.13	−0.13
[−10,−8]	−12.05	−0.38	−0.37	74.04	1.65	1.61	−80.61	−0.61	−0.60
[−10,−7]	−22.82	−0.72	−0.71	22.98	0.51	0.50	−159.34	−1.21	−1.19
[−10,−6]	4.15	0.13	0.13	−5.55	−0.12	−0.12	−158.84	−1.21	−1.19
[−10,−5]	0.42	0.01	0.01	−18.30	−0.41	−0.40	−149.72	−1.14	−1.12
[−10,−4]	−72.35	−2.30	−2.26	−46.54	−1.04	−1.02	−255.42	−1.94	−1.91
[−10,−3]	−3.97	−0.13	−0.12	19.43	0.43	0.42	−206.73	−1.57	−1.51
[−10,−2]	28.32	0.90	0.88	27.67	0.62	0.61	−207.60	−1.58	−1.55
[−10,−1]	6.78	0.22	0.21	−37.33	−0.83	−0.82	−129.02	−0.98	−0.96
[−10,0]	27.40	0.87	0.85	20.12	0.45	0.44	−100.01	−0.76	−0.74
[−10,1]	54.58	1.73	1.71	34.78	0.78	0.76	−4.27	−0.03	−0.03
[−10,2]	73.65	2.34	2.30	37.81	0.84	0.83	18.42	0.14	0.14
[−10,3]	82.44	2.62	2.56	27.67	0.62	0.60	27.92	0.21	0.21
[−10,4]	13.22	0.42	0.40	2.63	0.06	0.06	−152.73	−1.16	−1.10
[−10,5]	37.30	1.18	1.17	57.25	1.28	1.26	−130.50	−0.99	−0.98
[−10,6]	−2.36	−0.07	−0.07	77.33	1.73	1.70	−128.29	−0.97	−0.96
[−10,7]	19.64	0.62	0.61	45.04	1.00	0.99	9.32	0.07	0.07
[−10,8]	−8.67	−0.28	−0.27	46.25	1.03	1.02	−163.08	−1.24	−1.22
[−10,9]	−40.38	−1.28	−0.77	−46.82	−1.04	−0.63	−144.47	−1.10	−0.66
[−10,10]	33.77	1.07	1.03	145.33	3.24 *	3.11 *	22.96	0.17	0.17
[−10,11]	33.24	1.06	1.02	176.07	3.93 *	3.81 *	31.36	0.24	0.23
[−10,12]	72.28	2.30	2.24	217.51	4.85 **	4.74 **	27.66	0.21	0.21
[−10,13]	96.52	3.07 *	2.99 *	231.88	5.17 **	5.05 **	57.36	0.44	0.43
[−10,14]	75.16	2.39	2.34	210.81	4.70 **	4.61 **	−16.81	−0.13	−0.13
[−10,15]	8.23	0.26	0.26	155.46	3.47 *	3.41 *	−19.92	−0.15	−0.15
[−10,16]	5.45	0.17	0.17	130.98	2.92 *	2.88	21.34	0.16	0.16
[−10,17]	−6.66	−0.21	−0.21	85.37	1.90	1.88	23.51	0.18	0.18
[−10,18]	−38.59	−1.23	−1.20	29.29	0.65	0.64	52.51	0.40	0.39
[−10,19]	−49.77	−1.58	−1.52	13.92	0.31	0.30	−26.42	−0.20	−0.19
[−10,20]	−61.71	−1.96	−1.85	−34.58	−0.77	−0.73	−108.45	−0.82	−0.78

Note: ** and * denote significance at the 5% and 10% levels, respectively.

Table A23. Case VI: GJR(1,1)—Cumulative abnormal change rate of Chinese tourist arrivals.

Event Period $[\tau_1, \tau_2]$	Group-Type			Individual-Type			Medical-Type		
	CAR	t-Value		CAR	t-Value		CAR	t-Value	
		TM	SRM		TM	SRM		TM	SRM
[−10, −10]	−21.70	−0.33	−0.32	11.64	0.17	0.17	−61.71	−0.24	−0.23
[−10, −9]	15.06	0.23	0.22	63.98	0.93	0.91	−7.62	−0.03	−0.03
[−10, −8]	−3.67	−0.06	−0.05	76.55	1.11	1.08	−65.54	−0.25	−0.24
[−10, −7]	−13.08	−0.20	−0.19	26.72	0.39	0.38	−139.27	−0.53	−0.52
[−10, −6]	15.44	0.23	0.23	−0.62	−0.01	−0.01	−133.77	−0.51	−0.50
[−10, −5]	14.72	0.22	0.22	−12.60	−0.18	−0.18	−119.63	−0.46	−0.45
[−10, −4]	−55.71	−0.84	−0.83	−39.88	−0.58	−0.57	−220.31	−0.84	−0.83
[−10, −3]	17.24	0.26	0.25	26.42	0.38	0.37	−166.56	−0.64	−0.61
[−10, −2]	50.40	0.76	0.75	36.04	0.52	0.51	−162.44	−0.62	−0.61
[−10, −1]	29.98	0.45	0.45	−27.65	−0.40	−0.39	−78.88	−0.30	−0.30
[−10, 0]	52.02	0.79	0.77	31.02	0.45	0.44	−44.87	−0.17	−0.17
[−10, 1]	82.44	1.25	1.23	46.39	0.67	0.66	55.90	0.21	0.21
[−10, 2]	104.68	1.58	1.56	50.15	0.73	0.71	83.63	0.32	0.31
[−10, 3]	116.81	1.77	1.73	40.69	0.59	0.58	98.16	0.38	0.37
[−10, 4]	51.89	0.78	0.74	16.05	0.23	0.22	−77.44	−0.30	−0.28
[−10, 5]	75.31	1.14	1.12	72.48	1.05	1.03	−50.25	−0.19	−0.19
[−10, 6]	38.26	0.58	0.57	93.45	1.35	1.33	−43.02	−0.16	−0.16
[−10, 7]	62.89	0.95	0.93	62.04	0.90	0.88	99.61	0.38	0.37
[−10, 8]	36.60	0.55	0.54	64.30	0.93	0.92	−67.78	−0.26	−0.26
[−10, 9]	−7.40	−0.11	−0.07	−23.68	−0.34	−0.21	−44.44	−0.17	−0.10
[−10, 10]	86.06	1.30	1.25	164.65	2.38	2.29	128.34	0.49	0.47
[−10, 11]	87.35	1.32	1.28	196.49	2.84	2.76	141.74	0.54	0.53
[−10, 12]	128.18	1.94	1.89	239.06	3.46 *	3.38 *	143.05	0.55	0.53
[−10, 13]	154.92	2.34	2.29	254.35	3.68 *	3.59 *	177.76	0.68	0.66
[−10, 14]	135.56	2.05	2.01	234.33	3.39 *	3.32 *	108.60	0.42	0.41
[−10, 15]	70.57	1.07	1.05	180.05	2.61	2.56	110.50	0.42	0.42
[−10, 16]	69.35	1.05	1.03	156.75	2.27	2.23	156.76	0.60	0.59
[−10, 17]	59.59	0.90	0.89	112.11	1.62	1.60	163.95	0.63	0.62
[−10, 18]	31.29	0.47	0.46	56.62	0.82	0.80	197.99	0.76	0.74
[−10, 19]	23.83	0.36	0.35	41.82	0.61	0.58	124.09	0.47	0.46
[−10, 20]	15.18	0.23	0.22	−5.97	−0.09	−0.08	47.10	0.18	0.17

Note: * denotes significance at the 10% level.

Table A24. Case VI: EGARCH(1,1)—Cumulative abnormal change rate of Chinese tourist arrivals.

Event Period $[\tau_1, \tau_2]$	Group-Type			Individual-Type			Medical-Type		
	CAR	t-Value		CAR	t-Value		CAR	t-Value	
		TM	SRM		TM	SRM		TM	SRM
[−10, −10]	−21.43	−0.27	−0.26	11.60	0.16	0.16	−55.27	−0.12	−0.12
[−10, −9]	15.90	0.20	0.20	64.02	0.91	0.89	5.84	0.01	0.01
[−10, −8]	−2.74	−0.03	−0.03	76.48	1.08	1.06	−46.00	−0.10	−0.10
[−10, −7]	−11.11	−0.14	−0.14	26.91	0.38	0.37	−111.80	−0.25	−0.24
[−10, −6]	18.35	0.23	0.23	−0.20	0.00	0.00	−98.54	−0.22	−0.21
[−10, −5]	17.83	0.22	0.22	−12.24	−0.17	−0.17	−78.09	−0.17	−0.17
[−10, −4]	−52.06	−0.65	−0.64	−39.45	−0.56	−0.55	−171.82	−0.38	−0.37
[−10, −3]	20.29	0.25	0.24	26.46	0.37	0.36	−113.33	−0.25	−0.24
[−10, −2]	54.74	0.69	0.67	36.44	0.52	0.51	−100.79	−0.22	−0.22
[−10, −1]	35.49	0.45	0.44	−26.92	−0.38	−0.38	−9.04	−0.02	−0.02
[−10, 0]	58.54	0.73	0.72	32.00	0.45	0.44	32.86	0.07	0.07
[−10, 1]	89.04	1.12	1.10	47.26	0.67	0.66	139.69	0.31	0.30
[−10, 2]	111.40	1.40	1.38	50.92	0.72	0.71	173.55	0.38	0.37
[−10, 3]	123.55	1.55	1.52	41.32	0.58	0.57	194.05	0.43	0.42
[−10, 4]	58.17	0.73	0.69	16.35	0.23	0.22	23.45	0.05	0.05
[−10, 5]	83.67	1.05	1.03	73.47	1.04	1.02	60.61	0.13	0.13
[−10, 6]	47.02	0.59	0.58	94.45	1.34	1.32	74.54	0.16	0.16
[−10, 7]	72.04	0.90	0.89	63.04	0.89	0.88	223.83	0.49	0.48
[−10, 8]	46.46	0.58	0.57	65.44	0.93	0.91	63.72	0.14	0.14
[−10, 9]	10.50	0.13	0.08	−19.46	−0.28	−0.17	108.67	0.24	0.14
[−10, 10]	95.80	1.20	1.15	165.44	2.34	2.25	271.43	0.59	0.57
[−10, 11]	97.89	1.23	1.19	197.46	2.80	2.71	292.32	0.64	0.62
[−10, 12]	139.55	1.75	1.71	240.21	3.40 *	3.32 *	301.14	0.66	0.65
[−10, 13]	166.74	2.09	2.04	255.53	3.62 *	3.53 *	342.66	0.75	0.73
[−10, 14]	148.10	1.86	1.82	235.65	3.34 *	3.27 *	280.81	0.62	0.60
[−10, 15]	83.85	1.05	1.03	181.53	2.57	2.53	290.07	0.64	0.63
[−10, 16]	83.58	1.05	1.03	158.46	2.24	2.21	344.07	0.75	0.74
[−10, 17]	74.36	0.93	0.92	113.88	1.61	1.59	358.22	0.79	0.77
[−10, 18]	45.93	0.58	0.57	58.20	0.82	0.81	397.93	0.87	0.86
[−10, 19]	38.31	0.48	0.46	43.18	0.61	0.59	329.62	0.72	0.70
[−10, 20]	29.71	0.37	0.35	−4.74	−0.07	−0.06	258.64	0.57	0.54

Note: * denotes significance at the 10% level.

Table A25. Case VII: OLS—Cumulative abnormal change rate of Chinese tourist arrivals.

Event Period $[\tau_1, \tau_2]$	Group-Type			Individual-Type			Medical-Type		
	CAR	t-Value		CAR	t-Value		CAR	t-Value	
		TM	SRM		TM	SRM		TM	SRM
[0, 0]	−17.29	−0.88	−0.86	6.24	0.27	0.26	176.65	2.15	2.11
[0, 1]	−20.93	−1.06	−1.05	37.49	1.60	1.58	233.85	2.84	2.80
[0, 2]	0.56	0.03	0.03	47.07	2.01	1.98	53.96	0.66	0.65
[0, 3]	−28.25	−1.43	−1.41	23.73	1.02	1.00	227.76	2.77	2.73
[0, 4]	−34.92	−1.77	−1.74	11.10	0.47	0.47	138.31	1.68	1.66
[0, 5]	−9.64	−0.49	−0.48	20.04	0.86	0.84	256.74	3.12 *	3.07 *
[0, 6]	0.01	0.00	0.00	16.08	0.69	0.68	187.34	2.28	2.24
[0, 7]	6.44	0.33	0.32	13.94	0.60	0.59	281.62	3.42 *	3.37 *
[0, 8]	7.16	0.36	0.36	42.80	1.83	1.80	259.33	3.15 *	3.10 *
[0, 9]	16.77	0.85	0.84	52.25	2.24	2.20	309.96	3.77 *	3.71 *
[0, 10]	−21.75	−1.10	−1.09	20.16	0.86	0.85	213.71	2.60	2.56
[0, 11]	−23.03	−1.17	−1.15	11.32	0.48	0.48	265.44	3.23 *	3.18 *
[0, 12]	−4.07	−0.21	−0.20	10.95	0.47	0.46	110.16	1.34	1.32
[0, 13]	7.58	0.38	0.38	15.90	0.68	0.67	193.00	2.35	2.30
[0, 14]	16.32	0.83	0.82	19.06	0.82	0.80	198.66	2.41	2.38
[0, 15]	9.57	0.49	0.47	39.59	1.69	1.65	234.78	2.85	2.79
[0, 16]	21.61	1.10	1.08	37.16	1.59	1.56	282.05	3.43 *	3.37 *
[0, 17]	−30.99	−1.57	−1.55	3.80	0.16	0.16	222.94	2.71	2.67
[0, 18]	−18.37	−0.93	−0.92	−1.60	−0.07	−0.07	274.04	3.33 *	3.28 *
[0, 19]	−22.77	−1.16	−1.14	−11.07	−0.47	−0.47	303.07	3.68 *	3.62 *
[0, 20]	1.76	0.09	0.09	−4.33	−0.19	−0.18	327.69	3.98 *	3.92 *
[0, 21]	−5.85	−0.30	−0.29	−10.32	−0.44	−0.43	212.75	2.59	2.55
[0, 22]	7.78	0.39	0.39	2.08	0.09	0.09	177.01	2.15	2.12
[0, 23]	−0.50	−0.03	−0.02	−11.78	−0.50	−0.50	207.81	2.53	2.49
[0, 24]	−54.74	−2.78	−2.74	−30.23	−1.29	−1.27	231.82	2.82	2.77
[0, 25]	−77.00	−3.91 *	−3.85 *	−57.37	−2.45	−2.42	311.12	3.78 *	3.72 *
[0, 26]	−62.26	−3.16 *	−3.11 *	−74.21	−3.17 *	−3.12 *	188.75	2.29	2.26
[0, 27]	−43.88	−2.23	−2.19	−89.98	−3.85 *	−3.79 *	309.29	3.76 *	3.70 *
[0, 28]	−45.40	−2.30	−2.27	−75.29	−3.22 *	−3.17 *	284.92	3.46 *	3.41 *
[0, 29]	−42.96	−2.18	−2.14	−62.63	−2.68	−2.63	391.41	4.76 **	4.68 **
[0, 30]	−47.64	−2.42	−2.38	−62.01	−2.65	−2.61	357.44	4.34 **	4.28 *

Note: ** and * denote significance at the 5% and 10% levels, respectively.

Table A26. Case VII: GARCH(1,1)—Cumulative abnormal change rate of Chinese tourist arrivals.

Event Period $[\tau_1, \tau_2]$	Group-Type			Individual-Type			Medical-Type		
	CAR	t-Value		CAR	t-Value		CAR	t-Value	
		TM	SRM		TM	SRM		TM	SRM
[0, 0]	−18.31	−0.54	−0.53	5.71	0.20	0.20	176.75	2.11	2.08
[0, 1]	−23.24	−0.68	−0.67	36.48	1.29	1.27	234.01	2.80	2.76
[0, 2]	−2.57	−0.08	−0.07	45.51	1.61	1.58	54.24	0.65	0.64
[0, 3]	−32.35	−0.95	−0.94	21.63	0.76	0.75	228.14	2.73	2.69
[0, 4]	−39.96	−1.18	−1.16	8.46	0.30	0.29	138.78	1.66	1.63
[0, 5]	−16.17	−0.48	−0.47	16.95	0.60	0.59	257.26	3.08 *	3.03 *
[0, 6]	−7.72	−0.23	−0.22	12.49	0.44	0.43	187.93	2.25	2.21
[0, 7]	−2.18	−0.06	−0.06	9.80	0.35	0.34	282.33	3.38 *	3.32 *
[0, 8]	−2.75	−0.08	−0.08	38.18	1.35	1.33	260.11	3.11 *	3.06 *
[0, 9]	5.61	0.17	0.16	47.14	1.66	1.64	310.80	3.72 *	3.66 *
[0, 10]	−33.88	−1.00	−0.98	14.52	0.51	0.50	214.65	2.57	2.53
[0, 11]	−36.25	−1.07	−1.05	5.16	0.18	0.18	266.46	3.19 *	3.14 *
[0, 12]	−18.87	−0.56	−0.55	4.34	0.15	0.15	111.23	1.33	1.31
[0, 13]	−7.60	−0.22	−0.22	8.68	0.31	0.30	194.22	2.32	2.28
[0, 14]	−0.08	0.00	0.00	11.34	0.40	0.39	199.96	2.39	2.35
[0, 15]	−9.27	−0.27	−0.27	31.54	1.11	1.09	236.03	2.82	2.76
[0, 16]	1.98	0.06	0.06	28.56	1.01	0.99	283.41	3.39 *	3.33 *
[0, 17]	−51.32	−1.51	−1.49	−5.37	−0.19	−0.19	224.44	2.68	2.64
[0, 18]	−39.87	−1.17	−1.16	−11.28	−0.40	−0.39	275.61	3.30 *	3.25 *
[0, 19]	−46.02	−1.36	−1.33	−21.16	−0.75	−0.73	304.66	3.64 *	3.58 *
[0, 20]	−22.37	−0.66	−0.65	−14.97	−0.53	−0.52	329.39	3.94 *	3.88 *
[0, 21]	−30.93	−0.91	−0.90	−21.49	−0.76	−0.75	214.56	2.57	2.53
[0, 22]	−18.96	−0.56	−0.55	−9.53	−0.34	−0.33	178.85	2.14	2.10
[0, 23]	−28.40	−0.84	−0.82	−23.89	−0.84	−0.83	209.72	2.51	2.47
[0, 24]	−83.61	−2.46	−2.42	−42.88	−1.51	−1.49	233.84	2.80	2.75
[0, 25]	−106.71	−3.14 *	−3.09 *	−70.57	−2.49	−2.45	313.24	3.75 *	3.69 *
[0, 26]	−93.56	−2.76	−2.71	−87.85	−3.10 *	−3.05 *	190.91	2.28	2.25
[0, 27]	−76.17	−2.24	−2.21	−104.15	−3.67 *	−3.62 *	311.54	3.73 *	3.67 *
[0, 28]	−78.85	−2.32	−2.29	−89.97	−3.17 *	−3.13 *	287.26	3.43 *	3.38 *
[0, 29]	−78.12	−2.30	−2.26	−77.73	−2.74	−2.70	393.77	4.71 **	4.63 **
[0, 30]	−84.34	−2.48	−2.44	−77.56	−2.74	−2.69	359.84	4.30 *	4.23 *

Note: ** and * denote significance at the 5% and 10% levels, respectively.

Table A27. Case VII: GJR(1,1)—Cumulative abnormal change rate of Chinese tourist arrivals.

Event Period $[\tau_1, \tau_2]$	Group-Type			Individual-Type			Medical-Type		
	CAR	t-Value		CAR	t-Value		CAR	t-Value	
		TM	SRM		TM	SRM		TM	SRM
[0, 0]	−17.09	−0.81	−0.79	6.27	0.27	0.26	178.17	1.56	1.54
[0, 1]	−20.64	−0.97	−0.96	37.61	1.61	1.59	236.91	2.08	2.04
[0, 2]	1.12	0.05	0.05	47.19	2.02	1.99	58.52	0.51	0.50
[0, 3]	−27.47	−1.30	−1.28	23.87	1.02	1.01	233.84	2.05	2.02
[0, 4]	−33.91	−1.60	−1.57	11.25	0.48	0.47	145.90	1.28	1.26
[0, 5]	−8.62	−0.41	−0.40	20.32	0.87	0.86	265.89	2.33	2.29
[0, 6]	1.16	0.05	0.05	16.43	0.70	0.69	198.02	1.73	1.71
[0, 7]	7.84	0.37	0.36	14.30	0.61	0.60	293.81	2.57	2.53
[0, 8]	8.65	0.41	0.40	43.25	1.85	1.82	273.07	2.39	2.36
[0, 9]	18.37	0.87	0.85	52.77	2.26	2.23	325.24	2.85	2.81
[0, 10]	−19.94	−0.94	−0.93	20.71	0.89	0.87	230.50	2.02	1.99
[0, 11]	−21.05	−0.99	−0.98	11.91	0.51	0.50	283.75	2.49	2.45
[0, 12]	−2.11	−0.10	−0.10	11.68	0.50	0.49	130.05	1.14	1.12
[0, 13]	9.99	0.47	0.46	16.55	0.71	0.70	214.34	1.88	1.84
[0, 14]	18.85	0.89	0.88	19.77	0.85	0.83	221.55	1.94	1.91
[0, 15]	11.73	0.55	0.54	40.61	1.74	1.70	259.31	2.27	2.22
[0, 16]	24.06	1.13	1.12	38.17	1.64	1.61	308.08	2.70	2.66
[0, 17]	−28.21	−1.33	−1.31	4.79	0.21	0.20	250.47	2.19	2.16
[0, 18]	−15.45	−0.73	−0.72	−0.56	−0.02	−0.02	303.09	2.66	2.62
[0, 19]	−19.95	−0.94	−0.92	−9.85	−0.42	−0.41	333.71	2.92*	2.87
[0, 20]	4.84	0.23	0.22	−3.10	−0.13	−0.13	359.83	3.15*	3.10*
[0, 21]	−2.55	−0.12	−0.12	−9.07	−0.39	−0.38	246.41	2.16	2.13
[0, 22]	11.02	0.52	0.51	3.48	0.15	0.15	212.25	1.86	1.83
[0, 23]	2.89	0.14	0.13	−10.31	−0.44	−0.44	244.58	2.14	2.11
[0, 24]	−51.14	−2.41	−2.37	−28.74	−1.23	−1.21	270.10	2.37	2.33
[0, 25]	−73.13	−3.45 *	−3.39 *	−55.88	−2.39	−2.36	350.90	3.07 *	3.03 *
[0, 26]	−58.41	−2.75	−2.71	−72.58	−3.11 *	−3.06 *	230.10	2.02	1.98
[0, 27]	−39.82	−1.88	−1.85	−88.32	−3.78 *	−3.73 *	352.16	3.09 *	3.04 *
[0, 28]	−41.21	−1.94	−1.91	−73.57	−3.15 *	−3.10 *	329.32	2.89	2.84
[0, 29]	−38.85	−1.83	−1.80	−60.74	−2.60	−2.56	437.39	3.83 *	3.77 *
[0, 30]	−43.53	−2.05	−2.02	−59.98	−2.57	−2.53	404.99	3.55 *	3.49 *

Note: ** and * denote significance at the 5% and 10% levels, respectively.

Table A28. Case VII: EGARCH(1,1)–Cumulative Abnormal Change Rate of Chinese Tourist Arrivals.

Event Period $[\tau_1, \tau_2]$	Group-Type			Individual-Type			Medical-Type		
	CAR	t-Value		CAR	t-Value		CAR	t-Value	
		TM	SRM		TM	SRM		TM	SRM
[0, 0]	−16.75	−0.53	−0.53	6.32	0.27	0.27	178.17	0.51	0.50
[0, 1]	−19.62	−0.63	−0.62	37.74	1.61	1.58	236.91	0.67	0.66
[0, 2]	2.23	0.07	0.07	47.34	2.02	1.99	58.52	0.17	0.16
[0, 3]	−26.08	−0.83	−0.82	24.06	1.03	1.01	233.84	0.66	0.65
[0, 4]	−32.28	−1.03	−1.01	11.48	0.49	0.48	145.90	0.41	0.41
[0, 5]	−6.05	−0.19	−0.19	20.66	0.88	0.87	265.89	0.75	0.74
[0, 6]	4.30	0.14	0.14	16.85	0.72	0.71	198.02	0.56	0.55
[0, 7]	11.15	0.36	0.35	14.74	0.63	0.62	293.81	0.83	0.82
[0, 8]	12.64	0.40	0.40	43.77	1.87	1.84	273.07	0.77	0.76
[0, 9]	23.00	0.73	0.72	53.38	2.28	2.24	325.24	0.92	0.91
[0, 10]	−15.02	−0.48	−0.47	21.36	0.91	0.90	230.50	0.65	0.64
[0, 11]	−15.71	−0.50	−0.49	12.62	0.54	0.53	283.75	0.80	0.79
[0, 12]	4.28	0.14	0.13	12.52	0.53	0.53	130.05	0.37	0.36
[0, 13]	15.92	0.51	0.50	17.34	0.74	0.73	214.34	0.61	0.60
[0, 14]	25.36	0.81	0.80	20.64	0.88	0.87	221.55	0.63	0.62
[0, 15]	20.37	0.65	0.63	41.73	1.78	1.74	259.31	0.74	0.72
[0, 16]	32.76	1.05	1.03	39.31	1.68	1.65	308.08	0.87	0.86
[0, 17]	−19.58	−0.63	−0.61	5.92	0.25	0.25	250.47	0.71	0.70
[0, 18]	−6.29	−0.20	−0.20	0.65	0.03	0.03	303.09	0.86	0.85
[0, 19]	−9.52	−0.30	−0.30	−8.49	−0.36	−0.36	333.71	0.95	0.93
[0, 20]	15.44	0.49	0.49	−1.72	−0.07	−0.07	359.83	1.02	1.00
[0, 21]	8.30	0.26	0.26	−7.65	−0.33	−0.32	246.41	0.70	0.69
[0, 22]	23.01	0.73	0.72	5.04	0.22	0.21	212.25	0.60	0.59
[0, 23]	15.41	0.49	0.48	−8.69	−0.37	−0.36	244.58	0.69	0.68
[0, 24]	−38.34	−1.22	−1.21	−27.07	−1.15	−1.14	270.10	0.77	0.75
[0, 25]	−60.23	−1.92	−1.89	−54.19	−2.31	−2.27	350.90	0.99	0.98
[0, 26]	−44.44	−1.42	−1.40	−70.76	−3.02 *	−2.97 *	230.10	0.65	0.64
[0, 27]	−25.55	−0.82	−0.80	−86.46	−3.69 *	−3.63 *	352.16	1.00	0.98
[0, 28]	−26.42	−0.84	−0.83	−71.64	−3.05 *	−3.01 *	329.32	0.93	0.92
[0, 29]	−22.84	−0.73	−0.72	−58.66	−2.50	−2.46	437.39	1.24	1.22
[0, 30]	−26.52	−0.85	−0.83	−57.78	−2.46	−2.42	404.99	1.15	1.13

Note: ** and * denote significance at the 5% and 10% levels, respectively.

Table A29. Case VIII: OLS—Cumulative abnormal change rate of Chinese tourist arrivals.

Event Period $[\tau_1, \tau_2]$	Group-Type			Individual-Type			Medical-Type		
	CAR	t-Value		CAR	t-Value		CAR	t-Value	
		TM	SRM		TM	SRM		TM	SRM
[0, 0]	4.72	0.21	0.20	9.73	0.31	0.30	26.95	0.25	0.24
[0, 1]	5.36	0.23	0.23	27.43	0.86	0.85	161.67	1.48	1.45
[0, 2]	25.92	1.13	1.11	28.94	0.91	0.90	94.68	0.86	0.85
[0, 3]	−8.18	−0.36	−0.35	−25.21	−0.79	−0.78	159.44	1.46	1.43
[0, 4]	10.22	0.45	0.44	−75.97	−2.39	−2.35	103.78	0.95	0.93
[0, 5]	38.10	1.66	1.63	−6.14	−0.19	−0.19	14.05	0.13	0.13
[0, 6]	72.00	3.14 *	3.09 *	6.18	0.19	0.19	106.84	0.98	0.96
[0, 7]	94.02	4.09 *	4.03 *	42.28	1.33	1.31	243.60	2.22	2.19
[0, 8]	75.79	3.30 *	3.25 *	39.93	1.26	1.24	129.57	1.18	1.16
[0, 9]	78.19	3.41 *	3.35 *	39.50	1.24	1.22	262.72	2.40	2.36
[0, 10]	37.63	1.64	1.61	0.74	0.02	0.02	225.73	2.06	2.03
[0, 11]	54.47	2.37	2.34	−4.25	−0.13	−0.13	80.91	0.74	0.73
[0, 12]	69.67	3.03 *	2.99 *	18.10	0.57	0.56	120.24	1.10	1.08
[0, 13]	88.94	3.87 *	3.81 *	14.16	0.45	0.44	226.26	2.07	2.03
[0, 14]	83.04	3.62 *	3.56 *	10.67	0.34	0.33	286.53	2.62	2.58
[0, 15]	109.07	4.75 **	4.67 **	37.86	1.19	1.17	212.78	1.94	1.91
[0, 16]	86.05	3.75 *	3.69 *	33.31	1.05	1.03	194.44	1.78	1.75
[0, 17]	11.28	0.49	0.48	−33.07	−1.04	−1.02	313.07	2.86	2.81
[0, 18]	97.33	4.24 *	4.17 *	45.76	1.44	1.42	280.25	2.56	2.52
[0, 19]	80.53	3.51 *	3.45 *	10.36	0.33	0.32	230.22	2.10	2.07
[0, 20]	73.53	3.20 *	3.15 *	27.48	0.87	0.85	115.74	1.06	1.04
[0, 21]	58.35	2.54	2.50	60.78	1.92	1.88	358.75	3.28 *	3.22 *
[0, 22]	44.11	1.92	1.89	79.54	2.51	2.47	363.99	3.32 *	3.27 *
[0, 23]	54.46	2.37	2.34	102.67	3.23 *	3.19 *	276.45	2.52	2.48
[0, 24]	37.85	1.65	1.62	92.36	2.91	2.86	320.12	2.92 *	2.88
[0, 25]	82.27	3.58 *	3.53 *	127.84	4.03 *	3.97 *	251.14	2.29	2.26
[0, 26]	62.06	2.70	2.66	168.10	5.30 **	5.21 **	212.45	1.94	1.91
[0, 27]	97.53	4.25 *	4.18 *	188.72	5.95 **	5.85 **	211.11	1.93	1.90
[0, 28]	78.33	3.41 *	3.36 *	162.72	5.13 **	5.05 **	174.28	1.59	1.57
[0, 29]	31.03	1.35	1.33	121.60	3.83 *	3.77 *	284.24	2.59	2.55
[0, 30]	25.77	1.12	1.10	56.03	1.77	1.74	116.45	1.06	1.05

Note: ** and * denote significance at the 5% and 10% levels, respectively.

Table A30. Case VIII: GARCH(1,1)—Cumulative abnormal change rate of Chinese tourist arrivals.

Event Period $[\tau_1, \tau_2]$	Group-Type			Individual-Type			Medical-Type		
	CAR	t-Value		CAR	t-Value		CAR	t-Value	
		TM	SRM		TM	SRM		TM	SRM
[0, 0]	4.75	0.21	0.20	9.47	0.32	0.31	30.58	0.15	0.15
[0, 1]	5.60	0.25	0.24	26.91	0.90	0.88	168.37	0.82	0.80
[0, 2]	26.54	1.16	1.14	28.17	0.94	0.92	103.94	0.50	0.49
[0, 3]	−8.18	−0.36	−0.35	−26.25	−0.88	−0.86	174.31	0.84	0.83
[0, 4]	10.94	0.48	0.47	−77.26	−2.58	−2.53	120.20	0.58	0.57
[0, 5]	38.71	1.69	1.67	−7.69	−0.26	−0.25	34.50	0.17	0.16
[0, 6]	72.61	3.18 *	3.13 *	4.37	0.15	0.14	130.99	0.63	0.62
[0, 7]	94.80	4.15 *	4.08 *	40.22	1.34	1.32	270.95	1.31	1.29
[0, 8]	76.46	3.34 *	3.29 *	37.60	1.25	1.24	161.01	0.78	0.77
[0, 9]	79.04	3.46 *	3.40 *	36.92	1.23	1.21	297.33	1.44	1.42
[0, 10]	38.33	1.68	1.65	−2.11	−0.07	−0.07	264.49	1.28	1.26
[0, 11]	55.16	2.41	2.38	−7.36	−0.25	−0.24	123.40	0.60	0.59
[0, 12]	70.43	3.08 *	3.03 *	14.73	0.49	0.48	166.25	0.81	0.79
[0, 13]	89.73	3.93 *	3.87 *	10.54	0.35	0.35	275.87	1.34	1.32
[0, 14]	83.79	3.67 *	3.61 *	6.78	0.23	0.22	340.00	1.65	1.62
[0, 15]	110.11	4.82 **	4.74 **	33.72	1.13	1.11	269.11	1.30	1.28
[0, 16]	87.00	3.81 *	3.75 *	28.91	0.96	0.95	254.73	1.23	1.22
[0, 17]	11.97	0.52	0.51	−37.73	−1.26	−1.24	377.86	1.83	1.80
[0, 18]	98.32	4.30 *	4.24 *	40.84	1.36	1.34	347.88	1.69	1.66
[0, 19]	81.48	3.56 *	3.51 *	5.18	0.17	0.17	301.66	1.46	1.44
[0, 20]	74.66	3.27 *	3.22 *	22.04	0.74	0.72	190.36	0.92	0.91
[0, 21]	59.65	2.61	2.57	55.09	1.84	1.81	436.57	2.11	2.08
[0, 22]	45.22	1.98	1.95	73.59	2.46	2.42	446.12	2.16	2.13
[0, 23]	55.57	2.43	2.39	96.45	3.22 *	3.17 *	362.27	1.75	1.73
[0, 24]	38.89	1.70	1.67	85.89	2.87	2.82	409.86	1.99	1.95
[0, 25]	83.50	3.65 *	3.60 *	121.10	4.04 *	3.98 *	344.06	1.67	1.64
[0, 26]	63.23	2.77	2.72	161.11	5.38 **	5.29 **	309.24	1.50	1.47
[0, 27]	99.02	4.33 *	4.26 *	181.47	6.06 **	5.96 **	310.68	1.50	1.48
[0, 28]	79.89	3.49 *	3.44 *	155.21	5.18 **	5.10 **	277.36	1.34	1.32
[0, 29]	32.68	1.43	1.41	113.84	3.80 *	3.74 *	390.76	1.89	1.86
[0, 30]	27.01	1.18	1.16	48.00	1.60	1.58	227.88	1.10	1.09

Note: ** and * denote significance at the 5% and 10% levels, respectively.

Table A31. Case VIII: GJR(1,1)—Cumulative abnormal change rate of Chinese tourist arrivals.

Event Period $[\tau_1, \tau_2]$	Group-Type			Individual-Type			Medical-Type		
	CAR	t-Value		CAR	t-Value		CAR	t-Value	
		TM	SRM		TM	SRM		TM	SRM
[0, 0]	5.33	0.20	0.19	10.60	0.35	0.34	30.91	0.15	0.15
[0, 1]	6.76	0.25	0.24	29.14	0.96	0.94	169.08	0.82	0.81
[0, 2]	28.25	1.04	1.02	31.50	1.03	1.02	105.07	0.51	0.50
[0, 3]	−5.84	−0.21	−0.21	−21.72	−0.71	−0.70	175.61	0.85	0.83
[0, 4]	13.81	0.51	0.50	−71.68	−2.35	−2.31	122.01	0.59	0.58
[0, 5]	42.17	1.55	1.52	−0.97	−0.03	−0.03	36.60	0.18	0.17
[0, 6]	76.67	2.81	2.77	12.22	0.40	0.39	133.42	0.65	0.64
[0, 7]	99.43	3.65 *	3.58 *	49.18	1.61	1.59	273.75	1.33	1.30
[0, 8]	81.67	2.99 *	2.95 *	47.71	1.57	1.54	164.10	0.79	0.78
[0, 9]	84.83	3.11 *	3.06 *	48.14	1.58	1.55	300.80	1.46	1.43
[0, 10]	44.71	1.64	1.61	10.26	0.34	0.33	268.24	1.30	1.28
[0, 11]	62.13	2.28	2.24	6.14	0.20	0.20	127.48	0.62	0.61
[0, 12]	77.98	2.86	2.82	29.36	0.96	0.95	170.66	0.83	0.81
[0, 13]	97.87	3.59 *	3.53 *	26.29	0.86	0.85	280.62	1.36	1.34
[0, 14]	92.52	3.39 *	3.34 *	23.67	0.78	0.77	345.06	1.67	1.65
[0, 15]	119.40	4.38 **	4.31 **	51.71	1.70	1.67	274.56	1.33	1.31
[0, 16]	96.88	3.55 *	3.50 *	48.04	1.58	1.55	260.49	1.26	1.24
[0, 17]	22.45	0.82	0.81	−17.44	−0.57	−0.56	383.88	1.86	1.83
[0, 18]	109.36	4.01 *	3.95 *	62.23	2.04	2.01	354.31	1.72	1.69
[0, 19]	93.11	3.41 *	3.36 *	27.71	0.91	0.90	308.40	1.49	1.47
[0, 20]	86.87	3.19 *	3.14 *	45.68	1.50	1.48	197.47	0.96	0.94
[0, 21]	72.43	2.66	2.61	79.84	2.62	2.58	444.04	2.15	2.12
[0, 22]	58.59	2.15	2.12	99.49	3.26	3.22	453.87	2.20	2.16
[0, 23]	69.53	2.55	2.51	123.49	4.05 *	3.99 *	370.35	1.79	1.77
[0, 24]	53.44	1.96	1.93	114.06	3.74 *	3.68 *	418.25	2.03	1.99
[0, 25]	98.62	3.62 *	3.56 *	150.39	4.94 **	4.86 **	352.82	1.71	1.68
[0, 26]	78.95	2.89	2.85	191.53	6.29 **	6.19 **	318.31	1.54	1.52
[0, 27]	115.29	4.23 *	4.16 *	212.99	6.99 **	6.88 **	320.15	1.55	1.53
[0, 28]	96.74	3.55 *	3.49 *	187.86	6.16 **	6.07 **	287.17	1.39	1.37
[0, 29]	50.11	1.84	1.81	147.61	4.84 **	4.77 **	400.92	1.94	1.91
[0, 30]	45.06	1.65	1.62	82.95	2.72	2.68	238.27	1.15	1.13

Note: ** and * denote significance at the 5% and 10% levels, respectively.

Table A32. Case VIII: EGARCH(1,1)—Cumulative abnormal change rate of Chinese tourist arrivals.

Event Period $[\tau_1, \tau_2]$	Group-Type			Individual-Type			Medical-Type		
	CAR	t-Value		CAR	t-Value		CAR	t-Value	
		TM	SRM		TM	SRM		TM	SRM
[0, 0]	4.22	0.15	0.15	9.63	0.31	0.31	31.89	0.14	0.13
[0, 1]	5.42	0.19	0.19	27.20	0.88	0.87	171.50	0.73	0.72
[0, 2]	27.53	0.99	0.97	28.57	0.93	0.91	109.34	0.47	0.46
[0, 3]	−10.86	−0.39	−0.38	−25.57	−0.83	−0.81	179.26	0.77	0.75
[0, 4]	11.01	0.40	0.39	−76.54	−2.48	−2.44	128.32	0.55	0.54
[0, 5]	37.63	1.35	1.33	−6.78	−0.22	−0.22	43.58	0.19	0.18
[0, 6]	70.89	2.54	2.51	5.44	0.18	0.17	141.32	0.60	0.59
[0, 7]	93.21	3.35 *	3.29 *	41.43	1.34	1.32	282.97	1.21	1.19
[0, 8]	73.61	2.64	2.60	39.00	1.26	1.24	173.94	0.74	0.73
[0, 9]	76.39	2.74	2.70	38.46	1.25	1.23	311.99	1.33	1.31
[0, 10]	34.33	1.23	1.21	−0.37	−0.01	−0.01	280.00	1.20	1.18
[0, 11]	50.46	1.81	1.78	−5.45	−0.18	−0.17	140.13	0.60	0.59
[0, 12]	65.39	2.35	2.31	16.80	0.54	0.54	184.40	0.79	0.78
[0, 13]	84.20	3.02 *	2.98 *	12.76	0.41	0.41	295.36	1.26	1.24
[0, 14]	77.37	2.78	2.74	9.19	0.30	0.29	360.60	1.54	1.52
[0, 15]	104.36	3.75 *	3.69 *	36.24	1.17	1.16	291.70	1.25	1.23
[0, 16]	80.20	2.88	2.84	31.62	1.02	1.01	278.35	1.19	1.17
[0, 17]	3.26	0.12	0.11	−34.81	−1.13	−1.11	402.01	1.72	1.69
[0, 18]	90.32	3.24 *	3.19 *	43.88	1.42	1.40	374.06	1.60	1.57
[0, 19]	72.67	2.61	2.57	8.40	0.27	0.27	328.99	1.41	1.38
[0, 20]	66.04	2.37	2.33	25.40	0.82	0.81	219.41	0.94	0.92
[0, 21]	51.18	1.84	1.81	58.58	1.90	1.87	467.32	2.00	1.97
[0, 22]	35.14	1.26	1.24	77.28	2.50	2.47	477.58	2.04	2.01
[0, 23]	44.86	1.61	1.59	100.32	3.25 *	3.20 *	394.98	1.69	1.66
[0, 24]	27.18	0.98	0.96	89.93	2.91	2.87	443.63	1.90	1.87
[0, 25]	71.97	2.58	2.54	125.29	4.06 *	4.00 *	379.55	1.62	1.60
[0, 26]	50.80	1.82	1.80	165.47	5.36 **	5.28 **	345.83	1.48	1.46
[0, 27]	87.40	3.14 *	3.09 *	185.95	6.02 **	5.93 **	349.34	1.49	1.47
[0, 28]	67.93	2.44	2.40	159.85	5.18 **	5.10 **	317.45	1.36	1.34
[0, 29]	20.48	0.74	0.72	118.63	3.84 *	3.78 *	432.33	1.85	1.82
[0, 30]	12.26	0.44	0.43	53.03	1.72	1.69	269.62	1.15	1.13

Note: ** and * denote significance at the 5% and 10% levels, respectively.

Table A33. Case IX: OLS—Cumulative abnormal change rate of Chinese tourist arrivals.

Event Period $[\tau_1, \tau_2]$	Group-Type			Individual-Type			Medical-Type		
	CAR	t-Value		CAR	t-Value		CAR	t-Value	
		TM	SRM		TM	SRM		TM	SRM
[0, 0]	0.39	0.01	0.01	−12.89	−0.47	−0.46	−34.37	−0.42	−0.41
[0, 1]	−15.28	−0.56	−0.55	−26.34	−0.96	−0.95	−206.67	−2.51	−2.48
[0, 2]	−4.47	−0.16	−0.16	−25.11	−0.92	−0.90	−235.45	−2.86	−2.82
[0, 3]	3.48	0.13	0.12	−2.73	−0.10	−0.10	−75.79	−0.92	−0.91
[0, 4]	−13.91	−0.51	−0.50	−12.41	−0.45	−0.45	−68.70	−0.84	−0.82
[0, 5]	−7.10	−0.26	−0.25	−35.59	−1.30	−1.28	−154.55	−1.88	−1.85
[0, 6]	−16.97	−0.62	−0.60	−41.95	−1.53	−1.50	−103.91	−1.26	−1.23
[0, 7]	−26.45	−0.96	−0.95	−33.35	−1.22	−1.20	−131.33	−1.60	−1.57
[0, 8]	−65.79	−2.40	−2.35	−42.39	−1.55	−1.52	−145.12	−1.77	−1.73
[0, 9]	−62.43	−2.27	−2.23	−39.33	−1.44	−1.41	−94.88	−1.15	−1.13
[0, 10]	−59.72	−2.18	−2.13	−46.32	−1.69	−1.66	−149.71	−1.82	−1.78
[0, 11]	−61.38	−2.24	−2.13	−14.47	−0.53	−0.51	−30.49	−0.37	−0.35
[0, 12]	−46.84	−1.71	−1.67	2.17	0.08	0.08	60.71	0.74	0.72
[0, 13]	−52.86	−1.93	−1.89	4.84	0.18	0.17	55.12	0.67	0.66
[0, 14]	−59.78	−2.18	−2.02	−10.99	−0.40	−0.37	−176.64	−2.15	−2.00
[0, 15]	−25.70	−0.94	−0.92	46.52	1.70	1.68	−242.71	−2.95 *	−2.91
[0, 16]	6.29	0.23	0.22	58.06	2.12	2.05	−113.18	−1.38	−1.33
[0, 17]	−9.88	−0.36	−0.35	23.93	0.88	0.85	−73.47	−0.89	−0.87
[0, 18]	−35.13	−1.28	−1.26	3.26	0.12	0.12	23.43	0.28	0.28
[0, 19]	−37.25	−1.36	−1.34	−42.08	−1.54	−1.52	−1.48	−0.02	−0.02
[0, 20]	−22.02	−0.80	−0.76	−57.13	−2.09	−1.97	−93.89	−1.14	−1.08
[0, 21]	−17.07	−0.62	−0.60	−79.14	−2.90	−2.79	−108.85	−1.32	−1.27
[0, 22]	−38.23	−1.39	−1.37	−99.91	−3.66 *	−3.60 *	−155.53	−1.89	−1.86
[0, 23]	−49.72	−1.81	−1.78	−110.71	−4.05 *	−3.98 *	−288.68	−3.51 *	−3.45 *
[0, 24]	−57.53	−2.10	−2.06	−133.39	−4.88 **	−4.80 **	−33.24	−0.40	−0.40
[0, 25]	−108.41	−3.95 *	−3.88 *	−133.59	−4.89 **	−4.80 **	−213.51	−2.60	−2.55
[0, 26]	−111.51	−4.06 *	−3.96 *	−171.75	−6.28 **	−6.12 **	−195.14	−2.37	−2.31
[0, 27]	−132.55	−4.83 **	−4.67 **	−185.87	−6.80 **	−6.58 **	−367.89	−4.47 **	−4.33 *
[0, 28]	−128.69	−4.69 **	−4.61 **	−161.39	−5.91 **	−5.80 **	−341.62	−4.16 *	−4.08 *
[0, 29]	−164.70	−6.00 **	−5.90 **	−187.69	−6.87 **	−6.75 **	−290.17	−3.53 *	−3.47 *
[0, 30]	−108.27	−3.94 *	−3.88 *	−129.58	−4.74 **	−4.67 **	−281.02	−3.42 *	−3.37 *

Note: ** and * denote significance at the 5% and 10% levels, respectively.

Table A34. Case IX: GARCH(1,1)—Cumulative abnormal change rate of Chinese tourist arrivals.

Event Period [τ_1, τ_2]	Group-Type			Individual-Type			Medical-Type		
	CAR	t-Value		CAR	t-Value		CAR	t-Value	
		TM	SRM		TM	SRM		TM	SRM
[0, 0]	0.02	0.00	0.00	−11.31	−0.38	−0.37	−26.86	−0.34	−0.33
[0, 1]	−15.22	−0.71	−0.70	−24.82	−0.83	−0.82	−195.94	−2.47	−2.43
[0, 2]	−3.98	−0.19	−0.18	−23.66	−0.79	−0.78	−221.55	−2.79	−2.75
[0, 3]	4.34	0.20	0.20	−1.21	−0.04	−0.04	−58.36	−0.73	−0.72
[0, 4]	−12.89	−0.60	−0.59	−10.40	−0.35	−0.34	−46.62	−0.59	−0.58
[0, 5]	−5.53	−0.26	−0.25	−33.89	−1.13	−1.12	−129.97	−1.64	−1.61
[0, 6]	−14.29	−0.67	−0.65	−41.71	−1.39	−1.36	−79.83	−1.01	−0.98
[0, 7]	−23.82	−1.11	−1.09	−32.19	−1.08	−1.06	−101.45	−1.28	−1.25
[0, 8]	−62.27	−2.91	−2.86	−42.21	−1.41	−1.38	−114.51	−1.44	−1.41
[0, 9]	−58.93	−2.76	−2.71	−38.30	−1.28	−1.26	−58.65	−0.74	−0.73
[0, 10]	−56.45	−2.64	−2.58	−43.99	−1.47	−1.44	−106.69	−1.34	−1.31
[0, 11]	−56.42	−2.64	−2.52	−14.79	−0.49	−0.47	8.86	0.11	0.11
[0, 12]	−40.88	−1.91	−1.87	0.61	0.02	0.02	100.12	1.26	1.23
[0, 13]	−47.09	−2.20	−2.16	4.49	0.15	0.15	101.09	1.27	1.25
[0, 14]	−55.45	−2.59	−2.41	−7.55	−0.25	−0.23	−117.28	−1.48	−1.37
[0, 15]	−21.11	−0.99	−0.97	50.24	1.68	1.65	−179.26	−2.26	−2.22
[0, 16]	12.25	0.57	0.55	59.80	2.00	1.93	−51.64	−0.65	−0.63
[0, 17]	−2.74	−0.13	−0.12	24.06	0.80	0.78	−12.84	−0.16	−0.16
[0, 18]	−27.24	−1.27	−1.25	2.67	0.09	0.09	85.52	1.08	1.06
[0, 19]	−29.02	−1.36	−1.34	−42.55	−1.42	−1.40	64.25	0.81	0.80
[0, 20]	−14.95	−0.70	−0.66	−54.39	−1.82	−1.72	−16.30	−0.21	−0.19
[0, 21]	−10.75	−0.50	−0.48	−74.03	−2.47	−2.38	−21.63	−0.27	−0.26
[0, 22]	−31.41	−1.47	−1.45	−95.00	−3.18 *	−3.13 *	−65.49	−0.82	−0.81
[0, 23]	−42.12	−1.97	−1.93	−106.61	−3.56 *	−3.50 *	−197.43	−2.49	−2.44
[0, 24]	−49.19	−2.30	−2.26	−129.98	−4.34 *	−4.27 *	59.54	0.75	0.74
[0, 25]	−100.14	−4.68 **	−4.60 **	−129.22	−4.32 *	−4.24 *	−114.83	−1.45	−1.42
[0, 26]	−103.62	−4.85 **	−4.72 **	−165.76	−5.54 **	−5.40 **	−88.83	−1.12	−1.09
[0, 27]	−125.27	−5.86 **	−5.67 **	−177.79	−5.94 **	−5.75 **	−252.71	−3.18 *	−3.08 *
[0, 28]	−121.38	−5.68 **	−5.58 **	−152.56	−5.10 **	−5.01 **	−221.10	−2.78	−2.74
[0, 29]	−156.69	−7.33 **	−7.20 **	−179.50	−6.00 **	−5.90 **	−167.97	−2.12	−2.08
[0, 30]	−99.98	−4.68 **	−4.61 **	−121.12	−4.05 *	−3.99 *	−154.76	−1.95	−1.92

Note: ** and * denote significance at the 5% and 10% levels, respectively.

Table A35. Case IX: GJR(1,1)—Cumulative abnormal change rate of Chinese tourist arrivals.

Event Period $[\tau_1, \tau_2]$	Group-Type			Individual-Type			Medical-Type		
	CAR	t-Value		CAR	t-Value		CAR	t-Value	
		TM	SRM		TM	SRM		TM	SRM
[0, 0]	0.52	0.03	0.03	−11.51	−0.35	−0.34	−6.10	−0.02	−0.02
[0, 1]	−14.44	−0.74	−0.73	−25.22	−0.76	−0.75	−165.91	−0.48	−0.47
[0, 2]	−2.92	−0.15	−0.15	−24.26	−0.73	−0.72	−182.40	−0.53	−0.52
[0, 3]	5.69	0.29	0.29	−2.02	−0.06	−0.06	−9.13	−0.03	−0.03
[0, 4]	−11.19	−0.57	−0.56	−11.41	−0.34	−0.34	15.71	0.05	0.04
[0, 5]	−3.57	−0.18	−0.18	−35.11	−1.05	−1.04	−60.29	−0.17	−0.17
[0, 6]	−12.24	−0.63	−0.61	−43.14	−1.29	−1.26	−10.90	−0.03	−0.03
[0, 7]	−21.36	−1.10	−1.08	−33.82	−1.01	−1.00	−16.36	−0.05	−0.05
[0, 8]	−59.66	−3.06 *	−3.00 *	−44.06	−1.32	−1.30	−26.81	−0.08	−0.08
[0, 9]	−55.92	−2.87	−2.82	−40.34	−1.21	−1.19	44.74	0.13	0.13
[0, 10]	−52.98	−2.72	−2.66	−46.22	−1.39	−1.36	15.54	0.05	0.04
[0, 11]	−53.01	−2.72	−2.59	−17.26	−0.52	−0.49	121.83	0.35	0.34
[0, 12]	−37.35	−1.92	−1.87	−2.08	−0.06	−0.06	213.90	0.62	0.61
[0, 13]	−43.11	−2.21	−2.17	1.61	0.05	0.05	233.08	0.68	0.66
[0, 14]	−50.68	−2.60	−2.42	−10.61	−0.32	−0.30	51.23	0.15	0.14
[0, 15]	−16.01	−0.82	−0.81	46.99	1.41	1.39	0.87	0.00	0.00
[0, 16]	17.37	0.89	0.86	56.32	1.69	1.63	123.97	0.36	0.35
[0, 17]	2.46	0.13	0.12	20.36	0.61	0.59	160.94	0.47	0.45
[0, 18]	−21.86	−1.12	−1.10	−1.23	−0.04	−0.04	263.85	0.77	0.75
[0, 19]	−23.33	−1.20	−1.18	−46.67	−1.40	−1.38	252.98	0.73	0.72
[0, 20]	−8.54	−0.44	−0.41	−58.68	−1.76	−1.66	204.86	0.59	0.56
[0, 21]	−3.74	−0.19	−0.18	−78.51	−2.36	−2.27	225.97	0.66	0.63
[0, 22]	−24.14	−1.24	−1.22	−99.68	−2.99 *	−2.94 *	190.29	0.55	0.54
[0, 23]	−34.66	−1.78	−1.75	−111.51	−3.35 *	−3.28 *	62.21	0.18	0.18
[0, 24]	−41.54	−2.13	−2.09	−135.08	−4.05 *	−3.98 *	323.90	0.94	0.92
[0, 25]	−92.08	−4.72 **	−4.64 **	−134.52	−4.04 *	−3.96 *	166.00	0.48	0.47
[0, 26]	−95.05	−4.88 **	−4.75 **	−171.26	−5.14 **	−5.01 **	213.08	0.62	0.60
[0, 27]	−116.14	−5.96 **	−5.76 **	−183.47	−5.51 **	−5.33 **	73.60	0.21	0.21
[0, 28]	−111.86	−5.74 **	−5.64 **	−158.44	−4.75 **	−4.67 **	120.17	0.35	0.34
[0, 29]	−146.96	−7.54 **	−7.41 **	−185.59	−5.57 **	−5.47 **	178.42	0.52	0.51
[0, 30]	−89.93	−4.61 **	−4.54 **	−127.41	−3.82 *	−3.76 *	203.13	0.59	0.58

Note: ** and * denote significance at the 5% and 10% levels, respectively.

Table A36. Case IX: EGARCH(1,1)—Cumulative abnormal change rate of Chinese tourist arrivals.

Event Period $[\tau_1, \tau_2]$	Group-Type			Individual-Type			Medical-Type		
	CAR	t-Value		CAR	t-Value		CAR	t-Value	
		TM	SRM		TM	SRM		TM	SRM
[0, 0]	−2.24	−0.05	−0.05	−11.21	−0.35	−0.34	−2.21	−0.01	−0.01
[0, 1]	−18.52	−0.41	−0.40	−24.90	−0.77	−0.76	−159.93	−0.39	−0.39
[0, 2]	−8.30	−0.18	−0.18	−23.93	−0.74	−0.73	−174.35	−0.43	−0.42
[0, 3]	−1.10	−0.02	−0.02	−1.65	−0.05	−0.05	1.13	0.00	0.00
[0, 4]	−19.78	−0.43	−0.43	−10.93	−0.34	−0.33	28.66	0.07	0.07
[0, 5]	−13.24	−0.29	−0.29	−34.66	−1.07	−1.05	−45.55	−0.11	−0.11
[0, 6]	−21.96	−0.48	−0.47	−42.92	−1.32	−1.29	4.36	0.01	0.01
[0, 7]	−33.27	−0.73	−0.72	−33.41	−1.03	−1.01	2.08	0.01	0.01
[0, 8]	−72.04	−1.58	−1.55	−43.79	−1.35	−1.32	−7.33	−0.02	−0.02
[0, 9]	−70.42	−1.55	−1.52	−39.90	−1.23	−1.21	67.32	0.17	0.16
[0, 10]	−70.01	−1.54	−1.50	−45.54	−1.40	−1.37	41.71	0.10	0.10
[0, 11]	−69.02	−1.52	−1.45	−16.99	−0.52	−0.50	147.19	0.36	0.34
[0, 12]	−53.61	−1.18	−1.15	−2.00	−0.06	−0.06	240.02	0.59	0.58
[0, 13]	−61.81	−1.36	−1.33	1.92	0.06	0.06	262.69	0.64	0.63
[0, 14]	−74.13	−1.63	−1.51	−9.62	−0.30	−0.28	87.19	0.21	0.20
[0, 15]	−41.07	−0.90	−0.89	48.05	1.48	1.46	39.30	0.10	0.09
[0, 16]	−7.27	−0.16	−0.15	57.07	1.76	1.70	162.33	0.40	0.38
[0, 17]	−22.11	−0.49	−0.47	20.86	0.64	0.62	199.65	0.49	0.48
[0, 18]	−47.14	−1.04	−1.02	−0.83	−0.03	−0.03	303.91	0.75	0.73
[0, 19]	−50.07	−1.10	−1.08	−46.22	−1.42	−1.40	295.31	0.72	0.71
[0, 20]	−39.52	−0.87	−0.82	−57.66	−1.78	−1.68	252.91	0.62	0.59
[0, 21]	−38.20	−0.84	−0.81	−77.05	−2.37	−2.28	278.79	0.68	0.66
[0, 22]	−59.78	−1.31	−1.29	−98.24	−3.02 *	−2.98 *	245.04	0.60	0.59
[0, 23]	−70.93	−1.56	−1.53	−110.17	−3.39 *	−3.33 *	118.20	0.29	0.28
[0, 24]	−78.56	−1.73	−1.70	−133.84	−4.12 *	−4.05 *	381.27	0.93	0.92
[0, 25]	−131.31	−2.88	−2.83	−133.08	−4.10 *	−4.02 *	226.58	0.56	0.55
[0, 26]	−137.09	−3.01 *	−2.93 *	−169.52	−5.22 **	−5.09 **	277.60	0.68	0.66
[0, 27]	−161.40	−3.55 *	−3.43 *	−181.35	−5.58 **	−5.40 **	142.57	0.35	0.34
[0, 28]	−159.15	−3.50 *	−3.44 *	−156.17	−4.81 **	−4.73 *	192.13	0.47	0.46
[0, 29]	−195.05	−4.28 *	−4.21 *	−183.39	−5.65 **	−5.55 **	251.82	0.62	0.61
[0, 30]	−139.62	−3.07 *	−3.02 *	−125.14	−3.85 *	−3.79 *	278.97	0.68	0.67

Note: ** and * denote significance at the 5% and 10% levels, respectively.

Table A37. Case X: OLS—Cumulative abnormal change rate of Chinese tourist arrivals.

Event Period $[\tau_1, \tau_2]$	Group-Type			Individual-Type			Medical-Type		
	CAR	t-Value		CAR	t-Value		CAR	t-Value	
		TM	SRM		TM	SRM		TM	SRM
[0, 0]	18.83	0.54	0.53	−13.96	−0.49	−0.49	10.03	0.15	0.15
[0, 1]	3.86	0.11	0.11	12.71	0.45	0.44	9.46	0.14	0.14
[0, 2]	56.09	1.61	1.57	74.82	2.65	2.59	−108.42	−1.64	−1.61
[0, 3]	75.46	2.16	2.12	67.11	2.38	2.33	12.35	0.19	0.18
[0, 4]	80.23	2.30	2.26	49.13	1.74	1.71	20.73	0.31	0.31
[0, 5]	47.51	1.36	1.34	16.40	0.58	0.57	37.70	0.57	0.56
[0, 6]	47.67	1.37	1.33	9.08	0.32	0.31	3.11	0.05	0.05
[0, 7]	70.01	2.01	1.95	−20.97	−0.74	−0.72	11.20	0.17	0.16
[0, 8]	43.58	1.25	1.22	−59.91	−2.12	−2.07	−80.58	−1.22	−1.19
[0, 9]	63.34	1.81	1.79	−39.46	−1.40	−1.37	10.01	0.15	0.15
[0, 10]	60.68	1.74	1.70	−63.20	−2.24	−2.19	−36.33	−0.55	−0.54
[0, 11]	59.42	1.70	1.66	−95.49	−3.38 *	−3.29 *	−119.72	−1.81	−1.76
[0, 12]	29.16	0.84	0.81	−126.85	−4.49 **	−4.34 **	−46.99	−0.71	−0.69
[0, 13]	19.27	0.55	0.54	−122.76	−4.35 *	−4.21 *	−108.72	−1.64	−1.59
[0, 14]	27.11	0.78	0.75	−118.11	−4.18*	−4.06 *	−164.76	−2.49	−2.42
[0, 15]	−5.40	−0.15	−0.15	−153.50	−5.43 **	−5.26 **	−227.77	−3.44 *	−3.33 *
[0, 16]	12.31	0.35	0.34	−188.65	−6.68 **	−6.46 **	−287.11	−4.34 **	−4.20 **
[0, 17]	19.17	0.55	0.54	−131.37	−4.65 **	−4.55 **	−272.49	−4.12 *	−4.03 *
[0, 18]	39.32	1.13	1.10	−134.67	−4.77 **	−4.66 **	−116.81	−1.77	−1.73
[0, 19]	19.16	0.55	0.53	−147.38	−5.22 **	−5.06 **	−172.01	−2.60	−2.52
[0, 20]	20.69	0.59	0.58	−156.30	−5.53 **	−5.40 **	−188.53	−2.85	−2.78
[0, 21]	34.44	0.99	0.96	−149.10	−5.28 **	−5.13 **	−87.51	−1.32	−1.29
[0, 22]	26.75	0.77	0.75	−150.47	−5.33 **	−5.24 **	−87.63	−1.32	−1.30
[0, 23]	23.29	0.67	0.66	−155.27	−5.50 **	−5.41 **	−77.14	−1.17	−1.15
[0, 24]	20.42	0.58	0.57	−134.70	−4.77 **	−4.66 **	−49.66	−0.75	−0.73
[0, 25]	41.49	1.19	1.16	−130.28	−4.61 **	−4.51 **	−106.32	−1.61	−1.57
[0, 26]	20.13	0.58	0.56	−153.79	−5.44 **	−5.32 **	−32.29	−0.49	−0.48
[0, 27]	30.01	0.86	0.84	−137.81	−4.88 **	−4.77 **	−35.92	−0.54	−0.53
[0, 28]	56.25	1.61	1.58	−125.99	−4.46 **	−4.37 **	−174.26	−2.63	−2.58
[0, 29]	28.02	0.80	0.78	−156.93	−5.56 **	−5.43 **	−84.12	−1.27	−1.24
[0, 30]	56.56	1.62	1.58	−166.06	−5.88 **	−5.75 **	−85.31	−1.29	−1.26

Note: ** and * denote significance at the 5% and 10% levels, respectively.

Table A38. Case X: GARCH(1,1)—Cumulative abnormal change rate of Chinese tourist arrivals.

Event Period $[\tau_1, \tau_2]$	Group-Type			Individual-Type			Medical-Type		
	CAR	t-Value		CAR	t-Value		CAR	t-Value	
		TM	SRM		TM	SRM		TM	SRM
[0, 0]	23.11	0.55	0.55	−13.33	−0.34	−0.34	29.21	0.35	0.35
[0, 1]	7.16	0.17	0.17	12.21	0.32	0.31	23.92	0.29	0.29
[0, 2]	56.87	1.37	1.34	72.68	1.88	1.84	−105.60	−1.28	−1.25
[0, 3]	77.66	1.86	1.83	64.64	1.67	1.64	21.33	0.26	0.25
[0, 4]	82.66	1.98	1.95	45.95	1.19	1.17	30.55	0.37	0.36
[0, 5]	51.49	1.24	1.22	12.93	0.33	0.33	54.28	0.66	0.65
[0, 6]	49.00	1.18	1.15	3.93	0.10	0.10	7.45	0.09	0.09
[0, 7]	71.57	1.72	1.67	−26.84	−0.69	−0.68	16.31	0.20	0.19
[0, 8]	45.93	1.10	1.07	−66.32	−1.72	−1.67	−72.10	−0.87	−0.85
[0, 9]	70.78	1.70	1.67	−44.97	−1.16	−1.15	41.31	0.50	0.49
[0, 10]	70.56	1.69	1.66	−68.70	−1.78	−1.74	5.74	0.07	0.07
[0, 11]	70.86	1.70	1.66	−101.27	−2.62	−2.55	−70.82	−0.86	−0.83
[0, 12]	41.96	1.01	0.97	−132.97	−3.44 *	−3.33 *	7.84	0.09	0.09
[0, 13]	32.23	0.77	0.75	−129.63	−3.35 *	−3.25 *	−53.42	−0.65	−0.63
[0, 14]	40.36	0.97	0.94	−125.69	−3.25 *	−3.16 *	−108.39	−1.31	−1.27
[0, 15]	8.74	0.21	0.20	−161.58	−4.18 *	−4.04 *	−167.57	−2.03	−1.96
[0, 16]	26.84	0.64	0.62	−197.40	−5.11 **	−4.94 **	−225.40	−2.73	−2.64
[0, 17]	32.43	0.78	0.76	−141.33	−3.66 *	−3.58 *	−216.77	−2.62	−2.57
[0, 18]	53.02	1.27	1.24	−145.29	−3.76 *	−3.68 *	−59.33	−0.72	−0.70
[0, 19]	34.71	0.83	0.81	−158.19	−4.09 *	−3.97 *	−106.43	−1.29	−1.25
[0, 20]	35.62	0.86	0.83	−168.10	−4.35 **	−4.25 *	−125.97	−1.53	−1.49
[0, 21]	50.58	1.21	1.18	−161.31	−4.17 *	−4.06 *	−19.69	−0.24	−0.23
[0, 22]	40.64	0.98	0.96	−164.22	−4.25 **	−4.18 *	−30.26	−0.37	−0.36
[0, 23]	36.63	0.88	0.87	−170.01	−4.40 **	−4.33 **	−22.53	−0.27	−0.27
[0, 24]	37.17	0.89	0.87	−149.10	−3.86 *	−3.77 *	20.16	0.24	0.24
[0, 25]	58.13	1.40	1.37	−145.52	−3.76 *	−3.69 *	−37.23	−0.45	−0.44
[0, 26]	37.66	0.90	0.88	−169.53	−4.39 **	−4.29 **	40.60	0.49	0.48
[0, 27]	47.78	1.15	1.12	−154.26	−3.99 *	−3.90 *	37.79	0.46	0.45
[0, 28]	74.20	1.78	1.74	−143.19	−3.70 *	−3.63 *	−99.94	−1.21	−1.19
[0, 29]	46.88	1.13	1.10	−174.63	−4.52 **	−4.42 **	−5.96	−0.07	−0.07
[0, 30]	75.67	1.82	1.78	−184.47	−4.77 **	−4.67 **	−6.27	−0.08	−0.07

Note: ** and * denote significance at the 5% and 10% levels, respectively.

Table A39. Case X: GJR(1,1)—Cumulative abnormal change rate of Chinese tourist arrivals.

Event Period $[\tau_1, \tau_2]$	Group-Type			Individual-Type			Medical-Type		
	CAR	t-Value		CAR	t-Value		CAR	t-Value	
		TM	SRM		TM	SRM		TM	SRM
[0, 0]	7.00	0.10	0.10	−10.96	−0.17	−0.17	28.74	0.42	0.42
[0, 1]	−7.33	−0.10	−0.10	12.33	0.20	0.19	22.21	0.33	0.32
[0, 2]	49.14	0.69	0.68	69.21	1.10	1.08	−108.78	−1.61	−1.57
[0, 3]	63.49	0.89	0.88	61.03	0.97	0.95	17.27	0.26	0.25
[0, 4]	65.98	0.93	0.91	41.15	0.65	0.64	25.43	0.38	0.37
[0, 5]	27.92	0.39	0.39	8.11	0.13	0.13	48.30	0.71	0.70
[0, 6]	32.64	0.46	0.45	−4.60	−0.07	−0.07	−0.02	0.00	0.00
[0, 7]	52.75	0.74	0.72	−36.56	−0.58	−0.56	7.77	0.11	0.11
[0, 8]	22.74	0.32	0.31	−76.73	−1.22	−1.19	−81.62	−1.21	−1.17
[0, 9]	28.77	0.41	0.40	−52.30	−0.83	−0.82	31.45	0.46	0.46
[0, 10]	18.68	0.26	0.26	−75.29	−1.19	−1.17	−4.86	−0.07	−0.07
[0, 11]	12.02	0.17	0.16	−107.87	−1.71	−1.67	−82.28	−1.22	−1.18
[0, 12]	−23.15	−0.33	−0.32	−139.77	−2.22	−2.15	−4.52	−0.07	−0.06
[0, 13]	−35.11	−0.49	−0.48	−137.67	−2.18	−2.12	−66.86	−0.99	−0.96
[0, 14]	−29.65	−0.42	−0.41	−134.86	−2.14	−2.08	−122.88	−1.82	−1.76
[0, 15]	−65.99	−0.93	−0.90	−171.35	−2.72	−2.63	−183.02	−2.70	−2.62
[0, 16]	−50.89	−0.72	−0.69	−208.22	−3.30 *	−3.20 *	−241.89	−3.57 *	−3.46 *
[0, 17]	−42.73	−0.60	−0.59	−154.65	−2.45	−2.40	−234.54	−3.47 *	−3.39 *
[0, 18]	−25.33	−0.36	−0.35	−159.60	−2.53	−2.48	−78.13	−1.15	−1.13
[0, 19]	−51.52	−0.73	−0.70	−172.27	−2.73	−2.65	−126.06	−1.86	−1.81
[0, 20]	−50.25	−0.71	−0.69	−184.11	−2.92 *	−2.85	−146.78	−2.17	−2.12
[0, 21]	−41.07	−0.58	−0.56	−177.64	−2.82	−2.74	−41.42	−0.61	−0.59
[0, 22]	−45.13	−0.64	−0.63	−183.92	−2.92	−2.87	−53.42	−0.79	−0.78
[0, 23]	−48.97	−0.69	−0.68	−191.57	−3.04 *	−2.99 *	−46.86	−0.69	−0.68
[0, 24]	−61.61	−0.87	−0.85	−169.06	−2.68	−2.62	−4.76	−0.07	−0.07
[0, 25]	−41.98	−0.59	−0.58	−166.95	−2.65	−2.59	−63.26	−0.93	−0.92
[0, 26]	−67.14	−0.95	−0.92	−191.57	−3.04 *	−2.97 *	13.60	0.20	0.20
[0, 27]	−59.52	−0.84	−0.82	−177.49	−2.82	−2.75	9.73	0.14	0.14
[0, 28]	−35.41	−0.50	−0.49	−167.63	−2.66	−2.61	−129.07	−1.91	−1.87
[0, 29]	−67.47	−0.95	−0.93	−199.67	−3.17 *	−3.10 *	−36.05	−0.53	−0.52
[0, 30]	−41.21	−0.58	−0.57	−210.68	−3.34 *	−3.27 *	−37.42	−0.55	−0.54

Note: * denotes significance at the 10% level.

Table A40. Case X: EGARCH(1,1)—Cumulative abnormal change rate of Chinese tourist arrivals.

Event Period $[\tau_1, \tau_2]$	Group-Type			Individual-Type			Medical-Type		
	CAR	t-Value		CAR	t-Value		CAR	t-Value	
		TM	SRM		TM	SRM		TM	SRM
[0, 0]	12.98	0.29	0.28	−15.89	−0.16	−0.15	19.29	0.11	0.11
[0, 1]	−2.07	−0.05	−0.05	7.31	0.07	0.07	22.72	0.13	0.13
[0, 2]	51.73	1.15	1.13	65.49	0.65	0.63	−92.69	−0.54	−0.53
[0, 3]	68.40	1.52	1.49	55.01	0.54	0.53	34.48	0.20	0.20
[0, 4]	71.74	1.59	1.57	33.91	0.33	0.33	48.08	0.28	0.27
[0, 5]	36.17	0.80	0.79	−1.55	−0.02	−0.02	71.58	0.41	0.41
[0, 6]	38.06	0.85	0.82	−12.83	−0.13	−0.12	39.33	0.23	0.22
[0, 7]	58.99	1.31	1.27	−46.00	−0.45	−0.44	52.62	0.30	0.30
[0, 8]	30.52	0.68	0.66	−87.90	−0.87	−0.84	−33.37	−0.19	−0.19
[0, 9]	43.55	0.97	0.95	−69.14	−0.68	−0.67	67.27	0.39	0.38
[0, 10]	37.07	0.82	0.81	−95.35	−0.94	−0.92	28.34	0.16	0.16
[0, 11]	32.94	0.73	0.71	−130.37	−1.29	−1.25	−48.51	−0.28	−0.27
[0, 12]	0.02	0.00	0.00	−164.51	−1.62	−1.57	30.56	0.18	0.17
[0, 13]	−11.20	−0.25	−0.24	−163.56	−1.61	−1.56	−26.03	−0.15	−0.15
[0, 14]	−4.84	−0.11	−0.10	−162.02	−1.60	−1.55	−76.79	−0.44	−0.43
[0, 15]	−39.50	−0.88	−0.85	−200.33	−1.98	−1.91	−133.92	−0.77	−0.75
[0, 16]	−23.38	−0.52	−0.50	−238.55	−2.35	−2.28	−187.90	−1.09	−1.05
[0, 17]	−16.30	−0.36	−0.35	−184.82	−1.82	−1.78	−169.56	−0.98	−0.96
[0, 18]	2.20	0.05	0.05	−191.18	−1.89	−1.84	−8.45	−0.05	−0.05
[0, 19]	−21.13	−0.47	−0.46	−206.54	−2.04	−1.98	−56.83	−0.33	−0.32
[0, 20]	−20.11	−0.45	−0.44	−218.82	−2.16	−2.11	−68.98	−0.40	−0.39
[0, 21]	−8.85	−0.20	−0.19	−214.46	−2.12	−2.06	38.24	0.22	0.22
[0, 22]	−15.24	−0.34	−0.33	−219.67	−2.17	−2.13	40.86	0.24	0.23
[0, 23]	−19.26	−0.43	−0.42	−227.83	−2.25	−2.21	55.78	0.32	0.32
[0, 24]	−27.02	−0.60	−0.59	−209.43	−2.07	−2.02	91.64	0.53	0.52
[0, 25]	−7.00	−0.16	−0.15	−208.23	−2.05	−2.01	39.86	0.23	0.23
[0, 26]	−30.50	−0.68	−0.66	−234.67	−2.32	−2.26	119.76	0.69	0.68
[0, 27]	−22.04	−0.49	−0.48	−221.80	−2.19	−2.14	121.35	0.70	0.69
[0, 28]	2.83	0.06	0.06	−213.12	−2.10	−2.06	−11.82	−0.07	−0.07
[0, 29]	−27.55	−0.61	−0.60	−246.98	−2.44	−2.38	84.20	0.49	0.48
[0, 30]	−0.44	−0.01	−0.01	−259.23	−2.56	−2.50	88.25	0.51	0.50

Table A41. Case XI: OLS—Cumulative abnormal change rate of Chinese tourist arrivals.

Event Period $[\tau_1, \tau_2]$	Group-Type			Individual-Type			Medical-Type		
	CAR	t-Value		CAR	t-Value		CAR	t-Value	
		TM	SRM		TM	SRM		TM	SRM
[0, 0]	−15.18	−0.65	−0.64	37.05	1.66	1.63	−38.37	−0.40	−0.39
[0, 1]	−25.75	−1.11	−1.09	28.73	1.28	1.26	−76.77	−0.79	−0.78
[0, 2]	−16.16	−0.70	−0.68	15.61	0.70	0.69	−65.08	−0.67	−0.66
[0, 3]	−21.25	−0.91	−0.90	−5.39	−0.24	−0.24	−10.93	−0.11	−0.11
[0, 4]	−5.59	−0.24	−0.24	12.96	0.58	0.57	91.70	0.95	0.93
[0, 5]	2.68	0.12	0.11	8.99	0.40	0.40	−24.27	−0.25	−0.25
[0, 6]	−35.12	−1.51	−1.48	2.74	0.12	0.12	8.42	0.09	0.09
[0, 7]	−47.73	−2.05	−1.97	−43.28	−1.94	−1.85	48.04	0.50	0.47
[0, 8]	22.10	0.95	0.93	63.05	2.82	2.76	217.40	2.24	2.20
[0, 9]	9.98	0.43	0.42	36.07	1.61	1.59	123.78	1.28	1.26
[0, 10]	−11.06	−0.48	−0.47	29.23	1.31	1.29	60.51	0.62	0.61
[0, 11]	12.52	0.54	0.53	33.31	1.49	1.47	14.20	0.15	0.14
[0, 12]	15.91	0.68	0.67	29.51	1.32	1.30	−43.43	−0.45	−0.44
[0, 13]	−13.19	−0.57	−0.56	15.65	0.70	0.69	−10.34	−0.11	−0.11
[0, 14]	1.13	0.05	0.05	51.29	2.29	2.25	1.27	0.01	0.01
[0, 15]	1.18	0.05	0.05	35.71	1.60	1.56	−62.95	−0.65	−0.63
[0, 16]	22.49	0.97	0.95	26.35	1.18	1.16	151.59	1.56	1.54
[0, 17]	9.23	0.40	0.39	24.21	1.08	1.07	93.86	0.97	0.95
[0, 18]	14.84	0.64	0.63	32.07	1.43	1.41	36.54	0.38	0.37
[0, 19]	22.60	0.97	0.96	25.33	1.13	1.12	121.02	1.25	1.23
[0, 20]	6.75	0.29	0.29	18.06	0.81	0.79	−40.94	−0.42	−0.42
[0, 21]	12.30	0.53	0.52	42.30	1.89	1.86	42.88	0.44	0.44
[0, 22]	8.82	0.38	0.37	43.77	1.96	1.93	177.69	1.83	1.80
[0, 23]	12.65	0.54	0.54	24.49	1.09	1.08	20.75	0.21	0.21
[0, 24]	7.81	0.34	0.33	12.43	0.56	0.55	53.90	0.56	0.55
[0, 25]	5.87	0.25	0.25	9.74	0.44	0.43	150.81	1.56	1.53
[0, 26]	11.97	0.52	0.51	4.52	0.20	0.20	175.23	1.81	1.78
[0, 27]	−11.84	−0.51	−0.50	9.38	0.42	0.41	58.07	0.60	0.59
[0, 28]	8.80	0.38	0.37	27.92	1.25	1.23	37.34	0.39	0.38
[0, 29]	−1.65	−0.07	−0.07	31.26	1.40	1.37	186.99	1.93	1.89
[0, 30]	6.98	0.30	0.29	18.47	0.83	0.80	35.78	0.37	0.36

Table A42. Case XI: GARCH(1,1)—Cumulative abnormal change rate of Chinese tourist arrivals.

Event Period $[\tau_1, \tau_2]$	Group-Type			Individual-Type			Medical-Type		
	CAR	t-Value		CAR	t-Value		CAR	t-Value	
		TM	SRM		TM	SRM		TM	SRM
[0, 0]	−15.10	−0.82	−0.68	36.24	1.18	1.16	−41.43	−0.38	−0.38
[0, 1]	−25.42	−1.39	−1.14	27.41	0.89	0.87	−83.77	−0.78	−0.76
[0, 2]	−15.62	−0.85	−0.70	13.71	0.45	0.44	−75.86	−0.70	−0.69
[0, 3]	−20.56	−1.12	−0.92	−7.95	−0.26	−0.25	−25.20	−0.23	−0.23
[0, 4]	−5.03	−0.27	−0.23	9.22	0.30	0.29	75.49	0.70	0.69
[0, 5]	3.54	0.19	0.16	4.83	0.16	0.15	−44.73	−0.41	−0.41
[0, 6]	−35.04	−1.91	−1.56	−3.67	−0.12	−0.12	−10.70	−0.10	−0.10
[0, 7]	−48.38	−2.64	−2.11	−51.86	−1.68	−1.61	30.01	0.28	0.27
[0, 8]	24.15	1.32	1.08	58.11	1.89	1.85	182.77	1.69	1.66
[0, 9]	11.70	0.64	0.53	29.62	0.96	0.95	88.23	0.82	0.80
[0, 10]	−8.89	−0.49	−0.40	22.60	0.73	0.72	19.96	0.18	0.18
[0, 11]	14.36	0.78	0.64	25.19	0.82	0.81	−27.34	−0.25	−0.25
[0, 12]	17.96	0.98	0.81	20.82	0.68	0.67	−88.73	−0.82	−0.81
[0, 13]	−10.42	−0.57	−0.47	7.22	0.23	0.23	−61.98	−0.57	−0.57
[0, 14]	4.55	0.25	0.20	43.03	1.40	1.37	−56.38	−0.52	−0.51
[0, 15]	5.10	0.28	0.23	27.36	0.89	0.87	−125.86	−1.17	−1.14
[0, 16]	25.86	1.41	1.16	16.13	0.52	0.52	88.88	0.82	0.81
[0, 17]	12.64	0.69	0.57	13.14	0.43	0.42	28.23	0.26	0.26
[0, 18]	18.02	0.98	0.81	19.65	0.64	0.63	−30.55	−0.28	−0.28
[0, 19]	26.30	1.44	1.18	12.88	0.42	0.41	48.52	0.45	0.44
[0, 20]	11.03	0.60	0.50	5.65	0.18	0.18	−119.08	−1.10	−1.09
[0, 21]	16.89	0.92	0.76	29.47	0.96	0.94	−39.51	−0.37	−0.36
[0, 22]	13.52	0.74	0.61	30.19	0.98	0.97	92.06	0.85	0.84
[0, 23]	17.47	0.95	0.78	10.17	0.33	0.33	−68.14	−0.63	−0.62
[0, 24]	12.97	0.71	0.58	−2.25	−0.07	−0.07	−39.42	−0.37	−0.36
[0, 25]	10.89	0.59	0.49	−6.10	−0.20	−0.20	55.50	0.51	0.51
[0, 26]	17.48	0.95	0.78	−11.45	−0.37	−0.37	74.80	0.69	0.68
[0, 27]	−5.72	−0.31	−0.26	−6.49	−0.21	−0.21	−48.20	−0.45	−0.44
[0, 28]	15.12	0.83	0.68	11.46	0.37	0.37	−72.64	−0.67	−0.66
[0, 29]	4.98	0.27	0.22	14.39	0.47	0.46	72.72	0.67	0.66
[0, 30]	13.61	0.74	0.60	0.65	0.02	0.02	−81.10	−0.75	−0.73

Table A43. Case XI: GJR (1,1)—Cumulative abnormal change rate of Chinese tourist arrivals.

Event Period $[\tau_1, \tau_2]$	Group-Type			Individual-Type			Medical-Type		
	CAR	t-Value		CAR	t-Value		CAR	t-Value	
		TM	SRM		TM	SRM		TM	SRM
[0, 0]	−16.17	−0.37	−0.36	35.63	0.63	0.62	−26.36	−0.07	−0.07
[0, 1]	−27.80	−0.63	−0.62	25.65	0.45	0.45	−53.46	−0.14	−0.14
[0, 2]	−19.26	−0.44	−0.43	10.92	0.19	0.19	−30.33	−0.08	−0.08
[0, 3]	−25.38	−0.58	−0.57	−11.62	−0.21	−0.20	35.49	0.09	0.09
[0, 4]	−10.64	−0.24	−0.24	5.61	0.10	0.10	151.04	0.39	0.39
[0, 5]	−3.45	−0.08	−0.08	−0.10	0.00	0.00	46.12	0.12	0.12
[0, 6]	−41.93	−0.95	−0.93	−6.56	−0.12	−0.11	94.38	0.24	0.24
[0, 7]	−55.24	−1.26	−1.20	−52.87	−0.93	−0.89	149.37	0.39	0.37
[0, 8]	12.62	0.29	0.28	48.33	0.85	0.84	319.80	0.83	0.81
[0, 9]	−0.34	−0.01	−0.01	20.52	0.36	0.36	239.92	0.62	0.61
[0, 10]	−22.51	−0.51	−0.50	11.72	0.21	0.20	187.10	0.48	0.48
[0, 11]	0.22	0.00	0.00	14.95	0.26	0.26	154.48	0.40	0.39
[0, 12]	2.56	0.06	0.06	9.53	0.17	0.17	108.30	0.28	0.28
[0, 13]	−27.77	−0.63	−0.62	−6.65	−0.12	−0.12	150.75	0.39	0.38
[0, 14]	−14.66	−0.33	−0.33	26.77	0.47	0.46	171.99	0.45	0.44
[0, 15]	−15.76	−0.36	−0.35	9.16	0.16	0.16	118.01	0.31	0.30
[0, 16]	4.79	0.11	0.11	−0.72	−0.01	−0.01	347.20	0.90	0.89
[0, 17]	−9.46	−0.22	−0.21	−4.24	−0.07	−0.07	301.59	0.78	0.77
[0, 18]	−4.73	−0.11	−0.11	2.63	0.05	0.05	257.58	0.67	0.66
[0, 19]	1.86	0.04	0.04	−6.17	−0.11	−0.11	352.18	0.91	0.90
[0, 20]	−15.17	−0.35	−0.34	−15.56	−0.27	−0.27	200.15	0.52	0.51
[0, 21]	−10.70	−0.24	−0.24	6.92	0.12	0.12	295.02	0.76	0.75
[0, 22]	−15.19	−0.35	−0.34	6.93	0.12	0.12	441.70	1.14	1.13
[0, 23]	−12.37	−0.28	−0.28	−13.82	−0.24	−0.24	296.62	0.77	0.76
[0, 24]	−18.30	−0.42	−0.41	−27.68	−0.49	−0.48	340.67	0.88	0.87
[0, 25]	−21.16	−0.48	−0.47	−31.50	−0.56	−0.55	450.46	1.17	1.15
[0, 26]	−16.20	−0.37	−0.36	−38.70	−0.68	−0.67	485.23	1.26	1.24
[0, 27]	−41.21	−0.94	−0.92	−36.03	−0.64	−0.62	377.83	0.98	0.96
[0, 28]	−21.62	−0.49	−0.48	−19.09	−0.34	−0.33	368.60	0.96	0.94
[0, 29]	−33.15	−0.75	−0.74	−17.50	−0.31	−0.30	529.27	1.37	1.35
[0, 30]	−25.48	−0.58	−0.56	−31.59	−0.56	−0.54	390.43	1.01	0.99

Table A44. Case XI: EGARCH(1,1)—Cumulative abnormal change rate of Chinese tourist arrivals.

Event Period $[\tau_1, \tau_2]$	Group-Type			Individual-Type			Medical-Type		
	CAR	t-Value		CAR	t-Value		CAR	t-Value	
		TM	SRM		TM	SRM		TM	SRM
[0, 0]	−15.06	−0.35	−0.34	36.23	1.06	1.04	−27.65	−0.08	−0.08
[0, 1]	−26.85	−0.63	−0.61	27.21	0.80	0.78	−55.83	−0.16	−0.15
[0, 2]	−18.22	−0.42	−0.42	13.36	0.39	0.38	−33.83	−0.10	−0.09
[0, 3]	−23.86	−0.56	−0.55	−8.40	−0.25	−0.24	30.80	0.09	0.09
[0, 4]	−6.37	−0.15	−0.15	8.97	0.26	0.26	144.80	0.41	0.40
[0, 5]	0.21	0.00	0.00	4.34	0.13	0.13	38.86	0.11	0.11
[0, 6]	−30.78	−0.72	−0.70	−3.30	−0.10	−0.09	84.80	0.24	0.23
[0, 7]	−36.97	−0.86	−0.82	−50.69	−1.49	−1.42	137.52	0.39	0.37
[0, 8]	12.42	0.29	0.28	56.59	1.66	1.63	309.84	0.87	0.86
[0, 9]	3.66	0.09	0.08	28.52	0.84	0.82	228.17	0.64	0.63
[0, 10]	−20.19	−0.47	−0.46	21.11	0.62	0.61	174.51	0.49	0.48
[0, 11]	6.65	0.15	0.15	24.09	0.71	0.70	140.11	0.40	0.39
[0, 12]	9.10	0.21	0.21	19.56	0.57	0.56	92.81	0.26	0.26
[0, 13]	−24.86	−0.58	−0.57	5.31	0.16	0.15	134.74	0.38	0.37
[0, 14]	−14.91	−0.35	−0.34	40.52	1.19	1.16	155.39	0.44	0.43
[0, 15]	−18.07	−0.42	−0.41	24.40	0.72	0.70	100.63	0.28	0.28
[0, 16]	8.31	0.19	0.19	13.80	0.40	0.40	327.76	0.93	0.91
[0, 17]	−4.62	−0.11	−0.11	10.83	0.32	0.31	280.83	0.79	0.78
[0, 18]	3.55	0.08	0.08	17.65	0.52	0.51	235.15	0.66	0.65
[0, 19]	7.85	0.18	0.18	10.40	0.30	0.30	329.01	0.93	0.91
[0, 20]	−11.79	−0.27	−0.27	2.65	0.08	0.08	176.30	0.50	0.49
[0, 21]	−7.92	−0.18	−0.18	26.22	0.77	0.76	270.16	0.76	0.75
[0, 22]	−11.56	−0.27	−0.27	26.89	0.79	0.78	415.58	1.17	1.15
[0, 23]	−7.91	−0.18	−0.18	6.82	0.20	0.20	269.26	0.76	0.75
[0, 24]	−14.70	−0.34	−0.34	−5.88	−0.17	−0.17	312.35	0.88	0.87
[0, 25]	−14.90	−0.35	−0.34	−9.53	−0.28	−0.28	420.59	1.19	1.17
[0, 26]	−11.81	−0.28	−0.27	−15.30	−0.45	−0.44	454.55	1.28	1.26
[0, 27]	−39.72	−0.93	−0.91	−10.90	−0.32	−0.31	346.52	0.98	0.96
[0, 28]	−19.95	−0.46	−0.46	6.90	0.20	0.20	336.14	0.95	0.93
[0, 29]	−32.14	−0.75	−0.73	9.58	0.28	0.28	495.81	1.40	1.37
[0, 30]	−22.72	−0.53	−0.52	−4.08	−0.12	−0.12	355.58	1.00	0.98

Table A45. Case XII: OLS—Cumulative abnormal change rate of Chinese tourist arrivals.

Event Period $[\tau_1, \tau_2]$	Group-Type			Individual-Type			Medical-Type		
	CAR	t-Value		CAR	t-Value		CAR	t-Value	
		TM	SRM		TM	SRM		TM	SRM
[0, 0]	8.05	0.35	0.34	12.44	0.55	0.54	−53.37	−0.64	−0.62
[0, 1]	14.20	0.62	0.61	2.72	0.12	0.12	26.11	0.31	0.31
[0, 2]	−3.48	−0.15	−0.15	−7.99	−0.36	−0.35	−141.36	−1.68	−1.66
[0, 3]	1.66	0.07	0.07	15.48	0.69	0.68	−59.91	−0.71	−0.70
[0, 4]	−1.21	−0.05	−0.05	18.12	0.81	0.79	74.80	0.89	0.88
[0, 5]	3.22	0.14	0.14	−0.03	0.00	0.00	−82.26	−0.98	−0.96
[0, 6]	−2.22	−0.10	−0.09	−13.19	−0.59	−0.57	−51.88	−0.62	−0.60
[0, 7]	−2.27	−0.10	−0.10	−12.32	−0.55	−0.54	47.77	0.57	0.56
[0, 8]	2.53	0.11	0.11	−19.99	−0.89	−0.87	67.84	0.81	0.79
[0, 9]	−23.33	−1.01	−1.00	−18.95	−0.84	−0.83	−55.30	−0.66	−0.65
[0, 10]	−2.55	−0.11	−0.11	−0.14	−0.01	−0.01	−77.17	−0.92	−0.90
[0, 11]	−13.45	−0.59	−0.56	2.36	0.11	0.10	70.02	0.83	0.80
[0, 12]	−3.57	−0.16	−0.15	−8.07	−0.36	−0.35	−79.87	−0.95	−0.93
[0, 13]	−27.30	−1.19	−1.16	−8.14	−0.36	−0.36	−90.11	−1.07	−1.05
[0, 14]	−16.73	−0.73	−0.68	−4.12	−0.18	−0.17	−117.74	−1.40	−1.30
[0, 15]	−2.52	−0.11	−0.11	−12.69	−0.57	−0.56	−69.08	−0.82	−0.81
[0, 16]	−10.96	−0.48	−0.46	−14.44	−0.64	−0.62	−59.47	−0.71	−0.69
[0, 17]	7.21	0.31	0.31	23.28	1.04	1.01	−69.59	−0.83	−0.81
[0, 18]	−3.88	−0.17	−0.17	17.19	0.77	0.75	−76.65	−0.91	−0.90
[0, 19]	−14.73	−0.64	−0.63	−4.20	−0.19	−0.18	63.98	0.76	0.75
[0, 20]	−17.16	−0.75	−0.71	−12.63	−0.56	−0.53	−3.35	−0.04	−0.04
[0, 21]	−37.37	−1.63	−1.57	−19.16	−0.85	−0.82	−57.94	−0.69	−0.66
[0, 22]	−19.02	−0.83	−0.81	−23.06	−1.03	−1.01	−160.49	−1.91	−1.88
[0, 23]	−59.82	−2.60	−2.56	−35.14	−1.57	−1.54	7.46	0.09	0.09
[0, 24]	−55.08	−2.40	−2.35	−6.83	−0.30	−0.30	−10.33	−0.12	−0.12
[0, 25]	−25.88	−1.13	−1.10	2.68	0.12	0.12	−9.90	−0.12	−0.12
[0, 26]	−29.25	−1.27	−1.24	−25.59	−1.14	−1.11	−67.43	−0.80	−0.78
[0, 27]	−50.64	−2.20	−2.13	−32.17	−1.43	−1.39	−64.33	−0.77	−0.74
[0, 28]	−39.20	−1.71	−1.68	−28.83	−1.29	−1.26	74.36	0.89	0.87
[0, 29]	−25.79	−1.12	−1.10	−37.21	−1.66	−1.63	−16.04	−0.19	−0.19
[0, 30]	−32.86	−1.43	−1.41	−33.75	−1.50	−1.48	−56.65	−0.67	−0.66

Table A46. Case XII: GARCH(1,1)—Cumulative abnormal change rate of Chinese tourist arrivals.

Event Period $[\tau_1, \tau_2]$	Group-Type			Individual-Type			Medical-Type		
	CAR	t-Value		CAR	t-Value		CAR	t-Value	
		TM	SRM		TM	SRM		TM	SRM
[0, 0]	7.57	0.30	0.29	7.48	0.22	0.21	−53.62	−0.56	−0.54
[0, 1]	13.68	0.54	0.53	−0.17	0.00	0.00	24.05	0.25	0.25
[0, 2]	−4.03	−0.16	−0.16	−8.37	−0.25	−0.24	−145.33	−1.51	−1.49
[0, 3]	0.94	0.04	0.04	15.11	0.44	0.44	−65.23	−0.68	−0.67
[0, 4]	−2.22	−0.09	−0.09	15.97	0.47	0.46	68.53	0.71	0.70
[0, 5]	1.93	0.08	0.07	−3.93	−0.12	−0.11	−89.50	−0.93	−0.92
[0, 6]	−3.66	−0.14	−0.14	−16.76	−0.49	−0.48	−60.55	−0.63	−0.61
[0, 7]	−4.13	−0.16	−0.16	−19.91	−0.59	−0.58	38.64	0.40	0.39
[0, 8]	0.59	0.02	0.02	−25.99	−0.77	−0.75	57.02	0.59	0.58
[0, 9]	−25.26	−0.99	−0.97	−22.10	−0.65	−0.64	−68.10	−0.71	−0.70
[0, 10]	−4.72	−0.19	−0.18	−4.24	−0.12	−0.12	−91.11	−0.95	−0.93
[0, 11]	−15.79	−0.62	−0.59	−1.65	−0.05	−0.05	54.71	0.57	0.54
[0, 12]	−6.27	−0.25	−0.24	−14.98	−0.44	−0.43	−95.89	−1.00	−0.98
[0, 13]	−29.98	−1.18	−1.15	−12.10	−0.36	−0.35	−108.14	−1.13	−1.10
[0, 14]	−19.92	−0.78	−0.73	−13.43	−0.40	−0.37	−135.94	−1.41	−1.31
[0, 15]	−5.73	−0.22	−0.22	−19.57	−0.58	−0.57	−89.15	−0.93	−0.91
[0, 16]	−14.33	−0.56	−0.54	−20.98	−0.62	−0.60	−80.98	−0.84	−0.81
[0, 17]	3.53	0.14	0.13	14.33	0.42	0.41	−91.91	−0.96	−0.93
[0, 18]	−7.83	−0.31	−0.30	6.80	0.20	0.20	−100.00	−1.04	−1.02
[0, 19]	−18.89	−0.74	−0.73	−15.14	−0.45	−0.44	39.40	0.41	0.40
[0, 20]	−21.60	−0.85	−0.80	−25.28	−0.74	−0.70	−28.91	−0.30	−0.28
[0, 21]	−42.10	−1.65	−1.59	−33.61	−0.99	−0.95	−84.45	−0.88	−0.85
[0, 22]	−23.47	−0.92	−0.91	−30.21	−0.89	−0.88	−189.95	−1.98	−1.95
[0, 23]	−64.08	−2.52	−2.47	−36.36	−1.07	−1.05	−24.66	−0.26	−0.25
[0, 24]	−60.00	−2.36	−2.31	−15.87	−0.47	−0.46	−42.08	−0.44	−0.43
[0, 25]	−31.07	−1.22	−1.20	−8.04	−0.24	−0.23	−42.62	−0.44	−0.44
[0, 26]	−34.71	−1.36	−1.33	−37.69	−1.11	−1.08	−101.21	−1.05	−1.03
[0, 27]	−56.42	−2.21	−2.14	−46.83	−1.38	−1.33	−98.89	−1.03	−1.00
[0, 28]	−45.31	−1.78	−1.75	−45.91	−1.35	−1.33	38.99	0.41	0.40
[0, 29]	−32.05	−1.26	−1.24	−54.02	−1.59	−1.56	−52.82	−0.55	−0.54
[0, 30]	−39.31	−1.54	−1.52	−50.67	−1.49	−1.47	−94.76	−0.99	−0.97

Table A47. Case XII: GJR(1,1)—Cumulative abnormal change rate of Chinese tourist arrivals.

Event Period $[\tau_1, \tau_2]$	Group-Type			Individual-Type			Medical-Type		
	CAR	t-Value		CAR	t-Value		CAR	t-Value	
		TM	SRM		TM	SRM		TM	SRM
[0, 0]	7.92	0.34	0.33	8.95	0.38	0.37	−44.93	−0.18	−0.18
[0, 1]	15.00	0.64	0.63	1.31	0.06	0.06	43.30	0.17	0.17
[0, 2]	−1.69	−0.07	−0.07	−6.97	−0.30	−0.29	−115.41	−0.46	−0.46
[0, 3]	4.07	0.17	0.17	16.95	0.72	0.71	−25.30	−0.10	−0.10
[0, 4]	1.55	0.07	0.07	18.61	0.79	0.78	117.99	0.47	0.47
[0, 5]	6.33	0.27	0.27	−0.48	−0.02	−0.02	−30.49	−0.12	−0.12
[0, 6]	1.56	0.07	0.07	−12.94	−0.55	−0.54	8.56	0.03	0.03
[0, 7]	1.52	0.07	0.06	−14.81	−0.63	−0.62	116.69	0.47	0.46
[0, 8]	7.18	0.31	0.30	−20.78	−0.89	−0.87	145.49	0.58	0.57
[0, 9]	−17.64	−0.76	−0.74	−17.05	−0.73	−0.71	31.13	0.12	0.12
[0, 10]	3.61	0.16	0.15	1.45	0.06	0.06	17.87	0.07	0.07
[0, 11]	−6.66	−0.29	−0.27	4.46	0.19	0.18	173.72	0.70	0.67
[0, 12]	3.40	0.15	0.14	−7.82	−0.33	−0.33	32.36	0.13	0.13
[0, 13]	−19.27	−0.83	−0.81	−5.12	−0.22	−0.21	30.90	0.12	0.12
[0, 14]	−8.88	−0.38	−0.35	−4.90	−0.21	−0.19	11.70	0.05	0.04
[0, 15]	6.31	0.27	0.27	−11.10	−0.47	−0.47	69.13	0.28	0.27
[0, 16]	−1.47	−0.06	−0.06	−12.14	−0.52	−0.50	87.40	0.35	0.34
[0, 17]	16.97	0.73	0.71	24.11	1.03	1.00	85.84	0.34	0.34
[0, 18]	6.27	0.27	0.26	17.32	0.74	0.72	87.38	0.35	0.34
[0, 19]	−4.05	−0.17	−0.17	−4.06	−0.17	−0.17	236.64	0.95	0.94
[0, 20]	−6.11	−0.26	−0.25	−13.41	−0.57	−0.54	177.89	0.71	0.67
[0, 21]	−25.98	−1.11	−1.07	−20.93	−0.89	−0.86	131.88	0.53	0.51
[0, 22]	−5.92	−0.25	−0.25	−18.61	−0.79	−0.78	38.30	0.15	0.15
[0, 23]	−45.22	−1.94	−1.90	−25.56	−1.09	−1.07	215.15	0.86	0.85
[0, 24]	−41.03	−1.76	−1.73	−2.99	−0.13	−0.13	205.69	0.83	0.81
[0, 25]	−11.46	−0.49	−0.48	5.62	0.24	0.23	214.70	0.86	0.85
[0, 26]	−14.43	−0.62	−0.60	−23.29	−0.99	−0.97	165.77	0.67	0.65
[0, 27]	−35.58	−1.53	−1.48	−31.47	−1.34	−1.30	177.41	0.71	0.69
[0, 28]	−23.89	−1.02	−1.01	−29.60	−1.26	−1.24	324.66	1.30	1.28
[0, 29]	−9.81	−0.42	−0.41	−37.33	−1.59	−1.56	242.93	0.97	0.96
[0, 30]	−16.29	−0.70	−0.69	−33.52	−1.43	−1.41	210.96	0.85	0.83

Table A48. Case XII: EGARCH(1,1)—Cumulative abnormal change rate of Chinese tourist arrivals.

Event Period [τ_1, τ_2]	Group-Type			Individual-Type			Medical-Type		
	CAR	t-Value		CAR	t-Value		CAR	t-Value	
		TM	SRM		TM	SRM		TM	SRM
[0, 0]	7.52	0.34	0.33	9.07	0.32	0.31	−51.44	−0.62	−0.60
[0, 1]	14.31	0.65	0.64	2.88	0.10	0.10	27.08	0.33	0.32
[0, 2]	−2.66	−0.12	−0.12	−3.87	−0.14	−0.13	−141.52	−1.70	−1.67
[0, 3]	2.78	0.13	0.12	21.11	0.74	0.73	−60.17	−0.72	−0.71
[0, 4]	−0.10	0.00	0.00	23.49	0.82	0.81	75.17	0.90	0.89
[0, 5]	4.34	0.20	0.19	5.13	0.18	0.18	−81.28	−0.98	−0.96
[0, 6]	−0.75	−0.03	−0.03	−6.21	−0.22	−0.21	−51.15	−0.61	−0.60
[0, 7]	−1.17	−0.05	−0.05	−7.78	−0.27	−0.27	50.05	0.60	0.59
[0, 8]	4.18	0.19	0.19	−12.40	−0.43	−0.43	69.37	0.83	0.82
[0, 9]	−20.91	−0.95	−0.94	−7.06	−0.25	−0.24	−55.04	−0.66	−0.65
[0, 10]	0.01	0.00	0.00	12.31	0.43	0.42	−76.62	−0.92	−0.90
[0, 11]	−10.59	−0.48	−0.46	16.39	0.57	0.55	70.43	0.85	0.81
[0, 12]	−0.89	−0.04	−0.04	4.62	0.16	0.16	−78.38	−0.94	−0.92
[0, 13]	−23.84	−1.09	−1.06	8.94	0.31	0.31	−89.94	−1.08	−1.06
[0, 14]	−13.86	−0.63	−0.59	9.21	0.32	0.30	−115.48	−1.39	−1.29
[0, 15]	1.05	0.05	0.05	4.51	0.16	0.16	−67.91	−0.82	−0.80
[0, 16]	−7.05	−0.32	−0.31	4.60	0.16	0.16	−58.55	−0.70	−0.68
[0, 17]	11.03	0.50	0.49	41.46	1.45	1.41	−67.78	−0.81	−0.79
[0, 18]	−0.02	0.00	0.00	35.44	1.24	1.22	−74.35	−0.89	−0.88
[0, 19]	−10.66	−0.49	−0.48	15.02	0.53	0.52	66.40	0.80	0.79
[0, 20]	−13.08	−0.60	−0.56	6.41	0.22	0.21	−0.34	0.00	0.00
[0, 21]	−33.30	−1.52	−1.46	−0.40	−0.01	−0.01	−54.29	−0.65	−0.63
[0, 22]	−13.44	−0.61	−0.60	4.36	0.15	0.15	−159.93	−1.92	−1.89
[0, 23]	−52.97	−2.41	−2.37	−0.40	−0.01	−0.01	5.48	0.07	0.06
[0, 24]	−49.23	−2.24	−2.20	21.74	0.76	0.75	−9.21	−0.11	−0.11
[0, 25]	−20.00	−0.91	−0.89	31.09	1.09	1.07	−8.19	−0.10	−0.10
[0, 26]	−23.32	−1.06	−1.04	2.97	0.10	0.10	−65.27	−0.78	−0.76
[0, 27]	−44.83	−2.04	−1.98	−4.63	−0.16	−0.16	−61.22	−0.74	−0.71
[0, 28]	−33.50	−1.53	−1.50	−2.16	−0.08	−0.07	78.36	0.94	0.93
[0, 29]	−19.75	−0.90	−0.88	−8.78	−0.31	−0.30	−12.25	−0.15	−0.14
[0, 30]	−26.55	−1.21	−1.19	−3.93	−0.14	−0.14	−52.92	−0.64	−0.63

References

1. McAleer, M. The Fundamental Equation in Tourism Finance. *J. Risk Financ. Manag.* **2015**, *8*, 369–374. [CrossRef]
2. Dolley, J.C. Characteristics and Procedure of Common Stock Split-ups. *Harvard Bus. Rev.* **1933**, *11*, 316–326.
3. Ball, R.; Brown, P. An Empirical Evaluation of Accounting Index Numbers. *J. Acc. Res.* **1968**, *6*, 159–178. [CrossRef]
4. Fama, E.F.; Fisher, L.; Jensen, M.C.; Roll, R. The Adjustment of Stock Prices to New Information. *Int. Econ. Rev.* **1969**, *10*, 1–21. [CrossRef]
5. Fama, E.F. Efficient Capital Markets: A Review of Theory and Empirical Work. *J. Financ.* **1970**, *25*, 383–420. [CrossRef]
6. Boehmer, E.; Masumeci, J.; Poulsen, A.B. Event-study Methodology under Conditions of Event-induced Variance. *J. Financ. Econ.* **1991**, *30*, 253–272. [CrossRef]
7. MacKinlay, A.C. Event Studies in Economics and Finance. *J. Econ. Lit.* **1997**, *35*, 13–39.
8. Binder, J. The Event Study Methodology Since 1969. *Rev. Quant. Financ. Acc.* **1998**, *11*, 111–137. [CrossRef]
9. Corrado, C.J. A Nonparametric Test for Abnormal Security-price Performance in Event Studies. *J. Financ. Econ.* **1989**, *23*, 385–395. [CrossRef]
10. Mazzocchi, M.; Montini, A. Earthquake Effects on Tourism in Central Italy. *Ann. Tour. Res.* **2001**, *28*, 1031–1046. [CrossRef]
11. Patell, J. M Corporate Forecasts of Earnings Per Share and Stock Price Behavior: Empirical Test. *J. Acc. Res.* **1976**, *14*, 246–276. [CrossRef]

12. Tao, Z. Short-term Economic Effect of the M7. 0 Lushan Earthquake. *Nat. Hazards* **2014**, *70*, 1247–1261. [CrossRef]
13. Nicolau, J.L. Assessing New Hotel Openings Through an Event Study. *Tour. Manag.* **2002**, *23*, 47–54. [CrossRef]
14. Corrado, C.J. Event Studies: A Methodology Review. *Acc. Financ.* **2011**, *51*, 207–234. [CrossRef]
15. Chen, M.H.; Jang, S.S.; Kim, W.G. The Impact of the SARS Outbreak on Taiwanese Hotel Stock Performance: An Event-study Approach. *Int. J. Hosp. Manag.* **2007**, *26*, 200–212. [CrossRef]
16. Dick, C.D.; Wang, Q. The Economic Impact of the Olympic Games: Evidence from Stock Markets. *Appl. Econ. Lett.* **2010**, *17*, 861–864. [CrossRef]
17. Ogawa, R. *Using REIT Data to Assess the Economic Worth of Mega-events: The Case of the 2020 Tokyo Olympics*; MPRA Working Paper; University Library of Munich: Munich, Germany, 2017.
18. Szutowski, D.; Bednarska, M.A. Short-term Effects of Innovations on tourism Enterprise Market Value: Event Study Approach. In *New Trends in Tourism Research-A Polish Perspective*; Dias, F., Oliveira, S., Kosmaczewska, J., Pereira, Â., Eds.; GITUR-Tourism Research Group of Polytechnic Institute of Leiria: Leiria, Portugal, 2014; pp. 205–217.
19. Szyszka, A. *Efektywność Giełdy Papierów Wartościowych w Warszawie na tle Rynków Dojrzałych*; Efficiency of the Warsaw Stock Exchange in Comparison to Developed Markets, Wyd; Akademii Ekonomicznej w Poznaniu: Poznań, Poland, 2003; p. 64.
20. Johnson, M.; Singh, A.J.; Ma, Q. The impact of authorization of the travel promotion act on hotel firm stock returns. *Cornell Hosp. Q.* **2015**, *56*, 29–40. [CrossRef]
21. McWilliams, A.; Siegel, D. Event Studies in Management Research: Theoretical and Empirical Issues. *Acad. Manag. J.* **1997**, *40*, 626–657.
22. Sharpe, W.F. Capital Asset Prices: A Theory of Market Equilibrium under Conditions of Risk. *J. Financ.* **1964**, *19*, 425–442.
23. Engle, R.F. Autoregressive Conditional Heteroscedasticity with Estimates of the Variance of United Kingdom inflation. *Econometrica* **1982**, *50*, 987–1007. [CrossRef]
24. McAleer, M. Asymmetry and Leverage in Conditional Volatility Models. *Econometrics* **2014**, *2*, 145–150. [CrossRef]
25. Chang, C.L.; McAleer, M.; Wang, Y.A. Modelling Volatility Spillovers for Bio-ethanol, Sugarcane and Corn Spot and Futures Prices. *Renew. Sustain. Energy Rev.* **2018**, *81*, 1002–1018. [CrossRef]
26. Bollerslev, T. Generalized Autoregressive Conditional Heteroskedasticity. *J. Econ.* **1986**, *31*, 307–327. [CrossRef]
27. Tsay, R.S. Conditional Heteroscedastic Time Series Models. *J. Am. Stat. Assoc.* **1987**, *82*, 590–604. [CrossRef]
28. Ling, S.; McAleer, M. Asymptotic Theory for a Vector ARMA-GARCH Model. *Econ. Theory* **2003**, *19*, 280–310. [CrossRef]
29. Glosten, L.; Jagannathan, R.; Runkle, D. On the Relation Between the Expected Value and Volatility of Nominal Excess Return on Stocks. *J. Financ.* **1993**, *48*, 1779–1801. [CrossRef]
30. Nelson, D.B. Conditional Heteroscedasticity in Asset Returns: A New Approach. *Econometrica* **1991**, *59*, 347–370. [CrossRef]
31. McAleer, M.; Hafner, C.M. A One Line Derivation of EGARCH. *Econometrics* **2014**, *2*, 92–97. [CrossRef]
32. Brown, S.J.; Warner, J.B. Using Daily Stock Returns: The Case of Event Studies. *J. Financ. Econ.* **1985**, *14*, 3–31. [CrossRef]

9

A Sustainability-Oriented Enhanced Indexation Model with Regime Switching and Cardinality Constraint

Zhiping Chen [1,2,*], Xinkai Zhuang [1,2] and Jia Liu [1,2]

1 School of Mathematics and Statistics, Xi'an Jiaotong University, Xi'an 710049, China
2 Center for Optimization Technique and Quantitative Finance, Xi'an International Academy for Mathematics and Mathematical Technology, Xi'an 710049, China
* Correspondence: zchen@xjtu.edu.cn

Abstract: Enhanced indexation is an active portfolio management strategy aimed to find a portfolio outperforming a market index. To ensure stable returns and to avoid extreme losses, a sensible enhanced indexation model should be sustainable, where the parameters of the model should be adjusted adaptively according to the market environment. Hence, in this paper, we propose a novel sustainable regime-based cardinality constrained enhanced indexation (RCEI) model, where different benchmarks and cardinalities can be imposed under different market regimes. By using historical observations, the RCEI model is transformed into a deterministic optimization problem with an ℓ_0 norm constraint. We design a partial penalty method coupled with the proximal alternating direction method of multipliers (ADMM) to solve the deterministic optimization problem. Numerical results in UK and US financial markets confirm the superb performance of the sustainability-oriented RCEI model and the efficiency of the algorithm.

Keywords: enhanced indexation; regime switching; cardinality constraint; proximal ADMM

---

1. Introduction

As the global financial market is riddled with more and more uncertainty, there is a growing awareness of incorporating sustainability-relates insights into investment analysis and management; therefore, investors boost their chances for long-term and sustainable success. Incorporating sustainability insights can provide a more holistic view of the risks and opportunities associated with a given investment. In response to the increasing interest, there is a strong need to develop sustainable investing approaches and products.

The research on financial sustainability is in its infancy as only a handful of articles briefly touched on it [1–6]. Nurmakhanova et al. [3] claimed that a sustainable microfinance institution is the one that operates profitably and does not require subsidies to succeed. By integrating a composite sustainability index of a project into Markowitz mean-variance model, Dobrovolskienė and Tamošiūnienė [4] presented a sustainability-oriented model of financial resource allocation in a project portfolio. Li et al. [5] studied the Maslow portfolio selection model to meet the need of individuals with low financial sustainability who prefer to satisfy their lower-level needs first, and then look for higher-level needs. Nevertheless, the study of financial sustainability in portfolio management, especially in the enhanced indexation area, is far from adequate.

Financial portfolio management has long been of keen interest to fund managers, individual investors, and scholars. Relentless efforts have been made to quantify market dynamics and turn them into more strategic and sustainable investment tools. Enhanced indexation is an active portfolio management strategy, which is proposed to find a portfolio outperforming a market index [7–21].

Due to the existence of market frictions such as transaction costs and management expenses, the number of invested assets in the tracking portfolio should be limited. Nevertheless, finding a global optimal portfolio of a cardinality constrained optimization problem is generally NP-hard [22]. Therefore, some scholars investigated the enhanced indexation problems in the aspects of modeling and solution methods. Riepe and Werner [7] first studied the enhanced indexation problem and it became a fertile area of research. Dose and Cincotti [9] sought a relatively high excess return within a reduced tracking error by adopting the historical look-back approach. They solved the problem in a two-step heuristic method, while this method could not ensure the global optimality of the obtained portfolios. Canakgoz and Beasley [11] presented mixed-integer linear programs (MILP) for the enhanced indexation problem from the regression viewpoint. They adopted a two-stage approach to find the optimal solution, in which each stage can be solved by Cplex solver. Lejeune [13] formulated a stochastic enhanced indexation model whose goal is to maximize the excess return that can be attained, while ensuring that the semi-deviation risk does not exceed a specified limit. He provided the game theoretical framework when the distribution of the random return is known to belong to the ellipsoidal distribution family. Guastaroba and Speranza [15] illustrated mixed-integer linear programming models for index tracking and enhanced indexation, in which the enhanced indexation model was to maximize the over-performance with respect to the market index, while ensuring that the tracking error would not exceed a given threshold. In addition, the MILP is solved by a heuristic framework called kernel search. Roman et al. [16] studied the enhanced indexation problem based on a second-order stochastic dominance model. They adopted the cutting plane method to arrive at the optimal solution for the problem, whereas the number of selected stocks could not be restricted strictly due to the absence of a cardinality constraint. Xu et al. [19] showed a sparse enhanced indexation model with cardinality and chance constraints in the distributionally robust framework. The Fama–French three-factor model is used to reformulate the robust chance constraint of random variables. They applied a hybrid genetic algorithm to solve the NP-hard problem.

Nevertheless, all of these conventional enhanced indexation models referred to above—missing sustainability in scope—failed in capturing intrinsically dynamic market environments and thus only provided partial pictures. In particular, sustainability in enhanced indexation problem is a fundamental issue to ensure stable returns and to avoid extreme losses in a long-term investment process. In the scope of solution methods, the existing algorithms still have many defects. Even though some mixed integer programming [11,17] can be solved by standard software programs, which are not applicable in large-scale problems due to the curse of dimensionality. In addition, hybrid heuristic methods [8,15,19,20] based on genetic algorithms, kernel search or simulated annealing are not able to guarantee the optimality conditions of the obtained solutions. Therefore, more work are in great demand to establish scientific sustainability models to reflect the market environment and to design efficient algorithms that can solve the large-scale cardinality constrained enhanced indexation problem.

Inspired by the enhanced indexation models of Lejeune's [13], Guastaroba and Speranza [15], in this paper, we emphasize the standpoint of financial sustainability to avoid extreme losses when pursuing higher excess profits in a long-term investment process. Unlike the ellipsoidal distribution assumption by Lejeune or the heuristic framework by Guastaroba and Speranza, our proposed stochastic enhanced indexation model is determined by the historical observations' approximation, which is a universal framework to formulate the stochastic optimization problem into the deterministic form [11,17,20]. However, there is almost no literature on how to select the historical observations from the dataset, which will directly influence the performance of the enhanced indexation model. In fact, historical sample series sometimes have obvious random-effects in the historical dependence relationship [23]. Hence, for guaranteeing the sustainability of the enhanced indexation problem, in this paper, it is necessary to consider the nonlinear relationship between the forthcoming and historical return rates. In addition, the parameters of the enhanced indexation model should be adjusted adaptively according to the market environment. This idea is consistent with the regime switching technique [24], which has the strength of not only reflecting the change of the market environment but also demonstrating the nonlinear dynamic relationship among market environments in different time periods [25,26]. Therefore, in this paper, we properly select different risk thresholds and cardinality bonds in the enhanced indexation model according to different market regimes.

To help investors capitalize on opportunities in sustainable investing in this growing turbulent global market, this paper offers insights on how to integrate variable financial market environments with the investment process—from defining the objectives and approach for an investment strategy through developing the algorithms. More specifically, we propose a sustainable regime-based cardinality constrained enhanced indexation (RCEI) model. Incorporating the switching of market regimes into our analysis, we divide the historical observations with respect to different market regimes and introduce the regime-dependent threshold and cardinality upper bound to improve the model. In addition, we adopt a splitting algorithm based on the proximal alternating direction method of multipliers (ADMM). The new enhanced indexation model and proposed algorithm are examined by numerical tests for its sustainability and efficiency in different real financial markets. The main contributions of this paper can be summarized as follows:

- On account of the growing uncertainty in financial markets, we introduce a novel sustainability-oriented enhanced indexation model with the regime switching technique to avoid the extreme losses in the long-term assets management process, with the purpose of reflecting the fluctuations of the financial market timely and obtaining the sustainable investment profits.
- Considering the significant cardinality constraint in the deterministic formulation, we adopt a partial penalty method coupled with the proximal ADMM, which can solve the resulting nonsmooth and nonconvex problem effectively and efficiently.
- We conduct numerical tests in different financial markets for long-term processes. The evidence demonstrates the scientific soundness and the sustainability of the RCEI model as well as the efficiency of the proposed hybrid algorithm.

The paper is organized as follows: in Section 2, we establish the sustainable stochastic enhanced indexation model with regime switching and cardinality constraint, and then transform the formulation by using historical observations. In Section 3, we present a partial penalty method embedded with the proximal ADMM for solving the transformed deterministic optimization problem. In Section 4, we illustrate the numerical results about the applications of the RCEI model in the FTSE 100 and S&P 500 markets. We conclude this paper in Section 5.

2. Sustainability-Oriented Enhanced Indexation Model

In classic enhanced indexation problems, the main focus is to maximize the excess return and minimize the tracking error. However, a larger excess return is in contradiction with a lower tracking error if we consider the total deviation in the optimal portfolio. Therefore, we consider a stochastic optimization model where the expected excess return is maximized at the same time controlling the lower semi-absolute tracking error and the maximum number of assets being invested. The concrete cardinality constraint enhanced indexation problem is as follows:

$$\begin{array}{ll} \max\limits_{x} & \mathbb{E}[R^\top x - R_I] \\ \text{s.t.} & \mathbb{E}[(R^\top x - R_I)_-] \le \alpha, \\ & e_N^\top x = 1, \\ & \|x\|_0 \le K, \end{array} \tag{1}$$

where $x \in \mathbb{R}^N$ is a decision vector that denotes the portfolio. R is an N-dimensional random vector that denotes the random return rates of N assets. R_I is a random variable denoting the random return rate of the market index. $\alpha \in \mathbb{R}_+$ is a given threshold to constrain the lower semi-absolute tracking error. $e_N \in \mathbb{R}^N$ is an all-one vector with length N. $\|x\|_0$ is the cardinality of x, which denotes the number of nonzero components in x. The constraint $\|x\|_0 \le K$ means that the number of non-zero entries in the optimal portfolio is not larger than K. To deal with the general case in different financial markets, we do not restrict the short-selling in this paper. We should point out that our algorithm proposed later can also be applied to the no short-selling case.

In existing enhanced indexation models referred above, the benchmark is always a fixed scale or a given market index, while, as we pointed out in the Introduction, the market environment varies significantly according to different market regimes. Hence, for guaranteeing the financial sustainability, the benchmarks in an enhanced indexation model should be properly selected according to specific market regimes. Typically, in a bull market, the investor could choose higher benchmarks; in a bear market, the investor might set lower benchmarks in the hope of avoiding the absolute loss at the same time.

Before introducing the sustainable enhanced indexation model with regime switching, we present the basic setting for the regime switching. We assume that the current regime is s_0, and the regime during the next investment period is s. We assume that the regime switching is Markovian, and there are J possible regimes: $s^1, s^2, \dots, s^J$. $Q_{s^i s^j} := Q\{s_f = s^j : s_0 = s^i\}$ represents the transition probability from regime s^i in the current period to regime s^j in the next period. In this paper, we assume that the Markovian regime switching process is stationary. This means that, for any period, the transition probability matrix is

$$Q = \begin{bmatrix} Q_{s^1 s^1} & Q_{s^1 s^2} & \cdots & Q_{s^1 s^J} \\ Q_{s^2 s^1} & Q_{s^2 s^2} & \cdots & Q_{s^2 s^J} \\ \cdots & \cdots & \cdots & \cdots \\ Q_{s^J s^1} & Q_{s^J s^2} & \cdots & Q_{s^J s^J} \end{bmatrix}.$$

Under this setting, as an extension of the model (1), we can introduce the following sustainable regime-based cardinality constrained enhanced indexation model:

$$\text{(RCEI)} \qquad \begin{aligned} \max_{x} \quad & \mathbb{E}[R^\top x - R_I(s_f)] \\ \text{s.t.} \quad & \mathbb{E}[(R^\top x - R_I(s_f))_- : s_f = s^j] \le \alpha(s^j),\ j = 1, 2, \dots, J, \\ & e_N^\top x = 1, \\ & \|x\|_0 \le K(s_0), \end{aligned} \tag{2}$$

where $R_I(s_f)$ is the return rate of the market index whose distribution relies on the forthcoming market regime s_f. Meanwhile, we set the cardinality upper bound $K(s_0)$ according to the current market regime s_0. For example, in a bull market environment, investors can set a larger threshold of the lower semi-absolute tracking error and focus on fewer blue chip stocks in order to reap higher excess returns. On the contrary, in a bear market environment, investors opt for a more diverse investment strategy to secure financial sustainability. They can set a smaller threshold of the tracking error under the index to reduce the risk and avoid the absolute investment losses.

We use the historical observations for transforming the stochastic optimization problem (2). Concretely, the expectations in the problem are approximated by historical observations: we assume that there are T historical observations of R, $\{r_1, r_2, \dots, r_T\}$, the historical observations of R_I are $\{r_I(s(1)), r_I(s(2)), \dots, r_I(s(T))\}$, where $s(t)$, for $t = 1, 2, \dots T$, denotes the market regime to which the t-th observation belongs.

We define the historical observations' index set as $S = \{1, 2, \dots, T\}$, then we can divide S into J parts corresponding to the J market regimes. We denote the set of observations under the j-th market regime as S_j, then $S = \bigcup_{1,2,\dots,J} S_j$ and $S_i \bigcap S_j = \emptyset$ for $i, j = 1, 2, \dots, T$ and $i \neq j$. In S_j, we have T_j historical observations, and $\sum_{j=1}^{J} T_j = T$. We derive the sample reformulation of the RCEI model as:

$$\begin{aligned}
\max_{x} \quad & \sum_{j=1}^{J} \left(Q(s_0, s^j) \tfrac{1}{T_j} \sum_{t \in S_j} (r_t^\top x - r_I(s(t))) \right) \\
\text{s.t.} \quad & \tfrac{1}{T_j} \sum_{t \in S_j} [(r_t^\top x - r_I(s(t)))_-] \le \alpha(s^j),\ j = 1, 2, \dots, J, \\
& e_N^\top x = 1, \\
& \|x\|_0 \le K(s_0).
\end{aligned} \tag{3}$$

We notice that the term $r_I(s(t))$ in the objective function does not affect the optimal solution of the deterministic optimization problem, therefore we can get rid of this term in the following formulations. However, the negative part function in problem (3) leads the programming to a nonlinear optimization problem. By introducing an auxiliary vector $y = (y_1; y_2; \dots; y_T) \in \mathbb{R}^T$, problem (3) can be transformed into the following cardinality constrained linear programming problem:

$$\begin{aligned}
\max_{x,y} \quad & \sum_{j=1}^{J} \left(Q(s_0, s^j) \tfrac{1}{T_j} \sum_{t \in S_j} r_t^\top x \right) \\
\text{s.t.} \quad & \tfrac{1}{T_j} \sum_{t \in S_j} y_t \le \alpha(s^j),\ j = 1, 2, \dots, J, \\
& y_t \ge r_I(s(t)) - r_t^\top x,\ t = 1, 2, \dots, T, \\
& y_t \ge 0,\ t = 1, 2, \dots, T, \\
& e_N^\top x = 1, \\
& \|x\|_0 \le K(s_0).
\end{aligned} \tag{4}$$

Problem (4) is very often a large-scale optimization problem with linear and cardinality constraints since the number of stocks N and observations T are large enough. Fortunately, we notice that, in this formulation, the decision variables x and y can be divided into groups. This feature reminds us that the splitting methods, such as the proximal ADMM algorithm, can be adopted for solving this large-scale optimization problem.

3. Proximal ADMM Algorithm for Solving the Enhanced Indexation Model

In this section, we adopt the proximal ADMM algorithm for solving the sustainability-oriented enhanced indexation model. ADMM was first introduced in the early 1970s [27]. The Bregman modification of ADMM was recently proposed by Zhang et al. [28]; they showed the convergence for convex objective functions under the general Bregman distance. Chen et al. [29] demonstrated that the direct extension of the classic ADMM to the multi-block minimization problem is not necessarily convergent even if the objective function is the sum of separable convex functions. Following Chen and Zhuang [30], we adopt the partial penalty method embedded with the proximal ADMM algorithm for solving the deterministic RCEI model.

To adopt the proximal ADMM method better and express the formulation simply, we combine the decision variables x and y together, and represent it as $w = (x; y) \in \mathbb{R}^{N+T}$. Therefore, $x = Aw$, $y = Bw$, where $A = (I_N, 0) \in \mathbb{R}^{N \times (N+T)}$, $B = (0, I_T) \in \mathbb{R}^{T \times (N+T)}$, and I denotes the identity matrix. Then, $y_t = B_t w$, for $t = 1, 2, \dots, T$, where B_t is the t-th row of B, and $\sum_{t \in S_j} y_t = \sum_{t \in S_j} B_t w$. Then, problem (4) can be reformulated as:

$$\begin{aligned}
\max_{x,w} \quad & \sum_{j=1}^{J} \left(Q(s_0, s^j) \tfrac{1}{T_j} \sum_{t \in S_j} r_t^\top A w \right) \\
\text{s.t.} \quad & \tfrac{1}{T_j} \textstyle\sum_{t \in S_j} B_t w \le \alpha(s^j),\ j = 1, 2, \dots, J, \\
& B_t w \ge r_I(s(t)) - r_t^\top A w,\ t = 1, 2, \dots, T, \\
& B w \ge 0, \\
& e_N^\top A w = 1, \\
& A w - x = 0, \\
& \|x\|_0 \le K(s_0).
\end{aligned} \tag{5}$$

In order to simplify the deterministic RCEI model further, we treat the cardinality constraint individually and combine the other constraints of the same type together. Specifically, define the cardinality set $\mathcal{C}_{s_0} := \{x \in \mathbb{R}^N : \|x\|_0 \leq K(s_0)\}$, and let $\delta_{\mathcal{C}_{s_0}}(x)$ denote the indicator function of x with respect to $\mathcal{C}_{s_0}$, i.e., $\delta_{\mathcal{C}_{s_0}}(x) = 0$ if $\|x\|_0 \leq K(s_0)$, and $\delta_{\mathcal{C}_{s_0}}(x) = \infty$, otherwise. We should point out that $\delta_{\mathcal{C}_{s_0}}(x)$ can be abbreviated as $\delta_{\mathcal{C}}(x)$ as long as it will not cause any ambiguity. Let $A_1 = (A_1^1; A_1^2; \ldots; A_1^J) \in \mathbb{R}^{J\times(N+T)}$, where $A_1^j = \frac{1}{T_j}\sum_{t\in S_j} B_t \in \mathbb{R}^{1\times(N+T)}$ for $j = 1,\ldots,J$. $\bar{\alpha} = (\alpha(s^1); \alpha(s^2); \ldots; \alpha(s^J)) \in \mathbb{R}^J$. $A_2 = (A_2^1; A_2^2; \ldots; A_2^T) \in \mathbb{R}^{T\times(N+T)}$, where $A_2^t = -r_t^\top A - B_t \in \mathbb{R}^{1\times(N+T)}$ for $t = 1,\ldots,T$. $r_I = (r_I(s(1)); r_I(s(2)); \ldots; r_I(s(T))) \in \mathbb{R}^T$. $c = -(\frac{1}{T}\sum_{t=1}^T r_t^\top A)^\top \in \mathbb{R}^{N+T}$. Moreover, we joint some equality and inequality constraints together, respectively: $\bar{A} = (A_1; A_2; -B)$, $\bar{b} = (\bar{\alpha}; -r_I; 0)$, $\bar{C} = e_N^\top A$, $\bar{d} = 1$. Then, the reformulated problem (5) can be further simplified as

$$\begin{aligned} \min_{x,w} \quad & c^\top w + \delta_{\mathcal{C}}(x) \\ \text{s.t.} \quad & \bar{A}w \leq \bar{b}, \\ & \bar{C}w = \bar{d}, \\ & Aw - x = 0. \end{aligned} \tag{6}$$

Since the direct application of ADMM in problem (6) fails to preserve its convergence property [29], we consider the partial penalty method inspired by Chen and Zhuang [30]. By introducing auxiliary vectors $u \in \mathbb{R}^{J+2T}$ and $v \in \mathbb{R}$, the partial penalty enhanced indexation subproblem can be formulated as:

$$\begin{aligned} \min_{x,w,u,v} \quad & c^\top w + \mu(\|u_+\|^2 + \|v\|^2) + \delta_{\mathcal{C}}(x) \\ \text{s.t.} \quad & \bar{A}w - u = \bar{b}, \\ & \bar{C}w - v = \bar{d}, \\ & Aw - x = 0, \end{aligned} \tag{7}$$

where $\mu > 0$ denotes the penalty parameter of problem (6). For more concise expression of the constraints, we denote

$$\mathcal{A} = \begin{bmatrix} \bar{A} \\ \bar{C} \\ A \end{bmatrix}, \quad \mathcal{B} = \begin{bmatrix} -I & 0 \\ 0 & -I \\ 0 & 0 \end{bmatrix}, \quad \mathcal{D} = \begin{bmatrix} 0 \\ 0 \\ -I \end{bmatrix}, \quad b = \begin{bmatrix} \bar{b} \\ \bar{d} \\ 0 \end{bmatrix}, \tag{8}$$

then the constraints in problem (7) can be merged as:

$$\mathcal{A}w + \mathcal{B}\begin{bmatrix} u \\ v \end{bmatrix} + \mathcal{D}x = b. \tag{9}$$

Then, the augmented Lagrangian function of the enhanced indexation subproblem (7) is:

$$\begin{aligned} \mathcal{L}_\mu(x,w,u,v,\lambda;\beta) = \; & c^\top w + \mu(\|u_+\|^2 + \|v\|^2) + \delta_{\mathcal{C}}(x) \\ & + \lambda^T(\mathcal{A}w + \mathcal{B}\begin{bmatrix} u \\ v \end{bmatrix} + \mathcal{D}x - b) + \frac{\beta}{2}\|\mathcal{A}w + \mathcal{B}\begin{bmatrix} u \\ v \end{bmatrix} + \mathcal{D}x - b\|^2, \end{aligned} \tag{10}$$

where λ denotes the Lagrangian multiplier of constraint (9), and $\beta > 0$ denotes the penalty parameter of the partial penalty subproblem. Then, we can adopt the partial penalty method embedded with the proximal ADMM to solve the enhanced indexation problem. The concrete algorithm can be presented in Algorithm 1.

Algorithm 1: Partial penalty proximal ADMM for enhanced indexation problem

- **Step 1.** Given an initial point $(x^0, w^0) \in \mathbb{R}^N \times \mathbb{R}^{N+T}$, the outer tolerance $\epsilon_O > 0, \gamma > 1$. Let $k = 1, \mu^k > 0$;
- **Step 2.** Solve the enhanced indexation subproblem (7) by the proximal ADMM algorithm:
  - **Step 2.1.** Given $\mu = \mu^k$, the inner tolerance $\epsilon_I > 0, \sigma > 0$. Let $\beta > 0$, $(x^0, w^0) = (x^{k-1}, w^{k-1})$, $u^0 = \bar{A}w^0 - \bar{b}$, $v^0 = \bar{C}w^0 - \bar{d}$, $\lambda^0 \in \mathbb{R}^{J+2T+N+1}$, $i = 0$;
  - **Step 2.2.** Perform the $(i+1)$-th iteration as follows:

$$\begin{cases} x^{i+1} &= \arg\min_x \mathcal{L}_\mu(x, w^i, u^i, v^i, \lambda^i; \beta), \\ w^{i+1} &= \arg\min_w \{\mathcal{L}_\mu(x^{i+1}, w, u^i, v^i, \lambda^i; \beta) + \frac{\sigma}{2}\|w - w^i\|^2\}, \\ \begin{bmatrix} u^{i+1} \\ v^{i+1} \end{bmatrix} &= \arg\min_{u,v} \mathcal{L}_\mu(x^{i+1}, w^{i+1}, u, v, \lambda^i; \beta), \\ \lambda^{i+1} &= \lambda^i + \beta(\mathcal{A}w^{i+1} + \mathcal{B}\begin{bmatrix} u^{i+1} \\ v^{i+1} \end{bmatrix} + \mathcal{D}z^{i+1} - b), \end{cases}$$

  - **Step 2.3.** If the inner stopping criterion

$$\max\{\mu, \beta, 1\}(\|w^{i+1} - w^i\| + \|(\lambda^{i+1} - \lambda^i)/\beta\|) \le \epsilon_I$$

    is satisfied, stop the proximal ADMM algorithm and go to Step 3; otherwise, let $\beta = \gamma\beta$, $i = i + 1$ and go to Step 2.2;
- **Step 3.** If the outer stopping criterion

$$\|\mathcal{A}w^k + \mathcal{B}\begin{bmatrix} u^k \\ v^k \end{bmatrix} + \mathcal{D}x^k - b\| \le \epsilon_O$$

  is satisfied, stop the algorithm and return the approximate optimal solution (x^k, w^k); otherwise, let $\mu^{k+1} = \gamma\mu^k$ and go to Step 2 with $k = k + 1$.

Remark 1. *The proximal coefficient $\sigma > 0$ in Algorithm 1 controls the proximity of the new iteration point to the last one. It is obvious that the proximal regularized subproblem reduces to the classic ADMM algorithm if we set $\sigma = 0$.*

Remark 2. *Step 2.2 in Algorithm 1 can be further represented as:*

$$\begin{cases} x^{i+1} &= \text{Proj}_C(Aw^i + \lambda_x^i/\beta), \\ w^{i+1} &= H^{-1}\left(\sigma w^i - c - \bar{A}^\top\lambda_u^i - \bar{C}^\top\lambda_v^i - A^\top\lambda_x^i + \beta\bar{A}^\top(u^i + \bar{b}) + \beta\bar{C}^\top(v^i + \bar{d}) + \beta A^\top x^{i+1}\right), \\ u^{i+1} &= \text{Prox}^\beta_{\mu\|(\cdot)_+\|^2}(\bar{A}w^{i+1} - \bar{b} + \lambda_u^i/\beta), \\ v^{i+1} &= \text{Prox}^\beta_{\mu\|\cdot\|^2}(\bar{C}w^{i+1} - \bar{d} + \lambda_v^i/\beta), \\ \lambda^{i+1} &= \lambda^i + \beta(\mathcal{A}w^{i+1} + \mathcal{B}\begin{bmatrix} u^{i+1} \\ v^{i+1} \end{bmatrix} + \mathcal{D}x^{i+1} - b), \end{cases}$$

where $\lambda = (\lambda_u; \lambda_v; \lambda_x) \in \mathbb{R}^{(J+2T)\times 1\times N}$, $H = \beta\mathcal{A}^\top\mathcal{A} + \sigma I$. Given $z \in \mathbb{R}^N$ and $\rho > 0$, the proximal mapping of f with respect to z is defined as:

$$\text{Prox}_f^\rho(z) := \arg\min_s\{f(s) + (\rho/2)\|s - z\|^2 : v \in \mathbb{R}^N\}.$$

It is known that the proximal operator $\text{Prox}_{\delta_C}(\cdot)$ can be reduced to the projection operator $\text{Proj}_C(\cdot)$, as shown in the update step for x^{i+1}. Both proximal and projection operators have their closed form expressions in our proposed *problem, which means that each step in Algorithm 1 has their closed form, and, therefore, the computation time can be guaranteed to some extent.*

Remark 3. *The convergence of Algorithm 1 is ensured by the theoretical analysis in the work of Chen and Zhuang [30].*

4. Empirical Results

In this section, we carry out empirical tests to examine performances of the sustainability-oriented RCEI model in different financial markets. All formulations derived from enhanced indexation problems are solved by Algorithm 1 proposed in Section 3.

4.1. Data Sets and Model Settings

We consider two typical indices and different data sets correspondingly with different scales: the FTSE 100 index and the S&P 500 index, for testing the proposed RCEI model. These two indices represent the different financial markets in UK and US. The investment stocks are the corresponding components in the two indices: 100 stocks constituting the FTSE 100 index and 500 stocks constituting the S&P 500 index. All data are selected as the adjusted closing prices of stocks in every week: the FTSE 100 index data set is from 1 January 2004 to 27 December 2018; the S&P 500 index data set is from 1 January 2007 to 31 December 2018, which are used for computing each index's and stock's logarithmic weekly return rates. The original data are downloaded from Yahoo finance (http://finance.yahoo.com). We partition each data set into two subsets: a training data set and a testing data set. The training data set, also called the in-sample set, is used to determine the optimal enhanced indexation portfolio. The testing data set, also called the out-of-sample set, consists of the rest of the data and is used to test the performance of the resulting optimal portfolio. We adopt a rolling forward framework. For each week in the out-of-sample period, we find the optimal portfolio from the RCEI model with the historical data in the last 50 weeks before the week. This provides us 732 out-of-sample optimal portfolios, one per week, to track the FTSE 100 index, and 576 out-of-sample optimal portfolios to track the S&P 500 index. With the market price data in out-of-sample periods, we compute the return rates of these out-of-sample portfolios. All numerical tests are carried out with Matlab 9.2.0 (2017a) (MathWorks, Natick, MA, United States). Table 1 summarizes the settings of the tests.

Table 1. Test settings.

	Constituent Stocks	Benchmark	K	In-Sample Weeks	Out-of-Sample Period (Weeks)
Test 1	100	FTSE 100	5, 10, 20	50	2004.12.23–2018.12.27 (732)
Test 2	500	S&P 500	5, 10, 20	50	2007.12.24–2018.12.31 (576)

As common practice, we assume that there exist three market regimes: the bull regime, denoted as s^1, means that the market is going up; the consolidation regime, denoted as s^2, indicates that the market is in the transitional period between recovery and recession; and the bear regime, denoted as s^3, means that the market is going down. We use the method adopted in Liu and Chen [31] to determine market regimes based on the average values of the market index over a time window. By using the in-sample data, we estimate the transition probability matrices for the FTSE 100 and S&P 500 indices, respectively:

$$Q_{\text{FTSE}} = \begin{bmatrix} 0.9023 & 0.0951 & 0.0026 \\ 0.2482 & 0.5674 & 0.1844 \\ 0.0237 & 0.1361 & 0.8402 \end{bmatrix}, \quad Q_{\text{S\&P}} = \begin{bmatrix} 0.9342 & 0.0608 & 0.0051 \\ 0.2933 & 0.5467 & 0.1600 \\ 0.0310 & 0.0775 & 0.8915 \end{bmatrix}.$$

From the diagonal elements in Q_{FTSE} and $Q_{S\&P}$, we see that both markets are stable to stay in the bull or bear regime, but there is a relatively high possibility to switch from the consolidation regime into the bull or bear regime. This scenario is consistent with the real market situation.

Table 2 gives the mean and standard deviation of each index's out-of-sample return rates under different market regimes. It reflects the difference of weekly return rates in three market regimes.

Table 2. Mean and standard deviation of out-of-sample return rates under different market regimes.

Index	Mean (s^1)	Mean (s^2)	Mean (s^3)	Mean	Std (s^1)	Std (s^2)	Std (s^3)	Std
FTSE 100	0.0036	0.0010	−0.0063	0.0005	0.0187	0.0195	0.0318	0.0224
S&P 500	0.0033	0.0014	−0.0071	0.0009	0.0190	0.0240	0.0396	0.0254

We can see from Table 2 that both the expected return rates and the standard deviations are noticeably different among three different market regimes. Under the bull regime, the expected return rates are the highest and always positive; under the bear regime, they are the lowest and always negative; and, under the consolidation regime, they are in the middle. Correspondingly, the standard deviations of two indices under the bear regime are always higher than those under the bull or consolidation regime. These phenomena capture the real market well: the investment under the bear regime is usually active, which leads to a rather low return rate with large volatility; while the investment under the bull regime is less frequent, which leads to a high return rate with a relative small volatility.

4.2. Out-of-Sample Results

In practice, the primary concern is the out-of-sample performance of the determined portfolio. Therefore, we only demonstrate the out-of-sample results here. In the RCEI model, the lower semi-absolute tracking error thresholds $\alpha(s^1), \alpha(s^2), \alpha(s^3)$ are chosen as $0.007, 0.005, 0.003$, respectively. The cardinality upper bounds are set to $K(s^1) = 5$, $K(s^2) = 10$, $K(s^3) = 20$. That is to say, in a bull market, we prefer a more concentrated investment policy while we allow a larger tolerance of the losses under the index. In a bear market, we prefer a more diversified investment policy and set a smaller tolerance of the losses under the index, to reduce the risk. To elaborate whether the regime switching technique can improve the stability in enhanced indexation problems, we also test the cardinality constrained enhanced indexation model without regime switching, denoted by the CEI model for reference. We can obtain the optimal investment policy under the CEI model by solving the RCEI model with $J = 1$, $\alpha(s^1) = \alpha$ and $K(s^1) = K$. For the CEI model, we set the threshold $\alpha = 0.005$ and the cardinality upper bound $K = 10$. All parameters in the partial penalty proximal ADMM are set as: the initial penalty parameter $\mu^1 = 2$, the initial penalty in ADMM $\beta^1 = 2$, the growth coefficient $\gamma = 1.4$, the proximal coefficient $\sigma = 1.3$, the external and internal tolerances are 10^{-5} and 10^{-3}, respectively.

Figure 1 shows the out-of-sample cumulative return rates of the optimal tracking portfolios derived by the RCEI and CEI models in FTSE 100, compared with the cumulative return rates of the FTSE 100 index.

Figure 2 shows the out-of-sample cumulative return rates of the optimal tracking portfolios derived by the RCEI and CEI models in S&P 500, compared with the cumulative return rates of the S&P 500 index.

We can see from Figures 1 and 2 that both optimal portfolios obtained from the RCEI and CEI models can efficiently track the trend of the market index and even outperform the market index. Meanwhile, the out-of-sample performances of the RCEI models are better than those of the CEI models or the indices in FTSE 100 and S&P 500 markets, respectively. The cumulative return rates of the optimal portfolios from the RCEI models are substantially higher than those from the CEI models and the market indices in UK and US financial markets. In addition, the optimal portfolios obtained from the RCEI model secure more stable returns and thus avoid substantial losses in a long-term investment process.

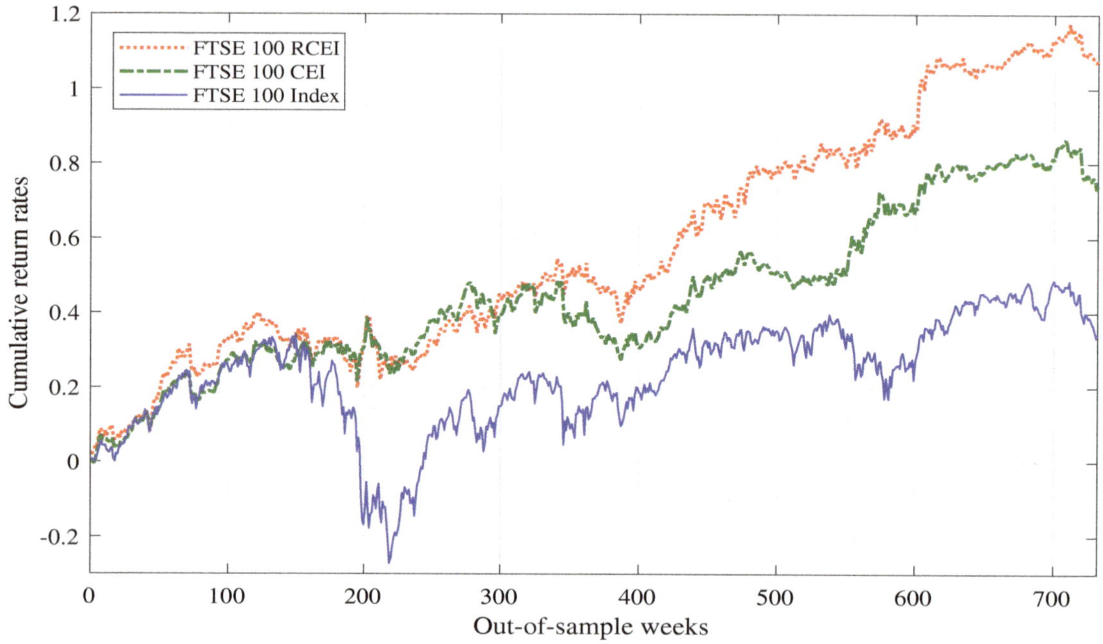

Figure 1. Out-of-sample performances of RCEI and CEI models in FTSE 100.

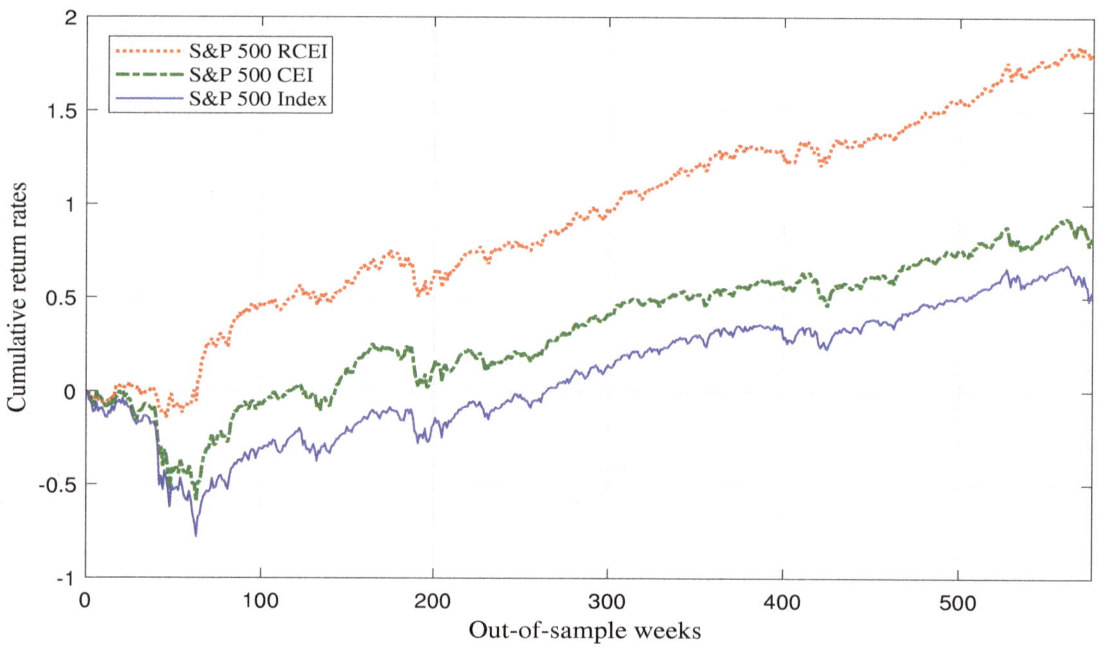

Figure 2. Out-of-sample performances of RCEI and CEI models in S&P 500.

For more details, we show typical statistics of weekly return rates of out-of-sample portfolios as well as the average CPU time in Table 3.

Table 3 shows that the means of the return rates of the RCEI and CEI models are much larger than that of the index, especially the RCEI model. In addition, the standard deviation of the RCEI and CEI models are smaller than that of the FTSE 100 index and close to that of the S&P 500 index, respectively. Sharpe ratio (SR) is a widely adopted indicator for calculating the risk-adjusted return, which can be used to evaluate a portfolio's performance. We can see from Table 3 that, in both financial markets, the Sharpe ratio value of the optimal portfolios from the RCEI models are larger than those of the CEI models or the market indices, respectively. It means that, in terms of the risk-adjusted return, the RCEI model also outperforms the CEI model and the market index.

Table 3. Statistics of out-of-sample portfolio return rates of RCEI and CEI models.

Index	Model	Mean	Std	SR	MDD	TE_+	TE_-	Time(s)
FTSE 100	RCEI	0.0015	0.0158	0.0931	0.2522	0.0067	0.0057	1.07
	CEI	0.0010	0.0143	0.0709	0.5918	0.0063	0.0057	1.10
	Index	0.0005	0.0224	0.0209	0.7717	-	-	-
S&P 500	RCEI	0.0031	0.0220	0.1425	0.1986	0.0060	0.0038	18.79
	CEI	0.0014	0.0258	0.0553	0.2104	0.0041	0.0036	18.94
	Index	0.0009	0.0254	0.0364	0.6117	-	-	-

Considering the financial sustainability in the long run, we calculate the maximum drawdown (MDD) [32] for each optimal portfolio of each model and the index in FTSE 100 and S&P 500. MDD is the maximum loss from a peak to a trough of a portfolio before a new peak is attained. It is an indicator of downside risk over a specific time period. We can see from Table 3 that the MDD value of the RCEI model is obviously smaller than those of the CEI model and the market index. It means that, when we obtain excess returns by the RCEI model, we can simultaneously avoid heavy losses for more than ten years. It is very important for the financial sustainability. In particular, a heavy loss is a big blow for any investor, which will result in the unsustainability in financial investments.

Table 3 also reveals that the expectation of the positive part of the tracking error i.e., $TE_+ = \mathbb{E}[(R^\top x - R_I)_+]$, and the expectation of the negative part of the tracking error, i.e., $TE_- = \mathbb{E}[(R^\top x - R_I)_-]$. In terms of TE_+ and TE_-, the performance of the RCEI model is better than that of the CEI model. Moreover, the proposed partial penalty proximal ADMM algorithm is highly efficient as the average CPU time is about 1 s in FTSE 100 enhanced problems and about 18 s in S&P 500 enhanced problems.

Furthermore, we divide the out-of-sample period of FTSE 100 and S&P 500 into three market regimes, respectively. Then, we compute the statistics of weekly return rates of the optimal portfolios under different market regimes, shown in Table 4.

In Table 4, we not only list the performance of the RCEI model under each market regime, but also that of the CEI model. We find that both RCEI and CEI models perform differently under different market regimes. Comparing with the CEI model, the RCEI model performs better in terms of the means, standard deviations and Sharpe ratios. In addition, the discrimination of the RCEI model in three market regimes are larger, which means that the RCEI model can describe the influence of different market regimes efficiently. In addition, in the bear market environment, the performance of the RECI model is better than that of the market index, which can avoid suffering a huge financial loss, and guarantee the sustainability of the investment consequently. It illustrates that the regime switching plays a fundamental role in financial sustainability.

Finally, we consider the effect of the cardinality constraint in the RCEI model. We test a reference of the RCEI model by removing the cardinality constraint, denoted by the REI model. We carry out the out-of-sample test for the REI model in a similar rolling forward way. Some statistics of out-of-sample weekly return rates of optimal portfolios determined by the RCEI and REI models are shown in Table 5. The average number of actually invested stocks in the corresponding optimal portfolios as well as the average CPU time are also shown in Table 5.

We can observe from Table 5 that, comparing with the REI model, the optimal portfolio obtained from the RCEI model could significantly reduce the number of really invested stocks without losing too much performance. Limiting the number of actually invested stocks is crucial in financial management due to the following reasons. Firstly, the transaction cost is high relative to the number of stocks we buy or sell. If we reduce the number of stocks in the indexation portfolio, we can save much capital in the transaction cost. Secondly, as fund managers or individual investors, it is impossible for them to manage dozens or hundreds of stocks at the same time, which can be regarded as another kind of manpower cost. This further proves that the RCEI model is sustainable in long-term financial investment problems if we take transaction costs into account.

Table 4. Statistics of the out-of-sample return rates under different market regimes.

Index	Model	State	Mean	Std	SR	TE_+	TE_-
FTSE 100	RCEI	Bull	0.0030	0.0142	0.2149	0.0053	0.0058
		Consolidation	0.0015	0.0147	0.1006	0.0056	0.0051
		Bear	−0.0014	0.0202	−0.0678	0.0118	0.0068
	CEI	Bull	0.0025	0.0120	0.2114	0.0048	0.0058
		Consolidation	0.0003	0.0136	0.0243	0.0049	0.0056
		Bear	−0.0001	0.0191	−0.0058	0.0122	0.0059
	Index	Bull	0.0036	0.0187	0.1902	-	-
		Consolidation	0.0010	0.0195	0.0518	-	-
		Bear	−0.0063	0.0318	−0.3328	-	-
S&P 500	RCEI	Bull	0.0040	0.0184	0.2148	0.0031	0.0031
		Consolidation	0.0032	0.0241	0.1343	0.0055	0.0028
		Bear	0.0005	0.0253	0.0193	0.0158	0.0088
	CEI	Bull	0.0032	0.0206	0.1579	0.0033	0.0034
		Consolidation	0.0024	0.0235	0.1017	0.0045	0.0035
		Bear	−0.0056	0.0393	−0.1419	0.0059	0.0044
	Index	Bull	0.0033	0.0190	0.1731	-	-
		Consolidation	0.0014	0.0240	0.0591	-	-
		Bear	−0.0071	0.0396	−0.1803	-	-

Table 5. Statistics of out-of-sample return rates of RCEI and REI models.

Index	Model	Mean	Std	SR	TE_+	TE_-	Stocks	Time(s)
FTSE 100	RCEI	0.0015	0.0158	0.0931	0.0067	0.0057	9.36	1.07
	REI	0.0017	0.0173	0.0974	0.0071	0.0061	88.75	0.06
S&P 500	RCEI	0.0031	0.0220	0.1425	0.0060	0.0038	9.67	18.79
	REI	0.0036	0.0282	0.1277	0.0104	0.0083	383.17	0.83

The average CPU time shows that the computational cost of the REI model is lower than that of the RCEI model. The reason is that we need to introduce some auxiliary variables and extra computation for dealing with the cardinality constraint, which not only increase the dimension of the problem but also increase the number of iterations for obtaining the optimal solution. Fortunately, the computation time of the RCEI model is quite acceptable even if we deal with 500 constituent stocks in the S&P 500 case.

5. Conclusions

In this paper, we propose a new sustainability-oriented enhanced indexation model with regime switching and cardinality constraint. By adopting the regime switching technique, we can flexibly set different risk thresholdsbenchmarks and cardinality bounds in different market environments, which can mirror the fluctuation of market environment in a timely manner. We solve the resulting deterministic optimization problem by the partial penalty proximal ADMM, which can deal with the cardinality constraint optimization problem in an acceptable computation time. In addition, we examine the performance of the proposed RCEI model in different financial markets and compare the out-of-sample results with FTSE 100 and S&P 500 indices, respectively. The numerical results show that the optimal portfolios obtained from the RCEI model have higher accumulative return and lower risk compared with those obtained from the CEI model and the market indices in the long-term investment process. At the same time, the invested stocks can be streamlined without losing much performance by adopting our proposed model and algorithm.

This innovative work fuels our conviction that the proposed model and algorithm are highly compatible with sustainable strategies, and investors can reap significant benefits from their joint cooperation. The accumulating evidence about the benefits of investment strategies would cultivate the growth of a sustainable investing market. Firstly, fund managers and individual investors can choose different threshold parameters and cardinality bounds in various financial markets. Risk-preference investors can set the semi-absolute tracking error threshold larger for higher excess returns. Risk-aversion ones who pursue a more secure return can set the threshold smaller. Fund managers and individual investors can also adjust the cardinality bounds according to their needs. Based on our experiences, cardinality bounds are suggested as no more than 20 for fund mangers and no more than 10 for individual investors. Secondly, our proposed model is more effective in mature financial markets. It should be used with caution in emerging financial markets which are less effective. To speak plainly, arbitrage opportunities will often occur in emerging markets; therefore, the optimal value may go to infinity. However, this is not consistent with the facts. In addition, mature financial markets provide more products that can be taken into account in our portfolios, such that investors can still maintain positive income by holding some short positions when the market is slow. In general, our method echoes sustainable growth in long-term investment processes.

This work can further be improved such as using another tracking error measure instead of the lower semi-absolute measure or extending the model to the multi-period case. These promising topics are left for future research.

Author Contributions: Methodology, Z.C., X.Z. and J.L.; software, X.Z.; formal analysis, X.Z. and J.L.; writing and editing, Z.C., X.Z. and J.L.; project administration, Z.C.

References

1. De Crombrugghe, A.; Tenikue, M.; Sureda, J. Performance analysis for a sample of microfinance institutions in India. *Ann. Public Coop. Econ.* **2008**, *79*, 269–299. [CrossRef]
2. Hermes, N.; Lensink, R.; Meesters, A. Outreach and efficiency of microfinance institutions. *World Dev.* **2011**, *39*, 938–948. [CrossRef]
3. Nurmakhanova, M.; Kretzschmar, G.; Fedhila, H. Trade-off between financial sustainability and outreach of microfinance institutions. *Eurasian Econ. Rev.* **2015**, *5*, 231–250. [CrossRef]
4. Dobrovolskienė, N.; Tamošiūnienė, R. Sustainability-oriented financial resource allocation in a project portfolio through multi-criteria decision-making. *Sustainability* **2016**, *8*, 485.
5. Li, Z.; Li, X.; Hui, Y.; Wong, W.K. Maslow portfolio selection for individuals with low financial sustainability. *Sustainability* **2018**, *10*, 1128. [CrossRef]
6. Wong, W.K.; Lean, H.; McAleer, M.; Tsai, F.T. Why Are Warrant Markets Sustained in Taiwan but Not in China? *Sustainability* **2018**, *10*, 3748. [CrossRef]
7. Riepe, M.W.; Werner, M.D. Are enhanced index mutual funds worthy of their name? *J. Invest.* **1998**, *7*, 6–15. [CrossRef]
8. Beasley, J.E.; Meade, N.; Chang, T.J. An evolutionary heuristic for the index tracking problem. *Eur. J. Oper. Res.* **2003**, *148*, 621–643. [CrossRef]
9. Dose, C.; Cincotti, S. Clustering of financial time series with application to index and enhanced index tracking portfolio. *Phys. A Stat. Mech. Appl.* **2005**, *355*, 145–151. [CrossRef]
10. Wu, L.C.; Chou, S.C.; Yang, C.C.; Ong, C.S. Enhanced index investing based on goal programming. *J. Portf. Manag.* **2007**, *33*, 49–56. [CrossRef]
11. Canakgoz, N.A.; Beasley, J.E. Mixed-integer programming approaches for index tracking and enhanced indexation. *Eur. J. Oper. Res.* **2009**, *196*, 384–399. [CrossRef]
12. Li, Q.; Sun, L.; Bao, L. Enhanced index tracking based on multi-objective immune algorithm. *Expert Syst. Appl.* **2011**, *38*, 6101–6106. [CrossRef]
13. Lejeune, M.A. Game theoretical approach for reliable enhanced indexation. *Decis. Anal.* **2012**, *9*, 146–155. [CrossRef]

14. Lejeune, M.A.; Samatlı-Paç, G. Construction of risk-averse enhanced index funds. *Inf. J. Comput.* **2012**, *25*, 701–719. [CrossRef]
15. Guastaroba, G.; Speranza, M.G. Kernel search: An application to the index tracking problem. *Eur. J. Oper. Res.* **2012**, *217*, 54–68. [CrossRef]
16. Roman, D.; Mitra, G.; Zverovich, V. Enhanced indexation based on second-order stochastic dominance. *Eur. J. Oper. Res.* **2013**, *228*, 273–281. [CrossRef]
17. Takeda, A.; Niranjan, M.; Gotoh, J.Y.; Kawahara, Y. Simultaneous pursuit of out-of-sample performance and sparsity in index tracking portfolios. *Comput. Manag. Sci.* **2013**, *10*, 21–49. [CrossRef]
18. Mezali, H.; Beasley, J. Quantile regression for index tracking and enhanced indexation. *J. Oper. Res. Soc.* **2013**, *64*, 1676–1692. [CrossRef]
19. Xu, F.; Wang, M.; Dai, Y.H.; Xu, D. A sparse enhanced indexation model with chance and cardinality constraints. *J. Glob. Optim.* **2018**, *70*, 5–25. [CrossRef]
20. Benidis, K.; Feng, Y.; Palomar, D.P. Sparse portfolios for high-dimensional financial index tracking. *IEEE Trans. Signal Process.* **2018**, *66*, 155–170. [CrossRef]
21. Goel, A.; Sharma, A.; Mehra, A. Index tracking and enhanced indexing using mixed conditional value-at-risk. *J. Comput. Appl. Math.* **2018**, *335*, 361–380. [CrossRef]
22. Bienstock, D. Computational study of a family of mixed-integer quadratic programming problems. *Math. Program.* **1996**, *74*, 121–140. [CrossRef]
23. Laird, N.M.; Ware, J.H. Random-effects models for longitudinal data. *Biometrics* **1982**, *38*, 963–974. [CrossRef] [PubMed]
24. Hamilton, J.D. A new approach to the economic analysis of nonstationary time series and the business cycle. *Econom. J. Econom. Soc.* **1989**, *57*, 357–384. [CrossRef]
25. Elliott, R.J.; Siu, T.K. Robust optimal portfolio choice under Markovian regime-switching model. *Methodol. Comput. Appl. Probab.* **2009**, *11*, 145–157. [CrossRef]
26. Ma, Y.; MacLean, L.; Xu, K.; Zhao, Y. A portfolio optimization model with regime-switching risk factors for sector exchange traded funds. *Pac. J. Optim.* **2011**, *7*, 281–296.
27. Gabay, D.; Mercier, B. A dual algorithm for the solution of nonlinear variational problems via finite element approximations. *Comput. Math. Appl.* **1976**, *2*, 17–40 [CrossRef]
28. Zhang, X.; Burger, M.; Osher, S. A unified primal-dual algorithm framework based on Bregman iteration. *J. Sci. Comput.* **2011**, *46*, 20–46. [CrossRef]
29. Chen, C.; He, B.; Ye, Y.; Yuan, X. The direct extension of ADMM for multi-block convex minimization problems is not necessarily convergent. *Math. Program.* **2016**, *155*, 57–79. [CrossRef]
30. Chen, Z.; Zhuang, X. Proxiaml Alternating Direction Method of Multipliers for Quadratic Programming with Sparsity Constraint. Working Paper. 2018. Available online: https://dwz.cn/Nvpn24Wp (accessed on 3 July 2019).
31. Chen, Z.; Liu, J.; Hui, Y. Recursive risk measures under regime switching applied to portfolio selection. *Quant. Financ.* **2017**, *17*, 1457–1476. [CrossRef]
32. Chekhlov, A.; Uryasev, S.; Zabarankin, M. Drawdown measure in portfolio optimization. *Int. J. Theor. Appl. Financ.* **2005**, *8*, 13–58. [CrossRef]

10

Why are Warrant Markets Sustained in Taiwan but not in China?

Wing-Keung Wong [1,2,3,4], Hooi Hooi Lean [5], Michael McAleer [6,7,8,9,10] and Feng-Tse Tsai [6,*]

[1] Department of Finance, Fintech Center, and Big Data Research Center, Asia University, Taichung City 41354, Taiwan; wong@asia.edu.tw
[2] Department of Medical Research, China Medical University Hospital, Taichung City 404, Taiwan
[3] Department of Economics and Finance, Hang Seng Management College, Hong Kong, China
[4] Department of Economics, Lingnan University, Hong Kong, China
[5] Economics Program, School of Social Sciences, Universiti Sains Malaysia, 11800 Gelugor, Malaysia; hooilean@usm.my
[6] Department of Finance, Asia University, Taichung City 41354, Taiwan; michael.mcaleer@gmail.com
[7] Discipline of Business Analytics, University of Sydney Business School, Sydney, NSW 2006, Australia
[8] Econometric Institute, Erasmus School of Economics, Erasmus University Rotterdam, 3062 PA Rotterdam, The Netherlands
[9] Department of Quantitative Economics, Complutense University of Madrid, 28040 Madrid, Spain
[10] Institute of Advanced Sciences, Yokohama National University, Yokohama 240-8501, Japan
* Correspondence: fttsai@gm.asia.edu.tw

Abstract: This paper uses moment analysis, capital asset pricing model (CAPM) statistics, stochastic dominance (SD) test, and volume analysis to investigating why the market for Taiwan warrants can be sustained but not in China. Our moment analysis shows that buying in China warrants has a higher likelihood of losses. Our CAPM analysis shows that both the Sharpe ratio and Jensen index for warrants from the Chinese market are too negative. The Treynor index shows that Chinese warrants are highly volatile. Our SD analysis shows that risk averters prefer to invest in Chinese warrants compared to Taiwanese warrants, implying that the warrant issuers prefer to issue Taiwanese warrants than Chinese warrants. Using volume analysis, the Chinese warrant market is much more active, implying more speculative activities in China than in Taiwan. All the above could lead to China's decision to close its warrant market. The findings in the paper are useful for academics, investors, and policy makers.

Keywords: moment analysis; CAPM statistics; stochastic dominance; volume analysis; arbitrage opportunity; market efficiency; warrants; China market; Taiwan market

---

1. Introduction

This paper compares investor preferences between the two largest warrant markets in Greater China, namely Mainland China and Taiwan. Both markets are politically, economically, and financially competitive, and always seem to be catching the eyes of the world. The comparison period was chosen such that China was experiencing reforms and opening up the securities market, while Taiwan was in the process of party rotation and economic transformation.

Warrants are one of the most commonly traded financial products in financial markets internationally. China has been developing its stock markets very well, to be one of the largest stock markets in the world, while the Taiwanese stock market is much smaller, being ranked in the top 20 stock exchanges, according to various international databases (see, for example, http://www.visualcapitalist.com/20-largest-stock-exchanges-world/). On the other hand, the market for warrants, which was initiated in 1997, is financially successful in Taiwan, while the market for warrants in China, which was initiated in 2004, was prevalent in Mainland China, especially in 2006, but closed in 2010. For this reason, among others, it is interesting to study why the market of warrants in China was prevalent in Mainland China, especially in 2006, but closed in 2010.

Most of the warrants traded in China by the end of 2008 were covered warrants, connected with the flotation of non-tradable shares (the Chinese share reform started in 2005, with two share types, tradable shares and non-tradable shares, before the reform). The unique characteristics of Chinese warrants and irrational investor behavior in the Chinese warrant market are important in the financial literature. Therefore, it is interesting to study investor performance and risk preference in the Chinese warrant market. In the case of warrants in China, the warrants can be calls or puts.

When call options are exercised by investors, non-tradable shares are issued by the Chinese company, leaving the total number of outstanding shares unchanged. Therefore, there is no issue about dilution of earnings when warrants are exercised. In this aspect, warrants in China are similar to covered warrants in Europe and Asia. However, covered warrants in Europe and Asia are issued by third parties, such as banks, whereas in China, most warrants are issued by separate companies.

After the stock reforms in 2005, China's equity warrants market became the second largest in the world in terms of trading value, after Germany, surpassing Hong Kong in 2006. The growth in the warrants market in China has been constrained by the gradual expiration of reform-related warrants, excessive speculation, and a lack of understanding of the warrants market by its participants. The mechanism for creating special warrants designed as a transition to the development of covered warrants has been under hot debate. A more refined regulatory framework and a stronger institutional investor base are needed, and are prerequisites for a smoothly-functioning warrants market.

In order to foster the long-term development of the warrants market in China, financial experts have argued that issuing covered warrants is crucial, together with proper regulation. Domestic brokerages and exchanges have been lobbying the Chinese government to approve the issuance of covered warrants in a more formal setting. Securities firms argue that allowing brokers to launch covered warrants will significantly boost supply. That is, it is expected that the covered warrants will help in pricing securities more efficiently, thereby increasing the market depth of both the warrant and underlying stock markets. At the same time, it may effectively help curb the current speculative sentiment in China's financial markets.

The split-share structure was a legacy of China's initial share issue privatization (SIP), in which state-owned enterprises (SOEs) went public to issue minority tradable shares to institutional and individual investors. On the other hand, the Chinese government withheld control of these listed SOEs by owning majority non-tradable shares. Although the split-share structure played a positive role in facilitating the SIP, it jeopardized China's continued privatization efforts by restricting the tradability of state-owned shares in the secondary market, and also caused serious corporate governance problems, encouraged speculation in the stock market, and blocked mergers and acquisitions.

In 2005, the Split-Share Structure Reform was initiated to dismantle the dual share structure by converting non-tradable shares into tradable shares. The reform effectively removed the legal and technical obstacles of transferring state-owned shares to public investors, opening up the gate to China's secondary privatization which, in contrast to the initial SIP, would further liberalize state-owned shares in full circulation.

However, there have been very few studies, if any, comparing the Chinese and Taiwanese warrant markets in which both the main participants of securities markets are individual investors or corporate investors. The Taiwanese warrant market was established in 1997, while the Chinese warrant market began in 2004. The background of the developing warrant market in Taiwan is to provide diversified investment and hedging tools compared with a tool of compensation in the share reforms in China. The Chinese warrant market became the largest warrant market in the world in terms of trading volume in 2006, shortly after its inception. In 2006, the Taiwanese warrant market was ranked at number 9 according to the total trading volume provided by the World Federation of Exchanges (WFE).

Although Greater China shares a common culture, the background of developing warrant markets are different in China and Taiwan. In the period 2004 to 2008, Taiwan's economy faced a huge problem because of industry transformation, with many entrepreneurs moving their factories to Mainland China. In addition, Taiwan experienced the first party transition and the ruling party was politically against Chinese authority, while Mainland China was devoted to the reform and opened its market at the same time. Therefore, in addition to political competition between Taiwan and Mainland China, the two economies were also facing industrial competition. Economic development will be reflected in the performance of the securities markets. Among other reasons, it will be interesting to compare the warrant markets in China and Taiwan.

In order to compare the Chinese and Taiwanese warrant markets, there are several differences that are worth mentioning. First, China developed its warrant market in 2004 mainly for the purpose of the share-split reform, which was intended to allow government-held non-tradable shares to become tradable in the market. In order to make up possible losses of original tradable shareholders, some corporations issued warrants and granted these warrants as compensation. However, the warrants in Taiwan and Hong Kong are issued by third parties, that is, securities corporations, and not by the corporations themselves. Securities corporations issue warrants, sell them to investors, and hedge by buying underlying stocks. Second, the Taiwanese warrant market was established in 1997, 7 years earlier than the Chinese warrant market.

In addition, they also play roles of market makers to facilitate market liquidity. In China, corporations themselves issue warrants based on their non-tradable stocks as underlying stocks, and neither hedge nor play as market makers. Third, the number of issued warrants in the two markets differs substantially. In China, there were only 55 warrants traded in the market, but the trading volume was once ranked as the largest in the world. In Taiwan, the warrant market experienced rises and falls, and currently there are more than 10 thousand warrants issued every year. Moreover, Taiwan has both vanilla and exotic types of warrants, while China has only vanilla-type warrants.

Finally, the transaction mechanism in the two markets are different. In Taiwan, trading warrants are similar to trading stocks in terms of trading rules and transaction costs. However, it is distinct from trade stocks and trade warrants in China. The detailed mechanism of the Chinese warrant market is described below.

The Chinese warrant market attracted a lot of funds from investors and became the largest in the world in terms of total trading volume, even though there were only 55 warrants in the market. The high turnover of warrants in China could be attributed to the warrants "T+0" trading rule, high volatility, and exemption from transaction taxes. Warrants were the only security in China with a "T+0" trading mechanism, that is, investors are able to sell warrants on the same trading day when they are purchased. On the other hand, stocks could only be sold on the next trading day (that is, the "T+1" rule).

Additionally, stock prices are restricted to fluctuate within 10% of the closing price on the previous trading day, while the range was usually over 25% of the closing price for the warrant on the preceding trading day. Moreover, trading in warrants was exempted from the 0.2% to 0.3% transaction tax or stamp duty, and hence trading warrants benefits from a tax advantage. These special characteristics provided greater flexibility for investors on trading warrants. Therefore, warrants were the only securities for intraday trading, and hence attracted significant trading activities.

In this paper, we bridge a gap in the literature by using moment analysis, CAPM statistics, SD test, and volume analysis to examine investor preferences for warrants between China and Taiwan, and investigate why the market for Taiwan warrants can be sustained but not in China. Using moment analysis, buying Chinese warrants has a much higher opportunity for making losses as compared with Taiwan. This could make investors avoid investing in Chinese warrants which, in turn, could lead to the closure of the market for warrants.

Using CAPM analysis, we conclude that, in general, both the Sharpe ratio and Jensen index for warrants from the Taiwanese market are more attractive financially, while the Chinese market is too negative. On the other hand, the Treynor index for Chinese warrants shows that they are highly volatile. Therefore, China closed its warrant market after the end of the share-split reform, where the warrants expired completely in 2010.

Based on SD analysis, it can be inferred that there are no arbitrage opportunities between the Chinese and Taiwanese warrant markets, the markets of Chinese and Taiwanese warrants are not efficient, and second- and third-order risk averters prefer to invest in China compared with Taiwan. This implies that warrant issuers prefer to Taiwanese warrants to their counterparts in China. This could be another reason why the market for Taiwanese warrants can be sustained but not in China.

Using volume analysis, the Chinese warrant market is clearly much more active than the Taiwanese warrant market. This could imply that there are more speculative activities in China than in Taiwan which, in turn, could lead to China's decision to close its warrant market. The findings in the paper are important for investors for their investment decisions regarding Taiwanese and Chinese warrants, challenging to academics for their study on modeling Taiwan and China warrants, and useful for policy makers for their policy making related to Taiwan and China warrants. In the future, China should seriously reconsider reopening its warrant market and learning from mature-covered warrant markets, such as Taiwan's, on how to inhibit excess speculation and to educate warrant investors.

The remainder of the paper is organized as follows. Section 2 briefly reviews the literature pertaining to covered warrants and the stochastic dominance rules, as well as the rationale behind the SD tests. The data, sample characteristics, and methodology are discussed in Section 3. The empirical results are analysed in Section 4, while Section 5 gives some concluding remarks.

2. Literature Review

Many studies have investigated Chinese and Taiwanese warrant markets. For example, Xiong and Yu [1] find that the daily trading volume of many warrants is more than 3 times that of the issuance volume, even though this put warrants extremely out of money between 2005 and 2008. The market is useful for examining price bubbles because of observable underlying stock prices and the limited life of the warrants to determine the values of the associated contingent claims. Bubbles can be used to test bubble theories, such as rational bubbles, agency problems, gambling behaviour, resale option theory, non-common knowledge of rationality, feedback loop theory, among other interesting topics. The authors conclude that short selling restrictions and heterogeneous beliefs drive bubbles.

Some previous studies have focused on issuance, hedging, and expiration effects of warrants on stock returns [2–5]. For example, Chung et al. [5] examine the impact of covered warrant hedging on underlying stocks on the Taiwan Stock Exchange. They find significant positive abnormal returns and trading volume before the announcement of issuing warrants, especially for large hedging demand warrants. Their findings show that stock return volatility is positively related to the price elasticity of hedging demand.

Additionally, the authors discover a significant negative effect on stock prices after a call warrant has expired in-the-money because of the liquidation of the hedging portfolio. In China, Liao and Chen [4] find that the expiration of call warrants has a significantly negative price effect during the last four days of the exercise period, whereas the expiration of put warrants exhibits no significant price effects. Overall, the trading activities of call warrants have a more profound effect than their put counterparts around the expiration day.

Previous studies have also compared the prices of warrants and options with the same underlying stocks. For instance, Li and Zhang [6] and Chan and Pinder [7] find derivative warrants generally have higher prices than corresponding options, with the price differences reflecting the liquidity premiums of derivative warrants over options in the Hong Kong and Australian markets, respectively. Horst and Veld [8] compare the price differences between 16 Euronext Amsterdam options and warrants, and find that investors may perceive warrants as another type of instrument, and that the warrants are over-priced over the first five trading days.

Bartram and Fehle [9] examine the degree of the bid-ask spread between warrants and options in Germany, and find that, with overlapped underlying, both warrants and options experienced lower bid-ask spreads due to competition between options and warrants. Petrella [10] examines the bid-ask spread of covered warrants in Italy, and finds that the reservation spread plays an important role in determining the warrant spreads that are connected with the underlying spreads.

As the Chinese warrant market is relatively young and speculative, investors have largely participated in the market for its special characteristics, namely the speculative behaviour of retail investors in Chinese warrant markets [1]. Additionally, speculative activities in the warrant market can be contagious and spill over across stock markets [11]. Tang and Wang [12] examine warrant return properties, volatility behaviour, and pricing errors, and document a stylized fact that call warrants have considerable linkage with their underlying financial assets, but put warrants have almost none.

The combination of the arbitrage pricing theory and the resale-option bubble theory proposed by Scheinkman and Xiong [13] is adopted to explain this stylized fact. In addition, Liao et al. [14] examine the incidence of two types of irrational exercise behaviour in the Chinese warrants market and find that 121.64 million shares of warrants were either exercised with an immediate loss, or failed to be exercised because of warrant holder ignorance and/or negligence of warrant mechanics.

Furthermore, several studies analysed pricing errors of warrants and hedging risks. For example, Chang et al. [15] find that the market price of warrants is far higher than the prices from Black–Scholes models using historical volatilities. In addition, warrant prices and their underlying stock prices are not monotonic, perfectly correlated, and follow option redundancy properties. Cumulative delta hedge profits for most mature warrants are negative, and these negative profits are mainly from volatility risks, trading value of put warrants, and market risk of call warrants.

Powers and Xiao [16] adopt three standard pricing models and document that put warrant market prices averaged 1.2 yuan more than model-generated prices (over-priced), while call warrant prices averaged 1.9 yuan less (under-priced). The authors explain the mispricing due to an implicit discount on the value of stocks when pricing warrants as investors take the potential burst of a stock market bubble into account and a premium on warrants to fulfill speculation purpose or tax advantage.

Liao et al. [17] observe that creation mechanics (that is, increasing the supply of securities) similar with the short-selling property is useful for reducing bubble issues in Chinese warrant markets but additional warrant supply can only reduce instead of eliminating bubbles. Fung et al. [18] review the development of the China warrants market, and highlight the issues of over-speculation and lacking of recognition of participants. The authors suggest that the market requires a more regulated structure and more institutional investors as the cornerstone of the market.

Some studies have applied mean variance (MV), CAPM, and SD to warrant markets. For example, Chan et al. [19] examine in the UK covered warrants market by using SD. Their empirical results show that neither covered warrants nor their underlying shares stochastically dominate each other, implying both markets are efficient. They also find that UK covered warrant returns efficiently reflect the return information of the underlying shares from a likelihood ratio (LR) test. As distinct from their analysis on warrants and their underlying shares, we compare warrants in the Chinese and Taiwanese markets with similarities (for example, retail investors are main market participants) and differences (for example, the issuers are share-reform companies in China and securities companies in Taiwan) in terms of stochastic dominance.

A variety of interesting papers have applied the MV rule, CAPM statistics, and SD tests to examine the performance of other markets. For example, applying the SD test and other techniques, Abid et al. [20] investigate the performance of different option strategies; Qiao et al. [21,22] and Lean et al. [23,24] evaluate the relationship between spot and futures prices; Bouri et al. [25] study the role of wine investment within a portfolio of different assets; Qiao and Wong [26] and Tsang et al. [27] examine whether the housing market in Hong Kong is efficient; Hoang et al. [28–30] and Khamlichi et al. [31] examine the role of gold in the diversification of portfolios; Vieito et al. [32] and Zhu et al. [33] investigate whether the financial crisis had any positive impacts on stock markets; Broll et al. [34,35] analyse banks behaviour; Egozcue and Wong [36], Egozcue et al. [37], Abid et al. [38], and Lozza et al. [39] examine investor behaviour in diversification; Fong et al. [40,41] and Lean et al. [42] study investor behaviour in stock markets; Ma and Wong [43], Alghalith et al. [44], Guo et al. [45], and Niu et al. [46] examine different risk measures; and Chiang et al. [47] and Lean et al. [48] evaluate the performance of different funds.

3. Data and Methodology

3.1. Data

The warrant data are obtained from the Taiwan Economic Journal (TEJ). There are 55 warrants listed in the Shanghai and Shenzen Stock Exchanges between 2005 and 2009 (65 warrants were issued in the period, but only 55 of them were listed). For comparison, we randomly select 44 covered warrants of which the underlying stocks are in the list of the Taiwan 50 index in the same period (from 2005 to 2009, 44 of the top 50 Taiwan companies were issued corresponding warrants) (Since the listed Chinese warrants belong to large firms in China, we choose the warrants of the largest 50 firms from Taiwan 50 index constituents for comparison. However, in the corresponding period of Chinese warrants, there were only 44 firms in Taiwan with warrants issued. Thus, we randomly select 1 warrant for each firm (in Taiwan, all securities companies can issue warrants for the same firm and hence one firm can have more than 1 warrant)). The daily data include tickers, warrant prices, underlying stock prices, adjusted strike prices, data dates, issuance dates, maturity dates, and others. The conclusions are drawn based on the selected data.

Chinese and Taiwanese warrants are denoted by C and T, respectively. As there are too many warrants in both the Chinese and Taiwanese markets, we follow Wong et al. [49] in selecting the most representative warrants that have the maximum and minimum values of the of mean, standard deviation, and Sharpe ratio for both China and Taiwan. In addition, we include the maximum and minimum of the beta value, Jensen index, and Treynor index for both China and Taiwan.

The China warrants are denoted as: C06 for the minimum Sharpe ratio; C12 for the maximum Treynor index; C14 for the minimum mean and the minimum Jensen index; C23 for the maximum mean, the maximum Sharpe ratio, and the maximum Jensen index; C44 for the minimum standard deviation; C47 for the maximum standard deviation and the minimum beta value; C52 for the maximum beta value; and C55 for the minimum Treynor index.

The Taiwanese warrants are denoted as: T1 for the minimum Jensen index; T12 for the maximum standard deviation; T13 for the minimum mean; T15 for the minimum Sharpe ratio; T17 for the minimum standard deviation, the maximum Sharpe ratio, the minimum beta value, and the maximum Treynor index; T25 for the minimum Treynor index; T26 for the maximum beta value; and T33 for the maximum mean and the maximum Jensen index.

3.2. Methodology

In this paper, we use the MV rule, CAPM statistics, SD test, and volume analysis to examine the investor preferences towards the warrants between China and Taiwan. We first discuss the MV rule in the following subsection.

3.2.1. Mean-Variance (MV) Criteria

Define U_j as the set of utility functions such that:

$$U_j = \{u : (-1)^{i+1} u^{(i)} \geq 0, i = 1, \cdots, j\} \tag{1}$$

where $u^{(i)}$ is the ith derivative of the utility function U.

For the returns Y and Z of any two assets or portfolios with means μ_y and μ_z and standard deviations σ_y and σ_z, respectively, the MV rule (Markowitz [50]; Bai, et al. [51]; Leung, et al. [52]) is such that Y is said to dominate Z if $\mu_y \geq \mu_z$ and $\sigma_y \leq \sigma_z$, and if the inequality holds in at least one of the two conditions. Wong [53] and Guo and Wong [54] show that if Y dominates Z by the MV rule, denoted by $Y \succ_{MV} Z$, then risk averters with $u^{(1)} > 0$ and $u^{(2)} < 0$ will attain higher expected utility by holding Y than Z under certain conditions. The theory can be extended to non-differentiable utilities (see Wong and Ma, [55]).

3.2.2. Stochastic Dominance (SD) Approach

Let Y and Z represent the returns of two assets or portfolios with a common support of $\Omega = [a, b]$ ($a < b$), cumulative distribution functions (CDFs), F and G, and corresponding probability density functions (PDFs), f and g, respectively, so that we define:

$$H_0 = h, H_j(x) = \int_a^x H_{j-1}(t)dt \tag{2}$$

for $h = f,\ g$; $H = F,\ G$; for any integer j.

We call the integral H_j the jth-order integral for $H = F,\ G$. Y is said to dominate Z by FSD (SSD, TSD), denoted by $Y \succ_1 Z$ ($Y \succ_2 Z$, $Y \succ_3 Z$), if $F_1(x) \leq G_1(x)$ ($F_2(x) \leq G_2(x)$, $F_3(x) \leq G_3(x)$) for all possible returns x, and the strict inequality holds for at least one small open interval of x, where FSD (SSD, TSD) denotes first-order (second-order, third-order) SD, respectively. For $Y \succ_3 Z$, we need a further condition: $\mu_Y \geq \mu_Z$ (see Sriboonchitta et al. [56], Levy [57], Guo and Wong [54]), and the references listed therein, for further information on the SD definitions for any order.

The SD tests have been well developed (Davidson and Duclos, DD, [58]; Bai, et al. [59,60]; Ng, et al. [61]) to allow statistical significance to be determined. The SD test developed by DD is found to be powerful, less conservative in size, and robust to non-iid and heteroscedastic data (Lean et al., [62]). As Bai et al. [59] derive the limiting process of the DD statistic when the underlying processes are dependent or independent, we use their SD tests in the empirical analysis.

Let $\{f_i\}$ $(i = 1, 2, \cdots n_f)$ and $\{g_i\}$ $(i = 1, 2, \cdots n_g)$ be observations drawn from the returns of any two assets or portfolios, Y and Z, with CDFs F and G, respectively. For a grid of pre-selected points x_1, $x_2, \ldots x_k$, the jth-order SD test statistic, $T_j(x)$ (j = 1, 2, and 3), is defined as:

$$T_j(x) = \frac{\hat{F}_j(x) - \hat{G}_j(x)}{\sqrt{\hat{V}_j(x)}} \tag{3}$$

where

$$\hat{V}_j(x) = \hat{V}_{F_j}(x) + \hat{V}_{G_j}(x) - 2\hat{V}_{FG_j}(x); \hat{H}_j(x) = \frac{1}{N_h(j-1)!}\sum_{i=1}^{N_h}(x - h_i)_+^{j-1}, \tag{4}$$

$$\begin{aligned} \hat{V}_{H_j}(x) &= \tfrac{1}{N_h}\left[\tfrac{1}{N_h((j-1)!)^2}\sum_{i=1}^{N_h}(x-h_i)_+^{2(j-1)} - \hat{H}_j(x)^2\right],\ H = F, G;\ h = f, g; \\ \hat{V}_{FG_j}(x) &= \tfrac{1}{N_h}\left[\tfrac{1}{N_h((j-1)!)^2}\sum_{i=1}^{N_h}(x-f_i)_+^{j-1}(x-g_i)_+^{j-1} - \hat{F}_j(x)\hat{G}_j(x)\right], \end{aligned} \tag{5}$$

F_j and G_j are defined in (2). For all $i = 1, 2, \ldots, k$, we test the following hypotheses:

Hypothesis 1 (H1). $F_j(x_i) = G_j(x_i),\ for\ all\ x_i.$

Hypothesis 2 (H2). $F_j(x_i) \neq G_j(x_i)\ for\ some\ x_i.$

Hypothesis 3 (H3). $F_j(x_i) \leq G_j(x_i)\ for\ all\ x_i,\ F_j(x_i) < G_j(x_i)\ for\ some\ x_i.$

Hypothesis 4 (H4). $F_j(x_i) \geq G_j(x_i)$ *for all* x_i, $F_j(x_i) > G_j(x_i)$ *for some* x_i.

Not rejecting either H1 or H2 implies the non-existence of any SD relationship between Y and Z. If H3 (H4) of order one is accepted, then $Y(Z)$ stochastically dominates $Z(Y)$ at first order, denoted by $Y \succ_1 Z$ $(Z \succ_1 Y)$. If H3 (H4) is accepted at order two [three], then $Y(Z)$ stochastically dominates $Z(Y)$ at second order, denoted by $Y \succ_2 Z$ $(Z \succ_2 Y)$, $[Y \succ_3 Z$ $(Z \succ_3 Y)]$. Readers may refer to Bai et al. [59] for the decision rules and further information on the tests, and Chan et al. [63] for testing the third-order SD.

Bai et al. [59] derive the limiting process of the SD statistic $T_j(x)$ so that the SD test can be performed by using $\max_x |T_j(x)|$ to account for the dependency of the partitions. We follow their recommendation in the empirical analysis. As Fong et al. [41], Lean et al. [48,62], among others, recommend a limited number (100) of grids for comparison, we adopt their suggestion. In order to minimize Type II errors and to accommodate the effect of almost SD (Leshno and Levy [64]; Guo, et al. [65–67]), we follow Gasbarro et al. [68], Clark et al. [69], among others, to use a conservative 5% cut-off point in examining the proportion of test statistics to draw inferences.

4. Empirical Results

This section discusses the empirical results. We use moment analysis, CAPM statistics, SD test, and volume analysis to examine investor preferences for warrants between China and Taiwan, and investigate why the market for Taiwanese warrants can be sustained but not in China. We note that the moment analysis (Chan et al. [70]) includes the mean-variance (MV) rule and the analysis of higher-order moments.

4.1. Moments Analysis

The MV rule is used to examine the performance between Chinese and Taiwanese warrants. In order to do so, we examine the descriptive statistics of daily excess returns in Table 1 and the results of the t and F tests in Table 2 for selected Chinese and Taiwanese warrants.

Table 1. Summary statistics and CAPM using daily excess returns for selected Chinese and Taiwanese warrants.

Warrant Code	Mean	Std. Dev.	Skewness	Kurtosis	JB	Sharpe	Beta	Treynor	Jensen
C06	−0.0201	0.0781	−3.7196	33.9411	10084.75	−0.2579	0.0150	−1.3384	−0.0186
C12	−0.0186	0.1440	−13.0898	242.2479	1160912.00	−0.1294	−0.0009	20.5741	−0.0183
C14	−0.0638	0.2956	−8.3235	80.9023	30407.42	−0.2157	−0.0059	10.8959	−0.0624
C23	0.0011	0.0555	0.4351	5.1238	52.02	0.0204	0.0175	0.0647	−0.0056
C44	−0.0057	0.0300	2.7879	24.6026	6885.69	−0.1527	0.0115	−0.4943	−0.0058
C47	−0.0365	0.3155	−13.5417	197.7772	377048.90	−0.1158	−0.0174	2.0965	−0.0298
C52	−0.0270	0.2297	−13.2963	195.6075	373322.80	−0.1175	0.0397	−0.6796	−0.0405
C55	−0.0189	0.1171	−2.2507	29.5247	7117.58	−0.1615	0.0003	−60.9548	−0.0190
T1	−0.0511	0.2409	−0.4242	12.6574	454.26	−0.2121	0.0814	−0.6280	−0.0565
T12	−0.0341	0.4486	−0.0494	20.9576	1679.60	−0.0760	0.0289	−1.1812	−0.0307
T13	−0.0573	0.2730	1.3731	15.5192	800.82	−0.2100	0.0232	−2.4702	−0.0560
T15	−0.0374	0.1388	−2.2828	22.0487	2925.68	−0.2693	0.0225	−1.6632	−0.0343
T17	0.0053	0.0588	1.9440	11.7270	475.41	0.0892	0.0056	0.9310	0.0037
T25	−0.0434	0.1742	0.2863	11.0227	336.94	−0.2491	0.0103	−4.2091	−0.0441
T26	−0.0032	0.2247	0.9245	5.1186	41.19	−0.0144	0.1324	−0.0245	−0.0109
T33	0.0128	0.1545	−1.0409	10.6930	320.22	0.0829	0.0523	0.2451	0.0094

Notes: C06—min Sharpe; C12—max Treynor; C14—min mean, min Jensen; C23—max mean, max Sharpe & max Jensen; C44—min s.d.; C47—max s.d., min beta; C52—max beta; C55—min Treynor; T1—min Jensen; T12—max s.d.; T13—min mean; T15—min Sharpe; T17—min s.d., max Sharpe, min beta, max Treynor; T25—min Treynor; T26—max beta; T33—max mean & max Jensen.

Table 2. MV Results for selected pairwise comparison.

Pairwise Comparison	*t* Test	*F* Test	MV Dominance
C14-T13	$\mu_C < \mu_T$ −0.1474	$\sigma_C > \sigma_T$ 1.1529	No
C23-T33	$\mu_C < \mu_T$ −1.041	$\sigma_C < \sigma_T$ 7.7611 ***	C23 $\succ_{MV}$ T33
C44-T17	$\mu_C < \mu_T$ −2.6106 ***	$\sigma_C < \sigma_T$ 3.8564 ***	No
C47-T12	$\mu_C < \mu_T$ −0.0597	$\sigma_C < \sigma_T$ 2.0222 ***	C47 $\succ_{MV}$ T12
C06-T15	$\mu_C > \mu_T$ 1.6191	$\sigma_C < \sigma_T$ 3.1598 ***	C06 $\succ_{MV}$ T15
C23-T17	$\mu_C < \mu_T$ −0.6578	$\sigma_C < \sigma_T$ 1.1249	No
C47-T17	$\mu_C < \mu_T$ −1.4663	$\sigma_C > \sigma_T$ 28.7523 ***	C47 $\succ_{MV}$ T17
C52-T26	$\mu_C < \mu_T$ −0.9425	$\sigma_C > \sigma_T$ 1.0449	No
C55-T25	$\mu_C < \mu_T$ 1.5869	$\sigma_C < \sigma_T$ 2.2131 ***	C55 $\succ_{MV}$ T25
C12-T17	$\mu_C < \mu_T$ −1.8125 *	$\sigma_C > \sigma_T$ 5.9872 ***	T17 $\succ_{MV}$ C12
C23-T01	$\mu_C > \mu_T$ 3.1743 ***	$\sigma_C < \sigma_T$ 18.8615 ***	C23 $\succ_{MV}$ T01
C14-T33	$\mu_C < \mu_T$ −2.4578 **	$\sigma_C > \sigma_T$ 3.5309 ***	T33 $\succ_{MV}$ C14

Notes: C14-T13 is the pair of mean min, C23-T33 is the pair of mean max; C44-T17 is the pair of s.d min, C47-T12 is the pair of s.d max; C06-T15 is the pair of Sharpe ratio min, C23-T17 is the pair of Sharpe ratio max; C47-T17 is the pair of beta min, C52-T26 is the pair of beta max; C55-T25 is the pair of Treynor ratio min, C12-T17 is the pair of Treynor ratio max; C23-T01 is the pair of Jensen ratio min, C14-T33 is the pair of Jensen ratio max. ***, ** and * denotes significant at 1%, 5% and 10% levels respectively.

We compare warrants with minimum daily excess returns from China and Taiwan, which are represented by C14 and T13, respectively. From Table 1, the mean excess return of T13 is higher than that of C14, while the standard deviation of the former is smaller. However, the insignificant t and F statistics in Table 2 conclude there is no MV dominance between T13 and C14 using the MV approach. We also compare warrants with maximum daily excess returns from China and Taiwan, which are represented by C23 and T33, respectively. Although T33 has larger mean excess returns, it also has a higher standard deviation than C23. Therefore, there is no MV dominance between T33 and C23 using the MV approach.

Next we compare warrants with minimum (maximum) daily standard deviations from China and Taiwan, which are represented by C44 and T17 (C47 and T12), respectively. It is found that T17 has significantly higher mean excess return and significantly higher standard deviation than C44, so there is no MV dominance between T33 and C23 using the MV approach. However, T12 has insignificantly higher mean excess return and significantly higher standard deviation than C47, implying that C47 dominates T12 using the MV approach. With the MV criterion, we find that five pairs of China warrants dominate Taiwan warrants, and three pairs of Taiwanese warrants dominate Chinese warrants. The other four pairs have not shown any dominance between Chinese and Taiwanese warrants.

Tables 1 and 2 indicate the following. First, the mean excess returns are, in general, higher for Taiwanese warrants, while most of the mean excess returns for both Chinese and Taiwanese warrants are negative, which implies that the mean excess returns of Chinese warrants are more negative.

This could make investors avoid investing in Chinese warrants which, in turn, could lead to the closure of the Chinese warrant market.

In addition, most of the Chin ese warrants are significant and negatively skewed, while most of the Taiwan ese warrants are either significantly and positively skewed or are not significantly skewed.

4.2. CAPM Analysis

For the CAPM statistics, the Sharpe ratio that measures the excess return per unit of risk is the conventional formula for stock evaluation where the risk is determined by the standard deviation. The higher the Sharpe ratio, the better the portfolio return is relative to risk, or the larger the excess return is per unit of risk in a portfolio. All Sharpe ratios are negative, except for C23, T17, and T33, while the Sharpe ratio of T17 is higher than all the eight selected warrants in China. Nearly all the Sharpe ratios are negative, which implies that, in general, investors are losing money in both Chinese and Taiwanese warrant markets.

The Sharpe ratio of T17 is higher than all the eight selected warrants in China. In general, the Sharpe ratio for warrants for Taiwan is higher than those in China, which indicates that Taiwanese warrants perform better than their counterparts in China. It can be concluded that, in general, the Sharpe ratio for warrants for Taiwan is more appealing, while that from China is too negative. This could make investors avoid investing in China warrants which, in turn, could lead to the closure of its market.

Similar to the Sharpe ratio, all Jensen indexes are also negative, except for T17 and T33. T33 has the highest Jensen index among all the warrants. A higher Jensen index suggests a higher level of return given the level of risk (systematic or market) on the investment. A low Jensen index, such as a negative number, indicates an inferior performance given the level of risk. The empirical findings that the values of the Jensen index for most warrants from both China and Taiwan are negative imply a poor performance of both warrant markets during the sample period. It is interesting that T33 is higher than all eight selected warrants in China. Nevertheless, the Jensen index of T1 (the Taiwan warrant with minimum Jensen index) is also larger than its counterpart in China, namely C14.

In general, the Jensen index for warrants for Taiwan is higher than in China, inferring that Taiwanese warrants perform better than Chinese warrants. Thus, we can conclude that, in general, the Jensen index for warrants for Taiwan is more appealing, while that from China is too negative. This could make investors avoid investing in Chinese warrants which, in turn, could lead to the closure of the market in China.

The Treynor ratio expresses the relationship of excess fund return, with the beta lying along the security market line taking account of the systematic risk or market volatility as its measure of risk, instead of the standard deviation, as in the Sharpe ratio. The Treynor index for China ranges from -61 to $+20$, indicating that Chinese warrants are very volatile. The higher volatility in the China warrants could make investors avoid investing in China warrants which, in turn, could lead to the closure of the market.

In summary, CAPM analysis demonstrates that Taiwanese warrants perform better than Chinese warrants in terms of the Sharpe ratio and Jensen index. In addition, the Chinese warrant market is volatile for investors according to the Treynor ratio. Therefore, China closed its warrant market after the end of the share-split reform, which expired completely in 2010. In the future, China might rethink reopening its warrant market and learning from mature-covered warrant markets, such as Taiwan, as to how it might be possible to inhibit excess speculation and to educate warrant investors.

4.3. SD Analysis

Table 3 reports the SD results based on the modified DD statistics. From the SD results, most of the Chinese warrants stochastically dominate Taiwanese warrants at the second and third orders, implying that risk averters prefer investing in Chinese warrants to Taiwanese warrants. However, there are still some pairs of Chinese and Taiwanese warrants that do not dominate each other. For example, for the pair of minimum mean return, C14 does not dominate T13 for any order. For the comparison among the maximum Jensen ratio, there is no SD between C14 and T33 for any order.

Table 3. SD Results for selected pairwise comparison.

Pairwise Comparison	Ascending SD
C14-T13	No SD
C23-T33	$C \succ_{2,3} T$
C44-T17	$C \succ_{2,3} T$
C47-T12	$C \succ_{2,3} T$
C06-T15	$C \succ_{2,3} T$
C23-T17	$C \succ_{2,3} T$
C47-T17	No SD
C52-T26	$C \succ_{2,3} T$
C55-T25	$C \succ_{2,3} T$
C12-T17	$C \succ_{2,3} T$
C23-T01	$C \succ_{2,3} T$
C14-T33	No SD

Notes: C14-T13 is the pair of mean min, C23-T33 is the pair of mean max; C44-T17 is the pair of s.d min, C47-T12 is the pair of s.d max; C06-T15 is the pair of Sharpe ratio min, C23-T17 is the pair of Sharpe ratio max; C47-T17 is the pair of beta min, C52-T26 is the pair of beta max; C55-T25 is the pair of Treynor ratio min, C12-T17 is the pair of Treynor ratio max; C23-T01 is the pair of Jensen ratio min, C14-T33 is the pair of Jensen ratio max.

In order to illustrate the SD relationship better, we plot the distributions of the excess returns, F and G, for Chinese and Taiwanese warrants, and the corresponding DD statistics for the pair of C23 and T33, as shown in Figure 1. From Figure 1, we find that F is below G for some negative returns, while G is below F for some positive returns, implying that the excess return in the Chinese warrant is preferred in the negative domain, while the excess return in the Taiwanese warrant is preferred in the positive domain. In addition, it is clear that the first-order DD statistic (T1) is negative when the returns are negative, and becomes positive when the returns are positive. These results imply that the excess return in the Chinese warrant is preferred in the negative return and the excess return in the Taiwanese warrant is preferred in the positive return. It is also worth noting that both the second- and third-order DD statistics (T2 and T3) are negative, with some regions being significant.

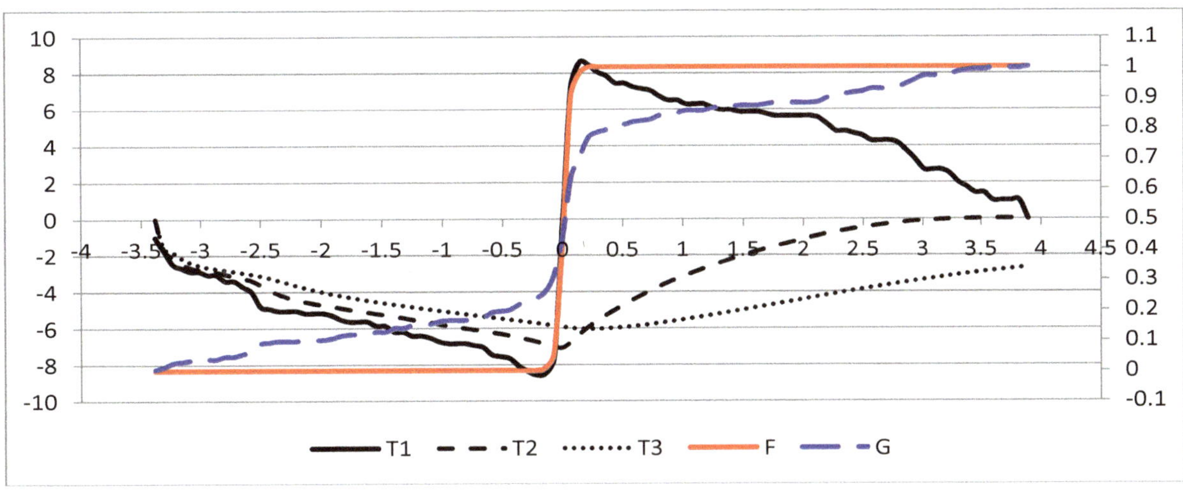

Figure 1. Ascending DD statistics distribution for C23-T33. Note: T_j is the test statistic defined in (3) for $j = 1, 2$ and 3. F and G are the CDFs of the excess warrant returns for C23 and T33, respectively.

In general, all investors with increasing utility functions prefer the negative excess return in Chinese warrants and prefer the positive excess return in Taiwanese warrants. For these reasons, there is no first-order SD between Chinese and Taiwanese warrants, and no arbitrage opportunity (see Guo et al. [71] and the references listed therein for further information) in the markets for Chinese and Taiwanese warrants.

However, Chinese warrants dominate Taiwanese warrants at the second and third orders, implying that second- and third-order risk averters prefer to invest in China as compared with Taiwan. This implies that the markets for Chinese and Taiwanese warrants are not efficient if investors are risk averters (see Qiao et al. [21], Clark et al. [69], and the references cited therein, for further information).

It can be concluded that Chinese warrants could be underpriced, so that it is more difficult for Chinese warrant issuers to make profits. This could be one of the main reasons why the market for Chinese warrants is not sustainable. Another reason that China presently has no warrant market is that the warrants issued by companies were used for compensation in the share reform from 2004 to 2008, and they expired in 1 to 2 years. China closed its warrants market because of the gradual expiration of reform-related warrants, excessive speculation, and lack of understanding of the warrants market by its participants.

4.4. Volume Analysis

We further examine the market activities between the Chinese and Taiwanese warrants. To do so, we analyse the daily trading volumes of Chinese and Taiwanese warrants that were selected in Section 3.1. In order to make the comparison practical, we convert both currencies in USD and exhibit the daily trading dollar value when the prices are in USD. These results are presented in Table 4 for Chinese and Taiwanese warrants.

Table 4. Summary statistics of trading volume (in USD) for selected Chinese and Taiwanese warrants.

Warrant Code	Mean	Std. Dev.	Skewness	Kurtosis	JB
C06	96,150.9500	73,283.1200	2.1843	10.0706	690.7704
C12	173,603.0000	324,388.6000	3.4949	17.0166	4926.9010
C14	46,306.6400	44,987.5000	1.8837	7.1179	150.5576
C23	55,458.4900	46,573.7300	1.9508	8.4068	440.8489
C44	214,101.4000	178,940.0000	1.9563	7.5217	718.0678
C47	40,012.9900	40,078.6000	2.3406	10.4683	760.7066
C52	59,475.6700	51,874.5500	2.4878	10.7968	848.3305
C55	48,996.5800	60,061.5300	3.2302	16.5166	2216.2940
T1	15.3537	103.6143	10.5616	113.3553	61,544.3700
T12	18.4588	72.0669	9.8558	105.4079	57,098.5700
T13	25.7770	127.7570	10.4158	111.5797	60,098.8800
T15	11.4235	75.4091	13.2409	178.1744	240,636.5000
T17	0.1405	0.4666	4.8718	29.5315	4194.0060
T25	37.7894	74.4648	2.3908	8.2631	265.4654
T26	79.8744	149.2158	7.2949	69.3507	24,230.2100
T33	107.3186	117.9072	2.8163	14.5546	839.9515

From Table 4, we find that the average daily trading volume of most Chinese warrants is of order 105, while that of most Taiwanese warrants are of the order 102. The average daily trading volume of individual Chinese warrants is 103 times greater than that of individual Taiwanese warrants. Thus, it can be concluded that the Chinese warrant market is much more active than its Taiwanese counterpart.

In China, there were only 55 warrants traded in the market, but the trading volume was once ranked the highest in the world. In Taiwan, the warrant market has experienced rises and falls, but there are currently more than 10 thousand warrants issued every year. Although the total trading volumes of warrants in China and Taiwan are the highest in the world, China had far fewer warrants than Taiwan. Thus, it is not surprising that the trading volume for "each warrant" in China is much greater than in Taiwan. Investors in China prefer warrants to stocks because of trading rules and transaction costs, as mentioned in Section 1. Thus, they are keen to trade fewer warrants available in the market, and hope to chase for the prices of warrants (Xiong and Yu, [1]). In other words, the Chinese warrant market is predominantly speculative, which can cause a greater number of trades.

5. Concluding Remarks

Academics, practitioners, and policy makers are interested in examining why the warrant market in China is not sustainable. In order to study this phenomenon, Fung et al. [18] point out the issues of over-speculation and lack of recognition of participants. Liao and Chen [4] determine that the expiration of call warrants have a significantly negative price effect during the last few days of the sample period. Xiong and Yu [1] find that the daily trading volume of many warrants is more than 3 times of the issuance volume.

Chang et al. [15] discovered that the market price of warrants is far higher than the prices from Black–Scholes models using historical volatilities. Liao et al. [14] find that 121.64 million shares of warrants were either exercised with an immediate loss, or failed to be exercised. Powers and Xiao [16] show that put warrant market prices averaged 1.2 yuan more than model-generated prices (over-priced), while call warrant prices averaged 1.9 yuan less (under-priced).

In this paper, we bridge a gap in the literature by using moment analysis, CAPM statistics, SD test, and volume analysis to examine investor preferences towards warrants between China and Taiwan, and investigate why the market for warrants in China is not sustainable while the market for Taiwanese warrants is succeeding.

Using moment analysis, we find that the mean excess returns are, in general, higher for Taiwanese warrants, while most of the mean excess returns for Chinese warrants are negative. In addition, most of the Chinese warrants have more significant and negative skewness, and significant and greater kurtosis than Taiwanese warrants. This information implies that buying Chinese warrants has a much higher chance for sustaining losses than Taiwanese warrants. This could make investors avoid investing in Chinese warrants which, in turn, could lead to the closure of the market for Chinese warrants.

Using CAPM analysis, the Sharpe ratio for warrants for Taiwan is higher than for China, and the Jensen index for warrants in Taiwan is higher than in China, inferring that Taiwan warrants perform better than China warrants. In general, both the Sharpe ratio and Jensen index for warrants for Taiwan are more attractive, while those for China are too negative. This could make investors avoid investing in Chinese warrants which, in turn, could lead to the closure of the market for Chinese warrants. On the other hand, the Treynor index for Chinese warrants shows that they are very volatile which, in turn, could also lead to the closure of the market of Chinese warrants.

In summary, CAPM analysis demonstrates that Taiwanese warrants perform better than Chinese warrants in terms of the Sharpe ratio and Jensen index. In addition, the Chinese warrant market is volatile for investors, according to the Treynor ratio. Therefore, China closed its warrant market after the end of the share-split reform and the warrants expired completely in 2010. In the future, China might think about reopening its warrant market and learning from mature-covered warrant markets, such as Taiwan's, how to inhibit excess speculation and to educate warrant investors.

Using SD analysis, there are no arbitrage opportunities between the Chinese and Taiwanese warrant markets, but the warrant markets in China and Taiwan are not efficient because the Chinese warrant market dominates Taiwan at the second and third orders, implying that second-order and third-order risk averters prefer to invest in China compared with Taiwan. This implies that the warrant issuers prefer to issue Taiwanese warrants than Chinese warrants, which could be another reason why the warrant market in China is not sustainable.

Based on volume analysis, the empirical findings show that the average daily trading volume of individual Chinese warrants is 103 times higher than individual Taiwanese warrants, so that the Chinese warrant market is much more active than its counterpart in Taiwan. This would seem to suggest that there are more speculative activities in the China warrant market than the Taiwanese warrant market which, in turn, could lead to China's decision to close its warrant market.

Another reason for China presently having no warrant market is that warrants issued by companies were used for compensation in the share reform during the period of 2004 to 2008, which expired in 1–2 years. China closed the warrant market because of the gradual expiration of reform-related warrants, excessive speculation, and lack of understanding of the warrants market by its participants.

The findings in the paper are important for investors for their investment decisions regarding Taiwanese and Chinese warrants, challenging for academics in modelling Taiwanese and Chinese warrants, and useful for policy makers for their policy making related to Taiwanese warrants and Chinese warrants. In the future, China might rethink reopening its warrant market and learning from mature-covered warrant markets such as Taiwan how to inhibit excess speculation and to educate warrant investors.

The paper investigated the preferences of risk averters to invest in warrants between China and Taiwan. Extensions include using other tools to compare the preferences for risk averters to invest in warrants between China and Taiwan, as well as investigate the preferences of other types of investors (see Chang et al. [72–76] for further information).

We note that this paper is studying whether the warrant market is sustainable. There are many other studies investigating whether other markets are sustainable, see, for example, Moslehpour, et al. [77] and Li, et al. [78,79]. We also note that there could be many directions for further studies. One of them is to study the preference of other types investors, for example, investors with S-shaped and reversed S-shaped utility functions, see, for example, Wong and Chan [80] and the references therein for more information.

Author Contributions: The authors contributed equally to this work.

Acknowledgments: Wing-Keung Wong is grateful to the Research Grants Council of Hong Kong, Asia University, Hang Seng Management College, Lingnan University, and the Ministry of Science and Technology (MOST), Taiwan, and would also like to thank Robert B. Miller and Howard E. Thompson for their continuous guidance and encouragement. Michael McAleer wishes to thank the Australian Research Council and the Ministry of Science and Technology (MOST), Taiwan. Feng-Tse Tsai is grateful to the Ministry of Science and Technology of Taiwan and Asia University.

References

1. Xiong, W.; Yu, J. The Chinese warrants Bubble. *Am. Econ. Rev.* **2011**, *101*, 2723–2753. [CrossRef]
2. Draper, P.; Mak, B.S.C.; Tang, G.Y.N. The Derivative Warrant Market in Hong Kong: Relationships with Underlying Assets. *J. Deriv.* **2001**, *8*, 72–83. [CrossRef]
3. Aitken, M.; Segara, R. Impact of warrant introductions on the behaviour of underlying stocks: Australian evidence. *Account. Financ.* **2005**, *45*, 127–144. [CrossRef]
4. Liao, X.-H.; Chen, K.C. Expiration Effects of Covered Warrants in China. *Chin. Econ.* **2010**, *43*, 54–75. [CrossRef]
5. Chung, S.-L.; Liu, W.-R.; Tsai, W.-C. The impact of derivatives hedging on the stock market: Evidence from Taiwan's covered warrants market. *J. Bank. Financ.* **2014**, *42*, 123–133. [CrossRef]
6. Li, G.; Zhang, C. Why Are Derivative Warrants More Expensive Than Options? An Empirical Study. *J. Financ. Quant. Anal.* **2011**, *46*, 275–297. [CrossRef]
7. Chan, H.W.-H.; Pinder, S.M. The value of liquidity: Evidence from the derivatives market. *Pacific-Basin Financ. J.* **2000**, *8*, 483–503. [CrossRef]
8. Horst, J.T.; Veld, C. An Empirical Analysis of the Pricing of Bank Issued Options versus Options Exchange Options. *Eur. Financ. Manag.* **2008**, *14*, 288–314. [CrossRef]
9. Bartram, S.M.; Fehle, F. Competition without fungibility: Evidence from alternative market structures for derivatives. *J. Bank. Financ.* **2007**, *31*, 659–677. [CrossRef]

10. Petrella, G. Option bid-ask spread and scalping risk: Evidence from a covered warrants market. *J. Futures Mark.* **2006**, *26*, 843–867. [CrossRef]
11. Liu, Y.-J.; Zhang, Z.; Zhao, L. Speculation Spillovers. *Manag. Sci.* **2014**, *61*, 649–664. [CrossRef]
12. Tang, K.; Wang, C. Are China warrants derivatives? Evidence from connections to their underlying stocks. *Quant. Financ.* **2013**, *13*, 1225–1240. [CrossRef]
13. Scheinkman, J.A.; Xiong, W. Overconfidence and Speculative Bubbles. *J. Political Econ.* **2003**, *111*, 1183–1219. [CrossRef]
14. Liao, L.; Li, Z.; Zhang, W.; Zhu, N. Exercise to Lose Money? Irrational Exercise Behavior from the China warrants Market. *J. Futures Mark.* **2014**, *34*, 399–419. [CrossRef]
15. Chang, E.C.; Luo, X.; Shi, L.; Zhang, J.E. Is warrant really a derivative? Evidence from the China warrant market. *J. Financ. Mark.* **2013**, *16*, 165–193. [CrossRef]
16. Powers, E.; Xiao, G. Mispricing of China warrants. *Pac.-Basin Financ. J.* **2014**, *30*, 62–86. [CrossRef]
17. Liao, L.; Li, Z.; Zhang, W.; Zhu, N. *Security Supply and Bubbles: A Natural Experiment from the China Warrants Market*; Working Paper; Hsinghua University: Beijing, China, 2010.
18. Fung, H.-G.; Zhang, G.; Zhao, L. China's Equity Warrants Market: An Overview and Analysis. *Chin. Econ.* **2009**, *42*, 86–97. [CrossRef]
19. Chan, C.Y.; de Peretti, C.; Qiao, Z.; Wong, W.K. Empirical test of the efficiency of UK covered warrants market: Stochastic dominance and likelihood ratio test approach. *J. Empir. Financ.* **2012**, *19*, 162–174. [CrossRef]
20. Abid, F.; Mroua, M.; Wong, W.K. The Impact of Option Strategies in Financial Portfolios Performance: Mean-Variance and Stochastic Dominance Approaches. *Financ. India* **2009**, *23*, 503–526. [CrossRef]
21. Qiao, Z.; Clark, E.; Wong, W.K. Investors' Preference towards Risk: Evidence from the Taiwan Stock and Stock Index Futures Markets. *Account. Financ.* **2012**, *54*, 251–274. [CrossRef]
22. Qiao, Z.; Wong, W.K.; Fung, J.K.W. Stochastic Dominance Relationships between Stock and Stock Index Futures Markets: International Evidence. *Econ. Model.* **2013**, *33*, 552–559. [CrossRef]
23. Lean, H.H.; McAleer, M.; Wong, W.K. Market Efficiency of Oil Spot and Futures: A Mean-Variance and Stochastic Dominance Approach. *Energy Econ.* **2010**, *32*, 979–986. [CrossRef]
24. Lean, H.H.; McAleer, M.; Wong, W.K. Preferences of risk-averse and risk-seeking investors for oil spot and futures before, during and after the Global Financial Crisis. *Int. Rev. Econ. Financ.* **2015**, *40*, 204–216. [CrossRef]
25. Bouri, E.; Gupta, R.; Wong, W.K.; Zhu, Z.Z. Is Wine a Good Choice for Investment? *Pac.-Basin Financ. J.* **2018**, *51*, 171–183. [CrossRef]
26. Qiao, Z.; Wong, W.K. Which is a better investment choice in the Hong Kong residential property market: A big or small property? *Appl. Econ.* **2015**, *47*, 1670–1685. [CrossRef]
27. Tsang, C.K.; Wong, W.K.; Horowitz, I. Arbitrage Opportunities, Efficiency, and the Role of Risk Preferences in the Hong Kong Property Market. *Stud. Econ. Financ.* **2016**, *33*, 735–754. [CrossRef]
28. Hoang, T.H.V.; Lean, H.H.; Wong, W.K. Is gold good for portfolio diversification? A stochastic dominance analysis of the Paris stock exchange. *Int. Rev. Financ. Anal.* **2015**, *42*, 98–108. [CrossRef]
29. Hoang, T.H.V.; Wong, W.K.; Xiao, B.; Zhu, Z.Z. The seasonality of gold prices in China: Does the risk-aversion level matter? *Account. Financ.* **2018**, *58*. [CrossRef]
30. Hoang, T.H.V.; Wong, W.K.; Zhu, Z.Z. Is gold different for risk-averse and risk-seeking investors? An empirical analysis of the Shanghai Gold Exchange. *Econ. Model.* **2015**, *50*, 200–211. [CrossRef]
31. Khamlichi, A.E.; Hoang, T.H.V.; Wong, W.K.; Zhu, Z.Z. Does the Shari'ah Screening Impact the Gold-Stock Nexus? A Sectorial Analysis. *Resour. Policy* **2018**. Available online: https://www.researchgate.net/publication/328073570_Does_the_Shari%27ah_Screening_Impact_the_Gold-Stock_Nexus_A_Sectorial_Analysis (accessed on 11 October 2018).
32. Vieito, J.P.; Wong, W.K.; Zhu, Z.Z. Could The Global Financial Crisis Improve the Performance of the G7 Stocks Markets? *Appl. Econ.* **2015**, *48*, 1066–1080. [CrossRef]
33. Zhu, Z.Z.; Bai, Z.D.; Vieito, J.P.; Wong, W.K. The Impact of the Global Financial Crisis on the Efficiency of Latin American Stock Markets. *Estudios de Economía* **2018**. Available online: https://www.researchgate.net/publication/326758644_The_Impact_of_the_Global_Financial_Crisis_on_the_Efficiency_and_Performance_of_Latin_American_Stock_Markets (accessed on 11 October 2018). [CrossRef]

34. Broll, U.; Guo, X.; Welzel, P.; Wong, W.K. The banking firm and risk taking in a two-moment decision model. *Econ. Model.* **2015**, *50*, 275–280. [CrossRef]
35. Broll, U.; Jack, E.; Wahl, J.E.; Wong, W.K. Elasticity of Risk Aversion and International Trade. *Econ. Lett.* **2006**, *92*, 126–130. [CrossRef]
36. Egozcue, M.; Fuentes García, L.; Wong, W.K.; Zitikis, R. Do Investors Like to Diversify? A Study of Markowitz Preferences. *Eur. J. Oper. Res.* **2011**, *215*, 188–193. [CrossRef]
37. Egozcue, M.; Wong, W.K. Gains from Diversification on Convex Combinations: A Majorization and Stochastic Dominance Approach. *Eur. J. Oper. Res.* **2010**, *200*, 893–900. [CrossRef]
38. Abid, F.; Leung, P.L.; Mroua, M.; Wong, W.K. International Diversification versus Domestic diversification: Mean-Variance Portfolio Optimization and stochastic dominance approaches. *J. Risk Financ. Manag.* **2014**, *7*, 45–66. [CrossRef]
39. Lozza, S.O.; Wong, W.K.; Fabozzi, F.J.; Egozcue, M. Diversification versus Optimal: Is There Really a Diversification Puzzle? *Appl. Econ.* **2018**, *50*, 4671–4693. [CrossRef]
40. Fong, W.M.; Lean, H.H.; Wong, W.K. Stochastic Dominance and Behavior towards Risk: The Market for Internet Stocks. *J. Econ. Behav. Organ.* **2008**, *68*, 194–208. [CrossRef]
41. Fong, W.M.; Wong, W.K.; Lean, H.H. International momentum strategies: A stochastic dominance. *J. Financ. Mark.* **2005**, *8*, 89–109. [CrossRef]
42. Lean, H.H.; Smyth, R.; Wong, W.K. Revisiting Calendar Anomalies in Asian Stock Markets Using a Stochastic Dominance Approach. *J. Multinatl. Financ. Manag.* **2007**, *17*, 125–141. [CrossRef]
43. Ma, C.; Wong, W.K. Stochastic dominance and risk measure: A decision-theoretic foundation for VaR and C-VaR. *Eur. J. Oper. Res.* **2010**, *207*, 927–935. [CrossRef]
44. Alghalith, M.; Guo, X.; Wong, W.K.; Zhu, L.X. A General Optimal Investment Model in the Presence of Background Risk. *Ann. Financ. Econ.* **2016**, *11*, 1650001. [CrossRef]
45. Guo, X.; Jiang, X.J.; Wong, W.K. Stochastic Dominance and Omega Ratio: Measures to Examine Market Efficiency. *Arbitr. Oppor. Anomaly Econ.* **2017**, *5*, 38.
46. Niu, C.Z.; Wong, W.K.; Xu, Q.F. Kappa Ratios and (Higher-Order) Stochastic Dominance. *Risk Manag.* **2017**, *19*, 245–253. [CrossRef]
47. Chiang, T.C.; Lean, H.H.; Wong, W.K. Do REITs Outperform Stocks and Fixed-Income Assets? New Evidence from Mean-Variance and Stochastic Dominance Approaches. *J. Risk Financ. Manag.* **2008**, *1*, 1–37. [CrossRef]
48. Lean, H.H.; Phoon, K.F.; Wong, W.K. Stochastic Dominance Analysis of CTA Funds. *Rev. Quant. Financ. Account.* **2013**, *40*, 155–170. [CrossRef]
49. Wong, W.K.; Phoon, K.F.; Lean, H.H. Stochastic dominance analysis of Asian hedge funds. *Pacific-Basin Financ. J.* **2008**, *16*, 204–223. [CrossRef]
50. Markowitz, H.M. Portfolio selection. *J. Financ.* **1952**, *7*, 77–91.
51. Bai, Z.D.; Liu, H.X.; Wong, W.K. Enhancement of the applicability of Markowitz's portfolio optimization by utilizing random matrix theory. *Math. Financ.* **2009**, *19*, 639–667. [CrossRef]
52. Leung, P.L.; Ng, H.Y.; Wong, W.K. An Improved Estimation to Make Markowitz's Portfolio Optimization Theory Users Friendly and Estimation Accurate with Application on the US Stock Market Investment. *Eur. J. Oper. Res.* **2012**, *222*, 85–95. [CrossRef]
53. Wong, W.K. Stochastic Dominance and Mean-Variance Measures of Profit and Loss for Business Planning and Investment. *Eur. J. Oper. Res.* **2017**, *182*, 829–843. [CrossRef]
54. Guo, X.; Wong, W.K. Multivariate Stochastic Dominance for Risk Averters and Risk Seekers. *RAIRO Oper. Res.* **2016**, *50*, 575–586. [CrossRef]
55. Wong, W.K.; Ma, C. Preferences over Meyer's location-scale family. *Econ. Theory* **2008**, *37*, 119–146. [CrossRef]
56. Sriboonchitta, S.; Wong, W.K.; Dhompongsa, S.; Nguyen, H.T. *Stochastic Dominance and Applications to Finance, Risk and Economics*; Chapman and Hall/CRC, Taylor and Francis Group: Boca Raton, FL, USA, 2009.
57. Levy, H. *Stochastic Dominance: Investment Decision Making under Uncertainty*; Springer: New York, NY, USA, 2015.
58. Davidson, R.; Duclos, J.Y. Statistical inference for stochastic dominance and for the measurement of poverty and inequality. *Econometrica* **2000**, *68*, 1435–1464. [CrossRef]
59. Bai, Z.D.; Li, H.; McAleer, M.; Wong, W.K. Stochastic dominance statistics for risk averters and risk seekers: An analysis of stock preferences for USA and China. *Quant. Financ.* **2015**, *15*, 889–900. [CrossRef]
60. Bai, Z.D.; Li, H.; Liu, H.X.; Wong, W.K. Test Statistics for Prospect and Markowitz Stochastic Dominances with Applications. *Econ. J.* **2012**, *14*, 278–303.

61. Ng, P.; Wong, W.K.; Xiao, Z.J. Stochastic dominance via quantile regression with applications to investigate arbitrage opportunity and market efficiency. *Eur. J. Oper. Res.* **2017**, *261*, 666–678. [CrossRef]
62. Lean, H.H.; Wong, W.K.; Zhang, X.B. The size and power of some stochastic dominance tests: A Monte Carlo study for correlated heteroskedastic distributions. *Math. Comput. Simul.* **2008**, *79*, 30–48. [CrossRef]
63. Chan, R.H.; Clark, E.; Wong, W.K. *On the Third Order Stochastic Dominance for Risk-Averse and Risk-Seeking Investors with Analysis of their Traditional and Internet Stocks*; MPRA Paper No. 75002; University Library of Munich: Munich, Germany, 2016.
64. Leshno, M.; Levy, H. Preferred by "all" and preferred by "most" decision makers: Almost stochastic dominance. *Manag. Sci.* **2002**, *48*, 1074–1085. [CrossRef]
65. Guo, X.; Post, T.; Wong, W.K.; Zhu, L.X. Moment Conditions for Almost Stochastic Dominance. *Econ. Lett.* **2014**, *124*, 163–167. [CrossRef]
66. Guo, X.; Wong, W.K.; Zhu, L.X. Almost Stochastic Dominance for Risk Averters and Risk Seeker. *Financ. Res. Lett.* **2016**, *19*, 15–21. [CrossRef]
67. Guo, X.; Zhu, X.H.; Wong, W.K.; Zhu, L.X. A Note on Almost Stochastic Dominance. *Econom. Lett.* **2013**, *121*, 252–256. [CrossRef]
68. Gasbarro, D.; Wong, W.K.; Zumwalt, J.K. Stochastic Dominance Analysis of iShares. *Eur. J. Financ.* **2007**, *13*, 89–101. [CrossRef]
69. Clark, E.; Qiao, Z.; Wong, W.K. Theories of Risk: Testing Investor Behaviour on the Taiwan Stock and Stock Index Futures Markets. *Econ. Inquiry* **2016**, *54*, 907–924. [CrossRef]
70. Chan, R.H.; Chow, S.C.; Guo, X.; Wong, W.K. *Central Moments, Stochastic Dominance, and The Moment Rules*; Social Science Research Network Working Paper Series 3034903; SSRN: Rochester, NY, USA, 2017.
71. Guo, X.; Wagener, A.; Wong, W.K.; Zhu, L.X. The Two-Moment Decision Model with Additive Risks. *Risk Manag.* **2017**, *20*, 77–94. [CrossRef]
72. Chang, C.L.; McAleer, M.; Wong, W.K. Behavioural, Financial, and Health & Medical Economics: A Connection. *J. Health Med. Econ.* **2016**, *2*, 1–4.
73. Chang, C.L.; McAleer, M.; Wong, W.K. Informatics, Data Mining, Econometrics and Financial Economics: A Connection. *J. Inform. Data Min.* **2016**, *1*, 1–5.
74. Chang, C.L.; McAleer, M.; Wong, W.K. Management Science, Economics and Finance: A Connection. *Int. J. Econ. Manag. Sci.* **2016**, *5*, 1–19.
75. Chang, C.L.; McAleer, M.; Wong, W.K. Management Information, Decision Sciences, and Financial Economics: A Connection. *J. Manag. Inf. Decis. Sci.* **2017**, *20*. Available online: https://ideas.repec.org/p/tin/wpaper/20180004.html (accessed on 11 October 2018). [CrossRef]
76. Chang, C.L.; McAleer, M.; Wong, W.K. Big Data, Computational Science, Economics, Finance, Marketing, Management, and Psychology: Connections. *J. Risk Financ. Manag.* **2018**, *11*, 15. [CrossRef]
77. Moslehpour, M.; Pham, V.K.; Wong, W.K.; Bilgiçli, İ. e-Purchase Intention of Taiwanese Consumers: Sustainable Mediation of Perceived Usefulness and Perceived Ease of Use. *Sustainability* **2018**, *10*, 234. [CrossRef]
78. Li, Z.; Li, X.; Hui, Y.C.; Wong, W.K. Maslow Portfolio Selection for Individuals with Low Financial Sustainability. *Sustainability* **2018**, *10*, 1128. [CrossRef]
79. Li, C.S.; Wong, W.K.; Peng, S.C.; Tsendsuren, S. The effects of health status on life insurance holding in 16 European countries. *Sustainability* **2018**, *10*, 3454.
80. Wong, W.K.; Chan, R. Prospect and Markowitz Stochastic Dominance. *Ann. Financ.* **2008**, *4*, 105–129. [CrossRef]

Permissions

All chapters in this book were first published in MDPI; hereby published with permission under the Creative Commons Attribution License or equivalent. Every chapter published in this book has been scrutinized by our experts. Their significance has been extensively debated. The topics covered herein carry significant findings which will fuel the growth of the discipline. They may even be implemented as practical applications or may be referred to as a beginning point for another development.

The contributors of this book come from diverse backgrounds, making this book a truly international effort. This book will bring forth new frontiers with its revolutionizing research information and detailed analysis of the nascent developments around the world.

We would like to thank all the contributing authors for lending their expertise to make the book truly unique. They have played a crucial role in the development of this book. Without their invaluable contributions this book wouldn't have been possible. They have made vital efforts to compile up to date information on the varied aspects of this subject to make this book a valuable addition to the collection of many professionals and students.

This book was conceptualized with the vision of imparting up-to-date information and advanced data in this field. To ensure the same, a matchless editorial board was set up. Every individual on the board went through rigorous rounds of assessment to prove their worth. After which they invested a large part of their time researching and compiling the most relevant data for our readers.

The editorial board has been involved in producing this book since its inception. They have spent rigorous hours researching and exploring the diverse topics which have resulted in the successful publishing of this book. They have passed on their knowledge of decades through this book. To expedite this challenging task, the publisher supported the team at every step. A small team of assistant editors was also appointed to further simplify the editing procedure and attain best results for the readers.

Apart from the editorial board, the designing team has also invested a significant amount of their time in understanding the subject and creating the most relevant covers. They scrutinized every image to scout for the most suitable representation of the subject and create an appropriate cover for the book.

The publishing team has been an ardent support to the editorial, designing and production team. Their endless efforts to recruit the best for this project, has resulted in the accomplishment of this book. They are a veteran in the field of academics and their pool of knowledge is as vast as their experience in printing. Their expertise and guidance has proved useful at every step. Their uncompromising quality standards have made this book an exceptional effort. Their encouragement from time to time has been an inspiration for everyone.

The publisher and the editorial board hope that this book will prove to be a valuable piece of knowledge for researchers, students, practitioners and scholars across the globe.

List of Contributors

Vasily E. Tarasov
Skobeltsyn Institute of Nuclear Physics, Lomonosov Moscow State University, Moscow 119991, Russia

Stefan Kremsner
Department of Mathematics, University of Graz, Heinrichstraße 36, 8010 Graz, Austria

Alexander Steinicke
Department of Mathematics and Information Technology, Montanuniversitaet Leoben, Peter Tunner-Straße 25/I, 8700 Leoben, Austria

Michaela Szölgyenyi
Department of Statistics, University of Klagenfurt, Universitätsstraße 65-67, 9020 Klagenfurt, Austria

Sergey Yevgenievich Barykin, Irina Vasilievna Kapustina and Sergey Mikhailovich Sergeev
Graduate School of Service and Trade, Peter the Great St. Petersburg Polytechnic University, 195251 St. Petersburg, Russia

Vladimir Konstantinovich Yadykin
Laboratory «Advanced Production Technologies» of the National Technological Initiative Center, Peter the Great St. Petersburg Polytechnic University, 195251 St. Petersburg, Russia

Rangan Gupta
Department of Economics, University of Pretoria, Pretoria 0002, South Africa

Zhihui Lv
KLASMOE & School of Mathematics and Statistics, Northeast Normal University, Changchun 130024, China

Wing-Keung Wong
Department of Finance, Fintech Center, and Big Data Research Center, Asia University, Taichung 41354, Taiwan
Department of Medical Research, China Medical University Hospital, Taichung 40402, Taiwan
Department of Economics and Finance, The Hang Seng University of Hong Kong, Shatin 999077, Hong Kong, China
Department of Economics, Lingnan University, Hong Kong, China

Chi Dong
School of Economics, Hebei University, Baoding 071002, China

Zamri Ahmad
School of Management, Universiti Sains Malaysia, Penang 11800, Malaysia

Massoud Moslehpour
Department of Business Administration, Asia University, Taichung 41354, Taiwan
Department of Business Administration, Saigon Institute of Technology, District 12, HCMC 70000, Vietnam

Purevdulam Altantsetseg
Law School, Mongolian National University, Ulaanbaatar 16060-0012, Mongolia

Weiming Mou
College of Economics and Management, Changzhou Institute of Technology, Changzhou 213022, China

Sayyed Sadaqat Hussain Shah
Department of Commerce and Finance, Faculty of Arts and Social Sciences, Government College University Lahore, Lahore 54000, Pakistan

Muhammad Asif Khan
School of Economics and Management, Yanshan University, 438, Hebei Avenue, Qinhuangdao City 066004, China
Department of Commerce, Faculty of Management Sciences, University of Kotli, Village Kurti, City Kotli, Azad Jammu and Kashmir 11100, Pakistan

Natanya Meyer
Work Well Research Unit, North-West University, Faculty of Economic and Management Sciences, School of Management, Vanderbijlpark 1900, South Africa

Daniel F. Meyer
TRADE Research Entity, North-West University, Faculty of Economic and Management Sciences, Vanderbijlpark 1900, South Africa

Judit Oláh
University of Debrecen, Faculty of Economics and Business, Institute of Applied Informatics and Logistics, 4032 Debrecen, Hungary

Shu-Han Hsu
Department of Applied Economics, National Chung Hsing University, Taichung 402, Taiwan

Chia-Lin Chang
Department of Applied Economics, National Chung Hsing University, Taichung 402, Taiwan
Department of Finance, National Chung Hsing University, Taichung 402, Taiwan
Department of Finance, Asia University, Taichung 41354, Taiwan

Michael McAleer
Department of Finance, Asia University, Taichung 41354, Taiwan
Discipline of Business Analytics, University of Sydney Business School, Sydney 2006, Australia
Econometric Institute, Erasmus School of Economics, Erasmus University Rotterdam, 3000 Rotterdam, The Netherlands
Department of Economic Analysis and ICAE, Complutense University of Madrid, 28040 Madrid, Spain
Institute of Advanced Sciences, Yokohama National University, Yokohama 240-8501, Japan

Zhiping Chen, Xinkai Zhuang and Jia Liu
School of Mathematics and Statistics, Xi'an Jiaotong University, Xi'an 710049, China
Center for Optimization Technique and Quantitative Finance, Xi'an International Academy for Mathematics and Mathematical Technology, Xi'an 710049, China

Hooi Hooi Lean
Economics Program, School of Social Sciences, Universiti Sains Malaysia, 11800 Gelugor, Malaysia

Feng-Tse Tsai
Department of Finance, Asia University, Taichung City 41354, Taiwan

Index

A
Aggregate Supply, 63-65, 70-72

C
Cardinality Constraint, 209-211, 219-220
Computer Simulation, 9, 60
Control Variables, 119-120, 125

D
Dependent Variable, 100, 119
Descriptive Statistics, 79-80, 101, 120, 230
Diagonal Elements, 66-68, 217
Digital Logistics, 47, 57-58
Discrete Time, 2-3, 22, 66
Dividend Payments, 29-30, 42

E
Econometrics, 14-15, 18, 208, 239
Economic Data, 3, 6, 13-14
Economic Theory, 1-3, 5, 7, 9, 14-15, 17, 21, 23
Econophysics, 1, 3, 5-6, 9, 20
Eigenvalues, 57
Endogenous Variables, 15, 67-68, 70, 100
Enhanced Indexation, 209-213, 215-217, 220-222
Event Study, 132, 134, 136-138, 158, 207-208
Exogenous Variable, 15, 100

F
Fading Memory, 3, 13, 15-16
Financial Crisis, 63-64, 67-68, 70, 72, 228, 237
Financial Liberalization, 67, 72
Financial Shocks, 63-64, 72
Financial Sustainability, 110, 209-210, 212, 219, 221, 239
Firm Value, 112-113, 117, 119, 125-126, 131
Fractional Calculus, 1-7, 9-17, 19-22, 24-27
Fractional Derivatives, 3-4, 6-7, 9-11, 13, 15, 18, 22, 26-28
Fractional Dynamics, 1, 5-6, 19-20, 24
Fractional Generalizations, 6-7, 9-11, 13
Fractional Operators, 10-12, 14, 16, 27
Fund Managers, 113-114, 116, 209, 219, 221

G
Gross Domestic Product, 6, 9, 13

I
Individual Investors, 91, 114, 129, 209, 219, 221, 224
Information Diffusion, 75-78, 80-83, 86-87, 89-94
Institutional Investors, 77, 91, 114, 130, 227
Insurance Mathematics, 29-31, 34, 39, 42-43
Interest Rate, 8, 65-70
Interim Storage, 49, 51
Intra-industry, 75-78, 80-83, 86-87, 89-92
Investor Herding Bias, 112-113, 118

J
Job Satisfaction, 95-100, 104-110

L
Leadership Style, 95-97, 99-100, 104-109
Logistics Network, 47-48, 51, 57-58, 60, 62
Logistics Processes, 47-48, 51, 57, 59
Long Memory, 1, 3, 10, 18-19, 25

M
Macroeconomic Shocks, 63-64, 73
Macroeconomics, 12-14, 22, 24, 27, 74
Market Condition, 75-77, 82-83, 86, 91-92
Market Efficiency, 77, 92, 94, 112, 116, 223, 237-239
Market Regimes, 209, 211-212, 216-217, 219-220
Mathematical Economics, 1-3, 5-7, 9, 12-15, 17, 23-25, 27
Mathematical Modeling, 2, 4, 47-48, 51, 57-58
Mathematical Tools, 2, 4, 58
Moment Analysis, 223, 225, 230, 235
Monetary Policy, 25, 63-69, 71-74

N
Network Logistics, 47-48, 54, 57, 59
Non-integer Orders, 1, 3, 9-10, 13

O
Optimal Control Problems, 29, 31
Organizational Climate, 95-100, 104-110

P
Poisson Equation, 30, 37
Probability Matrix, 66, 212

Q
Quadratic Growth, 31-32

R
Real Estate Market, 63-64, 66, 71-72
Regime Switching, 45-46, 74, 209-212, 217, 219-220, 222
Register Office, 96, 98-101, 104-106
Register Sector, 96, 104

S

Service Industries, 96-97
Sign-restrictions, 63-64, 72
Simulation Model, 47, 51, 59
Spread Yield Shocks, 63-64
Statistical Properties, 14, 63, 72
Stochastic Dominance, 210, 222-223, 226-227, 229, 237-239
Stock Exchange, 65, 94, 112-114, 130-131, 137-138, 208, 226, 237
Stock Market, 18, 75-78, 82, 86, 89-94, 112, 114-118, 129-131, 137-138, 223-224, 227, 236, 238

T

Terminal Time, 29-32, 34-35, 42, 44-45
Topology, 51-53, 56, 59
Tourism Finance, 132, 134, 139, 207
Transition Probability, 66-67, 212, 216

V

Volume Analysis, 223, 225-226, 228, 230, 234-235

W

Warrant Markets, 107, 110, 221, 223-227, 232, 235-236
Work Style, 95-100, 104-108, 110

www.ingramcontent.com/pod-product-compliance
Lightning Source LLC
LaVergne TN
LVHW081013210926
848485LV00004B/856